Contents

About your **BTEC Level 3 National Sport**   viii

Also available

There are many different optional units in your BTEC Level 3 National Sport qualification, which you may use to form specialist pathways or to build a broader programme of learning. This student book covers all the mandatory units for the Edexcel BTEC Level 3 National Extended Diploma in Sport across the two main pathways and some support for the Outdoor Adventure Pathway, but if you want a huge choice of optional units you may be interested in Student Book 2.

Written in the same accessible style with the same useful features to support you through your learning and assessment, *BTEC Level 3 National Sport Student Book 2* (ISBN: 9781846906503) covers the following units:

Unit number	Credit value	Unit name
10	10	Outdoor and adventurous activities
12	10	Current issues in sport
13	10	Leadership in sport
14	10	Exercise, health and lifestyle
15	10	Instructing physical activity and exercise
16	10	Exercise for specific groups
18	10	Sports injuries
19	10	Analysis of sports performance
20	10	Talent identification and development in sport
21	10	Sport and exercise massage
22	10	Rules, regulations and officiating in sport
23	10	Organising sports events
24	10	Physical education and the care of children and young people
25	10	Sport as a business
26	10	Work experience in sport

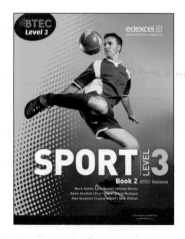

Available direct from www.pearsonfe.co.uk/BTEC2010 and can be ordered from all good bookshops.

Credits

The authors and publisher would like to thank the following individuals and organisations for permission to reproduce photographs:

Shutterstock/Julien Tromeur p. **1**; © Pearson Education Ltd. Jules Selmes p. **3**; Getty Images/Man Utd via Getty Images p. **9**; Getty Images p. **33**; © 2010 Photos.com p. **35**; Juice Images/Corbis p. **37**; Pearson Education Ltd. Gareth Boden p. **39**; Alamy/Enigma p. **43**; Shutterstock/Kurhan p. **48**; © Pearson Education Ltd. MindStudio p. **57**; John Foxx/Imagestate p. **59**; © Pearson Education Ltd. Jules Selmes p. **61**; Masterfile/Anders Hald p. **66**; Alamy/Radius Images p. **69**; Getty Images/ Jim Cummins p. **77**; Shutterstock/Alexander Kalina p. **81**; Shutterstock/tonobalaguerf p. **85**; Black 100/Getty p. **87**; © Pearson Education Ltd. Lord and Leverett p. **89**; Paul Lonsdale p. **90**; Shutterstock/Monkey Business Images p. **112**; Shutterstock/Yuri Arcurs p. **115**; Getty Images p. **117**; © Shutterstock.com/Andrey Shadrin p. **119**; Corbis / Sam Bagnall/AMA p. **121**; Corbis/Wally McNamee p. **126**; Dartfish p. **133**; Getty Images p. **133**; Getty Images p. **143**; © Pearson Education Ltd. Rob Judges p. **147**; Getty Images p. **149**; © Pearson Education Ltd. Jules Selmes p. **151**; Getty Images p. **152**; Getty Images p. **155**; Getty Images p. **157**; Getty Images/Bongarts p. **159**; © Shutterstock.com/Yuri Arcurs p. **177**; © Adrian Sherratt/Alamy p. **179**; JHershPhoto /Shutterstock p. **181**; Mike Park, University of Hull p. **183**; Press Association Images/AP p. **192**; Coventry University p. **198**; Shutterstock/Zsolt Nyulaszi p. **202**; © Shutterstock.com/Andresr p. **209**; Getty Images/ Chris Cole p. **211**; © Pearson Education Ltd. Gareth Boden p. **213**; © Shutterstock.com/ Monkey Business Images p. **214**; Getty Images/AFP p. **218**; Getty Images p. **218**; Corbis / CHRISTOPHE KARABA/epa p. **225**; Prozone p. **234**; Dartfish p. **235**; © Shutterstock.com/thefinalmiracle p. **243**; Shutterstock/Hannamariah p. **245**; © Pearson Education Ltd. Gareth Boden p. **247**; Shutterstock/ Morgan Lane Photography p. **248**; Shutterstock/Belova Larissa p. **249**; Getty Images/DEA/P.Martini p. **251**; Getty Images/Wire Image p. **261**; Corbis/Duomo p. **266**; Corbis / SRDJAN SUKI/epa p. **270**; © Shutterstock.com/Yuri Arcurs p. **277**; Steve Lipofsky/Corbis p. **279**; Clark Wiseman/© Pearson Education Ltd. 2006 p. **281**; Radius Images/Photolibrary p. **283**; actionplus p. **291**; Steve Lipofsky/ Corbis p. **298**; Shutterstock p. **319**; Hermann Erber/Getty p. **321**; © Pearson Education Ltd. Jules Selmes p. **323**; Getty Images/AFP p. **324**; Getty Images / Studio Paggy p. **332**; Corbis/Christian Liewig p. **340**; Getty Images/NBAE p. **341**; Corbis/Duomo p. **342**; © Shutterstock.com p. **357**; Roca/ Shutterstock p. **359**; Shutterstock/Tracy Whiteside p. **361**; Getty/2009 Eugene Gologursky p. 366; UK Sport p. **367**; Sport England p. **368**; Getty Images p. **369**; Getty Images p. **372**; Getty Images p. **378**; Shutterstock/ImageryMajestic p. **385**.

The authors and publisher would like to thank the following individuals and organisations for permission to reproduce their materials:

p. 124 Code of conduct: Coaches, Team Managers and Club Officials. The Football Association
pp. 160-161 Sport England
p.161 Case study. Bristol City Council
p. 168 Overview of long-term athlete-development stages. England Basketball
p. 173 Big Lottery Fund
p. 184 Example of an informed consent form for strength tests. Reprinted with permission from The Cooper Institute, Dallas, Texas from a book called "Physical Fitness Assessments and Norms for Adults and Law Enforcement". Available online at www.cooperinstitute.org
p. 187 Forestry non-adjusted aerobic fitness values for males table (ml/kg/min) for males. Adapted, with permission, from B. J. Sharkey, 1984, Physiology of fitness, 2nd ed. (Champaign, IL: Human Kinetics), 258

About the authors

Mark Adams is a Senior Verifier for Sport Levels 1 to 3 and has worked with Edexcel for seven years. He has taught for ten years at schools and colleges across all qualifications. Mark is a consultant with the Premier League education and learning team. He is the series editor for our BTEC Level 3 National Sport and BTEC Level 3 National Sport and Exercise Science resources and has written for our BTEC Level 2 First Sport books.

Ray Barker has worked as sports manager and lecturer in a number of contexts for 30 years for companies and colleges in Scotland, Wales, the USA and France. He has written extensively on Sport topics and has assisted in the development of awards for Edexcel and other exam boards. He currently lectures at the University of Hull and is external examiner at Loughborough College and Cardiff School of Sport.

Adam Gledhill has nine years experience teaching throughout Further and Higher education, has been involved with Edexcel's qualification development for five years and external verification for three years and was a co-author of the previous editions of this book for Heinemann. Alongside teaching, Adam is currently working towards a PhD in Sport Psychology around the area of talent development in football at Loughborough University and provides sport science support to youth athletes in a range of sports.

Chris Lydon is a department manager and senior sports lecturer currently teaching BTEC courses at a Further Education college. In this role he is involved in the professional development of new staff and introduces them to BTEC assessment and verification. He has wide-ranging experience of teaching Further Education and Higher Education programmes and has contributed to a number of BTEC Sport textbooks published by Heinemann.

Chris Mulligan has been teaching BTEC qualifications for the last ten years and has taught across all levels. He has worked for Edexcel for the last five years as an external verifier and has written unit specifications for the new First and National Diplomas in Sport. Chris was also an author of the previous BTEC National Sport student book as well as the BTEC Level 3 National Sport Teaching Resource Pack.

Pam Phillippo has played a key role in the redevelopment of Edexcel BTEC Sport qualifications and is an expert in psychophysiology. Formerly a lecturer in Further Education and Higher Education, and having worked with GB athletes, her specialist fields include fitness testing and training, exercise prescription, and experimental methods.

Louise Sutton is a principal lecturer in sport and exercise nutrition at Leeds Metropolitan University and currently manages the Carnegie Centre for Sports Performance and Wellbeing. She is a member of the Health and Fitness Technical Expert Group of SkillsActive, the Sector Skills Council for Active Leisure and Learning in the UK. In 2005 Louise was awarded the Re-Energise Fitness Professional of the Year award for her commitment and contribution to raising standards in nutrition training and education in the health and fitness industry.

About your BTEC Level 3 National Sport book

The sport and active leisure industry is very diverse and covers such aspects as coaching, fitness testing and sports development. Every year the sport and active leisure sector outperforms the rest of the UK economy and with the approach of the London 2012 Olympic and Paralympics Games the opportunities available within this sector are more varied than ever before. BTEC Level 3 National Sport will help you succeed in your future career within the sport and active leisure sector. It's designed to give you plenty of flexibility in selecting optional units so you can meet your interests and career aspirations. The principles of sport that you will learn here underpin many aspects of professional life within the sector and reflect the enormous breadth and depth of the subject – from principles of anatomy and physiology to talent identification and development, organising sports events and fitness testing for sport and exercise.

Your BTEC Level 3 National in Sport is a **vocational** or **work-related** qualification. This doesn't mean that it will give you *all* the skills you need to do a job, but it does mean that you'll have the opportunity to gain specific knowledge, understanding and skills that are relevant to your chosen subject or area of work. The qualification can also be used as an entry point to higher education qualifications and more specialist courses.

What will you be doing?

The qualification is structured into **mandatory units** (M) (ones you must do) and **optional units** (O) (ones you can choose to do). How many units you do and which ones you cover depend upon the type of qualification you are working towards.

- BTEC Level 3 National Certificate in Sport: three mandatory units plus optional units to provide a total of 30 credits
- BTEC Level 3 National Subsidiary Diploma in Sport: three mandatory units plus one mandatory specialist unit plus optional units to provide a total of 60 credits
- BTEC Level 3 National Diploma in Sport (Performance and Excellence – **PE**): nine mandatory units plus optional units to provide a total of 120 credits
- BTEC Level 3 National Diploma in Sport (Development, Coaching and Fitness – **DCF**): eight mandatory units plus optional units to provide a total of 120 credits
- BTEC Level 3 National Diploma in Sport (Outdoor Adventure – **OA**): seven mandatory units plus optional units to provide a total of 120 credits
- BTEC Level 3 National Extended Diploma in Sport (Performance and Excellence – **PE**): nine mandatory units plus optional units to provide a total of 180 credits
- BTEC Level 3 National Extended Diploma in Sport (Development, Coaching and Fitness – **DCF**): eight mandatory units plus optional units to provide a total of 180 credits
- BTEC Level 3 National Extended Diploma in Sport (Outdoor Adventure – **OA**): seven mandatory units plus optional units to provide a total of 180 credits

The table below shows how the units covered by the books in this series cover the different types of BTEC qualifications.

Unit no.	Credit value	Unit name	Cert	Sub Dip	Dip (PE)	Dip (DCF)	Dip (OA)	Ext Dip (PE)	Ext Dip (DCF)	Ext Dip (OA)
1	5	Principles of anatomy and physiology in sport	M	M	M	M	M	M	M	M
2	5	The physiology of fitness	M	M	M	M	M	M	M	M
3	10	Assessing risk in sport	M	M	M	M	M	M	M	M
4	10	Fitness training and programming		O	M	M	M	M	M	M
5	10	Sports coaching		O	O	M		O	M	O
6	10	Sports development		O		M			M	
7	10	Fitness testing for sport and exercise	O	M	M	M		M	M	
8	10	Practical team sports		O+	O	M*		O	M†	
9	10	Practical individual sports		O+		M*			M†	
10	10	Outdoor and adventurous activities		O+		O*			O	
11	10	Sports nutrition		O	M	O		M	O	O
12	10	Current issues in sport		O	O	O	O	O	O	O
13	10	Leadership in sport		O		O	M		O	M
14	10	Exercise, health and lifestyle		O		O			O	O
15	10	Instructing physical activity and exercise		O	O	O		O	O	
16	10	Exercise for specific groups							O	
17	10	Psychology for sports performance		O	M	O		M	O	
18	10	Sports injuries		O	O	O	O	O	O	O
19	10	Analysis of sports performance		O				O	O	
20	10	Talent identification and development in sport						O	O	
21	10	Sport and exercise massage		O	O			O	O	
22	10	Rules, regulations and officiating In sport		O	O			O	O	
23	10	Organising sports events			O	O	O	O	O	O
24	10	Physical education and the care of children and young people		O		O	O	O	O	O
25	10	Sport as a business			O	O	O	O	O	O
26	10	Work experience in sport		O	O	O	O	O	O	O
27	10	Technical and tactical skills in sport		O	M			M		
28	10	The athlete's lifestyle		O	M			M		

* Learners **must select either** Unit 8 or Unit 9 as a mandatory unit.

* Learners **may select**, as an optional unit, whichever of Unit 8 or Unit 9 that was not taken as a mandatory unit, **or** alternatively may select Unit 10.

* Learners **must not** select all three of Unit 8, Unit 9 and Unit 10.

+ Learners may select only **one** from Unit 8, Unit 9 or Unit 10.

† Learners must select **one** of these units (Unit 8 or Unit 9) as a mandatory unit, and may select the other as an optional unit.

Units in green are covered in this book. Units in yellow are covered in *BTEC Level 3 National Sport Student Book 2* (ISBN: 9781846906503)

How to use this book

This book is designed to help you through your BTEC Level 3 National Sport course.

It contains many features that will help you develop and apply your skills and knowledge in work-related situations and assist you in getting the most for your course.

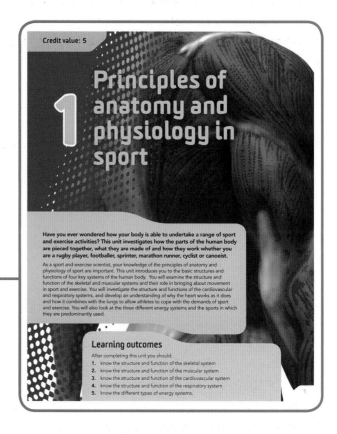

Credit value: 5

Principles of anatomy and physiology in sport

Have you ever wondered how your body is able to undertake a range of sport and exercise activities? This unit investigates how the parts of the human body are pieced together, what they are made of and how they work whether you are a rugby player, footballer, sprinter, marathon runner, cyclist or canoeist.

As a sport and exercise scientist, your knowledge of the principles of anatomy and physiology of sport are important. This unit introduces you to the basic structures and functions of four key systems of the human body. You will examine the structure and function of the skeletal and muscular systems and their role in bringing about movement in sport and exercise. You will investigate the structure and functions of the cardiovascular and respiratory systems, and develop an understanding of why the heart works as it does and how it combines with the lungs to allow athletes to cope with the demands of sport and exercise. You will also look at the three different energy systems and the sports in which they are predominantly used.

Learning outcomes

After completing this unit you should:
1. know the structure and function of the skeletal system
2. know the structure and function of the muscular system
3. know the structure and function of the cardiovascular system
4. know the structure and function of the respiratory system
5. know the different types of energy systems.

Introduction

These introductions give you a snapshot of what to expect from each unit – and what you should be aiming for by the time you finish it!

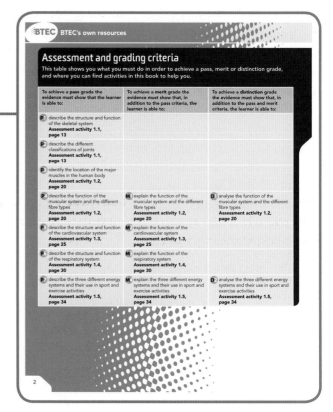

BTEC BTEC's own resources

Assessment and grading criteria

This table shows you what you must do in order to achieve a pass, merit or distinction grade, and where you can find activities in this book to help you.

To achieve a pass grade the evidence must show that the learner is able to:	To achieve a merit grade the evidence must show that, in addition to the pass criteria, the learner is able to:	To achieve a distinction grade the evidence must show that, in addition to the pass and merit criteria, the learner is able to:
P1 describe the structure and function of the skeletal system **Assessment activity 1.1, page 13**		
P2 describe the different classifications of joints **Assessment activity 1.1, page 13**		
P3 identify the location of the major muscles in the human body **Assessment activity 1.2, page 20**		
P4 describe the function of the muscular system and the different fibre types **Assessment activity 1.2, page 20**	M1 explain the function of the muscular system and the different fibre types **Assessment activity 1.2, page 20**	D1 analyse the function of the muscular system and the different fibre types **Assessment activity 1.2, page 20**
P5 describe the structure and function of the cardiovascular system **Assessment activity 1.3, page 25**	M2 explain the function of the cardiovascular system **Assessment activity 1.3, page 25**	
P6 describe the structure and function of the respiratory system **Assessment activity 1.4, page 30**	M3 explain the function of the respiratory system **Assessment activity 1.4, page 30**	
P7 describe the three different energy systems and their use in sport and exercise activities **Assessment activity 1.5, page 34**	M4 explain the three different energy systems and their use in sport and exercise activities **Assessment activity 1.5, page 34**	D2 analyse the three different energy systems and their use in sport and exercise activities **Assessment activity 1.5, page 34**

Assessment and grading criteria

This table explains what you must do in order to achieve each of the assessment criteria for each unit. For each assessment criterion, shown by the grade button **P1**, **M1**, **D1** there is an assessment activity.

Assessment

Your tutor will set **assignments** throughout your course for you to complete. These may take a variety of forms. The important thing is that you evidence your skills and knowledge to date.

Stuck for ideas? Daunted by your first assignment? These students have all been through it before…

Unit 1 Principles of anatomy and physiology in sport

How you will be assessed

This unit will be internally assessed by a range of assignments that will be designed and graded by your tutor. Your assessment tasks will be designed to allow you to demonstrate your understanding of the unit learning outcomes and relate to what you should be able to do after completing this unit. Your assignments could be in the form of:

- presentations
- practical tasks
- written assignments.

Gemma Stewart, a sports enthusiast

In this unit I learned that there are several systems that interact in a complex way to bring my body into action during sport and exercise. As a keen sports participant it has helped me to appreciate and understand how my body works and I have been able to apply what I have learned to understanding my performance in sport and exercise. I particularly enjoyed exploring the different energy systems and those involved in the different sports I take part in.

The practical activities for this unit have given me a better understanding of the muscle groups worked by the exercises in my gym programme.

There is a lot of complex information to learn in understanding the principles of anatomy and physiology in sport.

Over to you

- What aspects of the unit might you find most challenging?
- What preparation could you do to make the learning of these complex systems an easier task?

Activities

There are different types of activities for you to do: **Assessment activities** are suggestions for tasks that you might do as part of your assignment and will help you develop your knowledge, skills and understanding. **Grading tips** clearly explain what you need to do in order to achieve a pass, merit or distinction grade.

Assessment activity 1.1   P1 P2 BTEC

A fitness instructor regularly draws on anatomical knowledge to design and develop fitness programmes for clients.

1. Draw two large tables to describe the structure and function of the axial and appendicular

skeletons. Your descriptions should include the location of all the major bones of the skeleton and their different types. **P1**

2. Describe the different classifications of joints and the range of movement each provides. **P2**

Grading tips

P1 Describe the axial and appendicular skeletons and locate and name all the following major bones: cranium, clavicle, ribs, sternum, humerus, radius, ulna, scapula, ilium, pubis, ischium, carpals, metacarpals, phalanges, femur, patella, tibia, fibula, tarsals, metatarsals, vertebral column, vertebrae – cervical, thoracic, lumbar, sacrum and coccyx.

P2 You must be able to describe all three classifications of joint and the movement available at each, including the movement allowed at each of the synovial joints. Examine each of the three classifications of joints, including all six synovial joints, and explain how and why the range of movement allowed at these joints differs. Use sporting examples to support your explanation.

There are also suggestions for **activities** that will give you a broader grasp of the industry, stretch your understanding and deepen your skills.

Activity: Muscles at work

When your body is in action during sport and exercise, your muscles shorten, remain the same length or lengthen.

1. Pick up a dumb-bell (or a bag of sugar or a heavy book). Bend your arm at the elbow to bring your forearm up towards your shoulder in a bicep curl action.

2. Think about what your bicep muscle appears to be doing as you bring the weight closer to your shoulder. Has the muscle shortened, remained the same length or lengthened?

3. Return the dumb-bell to the starting position and consider what has to happen to your muscle to allow this action to take place. Do you think the bicep shortened, remained the same length or lengthened?

4. Curl the arm again, but this time only to a 90° angle. Hold your object in this position for a sustained period of time. What does the bicep muscle appear to be doing now? Do you think it is shortening, remaining the same length or lengthening?

Personal, learning and thinking skills

Throughout your BTEC Level 3 National Sport course, there are lots of opportunities to develop your personal, learning and thinking skills. Look out for these as you progress.

PLTS

Researching the structure and function of the skeletal system and examining the range of movement at joints using a variety of sporting examples will evidence your development as an **independent enquirer**.

Functional skills

It's important that you have good English, Mathematics and ICT skills – you never know when you'll need them, and employers will be looking for evidence that you've got these skills too.

Functional skills

Describing the structure and function of the axial and appendicular skeletons and the different classifications of joints and their range of movement will demonstrate your **English** skills.

Key terms

Technical words and phrases are easy to spot. You can also use the glossary at the back of the book.

Key term

Articulation – the meeting of two or more bones.

WorkSpace

Case studies provide snapshots of real workplace issues, and show how the skills and knowledge you develop during your course can help you in your career.

There are also mini-case studies throughout the book to help you focus on your own projects.

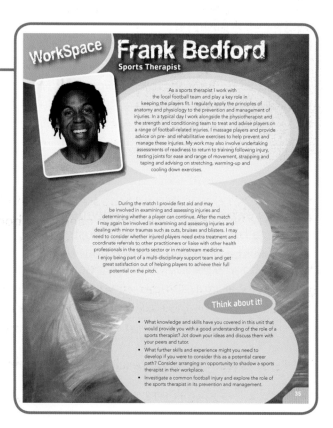

WorkSpace **Frank Bedford**
Sports Therapist

As a sports therapist I work with the local football team and play a key role in keeping the players fit. I regularly apply the principles of anatomy and physiology to the prevention and management of injuries. In a typical day I work alongside the physiotherapist and the strength and conditioning team to treat and advise players on a range of football-related injuries. I massage players and provide advice on pre- and rehabilitative exercises to help prevent and manage these injuries. My work may also involve undertaking assessments of readiness to return to training following injury, testing joints for ease and range of movement, strapping and taping and advising on stretching, warming-up and cooling down exercises.

During the match I provide first aid and may be involved in examining and assessing injuries and determining whether a player can continue. After the match I may again be involved in examining and assessing injuries and dealing with minor traumas such as cuts, bruises and blisters. I may need to consider whether injured players need extra treatment and coordinate referrals to other practitioners or liaise with other health professionals in the sports sector or in mainstream medicine.

I enjoy being part of a multi-disciplinary support team and get great satisfaction out of helping players to achieve their full potential on the pitch.

Think about it!

- What knowledge and skills have you covered in this unit that would provide you with a good understanding of the role of a sports therapist? Jot down your ideas and discuss them with your peers and tutor.
- What further skills and experience might you need to develop if you were to consider this as a potential career path? Consider arranging an opportunity to shadow a sports therapist in their workplace.
- Investigate a common football injury and explore the role of the sports therapist in its prevention and management.

Just checking

When you see this sort of activity, take stock! These quick activities and questions are there to check your knowledge. You can use them to see how much progress you've made.

Edexcel's assignment tips

At the end of each unit, you'll find hints and tips o help you get the best mark you can, such as the best websites to go to, checklists to help you remember processes and useful reminders to avoid common mistakes.

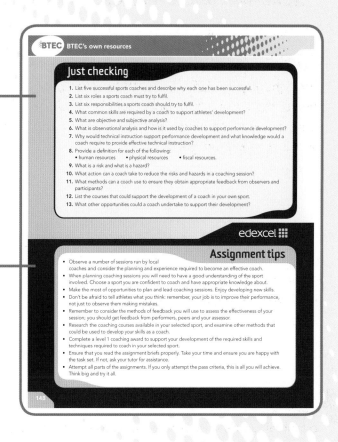

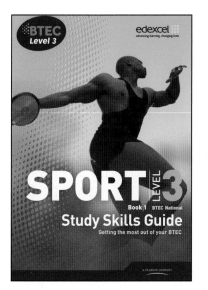

Don't miss out on these resources to help you!

Have you read your **BTEC Level 3 National Study Skills Guide?** It's full of advice on study skills, putting your assignments together and making the most of being a BTEC Sport student.

Your book is just part of the exciting resources from Edexcel to

 Ask your tutor about extra materials to help you through the course. **The Tutor Resource Pack** which accompanies this book contains interesting videos featuring Tottenham Hotspur, activities, PowerPoints, a Podcast and information about the Sport sector.

 Visit www.pearsonfe.co.uk/videopodcast to view or download a free video podcast that you can use at home or on the go via your mobile phone, MP3 player or laptop. Wherever you see the podcast icon in the book you'll know that the podcast will help you get to grips with the content. You can also access this podcast for free on the internet www.edexcel.com/BTEC or via the iTunes store.

Your book is just part of the exciting resources from Edexcel to help you succeed in your BTEC course.

Visit www.edexcel.com/BTEC or www.pearsonfe.co.uk/videopodcast for more details.

BTEC's own resources

1 Principles of anatomy and physiology in sport

Have you ever wondered how your body is able to undertake a range of sport and exercise activities? This unit investigates how the parts of the human body are pieced together, what they are made of and how they work whether you are a rugby player, footballer, sprinter, marathon runner, cyclist or canoeist.

As a sport and exercise scientist, your knowledge of the principles of anatomy and physiology of sport are important. This unit introduces you to the basic structures and functions of four key systems of the human body. You will examine the structure and function of the skeletal and muscular systems and their role in bringing about movement in sport and exercise. You will investigate the structure and functions of the cardiovascular and respiratory systems, and develop an understanding of why the heart works as it does and how it combines with the lungs to allow athletes to cope with the demands of sport and exercise. You will also look at the three different energy systems and the sports in which they are predominantly used.

Learning outcomes

After completing this unit you should:

1. know the structure and function of the skeletal system
2. know the structure and function of the muscular system
3. know the structure and function of the cardiovascular system
4. know the structure and function of the respiratory system
5. know the different types of energy systems.

Assessment and grading criteria

This table shows you what you must do in order to achieve a pass, merit or distinction grade, and where you can find activities in this book to help you.

To achieve a **pass** grade the evidence must show that the learner is able to:	To achieve a **merit** grade the evidence must show that, in addition to the pass criteria, the learner is able to:	To achieve a **distinction** grade the evidence must show that, in addition to the pass and merit criteria, the learner is able to:
P1 describe the structure and function of the skeletal system **Assessment activity 1.1, page 13**		
P2 describe the different classifications of joints **Assessment activity 1.1, page 13**		
P3 identify the location of the major muscles in the human body **Assessment activity 1.2, page 20**		
P4 describe the function of the muscular system and the different fibre types **Assessment activity 1.2, page 20**	**M1** explain the function of the muscular system and the different fibre types **Assessment activity 1.2, page 20**	**D1** analyse the function of the muscular system and the different fibre types **Assessment activity 1.2, page 20**
P5 describe the structure and function of the cardiovascular system **Assessment activity 1.3, page 25**	**M2** explain the function of the cardiovascular system **Assessment activity 1.3, page 25**	
P6 describe the structure and function of the respiratory system **Assessment activity 1.4, page 30**	**M3** explain the function of the respiratory system **Assessment activity 1.4, page 30**	
P7 describe the three different energy systems and their use in sport and exercise activities **Assessment activity 1.5, page 34**	**M4** explain the three different energy systems and their use in sport and exercise activities **Assessment activity 1.5, page 34**	**D2** analyse the three different energy systems and their use in sport and exercise activities **Assessment activity 1.5, page 34**

How you will be assessed

This unit will be internally assessed by a range of assignments that will be designed and graded by your tutor. Your assessment tasks will be designed to allow you to demonstrate your understanding of the unit learning outcomes and relate to what you should be able to do after completing this unit. Your assignments could be in the form of:

- presentations
- practical tasks
- written assignments.

Gemma Stewart, a sports enthusiast

In this unit I learned that there are several systems that interact in a complex way to bring my body into action during sport and exercise. As a keen sports participant it has helped me to appreciate and understand how my body works and I have been able to apply what I have learned to understanding my performance in sport and exercise. I particularly enjoyed exploring the different energy systems and those involved in the different sports I take part in.

The practical activities for this unit have given me a better understanding of the muscle groups worked by the exercises in my gym programme.

There is a lot of complex information to learn in understanding the principles of anatomy and physiology in sport.

Over to you

- What aspects of the unit might you find most challenging?
- What preparation could you do to make the learning of these complex systems an easier task?

1. Know the structure and function of the skeletal system

Analysis of sporting movements

In small groups, think of a range of sporting movements, for example, kicking a ball in rugby or football or shooting a goal in netball or basketball.

Identify the bones and muscles involved in these movements.

Discuss your findings to examine a wide range of sporting movements as a whole class.

1.1 Structure of the skeletal system

The skeletal system is made up of bones, cartilage and joints. Without bones, humans would be shapeless heaps of muscle and tissue, unable to get up off the floor. You need to know how the structure and function of the skeletal system contribute to the vast range of motion required to participate in sport.

Your skeleton provides a framework that supports your muscles and skin and protects your internal organs. It is made up of 206 bones, which are divided into two groups: 80 form your axial skeleton – the long axis of your body; the other 126 form your appendicular skeleton – the bones that are attached to this axis.

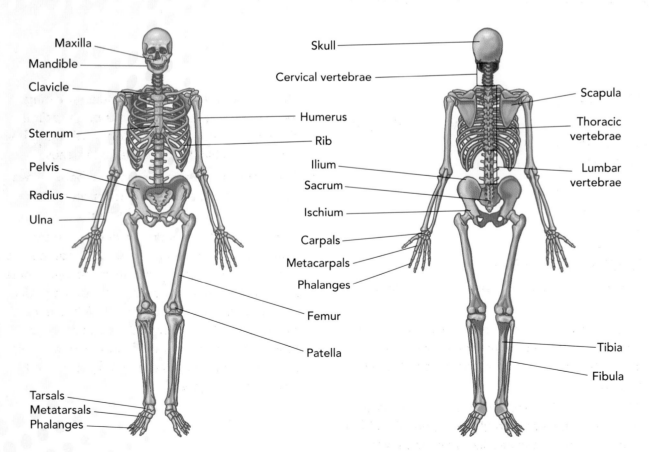

Figure 1.1: Bones of the human skeleton

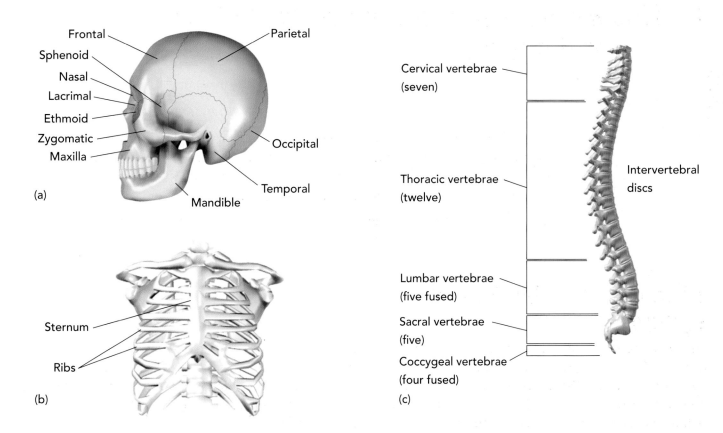

Figure 1.2: The axial skeleton: (a) the skull, (b) the thorax and (c) the vertebral column

Axial skeleton

This forms the main axis or core of your skeletal system and consists of the:

a) skull (cranium and facial bones)

b) thorax (sternum and ribs)

c) vertebral column.

See Figure 1.2 above.

Appendicular skeleton

The appendicular skeleton consists of the following parts (see Figure 1.3 on page 6).

a) 60 bones form the upper limbs. Each upper limb is made up of one humerus, one radius, one ulna, eight carpals, five metacarpals and fourteen phalanges.

b) 60 bones form the lower limbs. Each lower limb is made up of one femur (thigh bone), one tibia (shin bone), one fibula, one patella (kneecap), seven tarsals, five metatarsals and fourteen phalanges.

These bones are designed for weight-bearing, locomotion and maintaining an upright posture. They need to have a higher degree of strength and stability than the bones of the upper limbs.

c) The shoulder girdle consists of four bones – two clavicles and two scapulae – which connect the limbs of the upper body to the thorax.

d) The pelvic girdle is made of three bones: the ilium, pubis and ischium. These fuse together with age and are collectively known as the innominate bone. The principal function of the pelvic girdle is to provide a solid base through which to transmit the weight of the upper body. It also provides attachment for the powerful muscles of the lower back and legs, and protects the digestive and reproductive organs.

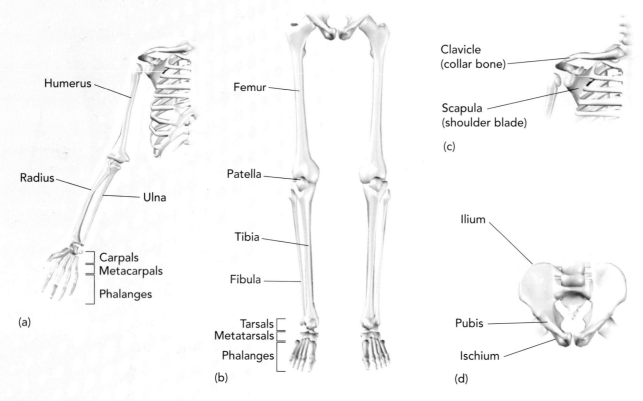

Figure 1.3: The appendicular skeleton: (a) the upper limbs, (b) the lower limbs, (c) the shoulder girdle and (d) the pelvis

Types of major bone

Bones vary in shape and size according to their location and function. They can be classified as follows:

- **Long bones** are found in the limbs. They have a shaft known as the diaphysis and two expanded ends known as the epiphysis (see Figure 1.4).
- **Short bones** are small, light, strong, cube-shaped bones consisting of cancellous bone surrounded by a thin layer of compact bone. The carpals and tarsals of the wrists and ankles are examples of short bones (see Figure 1.5).
- **Flat bones** are thin, flattened and slightly curved, and have a large surface area, examples include the scapulae, sternum and cranium (see Figure 1.6).
- **Sesamoid bones** have a specialised function. They are usually found within a tendon such as the patella in the knee.
- **Irregular bones** have complex shapes that fit none of the categories above. The bones of the spine are a good example (see Figure 1.7).

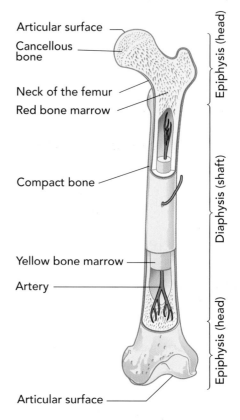

Figure 1.4: Long bones include the bones of the lower limbs, such as the femur, tibia and fibula

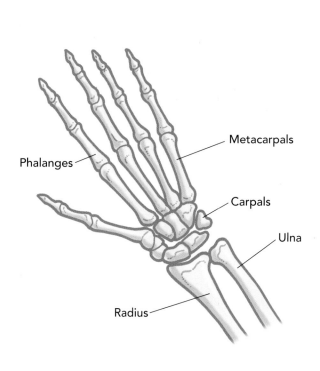

Figure 1.5: The carpals of the hand are examples of short bones

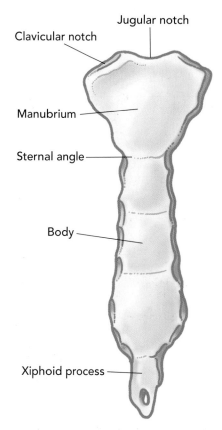

Figure 1.6: The sternum is an example of a flat bone

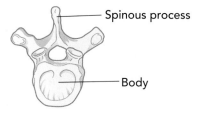

Figure 1.7: The vertebrae of the spine are examples of irregular bones

Location of major bones

Many terms are used to describe the position and location of anatomical structures; some are described in Table 1.1.

Term	Meaning
Anterior	To the front or in front
Posterior	To the rear or behind
Medial	Towards the midline
Lateral	Away from the midline
Proximal	Near to the root or origin
Distal	Away from the root or origin
Superior	Above
Inferior	Below

Table 1.1: Main anatomical terms

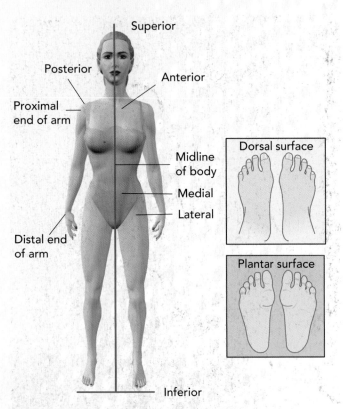

Figure 1.8: Anatomical positions

Cranium – a box-like cavity that contains and protects the brain. It consists of interlinking segments of bone that fuse together during the first few years of life.

Clavicles (collar bones) – the long, slim bones that form the anterior part of the shoulder girdle. This provides a strong and mobile attachment for the arms.

Ribs – long, flat bones. There are twelve pairs in all. The first seven are known as true ribs, as each is joined directly to the sternum. The remaining five pairs are known as false ribs.

Sternum (breast bone) – the elongated, flat bone that runs down the centre of the chest, from the base of the neck to the abdominal wall.

Humerus – the largest bone of the upper limbs. It is a long bone, the head of which articulates with the scapula to form the shoulder joint. The distal end **articulates** with the radius and ulna to form the elbow joint.

Key term

Articulation – the meeting of two or more bones.

Radius and ulna – the ulna is the longer of the two bones of the forearm. The ulna and radius articulate distally with the wrist. The convex shape of the radius allows it to move around the ulna to bring about pronation (turning) of the hand.

Scapulae (shoulder blades) – large, triangular, flat bones that form the posterior part of the shoulder girdle.

Ilium – the bony structure at the base of the spine that provides the sockets for the hip joints and supports the lower abdominal organs. There are three fused irregular pelvic bones collectively known as the innominate bone on each side of the pelvic girdle. The ilium is the upper and largest of these three bones. The upper edge of the ilium is known as the iliac crest.

Pubis (pubic bone) – forms the lower anterior part of the innominate bone.

Ischium – bone situated below the ilium that forms the lower posterior part of the innominate bone.

Carpals – the eight small bones that make up the wrist. They are irregular, small bones arranged in two rows of four. They fit closely together and are kept in place by ligaments.

Metacarpals – five long cylindrical bones in the palm of the hand, one corresponding to each digit. These run from the carpal bones of the wrist to the base of each digit in the hand.

Phalanges – the bones that make up the skeleton of the thumbs, fingers and toes. Most fingers and toes have three phalanges, but the thumbs and big toes have two. The phalanges at the tips of the fingers and toes are known as distal phalanges, whereas those that articulate with the bones of the hands and feet are called proximal phalanges.

Femur – the longest and strongest bone in the body. The head fits into the socket of the pelvis to form the hip joint; the lower end joins the tibia to form the knee joint.

Patella (kneecap) – the large, triangular sesamoid bone found in the quadriceps femoris tendon. It protects the knee joint.

Tibia and fibula – bones that form the long bones of the lower leg. The tibia is the inner and thicker bone, also known as the shin bone. The upper end of the tibia joins the femur to form the knee joint, while the lower end forms part of the ankle joint. The fibula is the outer, thinner bone of the lower leg; it does not reach the knee, but its lower end does form part of the ankle joint.

Tarsals – the foot and heel are formed from seven bones known collectively as the tarsals and often referred to as the midfoot and hindfoot. Along with the tibia and fibula, they form the ankle joint. They are short and irregular. The calcaneus, or heel bone, is the largest tarsal bone. It helps to support the weight of the body and provides attachment for the calf muscles via the Achilles tendon.

Metatarsals – five metatarsals form the dorsal surface of the foot, with 14 phalanges forming the toes. These collectively make up the forefoot. The base of each metatarsal articulates with one or more tarsal bones and the head of one phalange. The forefoot is responsible for bearing a great deal of weight and balances pressure through the balls of the feet. The metatarsals are a common site of fracture in sport.

Vertebral column

The vertebral column, also known as the spine or backbone, extends from the base of the cranium to the pelvis, providing a central axis for the body. It is made up of 33 irregular bones called vertebrae.

The vertebral column accounts for around 40 per cent of a person's overall height. The vertebrae are held together by powerful ligaments. These allow little movement between adjacent vertebrae, but afford a considerable degree of flexibility along the spine as a whole.

The vertebral column has many functions. It protects the spinal cord and supports the ribcage. The larger vertebrae of the lumbar region support a large amount of body weight. The flatter thoracic vertebrae offer attachment for the large muscles of the back and the curves of the spine – four in all. These, along with the intervertebral discs, receive and distribute impact associated with the dynamic functioning of the body in action, reducing shock.

Vertebrae

These increase in size from the top down, and can be classified as follows:

- cervical vertebrae (in the neck)
- thoracic vertebrae (in the chest region)
- lumbar vertebrae (in the small of the back)
- sacral vertebrae (fused vertebrae that form the sacrum)
- coccygeal vertebrae (fused vertebrae that form the coccyx).

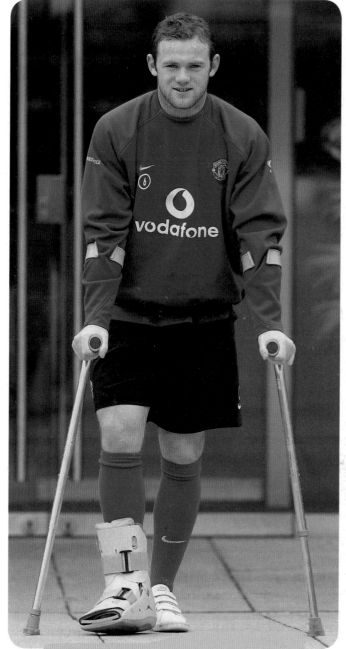

The metatarsals are often broken by football players.
Can you think of other sports where common injuries occur?

There are 24 movable vertebrae in all, separated by intervertebral discs. These padded discs act as shock absorbers and give the vertebral column a degree of flexibility. The cervical and lumbar regions of the spine are the most vulnerable to injury as a result of sport and exercise.

Cervical – the vertebrae of the neck. The first two are known as the atlas (C1) and the axis (C2). They form a pivot joint that allows the head and neck to move freely. These are the smallest and most vulnerable vertebrae of the vertebral column.

Thoracic – the vertebrae of the mid-spine, which articulate with the ribs. They lie in the thorax, a dome-shaped structure that protects the heart and lungs.

Lumbar – the largest of the movable vertebrae, situated in the lower back. They support more weight than other vertebrae and provide attachment for many of the muscles of the back. The discs between these vertebrae produce a concave curve in the back.

Sacrum – five sacral vertebrae are fused to form the sacrum, a triangular bone located below the lumbar vertebrae. It forms the back wall of the pelvic girdle, sitting between the two hip bones. The upper part connects with the last lumbar vertebra and the bottom part with the coccyx.

Coccyx – at the bottom of the vertebral column there are four coccygeal vertebrae, which are fused to form the coccyx or tail bone.

1.2 Function of the skeletal system

Your skeleton performs a number of mechanical and physiological functions.

Support – collectively, your bones give your body shape and provide the supporting framework for the soft tissues of your body.

Protection – the bones of your skeleton surround and protect vital tissues and organs in your body. Your skull protects your brain, your heart and lungs are protected by your thorax, your vertebral column protects your delicate spinal cord and your pelvis protects your abdominal and reproductive organs.

Attachment for skeletal muscle – parts of your skeleton provide a surface for your skeletal muscles to attach to, allowing you to move. Tendons attach muscles to bone, which provides leverage. Muscles pulling on bones act as levers and movement occurs at the joints so that you can walk, run, jump, throw etc., but you should remember that the type of joint determines the type of movement possible.

Source of blood cell production – your bones are not completely solid, as this would make your skeleton heavy and difficult to move. Blood vessels feed the centre of your bones and stored within them is bone marrow. The marrow of your long bones is continually producing red and white blood cells. This is an essential function as large numbers of blood cells, particularly red cells, die every minute.

Store of minerals – bone is a reservoir for minerals such as calcium and phosphorus, essential for bone growth and the maintenance of bone health. These minerals are stored and released into the bloodstream as required, facilitating the balance of minerals in your body.

Joints

You have seen that your skeleton is made up of bones that support and protect your body. For movement to occur, the bones must be linked. A joint is formed where two or more bones meet. This is known as an articulation. There are three types of joint, classified according to the degree of movement they allow: fixed, slightly movable and synovial.

Fixed

Fixed joints, also known as fibrous or immovable joints, do not move. They interlock and overlap and are held together by bands of tough, fibrous tissue. An example is between the plates in your cranium.

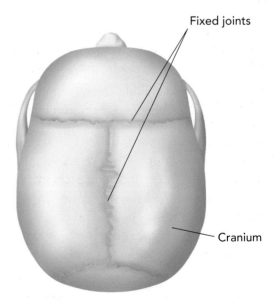

Figure 1.9: Fixed joints in the cranium

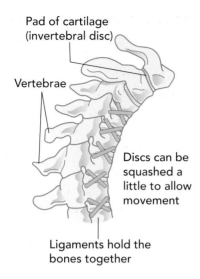

Figure 1.10: A slightly movable joint in the vertebral column

Slightly movable

Slightly movable or cartilaginous joints allow slight movement. The ends of the bone are covered in articular or hyaline cartilage (a smooth, shiny covering that reduces friction) which is separated by pads of white fibrocartilage (a tough cartilage that is capable of absorbing considerable loads). Slight movement at these articulating surfaces is made possible because the pads of cartilage compress, for example between most vertebrae (see Figure 1.10).

Synovial

Also termed freely movable, synovial joints offer the highest level of mobility at a joint. They consist of two or more bones, the ends of which are covered with articular cartilage, which allows the bones to move over each other with minimum friction. They make up most of the joints of your limbs. They are completely surrounded by a fibrous capsule, lined with a synovial membrane, whose purpose is to secrete fluid known as synovial fluid into the joint cavity to lubricate and nourish the joint. The joint capsule is held together by tough bands of connective tissue known as ligaments. This provides the strength to avoid dislocation, while being flexible enough to allow movement.

All synovial joints contain the following features:

- an outer sleeve or joint capsule to help to hold the bones in place and protect the joint

- a synovial membrane: the capsule lining that oozes a viscous liquid called synovial fluid: this lubricates the joint

- a joint cavity: the gap between the articulating bones where synovial fluid pools to lubricate the joint

- articular cartilage on the ends of the bones: to provide a smooth and slippery covering to stop the bones knocking or grinding together

- ligaments to hold the bones together and keep them in place.

Synovial joints can be divided into the following groups, according to the type of movement they allow.

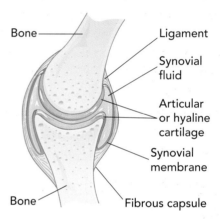

Figure 1.11: A synovial joint in the knee

Hinge

These allow movement in one direction only. Elbow and knee joints are typical examples.

Ball and socket

The round end of one bone fits into a cup-shaped socket in the other bone, allowing movement in all directions. Examples include hip and shoulder joints.

Ellipsoid

Also known as condyloid joints, these are a modified version of a ball and socket joint, in which a bump on one bone sits in the hollow formed by another. Movement is backwards and forwards and from side to side. Ligaments often prevent rotation. An example is the wrist joint.

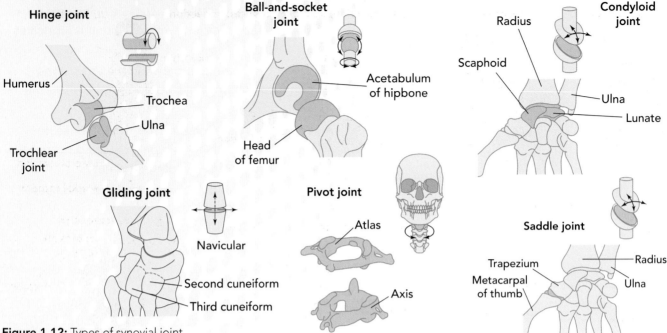

Figure 1.12: Types of synovial joint

Gliding

These joints allow movement over a flat surface in all directions, but this is restricted by ligaments or a bony prominence, for example in the carpals and tarsals of wrists and ankles.

Pivot

A ring of one bone fits over a peg of another, allowing controlled rotational movement, such as the joint of the atlas and axis in the neck.

Saddle

These are similar to ellipsoid joints but the surfaces are concave and convex. Movement occurs backwards and forwards and from side to side, like that at the base of the thumb.

Types of movement

When studying the body in action it is important to understand the range of movements that joints are capable of performing. The degree of movement at joints varies between individuals and depends on many factors, including: the shape and contour of the articulating surfaces, the tension of the supporting connective tissue and muscles that surround the joint, the amount of soft tissue surrounding the joint and the individual's age.

Flexion – bending a limb, reducing the angle at the joint, such as bending your arm in a bicep curl action or preparing to kick a football.

Extension – straightening a limb to increase the angle at the joint, such as straightening your arm to return to your starting position in a bicep curl action or taking a shot in netball.

Abduction – movement away from the body, such as at the hip in a side-step in gymnastics.

Adduction – movement towards the body, such as pulling on the oars while rowing.

Rotation – circular movement of a limb. Rotation occurs at the shoulder joint during a tennis serve.

Pronation – an inward rotation of the forearm so that the palm of the hand is facing backwards and downwards. This occurs at the wrist joint during a table tennis forehand topspin shot.

Supination – an outward rotation of the forearm so that the palm of the hand is facing forwards and upwards. This occurs at the wrist joint during a table tennis backhand topspin shot.

Plantar flexion – a movement that points the toes downwards by straightening the ankle. This occurs when jumping to shoot in basketball.

Dorsiflexion – an upward movement, as in moving the foot to pull the toes towards the knee in walking.

Hyper-extension – involves movement beyond the normal anatomical position in a direction opposite to flexion. This occurs at the spine when a cricketer arches his or her back when approaching the crease to bowl.

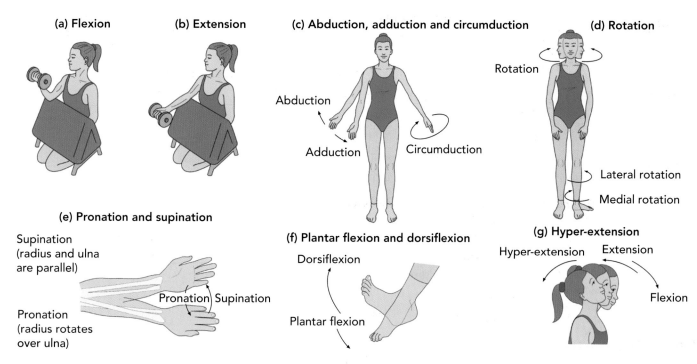

(a) Flexion

(b) Extension

(c) Abduction, adduction and circumduction

Abduction

Adduction

Circumduction

(d) Rotation

Rotation

Lateral rotation

Medial rotation

(e) Pronation and supination

Supination
(radius and ulna
are parallel)

Pronation Supination

Pronation
(radius rotates
over ulna)

(f) Plantar flexion and dorsiflexion

Dorsiflexion

Plantar flexion

(g) Hyper-extension

Hyper-extension Extension

Flexion

Figure 1.13: Anatomical and biomechanical terms relating to muscle action

Assessment activity 1.1   P1 P2 BTEC

A fitness instructor regularly draws on anatomical knowledge to design and develop fitness programmes for clients.

1. Draw two large tables to describe the structure and function of the axial and appendicular skeletons. Your descriptions should include the location of all the major bones of the skeleton and their different types. **P1**

2. Describe the different classifications of joints and the range of movement each provides. **P2**

Grading tips

P1 Describe the axial and appendicular skeletons and locate and name all the following major bones: cranium, clavicle, ribs, sternum, humerus, radius, ulna, scapula, ilium, pubis, ischium, carpals, metacarpals, phalanges, femur, patella, tibia, fibula, tarsals, metatarsals, vertebral column, vertebrae – cervical, thoracic, lumbar, sacrum and coccyx.

P2 You must be able to describe all three classifications of joint and the movement available at each, including the movement allowed at each of the synovial joints. Examine each of the three classifications of joints, including all six synovial joints, and explain how and why the range of movement allowed at these joints differs. Use sporting examples to support your explanation.

PLTS

Researching the structure and function of the skeletal system and examining the range of movement at joints using a variety of sporting examples will evidence your development as an **independent enquirer**.

Functional skills

Describing the structure and function of the axial and appendicular skeletons and the different classifications of joints and their range of movement will demonstrate your **English** skills.

2. Know the structure and function of the muscular system

2.1 The muscular system

Approximately 40 per cent of your body mass is muscle, whose key function is to move your bones. The muscles that move your bones during activity are skeletal muscles. There are over 640 named muscles in the human body. In this section you will learn about the principal skeletal muscles, their associated actions, and muscle fibre types.

Your muscles are generously supplied with arteries to convey nutrients and oxygen, and veins to remove waste products. Your skeletal muscles work to move either parts of your body or your body as a whole. Most sporting movements involve the coordinated action of muscles rather than muscles working in isolation.

Major muscles

Remembering the names, locations and actions of all the major muscles is a huge task. Therefore, from a sport and exercise perspective, the main ones you should remember are outlined in Table 1.2 on page 15.

Remember

To bring your body into action, different parts of your muscular skeletal system work under the influence of your nervous system to produce voluntary movements. Your skeletal muscles contract when stimulated via impulses from your nervous system. At the point of contraction your muscles shorten and pull on the bones to which they are attached. When a muscle contracts, one end normally remains stationary while the other end is drawn towards it. The end that remains stationary is known as the **origin**, and the end that moves is called the **insertion**.

Key terms

Origin – the end of a muscle that is attached to the immovable (or less movable) bone.

Insertion – the end of a muscle that is attached to the movable bone.

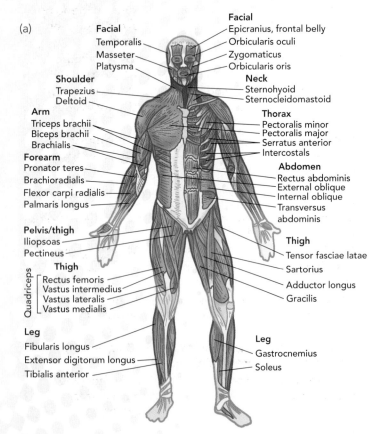

(a)

Facial
Temporalis
Masseter
Platysma

Shoulder
Trapezius
Deltoid

Arm
Triceps brachii
Biceps brachii
Brachialis

Forearm
Pronator teres
Brachioradialis
Flexor carpi radialis
Palmaris longus

Pelvis/thigh
Iliopsoas
Pectineus

Thigh
Quadriceps
Rectus femoris
Vastus intermedius
Vastus lateralis
Vastus medialis

Leg
Fibularis longus
Extensor digitorum longus
Tibialis anterior

Facial
Epicranius, frontal belly
Orbicularis oculi
Zygomaticus
Orbicularis oris

Neck
Sternohyoid
Sternocleidomastoid

Thorax
Pectoralis minor
Pectoralis major
Serratus anterior
Intercostals

Abdomen
Rectus abdominis
External oblique
Internal oblique
Transversus abdominis

Thigh
Tensor fasciae latae
Sartorius
Adductor longus
Gracilis

Leg
Gastrocnemius
Soleus

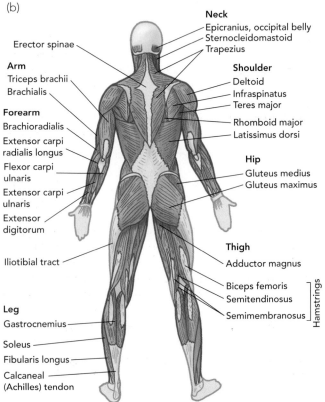

(b)

Erector spinae

Arm
Triceps brachii
Brachialis

Forearm
Brachioradialis
Extensor carpi radialis longus
Flexor carpi ulnaris
Extensor carpi ulnaris
Extensor digitorum

Iliotibial tract

Leg
Gastrocnemius
Soleus
Fibularis longus
Calcaneal (Achilles) tendon

Neck
Epicranius, occipital belly
Sternocleidomastoid
Trapezius

Shoulder
Deltoid
Infraspinatus
Teres major
Rhomboid major
Latissimus dorsi

Hip
Gluteus medius
Gluteus maximus

Thigh
Adductor magnus
Biceps femoris
Semitendinosus
Semimembranosus
Hamstrings

Figure 1.14: (a) Anterior muscular system and (b) posterior muscular system

Muscle	Function	Location	Origin	Insertion	Exercise/Activity
Biceps	Flexes lower arm	Inside upper arm	Scapula	Radius	Arm curls, chin-ups
Triceps	Extends lower arm	Outside upper arm	Humerus and scapula	Olecranon process	Press-ups, dips, overhead pressing
Deltoids	Abducts, flexes and extends upper arm	Forms cap of shoulder	Clavicle, scapula and acromion	Humerus	Forward, lateral and back-arm raises, overhead lifting
Pectorals	Flexes and adducts upper arm	Large chest muscle	Sternum, clavicle and rib cartilage	Humerus	All pressing movements
Rectus abdominis	Flexion and rotation of lumbar region of vertebral column	'Six-pack' muscle running down abdomen	Pubic crest and symphysis	Xiphoid process	Sit-ups
Quadriceps – rectus femoris – vastus lateralis – vastus medialis – vastus intermedius	Extends lower leg and flexes thigh	Front of thigh	Ilium and femur	Tibia and fibula	Knee bends, squats
Hamstrings – semimem-branosus – semitendinosus – biceps femoris	Flexes lower leg and extends thigh	Back of thigh	Ischium and femur	Tibia and fibula	Extending leg and flexing knee (running)
Gastrocnemius	Plantar flexion, flexes knee	Large calf muscle	Femur	Calcaneus	Running, jumping and standing on tip-toe
Soleus	Plantar flexion	Deep to gastrocnemius	Fibula and tibia	Calcaneus	Running and jumping
Tibialis anterior	Dorsiflexion of foot	Front of tibia on lower leg	Lateral condyle	By tendon to surface of medial cuneiform	All running and jumping exercises
Erector spinae	Extension of spine	Long muscle running either side of spine	Cervical, thoracic and lumbar vertebrae	Cervical, thoracic and lumbar vertebrae	Prime mover of back extension
Teres major	Rotates and abducts humerus	Between scapula and humerus	Posterior surface of scapula	Intertubercular sulcus of humerus	All rowing and pulling movements
Trapezius	Elevates and depresses scapula	Large triangular muscle at top of back	Continuous insertion along acromion	Occipital bone and all thoracic vertebrae	Shrugging and overhead lifting
Latissimus dorsi	Extends and adducts lower arm	Large muscle covering back of lower ribs	Vertebrae and iliac crest	Humerus	Rowing movements
Obliques	Lateral flexion of trunk	Waist	Pubic crest and iliac crest	Fleshy strips to lower eight ribs	Oblique curls
Gluteus maximus	Extends thigh	Large muscle on buttocks	Ilium, sacrum and coccyx	Femur	Knee-bending movements, cycling

Table 1.2: Major muscles and their functions

Types of muscle

There are three main types of muscle tissue in your body:

- **skeletal muscle** – also known as striated or striped muscle because of its striped appearance when viewed under a microscope. This type of muscle is voluntary, which means it is under conscious control.

- **smooth muscle** – an involuntary muscle that works without conscious thought, functioning under the control of your nervous system. It is located in the walls of your digestive system and blood vessels and helps to regulate digestion and blood pressure.

- **cardiac muscle** – found only in the wall of your heart. It works continuously. It is involuntary, which means it is not under conscious control. It is composed of a specialised type of striated tissue that has its own blood supply. Its contractions help to force blood through your blood vessels to all parts of your body. Each contraction and relaxation of your heart muscle as a whole represents one heartbeat.

2.2 Function of the muscular system

Muscles must cross the joints they move. When a muscle contracts, it exerts a pulling force on the bones, causing them to move together around the joint. The bones act like levers and the joint like the fulcrum. If a muscle did not cross a joint, no movement could occur.

Under normal circumstances, muscles are in a state of partial contraction, ready to react to a stimulus from your nervous system. Without this muscle tone, your body would collapse. When a stimulus from the nerve supply occurs, muscle fibres work on an 'all or nothing' basis – either contracting completely or not at all.

The strength of muscle contraction in response to the stimulus depends on the number of muscle fibres brought into use, a process known as muscle fibre recruitment. To bring about contraction, the muscle requires oxygen and a fuel source, either fat or glucose. Muscle cells use up much more energy than other cells in your body and convert chemical energy into mechanical energy. When you exercise, your muscles use energy at a rate that is directly proportional to the intensity of the exercise. If this energy is not replaced as it is used up, your muscles are unable to maintain their work rate and you have to reduce the intensity of the activity or stop it.

Antagonistic muscle pairs

Muscles do not work in isolation. They are assembled in groups and work together to bring about movement. They act only by contracting and pulling. They do not push, although they are able to contract without shortening, and so hold a joint firm and fixed in a certain position. When the contraction passes off, the muscles become soft but do not lengthen until stretched by the contraction of the opposing muscles. They can act in the following ways to bring about movement.

Activity: Muscles at work

When your body is in action during sport and exercise, your muscles shorten, remain the same length or lengthen.

1. Pick up a dumb-bell (or a bag of sugar or a heavy book). Bend your arm at the elbow to bring your forearm up towards your shoulder in a bicep curl action.

2. Think about what your bicep muscle appears to be doing as you bring the weight closer to your shoulder. Has the muscle shortened, remained the same length or lengthened?

3. Return the dumb-bell to the starting position and consider what has to happen to your muscle to allow this action to take place. Do you think the bicep shortened, remained the same length or lengthened?

4. Curl the arm again, but this time only to a 90° angle. Hold your object in this position for a sustained period of time. What does the bicep muscle appear to be doing now? Do you think it is shortening, remaining the same length or lengthening?

Agonist

The muscle that shortens to move a joint is called the agonist or prime mover. This is the muscle principally responsible for the movement taking place – the contracting muscle.

Antagonist

The muscle that relaxes in opposition to the agonist is called the antagonist. This is the muscle responsible for the opposite movement, and the one that relaxes as the agonist works. If it did not relax, movement could not take place. Antagonists exert a 'braking' control over the movement.

Synergist

Synergists are muscles that work together to enable the agonists to operate more effectively. They work with the agonists to control and direct movement by modifying or altering the direction of pull on the agonists to the most advantageous position.

Fixator

These muscles stop any unwanted movement throughout the whole body by fixing or stabilising the joint or joints involved. Fixator muscles stabilise the origin so that the agonist can achieve maximum and effective contraction.

Take a complex action like riding a bike: your quadriceps and calf muscles are the agonists, the contracting muscles. The antagonists are the muscles of your hamstrings and shins. Other leg muscles act as synergists and muscles of your back and abdomen act as fixators to stop you falling off.

Figure 1.15: Riding a bike involves a complex series of muscular movements

Remember

Each agonist must contract just sufficiently, and each antagonist must relax equally to allow movement to take place smoothly without jerking. This concerted action of many muscles is called muscle coordination.

📱 Types of contraction

Muscle contraction can be described as isometric, concentric, eccentric or isokinetic.

Isometric

During an isometric contraction the length of a muscle does not change and the joint angle does not alter. The muscle is actively engaged in holding a static position, for example when stopping halfway up in a press-up or squat, or holding an abdominal plank position. This type of muscle work is easy to undertake but rapidly leads to fatigue. It can cause sharp increases in blood pressure as blood flow is reduced. See Figure 1.16.

Concentric

This occurs when a muscle shortens against a resistance, for example in a bicep curl. The brachialis and bicep shorten, bringing your forearm towards your upper arm. Concentric contractions are sometimes known as the positive phase of muscle contraction. See Figure 1.17.

Eccentric

This occurs when a muscle returns to its normal length after shortening against resistance. Using the bicep curl as an example, this is the controlled lowering of your arm to its starting position. At this point your muscles are working against gravity and act like a braking mechanism. This contraction can be easier to perform, but it does produce muscle soreness. Eccentric contractions occur in many sporting and daily activities. Walking downstairs and running downhill involve eccentric contraction of your quadriceps muscles. Eccentric contraction can be a significant factor in the stimulus that promotes gains in muscle strength and size. Eccentric contractions are sometimes known as the negative phase of muscle contraction.

Isokinetic

During isokinetic contractions the muscle contracts and shortens at a constant speed. For this type of strength training you need specialised equipment that detects when the muscle is speeding up and can increase the load.

Figure 1.16: The rings in men's gymnastics demonstrate many isometric contractions

Figure 1.17: In a concentric contraction the muscle shortens

Activity: Movement and resistance

1. Lie on your back with both knees bent and both feet on the floor in a curl-up position. Place your hands on your thighs and slowly raise your head and shoulders, sliding your hands up your thighs until they touch your knees. Slowly return to the floor. Repeat this action six to eight times.

   a) Consider the type of movement you have just performed. What forms the resistance for this activity?

   b) There are two phases to this movement. Which phase can be described as the positive phase?

   c) Which joints and muscles are involved in this movement?

2. Hold a set of light dumb-bells or two small books at your sides. Keeping your elbows slightly bent but the arms long, with the palms facing downwards, raise your arms until your hands are at eye level. Slowly return the weights under control to your sides. Repeat this action six to eight times.

3. Consider the type of movement you have just performed. What forms the resistance for this activity?

4. Name the muscle groups targeted by this exercise. Are any other muscles working to bring about this movement?

Take it further

Health and fitness equipment targets specific muscle groups. Visit your local leisure centre or health club to analyse its fitness equipment. Draw up a table of your findings to include information on:

- the range of equipment available
- the muscle groups targeted by each piece of equipment and the actions they bring about.

metabolism and are recruited for higher-intensity, shorter-duration activities. They are important in sports that include many stop-go or change-of-pace activities.

Key terms

Aerobic – requiring oxygen.

Anaerobic – not requiring oxygen.

Case study: Peter, athletic sprinter

Peter is a member of his college's athletics sprint team. Before a race he spends some time warming up: he walks around the start area, shakes his arms and legs, and does a few strides and stretches. The starter calls the athletes to the line. Peter settles into his starting blocks, the starter announces the set position and Peter waits for the gun to sound. When it fires, he bursts out of the blocks and runs as hard as he can all the way through the tape, recording a 100 metres personal best time.

- What muscle fibres were creating the force required while Peter was walking around the start area?
- During the entire warm-up, were all muscle fibres recruited acting maximally?
- When Peter burst out of the blocks and sprinted towards the finish line, which muscle fibres were recruited?

Fibre types

All skeletal muscles contain a mixture of fibre types. The mix of fibres varies from individual to individual, and within the individual from muscle group to muscle group. To a large extent this fibre mix is inherited. However, training can influence the efficiency of these different fibre types. Two main types of striated skeletal muscle can be distinguished on the basis of their speed of contraction: Type 1 (slow twitch) and Type 2 (fast twitch).

Characteristics of Type 1 muscle fibres

Type 1 (slow-twitch) fibres contract slowly with less force. They are slow to fatigue and suited to longer duration **aerobic** activities. They have a rich blood supply and contain many mitochondria to sustain aerobic metabolism. Type 1 fibres have a high capacity for aerobic respiration. They are recruited for lower-intensity, longer-duration activities such as long-distance running and swimming.

Characteristics of Type 2a muscle fibres

Type 2a fibres (also called fast-twitch or fast-oxidative fibres) are fast-contracting and able to produce a great force, but are also resistant to fatigue. These fibres are suited to middle-distance events.

Characteristics of Type 2b muscle fibres

Type 2b fibres (also called fast-twitch or fast-glycolytic fibres) contract rapidly and have the capacity to produce large amounts of force, but they fatigue more readily, making them better suited to **anaerobic** activity. They depend almost entirely on anaerobic

Sports associated with each fibre type

All types of muscle fibre are used in all types of activity. Although Type 1 fibres are particularly adapted to low-intensity aerobic endurance work, they are generally employed at the beginning of exercise, regardless of the intensity of effort. Type 2 fibres adapt to high-intensity anaerobic exercise involving explosive or powerful movements, but are increasingly employed as fatigue sets in during low-intensity endurance work. Table 1.3 identifies the sports associated with the different fibre types.

Characteristic of muscle fibre types	Type 1	Type 2a	Type 2b
Colour	Red	Red	White
Contraction speed	Contract slowly	Contract rapidly (but not as fast as Type 2b)	Contract rapidly
Aerobic or anaerobic	Aerobic	Aerobic	Anaerobic
Type of activity	Endurance-based	Middle-distance	Speed- and strength-based
Endurance	Can contract repeatedly	Fairly resistant to fatigue	Easily exhausted
Force	Exert minimal force	Exert medium force	Exert great force
Type of sports associated with each fibre type	Endurance sports such as running, cycling, swimming, skiing	Middle-distance running such as 800 m and 1500 m	Explosive sports such as sprinting, jumping, throwing, weightlifting

Table 1.3: Characteristics of each muscle fibre type and sports associated with each fibre type

Assessment activity 1.2  **BTEC**

Continuing the theme from Assessment activity 1.1, design and develop a general fitness programme for a client that targets all of the major muscle groups outlined in this unit.

1. Write up the programme on client-friendly programme cards, identifying the location of the muscle groups exercised in the programme. **P3**

2. In a short written account, describe the function of the muscular system and the different types of muscle fibre. **P4**

3. Produce a short PowerPoint presentation to further explain the function of the muscular system and the different fibre types. **M1**

4. Develop your presentation further to analyse the function of the muscular system and the different fibre types. **D1**

Grading tips

P3 Make sure you identify the location of the biceps, triceps, deltoids, pectorals, rectus abdominis, quadriceps, hamstrings, gastrocnemius, soleus, tibialis anterior, erector spinae, teres major, trapezius, latissimus dorsi, obliques and gluteus maximus.

P4 You must be able to describe the function of the muscular system and the three different fibre types (Type 1, Type 2a and Type 2b).

M1 You must be able to explain the function of the muscular system and the three different fibre types (Type 1, Type 2a and Type 2b). Use sporting examples to support your explanations.

D1 Analysing requires you to take a more critical approach to your presentation. You may find it useful to undertake some practical research to support your answer.

PLTS

When you locate the muscle groups exercised in the fitness programme, you will be using your skills as a **reflective learner**.

Functional skills

When you develop and write the fitness programme and also write a short account on the function of the muscular system, you will be demonstrating **English** skills.
Creating a PowerPoint presentation will demonstrate your **ICT** skills.

3. Know the structure and function of the cardiovascular system

Also referred to as the circulatory system, the cardiovascular system consists of the heart, blood vessels and blood. It forms the major transport system in your body which carries food, oxygen and all other essential products to tissue cells, and takes waste products and carbon dioxide away. Oxygen is transported from the lungs to the body tissues, while carbon dioxide is carried from the cells to the lungs for excretion.

3.1 Structure of the cardiovascular system

Heart

The heart is the centre of the cardiovascular system. It is situated in the left-hand side of the chest beneath the sternum. An adult heart weighs approximately 255 grams and is about the size of a closed fist. It is a hollow muscular pump that drives blood into and through the arteries in order to deliver it to the tissues and working muscles.

The heart is surrounded by a twin-layered sac known as the pericardium. The cavity between the layers is filled with pericardial fluid, whose purpose is to prevent friction as the heart beats. The heart wall itself is made up of three layers: the epicardium (the outer layer), myocardium (the strong middle layer that forms most of the heart wall), and the endocardium (the inner layer).

The right side of the heart is separated from the left by a solid wall known as the septum. This prevents the blood on the right side coming into contact with the blood on the left side.

The heart can be thought of as two pumps: the two chambers on the right and the two chambers on the left function separately. The chambers on the right supply blood at a low pressure to the lungs via the pulmonary arteries, arterioles and capillaries, where gaseous exchange takes place. Here carbon dioxide passes from the blood to the alveoli of the lungs and oxygen is taken on board. This blood is then returned to the left side of the heart via the capillaries, **venules** and veins.

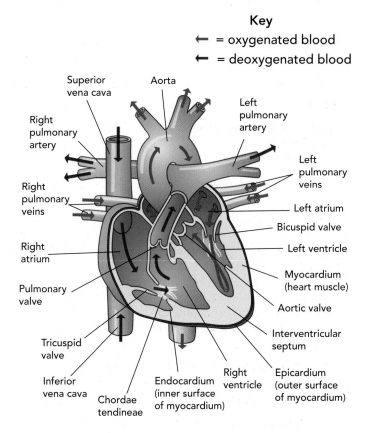

Key
← = oxygenated blood
← = deoxygenated blood

Labels: Superior vena cava, Aorta, Left pulmonary artery, Right pulmonary artery, Left pulmonary veins, Right pulmonary veins, Left atrium, Bicuspid valve, Left ventricle, Right atrium, Myocardium (heart muscle), Pulmonary valve, Aortic valve, Interventricular septum, Tricuspid valve, Inferior vena cava, Chordae tendineae, Endocardium (inner surface of myocardium), Right ventricle, Epicardium (outer surface of myocardium)

Figure 1.18: The heart

When the chambers of the left side of the heart are full, it contracts simultaneously with the right side, acting as a high-pressure pump. It supplies oxygenated blood via the arteries, arterioles, and capillaries to the tissues of the body such as muscle cells. Oxygen passes from the blood to the cells and carbon dioxide (a waste product of energy production) is taken on board. The blood then returns to the right atrium of the heart via the capillaries, venules and veins.

Key term

Venules – have thinner walls than arterioles. They collect blood leaving the capillaries and transport it to the veins.

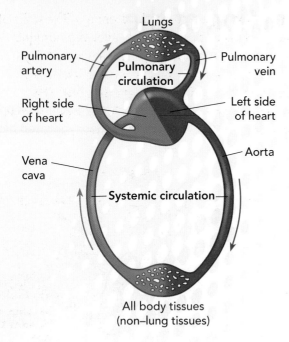

Figure 1.19: Double circulation of blood through the heart

Atria – the upper chambers of the heart. They receive blood returning to your heart from either the body or the lungs. The right atrium receives deoxygenated blood from the superior and inferior vena cava. The left atrium receives oxygenated blood from the left and right pulmonary veins.

Ventricles – the pumping chambers of the heart. They have thicker walls than the atria. The right ventricle pumps blood to the pulmonary circulation for the lungs and the left ventricle pumps blood to the systemic circulation for the body.

Bicuspid (mitral) valve – one of the four valves in the heart, situated between the left atrium and the left ventricle. It allows the blood to flow in one direction only, from the left atrium to the left ventricle.

Tricuspid valve – situated between the right atrium and the right ventricle, it allows blood to flow from the right atrium to the right ventricle.

Aortic valve – situated between the left ventricle and the aorta, prevents backflow from the aorta into the left ventricle.

Pulmonary valve – between the right ventricle and the pulmonary artery, prevents backflow from the pulmonary artery.

Aorta – the body's main artery. It originates in the left ventricle and carries oxygenated blood to all parts of the body except the lungs.

Superior vena cava – a vein that receives deoxygenated blood from the upper body to empty into the right atrium of the heart.

Inferior vena cava – a vein that receives deoxygenated blood from the lower body to empty into the right atrium of the heart.

Pulmonary vein – carries oxygenated blood from the lungs to the left atrium of the heart.

Pulmonary artery – carries deoxygenated blood from the heart back to the lungs. It is the only artery that carries deoxygenated blood.

Blood vessels

As the heart contracts, blood flows around the body in a complex network of vessels. Around 96,000 km of arteries, arterioles, capillaries, venules and veins maintain the blood's circulation throughout the body. The structure of these different vessels within the cardiovascular system is determined by their different functions and the pressure of blood within them.

Blood flowing through the arteries appears bright red, due to its oxygenation. As it moves through the capillaries it drops off oxygen and picks up carbon dioxide. By the time it reaches the veins it is much bluer.

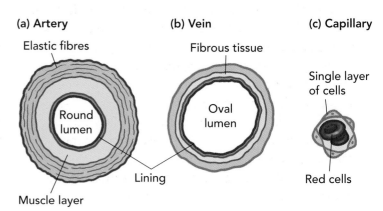

Figure 1.20: Major blood vessels

Arteries

Arteries carry blood away from the heart, and with the exception of the pulmonary artery they carry oxygenated blood. They have two major properties: elasticity and contractility. They have thick muscular walls to carry blood at high speeds under high pressure. When the heart ejects blood into the large arteries, the arteries expand to accommodate the extra blood. They do not require valves as the pressure within them remains high at all times, except at the point where the pulmonary artery leaves the heart.

The smooth muscle surrounding the arteries enables their diameter to be decreased and increased as required. This contractility of the arteries helps to maintain blood pressure in relation to changes in blood flow. The arteries are largely deep, except where they can be felt at a pulse point. These vessels branch into smaller arterioles that ultimately deliver blood to the capillaries.

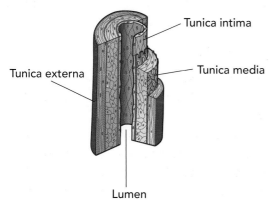

Figure 1.21: Structure of an artery

Arterioles

Arterioles have thinner walls than arteries. They control blood distribution by changing their diameter. This mechanism facilitates adjustment of blood flow to the capillaries in response to differing demands for oxygen. During exercise, muscles require an increased blood flow in order to get extra oxygen. To accommodate this, the diameter of arterioles leading to the muscles dilates. Other areas, like the gut, have their blood flow temporarily reduced to compensate for this, and the diameter of their arterioles is decreased. Arterioles are essentially responsible for controlling blood flow to the capillaries.

Capillaries

Capillaries form an extensive network that connects arteries and veins by uniting arterioles and venules. They are the smallest of all the blood vessels, narrow and very thin. They form an essential part of the vascular system as they bathe the tissues of the body with blood and allow the diffusion of oxygen and nutrients required by the body's cells. Capillaries that surround muscles ensure they get the oxygen and

nutrients they require to produce energy. The walls of capillaries are only one cell thick, allowing nutrients, oxygen and waste products to be transferred. The number of capillaries in muscle may be increased through frequent and appropriate exercise. The pressure of blood within the capillaries is higher than that in veins, but less than in the arteries.

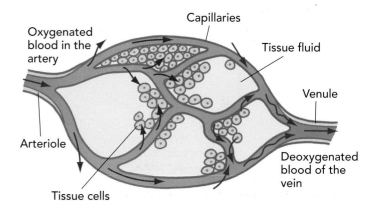

Figure 1.22: The capillary system

Veins

Veins facilitate venous return – the return of deoxygenated blood to the heart. They have thinner walls than arteries and a relatively large diameter. By the time blood reaches the veins, it is flowing slowly and under low pressure. Contracting muscles push the thin walls of the veins inwards to help squeeze the blood back towards the heart. As muscle contractions are intermittent, there are a number of pocket valves in the veins that assist in preventing any backflow when the muscles relax. Veins are mainly close to the surface and can be seen under the skin. They branch into smaller vessels called venules, which extend to the capillary network.

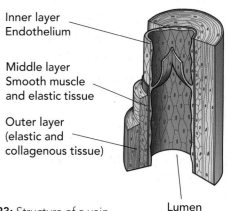

Figure 1.23: Structure of a vein

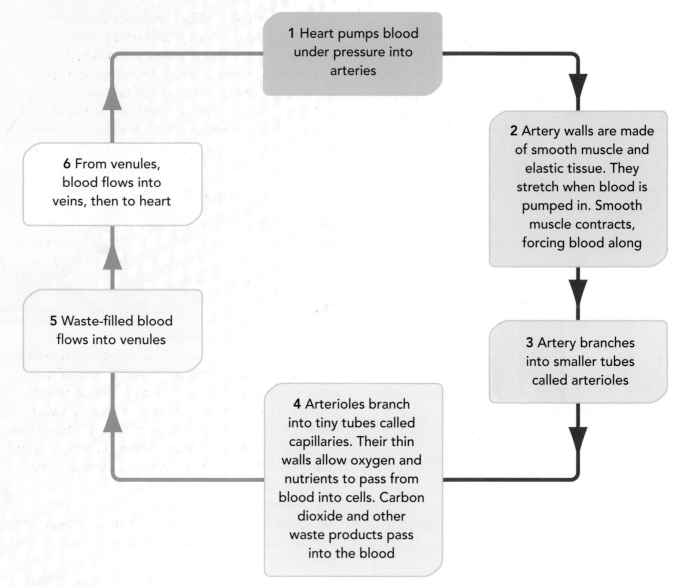

1 Heart pumps blood under pressure into arteries

2 Artery walls are made of smooth muscle and elastic tissue. They stretch when blood is pumped in. Smooth muscle contracts, forcing blood along

6 From venules, blood flows into veins, then to heart

5 Waste-filled blood flows into venules

3 Artery branches into smaller tubes called arterioles

4 Arterioles branch into tiny tubes called capillaries. Their thin walls allow oxygen and nutrients to pass from blood into cells. Carbon dioxide and other waste products pass into the blood

Figure 1.24: How is blood carried around your body?

Remember

- Arteries carry oxygenated blood away from the heart.
- Veins carry deoxygenated blood back to the heart.
- Capillaries connect the veins and arteries.

3.2 Function of the cardiovascular system

Delivery of oxygen and nutrients

The key function of the cardiovascular system is to supply oxygen and nutrients to the tissues of the body via the bloodstream.

Removal of waste products

As well as providing oxygen and nutrients to all the tissues in the body, the circulatory system carries waste products from the tissues to the kidneys and the liver and returns carbon dioxide from the tissues to the lungs.

Thermoregulation

Increased energy expenditure during exercise requires adjustments in blood flow that affect the cardiovascular system. The cardiovascular system is responsible for the distribution and redistribution of heat within your body to maintain thermal balance during exercise.

Vasodilation

During exercise the vascular portion of active muscles increases through dilation of arterioles. This process is known as vasodilation. Vasodilation causes an increase in the diameter of blood vessels to decrease resistance to the flow of blood to the area supplied by the vessels.

Vasoconstriction

Blood vessels can also temporarily shut down blood flow to tissues. This process is known as vasoconstriction and causes a decrease in the diameter of blood vessels. Contraction of involuntary muscle fibres in the vessel walls increases resistance to blood flow.

Function of blood

Blood provides the fluid environment for cells and is the medium by which many materials are carried to and from these cells. The average adult has approximately 4–5 litres of blood. Blood has four principle constituents: plasma, red blood cells (erythrocytes), white blood cells (leucocytes) of which there are different types, and platelets or cell fragments (thrombocytes).

Blood has a number of functions including distribution, regulation and protection. It helps to maintain the body's temperature by absorbing and distributing heat. Life-sustaining nutrients are transported from the intestines to the liver and body cells, and waste products from the tissues are transported to the kidneys. Protective white blood cells, antibodies, hormones and medicines are also transported in the blood.

Oxygen transport

Exercise increases the demand for oxygen. Blood transports oxygen from the lungs to the parts of the body that require it. It also transports metabolic waste from cells to areas of disposal.

Clotting

Clotting is a complex process during which white blood cells form solid clots. A damaged blood vessel wall is covered by a fibrin clot to assist repair of the damaged vessel. Platelets form a plug at the site of damage. Plasma components known as coagulation factors respond to form fibrin strands which strengthen the platelet plug. This is made possible by the constant supply of blood through the cardiovascular system.

Fighting infection

Blood contains antibodies and white blood cells which help defend against viruses and bacteria.

Assessment activity 1.3   BTEC

Part 1: Using detailed diagrams, describe the structure and function of the cardiovascular system. **P5**

Part 2: Using your detailed diagrams, explain the function of the cardiovascular system to an exercise client in the gym environment. Obtain witness statement testimony to evidence that you have successfully undertaken this activity. **M2**

Grading tips

P5 You must be able to label and describe the function of the constituent parts of the cardiovascular system and relate them to the exercise where appropriate.

M2 You must be able to examine the cardiovascular system and explain how each part is designed to meet its function.

4. Know the structure and function of the respiratory system

The respiratory system is responsible for providing oxygen and removing carbon dioxide, heat and water vapours. All living creatures require oxygen and give off carbon dioxide. Oxygen is required for every cell in your body to function.

4.1 Structure of the respiratory system

Air is usually drawn into your body via the nose, but sometimes via the mouth, and passes through a series of airways to reach the lungs. This series of airways is referred to as the respiratory tract, and can be divided into two main parts. The upper respiratory tract includes the nose, nasal cavity, mouth, pharynx and larynx; and the lower respiratory tract consists of the trachea, bronchi and lungs.

Nasal cavity

Your nose is divided into the external nose and the internal nasal cavity. When you breathe in, air enters the cavity by passing through the nostrils. Hairs within the cavity filter out dust, pollen and other foreign particles before the air passes into the two passages of the nasal cavity. Here the air is warmed and moistened before it passes into the nasopharynx. A sticky mucous layer traps smaller foreign particles, which tiny hairs called cilia transport to the pharynx to be swallowed.

Epiglottis

A small flap of cartilage at the back of the tongue, the epiglottis closes the top of the trachea when you swallow to ensure food and drink pass into your stomach and not your lungs.

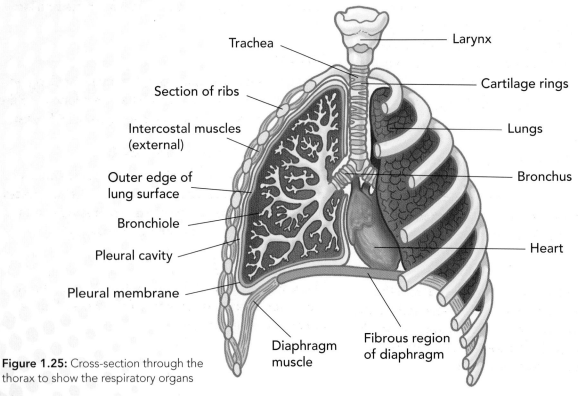

Figure 1.25: Cross-section through the thorax to show the respiratory organs

Pharynx

The funnel-shaped pharynx connects the nasal cavity and mouth to the larynx (air) and oesophagus (food). Commonly called the throat, the pharynx is a small tube that measures approximately 10–13 cm from the base of the skull to the level of the sixth cervical vertebra. The muscular pharynx wall is composed of skeletal muscle throughout its length. It is a passageway for food as well as air, so special adaptations are required to prevent choking when food or liquid is swallowed.

Larynx

The larynx or voice box has rigid walls of muscle and cartilage, contains the vocal cords and connects the pharynx to the trachea. It extends for about 5 cm from the level of the third to sixth vertebra.

Trachea

The trachea or windpipe denotes the start of the lower respiratory tract. It is about 12 cm long by 2 cm in diameter. It contains rings of cartilage to prevent it from collapsing and is very flexible. It travels down the neck in front of the oesophagus and branches into the right and left bronchi.

Bronchus

The right and left bronchi are formed by the division of the trachea. They carry air to the lungs. The right bronchus is shorter and wider than the left and is a more common site for foreign objects to become lodged. By the time inhaled air reaches the bronchi, it is warm, clear of most impurities and saturated with water vapour.

Once inside the lungs, each bronchus subdivides into lobar bronchi: three on the right and two on the left. The lobar bronchi branch into segmental bronchi, which divide again into smaller and smaller bronchi. Overall, there are approximately 23 orders of branching bronchial airways in the lungs. Because of this branching pattern, the bronchial network within the lungs is often called the bronchial tree.

Bronchioles

Bronchioles are small airways that extend from the bronchi. They are about 1 mm in diameter and are the first airway branches of the respiratory system that do not contain cartilage. Bronchioles end in clusters of thin-walled air sacs, known as alveoli.

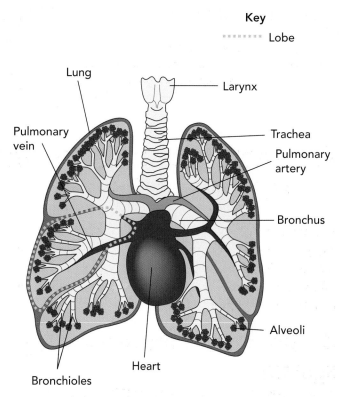

Figure 1.26: The lobes and pleural membranes of the lungs

Lungs

The paired right and left lungs occupy most of the thoracic cavity and extend down to the diaphragm. They hang suspended in the right and left pleural cavities straddling the heart. The left lung is smaller than the right.

Lobes

Each lung is divided into lobes; the right lung (lung on left when looking at Figure 1.26) has three lobes and the left (lung on right when looking at Figure 1.26) has two.

Pleural membrane and cavity

The lungs are surrounded by membranes known as pleura. These contain a cavity with fluid that lubricates the pleural surfaces as the lungs expand and contract, preventing friction and keeping them airtight.

Thoracic cavity

This is the chamber of the chest that is protected by the thoracic wall. It is separated from the abdominal cavity by the diaphragm.

Visceral pleura

The visceral pleura is the innermost of the two pleural membranes. It covers the surface of the lung and dips into the spaces between the lobes.

Pleural fluid

The pleural membranes produce pleural fluid which fills the space between them. This lubricating fluid allows the lungs to glide easily over the thoracic wall during respiration. Although the membranes slide easily over each other, their separation is resisted by the surface tension of the pleural fluid that keeps the lung surface in contact with the chest wall.

Alveoli

The bronchioles end in air sacs called alveoli. The 300 million gas-filled alveoli in each lung account for most of the lung volume and provide an enormous area for gaseous exchange – roughly the size of a tennis court. A dense network of capillaries surrounds the alveoli to facilitate this process. Together, the alveolar and capillary walls form the respiratory membrane that has gas on one side and blood flowing past on the other. Gaseous exchange occurs readily by simple diffusion across the respiratory membrane. Oxygen passes from the alveoli into the blood and carbon dioxide leaves the blood to enter the alveoli.

Diaphragm

The diaphragm separates the chest from the abdomen. It is the most important muscle involved in breathing. Contraction of the diaphragm increases the volume of the chest cavity, drawing air into the lungs during inspiration, while relaxation involves recoil of the diaphragm and decreases the volume of the chest cavity, pumping out air.

Internal and external intercostal muscles

The intercostal muscles lie between the ribs. To help with inhalation and exhalation, they extend and contract.

- The internal intercostal muscles lie inside the ribcage. They draw the ribs downwards and inwards, decreasing the volume of the chest cavity and forcing air out of the lungs during expiration.
- The external intercostal muscles lie outside the ribcage. They pull the ribs upwards and outwards, increasing the volume of the chest cavity and drawing air into the lungs during inspiration.

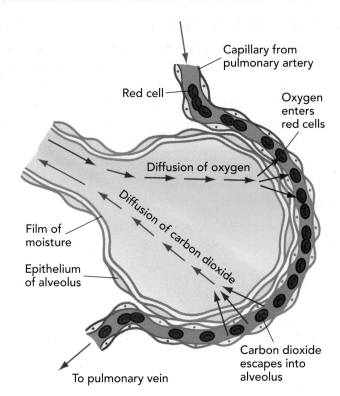

Figure 1.27: Gaseous exchange in the alveoli

4.2 Function of the respiratory system

Gaseous exchange

Gaseous exchange occurs by diffusion between air in the alveoli and blood in the capillaries surrounding their walls. The concept of partial pressure applies to the diffusion of gases from a gas mixture to a gas in solution and vice versa. Gases in contact with a liquid dissolve into solution by diffusion until equilibrium is achieved. At equilibrium, the partial pressure of the gases is the same in both gaseous and liquid states, and the gases are diffusing in and out of each state at the same rate. Blood entering the capillaries from the pulmonary arteries has a lower oxygen content and a higher carbon dioxide content than the air in the alveoli. Oxygen diffuses into the blood via the surface of the alveoli, through the thin walls of the capillaries, through the red blood cell membrane and finally latches on to haemoglobin. Carbon dioxide diffuses in the opposite direction, from blood into the alveoli.

Mechanisms of breathing

Pulmonary ventilation, or breathing, is the process by which air is transported into and out of the lungs, and it can be considered to have two phases. Breathing is regulated by the respiratory centres in the brain and stretch receptors within the air passages and lungs. It requires the thorax to increase in size to allow air to be taken in, followed by a decrease to allow air to be forced out.

Inspiration

With inspiration the intercostal muscles contract to lift the ribs upwards and outwards, while the diaphragm is forced downwards and the sternum forwards. This expansion of the thorax in all directions causes a drop in pressure below that of atmospheric pressure, which encourages air to flood into the lungs. At this point, oxygen is exchanged for carbon dioxide through the capillary walls.

Expiration

Expiration follows inspiration as the intercostal muscles relax, the diaphragm extends upwards and the ribs and sternum collapse. At that point, pressure within the lungs is increased and air is expelled. When the body is in action, greater amounts of oxygen are required, requiring the intercostal muscles and diaphragm to work harder.

Lung volumes

Your respiratory rate is the amount of air you breathe in one minute. For a typical 18-year-old, this represents about 12 breaths per minute at rest, during which time about 6 litres of air passes through the lungs. It can increase significantly during exercise, by as much as 30 to 40 breaths per minute.

Tidal volume

Tidal volume is the term used to describe the amount of air breathed in and out with each breath. Under normal conditions this represents about 500 cm³ of air breathed, both inhaled and exhaled. Of this, approximately two-thirds (350 cm³) reaches the alveoli in the lungs where gaseous exchange takes place. The remaining 150 cm³ fills the pharynx, larynx, trachea, bronchi and bronchioles and is known as dead or stationary air.

During exercise, tidal volume increases to allow more air to pass through the lungs. The volume of air passing through the lungs each minute is known as the minute volume and is the product of breathing rate and the amount of air taken in with each breath.

The lungs normally contain about 350 cm³ of fresh air, 150 cm³ of dead air and 2,500 cm³ of air that has already undergone gaseous exchange with the blood.

Inspiratory reserve volume

By breathing in deeply, it is possible to take in more than the usual 350 cm³ of fresh air that reaches the alveoli. This is especially important during exercise. In addition to the tidal volume, you can also breathe in up to an additional 3,000 cm³ of fresh air. This is known as the inspiratory reserve volume.

Expiratory reserve volume

This can be up to 1,500 cm³ and is the amount of additional air that can be breathed out after normal expiration. At the end of a normal breath, the lungs contain the residual volume plus the expiratory reserve volume. If you then exhale as much as possible, only the residual volume remains.

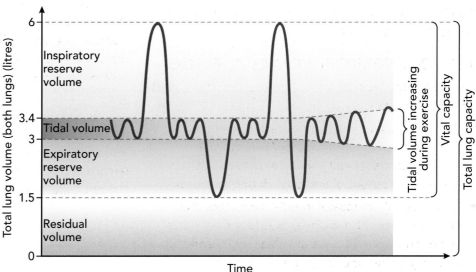

Figure 1.28: Lung volume and capacities of a healthy adult

Vital capacity

Vital capacity is the amount of air that can be forced out of the lungs after maximal inspiration. The volume is around 4,800 cm³.

Residual volume

The lungs are never fully emptied of air, otherwise they would collapse. The air that remains in the lungs after maximal exspiration, when you breathe out as hard as you can, is referred to as residual volume. The volume is around 1,200 cm³ for an average male.

Total lung capacity

This is your total lung capacity after you have inhaled as deeply and as maximally as you can, after maximal inspiration. It is normally around 6,000 cm³ for an average-sized male.

Control of breathing

Neutral control

Although breathing seems simple, its control is complex. It involves neurones, cells that conduct nerve impulses, in the **reticular formation** and **pons**, both parts of the brain stem. Neurones in two areas of the **medulla** are critical in respiration. These are the dorsal respiratory group (DRG) and the ventral respiratory group (VRG). The VRG is thought to be responsible for the rhythm generation.

Chemical control

Other factors that control breathing are the continually changing levels of oxygen and carbon dioxide. Sensors responding to such chemical fluctuations are called chemoreceptors. These are found in the medulla and in the **aortic arch** and **carotid arteries**.

Remember

It would not matter how efficient your cardiovascular system was at supplying blood to your tissues if your respiratory system could not keep pace with the demand for oxygen.

Assessment activity 1.4

P6 M3 **BTEC**

1. Create a short PowerPoint presentation to describe the structure and function of the respiratory system including gaseous exchange and the mechanisms of breathing. **P6**

2. In a short written account, examine the structure and functions of the respiratory system. **M3**

Grading tips

P6 You must be able to describe the structure and function of the constituent parts of the respiratory system outlined in this unit.

M3 You must be able to examine the respiratory system paying particular attention to how each part is designed to meet its function.

PLTS

When you create your PowerPoint presentation, you will be using your skills as a **creative thinker**.

Functional skills

Creating a PowerPoint presentation will demonstrate your **ICT** skills.

5. Know the different types of energy systems

All movement requires energy. The methods by which your body generates energy is determined by the intensity and duration of the activity being undertaken. Activities that require short bursts of effort like sprinting or jumping require the body to produce large amounts of energy over a short period, whereas marathon running or cycling require the body to provide continued energy production over a longer period and at a slower rate. The body's energy systems facilitate these processes.

5.1 Energy systems

The body's ability to extract energy from food and transfer it to the contractile proteins in the muscles determines your capacity to exercise for different durations at differing intensities. Thousands of complex chemical reactions are responsible for this energy transfer. The body maintains a continuous supply of energy through the use of **adenosine triphosphate (ATP)**, which is often referred to as the energy currency of the body.

Key term

Adenosine triphosphate (ATP) – a molecule that stores and releases chemical energy for use in body cells.

ATP consists of a base (adenine) and three phosphate groups. It is formed by a reaction between an adenosine diphosphate (ADP) molecule and a phosphate.

ATP is a versatile molecule that can be used for many things. Energy is stored in the chemical bonds in the molecules. When a bond is broken, energy is released. When a bond is made, energy is stored. When ADP binds with another phosphate, energy is stored for later use. When a molecule of ATP is combined with water, the last group splits off and energy is released.

The energy systems of the body can function aerobically (with oxygen) or anaerobically (without oxygen). Movements that require sudden bursts of effort are powered by energy systems that do not require oxygen – anaerobic systems – whereas prolonged activities are aerobic and require oxygen.

Energy is required in order to make the muscle fibres contract. It is obtained from the oxidation of foods in the diet, particularly carbohydrate and fat.

- **Carbohydrate** is broken down to a simple sugar called glucose, which if not required immediately by your body is converted into glycogen and stored in the liver and muscles.
- **Fat** is broken down to form free fatty acids.

When these substances are burned in the muscle cell, ATP is formed. When ATP is broken down, it gives energy for muscle contraction. It is the only molecule that can supply the energy used in the contraction of muscle fibres and can be made in three ways: the creatine phosphate energy system, the lactic acid energy system and the aerobic energy system.

Creatine phosphate energy system

ATP and creatine phosphate (or phosphocreatine, or PCr) make up the ATP–PCr system. It is the immediate energy system. Creatine phosphate (PCr) is a high-energy compound. When exercise intensity is high, or energy needs are instantaneous, creatine phosphate stored in muscle is broken down to provide energy to make ATP. When the high-energy bond in PCr is broken, the energy it releases is used to resynthesise ATP.

In this process, ATP is usually made without the presence of oxygen. Explosive work can be achieved, but only for up to about 10 seconds at maximum intensity, as the supply of PCr is limited.

Lactic acid energy system

This is the short-term energy system. To meet energy requirements of higher intensity over a longer period, such as during a 400-metre race, ATP can be made by the partial breakdown of glucose and glycogen. This is an anaerobic process that does not require oxygen and therefore is not sustainable over a long duration. Around 60–90 seconds of maximal work is possible using this system. See Figure 1.29 on page 32.

Anaerobic glycolysis

When the ATP–PCr system begins to fade at around 10 seconds, the process of anaerobic glycolysis begins. This system breaks down liver and muscle

(a) ATP is formed when adenosine diphosphate (ADP) binds with a phosphate

(b) A lot of energy is stored in the bond between the second and third phosphate groups, which can be used to fuel chemical reactions

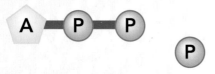

(c) When a cell needs energy, it breaks the bond between the phosphate groups to form ADP and a free phosphate molecule

Figure 1.29: ATP and energy released from the breakdown of ATP

glycogen stores without the presence of oxygen, which produces lactic acid as a by-product. This limits energy production via this process.

Lactic acid production

Lactic acid is the limiting factor of the anaerobic system. It accumulates and diffuses into the tissue fluid and blood. If this substance is not removed by the circulatory system, it builds up to impede muscle contraction and cause fatigue. You may have experienced this as an uncomfortable burning sensation in your muscles during intense exercise.

> **Remember**
>
> Glycolysis is the breakdown of glucose or glycogen to produce ATP.

Aerobic energy system

This is the long-term energy system. If plenty of oxygen is available, as it is during everyday movements and light exercise, glycogen and fatty acids break down to yield large amounts of ATP. This produces carbon dioxide and water, which do not affect the ability of muscles to contract.

Aerobic energy production occurs in the mitochondria of the cells. These are the power stations of the cells, responsible for converting food into energy. The production of energy within the aerobic system is slow to engage because it takes a few minutes for the heart to deliver oxygenated blood to working muscles. Long,

continuous and moderate exercise produces energy using this system.

During exercise the body does not switch from one system to the other – energy at any time is derived from all three systems. However, the emphasis changes depending on the intensity of the activity relative to the efficiency of your aerobic fitness, i.e. your ability to deliver and utilise oxygen.

Amounts of ATP produced by each system

Creatine phosphate energy system:
ADP + creatine phosphate → ATP + creatine

Lactic acid energy system:
Glucose → 2 ATP + 2 lactic acid + heat
Glycogen → 3 ATP + 2 lactic acid + heat

Aerobic energy system:
Glucose + oxygen →
38 ATP + carbon dioxide + water + heat

Fatty acids + oxygen →
129 ATP + carbon dioxide + water + heat

Figure 1.30: Amounts of ATP produced by each energy system

Types of sports that use each system

All three energy systems are active at any given time, but depending on the intensity and duration of activity undertaken, different energy systems will be the primary energy provider. Table 1.4 on page 33 shows the types of sport and the relative contributions made by the different energy systems.

Sport	Creatine phosphate energy system	Lactic acid energy system	Aerobic energy system
Archery	High	Low	–
Basketball	High	Moderate	Low
Hockey	High	Moderate	High
Netball	High	Moderate	Low
Soccer	High	Moderate	High
Track and field distance events	–	Moderate	High
Track and field jumping events	High	–	–
Track and field sprinting events	High	Moderate/high	–
Track and field throwing events	High	–	–

Table 1.4: Energy systems used for different sports

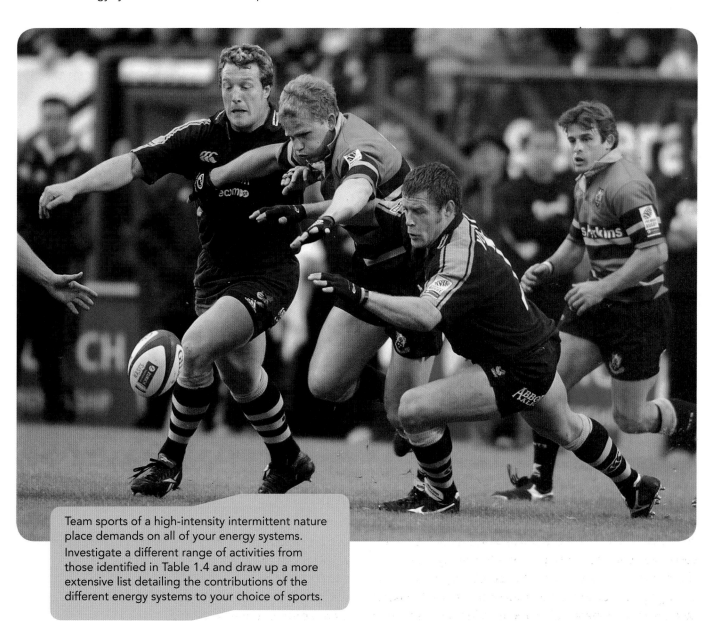

Team sports of a high-intensity intermittent nature place demands on all of your energy systems. Investigate a different range of activities from those identified in Table 1.4 and draw up a more extensive list detailing the contributions of the different energy systems to your choice of sports.

Recovery periods

Any exercise represents a stress to your body and disturbs its natural balance. The amount of disturbance depends on the intensity and duration of the activity or exercise. Your total recovery from exercise depends on a number of factors including the restoration of your immediate energy system, the removal of lactic acid and the restoration of muscle glycogen.

The creatine phosphate system can be restored almost as quickly as energy is released from the system. As a result, it is possible to repeat several short bursts of activity without becoming exhausted. However, once lactic acid is produced it will take around 45–60 minutes for it to be removed from the system. The rate of muscle glycogen restoration depends on the choice, speed and amount of carbohydrate consumption after exercise.

Take it further

Using the Internet and a selection of textbooks, investigate how an understanding of energy systems can help to facilitate the achievement of optimal sports performance.

Assessment activity 1.5 **P7** **M4** **D2** :BTEC

1. In a short written account, describe the different energy systems and their use in sport and exercise activities. **P7**

2. Consider the activity of running and examine the different energy systems and explain how they come in to play at different intensities and durations of running activity. **M4**

3. Using a wider variety of sport and exercise activities, analyse the different energy systems and explain their use in the sports you have chosen to examine. **D2**

Grading tips

P7 Make sure you describe each energy system and link each one to its use in different sport and exercise activities.

M4 Examine each energy system and explain its use in running and consider the implications of training.

D2 Analyse each energy system and explain its use in a variety of sport and exercise activities. Try to provide more complex sporting examples and consider the implications of training.

PLTS

Using a variety of sources to research the different energy systems to describe their use in sport and exercise activities will help you develop your skills as an **independent enquirer**.

Functional skills

Gathering information and formulating ideas and arguments by researching a variety of sources in describing, explaining and analysing energy systems in sport will provide you with evidence to demonstrate the development of your **English** skills.

Frank Bedford
Sports Therapist

As a sports therapist I work with the local football team and play a key role in keeping the players fit. I regularly apply the principles of anatomy and physiology to the prevention and management of injuries. In a typical day I work alongside the physiotherapist and the strength and conditioning team to treat and advise players on a range of football-related injuries. I massage players and provide advice on pre- and rehabilitative exercises to help prevent and manage these injuries. My work may also involve undertaking assessments of readiness to return to training following injury, testing joints for ease and range of movement, strapping and taping and advising on stretching, warming-up and cooling down exercises.

During the match I provide first aid and may be involved in examining and assessing injuries and determining whether a player can continue. After the match I may again be involved in examining and assessing injuries and dealing with minor traumas such as cuts, bruises and blisters. I may need to consider whether injured players need extra treatment and coordinate referrals to other practitioners or liaise with other health professionals in the sports sector or in mainstream medicine.

I enjoy being part of a multi-disciplinary support team and get great satisfaction out of helping players to achieve their full potential on the pitch.

Think about it!

- What knowledge and skills have you covered in this unit that would provide you with a good understanding of the role of a sports therapist? Jot down your ideas and discuss them with your peers and tutor.
- What further skills and experience might you need to develop if you were to consider this as a potential career path? Consider arranging an opportunity to shadow a sports therapist in their workplace.
- Investigate a common football injury and explore the role of the sports therapist in its prevention and management.

Just checking

1. Draw and label a simple diagram of the axial skeleton.

2. Describe five functions of the skeleton.

3. Draw and label a simple diagram of a synovial joint.

4. Describe the three types of muscle found in your body.

5. Describe the location and action of the following muscles:
   a) triceps
   b) erector spinae
   c) hamstrings
   d) tibialis anterior.

6. Define the functional roles of the following in relation to muscle movement:
   a) agonist
   b) antagonist
   c) synergist
   d) fixator.

7. Identify the main muscles working to bring about a bicep curl movement and analyse the type of contraction taking place.

8. Describe the major functional differences between arteries and veins.

9. Identify the key structures of the respiratory system and describe their functions.

10. Briefly describe the mechanics of breathing.

11. Describe and define three lung volumes.

12. Describe the three energy systems.

edexcel

Assignment tips

These are complex systems to understand in terms of structure and function. There are many interactive web-based resources to aid the development of your knowledge and understanding. E.g. www.bbc.co.uk/science/humanbody.

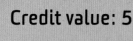

2 The physiology of fitness

As you sit reading this unit your body is doing little by way of physical exertion. Your oxygen and energy demands are easily met by your shallow breathing and resting heart rate. However, were you to get up and go for a run, significant changes would occur. Your body must adapt quickly to fuel this activity and to maintain its equilibrium, and it does so in a variety of ways involving many complex processes.

This unit explores the responses of the musculoskeletal, cardiovascular and respiratory systems to exercise. All three energy systems that provide energy for exercise participation are also covered, together with the energy continuum. You will have the chance to investigate the effects of exercise on each of your body systems by taking part in practical activities and conducting physiological tests.

Many jobs in sport require a good knowledge of how the body reacts to exercise, for example, personal training and fitness instruction, coaching and sports therapy.

Learning outcomes

After completing this unit you should be able to:

1. know the body's response to acute exercise
2. know the long-term effects of exercise on the body systems
3. be able to investigate the physiological effects of exercise on the body systems.

Assessment and grading criteria

This table shows you what you must do in order to achieve a pass, merit or distinction grade, and where you can find activities in this book to help you.

To achieve a **pass** grade the evidence must show that the learner is able to:	To achieve a **merit** grade the evidence must show that, in addition to the pass criteria, the learner is able to:	To achieve a **distinction** grade the evidence must show that, in addition to the pass and merit criteria, the learner is able to:
P1 describe the musculoskeletal and energy systems response to acute exercise **Assessment activity 2.1, page 46**	**M1** explain the response of the musculoskeletal, cardiovascular and respiratory systems to acute exercise **Assessment activity 2.1, page 46**	
P2 describe the cardiovascular and respiratory systems responses to acute exercise **Assessment activity 2.1, page 46**		
P3 describe the long-term effects of exercise on the musculoskeletal system and energy systems **Assessment activity 2.2, page 50**	**M2** explain the long-term effects of exercise on the musculoskeletal, cardiovascular, respiratory and energy systems **Assessment activity 2.2, page 50**	
P4 describe the long-term effects of exercise on the cardiovascular and respiratory systems **Assessment activity 2.2, page 50**		
P5 collect physiological data to investigate the effects of exercise on the musculoskeletal, cardiovascular, respiratory and energy systems, with tutor support **Assessment activity 2.3, page 56**	**M3** collect physiological data to investigate the effects of exercise on the musculoskeletal, cardiovascular, respiratory and energy systems, with limited tutor support **Assessment activity 2.3, page 56**	**D1** independently investigate the physiological effects of exercise on the musculoskeletal, cardiovascular, respiratory and energy systems **Assessment activity 2.3, page 56**
P6 review physiological data collected, describing the effects of exercise on the musculoskeletal, cardiovascular, respiratory and energy systems **Assessment activity 2.3, page 56**	**M4** review physiological data collected, explaining the effects of exercise on the musculoskeletal, cardiovascular, respiratory and energy systems **Assessment activity 2.3, page 56**	**D2** review physiological data collected, analysing the effects of exercise on the musculoskeletal, cardiovascular, respiratory and energy systems **Assessment activity 2.3, page 56**

How you will be assessed

This unit will be internally assessed by a range of assignments that will be designed and graded by your tutor. Your assignment tasks will be designed to allow you to demonstrate your understanding of the unit learning outcomes and relate them to what you should be able to do after completing this unit. Your assignments could be in the form of:

- presentations
- practical tasks
- written assignments and reports.

Emma Rashid, 18 years old, was relatively sedentary prior to studying this unit

This unit has taught me about the changes that occur as my body adapts to both short- and long-term exercise. Since giving up competitive sport a year ago I have been relatively sedentary. While undertaking the practical tasks associated with the unit I realised I am not as fit as I used to be and I have embarked on a regular programme of fitness training.

Undergoing physiological assessment made this unit more exciting for me. The bit I enjoyed most was reviewing my progress in certain aspects of fitness. I decided that if I was to stick to an exercise programme and gain long-term adaptations in terms of fitness and performance, the programme had to include activities I would enjoy, so I opted for a combination of strength training in the college gym and running that I could do either on the treadmill or outside in good weather.

Over to you

- **What might this unit teach you about your own levels of fitness and exercise performance?**
- **Do you feel there will be any challenges with meeting the assessment requirements for this unit?**
- **If so, how might you overcome them?**

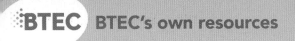

1.   Know the body's response to acute exercise

Warm-up

Paula Radcliffe set the women's marathon world record in the 2003 London Marathon with a time of 2 hours, 15 minutes and 25 seconds. A number of physiological processes occur when Paula competes in this gruelling event. What do you think is happening inside Paula's body to allow her to compete successfully in the marathon? Why would it be impossible for you to run a marathon in world record time?

Your body responds to the stress of exercise or physical activity in a variety of ways. Some of these are immediate and are often referred to as the **acute responses** to exercise, such as an increase in body temperature and heart rate. Others are long term, and are often referred to as **chronic responses** or adaptations that contribute to improved fitness for sports participation and reduced health risk.

Key terms

Acute responses – immediate responses to exercise, such as an increase in body temperature and heart rate.

Chronic responses – adaptations that contribute to improved fitness for sports participation and reduced health risk.

1.1 Musculoskeletal response

The musculoskeletal system consists of muscles, tendons, ligaments, bones and cartilage. These support your body and enable it to move. The different parts of your musculoskeletal system operate under the control of the nervous system to produce voluntary movement. Impulses from the nervous system cause muscles to contract: when a muscle contracts, it shortens, pulling on the bone to which it is attached. The skeletal system forms the framework of the body, while muscles form the fleshy part. They facilitate movement, maintain posture and produce heat.

Activity: Get active

Choose your favourite sporting or fitness activity, for example aerobics, running, cycling or swimming, or a team sport such as football, hockey, netball or basketball.

Take 5–6 minutes to warm up and then do your favourite activity at moderate intensity for about 15–20 minutes. At the end of the activity session, be sure to finish with a 5-minute cool down. At each stage of the fitness session (warm-up, main activity, cool down) you should pay close attention to how the different parts of your body respond and adapt to the activity.

1. List the bodily changes you experienced. How did your body adapt to the different stages of the workout?

2. Although you were asked to perform the activity at a moderate intensity, you could have chosen to walk at a low intensity, or run at a high intensity. How would different exercise intensities affect your body's reaction?

3. Taking account of your body's reaction to this bout of activity, how would you rate your current level of fitness?

Increased blood supply

The short-term effects of exercise on your muscles include an increase in temperature and metabolic activity. As a result of this increase in metabolic activity, there is a greater demand for oxygen met by an increase in blood supply through capillary dilation.

Increase in muscle pliability

The warming of your muscles during activity makes them more **pliable** and reduces the risk of injury.

Increased range of movement

The short-term effects of exercise on your skeletal system are demonstrated by changes within the joint. Movement of joints stimulates the secretion of synovial fluid. This fluid also becomes less **viscous** and the range of movement at the joint increases.

Key terms

Pliability – relates to the stretchiness of your muscles and connective tissue.

Viscous – the measure of resistance (thickness) of a fluid.

Muscle fibre micro tears

When you exercise, your muscles are put under stress to the point that tiny tears occur in the muscle fibres. These micro tears cause swelling in the muscle tissue which causes pressure on the nerve endings and pain. Training improvements will only be made if the body has sufficient fuel and rest to repair these micro tears, making the muscle a little bit stronger than it was before.

1.2 Energy systems

All movement requires energy. The methods by which the body generates energy are determined by the intensity and duration of the activity being undertaken. Activities that require short bursts of effort, such as sprinting or jumping, require the body to produce large amounts of energy over a short period, whereas activities like marathon running or endurance cycling require continued energy production over a longer period and at a slower rate. It is the energy systems of your body that facilitate these processes.

Energy is required in order to make the muscle fibres contract. This energy is obtained from the oxidation of foods in the diet, particularly carbohydrate and fat. When these substances are burned in the muscle cells, ATP is formed, which is rich in energy. When ATP is broken down, it gives energy for muscle contraction. It is the only molecule that can supply the energy used in the contraction of muscle fibres and can be made in three ways: the creatine phosphate energy system, the lactic acid energy system and the aerobic energy system.

Remember

The aerobic and anaerobic breakdown of nutrients provides the source of energy for the production of chemical energy to fuel work.

Creatine phosphate energy system

ATP and creatine phosphate (or phosphocreatine, or PCr) make up the ATP-PCr system. It is the immediate energy system. Creatine phosphate (PCr) is a high-energy compound. When exercise intensity is high, or energy needs are instantaneous, creatine phosphate stored in muscle is broken down to provide energy to make ATP. When the high-energy bond in PCr is broken, the energy it releases is used to resynthesise ATP.

In this process, ATP is usually made without the presence of oxygen. Explosive work can be achieved, but only for short periods (up to about 10 seconds) at maximum intensity, as the supply of PCr is very limited.

Lactic acid energy system

This is the short-term energy system. To meet energy requirements of higher intensity over a longer period, such as during a 400-metre race, ATP can be made by the partial breakdown of glucose and glycogen. This is an anaerobic process (it does not require oxygen) and therefore is not sustainable over a long duration. Around 60 to 90 seconds of maximal work is possible using this system.

Anaerobic glycolysis

When the ATP-PCr system begins to fade at around 10 seconds, the process of anaerobic glycolysis begins to occur. This system breaks down liver and muscle glycogen stores without the presence of oxygen, which produces lactic acid as a by-product. This limits energy production via this process.

Lactic acid production

Lactic acid is the limiting factor of the anaerobic system. It accumulates and diffuses into the tissue fluid and blood. If this substance is not removed by the circulatory system, it builds up to impede muscle contraction and cause fatigue. You may have experienced this during intense exercise as an uncomfortable burning sensation in your muscles.

(a) ATP is formed when adenosine diphosphate (ADP) binds with a phosphate

(b) A lot of energy is stored in the bond between the second and third phosphate groups, which can be used to fuel chemical reactions

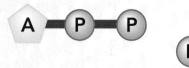

(c) When a cell needs energy, it breaks the bond between the phosphate groups to form ADP and a free phosphate molecule

Figure 2.1: ATP and energy released from the breakdown of ATP

Remember

Glycolysis is the breakdown of glucose or glycogen to produce ATP.

Aerobic energy system

This is the long-term energy system. If plenty of oxygen is available, as it is during everyday movements and light exercise, glycogen and fatty acids break down to yield large amounts of ATP. This produces carbon dioxide and water, which do not affect the muscles' ability to contract.

Aerobic energy production occurs in the **mitochondria** of the cells. These are the power stations of the cells, responsible for converting the food ingested by the cells into energy. The production of energy within the aerobic system is slow to engage because it takes a few minutes for the heart to deliver oxygenated blood to working muscles. Long, continuous and moderate exercise produces energy using this system.

Key term

Mitochondria – organelles containing enzymes responsible for energy production. Mitochondria are therefore the part of a muscle responsible for aerobic energy production.

Creatine phosphate energy system:

ADP + creatine phosphate → ATP + creatine

Lactic acid energy system:

Glucose → 2 ATP + 2 lactic acid + heat

Glycogen → 3 ATP + 2 lactic acid + heat

Aerobic energy system:

Glucose + oxygen →
38 ATP + carbon dioxide + water + heat

Fatty acids + oxygen →
129 ATP + carbon dioxide + water + heat

Figure 2.2: Amounts of ATP produced by each energy system

Energy continuum

The body's ability to extract energy from food and transfer it to the contractile proteins in the muscles determines your capacity to exercise for different durations at differing intensities. Thousands of complex chemical reactions are responsible for this energy transfer. The body maintains a continuous supply of energy through the use of adenosine triphosphate (ATP), which is often referred to as the energy currency of the body.

ATP consists of a base (adenine) and three phosphate groups. It is formed by a reaction between an adenosine diphosphate (ADP) molecule and a phosphate. ATP is a versatile molecule that can be used for many things. Energy is stored in the chemical bonds in the molecules. When a bond is broken, energy is released. When a bond is made, energy is stored. When ADP binds with another phosphate, energy is stored that can be used later. When a molecule of ATP is combined with water, the last group splits off and energy is released.

The energy systems of the body can function aerobically (with oxygen) or anaerobically (without oxygen). Movements that require sudden bursts of effort are powered by anaerobic systems, whereas prolonged activities are aerobic.

Energy requirements of different sport and exercise activities

All three energy systems are active at any given time, but depending on the intensity and duration of activity undertaken, different energy systems will be the primary energy provider. Table 2.1 shows the types of sport and the relative contributions made by the different energy systems.

Here's what happens when you start running:

- The muscle cells burn off the ATP they already contain in about 3 seconds.
- The creatine phosphate system kicks in and supplies energy for 8–10 seconds. This would be the major energy system used by the muscles of a 100-metre sprinter or weightlifter, where rapid acceleration, short-duration exercise occurs.

- If exercise continues longer, the lactic acid energy system kicks in. This would be true for short-distance exercises such as a 200- or 400-metre run or a 100-metre swim.
- If exercise continues, the aerobic energy system takes over. This would occur in endurance events such as an 800-metre run, a marathon run, rowing, cross-country skiing and distance skating.

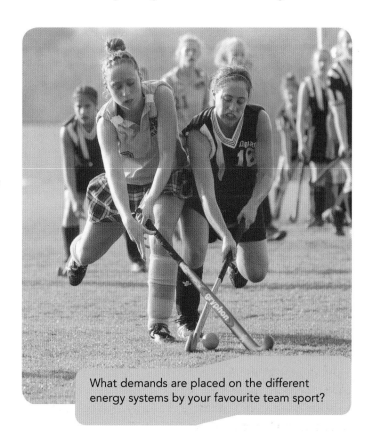

What demands are placed on the different energy systems by your favourite team sport?

Sport	Creatine phosphate energy system	Lactic acid energy system	Aerobic energy system
Archery	High	Low	
Basketball	High	Moderate	Low
Hockey	High	Moderate	High
Netball	High	Moderate	Low
Soccer	High	Moderate	High
Track and field distance		Moderate	High
Track and field jumping	High		
Track and field sprinting	High	Moderate/high	
Track and field throwing	High		

Table 2.1: Energy systems used for different sports

1.3 Cardiovascular response

During exercise your contracting muscles require a continual supply of nutrients and oxygen to support energy production. These requirements are over and above those required to support normal activities at work or rest. Your heart has to beat harder and faster to meet these increased demands. If these demands are repeated frequently as a result of a systematic training programme, over time your heart becomes stronger.

Heart rate anticipatory response

Nerves that directly supply your heart and chemicals in your blood can rapidly alter your heart rate. Before the start of exercise your heart rate usually increases above resting levels. This is known as anticipatory heart rate. The greatest anticipatory heart-rate response is observed in short sprint events.

Activity response

At the start of exercise, or even slightly before, nerve centres in your brain detect cardiovascular activity. This results in adjustments that increase the rate and pumping strength of your heart. At the same time regional blood flow is altered in proportion to the intensity of the activity undertaken.

Increased blood pressure

Blood pressure is the pressure of blood against the walls of your arteries and results from two forces. One is created by the heart as it pumps blood into your arteries and through your circulatory system, the other is the force of your arteries as they resist blood flow. During exercise, despite both cardiac output and blood pressure increases, these mechanisms act to restrict the blood pressure rise and eventually bring it down.

During aerobic exercise, oxygen consumption and heart rate increase in relation to the intensity of the activity. **Systolic blood pressure** rises progressively, while **diastolic blood pressure** stays the same or decreases slightly. Pulse rate rises and blood flow to your muscles increases.

Vasodilation

During exercise the vascular portion of active muscles increases through the dilation of arterioles, involving an increase in the diameter of the blood vessels and resulting in an increased blood flow to the muscles. This process is called **vasodilation**.

Vasoconstriction

Vessels can also shut down blood flow to tissues, which can temporarily lessen their blood supply. This involves a decrease in the diameter of the blood vessel, resulting in reduced blood flow to the muscles. This process is called **vasoconstriction**.

Key terms

Systolic blood pressure – the highest pressure within the bloodstream, which occurs during each beat when the heart is in systole (contracting).

Diastolic blood pressure – the lowest pressure within the bloodstream, which occurs between beats when the heart is in diastole (relaxing, filling with blood).

Vasodilation – when blood vessels widen in an attempt to increase blood flow.

Vasoconstriction – when blood vessels narrow and reduce blood flow.

1.4 Respiratory response

Your body is surprisingly insensitive to falling levels of oxygen, yet it is very sensitive to increased levels of carbon dioxide. The levels of oxygen in arterial blood vary little, even during exercise, but carbon dioxide levels vary in direct proportion to the level of physical activity. The more intense the exercise, the greater the carbon dioxide concentration in the blood. To combat this, your breathing rate increases to ensure the carbon dioxide can be expelled.

Increased breathing rate

Exercise results in an increase in the rate and depth of breathing. During exercise your muscles demand more oxygen and the corresponding increase in carbon dioxide production stimulates faster and deeper breathing. The capillary network surrounding the alveoli expands, increasing blood flow to the lungs and pulmonary diffusion.

A minor rise in breathing rate prior to exercise is known as an anticipatory rise. When exercise begins there is an immediate and significant increase in breathing rate, believed to be a result of receptors working in both the muscles and joints.

After several minutes of aerobic exercise, breathing continues to rise, though at a slower rate, and it levels off if the exercise intensity remains constant. If the exercise is maximal, breathing rate will continue to rise until exhaustion. After exercise the breathing rate returns to normal, rapidly to begin with and then more slowly.

Neural and chemical control

Breathing is a complex process that is largely under involuntary control by the respiratory centres of your brain. It involves two actions: inspiration (an active process), and expiration (a passive process). Breathing is controlled by neural and chemical factors. Increases in the rate and depth of breathing are detected by stretch receptors in the lungs. The respiratory centres of the brain (the medulla and pons) send nerve impulses to the respiratory muscles to control breathing frequency and tidal volume of each breath.

When altering depth and rate of breathing, these centres are responding to central and peripheral information. Other information comes from chemoreceptors, such as those in the aortic arch and carotid bodies, which respond to changes in partial pressure. Mechanoreceptors in the joints, tendons and active muscles that assess movement and metabolic status may also feed in information.

Remember

Athletes or highly trained individuals can tolerate higher breathing rates during exercise.

Increased tidal volume

Tidal volume is the amount of air breathed in and out with each breath, about $500 \, cm^3$ when the body is at rest. Of this, only two-thirds ($350 \, cm^3$) reaches the alveoli in the lungs where gaseous exchange occurs. During exercise, tidal volume increases to allow more air to pass through the lungs. The volume of air passing through the lungs each minute is known as the minute volume and is the product of breathing rate and the amount of air taken in with each breath.

Tidal volume is elevated by both aerobic and anaerobic exercise. During exercise, oxygen is depleted from your body, triggering a deeper tidal volume to compensate.

Remember

Inspiration is an active process. Expiration is a passive process.

Assessment activity 2.1

(P1) (P2) (M1) · BTEC

1. Taking account of your observations from undertaking practical tasks in this unit, produce a written report describing how the musculoskeletal and energy systems respond to acute exercise. **P1**

2. Again, taking account of your observations from undertaking practical tasks in this unit, produce a written report describing how the cardiovascular and respiratory systems respond to acute exercise. **P2**

3. Develop your report to further explain the response of the musculoskeletal, cardiovascular and respiratory systems to acute exercise, using a practical sporting example of your choice. **M1**

Grading tips

P1, **P2** You must describe the musculoskeletal, cardiovascular and respiratory systems' responses to acute exercises. Use practical examples to support your answer.

M1 A detailed explanation would include reasons or examples to support the statements you make.

PLTS

Researching the effects of exercise on the body develops you as an **independent enquirer**.

Functional skills

Producing a written report on your investigations will develop your **English** skills.

2. Know the long-term effects of exercise on the body systems

If you exercise regularly your body adapts and you become fitter and more able to cope with the demands of exercise. Responses to long-term exercise include changes in the heart, lungs, muscles and skeleton, but the extent of these changes depends on the type, intensity and frequency of exercise undertaken, and the overload achieved.

2.1 Cardiovascular system

The heart and blood vessels of the circulatory system adapt to repeated bouts of exercise in a number of ways.

Cardiac hypertrophy

Your heart increases in its size and blood volume. The wall of the left ventricle thickens, increasing the strength potential of its contractions.

Increase in stroke volume

Stroke volume at rest has been shown to be significantly higher after a prolonged endurance-training programme. The heart can therefore pump more blood per minute, increasing cardiac output during maximal levels of exercise. Blood flow increases

as a consequence of an increase in the size and number of blood vessels. This allows for more efficient delivery of oxygen and nutrients.

Increase in cardiac output

During participation in sport and exercise, cardiac output will be increased as a result of increases in heart rate and/or stroke volume. Stroke volume does not increase significantly beyond the light work rates of low-intensity exercise, so the increases in cardiac output required for moderate to high-intensity work rates are achieved by increases in heart rate. Your maximum attainable cardiac output decreases with increasing age, largely as a result of a decrease in maximum heart rate. Maximum heart rate can be calculated using the formula:
maximum heart rate = 220 – age (in years).

Remember

Cardiac output can increase 5–7 times to accelerate the delivery of blood to exercising muscles and meet their demand for increased oxygen.

Decreased resting heart rate

Your resting heart rate falls, reducing the workload on your heart and your heart rate returns to normal after exercise more quickly.

Capillarisation

Long-term exercise can lead to the development of the capillary network to a part of your body. Aerobic exercise improves the capillarisation of cardiac and skeletal muscle. Blood flow increases as a consequence of an increase in the size and number of blood vessels. This allows for more efficient delivery of oxygen and nutrients.

Increase in blood volume

Your blood volume represents the amount of blood circulating in your body. It varies from person to person, and increases as a result of training. Blood volume increases as a result of capillarisation.

Remember

It would not matter how efficient your circulatory system was at supplying blood to your tissues during exercise if your respiratory system could not keep pace with the demand for oxygen. Like the cardiovascular system, the respiratory system undergoes specific adaptations in response to a systematic training programme, which help to maximise its efficiency.

Reduction in resting blood pressure

Exercise causes your blood pressure to rise for a short time. However, when you stop your blood pressure should return to normal. The quicker it does this, the fitter you are likely to be. Research indicates that regular exercise can contribute to lowering blood pressure.

Decreased recovery time

Heart rate recovery is a measure of how much your heart rate falls during the first minute after exercise. The fitter your heart, the quicker it returns to normal after exercise. Fitter individuals generally recover more rapidly because their cardiovascular system can adapt more quickly to the imposed demands of exercise.

Increased aerobic fitness

When exercise is performed over a period of weeks or months, your body adapts. The physiological changes that occur with repeated exposure to exercise improve your body's exercise capacity and efficiency. With aerobic training, such as running and cycling, the heart and lungs become more efficient and endurance capacity increases, while with resistance modes of training such as weight training the muscles become stronger. Adaptations derived from training are highly specific to the type of exercise undertaken. To understand the responses and adaptation observed as a result of training it is necessary to understand the basic principles of training and exercise prescription, some of which can be applied to all forms of exercise training. This is covered in BTEC Level 3 National Student Book 2, Unit 14 Exercise, Health and Lifestyle.

2.2 Muscular system

Muscle tissue's response to exercise depends on the type of training undertaken and the degree of overload achieved. Muscle strength and size increase with high-intensity resistance training, while muscle endurance increases with repetitive low-intensity training. Stretching exercises improve flexibility and the range of motion around joints.

Hypertrophy

Increases in muscle size and bulk, hypertrophy, are the result of increases in the volume of contractile proteins within the muscle cells so that they can contract with greater force. In general, males have a greater potential to achieve increases in muscle bulk and size, due to higher levels of the hormone testosterone.

Increase in tendon strength

Tendons are tough bands of fibrous connective tissue designed to withstand tension. Like muscles, tendons adapt to the mechanical loading of regular exercise. A general adaptation is increased strength, but different types of training will exert differing effects on muscle–tendon complexes.

Ligaments and tendons, the connective tissue structures around joints, will increase in flexibility and strength with regular exercise. Cartilage also becomes thicker.

Increase in myoglobin stores and number of mitochondria and increased storage of glycogen and fat

Muscles increase their oxidative capacity with regular training. This is achieved by an increase in the number of mitochondria within the muscle cells, an increase in the supply of ATP and an increase in the quantity of enzymes involved in respiration. The ability of the muscles to store **myoglobin** is also increased, alongside the ability to store and use glycogen and fat.

Increased muscle strength

Muscles will only strengthen when forced to operate outside of their customary intensity, i.e. you need to overload them. Overload can be achieved by increasing the resistance they are required to overcome or the number of times a resistance is required to be overcome in repetitions or sets.

Increased tolerance to lactic acid

Anaerobic training stimulates the muscles to become better able to tolerate lactic acid, and clear it away more efficiently. With endurance training the capillary network extends, allowing greater volumes of blood to supply the muscles with oxygen and nutrients. The muscles are able to use more fat as a fuel source, and become more efficient at using oxygen, increasing the body's ability to work harder for longer without fatiguing. The net result is an increase in the body's maximal oxygen consumption.

2.3 Skeletal system

Regular exercise slows the rate of skeletal ageing. Regardless of age, those who maintain physically active lifestyles have greater bone mass compared to those who are sedentary.

Increase in bone calcium stores

Your bones are not static. They can become stronger and denser as a result of the demands placed on them through physical activity and exercise, which can increase their mineral content. The key factor regulating this is the mechanical force you apply during the activities you undertake. The types of exercise that help build stronger bones are strength-training and weight-bearing exercises that work against gravity with differing degrees of impact, for example tennis, netball, basketball, aerobics, dancing, walking and running. Bones are strengthened as a result of the stress exercise imposes on them, which results in greater quantities of calcium and **collagen** deposited within them, reducing the risk of **osteoporosis**. The supportive connective tissue surrounding your joints is also strengthened.

What impact might regular physical activity and exercise have on the strength of your bones?

Key terms

Myoglobin – the form of haemoglobin found in muscles that binds and stores oxygen. Myoglobin is responsible for delivering oxygen to the mitochondria.

Collagen – the main protein of connective tissue.

Osteoporosis – a disease characterised by the loss of bone mass and a change in bone structure that makes bones porous and increases the risk of fracture.

Remember

Bones are strengthened as a result of the stress exercise imposes on them, with greater quantities of calcium and collagen being deposited within them.

Increased stretch of ligaments

Ligaments, and also tendons (the connective tissue structures around a joint) will increase in flexibility and strength with regular exercise. Athletes require stronger tendons and more pliable ligaments to handle the demands of a progressive training programme. For example, if an athlete lifts progressively increasing weights as part of a strength-training programme, their muscles will get stronger. To accommodate this the tendons have to increase their load-bearing capacity, while the ligaments need to adapt their pliability. This adaptation occurs when **fibroblast** secretions increase the production of collagen fibres relative to the training load.

Increased thickness of hyaline cartilage

Hyaline cartilage is the most common type of cartilage in your body. It is found mainly on the articulating surfaces of your bones and protects them from wear and tear. It also provides a certain amount of elasticity to absorb shock. It becomes thicker with regular exercise.

Increased production of synovial fluid

Movement of joints stimulates the secretion of synovial fluid. With regular exercise, this becomes less viscous and the range of movement at the joint increases as connective tissue improves in its flexibility.

2.4 Respiratory system

In common with the cardiovascular system the respiratory system undergoes specific adaptations in response to a systematic training programme which help to maximise its efficiency. The muscles demand more oxygen and the corresponding increase in carbon dioxide production stimulates faster and deeper breathing.

Increased vital capacity

Vital capacity increases in response to physical training, to provide an increased and more efficient supply of oxygen to working muscles. During strenuous exercise, oxygen diffusion may increase by as much as threefold above the resting level.

Increase in minute ventilation

Minute ventilation depends on breathing rate and total volume. During exercise adults can generally achieve approximately 15 times resting values.

Increased strength of respiratory muscles

The diaphragm and intercostal muscles increase in strength, allowing for greater expansion of the chest cavity.

Increase in oxygen diffusion rate

An increase in diffusion rates in tissues favours oxygen movement from the capillaries to the tissues, and carbon dioxide from the cells to the blood. With regular training these rates increase, allowing oxygen and carbon dioxide to diffuse more rapidly.

Remember

When you exercise, your breathing rate increases to take in more oxygen and expel greater levels of carbon dioxide.

2.5 Energy systems

Increased aerobic and anaerobic enzymes

Long-term exercise brings about a number of cellular changes that enhance the ability of muscle tissue to generate ATP. Cellular adaptation such as the increase in size of mitochondria is usually accompanied by an increase in the level of aerobic system enzymes. A combination of these changes probably explains why an athlete can sustain prolonged periods of aerobic exercise as a result of longer-term training.

The anaerobic system also undergoes a number of changes, including an increase in enzymes that control the anaerobic phase of glucose breakdown.

Increased use of fats as an energy source

Fat is the primary energy source during low-intensity exercise. Fat combustion powers almost all exercise at approximately 25 per cent of aerobic power. Fat oxidation increases if exercise extends to long periods, as glycogen levels deplete. When considering the effects of long-term exercise the trained athlete has a greater opportunity to burn fat as a fuel than the non-trained athlete.

Assessment activity 2.2

1. You have been working alongside a cycling coach to support the training of his squad. One of the cyclists has requested an information sheet decribing how the musculoskeletal, cardiovascular, respiratory and energy systems respond to long-term exercise and training. **P3**, **P4**

2. In addition, the coach has asked you to prepare a PowerPoint presentation for the squad to explain the long-term effects of exercise on the musculoskeletal, cardiovascular, respiratory and energy systems. **M2**

Grading tips

P3, **P4** Use the example of a 6-week training programme to describe the adaptations to long-term exercise you would expect to see in the musculoskeletal, cardiovascular, respiratory and energy systems.

M2 Be sure to provide physiological evidence to support your explanation.

PLTS

Developing and formatting your PowerPoint presentation in a way that is fit for the intended audience will develop you as a **creative thinker**.

Functional skills

Developing and formatting your PowerPoint presentation in a way that is fit for the intended audience will evidence your **ICT** skills.

3. Be able to investigate the physiological effects of exercise on the body systems

Being physically fit is about having enough energy, strength and skill to cope with the everyday demands of your environment. Individual fitness levels vary greatly, from low levels required to cope with daily activities to optimal levels required by some performers at the top of their sport. Improving fitness will improve the physiological functioning of your body.

Key term

Fartlek (Swedish 'speed play') – a type of training that varies the pace at specific intervals and is usually applied to running. Continuous running at a steady pace is interspersed with changes in speed for varying durations.

3.1 Types of exercise

Aerobic

Endurance training is a generic term that refers to any low-intensity, long-duration activity such as running, rowing, swimming or cycling that aims to improve cardiorespiratory fitness. There are a number of techniques for developing this fitness component, including long, slow-distance training and varied pace or **Fartlek** training.

Long, slow-distance training is a popular continuous form of training undertaken at a steady pace. The exercise intensity is submaximal and usually set at around 70 per cent of maximum heart rate.

Fartlek training is similar to interval training but less fixed in its work to rest ratios and utilises a variety of terrains and gradients such as woodland trails, golf courses, sand dunes, uphill and downhill. Again, one of the key advantages of this mode of endurance training is that variety and motivation can be maintained. It can also be used to mimic the demands of sport such as the high-intensity intermittent bursts required to keep up with play on the football or hockey pitch.

Resistance

The fitness of muscles relates to their strength, size, power and endurance capacity. To develop muscular strength and endurance, the concept of progressive resistance overload must be applied to the training process. Muscle improvements are gained as they respond and adapt to overload. Progressive resistance overload means that as the muscles' strength and endurance increases, the load against which they are working must be increased periodically for continued gains to be realised. The training programme may be planned to emphasise muscular strength, muscle bulk, muscular endurance or explosive power. Muscular strength is achieved by using high resistance with low repetitions. Muscle strength and muscle bulk are interrelated in that as strength increases, so does bulk. Resistance training undertaken to result in muscle bulking should include sessions focused on maximal lifting.

Circuit training

In circuit training, exercises are organised and performed in a particular sequence. Each exercise usually targets a different muscle or muscle group. Circuit-training sessions can be planned to focus on the development of cardiorespiratory or muscular endurance and as a result are useful for improving overall fitness. Exercises aimed at the development of muscular endurance such as curl-ups, squats and press-ups can be interspersed with aerobic activities such as running, stepping and skipping. The resistance, number of repetitions, and recovery period between exercises will be determined by the fitness level of the participants. This mode of training can be adapted for use with individuals as well as groups, and is a useful mode of team training for many sports. It has the advantage of offering a variety of possibilities: it can be undertaken indoors, outdoors, with free weights or fixed weights in the gym, and can be tailored to meet the fitness demands of particular sports.

Interval training

This is a common form of endurance training for athletes who have already established a good base of endurance and wish to attain higher levels of fitness. Set periods of work, usually at a relatively high intensity, are followed by periods of recovery. The interval can vary from 30 seconds to 5 minutes and the recovery phase may be complete rest, a walk or jogging. The recovery periods, especially active forms of recovery, allow for the oxygen debt incurred during the work interval to be repaid. This mode of training develops both aerobic and anaerobic systems.

3.2 Methods of investigation

Physiological assessment and fitness testing can be used as a means of monitoring how the body adapts to long-term exercise.

Comparison of pre-exercise, exercise and post-exercise physiological readings

The most accurate measure of aerobic fitness is the laboratory assessment of maximal oxygen consumption known as the **VO_2 max** test. The test usually consists of walking or running on a treadmill, or cycling on a cycle ergometer for approximately 15 minutes with increasing loads with maximal effort. The oxygen used during the maximal effort is the maximal oxygen uptake. The higher the VO_2 max score, the fitter the individual.

> **Key term**
>
> **VO_2 max** – the maximum amount of oxygen that can be taken in by and be utilised by the body. Also, a measure of the endurance capacity of the cardiovascular and respiratory systems and exercising skeletal muscles.

Direct measurement of VO_2 max is time-consuming and requires expensive laboratory equipment, making it impractical for general use. As a result, researchers have developed several methods of estimating VO_2 max using simple field techniques, such as the Rockport walk test, Cooper's 1.5 mile run and the three-minute step test.

Rockport 1-mile walk test

This is a simple weight-bearing field test to determine cardiorespiratory fitness, which is particularly useful for sedentary subjects or those about to embark on a training programme. The objective is to complete the mile walk in as fast a time as possible. It involves a timed 1-mile walk on a smooth, level surface, preferably a running track in good weather conditions with the subject aiming to maintain a steady even pace throughout. The test procedure is as follows:

- Prior to commencing the test, the subject should undertake a 5–10-minute warm-up.

- The subject should be informed that the test requires maximum effort, but that if any distress is suffered during the test they should slow their pace, inform the researcher and seek medical advice as soon as possible.
- Activate the stop watch at the start of the measured mile and on completion of the test record the time taken.
- The subject should then undertake a 5–10-minute cool down.

Cooper's 1.5-mile run

This is another simple weight-bearing field test designed to evaluate cardiorespiratory endurance which can be more readily applied to physically active subjects. The objective is to complete the distance in the shortest time possible. It involves a timed 1.5-mile run on a smooth level surface, preferably a running track in good weather conditions. Again a useful strategy is to maintain a steady even pace throughout. The test procedure is as follows:

- Prior to commencing the test, the subject should undertake a 5–10-minute warm-up.
- The subject should be informed that the test requires maximum effort, but that if any distress is suffered during the test they should slow their pace, inform the researcher and seek medical advice as soon as possible.
- Activate the stop watch at the start of the measured 1.5 mile and on completion of the test record the time taken.
- The subject should then undertake a 5–10-minute cool down.

Take it further

Using the Internet and sources identified at the end of this unit, identify the fitness scores and classifications for the Cooper 1.5-mile run test.

Three-minute step test

The 3-minute step test is another submaximal test to determine aerobic fitness. The basic principle is that subjects with a higher level of aerobic fitness will recover more rapidly and have a lower heart rate during recovery from a 3-minute standardised bench-stepping test. One advantage of this test is that it can be performed indoors. The standardised height of the step is 45 cm (18 inches) and cadence 60 beats per minute (bpm) for both male and female subjects. Thirty complete steps in a four-beat cycle (up, down, up, down) should be completed during each minute of the test. The test procedure is as follows:

- Prior to commencing the test, the subject should undertake a 5–10-minute warm-up.
- The subject should be informed that the test requires maximum effort, but that if any distress is suffered during the test they should slow their pace, inform the researcher and seek medical advice as soon as possible.
- Set the metronome to 60 bpm.
- The subject starts stepping, ensuring that the knee is straightened during the up phase of the step.
- On completing the test the subject sits on the bench and the pulse is located and counted for a 30-second period during three separate recovery times: 1–1.5 minutes, 2–2.5 minutes and 3–3.5 minutes post-exercise.
- The subject's fitness category is determined by adding the three values obtained for the 30-second heart rates during recovery and referring to Table 2.2.
- The subject should then undertake a 5–10-minute cool down.

See Unit 7 Fitness testing for sport and exercise, pages 186–89 for information on the Forestry step test.

Take it further

There are a number of different protocols for the step test. Undertake your own research into three different step tests and compare and contrast their protocols and normative score data.

Activity: Try a fitness test

Working in pairs in the roles of subject and researcher, undertake one of the test protocols for establishing aerobic fitness and determine each other's fitness scores.

Remember

This test should only be attempted if the participant meets all the criteria on the pre-exercise health questionnaire. See Unit 4 Fitness training and programming, page 109, for an example of a pre-exercise health questionnaire.

Resting heart rate

Coinciding with every heartbeat a pulse can be felt wherever an artery can be compressed gently against a bone. It is possible to feel the movement of the blood by placing two or three fingers over the artery. Common sites for measurement of the pulse are the wrist (radial artery), the neck (carotid artery) or the elbow (brachial artery).

Counting the 'pulse' of the blood at these points is a simple method that is often used to estimate heart rate. It can provide a useful estimate for training purposes, but it is important to note that the true maximum heart rate can vary by plus or minus 15 bpm. The average range of pulse in healthy adults is between 60–80 bpm. Increases in temperature, exercise and intense emotion can all raise pulse rate.

Exercise heart rate

While exercising you will need to elevate your heart rate to produce a training effect. Target heart-rate zone charts can be used to identify working heart-rate ranges.

Percentage of heart rate maximum

Percentage of heart rate maximum can be used to calculate target heart rate zones. One simple formula for obtaining target heart rate is 220 minus age (to determine theoretical maximum heart rate) multiplied by a percentage depending on physical condition and fitness goals (usually 60–85 per cent for developing aerobic fitness).

Percentage of heart rate reserve maximum

Your heart rate reserve is your theoretical maxiumum heart rate minus your resting heart rate. Once you know your heart rate reserve, you can calculate your training heart rate zones based on a percentage.

Target Heart Rate Zones should only be used as a guide. How an individual feels while exercising (the perceived exertion) is also important. While exercising aerobically you should be able to hold a conversation and feel puffed rather than exhausted.

Rating of Perceived Exertion (RPE)

The best way to monitor intensity during exercise is to use a combination of heart-rate measures and ratings of perceived exertion (RPE). Heart rates can be taken manually or by wearing a heart-rate monitor. RPE is a ten-point scale that focuses on tuning the body into physical cues for recognising intensity of effort, such as a quickened breathing rate, breathlessness or flat-out effort. The RPE scale provides a way of quantifying subjective exercise intensity, but has been shown to correlate well with heart rate and oxygen uptake.

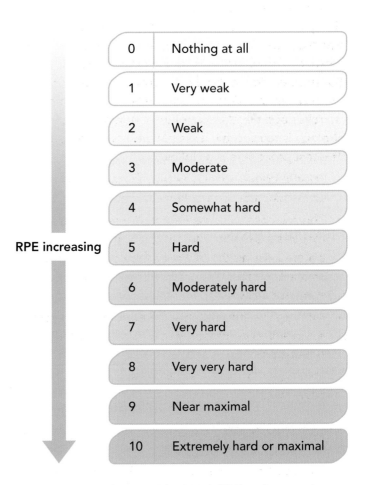

0	Nothing at all
1	Very weak
2	Weak
3	Moderate
4	Somewhat hard
5	Hard
6	Moderately hard
7	Very hard
8	Very very hard
9	Near maximal
10	Extremely hard or maximal

RPE increasing

Figure 2.3: Rate of perceived exertion (RPE) scale

Blood pressure

The blood in the circulatory system is always under pressure. Without blood pressure, blood would gravitate to the lowest parts of the body. Blood pressure therefore enables some of the circulatory blood to gravitate upwards to supply the brain, and to flow through the tiny capillaries.

Blood pressure in the large arteries varies with the heartbeat. It is highest when the ventricle contracts (the systolic pressure), and lowest when the ventricle relaxes (the diastolic pressure). Blood pressure can be measured using a sphygmomanometer and is measured in millimetres of mercury. Normal blood pressure is considered to be anything between 100–140 mmHg for systolic and 60–90 mmHg for diastolic pressure. Blood pressure will be affected by anything that makes the heart beat faster. Exercise, along with a wide range of other factors such as stress, anger, excitement, pain and even smoking can cause blood pressure to rise. Low blood pressure is considered as values less than 99 mmHg systolic and 58 mmHg diastolic. High blood pressure (or hypertension), results when resting pressure is above normal values.

Remember

Blood pressure is measured in mmHg, which stands for millimetres of mercury.

Flexibility tests

Flexibility is the ability to work a joint and its associated soft tissue structures freely through its full range of movement. In the absence of routine stretching, muscles and tendons shorten, becoming tight and impairing the range of movement. Good flexibility allows you to perform daily activities with ease, such as dressing and bending to pick things up from the floor. Flexibility is often undervalued and undertrained. Sport, health and lifestyle benefits of good flexibility include:

* maintenance of healthy joints
* good posture and prevention of lower back pain
* reduced risk of injury
* better balance and coordination.

Take it further

Working in pairs under the guidance of your tutor measure your blood pressure, flexibility and peak flow.

The sit-and-reach test is the most common measure of flexibility, and is designed to assess the flexibility of the lower back and hamstring muscles. It requires minimal equipment (a bench and a large measuring stick or ruler). The client sits on the floor with their feet 30 cm apart, with their heels touching the bench. The ruler should protrude 15 cm over the bench towards the client. They should reach forward slowly and as far as possible, without forcing the movement and keeping the backs of their knees in touch with the floor and their hands parallel. A score is obtained by measuring the furthest point reached by the fingertips before or beyond the toes.

Spirometry

Lung function can be measured using a technique called spirometry. This measures how efficiently the lungs work and determines how much air they can hold and how efficiently they transfer oxygen into the blood. For this test you need to breathe into a mouthpiece attached to a recording device where the information collected is printed out on to a chart known as a spirogram.

A more common measure of lung function is the measurement of peak flow. This is a simple measurement of how much air can be pushed out of the lungs in one fast blast, using a portable, inexpensive hand-held meter.

When measuring peak flow it is important to use the correct procedure:

* attach a mouthpiece to the meter and make sure it is set to zero
* if possible, the subject should stand
* the subject takes a deep breath and places their lips tightly around the mouthpiece
* the subject breathes out as hard and as long as they can
* the process is repeated a maximum of three times, taking the highest value attained.

Peak flow scores are dependent on age, height and sex, for example a young boy who is 1.50 metre tall should have a peak flow of approximately 350 litres per minute, while a 50-year-old who is 1.75 metre tall should have a peak flow of approximately 600 litres per minute. Scores should always be evaluated in line with previous test scores.

3.3 Review

Recording results from testing sessions will allow you to analyse and interpret your data with the aim of making an assessment of the client's fitness, either as a baseline score or as a measure of progress.

You can compare scores against normative data for specific tests. This allows you to compare your client's performance with others of the same age and sex.

Effects of exercise on the body systems

There are differences between your body's responses to exercise and how it adapts to long-term exercise. The immediate changes that occur to the energy and neuromuscular systems are called **acute responses**. **Long-term responses** following repeated bouts of activity and training are referred to as adaptations to exercise.

> ### Remember
>
> **Acute responses (to exercise)** – the immediate changes that occur in your body as a result of the increased demands placed upon it by exercise.
>
> **Long-term responses (to exercise)** – adaptations that contribute to improved fitness for sports participation and reduced health risk.

Pre-exercise, exercise and post-exercise physiological data

Pre-exercise, exercise and post-exercise testing can be used to measure and evaluate components of fitness for a variety of reasons:

- to identify components of fitness that require improvement
- to provide **benchmark scores** against which improvements can be measured
- to allow for the development of a more targeted programme of fitness training
- to educate the client about health and fitness.

> ### Remember
>
> It is important that health and safety issues are considered before, during and after a testing session in order to maintain the safety of the client and tester.

> ### Key term
>
> **Benchmark scores** – give a current fitness status against which to monitor adaptation within a fitness programme.

Normative data tables can be used to analyse fitness testing results. Normative tables have been devised by researchers testing hundreds of subjects. When using normative data you need to consider that:

- most are age-specific
- they can be gender-specific
- some may specify a level of performance or be population-specific (e.g. sedentary, elite).

Practicality of exercise activities selected

It may be necessary to reset goals and targets based on results reviewed. To complete the evaluation process you need to offer recommendations to the client to either improve or maintain their fitness. In the design of a training programme, appropriate exercises must be considered that take account of the client's preferences and circumstances in terms of affordability and ease of access and whether they can be easily incorporated into their fitness regime.

Advantages and disadvantages of different tests

Whether you use a laboratory- or a field-based test, you will need to consider its advantages and disadvantages. General issues for consideration include cost, time, equipment and facility requirements, skills level and issues of test validity and reliability.

Strengths and areas for improvement

In any feedback to a client you will need to identify strengths and areas for improvement. This allows for possible recommendations for future training plans and activities. Where possible it is useful to provide normative data for reference if this will be motivating to the client.

Assessment activity 2.3

1. Working in pairs under the supervision of your tutor, choose two different types of exercise and obtain physiological data to investigate the acute and long-term responses of a fellow class member (your client).

2. Record and review the data you have collected pre-, during and post-exercise and write this up in a short report. In your report, give consideration to the practicality of exercise activities you selected and any advantages and disadvantages encountered during data collection. You should also describe the strengths and any areas for improvement in your investigation. **P5**, **P6**

3. Provide a 6-week training plan for your client, identifying appropriate training activities to improve their fitness. You will need to explore their exercise preferences and different training modes as well as carrying out repeat physiological assessments at the end of the training period.

4. Write a report on your client's progress and adaptations to your training programme. Did you observe the results you where expecting? **M3** **M4**

5. To achieve D1 and D2, carry out the tasks above without tutor support. **D1**, **D2**

Grading tips

P5 Explain how the different types of exercise result in differing reponses and adaptations to acute and chronic exercise.

P6 Examine the practicality of exercise activities selected and any advantages and disadvantages encountered during data collection. Consider the strengths and any areas for improvement in your investigation, for example the reliability and validity of the tests you have used.

M3 Examine how different types of exercise result in differing reponses and adaptations to acute and chronic exercise.

M4 Justify the practicality of activities selected and any advantages and disadvantages encountered during data collection. Consider the strengths and areas for improvement in

your investigation, for example the suitability, reliability and validity of the tests you have used.

D1 As part of your written report, evaluate the test you have used and adaptations you have found. Support your findings with reference to appropriate literature.

D2 Critically evaluate the results of your investigation against normative data. Analyse the practicality of exercise activities selected and any advantages and disadvantages encountered during data collection, and analyse the strengths and areas for improvement in your investigation, for example the suitability, reliability and validity of the tests you have used. What do the results mean in relation to your client's level of fitness and performance?

PLTS

Independently conducting physiological investigations and collecting data to provide a training plan for a selected individual will develop your skills as an **independent enquirer**. Reviewing the results and analysing how the individual responds to exercise in both the short and long term will develop your skills as a **reflective learner**.

Functional skills

Developing and formatting data to provide a clear and accurate record of your investigations will develop your **ICT** skills. Presenting information in a client-friendly manner will develop your **English** skills in both written and verbal forms of communication.

Kate Jenkins
Health and Fitness Instructor

I work in a health club chain as part of a team who deliver health and fitness services to a range of clients. All of our team are qualified fitness instructors and are members of the Register of Exercise Professionals (REPs).

My work responsibilities include:

- health and fitness assessments
- exercise prescription and programming
- ensuring health and safety standards are met.

My typical day involves undertaking individual lifestyle and fitness assessments. I may spend 2–3 hours each day developing and reviewing health-related exercise programmes for clients, instructing clients on new programmes or new equipment. Out of work hours I try to find time to fit in my own gym training sessions or occasional run.

The best thing about my job is seeing how people respond to positive changes in the assessment of their fitness and how they are adapting to their fitness programmes. Many people are apprehensive about fitness assessment, and struggle with some of the immediate responses to exercise, e.g. increased shortness of breath on exertion. With a carefully planned programme appropriate to current level of fitness, these challenges can be overcome. I find it satisfying to know that I have helped clients overcome these challenges and improved their fitness.

Think about it!

- What knowledge and skills have you covered in this unit that would provide you with an understanding of the role of the health and fitness instructor? Jot your ideas down and discuss with your peers.
- How would you rate your current level of competency at using the knowledge and skills you have developed in this unit? What further knowledge and skills might you need to develop to pursue a career in the fitness industry?
- Investigate further the range of tests you can undertake to assess fitness and monitor the body's acute and chronic responses to exercise.

Just checking

1. Describe the short- and long-term effects of exercise on the cardiovascular system.
2. Identify two of the respiratory system's short-term responses to exercise.
3. Describe the three energy systems.
4. Explain the difference between responses and adaptations to exercise.
5. Explain how your heart and lungs work together to respond to steady-state exercise such as running on a treadmill for 30 minutes.
6. What is normative data and how can it be used in the evaluation of fitness?
7. Identify two tests that can be used to assess aerobic endurance.
8. Describe vasodilation and vasoconstriction.
9. Briefly describe factors that might raise heart rate but are not exercise-related.
10. Explain the concepts of reliability and validity.

Assignment tips

- You will enhance your learning in this unit by practical experience, so when taking part in sport and exercise, reflect on your theoretical learning to discuss and identify through experience the effects that exercise and activity have on your different body systems.

- When undertaking the practical activities in this unit, keep a notebook at hand to facilitate your data collection, and consider the advantages and disadvantages encountered in your data collection to evidence critical evaluation.

- You may find it useful to shadow the work of a health and fitness instructor, personal trainer or exercise physiologist to observe the practical application of field- and laboratory-based assessments.

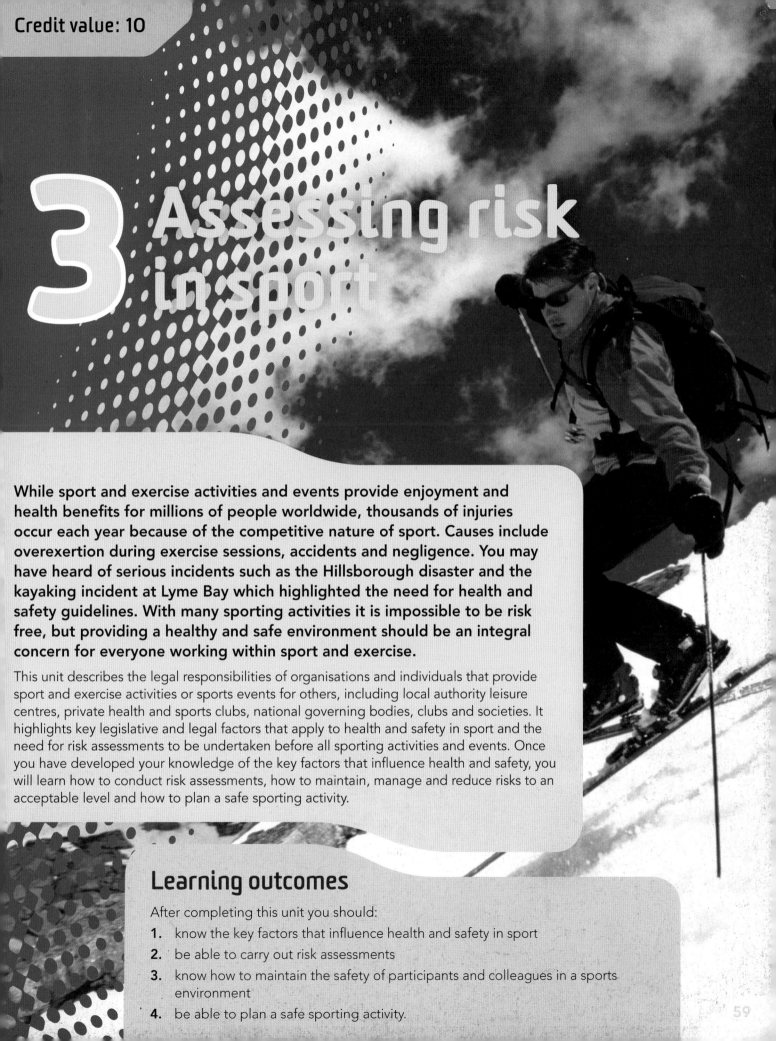

3 Assessing risk in sport

While sport and exercise activities and events provide enjoyment and health benefits for millions of people worldwide, thousands of injuries occur each year because of the competitive nature of sport. Causes include overexertion during exercise sessions, accidents and negligence. You may have heard of serious incidents such as the Hillsborough disaster and the kayaking incident at Lyme Bay which highlighted the need for health and safety guidelines. With many sporting activities it is impossible to be risk free, but providing a healthy and safe environment should be an integral concern for everyone working within sport and exercise.

This unit describes the legal responsibilities of organisations and individuals that provide sport and exercise activities or sports events for others, including local authority leisure centres, private health and sports clubs, national governing bodies, clubs and societies. It highlights key legislative and legal factors that apply to health and safety in sport and the need for risk assessments to be undertaken before all sporting activities and events. Once you have developed your knowledge of the key factors that influence health and safety, you will learn how to conduct risk assessments, how to maintain, manage and reduce risks to an acceptable level and how to plan a safe sporting activity.

Learning outcomes

After completing this unit you should:

1. know the key factors that influence health and safety in sport
2. be able to carry out risk assessments
3. know how to maintain the safety of participants and colleagues in a sports environment
4. be able to plan a safe sporting activity.

Assessment and grading criteria

This table shows you what you must do in order to achieve a pass, merit or distinction grade, and where you can find activities in this book to help you.

To achieve a **pass** grade the evidence must show that the learner is able to:	To achieve a **merit** grade the evidence must show that, in addition to the pass criteria, the learner is able to:	To achieve a **distinction** grade the evidence must show that, in addition to the pass and merit criteria, the learner is able to:
P1 describe four legislative factors that influence health and safety in sport **Assessment activity 3.1, page 73**	**M1** compare and contrast the influences of legislation, legal factors and regulatory bodies on health and safety in sport **Assessment activity 3.1, page 73**	
P2 describe the legal factors and regulatory bodies that influence health and safety in sport **Assessment activity 3.1, page 73**		
P3 carry out risk assessments for two different sports activities, with tutor support **Assessment activity 3.2, page 76**	**M2** independently carry out risk assessments for two different sports activities **Assessment activity 3.2, page 76**	**D1** review the risk assessment controls and evaluate their effectiveness **Assessment activity 3.2, page 76**
P4 describe three procedures used to promote and maintain a healthy and safe sporting environment **Assessment activity 3.3, page 80**	**M3** explain three procedures used to promote and maintain a healthy and safe sporting environment **Assessment activity 3.3, page 80**	**D2** analyse three procedures used to promote and maintain a healthy and safe sporting environment **Assessment activity 3.3, page 80**
P5 produce a plan for the safe delivery of a selected sports activity and review the plan **Assessment activity 3.4, page 84**	**M4** explain the plan for the safe delivery of a selected sports activity and review the plan **Assessment activity 3.4, page 84**	

How you will be assessed

This unit will be assessed by internal assignments designed and marked by the tutors at your centre. Your assessments could be in the form of:

- written reports
- posters
- presentations
- risk assessments
- activity plans.

Maria Conti, 19-year-old sports massage therapist

This unit was really useful for me as it taught me about the different legislation that is important for my part-time job, different aspects of insurance that I needed and who I could go to for more advice regarding different health and safety issues. This unit has also been really useful as it has made me reflect on my own work and made me think about whether the way that I work is safe. As well as the legal elements and my responsibilities with other people, I now consider the less obvious things that relate to protecting myself, such as using the correct stance and techniques in massage treatments and having the correct protective equipment.

The part of the unit that I enjoyed the most was looking at duty of care and negligence. This was really interesting when I was looking at the different cases and trying to decide whether people were negligent or not, and why. It really challenged my thinking skills and I could apply it to the career that I wanted to progress into.

Over to you

- **Which elements of the unit are you looking forward to learning about?**
- **Which parts do you think are the most applicable to the careers that you want to progress into?**

1. Know the key factors that influence health and safety in sport

How aware are you of health and safety?

Think about the number of stewards and security staff that you see at professional sports events – why do you think they have to be there? What about all the first-aid boxes and therapist bags that you will have seen at games that you have played in?

There are a number of legislative factors, legal factors and regulatory bodies that are the underpinning factors associated with health and safety within sport activities and events.

1.1 Legislative factors

A legislative factor relates to making or enforcing the law. Due to the ever-changing nature of sport and the number of hazards and risks associated with it, there is key legislation that impacts on sport within the UK.

Health and Safety at Work Act (1974)

The main health and safety legislation is the Health and Safety at Work Act (1974). This sets out the general duties that employers, self-employed people and those in control of premises have towards their employees and others who could be affected by their work activities (such as customers and clients). It gives employees the duty to ensure the health and safety of themselves and each other.

The principles of the Health and Safety at Work Act are to:

- secure the health, safety and welfare of people at work
- protect people other than those at work against risks to health and safety arising from the activities of people at work
- control the handling and storage of dangerous substances
- control the emission into the atmosphere of noxious or offensive substances from premises.

It is the duty of the employer, as far as is reasonably practicable, to safeguard the health, safety and welfare of the people who work for them as well as that of non-employees (for example, customers, visitors and members of the general public) while they are on the premises. The term 'reasonable and practicable' means what could reasonably be expected to ensure that everybody you are responsible for is safeguarded. It means that in any situation you must use your own judgement before taking a course of action. You should carefully consider all the options, thinking about the consequences (i.e. what could happen as a result of this decision?), how quickly you can decide to do something and the available resources. At that time, you need to decide what you consider to be reasonable and practicable.

Under the Health and Safety at Work Act the employee also has responsibilities. Employees are responsible for:

- taking care of their own health and safety
- taking care of the health and safety of others who may be affected by their actions
- cooperating with the employer and other relevant organisations to ensure that the requirements of the act are met (including notifying supervisors of unsafe equipment or practices)
- not misusing equipment provided to maintain health and safety.

Remember

The main aim of the Health and Safety at Work Act is to ensure the health and safety of everybody in the workplace.

Reporting of Injuries, Diseases and Dangerous Occurrences Regulations (RIDDOR, 1995)

The regulations relating to reporting accidents and incidents are covered under the Reporting of Injuries, Diseases and Dangerous Occurrences Regulations (1995). These regulations are also known as RIDDOR. RIDDOR places a legal duty on employers, self-employed people and people in control of premises to report:

- work-related deaths
- major injuries or over-three-day injuries
- work-related diseases
- dangerous occurrences (near-miss accidents).

RIDDOR is in place to allow the **Health and Safety Executive (HSE)** to:

- follow up, report and check safety practices and operational procedures
- ensure a standardised report form is used
- allow officers from the HSE to advise organisations on prevention of further accident and illness
- allow an investigation to prosecute, prohibit and make improvements where necessary.

Key term

Health and Safety Executive (HSE) – the organisation responsible for proposing and enforcing safety regulations throughout the UK.

HSE Health & Safety Executive

Health and Safety at Work etc Act 1974

The Reporting of Injuries, Diseases and Dangerous Occurrences Regulations 1995

Report of an injury or dangerous occurrence

Filling in this form

This form must be filled in by an employer or other responsible person.

Part A

About you

1 What is your full name?

2 What is your job title?

3 What is your telephone number?

About your organisation

4 What is the name of your organisation?

5 What is its address and postcode?

6 What type of work does the organisation do?

Part B

About the incident

1 On what date did the incident happen?

2 At what time did the incident happen? (Please use the 24-hour clock eg 0600)

3 Did the incident happen at the above address?

Yes ☐ Go to question 4

No ☐ Where did the incident happen?

☐ elsewhere in your organisation – give the name, address and postcode

☐ at someone else's premises – give the name, address and postcode

☐ in a public place – give details of where it happened

If you do not know the postcode, what is the name of the local authority?

4 In which department, or where on the premises, did the incident happen?

F2508 (05.00)

Part C

About the injured person

If you are reporting a dangerous occurrence, go to Part F. If more than one person was injured in the same incident, please attach the details asked for in Part C and Part D for each injured person.

1 What is their full name?

2 What is their home address and postcode?

3 What is their home phone number?

4 How old are they?

5 Are they

☐ male?

☐ female?

6 What is their job title?

7 Was the injured person (tick only one box)

☐ one of your employees?

☐ on a training scheme? Give details:

☐ on work experience?

☐ employed by someone else? Give details of the employer:

☐ self-employed and at work?

☐ a member of the public?

Part D

About the injury

1 What was the injury? (eg fracture, laceration)

2 What part of the body was injured?

3 Was the injury (tick the one box that applies)

☐ a fatality?

☐ a major injury or condition? (see accompanying notes)

☐ an injury to an employee or self-employed person which prevented them doing their normal work for more than 3 days?

☐ an injury to a member of the public which meant they had to be taken from the scene of the accident to a hospital for treatment?

4 Did the injured person (tick all the boxes that apply)

☐ become unconscious?

☐ need resuscitation?

☐ remain in hospital for more than 24 hours?

☐ none of the above.

Part E

About the kind of accident

Please tick the one box that best describes what happened, then go to Part G.

☐ Contact with moving machinery or material being machined

☐ Hit by a moving, flying or falling object

☐ Hit by a moving vehicle

☐ Hit something fixed or stationary

☐ Injured while handling, lifting or carrying

☐ Slipped, tripped or fell on the same level

☐ Fell from a height

How high was the fall? metres

☐ Trapped by something collapsing

☐ Drowned or asphyxiated

☐ Exposed to, or in contact with, a harmful substance

☐ Exposed to fire

☐ Exposed to an explosion

☐ Contact with electricity or an electrical discharge

☐ Injured by an animal

☐ Physically assaulted by a person

☐ Another kind of accident (describe it in Part G)

Part F

Dangerous occurrences

Enter the number of the dangerous occurrence you are reporting. (The numbers are given in the Regulations and in the notes which accompany this form)

Part G

Describing what happened

Give as much detail as you can. For instance

- the name of any substance involved
- the name and type of any machine involved
- the events that led to the incident
- the part played by any people.

If it was a personal injury, give details of what the person was doing. Describe any action that has since been taken to prevent a similar incident. Use a separate piece of paper if you need to.

Part H

Your signature

Signature

Date

If returning by post/fax, please ensure this form is signed, alternatively, if returning by E-Mail, please type your name in the signature box

Where to send the form

Incident Contact Centre, Caerphilly Business Centre, Caerphilly Business Park, Caerphilly, CF83 3GG.

or email to riddor@connaught.plc.uk or fax to 0845 300 99 2

For official use

Client number Location number Event number

☐ INV REP ☐ Y ☐ N

Figure 3.1: Why do you think that you need to report such depth of detail on a RIDDOR form?

Personal Protective Equipment (PPE, 2002)

The Personal Protective Equipment (2002) regulations cover all aspects concerned with the use of **personal protective equipment (PPE)**. The regulations require PPE (such as safety helmets, gloves, eye protection and high-visibility clothing) to be supplied and used at work wherever there are risks to workers' health and safety that cannot be adequately controlled in other ways. The regulations require that PPE is:

- properly assessed before use to ensure its suitability for the work being done
- maintained and stored correctly
- supplied with adequate instructions so that users know how to use it safely
- worn correctly by the user.

Control of Substances Hazardous to Health (COSHH, 2002)

Hazardous substances include all substances or mixtures of substances classified as dangerous to health under the Chemicals (Hazard Information and Packaging for Supply) Regulations 2002 (CHIP), such as:

- substances used directly in work activities (for example, adhesives, paints and cleaning agents such as markings used for sports pitches)
- substances generated during work activities (for example, fumes from soldering and welding)
- naturally occurring substances (for example, grain dust)
- biological agents (for example, bacteria and other micro-organisms such as those in swimming pools or spas).

The COSHH regulations can be enforced by following an eight-step process. The steps and example activities associated with each step can be seen in Table 3.1 on page 65.

COSSH is important in a leisure centre swimming pool, which contains different chemicals. Under COSHH, bacteriological testing should be carried out regularly. In public leisure centres such tests are checked by the HSE while in private leisure pools this responsibility often falls on the Environmental Health Officer to take random bacteriological tests.

Health and Safety (First-aid) Regulations (1981)

The Health and Safety (First-aid) Regulations (1981) require that, in order to provide first-aid to their

Key terms

Personal Protective Equipment (PPE) – all equipment (including clothing affording protection against the weather) which is intended to be worn or held by a person at work and which protects them from one or more risks to their health or safety, for example, safety helmets, gloves, eye protection, high-visibility clothing and safety footwear.

Health surveillance – a strategy and method for employers to detect and assess systematically the adverse effects of work on the health of workers.

employees who are injured or become ill at work, employers must have adequate and appropriate equipment, facilities and personnel. The regulations also state that an organisation must provide:

- first-aid equipment, including first-aid boxes, a list of controls and their locations and supplementary equipment such as a spine board and resuscitation kit
- a first-aid room (the regulations also specify the size, design and location)
- first-aiders and any necessary training programmes (this includes a list of those people who have received a certificate from an authorised training body – certificates are normally valid for at least one year).

Manual Handling Operations Regulations (1992)

The Manual Handling Operations Regulations (1992) apply to any situation where employees are carrying, lifting or moving loads. Loads are not identified with a maximum weight so each requires a risk assessment of the task, the weight to be lifted or carried and the working environment.

Employers are required to 'avoid hazardous manual handling operations' as far as is reasonably practicable. This can be done in several ways.

Activity: Manual handling guidelines

In groups, research the guidelines for correct posture while lifting heavy loads. Produce a poster that shows a series of images demonstrating correct lifting technique with an explanation of each image.

Step	Example activities
Undertake a risk assessment (to be carried out by appropriately trained individual)	• Identify hazardous substances • Consider the risks these substances present
Decide what precautions are needed	• Decide on all actions, such as measures to prevent hazardous substances being absorbed through the skin
Prevent or adequately control exposure (do what is reasonably practicable)	• Change the process or activity so that hazardous substances are not needed or generated • Replace hazardous substances with a safer alternative • Use in a safer form, for example, cones instead of markings
Ensure that control measures are used and maintained	• Staff training • Display notices • Checks by managers or supervisors
Monitor exposure	• Measure the concentration of hazardous substances
Carry out appropriate **health surveillance**	• Monitor any adverse effects of exposure to hazardous substances
Prepare plans and procedures to deal with accidents, incidents and emergencies	• Set up warning systems • Set up lines of communication in the case of an incident
Ensure that employees are properly informed, trained and supervised	• Provide suitable and sufficient information, instruction and training, which should include: o the names of the substances they work with or could be exposed to and the risks o the main findings of the risk assessment o the precautions that should be taken to protect themselves and others o how to use personal protective equipment and clothing o the results of any exposure monitoring and health surveillance (without giving individual employees' names) o any emergency procedures that need to be followed.

Table 3.1: The eight steps of the COSHH regulations

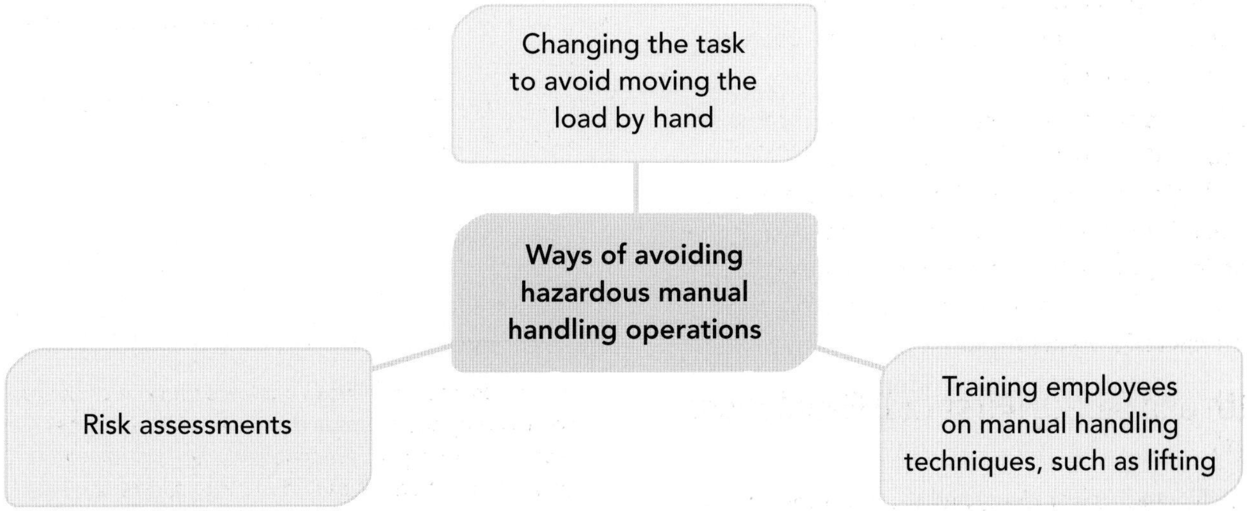

Figure 3.2: Ways of avoiding hazardous manual handling operations

Management of Health and Safety Regulations (1999)

These regulations came into place to make more explicit what employers were required to do to manage health and safety under the Health and Safety at Work Act. The major change in these regulations was the necessity for employers to conduct risk assessments. This major change included specific regulations for the employment of young people. Under these regulations, every employer and anyone who is self-employed, such as a football coach, should make a suitable and sufficient assessment of the risks to the health and safety of employees or himself/herself while at work; and the risks to the health and safety of people not in employment, such as visitors to a leisure centre or participants with a coaching session. An employer with five or more employees needs to record the significant findings of the risk assessment.

In addition to the general guidelines given on assessing risk in the workplace, these regulations provide specific information relating to young people (people under the age of 18). Under these regulations, an employer should:

Why do you think manual handling guidelines could be important in jobs such as fitness instructing?

- assess the risk to the young person before they begin employment
- take into consideration a young person's psychological or physical immaturity, inexperience, and lack of awareness of existing or potential risks
- introduce control measures to eliminate or minimise the risks, so far as is reasonably practicable.

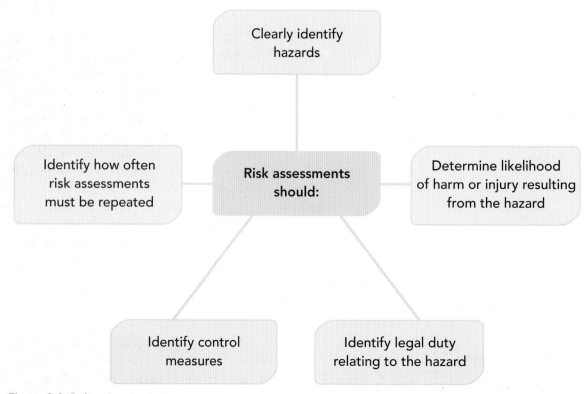

Clearly identify hazards

Identify how often risk assessments must be repeated

Risk assessments should:

Determine likelihood of harm or injury resulting from the hazard

Identify control measures

Identify legal duty relating to the hazard

Figure 3.3: Risk assessments

Fire Safety and Safety of Places of Sport Act (1987)

This legislation was brought into effect as a result of the Popplewell Inquiry, which examined the safety of sports grounds following the devastating fire at Bradford City Football Club in May 1985 in which 56 people died. This act is in five main parts:

1. Fire safety
2. The safety of sports grounds
3. The safety of stands at sports grounds
4. Indoor sports licences
5. Miscellaneous and general section relating to fees and exemption.

Adventurous Activities Licensing Authority Regulations (2004)

These regulations arose from the tragedy at Lyme Bay in 1993 when four teenagers died while on a kayaking trip. This event accelerated governmental discussions until the Activity Centres (Young Persons' Safety) Act (1995) was passed through parliament in January 1995 and an independent licensing authority, the Adventurous Activities Licensing Authority (AALA), was created to bring the act into reality. It is a legal requirement under the Activity Centres (Young Persons' Safety) Act (1995) for providers of certain adventure activities to undergo inspection of their safety management systems and become licensed. This licensing scheme only applies to those who offer activities to young people under the age of 18 and who operate these activities commercially. Generally, licensing only applies to these activities when they are done in remote or isolated environments, for example, climbing on natural terrain requires a licence whereas climbing on a purpose-built climbing wall does not.

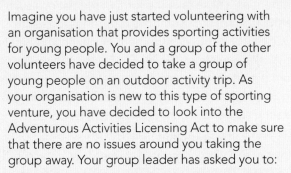

1.2 Legal factors

Law

- **Statutory** – legislation has become the common source of new laws or law reform since the seventeenth century. When thinking of modern laws, you may think of sections in an **Act of Parliament** such as the Health and Safety at Work Act (1974). **Statutes** can be applied to all or any combination of **jurisdictions** within the UK, whereas common law jurisdictions are more limited. Acts of Parliament which apply to everyone throughout one or more jurisdiction are called public general acts. But acts may be limited to geographical locations within a jurisdiction (such as local bye-laws) or to specific people or companies. They are designed to regulate the behaviour of organisations and individuals and are enforced by representatives of the government (mainly the police). The courts, magistrates and crown courts impose penalties on those found to have criminal liability, such as fines, improvement and remedial liabilities.

Statutory legislation comes with a number of instruments that relate closely to the act. These are put forward by the Health and Safety Commission following discussions and advice provided by relevant organisations that represent the industry such as national governing bodies of sport and local authorities. These take the form of regulations such as the Control of Substances Hazardous to Health (COSHH) and the Management of Health and Safety at Work Regulations (1999). Guidelines and codes of conduct often produced by specialists and governing bodies of sport also play a major role in providing a healthy, safe and secure environment by determining standards and approved codes of practice.

Any person who commits a crime does so against the state. This means they have made a breach of criminal law. The police will make a criminal charge and have to prove that the person accused is guilty beyond reasonable doubt. If the person is guilty, the courts impose a punishment that could be in the form of a fine or a prison sentence.

Remember

Codes of practice are not legislation but are often considered by the law to be developed by experts in their field and hence are often referenced when people take civil action.

- **Civil law** – there is an increasing awareness of individuals' legal rights and willingness to seek compensation for damages caused by the acts or omissions of others. This is especially so within a sporting environment where one person suffers a sports injury caused by another player. For example, there are several cases where a professional footballer has won a case for injuries caused by the poor tackle of another player. These cases are normally heard in county and high courts. An individual (plaintiff) brings an action against another party (defendant) to claim damages for losses incurred. The penalties that can be imposed by the courts are known as civil liability and the action taken by the plaintiff is called civil action. The most important common law duty for providers of sport and leisure in terms of health and safety is the duty of care. For employers this means that they have to take reasonable care to protect their employees from the risk of foreseeable injury or death at work.

- **Case law** – the legal system within the UK was based largely on case law (law developed through decisions by judges on cases brought before them, sometimes called common law) until around the seventeenth century. Each jurisdiction developed its own forms of common law. Since then, new laws and law reform have increasingly been brought about through Acts of Parliament. A statement of law made by a judge in a case can become binding on later judges and can in this way become the law for everyone to follow. This is called a precedent and has an important role in case law. It ensures certainty, consistency, logical progression and development in the law. At the same time it can be rigid and complex. Nevertheless, common law has advantages over **codified systems**. It is more flexible and practical as it is derived from real-life dramas played out before the courts.

Key terms

Act of Parliament – these originate from a bill, which is considered by both houses of parliament. Once the content of the bill has been agreed, it receives Royal Assent and becomes an Act of Parliament.

Statute – a written law passed by a legislative body.

Jurisdiction – the right and power to apply the law.

Codified systems – general and permanent laws or regulations that are arranged in subject matter order by title or other major subdivision and section.

In loco parentis

According to the courts, when parents send a child to school or college they delegate their authority to the tutor (so far as is necessary for the child's welfare and so far as is reasonable to maintain discipline) both in the interests of the school or college as a whole and (above all) of the individual student. As a result, a tutor supervising or accompanying a student on a school or college trip has responsibility for the student's health and safety and is said to act 'in loco parentis'. The tutor is expected to apply the same standard of care as a 'reasonable parent' acting within a range of reasonable responses. The standard of care that a court expects might vary according to the type of activity, the age and maturity of the students and changing conditions. A tutor who takes a party away from school or college remains 'in loco parentis' throughout the trip – the responsibility cannot be delegated to anyone else. Tutors could be liable for negligence if a student or other person suffers injury or damage as a consequence of their carelessness, or their failure to act within the range of reasonable responses.

Duty of care

All those involved in sport have a duty of care for the health and safety of others who may be affected by their actions. These include owners, event organisers, staff, agents, contractors, officials, coaches, administrators and participants. All these groups need to have some understanding of the law of negligence and how it applies to them. Duty of care is based on common sense, reason and foresight. You are said to have a duty of care when it is 'reasonably foreseeable' (predictable) that your actions may cause harm. The principles for duty of care were laid down in the case of Donoghue versus Stevenson (1932). These principles form the basis for establishing a duty of care under UK law. The general principles for duty of care were highlighted in this case as follows:

- Does a duty of care exist? This depends on the relationship between the parties, as a duty of care is not owed to everybody but only to those who have a sufficiently close relationship. The courts have found that there is no liability if the relationship between the parties is too remote.
- Is there a breach of that duty? Liability will only arise if the action breaches the duty of care and causes

Why do you think that duty of care is an important concept for sports coaches?

a loss or harm to the individual which would have been reasonably foreseeable in all the facts and circumstances of the case.

- Did the breach cause damage or loss to an individual's person or property? When this case was decided it was thought that duty of care would only be applicable to physical injury and damage to property. However, this has been extended in some circumstances to include economic loss.

All those involved in sport, including participants, need to comply with legislation as a minimum standard and be aware of relevant codes of practice, regulations and the issue of 'forseeability'. This extends to those involved on the field of play such as players, coaches and officials. Duty of care is said to be breached when the standard of care falls short of the 'accepted standard'. The accepted standard is that of the 'ordinary skilled person' working within that position, for example, a personal trainer has a higher standard of care than an assistant fitness instructor. You should also note that the accepted standard is not variable within the same profession, for example, a personal trainer on their first day with their first client has the same standard as a personal trainer with ten years' experience.

Higher duty of care

It is recognised that there is a higher duty of care owed to children and young people and this is something that those working in sport with children and young people must reflect. An example of this is the Occupier's Liability Act (1957). This requires that 'an occupier must be prepared for children to be less careful than adults would be in a similar situation'. This consideration should be even greater if a child is known to have learning difficulties or a medical condition that may make them more vulnerable than the average child to foreseeable risk of harm.

Negligence

Negligence is a term used in civil law when breaches in health and safety have occurred and have resulted in injury or harm to another person or to property. Negligence claims are closely related to duty of care. To be able to win a claim for negligence, you need to have been owed a duty of care by the person who caused the harm or damage; you must be able to show that the duty of care was breached and that the injury or damage was a result of the breach of duty of care. The common defences that are used against negligence claims are that the injury or damage was caused by an unforeseen accident or that the injury or damage occurred when the claimant volunteered to take the risk or when the claimant was also responsible for the damage.

Recently there has been an increased interest in negligence in sports events where players have been injured and made claims against other players. As a general rule of thumb, anything that occurs within the rules of the game as stated by that sports' governing body cannot be classed as negligent. Anything that occurs outside the rules of the governing body, but within the accepted playing culture for the sport, cannot be classed as negligent. Any incident that occurs outside the rules of the sport and outside the accepted playing culture would be classed as negligent.

1.3 Regulatory bodies

There are regulatory bodies that are appropriate to all activities and some that are appropriate to specific activities. It is important for everybody working in sport to have a knowledge of the different regulatory bodies.

Appropriate to all activities

A regulatory body or competent authority is an organisation recognised by a national government as being the body responsible for the regulation and/ or approval of processes in a specific area. There are many regulatory bodies appropriate to sport and safety, some of which may work together to ensure that safety in sports activities is achieved.

The Health and Safety Executive (HSE) looks at people's health and safety at work. The different roles of the HSE can be seen in Figure 3.4 on page 71.

The HSE visits properties and facilities owned by local authorities such as sports arenas and swimming pools, and works with local authorities to enforce health and safety legislation.

Other regulatory bodies

- **Local authorities** – a typical local authority will have a role in the health and safety in sports facilities such as leisure centres. The roles can be seen in Figure 3.5 on page 71.

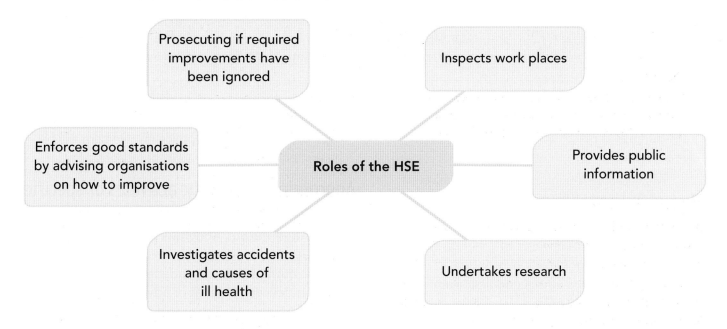

Figure 3.4: Roles of the HSE

Figure 3.5: Roles of the Local Authority

- **Local education authorities** – there are 150 local education authorities (LEAs) in England. They are part of a local council or local authority and are responsible for education within that council's area.

  LEAs have responsibility for all state schools in their area. They organise funding for the schools, allocate the number of places available and employ all teachers. LEAs have three roles:

  1. To guarantee the infrastructure of a universal school system. This means ensuring that:
     o every child has a school place
     o children with special needs receive appropriate education and support
     o changes in the school population are planned for
     o children entitled to free school travel receive it
     o large school building projects can be managed and funded.
  2. To lead the local education community, to set a vision for education, and to bring different partners together to achieve change and improvement.
  3. To offer support to heads, governors and teachers and to monitor and challenge performance in schools.

- **Police** – the main purpose of the police force is to
  o uphold the law fairly and firmly
  o prevent crime
  o pursue and bring to justice those who break the law.

  For many people working in the sporting community, having a good working relationship with the local police force is essential. For example, a voluntary sports soccer club which wanted to stage a charity run would certainly contact the police for advice and cooperation if roads were involved in the course. The assessment of the need for police attendance and action at an event is mainly based on the need to discharge the police service's core responsibilities, which are to:
  o protect life and property
  o prevent and detect crime
  o prevent or stop breaches of the peace
  o regulate traffic (within the legal powers provided by statute)

  o activate a contingency plan where there is an immediate threat to life and coordinate the resulting emergency service activities.

  The level of police resources committed to any event and the action undertaken should be proportionate to the assessment of risks posed by the event. Normally, police involvement will be restricted to these core areas of responsibility.

Appropriate to specific activities or specific types of activities

- **The Adventurous Activities Licensing Authority (AALA)** is an independent, cross-departmental public authority. It is an independent watchdog for the delivery of outdoor adventure activities for young people. The aim of the licensing scheme is to provide assurances to the public about the safety of those activity providers who have been granted a licence. In this way it is hoped that young people can continue to enjoy exciting and stimulating outdoor activities without being exposed to avoidable risks of death or disabling injury. A licence indicates that the provider has been inspected by the organisation, with particular attention being paid to their safety management systems, and demonstrates compliance with nationally accepted standards of good practice in the delivery of adventure activities to young people.

- **National governing bodies of sport** – each sport is represented by a governing body of sport that defines the way in which the sport operates through its affiliated clubs and societies. Employed and/or voluntary workers within governing bodies of sport, clubs and societies accept a responsibility to take reasonable steps to identify and control the risks associated with the sport. These responsibilities, however, do not extend to providing an absolute guarantee to all participants, spectators and members of the public that accidents or injuries will not occur. Most activities involve a certain level of risk, even when the risks have been identified and all reasonable precautions have been implemented. Governing bodies must, however, demonstrate that they have identified these risks and provided adequate guidance to associated clubs and societies on how to assess and control them in order to meet their legal obligations.

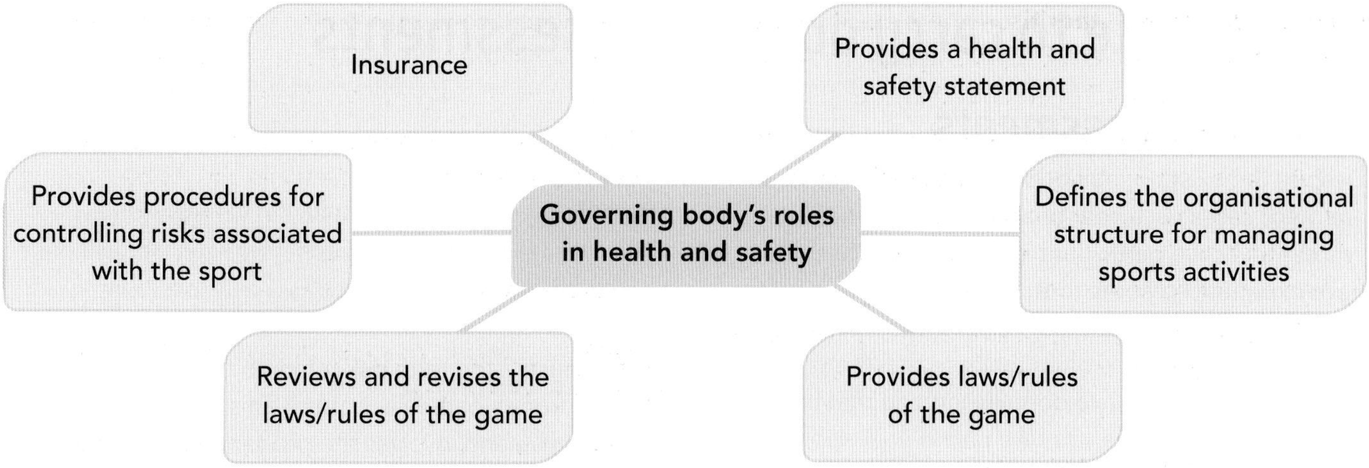

Insurance

Provides a health and safety statement

Provides procedures for controlling risks associated with the sport

Governing body's roles in health and safety

Defines the organisational structure for managing sports activities

Reviews and revises the laws/rules of the game

Provides laws/rules of the game

Figure 3.6: Governing body's roles in health and safety

Take it further

National governing bodies and health and safety

In small groups, select a governing body for your favourite sport. Identify all of the provisions that they have in place for health and safety including policies, advice and guidance.

Assessment activity 3.1

P1 P2 M1   BTEC

You are working as the health and safety officer for a local cricket club. The club has recently achieved Clubmark status and is reviewing all of its policies in preparation for the coming season. It employs a range of staff including coaches, groundsmen, catering staff, a sports therapist, a physiotherapist, an assistant fitness instructor, a personal trainer and some players. You have been asked to prepare a presentation for the different staff in order to brief them on the key factors in health and safety that are important for their job roles.

1. Describe four legislative factors that influence health and safety and say how they are relevant to the cricket club. **P1**

2. Compare and contrast the influences of legislation, legal factors and regulatory bodies on health and safety in sport. **M1**

3. Describe the legal factors and regulatory bodies that influence health and safety in sport. **P2**

Grading tips

P1 To attain P1 you may want to try to relate specific legislative factors to specific employees within the club.

M1 To attain M1 you need to demonstrate how the influence of the different legislative factors, legal factors and regulatory bodies could be similar or different for the different job roles, using specific examples.

P2 To attain P2 list and describe the different regulatory bodies that will apply to the cricket club; and describe each of the legal factors that are relevant to the club.

PLTS

When looking at the application of legislative factors, legal factors and regulatory bodies and their application to the cricket club, you could provide evidence of your skills as an **independent enquirer**.

Functional skills

When researching legislative, legal and regulatory body information, you could provide evidence of your **ICT** skills by selecting and using a variety of sources of information independently.

2. Be able to carry out risk assessments

2.1 Risk assessments

Despite the existing legislation and regulations, there are many cases each year of accidents and injuries. If you are an active participant in sport or exercise you may have experienced some form of injury, but this is often due to the inherent nature of injury risks associated with sport and exercise. It is often the case that the organisers of the sports events have done everything that they can to safeguard you while you take part in your sport. The main element of this safeguarding comes through the completion of risk assessments.

Aims

The overall aim of a risk assessment is to prevent accidents and injury and thus maintain the health, safety and welfare of all concerned with an activity, company or location.

- **Eliminate** – a **hazard** is something that has the potential to cause harm. It may be something you are aware of, such as water in a swimming pool, whereas other hazards may be unknown. An example could be a loose collar on a bar with free weights. Hazards must be eliminated wherever possible.

Key terms

Hazard – something with the potential to cause harm.

Risk – the likelihood and severity of the harm that could occur as a result of the hazard.

- **Minimise** – the term **risk** refers to the likelihood of harm from a particular hazard. This tends to be more subjective and involves the probability of future events taking place. A trampoline can be viewed as a hazard. Putting a novice on a trampoline without safety mats or 'spotters' and without anyone with coaching qualifications supervising increases the risk of injury. Providing these precautions will help to minimise the risk to an acceptable level.

- **Protect participants from harm** – this is the most important aim of risk assessment and can be achieved by following the risk assessment process. There are many variations and formats of risk assessments which could be adapted to meet the needs of the situation, the sports environment and the employer. However, Table 3.2 shows steps that could be used to eliminate or minimise hazards and risks.

Steps	Examples/comments
Look for different types of hazards within the workplace	Chemicals, work equipment and work activities
Decide who might be harmed and to what extent	Consider participants, employees, visitors, contractors and members of the public. Pay particular attention to young workers, trainees and new or expectant mothers
Assess the risk of the hazard causing harm	This helps to determine whether or not anything else can be done to reduce the likelihood further. This may involve monitoring and reviewing existing control measures and practices. A risk of harm will always exist and the risk assessment process helps you decide whether any further action needs to be taken to reduce it. A useful way of carrying out a risk assessment is to prioritise these remaining risks. They could be categorised as high, medium or low. The risk assessments need to be suitable and sufficient to address the category of risk. Staff should be made aware of and trained in the procedures in place for controlling the hazard
Undertake a written risk assessment	This ensures that the process is systematic and consistent and gives you a record of the process you have used to reach your conclusions. This helps you to monitor systems in place to reduce the likelihood of injury occurring. One method might include a daily checklist for a particular piece of sports equipment or activity, especially in sports halls where the equipment being used can change regularly
Review the risk assessment	The hazards associated with your sports environment or the nature of your business may change from time to time, and you should periodically review your risk assessment to keep it current. If any changes occur, staff should be made aware of the detail of the changes. This may result in the need for additional training

Table 3.2: Steps that can remove or minimise hazards and risks

Objectives

The objectives of risk assessment are the things that you need to do to be able to achieve the aims.

- **Identify hazards** – having a good understanding of the areas where hazards are likely to occur will help to prevent accidents and improve safety awareness. It is often preferable to undertake hazard identification as a group rather than individually as this increases the likelihood of hazards being isolated.

- **Identify those at risk** – you should identify those who may be at risk from the hazards identified. As well as identifying those at risk, some risk assessment systems consider how many people may be at risk and how potential incidents could happen.

- **Assess chance of hazard causing harm and grade risks** – this process develops the degree of risk that is perceived. It involves looking at each hazard and attempting to foresee the potential risks that could happen. This is sometimes given in numerical scores or simply as low, medium or high risk. A thorough process would also include a grading on the severity of injury that may occur from the risk.

Risk controls

Any risks that have been identified as high risk require immediate action to move the risk to an appropriate level. This action forms the risk management proposal, which needs to be recorded. The measures proposed should allocate people and resources clearly.

- **Do not do the activity** – where the risks are deemed too high, stop the activity or do not let it start.

- **Modify the activity** – this can be done in several ways such as moving the activities away from unsafe areas or altering sports activities to make them non-contact.

- **Protect participants from hazard** – once a hazard has been identified, action should be taken to protect participants wherever possible. For example, if a light is not working in an area of a sports hall, that area should not be used.

- **Provide appropriate safety equipment** – these needs should have been identified following the risk assessment. For example, a hockey player has the hazard of a hard ball hitting them and the person most likely to be injured is the goalkeeper. Therefore, the goalkeeper should be provided with the appropriate safety equipment before starting the activity.

- **Provide appropriate training** – regular training of staff and reviewing risk assessments are part of the risk assessment process. All employees should be aware of changes in conditions that might affect risks. If it is found that systems and procedures need to be revised, this must be communicated to any internal and external customers who may be affected.

- **Provide appropriate supervision for participants** – when leading or coaching activities, or when supervising field trips, local authorities and sports governing bodies have guidelines on the ratios of leaders to the number of participants. This ratio depends on the age, ability, number and disability of participants and the nature and location of the activity. An example of this would be employing more lifeguards if more people use a swimming pool.

Conducting risk assessments

When you conduct a risk assessment, you could use a form similar to the one shown in Table 3.3. Why do you think it is important to provide as much detail as possible when completing these forms?

Hazard	Risk	Scoring the risk			Control measures
What is the hazard?	What is the risk and who is at risk?	Likelihood of harm (0–10)	Severity of harm (0–10)	Overall risk level (low/medium/high?)	What can be/ has been done to eliminate or reduce the risks?

Table 3.3: Sample risk assessment form

Assessment activity 3.2

1. Before you take part in your next sports event, conduct a risk assessment. When you have done this, find a friend that plays a different sport and conduct a risk assessment before they start their event. You could reproduce the form in Table 3.3 to help you to complete the risk assessments. Ask your tutor for support. **P3**

2. To meet the merit criterion, you need to carry out both risk assessments independently. **M2**

3. After you have completed your two risk assessments, review your risk assessment controls and evaluate their effectiveness. **D1**

Grading tips

P3 To attain P3 ask your tutor for help if you need it (for example, understanding the differences between hazards and risks).

M2 To attain M2, if you are confident of your understanding, complete your risk assessments independently.

D1 To attain D1 write a short report to accompany your risk assessments that reviews the control measures and evaluates their effectiveness. You should try to link specific control measures to specific hazards and risks, saying how the control measure can reduce the level of risk.

PLTS

If you start to ask questions to extend your thinking about why and how the control measure would be effective, you could provide evidence of your skills as a **creative thinker**.

Functional skills

If you produce your risk assessments using appropriate forms that are fit for purpose and appropriate for the intended audience, you could provide evidence towards **ICT**.

3. Know how to maintain the safety of participants and colleagues in a sports environment

Throughout this unit, you have studied the legislation and regulations that affect sports providers, organisers and facility managers. Now you will look at the different procedures that are in place as a result of the legislation that you have covered.

3.1 Procedures

Operating procedures and good practice

Many sports facilities produce a set of operating procedures known as standard/normal operating procedures (S/NOPs). These procedures contain the safety programme as well as health and safety issues, such as daily alarm testing. They also cover operational procedures for maintenance and dealing with customer complaints.

A safety programme is a document produced by the organisation in accordance with relevant legislation and approved guidelines and practices. It should contain methods of raising the awareness of the importance of health and safety to all staff and customers. This involves having clear methods of communicating essential information to employees as well as allowing time for the safety programme to be effective. It is good practice for coaches and fitness instructors to be aware of the correct operating procedures. It is their responsibility to ensure the health and safety of participants.

- **Staff training and development** is a method used by organisations to keep their staff up to date with the latest regulations, policies and procedures. It involves sending staff on appropriate courses, seminars and conferences; or holding internal training to increase

What are the different factors that sports leaders and coaches need to consider when running sports sessions?

• **Emergency procedure protocols** – your school, college or sports club has protocols that relate to different emergencies. These could include fire evacuation, bomb alerts and injury or first-aid protocols. These procedures are designed to provide safe and efficient help to everybody involved in the event of an emergency. It is good practice to refer to these in your risk assessments when you are looking at control measures to minimise the level of risk. If you are working as part of a sports club committee, all committee members should be clear about the procedures to follow in the event of an emergency. It is good practice to make everybody associated with different activities aware of the procedures to be followed. You could do this by placing them on a club website or taking a laminated copy of the protocols away with you if you go on a field trip.

Take it further

Key emergency procedures

Research key emergency procedures (such as fire evacuation procedure) for a major sports venue and then research the same procedure for your school, college or local sports team (this could be done by asking your tutor or sports coach); and answer the following questions:

1. What is the procedure to be followed in the event of the emergency?
2. Are there any differences in the procedures for the different settings?

the knowledge and skills of staff members. All safety representatives have the right to be paid for time taken off work in order to carry out their safety duties. This training could vary from performance analysts being trained in the use of display screen equipment, to sports coaches receiving first-aid training, to newly qualified fitness instructors being trained on conducting risk assessments.

• **Risk assessments** are there to identify hazards, the risks and level of risk associated with those hazards, and control measures that can be put in place to eliminate or reduce the risk (see page 74 for more information on risk assessments).

Remember

The control measures used must be linked to specific hazards and risks and should aim to either eliminate or minimise the level of risk for the affected individuals.

• **First-aid** – the Health and Safety (First-aid) Regulations (1981) require that, in order to provide first-aid to their employees who are injured or become ill at work, employers must have adequate and appropriate equipment, facilities and personnel. First-aid procedures generally state that how badly the person is injured determines whether first-aid can be administered on the premises or if a visit to hospital is required. Certificates to identify who can administer first-aid and where they are located should be clearly visible and accessible to all staff. The duties of someone administering first-aid are to:

o preserve life
o prevent the condition worsening
o promote recovery
o provide information to more qualified people, such as the patient's history, symptoms and treatment.

The Health and Safety at Work Act (1974) influences first-aid in the workplace as it recognises the requirement for employers to provide first-aid. In order to do this they should consider:

o the nature of the workplace

o any hazards and risks

o the size of the premises

o the organisation and where workers are situated

o previous information on accidents

o annual leave of first-aiders and any cover that is required

o the proximity to emergency services.

Remember

If you are not qualified to handle first-aid incidents, do not attempt to do so as you could do more harm than good! Always make sure that you know the first-aid procedure for any organisation that you work for.

- **Communications cascade system for notification of incidents** – if an incident has occurred, the first course of action is to ensure that no further incidents can occur. For example, if a footballer is injured during a game, the match should be stopped to deal with the incident and to prevent further accidents. Once the incident has been dealt with, the next stage is to report it. This can be done verbally at first to a supervisor. This may then have to be formally documented in written form in an accident or incident book. You should always make a note of the time and location as well as the nature of the incident, who was involved and what action was taken. It is good practice to identify any reliable witnesses who can support your statement.

Safety procedures and protocols

Safety procedures and protocols are often recorded in the organisation's operating procedures. The procedures should cover different areas of work and focus on establishing and maintaining a safe environment to work in. This should ensure everyone's safety.

- **Established to maintain a safe environment** – the first step to establishing safety procedures and protocols is to produce a written commitment to providing a safe and inviting sports environment.

Copies of the policy should be distributed widely and distributed throughout the organisation. Information about the procedures should flow from all those who work and enjoy the use of the sports facilities. Preventative measures are essential but they cannot keep all dangerous situations from occurring. Everyone must work hard to create a safe sports environment. However, if problems arise, the response should be immediate.

Case study: FA Coaches Association Code of Conduct

Coaches are key to the establishment of ethics in football. Their concept of ethics and their attitude directly affects the behaviour of players under their supervision. Coaches are, therefore, expected to pay particular care to the moral aspect of their conduct.

Coaches have to be aware that almost all of their everyday decisions and choices of actions, as well as strategic targets, have ethical implications.

It is natural that winning constitutes a basic concern for coaches. This code is not intended to conflict with that. However, the code calls for coaches to disassociate themselves from a 'win-at-all-costs' attitude.

Increased responsibility is requested from coaches involved in coaching young people. The health, safety, welfare and moral education of young people are a first priority, before the achievement or the reputation of the club, school, coach or parent.

See Unit 5 Sports coaching, page 124 for the FA Coaches Association Code of Conduct, which forms the benchmark for all involved in coaching. Read the code of conduct and answer the questions below so that you can discuss the issues with a group of your friends.

1. What consideration does the code of conduct give to the health, safety and well-being of players?

2. Are there any areas relating to health, safety and well-being that you think are not adequately covered?

3. How would you change the code of conduct to incorporate other important areas of health, safety and well-being, and why?

- **Governing body guidelines** – the governing bodies of sport, with the support of Sports Coach UK, have guidelines to help support sports leaders and coaches. These guidelines will usually be (or form part of) a code of conduct or code of practice for your governing body.

- **Equipment manufacturers' guidelines** – most sports equipment is simple to use and needs few instructions. However, there are many items of sports equipment that may need to be assembled such as a basketball post or football posts. Each of these items will have instructions of assembly and guidelines for use that should have the EU approval mark. You will also find instructions and guidelines of use on smaller items such as balls, which will have inflation pressure suggestions and instructions on how to insert the needle to inflate the ball.

- **When to consult with others and who to consult with** – there are people that you can consult to maintain the safety of participants and colleagues (see Figure 3.7). How do you think each of these people can influence the health and safety of participants and colleagues?

- **Local and national requirements** – earlier in this unit, you learned about the major legal and legislative factors that influence health and safety in sport as well as the role of many national governing bodies. However, local requirements relating to the safety of sports participants may vary from region to region. You should check with your local authority and regional governing body of sport before starting any activity to ensure you are following approved guidelines.

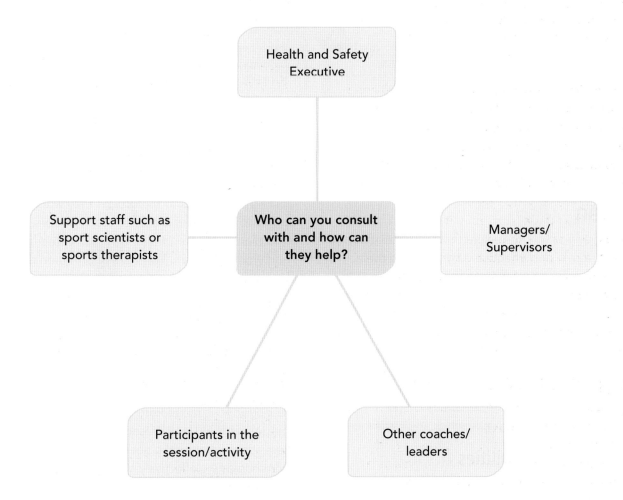

Figure 3.7: Who can you consult with and how can they help?

Assessment activity 3.3

P4 **M3** **D2**

You are working as an assistant sports coach and you have been asked to provide an information leaflet for parents of youth athletes at your club that looks at the procedures used to promote and maintain a health and safe sporting environment within your club.

1. In your leaflet, describe three procedures used to promote and maintain a healthy and safe sporting environment. **P4**
2. Explain these three procedures. **M3**
3. Analyse the three procedures. **D2**

Grading tips

P4 To attain P4 use procedures that are applicable to your favourite sport so that you can see how they are used.

M3 To attain M3 explain the procedures by providing examples from your chosen sport.

D2 To attain D2 consider how successful these procedures would be for your chosen sport and provide evidence to support your answer.

PLTS

When you are discussing how successful your chosen procedures would be, you could provide evidence of your skills as an **independent enquirer** if you use reasoned arguments and support your answers.

Functional skills

If you present your leaflet in a manner that is fit for purpose, you could provide evidence of your **ICT** skills.

4. Be able to plan a safe sporting activity

4.1 Plan

The only way you will make sure that your activities and sessions are safe and effective is by planning them. This planning should take place long before the start of the session. In the first instance, it can take a while to plan sessions until you get used to the different factors that you have to take into account; but once you are familiar with these, your session planning will be easier. The different factors that you have to take into account are roles and responsibilities, equipment, the suitability of the site, the suitability of the participants to the activity, guidelines and insurance.

Roles and responsibilities

When working within sport sessions, you could be expected to take on a variety of roles including leader, coach or first-aider. You should understand the responsibilities that come with each of these roles.

- **Leader** – a sports leader helps participants to develop vital skills for life and to make real and

lasting differences to the groups they work with. A good sports leader is able to teach people, organise and plan, motivate others, communicate effectively and work as a team. For more information about becoming a sports leader and the training required, see BTEC Level 3 National Student Book 2, Unit 13 Leadership in sport. You could also visit the Sports Leaders UK website at www.bst.org.uk.

- **Coaches** – one of the roles that you are likely to fulfil during your sessions is that of the coach. With this role comes a range of rights and responsibilities. These responsibilities range from basic elements (such as making sure you look presentable) to structuring your sessions to cater for the needs of everybody and communicating effectively. When you are planning your sessions, you will want to consider the Sports Coach UK Code of Practice for Sports Coaches, which can be downloaded from the Sports Coach UK website at www.sportscoachuk.org. For more information on the role of coach, please see Unit 5: Sports coaching on page 117.

How can keeping an up-to-date knowledge of health and safety guidelines help you when you are planning sessions?

- **First-aid** – as the person in charge of the session, it is your responsibility to ensure that adequate first-aid provision is available for the duration. You should check that your first-aider or first-aid team are available in advance of your session, or if you are the first-aider for the session, your first-aid qualifications must be up to date.

Remember

It is standard practice to have a qualified first-aider on hand when you are leading or coaching sports sessions.

Equipment

All sports have recommendations and guidelines relating to the equipment that can be used for a sport. These recommendations will often relate to the **type** of equipment that can be used and the **appropriate use** of that equipment.

The type of equipment to be used in your sport ranges from the clothes that you wear through to whether or not equipment is fit for use. For example, nearly all sports have recommended dress codes, some involving safety equipment to prevent illness and injury. Proper dress may range from the usual sturdy, loose-fitting clothing made of breathable fabric to heat-preserving wetsuits or running shoes with a list of essential features. This depends on the type of sport and the environmental conditions in which the sport is played. Protective equipment for contact sports – or those with a high risk of falling – is also specific to the activity. It may include guards or pads for specific body areas and may need to be professionally fitted. It should be worn at all times during participation, including practice and matches.

Equipment should be fit for purpose. This relates to the guidelines of sports equipment and recommendations such as size of footballs and goals in relation to the age group. When deciding if the equipment for your session is fit for use, ask yourself the following questions:

- What is the age of the equipment?
- What is its quality and condition?
- Is the equipment being maintained correctly, including regular services and inspections?
- How suitable is it for use by the age group involved?

Suitability of site

One of the key health and safety factors for your session is the suitability of the site. This depends on a number of factors including the space available, whether the facility was designed for that sporting activity, accessibility of emergency exits, noise/acoustics (for example, is there a lot of echo that could make instructions difficult to hear) and accessibility and suitability for people with particular needs such as wheelchair users.

Suitability of participants to activity

As well as planning for the suitability of the site for the activity, decide whether the participants in your session are suitable for the activity. If you have planned well, you will have planned your session around the needs of the people that you are working with, not vice versa. When planning your sessions, consider factors such as:

- the age and experience of participants
- the number of participants
- how well you know the group and how well they know you
- any specific learning needs
- any behavioural issues

and how all of these factors may affect the level of risk within the session.

Remember

Under section 7 of the Health and Safety at Work Act (1974), employees are required to take reasonable care for the health and safety of themselves and others who may be affected by their acts or omissions at work. This means that sports leaders can legitimately refuse to participate in activities that risk their own health and safety and/or that of their class, including in sites that are too small for the group or in sessions that involve activities that are not age or ability appropriate. Advice should be sought from the sport's governing body on matters such as these.

Guidelines

Sessions have guidelines that both participants and leaders need to follow. These guidelines will be specific to the type of session that you are running but will range from ensuring that all participants:

- complete a warm-up and cool down
- play within the rules of the activity
- have any appropriate personal and protective equipment
- are fit to take part in the session.

There are some useful tips for different types of session available at www.safesport.co.uk.

Insurance

All coaches must have insurance. If you are a member of the national governing body you may have insurance cover as part of this membership. However, check that your insurance covers public liability, products, professional indemnity, officers and officials and libel and slander.

4.2 Review

The only way to improve the overall quality of your work is by reviewing what you have done and looking at ways you could improve. This is just as important when reviewing the health and safety of your sessions.

Effectiveness of risk management

Sports organisers must consider action that is preventative and is documented in the risk assessment. However, the risk assessment should be reviewed to find out how effective it has been. You could use Table 3.4 on page 83 as a guide for reviewing your risk management.

Injuries, near misses and dangerous occurrences

Always keep health and safety in mind. Allow time for evaluating the effectiveness of your risk management strategies. Collecting data on the type, frequency and nature of any injuries helps you to evaluate if your activities are appropriate and safe. Note any near misses that have occurred and the situation that led to these. Subsequent action to prevent further near misses and dangerous occurrences is a sign of a good sports organiser.

Did you:	Yes/no	Comments
avoid risks altogether?		
evaluate unavoidable risks?		
combat risks at source?		
adapt your work to an individual?		
adapt equipment as necessary?		
provide/receive adequate health and safety training?		
provide appropriate PPE for workers and participants?		

Table 3.4: Reviewing your risk assessment

Suitability of group for activity and effectiveness of briefings

Any good sports leader or coach reviews the effectiveness of each session to find out if the session's goals were achieved and whether the activity was suitable for the participants. Most sessions start with a briefing for the participants. This outlines the key safety factors including what to do in case of an emergency and what the session will entail, as well as any discipline and behavioural rules. The review of whether or not the participants have understood what has been said should occur during the session and not at the end. At the end of the session there should be an overall review of suitability of the activity.

Suitability of equipment

Before the session starts, select the appropriate equipment for your participants, such as the correct size basketball and height of ring for the given age group (guidelines on this are available from the English Basketball Association). The review should take place during the activity through observation and asking participants to ensure they are using the equipment safely.

Support of other agencies

You may have sought support from agencies such as governing bodies, local authorities or managers and it is a useful exercise to see if that advice and support was effective.

Strengths and areas for improvement

When reviewing your session, consider the strengths and weaknesses of the session. While there are no set criteria for reviewing strengths and weaknesses (as they will depend on the type of session you are running), there are areas to consider.

- Did you assess the facility prior to the session?
- Did you observe the session for health and safety issues as well as monitoring performance?
- Was your plan detailed enough?
- Did you brief participants at the start on the health and safety arrangements?
- Was all of your equipment appropriate for the session?
- Was your facility appropriate for the session?
- Did all of your participants understand the instructions for the session?
- Did any injuries/accidents/emergencies/near misses occur during the session? If so, how did you deal with them?
- Were your risk management strategies effective? Do they need adapting for future sessions of this type?

Assessment activity 3.4

You are applying for a job at a sports coaching firm that goes into schools and runs holiday courses for a range of sports.

1. As part of your application, produce a session plan for the safe delivery of your chosen sports activity and a review of your session plan that shows its strengths and any areas that you feel you need to improve upon. **P5**
2. Explain your plan for the safe delivery of your sports activity and review it. **M4**

Grading tips

P5 To attain P5 plan your session based around roles and responsibilities, equipment, suitability of the site, suitability of the participants to the activity, guidelines and insurance.

M4 To attain M4 explain how your session plan will ensure the health and safety of your participants. When you review each of the strengths and areas for improvement, state how the strengths will benefit the participants and recognise any issues that could arise from the areas for improvement.

PLTS

If you organise your time and resources and place your actions for completion of your session plan in order of priority, you could provide evidence of your skills as a **self-manager**.

Functional skills

If you present your session in a format that is fit for purpose, you could provide evidence of your **ICT** skills.

Jack Marsh
Rugby coach

Jack is 18 and works as a rugby coach for the youth team at his local rugby club. He is responsible for a range of duties including conducting risk assessments, checking facilities (such as pitch inspections before games), checking equipment (making sure balls are pumped up and the right size, etc.) and organising the first-aiders.

'Rugby is a great sport for young people to play as it helps to develop a number of important components of fitness. It can develop a number of interpersonal skills and life skills and provides an opportunity for young people to become more active in sports. Due to the nature of rugby, I need to get all the health and safety elements of matches and practice right because if I don't, I'm going to increase the level of risk for the players involved.

Normally when I get to work, I'll check to make sure that all of the equipment and facilities are safe for use. Then when the players arrive I'll make sure that they are all fit to train before we start. With the younger players this includes making sure that they have all of their equipment as well as not having any injuries. After this, it is a case of running the sessions and making sure that everybody is getting everything out of the session that they need.

One of the biggest problems I face is that, regardless of their level, a lot of people don't seem to pay that much attention to health and safety elements of sport. This could range from people not doing warm-ups properly before games, to forgetting to bring their gum shields, to not giving me the information I need to be able to do my risk assessments properly. No matter how much I try to encourage people to take health and safety seriously, people don't seem too interested because they don't see it as directly involved with rugby.'

Think about it!

- If you were in Jack's position how would you try to get people to increase their involvement in health and safety?
- Why do you think it is important for all people associated with sport to understand the health and safety elements of sport?
- If you could give people one piece of advice regarding their flexibility training, what would it be?

Just checking

1. Name four key legislative factors associated with health and safety in sport.
2. What are the key legal factors associated with health and safety in sport?
3. What are the differences between statutory law, civil law and case law?
4. What are the different regulatory bodies associated with health and safety in sport?
5. What is the purpose of conducting a risk assessment?
6. What are the aims of risk assessments?
7. What is the difference between a hazard and a risk?
8. What are the different procedures that can be followed in order to maintain the safety of participants and colleagues?
9. What are the different factors to consider when planning safe sporting activities?
10. What are the key factors to consider when reviewing the effectiveness of sessions?

edexcel

Assignment tips

- When you are researching different areas of health and safety, it will be useful to research individual legislative factors so you may want to use websites such as the Health and Safety Executive (www.hse.gov.uk) and the Office of Public Sector Information (www.opsi.gov.uk).

- You may also want to look at advice and guidance that is specific to sport and exercise, so websites such as www.safesport.co.uk, www.sportscoachuk.org and national governing body websites such as www.thefa.com could be useful for you. These could be particularly useful when planning sports activities, for example gaining specific information on goal post safety in football.

- When you are in different sporting settings, or when you are watching sport, try to think about them with your health and safety head on. Start thinking about different risks and hazards and how they could be minimised so that you can bring the topic to life.

- If you know any sports coaches or health and safety officers at different clubs, speak to them about their health and safety roles and responsibilities so that you can develop your knowledge further.

- You may have a particular aspect of study that you are interested in, for example sports injuries; so why not try to contextualise the information in this unit to your favourite topic so that you can develop your applied understanding further?

4 Fitness training and programming

What does it takes for Wayne Rooney to be able to sprint for a football in the final minute of a football match? Consider the novice marathon runner and what they put their body through to complete the London Marathon and raise money for charity, or the injured youth basketball player entering the later stages of rehabilitation and training more purposefully – what must they do to get back to competition? Regardless of your ability in sport, you need certain levels of fitness to perform at your best. It is important for health, self-confidence, injury prevention and peak performance in sport that you have the required level of fitness. The role of people such as sports conditioning specialists, fitness instructors or personal trainers is to help different people improve or maintain their fitness level.

Throughout this unit, you will examine a range of topics within fitness training and programming. These range from understanding different components of fitness, and the training methods used to improve them, to being able to plan, take part in and review training sessions and programmes; these are useful for you if you wish to progress into fitness instructing, personal training, sports coaching or sports therapy.

Learning outcomes

After completing this unit you should:

1. know different methods of fitness training
2. be able to plan a fitness training session
3. be able to plan a fitness training programme
4. be able to review a fitness training programme.

Assessment and grading criteria

This table shows you what you must do in order to achieve a pass, merit or distinction grade, and where you can find activities in this book to help you.

To achieve a **pass** grade the evidence must show that the learner is able to:	To achieve a **merit** grade the evidence must show that, in addition to the pass criteria, the learner is able to:	To achieve a **distinction** grade the evidence must show that, in addition to the pass and merit criteria, the learner is able to:
P1 describe one method of fitness training for six different components of physical fitness **Assessment activity 4.1, page 99**	**M1** explain one method of fitness training for six different components of physical fitness **Assessment activity 4.1, page 99**	
P2 produce training session plans covering cardiovascular training, resistance training, flexibility training and speed training **Assessment activity 4.2, page 107**	**M2** produce detailed session plans covering cardiovascular training, resistance training, flexibility training and speed training **Assessment activity 4.2, page 107**	**D1** justify the training session plans covering cardiovascular training, resistance training, flexibility training and speed training **Assessment activity 4.2, page 107**
P3 produce a six-week fitness training programme for a selected individual that incorporates the principles of training and periodisation **Assessment activity 4.3, page 113**		
P4 monitor performance against goals during the six-week training programme **Assessment activity 4.4, page 114**		
P5 give feedback to an individual following completion of a six-week fitness training programme, describing strengths and areas for improvement **Assessment activity 4.4, page 114**	**M3** give feedback to an individual following completion of a six-week fitness training programme, explaining strengths and areas for improvement **Assessment activity 4.4, page 114**	**D2** give feedback to an individual following completion of a six-week fitness training programme, evaluating progress and providing recommendations for future activities **Assessment activity 4.4, page 114**

How you will be assessed

This unit will be assessed by internal assignments designed and marked by the tutors at your centre. Your assessments could be in the form of:

* written reports
* posters
* presentations
* session plans
* training diaries
* practical observations of performance.

Paul Cooke, 17-year-old gym enthusiast

This unit has been really beneficial because it has taught me all sorts of things about fitness and training that I didn't know before. I really like being physically active and exercising so I spend a lot of my time in the gym which means this unit was tailor-made for me!

The parts of the unit that I really enjoyed were the ones where I learned about the different methods of training, how to plan sessions correctly and how to plan training programmes effectively. I go to the gym a lot but up until starting this unit I didn't really know what I was doing in there – I just went in and lifted weights after doing some cardio work but I didn't really structure anything or have any specific goals. This unit has helped me to improve the quality of my own training and I'm starting to see the benefit of it now. I've also just started fitness instructing for my part-time job and I want to be a personal trainer so this unit has helped me out a lot with that too!

Over to you

* How do you think this unit can help you?
* What are you looking forward to learning about?
* What might you find especially challenging?

1. Know different methods of fitness training

The importance of fitness training

Consider how athletes meet the physical demands of their sport at an elite level. Now consider the rising levels of obesity in the world, particularly in the UK. These examples tell you about the importance of fitness training and programming. How can a knowledge of fitness training and programming help in these different scenarios?

When designing training programmes, there are two key questions:

- What am I trying to improve?
- How am I going to improve it?

You need detailed knowledge of the different components of fitness, and the different training methods used to improve them, to answer these two questions.

1.1 Components of fitness

When you think about fitness, different things spring to mind, such as people who can run far, people with big muscles and people that are slim and toned. Fitness is the ability to meet the demands of your environment. It relates to an optimal quality of life and includes social, spiritual, psychological, emotional and physical well-being and can be classified under the following areas:

- Physical/health-related fitness: this focuses on your health-related aspects of fitness, with good scores in components in this area meaning you have only a small chance of developing health problems.
- Skill-related fitness: this is a level of fitness that allows the individual to perform an activity, task or sport (this is also sometimes known as motor fitness).

Fitness involves six main components:

- **aerobic endurance**
- **muscular endurance**
- **flexibility**
- **strength**
- **speed**
- **power**.

What do you think are the main reasons behind people starting training programmes?

Key terms

Aerobic endurance – the ability of the cardiovascular and respiratory systems to supply the exercising muscles with oxygen to maintain the aerobic exercise for a long period of time, for example over two hours during a marathon.

Muscular endurance – the ability of a specific muscle or muscle group to sustain repeated contractions over an extended period of time.

Flexibility – the ability of a specific joint, for example the knee, to move through a full range of movement. As with muscular endurance, an athlete can have different flexibility levels in different joints.

Strength – the ability of a specific muscle or muscle group to exert a force in a single maximal contraction to overcome some form of resistance.

Speed – the ability to move a distance in the shortest time.

Power – the ability to generate and use muscular strength quickly over a short period of time.

Aerobic endurance

A physical-related aspect of fitness, this is also known as stamina or cardiorespiratory endurance. It is the ability of the cardiovascular and respiratory systems to supply the exercising muscles with oxygen to maintain the exercise. It is important for daily tasks such as walking to work or doing the gardening and housework, but is also important for a range of sport, leisure and recreational activities. There are a number of events that rely almost exclusively on aerobic endurance, such as marathon running, long-distance swimming and cycling. Aerobic endurance forms the basis of fitness for most sports. If an athlete has a reduced aerobic endurance, possibly due to a long-term injury, this leads to a decrease in other fitness components such as muscular endurance. Poor aerobic endurance leads to poor sporting performance in some sports.

Muscular endurance

Another physical-related aspect of fitness, muscular endurance is needed where a specific muscle or muscle group makes repeated contractions over a significant period of time (possibly over a number of minutes). Examples include:

- a boxer making a repeated jab
- continuous press-ups or sit-ups
- 400-metre sprint in athletics.

Flexibility

Another physical-related aspect of fitness, flexibility is important for all sports and for health. There are two main types of flexibility: **static flexibility** and **dynamic flexibility**. Static flexibility is the range of movement that a muscle or joint can achieve and is limited by the structure of bones and joints, as well as factors such as muscle size and muscle tone. Dynamic flexibility is the range of movement that a muscle or joint can achieve while you are moving and is limited by your levels of static flexibility and coordination.

Key terms

Static flexibility – the range of movement that a muscle or joint can achieve.

Dynamic flexibility – the range of movement that a muscle or joint can achieve when in motion.

Poor flexibility may lead to:

- a decrease in the range of possible movement
- an increased chance of injury and stiffness
- a decrease in sporting performance.

Possible improvements in flexibility are limited by an individual's:

- body composition (for example, the percentage of body fat)
- genetics (characteristics inherited from parents)
- age (flexibility levels generally decrease with age)
- gender (females tend to be more flexible than males)
- muscle and tendon elasticity (the capacity to stretch before injury occurs).

While flexibility is important for all sports, any joint should not become too flexible because an excessive range of movement can lead to injury.

Strength

A physical-related aspect of fitness, strength is the ability of a specific muscle or muscle group to exert a force in a single maximal contraction. When you think about strength, you may think about athletes such as weightlifters or boxers, but strength is required in most sports, just in varying degrees.

Speed

A skill-related component of fitness, speed is required by an athlete to maximise performance. It is the ability to move over distance in the quickest possible time. Athletic sports such as the 100-metre sprint and long jump require high levels of speed. Speed endurance is a secondary element to speed and combines with anaerobic endurance. It is the ability of an athlete to make repeated sprints over a period of time and is important in different team sports. For example, a midfield player in football often has to make 10–30 metre sprints continuously throughout the game.

Power

Power is also a skill-related component of fitness. It is the ability to generate and use muscular strength quickly. Athletes who are stronger tend to produce a greater amount of power during an action. Generally, an athlete interested in health-related fitness does not train for power as it is needed more by athletes in specific sports and can only be developed by using advanced training methods. Power is important for sprinters when pushing away from the blocks, footballers striking a long range drive and boxers delivering a punch, as well as other sports.

Other components of physical fitness

In addition to the components above relating to skills and physical fitness, there are others:

- **Body composition** – the amount of body fat and lean body tissue the athlete has. It is important from a health and a sports performance perspective.
- **Agility** – the ability of an athlete to change direction many times quickly and accurately during sporting performance while maintaining control of the movement.
- **Balance** – being able to maintain stability or equilibrium while performing. There are two forms of balance: static balance, where the athlete is stationary, for example, in a handstand in gymnastics; dynamic balance, where the athlete is moving, for example, a footballer sprinting with the ball.

- **Coordination** – most sporting movements require athletes to use different joints and muscles in a specific order or sequence.
- **Reaction time** – the time between a stimulus to move and the start of a movement, such as a starting pistol (the stimulus) and the sprint start (the movement) in sprint events.

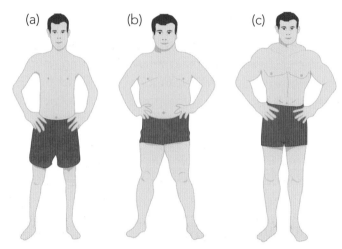

Figure 4.1: The three types of body frame: (a) ectomorph, (b) endomorph and (c) mesomorph. Which appears to be the most athletic and why?

Activity: Components of fitness in sport

- Complete the table that examines the importance of the different components of fitness in different sports. Give each component of fitness a rating from 1 to 10, with 1 being not important and 10 being very important.
- On a separate sheet of paper, choose your favourite sport out of the three and justify why the components of fitness are important: for example 'reaction time is important in goalkeeping because the quicker the goalkeeper reacts, the more chance they have of saving the ball and then distributing it to their teammates'.

Components of fitness	Boxing	Goalkeeper in football	100-metre sprinter
Aerobic endurance			
Muscular endurance			
Flexibility			
Speed			
Strength			
Power			
Body composition			
Agility			
Balance			
Coordination			
Reaction time			

1.2 Methods of training

Consider all the components of fitness and the different sports that you have covered so far. To develop each of these components of fitness to meet the needs of different sports, athletes, coaches and personal trainers can't just use one type of training – they need to use a range of appropriate training methods.

Aerobic endurance

The three most common methods used to improve aerobic endurance (also known as **VO$_2$ max**) are:

- continuous training
- fartlek training
- interval training.

There is not enough evidence to determine which method is best, but all will lead to improvements in aerobic endurance. Aerobic endurance training is often used by people who want to lose or manage their weight by reducing their body fat content, which is why aerobic training is often used during the pre-season by football teams and rugby teams. Body fat is reduced by aerobic endurance training because training results in increased levels of hormones, **epinephrine** and **norepinephrine**, which then activate enzymes which break down **triglycerides** into **free fatty acids**. These are used as an energy source. This reduces your body fat levels. As well as the health-related benefits of aerobic endurance training methods, they have different benefits for sport performance. They can help to improve blood volume, mitochondrial size and density, develop neuromuscular patterns and improve muscle tone; all of which benefits performance levels in a range of sports.

Key terms

VO$_2$ max – the maximum amount of oxygen that can be taken in by and be utilised by the body. Also, a measure of the endurance capacity of the cardiovascular and respiratory systems and exercising skeletal muscles.

Epinephrine – a chemical in the body used for communication between cells in the nervous system and other cells in the body. It works with norepinephrine to prepare the body for the 'fight or flight response'.

Norepinephrine – a chemical in the body used for communication between cells in the nervous system and other cells in the body. It works with epinephrine to prepare the body for the 'fight or flight response'.

Triglycerides – the most concentrated energy source in the body. Most fats are stored as these.

Free fatty acids – the parts of fat that are used by the body for metabolism.

- **Continuous training** is also known as steady-state or long, slow, distance training. It involves the athlete training at a steady pace over a long distance. The intensity of continuous training should be moderate intensity (approximately ≤70% VO$_2$ max) over a long distance and time.

This method of training is suited to long distance runners or swimmers. Due to the lower level of intensity, an athlete can train for longer. It can also be useful for:

- o   beginners who are starting structured exercise
- o   athletes recovering from injury
- o   'specific population' individuals such as children or elderly people.

Some of the disadvantages of this type of training include a higher risk of injury when running long distances on harder surfaces, it can be boring and it is not always sport specific; the sport specific benefits are small.

- **Fartlek training** is designed to improve an athlete's aerobic endurance. It is based on running outdoors, and varies the intensity of work according to the athlete's requirements. The intensity of training is changed by varying terrain, such as sand, hills, soft grassland or woodland. Some of the benefits of this training method include improving aerobic endurance, improving muscular endurance and improving balance and proprioception in the ankle, knee and hip; all of which have a variety of benefits ranging from improved sport performance during a game to helping with injury rehabilitation. Fartlek training can be more useful than continuous training for some people because it can be individual and sport specific. In addition, this training method uses both aerobic and anaerobic energy systems to improve aerobic endurance and can involve changes in direction, so it is useful for team sports players as it can closely mimic the requirements of the sport. In fartlek training there is no rest period, but the athlete has more control and is able to decrease intensity at any time to rest. The benefits of fartlek training are:

- o   it is less technical than other methods (such as interval training) making it easier to use
- o   athletes control their own pacing
- o   the boredom of conventional training is reduced.

Some common examples of fartlek sessions include Astrand, Gerschler, Saltin and Watson methods.

- **Interval training** improves anaerobic endurance components and aerobic endurance by varying the intensity and length of the work periods. In interval training, athletes perform a work period, followed by a rest or recovery period, before completing another work period. When designing an interval training programme, you should consider:

  o the number of intervals (rest and work periods)

  o the intensity of the work interval

  o the duration of the work interval

  o the duration of the rest interval

  o the intensity of the rest interval.

An example of an interval training prescription for aerobic endurance could be 1 set of 3 repetitions of 5 minute runs interspersed with 2 minutes and 30 seconds of rest. This would be written in a training diary as 1 x 3 x 5:00 Work:Rest 2:30. This method of training allows clear progression and overload to be built into the programme by increasing the intensity of work periods, increasing the number of intervals, decreasing the duration of the rest period or increasing the intensity of the rest period (for example, using a slow jog rather than a walk).

Activity: Benefits of training methods

You are applying for the position of strength and conditioning coach at a multi-sport organisation. The head of athlete support would like you (as part of the interview process) to produce a presentation that describes different aerobic training methods and the physiological benefits of each of the different methods. You should use the Internet, books and journals to produce your presentation. Your presentation should include:

- the names of the different training methods
- a description of each of the training methods (including strengths and limitations)
- an example of different training routines that could be used
- a general description of the physiological benefits of aerobic training
- the specific physiological changes that can occur as a result of each type of training so that you can justify the use of the different training methods with your specific sport.

Muscular strength and muscular endurance training

Think about when you have been in your gym or your fitness suite at school or college. You will have seen people lifting different weights at different speeds. Have you ever looked around and not known what to do or why? This is because a number of the training methods used to improve muscular strength can also be used to improve muscular endurance simply by doing the training differently, for example by altering the weight, the number of repetitions and the number of sets. Common training methods used to improve muscular strength and muscular endurance include:

- resistance machines
- free weights
- medicine ball training
- circuit training
- core stability training.

- **Resistance machines** – your local fitness centre will have a number of fixed resistance machines, which allow individuals to change the load based on their training programme schedule. The variable resistance ranges from 0–100 kg on most machines, allowing the programme to include overload and progression. These machines are expensive, making them impractical for use at home. Due to their design they are limited to specialist exercises such as a bench or leg press. On the positive side, they have an increased safety element compared to free weights, they can be useful for novice trainers who are still learning different movement patterns and an individual can change the range of movement at a specific joint by adjusting the machine's settings.

- **Free weights**, such as barbells or dumb-bells, allow an individual to have a constant resistance during a dynamic action. Free weights increase strength in the short term, increase range of movement, specialise in certain movements or muscle groups and some movements aid the training of balance and coordination. Fixed resistance machines and free weights are used to improve muscular strength. Both produce positive results. However, there is a greater chance of injury while using free weights. For safety reasons when using larger weights, helpers (or 'spotters') are required to oversee (or 'spot') for an individual.

- **Medicine balls** – volleyball players throw and catch medicine balls (heavy balls weighing from 1 to 7 kg) to upgrade their spiking ability; basketball players use the balls to improve their passing and rebounding capacities; baseball players toss medicine balls to improve their throwing speed; and all-round athletes cavort with the balls in the hope of enhancing their 'core strength' (muscle strength in the hips, abdomen and back).

- **Circuit training** – in a circuit training session, a number of different exercises (or stations) are organised in rotations. Individuals are set a time period to perform these exercises, such as one minute per station. Between the stations there should be a rest period dependent on the individual or groups completing the circuit.

  A circuit can be designed to improve aerobic endurance, muscular endurance or strength, or a combination of all three. To avoid fatigue, the stations should be structured in a way that consecutive exercises use different muscle groups, for example, repeated sprints (legs) may be followed by press-ups (upper body). To increase progression and overload, the individual may wish to:

  o decrease the rest period

  o increase the number of stations

  o increase the number of circuits

  o increase the time spent at each station

  o increase the number of circuit sessions per week.

- **Core stability training** exercises the deep muscles of the torso all at the same time. It is vital to most sports because the core muscles stabilise the spine and provide a solid foundation for movement in the arms and legs. The core is the centre point for all sporting actions – it reduces postural imbalance and plays an important role in injury prevention.

Benefits of strength training

If you think about how a person's appearance changes after they have been using the gym a lot, you will be able to identify some changes that are a result of strength training and may say that somebody looks 'built' or 'pumped'. These changes in appearance are known as increased muscle tone and muscle hypertrophy. Muscle tone is where muscles have a more defined appearance; whereas muscle hypertrophy is the growth of the muscle and happens when the **muscle fibres** and **myofibrils** increase in size.

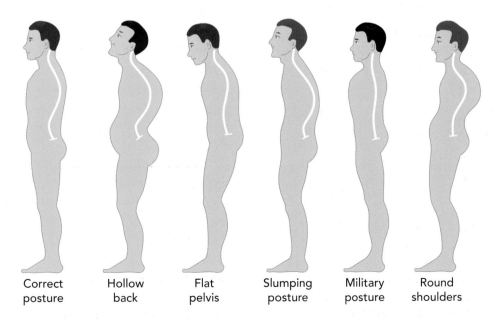

| Correct posture | Hollow back | Flat pelvis | Slumping posture | Military posture | Round shoulders |

Figure 4.2: How do you think core stability training could help these postural deviations?

Benefits of muscular endurance training

Muscular endurance training has similar benefits to muscular strength training in that muscle tone can increase and muscles will experience hypertrophy (although to a lesser extent). The benefits of muscular endurance training are ones that you can't see as they happen within the muscle cell.

The first benefit is that muscular endurance training places stress on the slow twitch muscle fibres and as a result they can increase in size. This means that there is more space for mitochondrial activity. The increase in size and number of the **mitochondria** is important because they are the part of the muscle that produces aerobic energy. By increasing the size and number of mitochondria, you can increase aerobic performance. Another important change within the muscle is that there is a large increase in **myoglobin** content. This is important for aerobic performance as the myoglobin carries oxygen to the mitochondria. If you have more myoglobin you can produce more aerobic energy in the mitochondria. These changes within the muscle can increase VO_2 max by up to 20 per cent which is important in a number of sports.

Key terms

Muscle fibres – the contractile element of a muscle.

Myofibril – the contractile element of a muscle fibre.

Mitochondria – organelles containing enzymes responsible for energy production. Mitochondria are therefore the part of a muscle responsible for aerobic energy production.

Myoglobin – the form of haemoglobin found in muscles that binds and stores oxygen. Myoglobin is responsible for delivering oxygen to the mitochondria.

Flexibility training

Both static and dynamic flexibility can be developed using a range of training methods. The main methods of flexibility training are:

- static stretching
- dynamic stretching
- ballistic stretching
- proprioceptive neuromuscular facilitation (PNF) stretching.

The general principle of flexibility training is to overload the specific muscle group by stretching the muscles beyond what they are used to. The aim is to increase the range of movement, and work must be targeted towards the joints and muscle groups requiring improvement. The movement should not exceed the tolerance level of the tissue. For improvements in flexibility, an individual should increase the time (duration) of stretching and the number of repetitions to allow overload to take place. As flexibility is significantly affected by the temperature of muscles and connective tissues, flexibility training is best completed at the end of a training session or after some form of aerobic training. If using stretching activities as part of a warm-up, you should make sure that the stretching is low intensity and doesn't stretch the muscle or joint too far, too soon.

- **Static stretching** – if you want to improve your flexibility, you could use static stretching. Static stretches are controlled and slow. There are two types: passive and active. Passive stretching is also known as assisted stretching as it requires the help of another person or an object such as a wall. The other person would apply an external force (push or pull) to force the muscle to stretch. Unlike passive stretching, active stretching can be achieved by an individual. It involves voluntary contraction of specific muscles.

- **Dynamic stretching** – think about when you have watched football players, rugby players or basketball players going through their warm-up. You will see them performing a range of movements that are like the sports movements they need during the game. These are dynamic flexibility exercises. Dynamic flexibility is important for sports that have high speed movements and movements that take a muscle or joint past its normal range of static flexibility.

- **Ballistic stretching** improves an individual's flexibility. The individual has to make fast, jerky movements, usually taking the form of bouncing and bobbing through the full range of motion. Ballistic stretching should be specific to the movement pattern experienced in the relevant sporting activity. These stretches can lead to soreness or may cause injury such as strains, so must be undertaken carefully and with the correct technique.

- **Proprioceptive neuromuscular facilitation (PNF) stretching** is an advanced form of passive stretching and is one of the most effective forms of increasing flexibility. The types of movement vary between muscles and muscle groups, but the processes are generally the same:

    o stretch the target muscle group to the upper limit of its range of movement

    o isometrically contract the muscle or muscle group against a partner for 6–10 seconds

    o relax the muscle or muscle group as your partner stretches it to a new upper limit of range of movement (you should be able to stretch it further this time).

    When using this type of stretching remember that pain is the body's signal that you are working it too hard in some way, so when this activity hurts too much you have taken it too far.

Responses to stretching

The improvements that occur because of flexibility training occur because when you stretch a muscle, you stretch the muscle spindle. When you stretch the muscle spindle, a series of signals are sent to your spinal cord. Signals are then sent back, telling the muscle to resist the stretch. After this, your Golgi tendon organ is activated which makes your muscle relax, which allows the muscle to be stretched further the next time. To get this series of reactions, the stretch needs to be held for at least 7 seconds.

Power

There are two common methods of power training:

- plyometrics
- hill sprints.

- **Plyometrics** is designed to improve explosive leg power and is regularly used to increase power in sports. Plyometrics is a useful training method because it engages and stretches the target muscle or muscle groups at the same time. If you stretch a contracted muscle it becomes stronger. Like most elastic tissues, muscles produce more force if they have been previously stretched. Think of your muscle as an elastic band – the elastic band will fire further if you stretch it further back before letting it go. Plyometric activities facilitate this process of force production by taking the muscle through an **eccentric muscle action** before a powerful **concentric muscle action**. This process causes the muscle spindles to cause a **stretch reflex**, preventing any muscle damage and producing maximum force at a rapid rate. Plyometric training is ideal for sports and activities that involve explosive actions, such as a slam dunk in basketball or a sprint start for the 100 metres.

    Different activities are used in plyometric training sessions. Lower body activities include hurdle jumps, single leg bounds, alternate leg bounds, box drills and depth jumps. Upper body activities include plyometric press-ups and medicine ball throws.

- **Hill sprints** – athletes use hill sprints to increase speed, coordination and acceleration. These sprints can be up or down a hill, depending on the content and aims of the session. Hill sprints help to develop

Key terms

Eccentric muscle action – the muscle increases in length while still producing tension.

Concentric muscle action – the muscle gets shorter and the two ends of the muscle move closer together.

Stretch reflex – the body's automatic response to something that stretches the muscle.

Standing calf stretch

Pectoralis stretch

Quadriceps stretch

Standing hamstring stretch

Hip flexor stretch

Double knee to chest

Hip adductor stretch

Piriformis stretch

Trunk rotation

Upper trapezius stretch

Wrist stretch

Figure 4.3: Which athletes would benefit from these types of stretches?

Activity: Plyometrics

Imagine you are working as an assistant to the strength and conditioning coach of your local athletics club. The coach has asked you to produce an information booklet that shows and explains different plyometric exercises that can be used by a range of track and field athletes including jump, sprint and throwing athletes. The coach has asked you to provide:

- a range of both upper and lower body activities
- an image (or series of images) of the different activities
- a step-by-step instruction list for each activity.

power for different reasons. Hill sprints involve a shorter stride length and a longer contact time with the ground than flat sprints; the knee, hip and ankle joints are more flexed during hill sprints and there is greater muscle activity in the gastrocnemius, quadriceps muscle group and gluteus maximus muscle. All of these play a key role in sporting activities that involve sprinting and jumping.

Speed training

Speed is an essential component of fitness in most sports, and good acceleration is vital. Acceleration from a standing position is critical for success in sports such as sprinting and in team-based sports such as rugby league, where a player has to accelerate with the ball past opponents, changing pace rapidly. Interval training and sport-specific speed training benefit speed and acceleration.

- **Interval training** can improve anaerobic endurance. The work intervals for aerobic endurance training tend to be long in duration and low in intensity in order to train the aerobic system. By contrast, for anaerobic endurance, the work intervals will be shorter but more intense (near to maximum). Interval training can help an athlete improve speed and anaerobic endurance (speed endurance). An athlete should work at a high intensity. The principles of overload and progression can be brought into the programme by making changes such as decreasing the rest period (see Table 4.1 on page 96).

- **Sport-specific speed training** – some sports require specific types of speed training to improve performance. For team-based sports you need to concentrate on different distances as players sprint over varying distances and movement patterns by sprinting in different directions to aid agility.

Take it further

Speed training techniques

Using books and the Internet, research the following speed training techniques:

- interval training
- sport-specific speed training
- parachute runs
- hill sprints
- ladders and hurdles

For each one, provide a description of the training method, an example of a training session using that method and a summary of the benefits and limitations of each method.

Assessment activity 4.1

  BTEC

You are working as a fitness trainer for a youth sports team. Your club is launching a new website and would like you to produce some information for the new website that can be accessed by players and coaches of the sports club.

The information for the website needs to include:

1. a description of one method of fitness training for six different components of physical fitness (so six training methods in total). **P1**
2. an explanation of one method of fitness training for six different components of physical fitness (again, six training methods in total). **M1**

Grading tips

P1 To attain P1 provide a general description of each of the different training methods.

M1 To attain M1 give a detailed explanation of each of the training methods that provides examples of exercises that can be used in the different training methods and highlights the benefits of the training methods for the athlete.

2. Be able to plan a fitness training session

2.1 Plan

When planning sessions, you should consider a number of different factors. One of the most important principles when planning individual sessions and full training programmes is the FITT principle.

Frequency, intensity, time and type (FITT principle)

FITT stands for:

Frequency – the number of session(s)

Intensity – how hard the session(s) are

Time – how long the session(s) last for

Type – the activities that you will include in your session(s).

- **Frequency** of a training session or programme refers to the number of training sessions per week. While the frequency of sessions is important, intensity and duration of training are more important. Novice trainers should not train more than three times per week until their levels of fitness can cope with the increased training load. Once your levels of fitness have increased, you could progress to five times per week.

- **Intensity** of a programme is closely linked with the training principle of overload – it is how hard you are working during your training. Intensity is one of the most important factors when designing a training programme and relates to factors such as weight, distance, heart rate percentages and speed.

- **Time** relates to the length of your training session.

- **Type** of exercise you complete will be related to your individual needs. It is the mode of training you will complete, for example free weight training.

2.2 Individuals

When planning your sessions, you need to take into account the type of individual that you are working with. It is not uncommon for personal trainers to work with a combination of elite athletes, trained individuals, untrained individuals or even teams. You need knowledge of each of their circumstances to plan the right type of session for each client.

2.3 Cardiovascular training

Exercise intensities

See Table 4.1 for some general guidelines for cardiovascular exercise intensities.

Guidelines for aerobic training			
Level	Percentage of age predicted maximum heart rate	Duration (per session)	Frequency
Beginner	60	20 minutes	3
Advanced	90	20–50 minutes	5

Table 4.1: Guidelines for aerobic training

Another way of looking at cardiovascular exercise intensities is to see them as zones of training.

- **Warm-up or cool down zone** – the first cardiovascular training intensity is often known as the warm-up/cool down zone. This zone is at around 50 per cent of your maximum heart rate and is mainly for the sedentary or unfit person that wants to start training.

- **Active recovery zone** – this zone is approximately 60 per cent of your maximum heart rate. It is useful for aiding recovery, removing waste products and provides a good next step for those new to cardiovascular training.

- **Fat burning zone** – the fat burning (or weight management) zone is at 60–70 per cent of your maximum heart rate. It is a progression for people from the moderate aerobic zone once they have increased their fitness levels, but is also used by athletes training for long distance events such as a marathon. You may use continuous training when training in this zone.

- **Aerobic fitness zone** – this zone is at 70–80 per cent of your maximum heart rate and is the zone where you develop your aerobic endurance. This zone is suitable for more active or trained individuals.

- **'Target heart rate' zone** – this zone occurs at approximately 60–75 per cent of your maximum heart rate (but has sometimes been known to go as high as 85 per cent). This is the zone that has the greatest benefits for cardiovascular health and for improving the body's ability to use fat as an energy source.

- **Peak performance zone** – this zone occurs at 80–90 per cent of your maximum heart rate and is your highest zone of cardiovascular training. This training zone is geared towards competitive sport and will help you develop speed. It is at this training zone that you will alter your anaerobic threshold. You will often use up-tempo methods such as fartlek and interval training when training through the aerobic fitness and peak performance zones.

- **Anaerobic threshold** – have you ever run for a while and your legs have started to get hot, tight and achy? These are signs that you are close to your anaerobic threshold. Your anaerobic threshold is the point where you can no longer meet your energy requirements of exercise using your aerobic energy system, so your body produces energy using your anaerobic systems. This is the point that your blood lactate levels increase significantly. Training at high percentages of your maximum heart rate helps to increase this threshold, allowing you to train at higher intensities and longer durations while still using your aerobic energy system. Training close to your **anaerobic threshold** significantly stresses your cardiovascular system so is not suitable for inexperienced trainers.

Key term

Anaerobic threshold – the point at which aerobic energy sources can no longer meet the demand of the activity being undertaken, so there is an increase in anaerobic energy production. This shift is also reflected by an increase in blood lactate production.

Monitoring intensity

When training yourself or working with a client, you must monitor the intensity of the session to ensure that it is as effective as possible and so that your client is not at any risk. Common methods of monitoring intensity include:

- observing your client
- the talk test
- the rating of perceived exertion (RPE)
- age predicted maximum heart rate
- the Karvonen (or heart rate reserve) formula.

- **Observation** – how many times have you been training and ended up tired and red-faced? This is just one of the things that you can look for when observing people while training. Observing people is a subjective way of monitoring progress, but can be very useful. When observing people, look for changes in exercise technique, skin colour, changes in breathing patterns and excessive sweat levels.

- **Talk test** – think about when you're exercising and how much harder it becomes to talk to people as the exercise time continues. The American College of Sports Medicine states that if you are able to hold a conversation at the same time as breathing rhythmically while exercising, you are probably working at an acceptable level for cardiovascular training.

- **Rating of Perceived Exertion (RPE)** is a scale (see Table 4.2) that runs from 6–20 and reflects heart rates that range from 60–200 beats per minute. For example, if you are exercising and you give a rating of 13 (somewhat hard), this gives an equivalent heart rate of 130 beats per minute.

Rate of Perceived Exertion	Intensity	Heart rate equivalent
6		60
7	very, very light	70
8		80
9	very light	90
10		100
11	fairly light	110
12		120
13	somewhat hard	130
14		140
15	hard	150
16		160
17	very hard	170
18		180
19	very, very hard	190
20		200

Table 4.2: Rating of Perceived Exertion (RPE)

It can take some time to learn how to use this rating correctly, so use it with other methods of assessment until you and your client are used to it. One problem with the RPE scale is that it is based on you having a maximum heart rate of 200 beats per minute, which won't always be the case.

- **Maximum heart rate** – monitoring heart rate during cardiovascular training sessions helps you see if you're working hard enough or should work harder. You can use your maximum heart rate and the Karvonen formula to set target training zones and use heart rate monitors to monitor your heart rate and ensure you are within the correct training zone.

You can calculate your maximum heart rate (MHR) by using the simple equation:

maximum heart rate = 220 – age (in years)

This can then be used as part of the Karvonen formula to calculate appropriate training zones (see below).

Activity: Calculating your heart rate zones

For each of the different training zones highlighted above, calculate your training zone based on the percentage of your maximum heart rate.

- **Karvonen formula (heart rate reserve)** was suggested to find target heart rates and training zones for people in cardiovascular training. It uses MHR and resting heart rate (RHR) to calculate your heart rate reserve in the following equation:

heart rate reserve (HRR) = MHR – RHR

Karvonen suggested that a training intensity between 60 and 75 per cent of MHR is suitable for the average athlete. The training heart rate intensity (or zone) is calculated using the equation:

training heart rate % x (HRR) + RHR

This case study below demonstrates how training zone could be used.

Case study: Mike, 20-year-old swimmer

Mike is a 20-year-old swimmer with a RHR of 60 beats per minute. He has been instructed by his coach to train at 60–75 per cent of MHR.

- Training heart rate = 60 per cent
  = 0.60 (HRR) + RHR
  = 0.60 (200 – 60) + 60
  = 84 + 60
  = 144 beats per minute
- Training heart rate = 75 per cent
  = 0.75 (HRR) + RHR
  = 0.75 (200 – 60) + 60
  = 105 + 60
  = 165 beats per minute

From this, you would be able to tell Mike that he needs to be working at an intensity of 144–165 beats per minute and would be able to monitor this intensity using a heart rate monitor.

What are the benefits for Mike of training at this intensity?

If you were in Mike's position and had to train at 60–75 per cent of your MHR, what would your training heart rate be?

Anaerobic threshold

Refer back to page 101 for a description of anaerobic threshold.

Work/rest ratios

You need to get the right work/rest ratio when using training methods such as interval training. Table 4.4 on page 106 demonstrates guidelines for interval training for different type of training sessions.

> ### Remember
>
> You have to work at the correct intensity for the correct period of time to be able to get the correct training effect.

2.4 Resistance training

When designing your resistance training session, find out your primary goal as there are different training sessions for improving strength, power, muscle size or muscle endurance. Try to work on one training outcome per session/programme as this will give you the best results (for example, working on power and muscular endurance produces fewer gains than working on endurance alone).

Choice of exercises

When designing resistance sessions, there are hundreds of exercises to choose from. Make sure that you choose activities that meet the needs of the individual and the sport and keep them as simple as possible. Generally, resistance exercises fall into one of two categories: **core exercises** and **assistance exercises**.

Core exercises:

- focus on large muscle areas such as the chest, back or thigh
- involve two or more joints (called multi-joint activities)
- have more impact on sporting movements.

Assistance exercises:

- focus on smaller muscle areas (such as the upper arm or lower leg)
- involve one joint (single joint exercises)
- have less importance when you are trying to improve sport performance.

Key terms

Core exercises – focus on large muscle areas, involve two or more joints and have more direct impact on sport performance.

Assistance exercises – focus on smaller muscle areas, only involve one joint and have less importance when trying to improve sport performance.

Number of exercises

The number of exercises you will do during a resistance training session depends on your training goals. Generally you need to ensure that there aren't too many exercises as this could lead to injury. Where you use more than one exercise for an area or muscle group, make sure that you alternate these exercises with other areas or muscles.

Order of exercises

There are different ways to structure your resistance training session but structure exercises so you can create as much force as possible in each exercise, while maintaining correct technique and allowing adequate rest between exercises. Three common techniques used to order exercises are to:

- complete core exercises before assistance exercises
- have exercises that alternate between upper and lower body exercises
- alternate push and pull activities.

Rest between sets

Think about when you have attempted any exercise feeling fine and then when you are tired. You will probably have made more mistakes in technique and performance, had lower effort levels and may have been injured when trying to exercise while fatigued. Allow adequate recovery between sets for performance reasons and health and safety reasons.

Speed of movement

With resistance training, it is not only the repetitions, sets, load and rest that influence the adaptations that the body will experience, the speed of movement is also important. When performing the exercise in a slow and controlled fashion, you will move the joint through the full range of motion and develop the highest force through the full range. This results in the greatest strength gains. Take 4 seconds from the start point of the exercise to the end of the range of motion and 2 seconds to return the resistance to the start point.

Systems of training

There are different systems of training designed to be used by all trainers from novice to experienced. For example, a simple circuit could be used with a novice trainer whereas pyramid training could be used for somebody who wants to increase their power. You should use these systems when planning resistance training sessions for yourself or your clients; and you should use your goals (or the goals of your client) as one of the key factors in your choice of training system. While each of the systems has different benefits and is aimed at people of different levels, one thing that they all share is an aim to help you reach overload which will help you meet your training goals.

- **Simple circuit** – this normally consists of 8–10 exercises, of 15–25 repetitions and with a resistance of 40–60 per cent of your repetition max. It uses a range of multi-joint exercises and works the major muscle groups. This training system is useful for beginners as, through using multi-joint exercises and the major muscles, you will work the smaller muscle groups and develop exercise technique. You can adjust this system of training by altering the number of times the circuit is performed, the number of repetitions, the resistance used and the number of exercises.

- **Pyramids** – pyramid training is a form of multiple set training and develops different components of fitness, depending on whether you use light-to-heavy (ascending pyramid) or heavy-to-light (descending pyramid) methods. Using a descending pyramid is a more advanced training method so is more suited to experienced strength trainers.

- **Super sets** involve performing two or more exercises for the same muscle group in a row or working opposite muscle groups or muscle areas. Performing two or more exercises on the same muscle group (known as compound super sets) increases the stress placed on the working muscle as you can work it from different angles. The benefit of this is that you use more muscle fibres and increase the blood flow to the muscle. Some of the negative elements of this

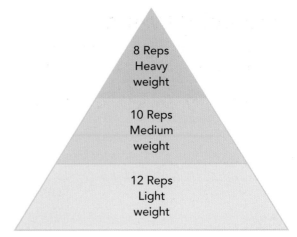

Figure 4.4: Why do you think descending pyramid training is a more advanced method?

training are that it cannot be used in every training session because of the intensity of training and it can carry a high risk of injury and overtraining if you don't know how to do it correctly. Working opposite muscle groups or muscle areas has the advantage that blood is kept in the same area which increases blood flow, carrying more nutrients and oxygen to the working muscle. It is more time-efficient than other training methods as the rest periods are built in to the training (because you are working opposite muscle groups) reducing the overall training time. One key limitation of this training system is that it doesn't increase the overload in the same way as a compound set does, but an advantage is that it increases the demand on the cardiovascular system which helps increase your anaerobic threshold, lactate tolerance and muscular endurance.

Take it further

Research advanced training methods

Using books and the Internet research the following advanced training methods:

- forced rep training
- drop sets
- pre-exhaust
- eccentric training
- split training.

When you are researching, try to find for each method:

1. a description
2. a sample session plan
3. the strengths and limitations.

2.5 Flexibility training

Flexibility training sessions often complement resistance training sessions (and vice versa) because they both improve muscle shape and size. Different factors to consider when designing flexibility training sessions include:

- the choice of exercises
- the number of exercises
- the order of exercises
- the number of repetitions
- the time.

Choice of exercises

When designing flexibility training sessions, relate your choice of exercises to your aims or the aims of your client. Choose from static, dynamic and ballistics flexibility training exercises. A well-designed flexibility session bases the choice of exercises on the results of flexibility tests. If you identify areas of weakness, you will want to focus on these.

Number of exercises

Your flexibility session should include approximately 10–12 exercises.

Order of exercises

Structure your exercises so that your session works different areas of the body to reduce the risk of injury and so that your exercises get progressively harder to help overload the body. For example, dynamic flexibility sessions should start with low speed movements that replicate the sporting actions but don't stretch the muscle or joint to the maximum range of movement. The sessions should then get progressively faster and the range of movement should be pushed further gradually until you reach full speed movement that pushes the limits of flexibility.

Repetitions

If you are a beginner starting a flexibility training programme, start by using three repetitions per exercise. As your flexibility increases, aim to increase this to five repetitions per exercise.

Time

On average, you will spend about 15–30 minutes on a flexibility session depending on the type and number of exercises to be performed. Each stretch should be held for between 6 seconds and 60 seconds, depending on the type of stretch you are doing. For example, static stretching could be held for up to 60 seconds. PNF stretching (see page 97) should have a 6 second contraction followed by 10–30 seconds of assisted stretching.

Activity: Planning flexibility training

Using the guidelines for flexibility training, plan your own flexibility training session. Your session should allow you to improve flexibility in important body parts for your particular sport or activity. When you have done this, ask somebody (for example, a tutor or fitness instructor) to look over your plan to make sure that it is safe and then take part in your session. On completion, write down the good and bad points about your session and try to suggest ways to improve it.

2.6 Speed training

Although there are general guidelines (see Table 4.4 on page 106) for speed-based interval training, the more specific requirements are geared towards the requirements of specific sports and specific positions within those sports. During the training week, speed training should take place after a rest period or low intensity training to reduce the risk of injury or over-training. Within a training session, speed training should take place after the warm-up and any other training within the session should be low intensity.

Time/distance

The time or distance of the sprint is dependent upon your particular sport. In most team sports, acceleration is more important than speed as you don't often hit maximum speed until approximately 50 metres, so most team sports will do speed training over distances of 10–30 metres; whereas an extended sprint athlete, such as an 800-metre runner, may use speed training distances of up to 400 metres at 2–3 seconds faster than their race pace.

Repetitions

As with the time/distance, the number of repetitions is dependent on your sport. Team sports players may use up to 10 repetitions per set but extended sprint athletes, such as 800-metre runners, may only use up to 4 repetitions. A typical speed training session will consist of 5–10 repetitions when aiming to develop maximal speed.

Sets

Depending on the time, distance and repetitions, you will use between 1–5 sets during a speed training session.

Rest between sets

Depending on the intensity, repetitions and sets you are using as part of your training programmes, you may require rest periods of between 1–3 minutes in between sets. These rest periods will be essential for you to replenish energy stores, maintain correct technique and reduce the risk of injury.

Work/rest ratio

A general guideline for maximal speed training is that there should be a work to rest ratio of 1:5, so if you were to have a 10-second maximal sprint, this would be followed by a 50-second rest period. As interval training is used in both running-based cardiovascular training and speed training, you could use the table below to plan training sessions for different energy systems.

Energy system	Time (min:sec)	Sets	Reps per set	Work: relief ratio	Relief interval type
ATP – PC	0:10	5	10	1:3	walking
	0:20	4	10	1:3	
ATP – PC – LA	0:30	5	5	1:3	jogging
	0:40	4	5	1:3	
	0:50	4	5	1:3	
	1:00	3	5	1:3	
	1:10	3	5	1:3	
	1:20	2	5	1:2	
LA – O_2	1:30 – 2:00	2	4	1:2	jogging
	2:00 – 3:00	1	6	1:1	
O_2	3:00 – 4:00	1	4	1:1	walking
	4:00 – 5:00	1	3	1:0.5	

Table 4.3: Guidelines for interval training

PLTS

If you generate ideas and explore different possibilities that could be used in your different sessions (see Assessment activity 4.2 opposite), you could provide evidence of your skills as a **creative thinker**.

Functional skills

If you bring together information regarding different training methods to suit the training programme (see Assessment activity 4.2 opposite), you could provide evidence of your **ICT** skills.

Assessment activity 4.2

BTEC

You are starting your first day as a personal trainer at your local health club which is used by several types of individuals ranging from elite athletes to individuals on the GP referral scheme.

1. Your manager has asked you to prepare four training session plans, one for each of the following session types:
   - a cardiovascular training session for a trained recreational runner
   - a resistance training session for a boxer
   - a flexibility training session for a youth football player that suffers from tight hamstrings and has been referred to you by the resident sports therapist
   - a speed training session for a 200-metre sprinter. **P2**
2. To meet the merit grade, you must ensure that each of your training session plans is detailed. **M2**
3. Finally, you must justify each of your training session plans. **D1**

Grading tips

P2 To attain P2 produce a session plan for each type of session that says who the session is aimed at, the FITT of activities and shows how you could develop the required components of fitness.

M2 To attain M2 produce detailed session plans plus a range of activities and alternate activities that would benefit each individual.

D1 To attain D1 say why you would use each of the different activities that you have suggested on your session plan. This could be achieved by using physiological and performance related benefits of the different activities.

Use websites such as www.sport-fitness-advisor.com and www.pponline.co.uk to help you with this activity.

3. Be able to plan a fitness training programme

3.1 Collect information

One of the biggest problems for anybody trying to improve their fitness is that they often do the wrong type of training or their training programme is not structured properly. This leads to a lack of motivation for the individual as well as few training gains which will make the training programme useless. Collecting appropriate information about your client, such as goals, lifestyle information, medical history and physical activity history, means you will produce a more effective programme for your client.

Remember

Collecting information about your client is important, not only for the effectiveness of your programme, but also for health and safety reasons and (if you are working as a self-employed personal trainer or fitness instructor) your own insurance purposes.

Short-, medium- and long-term goals

An important part of designing training programmes is the individual's goals – without knowing these, you will not know what to direct your training towards. The programme must be flexible but capable of meeting these goals and personal needs. Each individual has different ambitions and aspirations, and your programme should reflect these. The athlete's goals should be broken up into short-term (up to one month) medium-term (one to three months) and long-term goals (three months to one year).

SMART targets

When designing the training programme, set goals that are based on SMART targets:

Specific – they say exactly what you mean (for example, to improve flexibility in the hamstring muscle group)

Measurable – you can prove that you have reached them (for example, increase flexibility by 5 cm using the sit and reach test)

Achievable – they are actions you can in fact achieve (for example, you can practise and improve flexibility through training)

Realistic – you will be able to achieve them but they will still challenge you (for example, the increase in flexibility must be manageable – a 20 cm increase in two weeks is not achievable)

Time-bound – they have deadlines (for example, to reach the target within six weeks).

Lifestyle

When designing a training programme, you need to know about different lifestyle factors such as alcohol intake, diet, time availability, occupation, family and financial situation; all of these will influence how you design a training programme for clients. The training programme should be built into a routine rather than becoming an extra stress as this will help adherence to the programme and will produce the best results.

Take it further

Why do you think that it is important for the fitness instructor or personal trainer to know about all of the different lifestyle factors?

Medical history

Before you design the programme, find out about the athlete's medical history. Ask them to complete a pre-exercise health questionnaire like the one shown in Figure 4.5 on page 109.

Physical activity history

When designing a training programme, the fitness trainer must gain a picture of the athlete's history, including any health-related issues, asthma or recent illnesses. Previous activity levels are part of this picture. If the athlete has been involved in a structured programme and has a good level of fitness, assessed through fitness tests, then the programme should reflect this. The exercises prescribed should be at a moderate to high intensity. Another athlete may not

have exercised for a long time (one month or more) for reasons such as injury, illness or loss of motivation. In this case, the programme should initially be set at a lower level, in terms of number of sessions per week, duration and intensity.

3.2 Principles of training

Any fitness programme is based on the principles of training. Following these principles results in the greatest gains through your training. The principles of training can be remembered using the acronym SPORTI, which stands for:

Specificity

Progression

Overload

Reversibility/recovery

Tedium

Individual differences.

Specificity

The principle of specificity means that you should plan your training programme around the needs of the sport or activity (such as specific muscle groups, components of fitness or sporting actions) and your individual needs (such as targets that are specific to you rather than just general targets).

Progression

Have you ever heard the phrase 'if you always do what you've always done, you'll always get what you've always got'? This is where progression is important because the only way your body adapts to training is if you keep making training progressively harder (increasing the levels of overload). Without correct levels of overload and progression, your training gains would start to level off (plateau). Be careful when planning progression because poor performances may result from too little progression or a training programme that overloads the system. As well as poor performance, excessive overloading may lead to injury or illness through over-training.

Overload

Overload is stretching the body systems beyond their normal functional level and is an essential aspect of gaining training effects. The following areas can be adapted (increased or decreased) to control the level of overload:

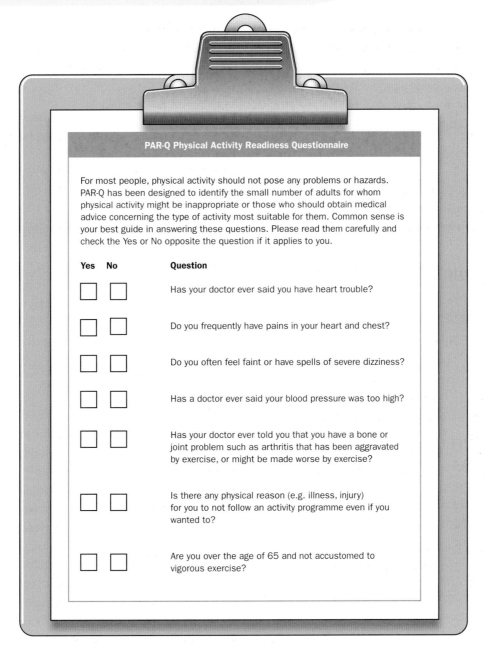

PAR-Q Physical Activity Readiness Questionnaire

For most people, physical activity should not pose any problems or hazards. PAR-Q has been designed to identify the small number of adults for whom physical activity might be inappropriate or those who should obtain medical advice concerning the type of activity most suitable for them. Common sense is your best guide in answering these questions. Please read them carefully and check the Yes or No opposite the question if it applies to you.

Yes	No	Question
☐	☐	Has your doctor ever said you have heart trouble?
☐	☐	Do you frequently have pains in your heart and chest?
☐	☐	Do you often feel faint or have spells of severe dizziness?
☐	☐	Has a doctor ever said your blood pressure was too high?
☐	☐	Has your doctor ever told you that you have a bone or joint problem such as arthritis that has been aggravated by exercise, or might be made worse by exercise?
☐	☐	Is there any physical reason (e.g. illness, injury) for you to not follow an activity programme even if you wanted to?
☐	☐	Are you over the age of 65 and not accustomed to vigorous exercise?

Figure 4.5: Why is using a pre-exercise health questionnaire important for a fitness instructor or personal trainer?

- frequency: the number of sessions a week, for example, increasing from two to four
- intensity: the amount of energy needed to perform a particular exercise or activity
- duration: the total time an exercise session or activity takes, for example, a 20-minute session could be increased to a 30-minute session.

During your training, you will normally be trying to progress the overload to make sure that you keep seeing training effects, but there are times when you would want or need to reduce the overload.

These include:

- signs of over-training or burnout, such as injury, illness or severe decrease in motivation
- different times of the season (for example, off season or close to a major competition).

Recovery and reversibility

Recovery time is essential within any athlete's training programme to allow for repair and renewal of the body's tissues. If you don't give the physiological system that you have been training the time that it needs to recover, you reduce your progression rate. However, a marked decrease in training or complete inactivity (for example during an illness, the off season or a long-term injury) leads to a decrease in functional capacity which is detrimental to performance. This decrease in performance is due to the principle of training called reversibility, which is sometimes known as detraining.

> **Remember**
>
> Reversibility leads to a dramatic and rapid reduction in fitness levels – faster than the improvements gained through overloading over a period of time.

Tedium/variation

One of the biggest reasons for stopping a training programme is if it becomes tedious (boring). This is often caused by following the same style of training on a regular basis. This principle is also known as the principle of variation because, to avoid tedium, you need to vary the training methods used in the programme.

Individual differences

All individuals have different needs, abilities, goals, skills, physical attributes, lifestyles, medical history and exercise preferences. Therefore a training programme should be tailor-made for each individual. Your expectations should be specific to different individuals. Athletes with low levels of fitness will show greater improvement than elite athletes because they have scope for larger amounts of improvement. However, even though elite athletes will show a minimal improvement, it could prove significant. For example, if you have never trained before, you could improve your 1 repetition max by 60 kg after a long period of resistance training. An Olympic weightlifter, however, might increase their personal best by only 1 kg during the same time frame, but this could mean breaking the world record.

FITT

In addition to the SPORTI principles, you also need to consider the FITT (frequency, intensity, time and type) principles (refer back to page 100).

3.3 Periodisation

Most people in sport use a training programme based on a structured cycle. This is known as periodisation. The training cycle is split into:

- **macrocycles** – 1-year to 4-year training cycles
- **mesocycles** – monthly training cycles
- **microcycles** – weekly or individually planned training sessions.

Periodisation can benefit you because it ensures continued physiological and psychological changes, it prevents over-training injuries and boredom and helps to achieve peak performance for key events.

Macrocycle

The first layer of a training programme may be based on a 1-year to 4-year cycle, which is known as a macrocycle. For example, a football player will train based on a 1-year cycle, from June to May, aiming to peak for a weekly or bi-weekly match, whereas an Olympic athlete will have a 4-year macrocycle, aiming for peak performance to coincide with the Olympic games.

Mesocycle

The macrocycle is divided into a number of mesocycles. These normally consist of a medium-term process of 4–24 weeks. The mesocycle is the main method of controlling the work to rest ratios; for example if you had a work to rest ratio of 3:1, this means you would have three working weeks followed by one active rest week. If you are an inexperienced trainer, you would have a ratio of 2:1 but if you are an advanced trainer, you could have a ratio of up to 6:1. Mesocycles can be step loaded. This technique uses a repetitive work to rest ratio; for example, with a 4-week mesocycle, you could have a ratio of 3:1 and repeat this cycle three times but increasing the intensity of the work weeks at the start of each cycle.

Microcycle

Each mesocycle is divided into a number of microcycles. The microcycle is planned with a specific adaptation in mind and should show the details of FITT training. Microcycles typically last for one week, but can range from 5–10 days.

A typical periodised training programme would look like the one in Table 4.4 (opposite).

Individual training sessions

Each microcycle consists of a number of individual training sessions. A training session should include three basic components: the warm-up, the main workout and the cool down.

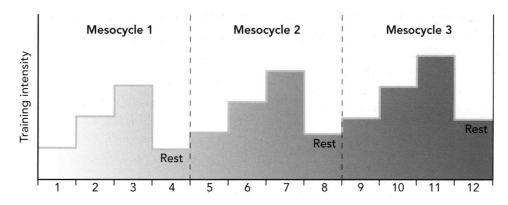

Figure 4.6: Why do you think that step loading mesocycles can improve fitness?

Macrocycle											
Mesocycle 1				Mesocycle 2				Mesocycle 3			
Microcycle 1	Microcycle 2	Microcycle 3	Microcycle 4	Microcycle 1	Microcycle 2	Microcycle 3	Microcycle 4	Microcycle 1	Microcycle 2	Microcycle 3	Microcycle 4
work	work	work	rest	work	work	work	rest	work	work	work	rest

Table 4.4: A typical periodised training programme. What level of athlete do you think that this structure of programme would be suitable for and why?

The warm-up is performed before the main exercise period to prepare you for the main session and to ensure your health and safety. A warm-up is required to:

- lubricate the joints with synovial fluid
- increase the temperature of the body generally, but specifically muscles and connective tissues
- increase blood flow
- take muscles and connective tissues through the full range of movement
- prepare you psychologically for the activity, focusing attention and increasing arousal.

A warm-up consists of: mobility exercises for joints; aerobic activity to increase body temperature and raise the pulse; preparatory stretches for the muscles and groups used in the main session; specific rehearsal activities that mimic the main session content.

The main session – the content of the main session is dependent on the session aims. However, make sure that your session is designed to meet your individual needs and ensure health, safety and welfare.

The cool down is shorter than the warm-up and is based on low-intensity exercises. The main aim of the cool down is to return the body to its resting state, and the main focus is on the aerobic component. Reasons why the athlete should perform a cool down include:

- to remove waste products from the working muscles, which are still receiving the oxygenated blood
- to stretch in order to decrease the chance of muscle stiffness
- to reduce the chances of fainting after an intense session.

3.4 Training diary

When working with athletes, maintain a training diary on a regular basis. The need to keep records of the training programme is often overlooked in the fitness industry, possibly because it is time-consuming. However, it is important for:

- **health and safety** – records can increase a trainer's awareness of previous injuries or illnesses
- **progression** – records allow the fitness trainer to see whether there is progression in the programme

- **communication** – records allow the trainer to gain an understanding of the athlete's history, which should aid communication
- **evaluation** – the information stored can be used as a part of the evaluation process
- **professionalism** – keeping records shows the fitness trainer has a level of competence and is following good practice
- reviewing your training programme.

Date and details of the session

Keeping the dates and details of the different training sessions helps you organise your time and monitor your progression more effectively, and allows you to alter future plans when necessary.

Progression

Progress should be logged so that you can monitor the programme regularly. You may make comments on the following:

- How did you find the intensity?
- Could you have performed more repetitions or sets?
- What were your thoughts on the types of exercises you were performing?
- Do you feel you have progressed from the previous session?
- Any other relevant thoughts.

Attitude

A major part of a training session is based on your attitude or approach to training. You should use the diary to make comments on your attitude so that you can explain the reason for good or poor sessions. To gain a wider picture, the fitness trainer should make comments on the attitude shown.

Why do you think having the correct attitude is important for training benefits?

Motivation

Motivation is the most important ingredient for success when carrying out a training programme. An athlete needs to be motivated in the sessions to maximise training effects. The motivation of an athlete may decrease due to:

- lack of improvement in fitness
- boredom due to repetitive exercise
- poor sporting performances
- external pressures, for example, college work.

Links to goals

Within the diary try to comment on your goal, which you identified at the start of the programme. Consider the following questions:

- How close are you to your goals?
- Are the goals still SMART targets?
- Do the goals need to be revised?
- Is the training too focused on one particular goal?

Competition results

For athletes at all levels, keeping competition results as part of the training diary is an important part of monitoring progress. It has a number of benefits:

- **Motivation:** if you can see improvements then you are more likely to want to experience more success. Alternatively, if you aren't seeing improvements it is more likely to motivate you to review your training to see if it is as effective as it could be.
- **Progression:** if you are seeing an improvement in performance results, this can act as a catalyst for progression in your training programme as the only way to keep improvements going is to keep progressing your training in the correct way.

PLTS

If you generate ideas and explore possibilities for your training programme, you could provide evidence of your **creative thinker** skills (see Assessment activity 4.3 on page 113).

Functional skills

If you present your information in an appropriate manner, you could provide evidence of your **ICT** skills (see Assessment activity 4.3 on page 113).

Assessment activity 4.3 BTEC

Plan a 6-week training programme for an individual of your choice, such as a friend or family member, that will help them to improve important components of fitness for their activity. Make sure that you incorporate the principles of training and use the periodisation model to structure your programme. **P3**

Grading tips

P3 To attain P3 make sure that your training programme is geared towards individual needs and the fitness requirements of their specific activity. Use each of the principles of training and periodisation to structure the training.

4. Be able to review a fitness training programme

To find out the effectiveness of a training programme, monitor and review your progress throughout it. There are different techniques that you can use.

4.1 Monitor

A training programme is useless unless you know if (and how) it is working. Ways of monitoring your training programmes include the use of training diaries and fitness tests and gaining feedback from your coach or fitness instructor.

Training diaries

Training diaries should be as detailed as possible when used for monitoring. You may want to include some of the details discussed earlier. If you are the fitness instructor or personal trainer, include some of the following in your diary for your client:

- personal contact details in case of emergency – stored confidentially in accordance with the Data Protection Act
- health questionnaires
- accident, injury or illness forms
- copies of any quality check questionnaires given to the athlete to assess the quality of service.

Fitness test results

The only way of monitoring physiological changes is to conduct repeated fitness tests. Record the following details in your training diary to monitor your progression:

- the name of the test
- the component of fitness
- the result

- units of measurement, for example, metres or kilograms
- the comparison of results to normative data rating, for example, very good.

To effectively monitor and evaluate a training programme, fitness testing should take place at the start, during and at the end of the training programme (see Unit 7 Fitness testing for sport and exercise, on page 179).

Coach/instructor feedback

A coach or fitness instructor must record, monitor and review an individual's progress on a regular basis so that they can interpret the effectiveness of the training programme. It is commonplace for fitness trainers to record training details using ICT such as databases, spreadsheets, tables and online journals. Feedback and reviews should take place regularly so that any issues with the training programme can be identified and rectified quickly.

4.2 Review

An individual's training programme should be reviewed regularly to gauge its effectiveness. Through the appropriate fitness tests, the programme should be evaluated to assess whether personal goals and objectives have been met. The review process should involve both the coach/fitness instructor and the athlete. When reviewing training programmes consider:

- the overall suitability of the programme in terms of structure, goals, time and equipment
- achievements – physical, psychological, social and health-related

- negative aspects – issues such as boredom and lack of motivation
- future needs – new or modified goals
- whether the individual has received value for money.

Extent to which programme is achieving set goals

To discover how the training programme is working, fitness test the individual halfway through the programme. To read more about the fitness tests you could use with the individual, see Unit 7 Fitness testing for sport and exercise. If things are going well, maintain the programme or even increase the intensity/frequency of exercise. However, if the individual is unlikely to achieve the goals set, adapt the training programme and/or goals.

Remember

A review halfway through a programme can help to pinpoint any problems and indicate where valuable changes could be made.

Modification of programme to achieve planned goals

The main function of reviewing the training programme is to monitor its effectiveness against achievement of the planned goals. To make the training programme more effective you may need to modify it. This could be for a variety of reasons including:

- injury to the individual
- change in facilities or equipment
- change in motivation level
- lack of progress
- boredom
- achieving goals too quickly.

In these cases, it is important that you consider changing the:

- frequency of sessions or exercises
- intensity of exercises
- type of exercises being performed
- location of training
- overload and progression within the programme.

Assessment activity 4.4

 P4 P5 M3 D2 **BTEC**

Ask your client to complete the 6-week training programme that you designed as part of Assessment activity 4.3.

1. In order to make sure that your training programme is effective, monitor performance against goals during the six weeks. **P4**

2. At the end of the training programme, write a letter of feedback to your client that describes their strengths and areas for improvement. **P5**

3. In your feedback, make sure that you explain their strengths and areas for improvement. **M3**

4. Finally, evaluate your client's progress and provide them with recommendations for future activities. **D2**

Grading tips

P4 To attain P4 use a range of techniques to monitor progress against the goals of the training programme.

P5 To attain P5 include the client's key strengths and areas for improvement in order of priority.

M3 To attain M3 give specific details of strengths and areas for improvement of your client that are related to specific training goals and norm data for fitness tests.

D2 To attain D2 inform your client how the future recommendations will benefit them. You could suggest how the future recommendations will improve components of fitness further and look at any general sport or health-related benefits that will result from this.

PLTS

If you support your conclusions relating to the success of the training programme using reasoned arguments and supporting evidence, you could provide evidence of your skills as an **independent enquirer**.

Functional skills

If you provide feedback to your client in the correct manner, you could provide evidence of your **English** skills.

Amy Done
Fitness instructor

Amy is 19 and works as a fitness instructor at a local health club. She is responsible for a range of duties including: inducting people into the health club, conducting health screening with new members, setting training programmes for new members, reviewing current training programmes for existing members and providing general training advice for club members.

'Training is really important for both health and sport performance, so I need to make sure the advice that I give is up to date and correct so my clients get the best out of their sessions with me. I get to work with lots of different people as part of my job role which I find really interesting and challenging. On any day, it's quite common for me to be working with clients that range from obese people that need guidance on starting their exercise programmes so that they can lose weight and reduce their risk of associated conditions and diseases, all the way up to experienced weight trainers that just want somebody there to spot them or watch their technique for them. Quite often I'll get to see people develop their training habits over a long period of time and it's good to see that I've helped people to progress.

One of the biggest problems that I face is that, regardless of their level, one aspect of training that people always neglect is their flexibility training. No matter how much I try to encourage them to do it, most people don't bother with it because it doesn't involve lifting weights, running on the treadmill or swimming in the pool, so they don't see it as an actual method of training.'

Think about it!

- If you were in Amy's position how would you try to get people to increase their levels of flexibility training?
- Why do you think it is important for all gym users to understand flexibility training?
- If you could give people one piece of advice regarding their flexibility training, what would it be?
- Is fitness instructing a career you would be interested in and why?

Just checking

1. What are the health-related components of fitness?
2. What are the skill-related components of fitness?
3. Name one training method that can be used to increase each of the components of fitness
4. What does FITT stand for?
5. What does SPORTI stand for?
6. What types of information should you collect from a client before designing a training programme for them?
7. What is periodisation?
8. What are the different cycles within a periodised training programme?
9. Why should you use a training diary?
10. What are the different ways that you can monitor and review a training programme?

edexcel

Assignment tips

- Visit www.pponline.co.uk and www.sport-fitness-advisor.com. You can also use e-journals such as the American College of Sports Medicine Fit Society Newsletter which can be found at www.acsm.org.

- Use a range of specific textbooks for support when you are completing this unit. You may be really interested in a specific aspect of training and would like to read about it in more depth.

- If you know any fitness instructors, personal trainers or strength and conditioning coaches, talk to them about the content of this unit and how it fits in an applied setting.

- When you are completing assessments, provide as many appropriate examples, recommendations and justifications as you can on top of the more general information – this will help you to work at a higher level.

- Check your work with your tutor. They will be able to tell you how close you are to achieving the high grades and offer advice on how to improve your work.

- When you are learning about the different training methods, take part practically in the classes and even outside class. If you are experiencing the different training methods, you will get an understanding of their benefits.

- There are several professional bodies that are associated with fitness training and programming, including the British Association of Sport and Exercise Sciences (BASES), Register of Exercise Professionals (REPS), UK Strength and Conditioning Association (UKSCA) and British Weightlifting Association (BWLA). Visit their websites to investigate careers within fitness training and programming.

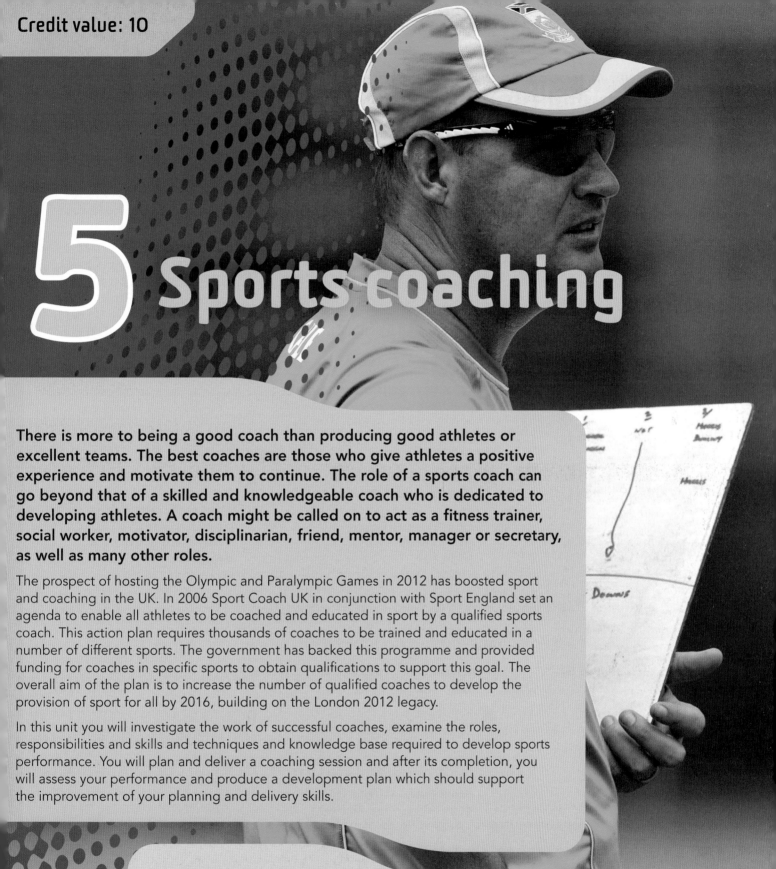

5 Sports coaching

There is more to being a good coach than producing good athletes or excellent teams. The best coaches are those who give athletes a positive experience and motivate them to continue. The role of a sports coach can go beyond that of a skilled and knowledgeable coach who is dedicated to developing athletes. A coach might be called on to act as a fitness trainer, social worker, motivator, disciplinarian, friend, mentor, manager or secretary, as well as many other roles.

The prospect of hosting the Olympic and Paralympic Games in 2012 has boosted sport and coaching in the UK. In 2006 Sport Coach UK in conjunction with Sport England set an agenda to enable all athletes to be coached and educated in sport by a qualified sports coach. This action plan requires thousands of coaches to be trained and educated in a number of different sports. The government has backed this programme and provided funding for coaches in specific sports to obtain qualifications to support this goal. The overall aim of the plan is to increase the number of qualified coaches to develop the provision of sport for all by 2016, building on the London 2012 legacy.

In this unit you will investigate the work of successful coaches, examine the roles, responsibilities and skills and techniques and knowledge base required to develop sports performance. You will plan and deliver a coaching session and after its completion, you will assess your performance and produce a development plan which should support the improvement of your planning and delivery skills.

Learning outcomes

After completing this unit you should:

1. know the roles, responsibilities and skills of sports coaches
2. know the techniques used by coaches to improve the performance of athletes
3. be able to plan a sports coaching session
4. be able to deliver and review a sports coaching session.

Assessment and grading criteria

This table shows you what you must do in order to achieve a pass, merit or distinction grade, and where you can find activities in this book to help you.

To achieve a **pass** grade the evidence must show that the learner is able to:	To achieve a **merit** grade the evidence must show that, in addition to the pass criteria, the learner is able to:	To achieve a **distinction** grade the evidence must show that, in addition to the pass and merit criteria, the learner is able to:
P1 describe four roles and four responsibilities of sports coaches, using examples of coaches from different sports **Assessment activity 5.1, page 130**	**M1** explain four roles and four responsibilities of sports coaches, using examples of coaches from different sports **Assessment activity 5.1, page 130**	**D1** compare and contrast the roles, responsibilities and skills of successful coaches from different sports **Assessment activity 5.1, page 130**
P2 describe three skills common to successful sports coaches, using examples of coaches from different sports **Assessment activity 5.1, page 130**	**M2** explain three skills common to successful sports coaches, using examples of coaches from different sports **Assessment activity 5.1, page 130**	
P3 describe three different techniques that are used by coaches, to improve the performance of athletes **Assessment activity 5.2, page 135**	**M3** explain three different techniques that are used by coaches to improve the performance of athletes **Assessment activity 5.2, page 135**	**D2** evaluate three different techniques that are used by coaches, to improve the performance of athletes **Assessment activity 5.2, page 135**
P4 plan a sports coaching session **Assessment activity 5.3, page 146**		
P5 deliver a sports coaching session, with tutor support **Assessment activity 5.3, page 146**	**M4** independently deliver a sports coaching session **Assessment activity 5.3, page 146**	
P6 carry out a review of the planning and delivery of a sports coaching session, identifying strengths and areas for improvement **Assessment activity 5.3, page 146**	**M5** evaluate the planning and delivery of a sports coaching session, suggesting how improvements could be reached in the identified areas **Assessment activity 5.3, page 146**	**D3** justify suggestions made in relation to the development plan **Assessment activity 5.3, page 146**

How you will be assessed

Your assessment could be in the form of:

- video recordings
- session plans completed for a sports activity session
- observation records of your performance while leading a sports coaching session
- assessment of your own performance while coaching a session
- a development plan which identifies and describes methods for improving performance.

Wayne Pybus, 22-year-old football coach

I have always wanted to pursue a career in sport. When I was younger I thought I would be a professional footballer, but realised when I was released from a football club that professional sport was not for me. After this, I enrolled on a BTEC National Diploma course at my local college. I really enjoyed the course, especially the sports coaching unit. Through completing this unit I developed a greater understanding of the roles, responsibilities, skills and techniques required to be a successful coach. This was very useful when I went on to complete coaching qualifications in a variety of sports.

The coaching unit was practical and very hands on and enabled me to plan and lead coaching sessions to a variety of groups of athletes. I really enjoyed this part of the unit, especially when we went into a local school and I led a football session and improved the performance of every participant.

Over to you

- **What are your reasons for wanting to play sport?**
- **What could a sports coach do to ensure that all your needs are met in a coaching session?**

1. Know the roles, responsibilities and skills of sports coaches

1. List the different roles of a sports coach.
2. Are some of these roles more appropriate than others? List your top five roles for a sports coach.
3. List the skills a good coach will need to coach athletes.
4. List the qualities a good coach needs to coach athletes.

In this unit you will examine the roles, responsibilities and skills of a sports coach. You will reflect on how coaches should and do meet the requirements of each of these roles, responsibilities and skills. Remember that in order to be an excellent coach you don't have to fulfil every role, responsibility and skill covered in this unit. Even the greatest coaches may not demonstrate excellence in all the areas covered. As a sports coach you can always improve and should always seek to develop in order to support the athletes you work with.

1.1 Roles

In sports coaching, the desired roles should support the development of athletes at a variety of levels.

Innovator

The term innovation means a new or original way of doing something. As a sports coach you need to search for new techniques to enhance performance or to generate greater enjoyment in a session.

During his management of Bolton Wanderers FC (1999–2007), Sam Allardyce examined methods of measuring and improving players' performance. He introduced the use of Prozone technology to assess players' effectiveness and based training programmes on the results. Allardyce also added nutritionists, sports psychologists, fitness coaches, defensive coaches and attacking coaches to his coaching squad. He turned Bolton Wanderers from a Premier League yo-yo club to an established top ten Premier League team.

Another innovator is Shane Sutton, a coach with the British cycling team in Beijing 2008. Sutton combined scientific, data-based technology with specific training methods, developing a team mentality in a predominantly individual sport that led the British cycling team to enormous success.

Friend

An athlete and coach may spend considerable amounts of time together. Friendships develop, athlete and coach may share positive and negative experiences and because of these common experiences a bond evolves.

When developing a relationship with anyone you learn more about their personality and a sports coach can use this knowledge to help them. Increased understanding of an athlete's personality will support the coach in developing an effective training plan.

When developing friendships with athletes it is important that the coach is aware of their role and clearly states the boundaries of the relationship at the start of the friendship. The athlete's development must be the priority. At times a coach may have to criticise an athlete's performance; as a friend, this information may be easily shared, although athletes may react negatively to criticism.

Manager

You may think of managing a team when you consider sports coaching. It is often the manager's responsibility to coach the team and individual players as well as to manage the fixtures, prepare the equipment and organise transport to the competition or training venues. The principle role of a manager is to lead. Their leadership style will depend on the athletes they are managing.

Coaching style	Characteristics	Advantages	Disadvantages
Command style	Coach makes all the decisions Leader tells the athletes what to do and how to do it	Good for beginners when explaining basic skills and techniques Good method of controlling a group and keeping large groups safe	Only works on single skills in isolation Difficult to examine athletes' prior knowledge and understanding, as session controlled solely by coach
Reciprocal style	Coach decides what is to be delivered in the session, but involves athletes in decision-making process	Good for developed athletes Develops close relationships with athletes Develops communication and athletes' confidence	Time-consuming Problems may occur in large teams when everyone has different opinions and ideas
The guided discovery style	Athletes are in control of the session and make the decisions Coach is a mentor for the athletes when appropriate	Often used with experts or professional athletes Helps develop self-confidence Can increase understanding and develop athletes' decision-making skills Can increase athletes' motivation	Lack of structure to the session Can develop bad techniques without coach's intervention Can take time to meet a desired goal or target

Table 5.1: Different coaching styles and which athletes they are best suited to

Take it further

Think of the different coaches you have worked with as an athlete. Can you identify a coach who used any of the leadership styles described in Table 5.1? Can you evaluate the effectiveness of their coaching for you as an athlete?

The photo shows England team manager Fabio Capello giving instructions to David Beckham during an international football match.

1. List the other roles and responsibilities Capello will have to meet in his role as England football manager.
2. Identify your own sports manager or another team manager from your school or college. List the roles and responsibilities they will have to meet.

A good manager should motivate their team, learn from mistakes, and gain respect from the athletes who play for them. The managers who attain excellence are those whose players want to play for them. Managers generate this desire through a mixture of motivation and respect, which could stem from coaching sessions, team talks, previous successes and their reputation. For an individual sport the manager's role is to monitor the individual's development and do everything possible to obtain their optimum performance. In team sports the manager's role involves team selection and could include choosing the best team from a squad of players, or the best combination of players to beat the opponents. When working with teams the manager has to oversee the relationship between players. Good managers create team cohesion to help players perform to the best of their ability.

In some sports and at the highest levels, a variety of coaches may be employed to develop skills, fitness and tactical awareness, while the manager's role is to organise and coordinate training programmes.

Trainer

When a coach takes up a role as trainer they need to be aware of the physical, technical and tactical demands of the specific sport. They should have a bank of activities that can be drawn on to develop the athlete's ability to perform to their optimum. The most common trainer is probably a fitness trainer.

Coaches need to have a good knowledge of health and fitness and training principles (see Unit 4: Fitness training and programming, page 87). As a trainer, a coach should be able to design and implement programmes that are appropriate for the athletes and reflect the sports they compete in. When planning fitness development sessions, coaches should consider the athletes':

- age
- ability
- interests
- experience.

Role model

When leading a sport or physical activity session, a coach is representing that particular sport or activity, and should set an example to the participants. A good coach will demonstrate appropriate behaviour and use appropriate language with athletes at all times. Coaches should accept responsibility for the conduct of the athletes they coach and encourage positive and non-discriminatory behaviour.

To be an effective role model, a coach must set an example with the clothes they wear when coaching. A coach should have sports clothing and footwear and the appropriate equipment to coach the session.

A coach will sell the sport or physical activity session to the athletes, and the more enthusiastic the coach is, the more enthusiastic the athletes are likely to become.

Educator

A coach will educate athletes so that they can develop as performers. When coaching young children and beginners, a coach will start by educating them about the basic skills of the game. As a performer develops in the basic skills, the coach will provide support and develop their skills to enhance their efficiency and effectiveness. A coach needs to understand how people learn. Athletes learn best when:

- they are actively involved, rather than listening and watching the coach playing

- they recognise how, when and where new techniques, skills or tactics can be used
- they are encouraged to build on experiences and skills learned in previous sessions or other sports (for example, catching in cricket could be transferred to basketball, netball or rugby)
- they are interested, enjoying themselves and motivated
- they can see or feel improvements in their performance.

A coach will be aware that athletes develop differently and require a mixture of coaching styles. An effective coach develops a range of styles to deal with a variety of learners.

1.2 Responsibilities

A coach has responsibilities to the participants in their coaching session and also to:

- the participants' parents or guardians
- the club or school that the coach is representing
- other coaches who may be involved in the delivery of the session
- the sport that the coach is representing, for example in a football session a coach will be representing the Football Association and the sport of football.

Legal obligations

Child protection

Children are introduced to sport at very early ages, and coaches must be aware of child-protection procedures. See also BTEC Level 3 National Sport Student Book 2, Unit 24, pages 349–54.

Prior to working with children in any capacity a coach must be the subject of a Criminal Records Bureau (CRB) check to check the criminal records of a potential employee. Any previous convictions will be listed and a decision will be made by the organisation after they have viewed the CRB's feedback. This will determine whether or not the candidate is appropriate for the work. In some instances those with criminal records will not be able to work with children (this includes people on the sex offenders' registers and those with violent criminal records).

The Children Act (2004)

A coach must be aware of the Children Act (2004) and of the signs and symptoms of child abuse. This act provides a legislative framework for services working with children and young people to improve their health, development and well-being.

The Children Act makes it a responsibility of all agencies working with children and young people to work together and adopt a multi-agency approach when offering services. The act enforces specific duties which must be carried out by the service providers. These include:

- providing care, planned and supervised activities for all children at all times
- publishing adequate information about the services
- reviewing and monitoring the services on offer and consulting with the appropriate bodies, for example professionals who deal with the protection of children
- ensuring that registration is completed for all organisations which supervise activities for children under the age of 18 years.

Before a service can be registered, the suitability of the organisation, all its employees and its premises need to be assessed.

Coaches must be able to recognise the main forms of child abuse, which include:

Physical abuse – physical hurt or injury caused by an adult to a child (could be displayed when a child displays unexplained bruising, cuts or burns)

Sexual abuse – adults, both male and female, using children to meet their own sexual needs (could be displayed when a child demonstrates over-sexualised behaviour)

Emotional abuse – could be a persistent lack of love and affection (this could be displayed when a child becomes reserved and withdrawn from social contact with others)

Neglect – failure to meet the child's basic needs like food and warm clothing (this could be evident from a child's appearance and clothing).

If a child says or indicates that he or she is being abused, or information is obtained which raises concerns that a child is being abused, the coach or anyone receiving the information should:

- react calmly so as not to frighten the child
- tell the child they are not to blame and they are right to tell
- take what the child says seriously
- keep questions to an absolute minimum
- reassure the child
- make a full record of what the child has said
- not promise the child that no one else will be informed

- as soon as the conversation has ended, the person receiving the information should report the findings to a designated child-protection officer at the school or sports centre, or report the information directly to the police.

As a sports coach you should be aware that coaches have caused harm to children through over-training, bullying and other forms of mistreatment, and that it is vital that a coach always treats children fairly and with respect.

Insurance

Sports coaches are required to have appropriate insurance cover to participate in physical activity as well as to lead a sport or physical activity session. A coach is responsible for the safety of the athletes while they are under his or her supervision. If an athlete is injured during a coaching session, the coach is considered liable and could be deemed negligent.

Professional conduct

A coach should always behave appropriately. As a coach your conduct and behaviour will determine the experience and future behaviour of the athletes you coach. A good coach will:

- demonstrate clear knowledge and experience of the sport
- have appropriate coaching qualifications and relevant experience
- dress appropriately for the coaching session
- speak clearly, using appropriate language at all times
- respect all athletes of all abilities and treat them all equally
- respect and support all officials and their decisions
- promote **fair play**
- promote honesty
- reward effort.

Key term

Fair play – playing as competitively as possible, but always within the rules of the sport as determined by the national governing body.

Many national governing bodies (NGBs) have set specific codes of conduct to promote appropriate behaviour for coaches who are qualified under their coach-education schemes. These codes of conduct determine whether or not a coach is acting professionally.

Take it further

Below is an example of a code of conduct provided by the Football Association for all football coaches, team managers and club officials. For more information about codes of conduct see www.TheFA.com/Respect.

Code of conduct: Coaches, team managers and club officials

We all have a responsibility to promote high standards of behaviour in the game.

In the Football Association's survey of over 37,000 grassroots participants, behaviour was the biggest concern in the game. This included the abuse of match officials and the unacceptable behaviour by over competitive parents, spectators and coaches on the sideline.

Play your part and observe the FA's Respect Code of Conduct in everything you do.

On and off the field, I will:
- Show respect to others involved in the game including match officials, opposition players, coaches, managers, officials and spectators
- Adhere to the laws and spirit of the game
- Promote Fair Play and high standards of behaviour
- Always respect the match officials' decision
- Never enter the field of play without the referee's permission
- Never engage in public criticism of the match officials
- Never engage in, or tolerate, offensive, insulting or abusive language or behaviour

When working with players, I will:
- Place the well-being, safety and enjoyment of each player above everything, including winning
- Explain exactly what I expect of players and what they can expect from me
- Ensure all parents/carers of all players under the age of 18 understand these expectations
- Never engage in or tolerate any form of bullying
- Develop mutual trust and respect with every player to build their self-esteem
- Encourage each player to accept responsibility for their own behaviour and performance
- Ensure all activities I organise are appropriate for the players' ability level, age and maturity
- Co-operate fully with others in football (e.g. officials, doctors, physiotherapists, welfare officers) for each player's best interests

I understand that if I do not follow the Code, any/all of the following actions may be taken by my club, County FA or The FA.

I may be:
- Required to meet with the club, league or County Welfare Officer
- Required to meet with the club committee
- Monitored by another club coach
- Required to attend a FA education course
- Suspended by the club from attending matches
- Suspended or fined by the County FA
- Required to leave or be sacked by the club

In addition:
- My FACA (FA Coaches Association) membership may be withdrawn

Activity: Code of conduct

Produce a code of conduct with your peers for when you are coaching – as a class, make it clear what expectations you have of everyone who coaches at your school/college/sports club.

To support the completion of your code of conduct, each group member should identify what makes a good coach and what makes a bad coach – share and discuss your findings.

Activity: Intrinsic or extrinsic injuries?

Classify each of the following causes of injury as intrinsic or extrinsic.

- overuse
- age
- inappropriate coaching
- environmental conditions, e.g. rain, snow, ice
- poor preparation
- poor technique
- clashes with opponents
- clashes with teammates
- postural defects
- muscle imbalance
- equipment failure
- loose clothing
- inappropriate clothing.

Health and safety

A key responsibility of a sports coach is managing the safety of everyone involved in a coaching session. When working anyone under the age of 18 this responsibility becomes a legal obligation of a **duty of care**. A coach should consider the health and safety of the participants before, during and after the session as a priority. It is often the head coach's responsibility to lead on health and safety, although assistant coaches must also maintain a safe coaching environment at all times.

All sports carry an element of risk of injury; it is the role of the sports coach to:

- assess risk
- protect athletes from injury and reduce the likelihood of risk
- deal with injuries and accidents when they occur.

Although a coach may assess every risk and hazard and implement methods of reducing injury and keeping harm to a minimum, injuries can and will occur during sport and physical activity sessions. There are two major causes of injuries – **extrinsic risks** and **intrinsic risks**.

Sports coaches may benefit from obtaining a first-aid qualification to ensure they know what action to take if an athlete is injured. If you are not a qualified first-aider, you should make provision for first-aid during coaching sessions, for example by ensuring that a qualified first-aider is present. A coach should ensure that athletes seek professional advice as soon as possible if:

- a major injury is sustained during a session – fracture, severe bleeding, head injury, severe swelling or bruising with pain
- a minor injury is sustained during a session – muscle strain, muscle contusion (bruising), minor cuts or bleeding
- they become ill – vomiting, headache, sore throat, dizziness.

It is vital to ensure that the coaching and playing environment is safe and to know what to do in the event of a serious accident. If you are not sure about anything regarding the health and safety of the participants of your session, you should seek advice from a senior coach or a senior member of staff prior to starting your session.

Key terms

Duty of care – a legal obligation imposed on an individual, requiring that they adhere to a standard of reasonable care while performing any acts that could possibly harm others.

Extrinsic risk – something outside the body that may cause an injury.

Intrinsic risk – a physical aspect of the body that may cause an injury.

The photo shows an athlete receiving first-aid. Often the coach is first on the scene of an injury, therefore they must have knowledge of first-aid.

- Identify an appropriate first-aid course that would be suitable for you to complete as a coach.
- Identify the location of the next available first-aid course and the cost of the qualification.

Activity: Dealing with accidents and illnesses

During a coaching session, you may be presented with any of the following:

- a player suffers a minor injury, e.g. cut/bruise/strain
- a player suffers a major injury, e.g. broken bone/concussion/severe bleed
- a player becomes ill, e.g. vomiting/headache.

1. For each scenario, explain what action(s) you would take to deal with the problem.

2. Imagine each scenario occurring in your sports hall – identify the qualified contact at the school/college and explain how they would be contacted and what procedure would need to be followed.

3. Find the nearest first-aid bag at your sports hall – assess the effectiveness of its contents and discuss with your group how they could be improved.

Equal opportunities

A competent coach will ensure that equal opportunities are given to all athletes, spectators, parents and match officials. Ensuring equal opportunities is about recognising inequalities and addressing and solving the issues that surround each one. To achieve equality, coaches should make sure that coaching sessions are accessible to all, without prejudice to age, gender, race, ethnicity, religion, sexuality, socio-economic status or ability.

When planning coaching sessions you as a coach will need to cater for participants with different motives, needs and goals. In order for all groups to achieve what they want, you must be willing and able to adapt the session.

Knowledge of the coaching environment

Sports coaches familiarise themselves with the environment in which they deliver their sessions. This can take many forms, including:

- outdoor pitches
- indoor pitches
- sports halls
- indoor courts
- outdoor courts
- multi-use game areas
- astroturf pitches
- third-generation grass pitches
- gymnasiums
- school halls.

A coach will be aware of the size of the environment and how it can be best used. For example, if a coach is delivering a basketball session in a sports hall and the basketball nets are folded away, the coach will need to know how to unfold them or where to find a member of staff who can help.

The coach should also be aware of the location of changing rooms, toilets, showers, first-aid box or designated first-aid room and member of staff if appropriate. This knowledge will demonstrate to the participating athletes that their coach is well prepared.

The more a coach knows about the coaching environment, the more organisation and professionalism they can demonstrate when running a session. This in turn will increase the athletes' confidence in their coach.

1.3 Skills

Communication

Communication is possibly the most important skill required to coach athletes effectively. Coaches have to exchange information not only with athletes, but also with parents, other coaches, officials, other staff at a sports club, teachers, spectators and many other people. The three main forms of communication used by sports coaches are verbal communication, non-verbal communication, and listening skills.

In **verbal communication** it is important to keep language simple and free from technical and complex jargon. A coach should ensure that what they are to say is correct and appropriate, and that they have the attention of the person/people they are speaking to. After providing the information, they should check for understanding by questioning the audience or observing the performance of the athlete.

Non-verbal communication can take many forms, for example body language. Most body language is unconscious (done without thinking). An athlete will be able to read positive and negative body language and this information will indicate the coach's mood.

Other forms of non-verbal communication used by coaches are hand signals and demonstrations. Hand signals can direct athletes or provide instructions during training and competitions. Demonstrations are used to show the correct technique and model each component of a skill, technique or tactic.

As well as sending out communication, it is important that a coach can receive information. In order to improve their listening skills a coach should:

- concentrate when someone is talking to them
- make eye contact with the speaker
- avoid interrupting the speaker
- ask questions or summarise what has been said to confirm understanding.

Organisation

When planning training programmes and sessions, a coach needs to demonstrate high levels of organisation. An organised session will motivate athletes and maintain interest. In order to be fully prepared and organised for a session a coach should:

- ensure they know how many participants are taking part
- ensure that the activities are appropriate for all the participants (to do this the coach will need to know the ability levels of each participant)
- decide what equipment they will need prior to the event and ensure that it is available and ready for use on the day of the session
- ensure that the facility where the session is taking place is booked well in advance and that they are aware of its safety procedures
- ensure at the end of the session that the facility and equipment are left as they were when the session started
- ensure that they have clear methods of stopping and starting the session. This could be discussed with participants at the start of the session, for example, when the coach blows the whistle, all participants must stop.

When they first start coaching, many sports coaches record each session they deliver and collate their records to make a logbook to which they can refer when planning future sessions. Although these session plans and logbooks are important to demonstrate organisation for the planning and delivery of coaching sessions, coaches need to know how to adapt sessions if activities are not working. It is in these situations that a coach's knowledge, experience and organisational skills will be pushed to the limit.

Analysing

Spectators watching sports live or on television make judgements on what they see. Everyone has their own ideas, which sometimes go against those of the coach of the team they are observing. A coach makes similar judgements, but they are often based on more objective data.

A coach must demonstrate effective analysis skills. Analysis of sports performance is the ability to observe and make appropriate judgements about performers' technical and tactical ability. A coach should assess individual players and/or teams in action and should identify and prioritise performance targets for them.

In order to complete an effective analysis of a player's and/or team's performance, a coach needs to have a clear expectation of the performers at their stage of development. The ability to analyse requires a coach to observe and assess any faults in what they see. This skill takes time and experience to develop. Even the greatest athletes have weaknesses and sometimes these are not spotted by every coach. That is why elite athletes change coaches or seek support from others, or build a team of coaches to work on specific parts of their overall performance.

As well as analysing ability, a coach must be able to analyse the personality and motivation of the athletes they will be coaching. A coach will do the majority of their analysis by watching athletes' performance, behaviour and actions to learn about their personality and motivation, and should be able to read their mood through their body language and gestures while training or competing.

Problem-solving

The coaching environment can be very inconsistent: problems may arise suddenly which will require the coach's attention. Problems can take many forms including:

- participants
- equipment
- facility
- opponents
- transport.

Athletes expecting to participate in a coaching session will often expect any problems to be solved in advance so that the session can proceed according to plan. It is a coach's job to spot when things are going wrong, determine the nature of the problem and find a solution. Often they will have to find a solution on the spot, to allow things to continue as normal.

Activity: Problem-solving

Imagine you are a sports coach and explain what actions you would take to resolve the following problems:

- You have planned a football coaching session with the aim of improving dribbling. The majority of the activities you have planned require each player to dribble with a ball – you have 12 balls but 18 players – what should you do?

- You are coaching a tennis session. You arrive at the local tennis centre and all the tennis courts are booked, but the receptionist tells you that there are two squash courts free – what should you do?

- You are coaching a basketball session; on arrival at the sports hall you find the storage room is locked and no key is available. There are 14 players waiting to participate – what should you do?

Evaluating

Evaluation is observing yourself or someone else and assessing the effectiveness of your, or their, performance. To do this, you need to compare the performance with an exemplar performance at an equivalent level or with equivalent experience and qualifications.

The skills of evaluation should be used by a coach in two different ways. First, they should evaluate their own performance to form the basis of future coaching session plans. An evaluation of every session should enable them to assess what went well and could be used again and what was less successful. The way a coach deals with identified areas of weakness depends on how they develop as a coach. A good coach should be able to reflect on any areas of weakness and plan short-, medium- and long-term targets for their development.

Second, a coach should evaluate the performance of an athlete or a team, and produce a training programme based around their evaluation.

Time-management

The tasks a coach has to carry out prior to delivering a coaching session can demand a lot of time and effort. Many coaches are not professional, so may be juggling the demands of planning and delivering a coaching session around full- or part-time employment. Due to the demands that can be placed on a coach, it is important that they manage their time effectively.

Prior to a coaching session a coach will need to ensure that:

- all athletes attending the session are aware of the location and timing of the session
- the facility is booked
- the equipment required is prepared and ready for use
- the session is planned and all appropriate arrangements are made.

During the session the coach must also ensure that:

- an appropriate amount of time is dedicated to each component of the session
- weaknesses previously observed are worked on
- all athletes will develop technically and tactically (depending on the aims of the session)
- the session is fun and enjoyable
- time is allocated for athletes in a competitive situation to apply the skills covered in the session
- feedback is completed for players and parents or spectators as appropriate
- athletes are aware of future competitions or training.

Assessment activity 5.1

(P1) (P2) (M1) (M2) (D1)   :BTEC

1. You have been asked to produce a leaflet for prospective volunteer coaches at a local sports club. Your leaflet must describe four roles and four responsibilities of sports coaches, using examples from different sports. **P1**

2. In order to meet the requirement for M1 in your leaflet, in addition to the requirements for P1, you must explain four roles and four responsibilities of sports coaches, using examples from different sports. **M1**

3. In your leaflet you must also describe three skills common to successful sports coaches, using examples from different sports. **P2**

4. In order to meet the requirements of M2, in addition to the requirements for P2, you must explain three skills common to successful sports coaches, using examples from different sports. **M2**

5. If you would like to achieve D1 in this activity, in addition to the requirements for P1, P2, M1 and M2, you must compare and contrast the roles, responsibilities and skills of successful coaches from different sports. **D1**

Grading tips

P1 Select four roles and four responsibilities and define each one, stating how sports coaches use each role and responsibility effectively.

P2 Select three skills.

M1, M2 Use examples of at least three coaches from different sports to discuss the effective application of each role, responsibility and skill.

M1 Explain how each coach selected meets the requirement of each role, responsibility and skill successfully.

D1 Compare the roles, responsibilities and skills of the selected sports coaches. Say which roles, responsibilities and skills they all use (similarities) and which roles, responsibilities and skills some, but not all, of the coaches use (differences).

PLTS

Researching sports coaches who have fulfilled each role, responsibility and skill selected will help you to develop your skills as an **independent enquirer**.

Functional skills

Describing the roles, responsibilities and skills of sports coaches will help you develop your **English** writing skills.

2. Know the techniques used by coaches to improve the performance of athletes

2.1 Techniques

Observation analysis

A popular technique used by coaches to assess the performance and effective application of the skills, techniques and tactics required in a specific sport is observation analysis. Coaches need to be effective observers to enable them to identify strengths and weaknesses during performance.

Observation analysis is a crucial part of the coach's role, since coaching plans should be informed by analysis. Observation analysis should be used to identify an athlete's needs, with the coach completing a full analysis of their overall performance and then developing a training programme around it, aiming to improve the most significant weaknesses observed.

There are two basic ways of formulating judgements through observation analysis: subjective and objective analysis. Subjective analysis is based on observational judgements, personal interpretations and opinions. Objective analysis involves the measurement and comparison of performance data, for example the ability to perform a basketball free throw could be assessed objectively by counting how many free throws a player scores out of ten. The same assessment could be carried out objectively if a coach compares the player's technique and skill against a mental image of an ideal technique.

The most commonly used method of observation analysis is notational analysis. This requires the coach to record the number of skills completed effectively in a competitive situation. On completion of an objective analysis the coach is able to make subjective observations on the outcome of the athlete's overall performance.

When carrying out observation analysis, a coach must be careful not to be biased. They will have built up a relationship with the athlete they work with, but must view their performance in as unbiased a light as possible.

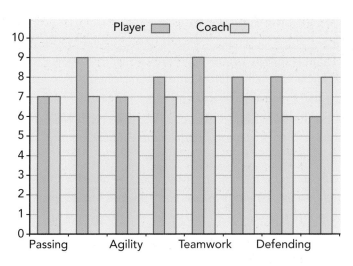

Figure 5.1: A performance profile completed by a coach and an athlete

a subjective assessment which is completed using a variety of methods including notational analysis and performance observation. After such an assessment the coach will award the athletes or themselves a grade or mark which should be set against a specific target or goal with regard to development.

For example, a golfer who has a handicap of 16 may compare their performance against a golfer who has an 8 handicap, so on a scale of 1 to 10, 1 may be the attribute of a 16 handicap while 10 may be compared to the skills and attributes of a 4 handicap golfer. It would not be realistic to compare their performance to Tiger Woods because of the difference in ability and skill levels. It is therefore important for a coach to have realistic expectations regarding the developmental goals of athletes.

When coaching a beginner, a coach will complete a performance profile to determine which elements of the performance require development. At this stage of the athlete's career there will be little conversation between the athlete and the coach, as only the coach has the knowledge and experience required to develop performance.

As an athlete develops, the performance profiling should be completed by both the coach and the performer. After the completion of the performance profile, they should discuss the findings and agree a development plan that aims to address any technical, tactical, psychological or physical weaknesses in their performance.

Activity: Observation analysis

Produce a checklist that you could use to assess the performance of an athlete/team from your chosen sport.

Ensure that you allow room to assess the technical and tactical ability of the athlete/team.

Performance profiling

In order to complete a full assessment of an athlete's overall performance, a coach needs to carry out a full assessment of the technical, tactical, physical and psychological requirements of the sport. This is called a performance profile.

A performance profile is used by a coach to assess the technical and tactical ability of an athlete. It is

Fitness assessment

Unit 7: Fitness testing for sport and exercise (page 179) introduces a variety of methods of assessing the physical and skill-related fitness components. A coach will use these to assess an athlete's fitness.

After the completion of such tests, the coach will be able to plan a training programme to work on any identified areas for improvement.

Following the training programme, the coach can also use fitness tests to reassess the athlete's fitness and compare the results to see whether improvements have been made.

Goal-setting

Goal-setting should be used by coaches to increase athletes' motivation and confidence. It should be the first stage of the planning process for any coach, as goals should provide both direction and motivation for athletes. Goals may be **short-term**, **medium-term**, or **long-term**.

Short-term goals could extend from one day to one month, for example a target that an athlete wishes to achieve after the next training session, or a specific technique they would like to develop by the end of the next month.

Medium-term goals should progressively support the progress of the athlete and their coach towards achieving the long-term goals. These goals can be measured at specific points in an athlete's season.

Long-term goals are set for and with athletes to help determine what their aims are and the best way of achieving them. A coach should use these to shape their coaching schedule for a season or longer if appropriate. The goals are often set for a season, for example a team may aim to finish the season in the top two positions in the league and achieve promotion. Long-term goals can also run over a number of years, as with an elite athlete who sets themselves a target of competing in the next Olympic Games, which may not take place for the next three years.

Simulation

When athletes have mastered the technical components in coaching sessions, the coach may use simulated practices as a means of advancing the skills developed in the session or previous sessions. Such practices may simulate a competitive environment, for example a simulated practice in a team game would be a conditioned game that would replicate some elements of the game, but where the coach would adapt the rules, number of players, or size of the pitch to try to support the development of specific skills.

Conditioned games will enable athletes to develop more of an understanding of the skills they are working on. If a coach limits the number of defenders when working on an attacking skill, the attackers are more likely to succeed, which will support their motivation. The coach can increase the number of defenders when they feel the performers are ready to be tested, and this will show how the performers cope in a realistic situation.

Simulation can also be used to support athletes to prepare for a specific event. For example, an athlete who is going to compete at a certain time of day at a certain altitude could simulate the environment by training at the same time of day and at the same altitude as the location of the competition.

Modelling

When introducing new skills to athletes, coaches often use modelling to demonstrate exactly what they expect the athletes to achieve. Modelling can be delivered in two forms:

- coach or performer demonstration
- video demonstration.

The model is an example of the skill, technique or activity which the coach would like the athletes to master. For example, when delivering a session with the aim of improving a player's ability to correctly and safely administer a rugby tackle, a coach may use a model of the action to show learners what is expected of them.

Modelling skills should be used to paint a picture in the minds of athletes, and to point out key technical instructions for the skill or activity the coach would like them to achieve.

Dartfish technology provides an opportunity to slow down movements and freeze actions, allowing coaches to demonstrate complex skills. It can also show two performances simultaneously to compare techniques.

Take it further

Dartfish is a video analysis program that can slow down and freeze-frame sporting actions. It is used to analyse sport skills and techniques in action.

This image demonstrates how Dartfish is used to analyse performance and the application of skills.

Can you think of other sports where this technology could be used to develop performance?

Effective demonstration

Demonstrations are an important tool which should be used by coaches to support and develop athletes of all abilities. One of the first considerations a coach will have to make is whether to use video or still images to support the athlete's development.

For example, when working with a group of children or beginners, the coach should demonstrate the skill they would like the group to achieve during the session. At this stage the group's knowledge of the skill is limited and therefore if the coach has any bad habits these could be amended at a later stage in their development. On the other hand, when coaching elite athletes a coach may choose to use still images or video demonstrations because their own demonstrations at this level may display an inaccurate model. A video can be slowed down and replayed, with the coach highlighting the key factors for the athlete to address in their own application of the skill.

When demonstrating a skill to athletes a coach should:

- determine the purpose and type of demonstration to be used
- ensure that the image the demonstration paints in the athletes' minds is correct and appropriate
- ensure all athletes can see the demonstration
- only demonstrate one or two coaching points at a time
- repeat the demonstration more than once
- invite questions from the athletes at the end of the demonstration

The photo shows an international coach describing and demonstrating a skill to an England cricketer. Why is it important for the coach to demonstrate a skill or technique? Do you think it is ever inappropriate for a coach to demonstrate a skill? If so, when?

- let the athletes practise the skill
- observe the application of the skill and work individually with athletes if possible.

> **Remember**
>
> Demonstration: 'A picture paints a thousand words.'

Technical instruction

As mentioned earlier in this unit (page 127), verbal communication in coaching sessions should be clear and concise. A coach will often convey technical instructions to athletes using both verbal and non-verbal means. Non-verbal communication usually consists of some form of demonstration, while verbal communication involves providing instructions and guidance during and after demonstrations.

An effective coach should have a good knowledge of the technical requirements of the sport they are coaching. They should know how to break down the components of each skill or technique in order to share it with the participants in the session. When instructing athletes it is important to explain the significance and relevance of the instruction in relation to their overall development.

When providing technical instructions a coach should:

- plan what they are going to say and how they are going to deliver the information (this may depend on the audience)
- gain the attention of all the athletes prior to speaking
- keep the instructions simple but ensure the information is accurate
- when possible, use demonstrations/visual examples to reinforce the instructions
- check at the end of the instructions that all members of the group have understood.

As with any learning process, an athlete's ability to take in information will depend on what stage of learning they are at. For each stage, a coach should provide different levels of instructions and support (see Table 5.2).

> **Remember**
>
> When giving instructions, KISS – Keep It Simple.

The stages of learning		
Cognitive	**Associative**	**Autonomous**
Athletes are trying to grasp the basics of the skills/tasks set; they often have few experiences to relate to in the sport being coached. They will demonstrate a lot of errors and technical inefficiencies.	Athletes try to develop skills and techniques. They do this through practice. As they develop, they make fewer errors, although there will still be errors in the application of skills.	Athletes can produce skills with little effort almost 100% accuracy and success. At this stage they should be able to apply skills successfully in competitive situations.
Coach should: • use simple technical explanations and demonstrations • use simple basic drills and practices to develop skills • create fun and enjoyable sessions • encourage performers to practise unopposed • use lots of positive feedback.	Coach should: • use instructions and demonstrations to give athletes more information on the correct application of the skills • simulate training sessions and activities to develop specific skills • provide constructive feedback and promote peer- and self-analysis to assess performance.	Coach should: • use video demonstrations to demonstrate perfect application of skills • use complex technical instructions to fine-tune skills • discuss tactical application of the skills mastered.

Table 5.2: Matching instructions to the appropriate stage of learning

Developing performer coaching diaries

At the start of their career, sports coaches are always encouraged to keep a log of every session they complete and to collate all their session plans. At the end of each session they should reflect on what they and the participants have achieved. This process should continue as a coach develops.

A coach who records the development of each participant in each session will have a record of progress over a season. This can be useful when an athlete and coach reflect on the last season or look ahead and start to plan short-, medium- and long-term goals.

Adapting practices to meet individual needs

A coach must be able to support the varying needs and aspirations of all athletes who attend their sessions, all of whom have different methods of learning. This does not mean producing different session plans for each athlete, but it does mean that a coach should know their athletes, how they learn and which components of their game need support. A coach should be tactful, so that no one feels embarrassed or uncomfortable.

Designing effective practice sessions

A coach should aim to maintain athletes' interest, enjoyment and motivation. To achieve this aim, sessions should balance technical development, simulated practices and competitive situations. Although athletes should enjoy the sessions, it is also vital that the coach develops the application of skills, techniques and tactics in every session that they plan and deliver. Coaching sessions should differ for athletes of different ages or ability levels. However, a coach should also consider individual needs, as mentioned above.

Assessment activity 5.2

1. You have been asked to produce a presentation for all the volunteer coaches who have responded to an advertisement placed by your local sports club. Your presentation must describe three different techniques used by coaches to improve athletes' performance. **P3**

2. In order to meet the requirements of M3 in your presentation you must, in addition to the requirements for P3, explain three different techniques that are used by coaches to improve athletes' performance. **M3**

3. Finally, to meet the requirements of D2 in addition to the requirements of P3 and M3, your presentation must evaluate three different techniques that are used by coaches to improve athletes' performance. **D2**

Grading tips

P3 Select the three techniques you know most about. Describe what each one is and how it is used by coaches to improve performance.

M3 Give examples of coaches who use this technique successfully to develop athletes.

Give examples of coaches who have used these techniques and failed to develop athletes' performance.

D2 Assess the strengths and weaknesses of each technique, commenting on the reliability, subjectivity and validity of each one, as appropriate.

PLTS

Describing techniques used by coaches to improve athletes' performance will develop your skills as a **creative thinker**.

Functional skills

Describing techniques used by coaches to improve athletes' performance will develop your **English** writing skills.

3. Be able to plan a sports coaching session

3.1 Plan

Aims and objectives

All coaching sessions should have a clear **aim**. This should be clearly stated on the coach's session plan and agreed before the start of the session, for example for everyone to be able to execute a chest pass in netball by the end of the session.

In order to achieve your aims, you will need to have **objectives** (one per aim). These should be clearly written on your session plan and should express how you will meet each of them, for example 'In order for everyone in the group to execute a chest pass effectively I must introduce, demonstrate and develop the required technique for the chest pass.'

SMART (specific, measurable, achievable, realistic, time-bound) targets

A coach uses targets to develop athletes. They should be set around each individual's strengths and areas for improvement. The coach's session plan should focus on particular performers and set realistic targets. Coaches could use the SMART model for setting targets for participants in their session:

Specific – make the target as precise and detailed as possible.

Measurable – define a method of measuring the success of the athlete – set achievement targets – what by when?

Achievable – goal should be able to be attained within a set period of time and should be relevant for the athlete.

Realistic – appropriate for the athlete.

Time-bound – ensure you agree a timescale, even if it includes mini-targets for athlete development.

Roles and responsibilities

When planning a session with more than one coach, it is important to share roles and responsibilities equally. The plan should be recorded and the coaches should meet regularly to discuss the planning and preparation for the session/event and ensure that each coach is fulfilling their designated role and responsibility.

When planning a coaching session on your own, you should consider how you will meet each of your roles and responsibilities; you will be able to prepare for some of these beforehand, others you will have to apply during the delivery of your session.

3.2 Participants

When planning coaching sessions, the coach must consider the participants. They may determine the types of activities and the method of delivery and instruction (as discussed earlier in this unit). All information regarding the participants should be highlighted on the session plan (see Figure 5.3 pages 138–39).

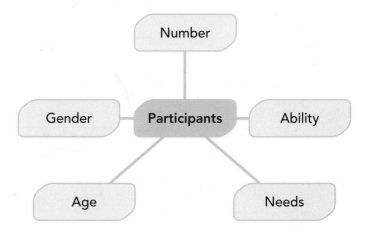

Figure 5.2: Participants

3.3 Resources

Highlight on a session plan the resources required in each component of the session and how they will be used. There are three different types of resources in coaching sessions: **human, physical** and **fiscal**.

Key terms

Human resources – people involved in the delivery of a coaching session, e.g. coaches, assistant coaches, parents, spectators.

Physical resources – the facility and equipment required to deliver the session.

Fiscal resources – the financial costs of running coaching sessions, this may include facility and or equipment hire and could include depreciation costs or loss or damage costs to the equipment or facility.

3.4 Health and safety

Risk assessment

Sports coaches must exercise their duty of care at all times to provide a safe environment for the athletes who participate in their sessions, in order to comply with all relevant health and safety legislation, e.g. the Health and Safety at Work Act (1974). Assessing risk is not new: every time you cross the road you assess the risks. Risk assessment is an examination of everything that could cause harm and what can be done to reduce the risk of harm or injury to players, spectators and coaches.

Risk assessment requires the coach to examine all equipment and the facility/playing surface where the activity is taking place. Once a hazard has been identified, the coach must eliminate the hazard and/or risk. If the hazard can be eliminated then the session can proceed; if not, the coach must classify the degree of risk. Risks are usually classified as:

- low – no or minimal risk of injury
- medium – some risk of injury
- high – high risk of injury.

If the risk is anything higher than low, the coach must take action to eliminate the hazard, where possible, or reduce it to an acceptable level by reviewing and adding precautions. If a coach encounters such hazards, they must consult a more senior coach or member of staff and discuss whether the session should proceed.

Emergency procedures

When coaching a sports session, a coach needs to be aware of all the emergency procedures for the facility. They should follow these procedures and should also share their knowledge of them with athletes at the start of every session. A coach will therefore need to familiarise themselves with:

- the fire drill at a facility/organisation
- the evacuation procedures at a facility/organisation
- the first-aid procedure at a facility/organisation
- the location of qualified first-aid staff at a facility/organisation
- the location of telephones at a facility/organisation in the event of the emergency services being needed
- the risk-assessment procedure at a facility/organisation.

Prior to a coaching session a coach should carry out last-minute health and safety checks to ensure the facility is prepared and safe for physical activity to commence.

Contingencies

A good coach should be prepared for every eventuality, this is known as contingency planning. When undertaking a contingency plan it is important to:

- consider everything that could possibly go wrong
- do everything you can to ensure that none of these things does happen, so check all equipment, the availability of the facility, the number of participants and specific needs of participants at least the night before the event
- have an alternative plan and be prepared in case something does go wrong.

Figure 5.3 shows a session plan.

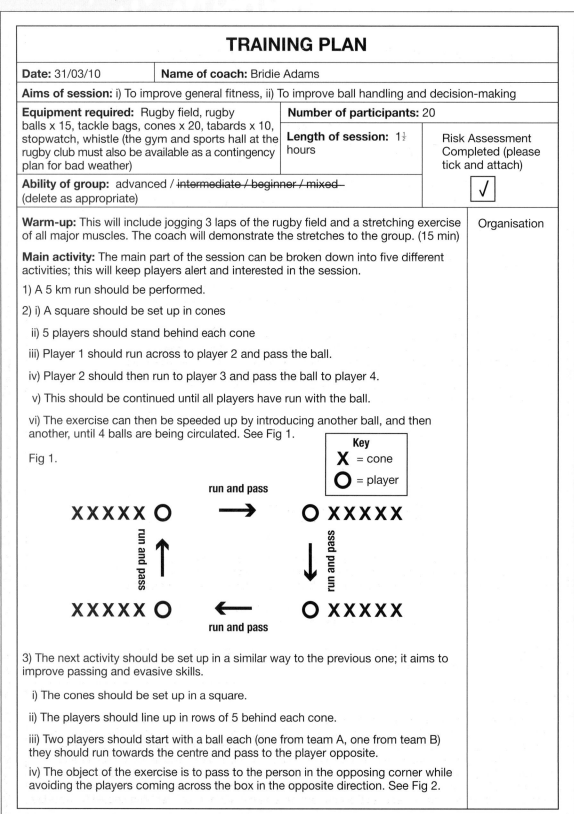

TRAINING PLAN

Date: 31/03/10	**Name of coach:** Bridie Adams

Aims of session: i) To improve general fitness, ii) To improve ball handling and decision-making

Equipment required: Rugby field, rugby balls x 15, tackle bags, cones x 20, tabards x 10, stopwatch, whistle (the gym and sports hall at the rugby club must also be available as a contingency plan for bad weather)	**Number of participants:** 20	
	Length of session: 1½ hours	Risk Assessment Completed (please tick and attach)
Ability of group: advanced / ~~intermediate / beginner / mixed~~ (delete as appropriate)		☑

	Organisation
Warm-up: This will include jogging 3 laps of the rugby field and a stretching exercise of all major muscles. The coach will demonstrate the stretches to the group. (15 min)	
Main activity: The main part of the session can be broken down into five different activities; this will keep players alert and interested in the session.	
1) A 5 km run should be performed.	
2) i) A square should be set up in cones	
ii) 5 players should stand behind each cone	
iii) Player 1 should run across to player 2 and pass the ball.	
iv) Player 2 should then run to player 3 and pass the ball to player 4.	
v) This should be continued until all players have run with the ball.	
vi) The exercise can then be speeded up by introducing another ball, and then another, until 4 balls are being circulated. See Fig 1.	

Key
X = cone
O = player

Fig 1.

run and pass

XXXXX O → O XXXXX

run and pass ↑   ↓ run and pass

XXXXX O ← O XXXXX

run and pass

3) The next activity should be set up in a similar way to the previous one; it aims to improve passing and evasive skills.
i) The cones should be set up in a square.
ii) The players should line up in rows of 5 behind each cone.
iii) Two players should start with a ball each (one from team A, one from team B) they should run towards the centre and pass to the player opposite.
iv) The object of the exercise is to pass to the person in the opposing corner while avoiding the players coming across the box in the opposite direction. See Fig 2.

Figure 5.3: A plan for a rugby training session

Fig 2.

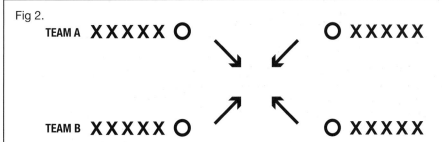

4) This exercise aims to improve defending and decision-making skills.

i) During this exercise two players must attempt to score a try at the other side of a marked-out box. The defender who is positioned in the box will attempt to stop the try being scored. The two ball carriers are not permitted to stray outside the box.

ii) When the two players enter the marked-out defender s box, they must pass to each other.

iii) The aim of the exercise is for the ball carrier to draw the defender in and either pass/dummy and score a try at the other side of the box without the defender intercepting the pass or tackling the ball carrier.

iv) Two sets of boxes can be set up in different parts of the field, allowing two exercises to be carried out in sequence. When everyone has had a turn, the exercise can be adapted and two defenders can be stationed in the box, then three, etc.

v) Tackle bags can then be introduced for the defenders to hold, this will encourage more physical contact.

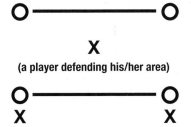

(a player defending his/her area)

5) The next exercise uses the whole pitch. The players must be split into two teams; they can then practise match plays and moves on their own with no opposition. Coaches must observe the players and give feedback and advice on their performance.

6) Finally, a friendly game of tag rugby can be played. This should help strengthen team spirit, help the players to interact well together and should also be relaxed and fun.

Cool down: The cool down will include a further 2 laps of the field and stretching out of all muscles and joints. (10 min)

Contingencies

This coaching plan can take place in most weather conditions. If it is raining, slippery or too cold to catch and throw properly, the plan can be adjusted. If necessary, more emphasis can be placed on the physical fitness aim of the session, a longer run could be incorporated which will improve fitness and warm the players up, the gym at the club can also be used. In order to practise ball skills and decision-making, the hall at the club is available and scaled exercises in smaller groups can be performed safely within this space. The exercises that involve physical contact should be eliminated, as these could be dangerous; also as the floor will be a harder surface, any tackling should be avoided.

Figure 5.3: A plan for a rugby training session (continued)

3.5 Components of a session

Having set clear aims and objectives for your coaching session, you can begin to devise the activities that will make up the session itself. Any session you devise will follow a structure broadly similar to the one below.

Warm-up – every coaching session should start with a warm-up to prepare the athletes both physically and mentally. This should last for at least 10 minutes. It should take a methodological approach which:

- initially increases body heat and respiratory and metabolic rates
- stretches the muscles and mobilises the joints that will be used in the session
- includes rehearsal and practice of some of the activities that are required in the sport.

Main body – this could include a variety of activities, depending on the aims and objectives of the session. If the aims and objectives are to develop a technical component of a sport, then the coach will need to include technical drills and skill practices. If the aims and objectives are to develop a specific aspect of fitness, then the session will have to include appropriate fitness activities. The main body of the session often includes a competitive element, which some coaches use to develop the skill or component of fitness covered earlier in the session. To do this a coach may choose to condition the game. For example, if the aim of the session is to develop short passing in football, the coach may choose to condition a competitive game at the end where a team score a goal for completing ten or more consecutive passes.

Cool down – at the end of the session a coach should ensure that all participants spend an appropriate amount of time cooling down. The aim of this is to bring the body gradually back to the pre-exercise condition. It should prevent muscle stiffness, injury and improve flexibility, provided stretches are performed correctly and controlled effectively by the coach.

Sequencing

When teaching a new skill or technique, the coach should consider how the delivery of the skill or technique will be best understood and learned by each athlete. To ensure that participants achieve optimum results in a session, the coach should consider:

- when to introduce skills and techniques
- whether to deliver a skill or technique as a whole practice or by breaking it down into parts
- the method of competition in which performers will be required to apply the skill or technique covered in the session.

Coaching skills and techniques

As mentioned earlier in this unit, a coach can use a number of skills and techniques to develop athletes' performance and ability. When planning coaching sessions a coach should consider the appropriate techniques and skills to use and when to use them.

Feedback

At the end of each activity and throughout a session, time should be allocated for the coach and athletes to feed back regarding the performance of each skill or technique covered.

Coaches are always providing feedback to athletes. This is usually given verbally, although with the development of technology and sports-analysis software, more coaches are using video and objective data.

It is essential for a coach to discuss with the athletes how well they have done in a session and what areas they can develop in future sessions. Inexperienced performers and children are less able to make sense of what happened during the session, so have a greater need for feedback. As athletes gain experience, they are more able to compare their own experiences and actions with previous attempts and thus more able to contribute to a coach-led discussion.

Assessment activity 5.3

The assessment activity for this section of Unit 5 is on page 146.

4.   Be able to deliver and review a sports coaching session

When delivering coaching sessions the sports coach has to demonstrate appropriate roles, responsibilities, skills and techniques to support the development of the participants. The coach should ensure that they deliver the session they planned, only making changes when these are demanded by external factors.

The final part of this unit will require you as the coach to be assessed; the delivery of your session will be assessed against the criteria shown in Figure 5.4.

Methods of assessment will vary, but for an exemplar assessment observation sheet used by an assessor, look at Figure 5.7 on page 144. When being assessed it is important that learners fulfil the requirement of each role, responsibility, skill and technique as appropriate.

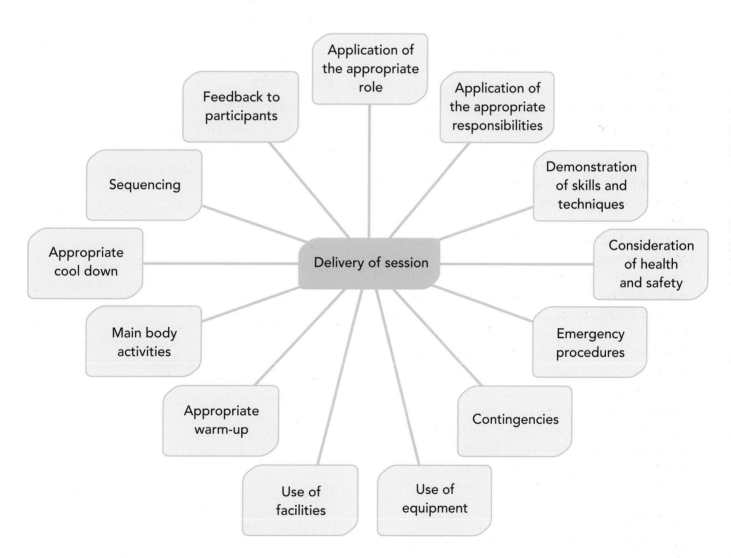

Figure 5.4: Vital factors in planning and delivering a coaching session

4.1 Review

Figure 5.5 shows the process every coach should follow to support their development and future sessions that they deliver. Even top coaches like Arsene Wenger constantly evaluate their own performance while delivering coaching sessions and look for other ways to develop the players they coach and their own practices as a coach. This is part of Wenger's coaching philosophy and one of the reasons why Arsenal have been so successful in spite of having limited resources in comparison to other Premier League teams.

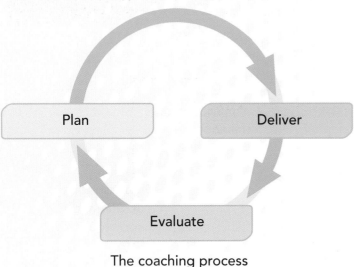

The coaching process

Figure 5.5: The coaching process

The evaluation stage of the coaching process is an important stage where the coach should assess the effectiveness of each session. It should influence the planning of future sessions. The cycle should continue, each time benefiting from the experience of the previous stage.

Following each session, a coach should find time to evaluate how the session went. The questions below should help in assessing the success of a session.

1. Did the session meet the aims and objectives set at the start?
2. Did you meet the SMART targets that you set the athletes?
3. What went well in the session and why?
4. What did not go well in the session and why?
5. What lessons have you learnt as a coach and why?
6. What would you do to improve the session if you had to deliver it again?

Formative and summative assessment

A coach should review their performance at different stages in their development. In a **formative assessment** they will assess their coaching bit by bit and use feedback from learners and observers to assess their effectiveness. This will help a developing coach to plan short- and medium-term goals. **Summative assessment** could come from an external coach or assessor to award a coaching qualification or as a judgement about a coach's overall performance. When any form of assessment takes place the coach should use the feedback to support their development. Even negative feedback is useful: the best coaches are those who respond and come back improved after listening to the advice.

Key terms

Formative assessment – takes place informally and should support the development of a coach.

Summative assessment – takes place formally to assess the performance of a coach. It is often used to assess ability – for example, when trying to attain a coaching qualification.

Feedback

A developing coach should use feedback from participants and spectators regarding the delivery of their coaching sessions. A coach could ask athletes to complete a brief questionnaire like the one in Figure 5.6 on page 143.

Feedback from another coach can provide greater objectivity. See Figure 5.7 on page 144 for an example of an observation checklist that could be used by an experienced coach to assess another's performance.

Strengths

Feedback from participants and observers should enable the coach to identify the strengths of a session. The feedback should consist of summative feedback, plus the athletes' body language and responses during the session.

Areas for improvement

A coach should be able to ascertain which elements of their performance require improvement. This is the basis on which they should build their efforts to improve their performance. Every coach should seek to improve at every stage of their career.

Even Glenn Mills, the coach of the greatest sprinter of all time, will sometimes reflect on his own development as a coach and set targets for improvement.

- What areas do you think your own sports coach could improve on?
- What advice would you give your coach to develop these identified areas of weakness?

Performer Feedback Sheet

Please circle your answers.

Did you enjoy the session?

Did you enjoy the warm-up?

Did you enjoy the drills in the session e.g. the dribbling between the cones, the shooting into the hockey net?

Did the sports leader communicate clearly?

Did the sports leader demonstrate clearly what you had to do in the session?

Did you feel that your performance improved in the session?

What extra activities would you like to have done in the session?

....

Figure 5.6: An example of a questionnaire on a coach's performance

Assessment of:

Session Plan

Did the learner produce a lesson plan (prior to the start of the session/event?)	YES/NO
Was the session planned appropriately for the needs of the participants?	YES/NO
Will the session/event meet the aims and objectives of the session?	YES/NO

Targets

Did the learner set targets for participants?	YES/NO
Were these targets met during the session/event?	YES/NO

Before the session:

Did the learner carry out a safety check of the participants and of the venue and equipment prior to the session/event?	YES/NO
Did the learner produce a risk assessment for the event/session?	YES/NO

Delivery

Did the learner communicate effectively throughout the session/event?	YES/NO
Did the learner use the facility and equipment effectively throughout the session?	YES/NO
Did the learner organise the session effectively?	YES/NO
Did the learner demonstrate effective application of the roles and responsibilities of a sports coach?	YES/NO
Did the learner demonstrate appropriate knowledge and language of the sport and the techniques and skills covered in the session?	YES/NO

Which techniques did the learner use to develop the performers within the session?

Did the learner wear appropriate clothing for the session?	YES/NO
Did the learner motivate the performers throughout the session?	YES/NO
Were the components of the session delivered effectively and appropriately?	YES/NO
Did the learner demonstrate effective sequencing within the session?	YES/NO
Did the learner provide feedback throughout the session?	YES/NO
Did the learner conclude the session with a summary and provide opportunities for feedback to all performers?	YES/NO

Which areas could be improved?

Signed _____ (assessor) Date _____

Figure 5.7: An example of the observation record that the assessor may use when assessing your delivery skills of the coaching session for this unit

4.2 Development plan

After completing the coaching process (see Figure 5.5) a coach should reflect on their performance and consider how to address the feedback obtained. Their conclusions should form the basis of a development plan, consisting of targets they have set themselves.

Opportunities

In their development plan the coach should identify specific goals, for example:

- completing specific coaching qualifications
- working with specific sports coaches
- observing sports coaches working with specific groups.

The plan should clearly identify the methods the coach wishes to use to improve their performance, with a justification of how and why.

Further qualifications

National governing bodies (NGBs) of sport have developed coaching and leadership awards to support developing coaches. Almost all NGBs now have a coach-education structure which produces qualifications from assistant coach level (level 1) up to elite coach level (levels 4 and 5).

A coach should aim to gain the qualifications required to coach and lead the athletes they work with, to ensure that they receive the support and experience recommended by the NGB.

Potential barriers

When producing a development plan a coach must be aware of the barriers that could prevent some of their targets being met. A coach, unlike an athlete, will be left to their own devices to overcome potential barriers and therefore must be aware of what may stand in their way, for example:

- geographical location
- cost
- time
- gender
- ethnic minority.

Activity: Further qualifications

As part of your development as a coach, you should be aware of the location of the NGB for your chosen sport.

1. Research the address and contact details (phone number, email address and website) of the national headquarters of the NGB for your chosen sport.

2. Find out if there are regional offices for the NGB for your chosen sport, make a note of the contact details if appropriate (telephone number, email address and website).

3. Now you have the contact details, research the coach-education structure for your chosen sport:
   - make a note of the title of each qualification
   - make a note of the level of each qualification
   - make a note of the learning hours required to complete each qualification
   - make a note of the location of the next available appropriate course for a delegate with similar experience to you
   - make a note of the cost of the course.

Despite such barriers, Sport England and NGBs are working with community groups to increase the number of coaches. Initiatives such as the McDonalds Coaching Scheme run in conjunction with the Football Association to increase the number of qualified coaches. The scheme offers football coaches an opportunity to gain a coaching qualification for free and is run through the regional FAs to support coaches who may have not been able to access such qualifications in the past.

Assessment activity 5.3

(P4) (P5) (P6) (M4) (M5) (D3)

BTEC

You have been asked to demonstrate to volunteers how to plan and deliver a sports coaching session.

1. You should provide the volunteers with a session plan for a specific sports coaching session. **P4**

2. You will then deliver the coaching session with support. **P5**

3. In addition to the requirement of P5, if you complete it independently you will attain M4 criteria. **M4**

4. After you have completed the session you must demonstrate to the volunteers how to review the planning and delivery of a sports coaching session, identifying strengths and areas for improvement. You will do this in the form of a written report which will be sent to each volunteer after the event. **P6**

5. In order to meet the requirements for M5, in addition to the requirements for P6, in your feedback to the volunteers you should also evaluate the planning and delivery of a sports coaching session, suggesting how improvements could be made in the areas identified for improvement. **M5**

6. To meet the requirements of D3, in addition to the requirements of P6 and M5, you must justify suggestions made in relation to the development plan. **D3**

Grading tips

P4 Complete your session plan in a clear format, ensuring that it includes the aims and objectives of the session, coaching pointers and methods of managing health and safety.

Prior to the session, ensure you have arranged questionnaires for the athletes and observers to complete regarding the delivery of the session.

P5 Ensure that your assessor observes your performance and completes an observation record.

M4 Lead your session independently.

P6 Ensure that someone records your coaching session so you can look back on it to develop a self-assessment of your performance.

Observe your coaching session and list your strengths and areas for improvement.

Look through the feedback obtained from the participants and performers and list the strengths and areas for improvement.

M5 Summarise the planning and delivery of the session, what you did well, what you did less well and what you would do if you had the opportunity to deliver the session again.

Produce a development plan, stating how you plan to develop as a coach.

D3 Identify specific coaching qualifications which you could complete to support your development, describing what components of your performance as a coach these will develop.

For each selected coaching course and planned development opportunity, identify how this will support your development as a coach.

PLTS

Reviewing your performance after the coaching session will improve your skills as a **reflective learner**.

Functional skills

Planning a sports coaching session using a computer will develop your **ICT** skills.

Teresa Dodd
Head Netball Coach, Wilberforce Academy

Teresa's team have been consistently high achievers for 5 years, winning the league twice and the cup competition once. This year their form has dipped significantly and they are currently bottom of the Hull and East Riding District League. This is mainly because the team lost a number of players at the end of the last season to another team in the Northern League. These have been replaced with young players with limited competitive experience at this level but exceptional technical skills.

During the last competitive match Teresa carried out an observational analysis of the team's performance. She concluded that a number of players lacked the required aerobic endurance to complete the game. She also noticed that technically all the members of the team matched their opponents. However, their application of the required tactical components was weak, especially when attacking with the ball.

In the past Teresa has allowed the club captain to take the training sessions, as she is an experienced player. However, she noticed that the last training session consisted of a competitive match between the old team members and the players who have recently joined the club. Many players have spoken with Teresa, expressing their lack of motivation to train.

Teresa has decided to take over the training sessions to try to improve the team's performance. Teresa has not coached a session for a long time and is seeking advice on how to support the team and tackle some of the areas for improvement.

Think about it!

- Give Teresa some advice regarding the types of activities she could use to develop team cohesion.
- Advise her on the types of activities she could use to develop the weak areas she noticed in the team's fitness.
- Guide Teresa on types of activities used to support the development of tactical knowledge and its application in competitive situations.
- Produce a session plan for Teresa's first training session that identifies different types of activities and coaching tips she could use.

Just checking

1. List five successful sports coaches and describe why each one has been successful.

2. List six roles a sports coach must try to fulfil.

3. List six responsibilities a sports coach should try to fulfil.

4. What common skills are required by a coach to support athletes' development?

5. What are objective and subjective analysis?

6. What is observational analysis and how is it used by coaches to support performance development?

7. Why would technical instruction support performance development and what knowledge would a coach require to provide effective technical instruction?

8. Provide a definition for each of the following:
   • human resources   • physical resources   • fiscal resources.

9. What is a risk and what is a hazard?

10. What action can a coach take to reduce the risks and hazards in a coaching session?

11. What methods can a coach use to ensure they obtain appropriate feedback from observers and participants?

12. List the courses that could support the development of a coach in your own sport.

13. What other opportunities could a coach undertake to support their development?

edexcel ▦

Assignment tips

• Observe a number of sessions run by local coaches and consider the planning and experience required to become an effective coach.

• When planning coaching sessions you will need to have a good understanding of the sport involved. Choose a sport you are confident to coach and have appropriate knowledge about.

• Make the most of opportunities to plan and lead coaching sessions. Enjoy developing new skills.

• Don't be afraid to tell athletes what you think: remember, your job is to improve their performance, not just to observe them making mistakes.

• Remember to consider the methods of feedback you will use to assess the effectiveness of your session; you should get feedback from performers, peers and your assessor.

• Research the coaching courses available in your selected sport, and examine other methods that could be used to develop your skills as a coach.

• Complete a level 1 coaching award to support your development of the required skills and techniques required to coach in your selected sport.

• Ensure that you read the assignment briefs properly. Take your time and ensure you are happy with the task set. If not, ask your tutor for assistance.

• Attempt all parts of the assignments. If you only attempt the pass criteria, this is all you will achieve. Think big and try it all.

6 Sports development

This unit introduces the principles of sports development and the key organisations involved. It also aims to give you an understanding of the work that goes on in this area.

The work of sports developers cuts across and integrates with many other current issues, such as healthy living, improving athletic performance, and participation in sport for less able people. Many of the schemes described in this unit show that sports development can be an agent for positive change, and that social, cultural and political agendas are involved as key agencies seek to further their aims using sport as a theme for their goals.

You will explore the key concepts that professional staff use in their planning, such as the sports-development continuum, identification of target groups and their needs, management of projects, plus the barriers that may hinder participation in sport. The importance of quality and evaluation will also be brought out.

Investigation of schemes and strategies for sport will show you the importance of 'inclusion' in the design, implementation and goals of sports development.

Learning outcomes

After completing this unit you should be able to:

1. know key concepts in sports development
2. know the key providers of sports development
3. understand how quality is measured in sports development
4. know about sports development in practice.

Assessment and grading criteria

This table shows you what you must do in order to achieve a pass, merit or distinction grade, and where you can find activities in this book to help you.

To achieve a **pass** grade the evidence must show that the learner is able to:	To achieve a **merit** grade the evidence must show that, in addition to the pass criteria, the learner is able to:	To achieve a **distinction** grade the evidence must show that, in addition to the pass and merit criteria, the learner is able to:
P1 describe three examples of the sports-development continuum, from three different sports **Assessment activity 6.1, page 155**	**M1** compare and contrast three examples of the sports-development continuum, from three different sports, identifying strengths and areas for improvement **Assessment activity 6.1, page 155**	
P2 describe barriers to participation for individuals from three different target groups at different levels of the sports-development continuum **Assessment activity 6.2, page 160**	**M2** explain barriers to participation for individuals from three different target groups at different levels of the sports-development continuum **Assessment activity 6.2, page 160**	**D1** analyse the barriers to participation for individuals from three different target groups at different levels of the sports-development continuum, providing effective and realistic solutions **Assessment activity 6.2, page 160**
P3 describe the structures and roles of three sports development providers in the UK **Assessment activity 6.3, page 169**		
P4 explain two methods of measuring quality in sports development **Assessment activity 6.4, page 172**	**M3** evaluate two methods of measuring quality in sports development **Assessment activity 6.4, page 172**	
P5 describe two different sports development initiatives **Assessment activity 6.5, page 176**	**M4** compare and contrast two different sports development initiatives, identifying strengths and areas for improvement **Assessment activity 6.5, page 176**	**D2** analyse two different sports development initiatives, offering realistic recommendations for improvement **Assessment activity 6.5, page 176**

How you will be assessed

Assessment for the unit will require you to cover examples of projects, barriers to be overcome, roles of professionals and how the quality and outcomes of sports-development initiatives can be measured. This could be in the form of:

- evidence from local sports developers and schemes
- making presentations and observations on projects
- using worksheets and project logbooks
- collating personal evidence and records
- writing reports or creating promotional materials
- researching your own case studies.

Valentina Raymond, 18 years old: Help from a professional

My assignment asked me to identify some sports-development agencies, analyse their programmes and initiatives and evaluate what I found.

I wanted to talk to a professional to get the inside story and maybe some contacts in schemes in my area, so I contacted my local sports-development unit and spoke to an experienced sports-development officer. He put me in touch with a club that was running development schemes in swimming and tennis. I interviewed some of the members, who helped me to understand how their club was run and structured. They also talked about their plans to try to achieve a Clubmark award. I also visited some local schools to ask staff and pupils what the main barriers to participation were for the children.

This structured approach and the networking gave me all the material I needed – I passed with flying colours. 'What's so special about that?' you may ask – well, I am French and did all of this in English, after being in the UK for only a few months!

Over to you

- **Would this approach suit you?**
- **What key things did Valentina do that made her successful?**

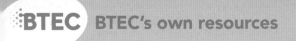

1. Know key concepts in sports development

Warm-up

Taking part

Not everyone who wants to can take part in sport. With a partner, list reasons why this might be the case, based on your experience or people you know.

Group your reasons under the following headings to help you identify the most common reason: family, social group, personal or cultural reasons, financial or time restraints.

Now think about how you would try to overcome difficulties if you worked in the sports-development sector.

Sports development is all about getting people into sport and enjoying it, whatever their age or capabilities.
Some initiatives are sponsored – can you identify who it is in this case?
What do you think the motives of the sponsors are?

1.1 The sports-development continuum

Sports development has evolved over the last 30 years, for although it originally focused on sport and exercise, it has become a flexible concept that has brought a variety of benefits to different areas, people and sports. Big sports-development schemes can help drive regeneration projects, bringing community pride, improved local image, new facilities and improved training for athletes – this is certainly part of the legacy hoped for with the London Olympics in 2012 and for Rio de Janeiro in 2016.

Many sports-development schemes have to tie their aims and objectives into local, regional and national strategies. This may involve several agencies (**stakeholders**) collaborating to manage, fund and implement sports development in a locality.

There are four levels in the **sports-development continuum**: foundation, participation, performance and excellence (see Figure 6.1).

Key terms

Stakeholders – people who have an important share in something.
Sports-development continuum – a model that shows the different levels of sports development.

Figure 6.1: A simple sports-development continuum. Arrows show the movement between levels that can be taken

Foundation

Sports-development programmes at foundation level are mainly aimed at primary school children or complete beginners. They tend to provide basic skills education such as catching or throwing and simple rules, but there is much emphasis on fun, so that youngsters enjoy their sessions and continue the activity, such as Brazilian soccer schools.

Remember

The foundation level focuses on young people gaining key movement and coordination skills, learning the basics of the game safely, making friends and having fun. It is mainly found in school-age sports schemes, teams and clubs.

Participation

This level is less easy to define, with many different schemes and participants of all ages and types. However, the schemes tend to focus on community participation by trying to get people to take part more regularly, especially those who do not take regular exercise or play sport at all.

Take it further

You can learn more of real schemes using the community approach by logging onto most local government websites.

Performance

This level in the continuum emphasises improvement through regular practice, competition or skills training. A feature of this level would be the selection of participants to take part in trials or take up a place at an academy or perhaps obtain sponsorship to train. An example would be a county scheme that helps to identify players who can gain representative honours and possibly move on to the excellence level for talent development.

Take it further

British cycling

Visit British Cycling's website to read about their approach: www.britishcycling.org.

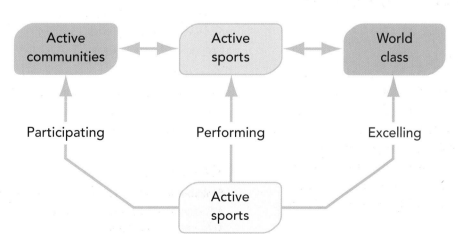

Figure 6.2: Sport England's sport-development model reflecting their interpretation of the continuum

153

Excellence

This is national and international level, and might involve preparation for competition at championship levels around the world. From April 2006, UK Sport took over the running of a range of sports at this level, at least until the London Olympics in 2012. UK Sport has set out three new aspects of the world-class programme (WCP), the excellence level of the continuum that supports top athletes in their training and funding:

- WCP Talent supports athletes who have the potential to progress through to the next two stages
- WCP Development supports athletes building up to Podium level
- WCP Podium supports athletes with realistic medal potential (see Figure 6.3).

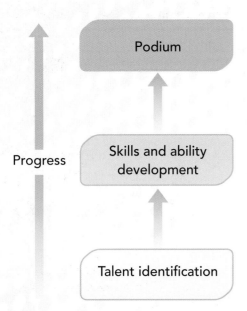

Figure 6.3: The world-class programme model used by UK Sport

Purpose

Show progression

Most sports-development schemes focus on helping participants to progress with skills, tactics and training. These are programmes that show progression, either through the levels of the continuum or higher within a level itself, such as when a regular participant becomes good enough to be picked for a club team. Such programmes have sport at their heart but tend to have social and confidence-building purposes too, and may focus equally on participation and progression.

Appropriateness

Some sports-development schemes take a more specific approach and are designed so that their content and delivery are specific to the participants.

Target groups

Some schemes are tailor-made for youngsters wishing to learn football skills or targeted at overweight adults who have a low-activity lifestyle.

Communities

Some schemes are based around community events, such as a charity fun run, e.g. 'sports relief'.

Cross-cutting agendas

In addition to sports development, some complex schemes incorporate areas such as health, social, cultural and economic benefits. These diverse aims and purposes are called **cross-cutting agendas** and projects focus on **inclusiveness**.

> ### Key terms
> **Cross-cutting agendas** – sports development schemes can have more than one purpose, mixing sports aims with social or cultural ones.
> **Inclusiveness** – bringing in those who are not usually included.

Pro-health

This area has a health bias, such as guiding young people into participating in an activity, and promoting healthy eating and regular exercise.

Pro-education

This agenda might be based on helping people to understand fair play and follow the rules, or it might try to show how to work together in multicultural teams.

Anti-drug

This area might be aimed at highlighting the dangers of drug-taking or helping those with a drug problem to find a way back into normal activities, such as sport.

Anti-crime

This aspect aims to encourage young people to avoid criminal activity and to take part in more constructive sports and activities.

Regeneration

Areas of East London are currently undergoing regeneration in order to host the Olympic Games in 2012 (see the photo opposite). Glasgow is preparing to create new areas in the city centre for the Commonwealth Games in 2014.

Regeneration creates new sports venues, creating a legacy for others to use.
- Has there been a small or large regeneration scheme in your area?
- What did it focus on?
- Was it successful and what is run there now?

Take it further

Football in the Community

A scheme called Football in the Community exists at many football clubs. Do some research to find the nearest one to you. Evaluate what benefits it brings.

Assessment activity 6.1

P1 **M1**   **BTEC**

You are preparing for an interview for a sports-development job. You have been asked to prepare a short PowerPoint presentation for the interview panel.

1. Using three different sports and making links to the sports-development continuum, describe three sports-development schemes in action. **P1**

2. Compare and contrast three examples of the sports-development continuum, involving three different sports, identifying strengths and areas for improvement. **M1**

Grading tips

P1 You could describe local or national schemes, but ensure they are clearly presented and there is plenty of data to use.

M1 To meet the requirements of M1, make sure you make links to the sports-development continuum, evaluate cross-cutting agendas and highlight complementary aims. Select your criteria for comparing and contrasting carefully and ensure there is plenty of data to use.

PLTS

Researching your schemes will develop your skills as an **independent enquirer**, describing the initiatives and making the links will give you practice as a **creative thinker**, and if you meet deadlines and criteria well you will have developed as a **self-manager**.

Functional skills

Evidence for **ICT** skills could be generated as you use software to prepare your PowerPoints and research the schemes.

1.2 Barriers to participation

Not everyone can take up a sport or get involved when an activity is taking place. There are many reasons for this, which are called **barriers to participation**. You may have discussed some of these in your opening task. In this section we shall explore these in more depth.

> ### Key term
>
> **Barriers to participation** – factors that prevent people from participating.

Cultural

The UK includes people from many different nationalities and cultures. Some cultures have rules or traditions about the right of women to participate in sport, or about women playing sport in the same place or way as men. Some cultures will not be familiar with British sports, or may have different games, e.g. thoda, kabaddi or korfball, but no place, coaches or players to play with.

Social

Social barriers might be based on what your peers think and do, and taking part in sport might not be considered 'cool'. People might feel a bit inept or embarrassed to try a sport in front of others. There might also be social barriers created by circumstances such as age differences, family influence or pressure, or maybe an over-competitive coach.

> ### Take it further
>
> #### Social pressures
>
> Try to identify examples of social barriers to participation caused by:
>
> - image
> - lifestyle
> - pressure from others.

Economic

These are usually created by an inability to meet the costs of participation, such as bus fares, entry fees or club membership. Economic barriers could apply to a whole community if an area is run down and has had little investment to create sports play spaces or many people are jobless or on low incomes. You may know of inner-city areas or residential estates like this. This creates what is called 'social exclusion'.

Historical

The UK has many sports, and these have spread around the Commonwealth. However, traditionally most sports have been male-dominated, and women's participation has been limited to hockey, tennis and netball. These traditions may have limited certain groups' involvement, such as Asians in football or females in contact sports. Although sports still have to combat stereotypes, equality and access no longer seem unattainable. In recent years, a great deal of the gender imbalance has been redressed, and women are finding more opportunities to participate.

> ### Activity: Breaking through barriers
>
> 1. a) As a class, list the things that you think should be done to help develop sport in economically run-down areas.
>   b) Try to identify what barriers there might be to funding your suggestions.
> 2. Name two sports that are beginning to be played by women.
> 3. Identify two sports where different ethnic groups are beginning to break through or dominate.

Educational

Through sport, young people often first encounter their own weaknesses in performance and become less confident and more self-conscious about their body shape and size. This leads to poor attitudes to PE and even poorer skills (both mental and physical) to help progress. PE teachers have the challenge of rebuilding that confidence or finding a sport that the individual can enjoy. Other educational factors that might cause barriers include:

- lack of facilities or choice of sports
- no after-school clubs or teams
- lack of funding to pay for extra sessions, courses or trips.

In an attempt to halt the trends of low participation rates and increasing obesity among schoolchildren, the government has pumped funding into schools to boost activities.

In February 2009 the Secretary of State for Children, Schools and Families announced that 75 sports colleges across the country would share over £21 million in extra funding. The scheme is called Sports Unlimited and aims to ensure that facilities can be used in the evenings and through the winter by installing floodlights, artificial turf and new tented-style sports halls.

1.3 Target groups

Target groups include women, young people, the over-50s, disabled people, black and minority ethnic groups (BMEs). These groups may also have other characteristics, such as low income or a disability, which increase the barriers to participation. They are generally those groups that would benefit most.

Women

Women have traditionally participated less in sport than men. Sports-development schemes aimed specifically at women, such as single-sex exercise classes in pilates and aerobics, plus more female teams playing male-dominated sports (rugby, soccer and cricket) ought to help to overcome inhibitions and spread opportunities. Statistics gathered by Sport England (Active People surveys begun in 2005 and continuing) show that overall female participation rates have indeed increased from 2.57 million (12.3 per cent) to 2.81 million (13.2 per cent) between 2005/6 and the end of 2008. The survey continues and you can get more detailed statistics and trends at www.sportengland.org.

Women have pushed their playing boundaries into many traditionally male-dominated sports.
• Do you know what the fastest-growing women's sport is in the USA?
• What kind of sponsors does women's sport attract?

The efforts globally of England's female teams have sometimes surpassed those of the men's teams. They were World Cricket Cup winners and finalists in the European Football Championships 2009. However, in some segments of society the imbalance still exists, so women will remain a target group for some time to come.

Young people

This is a key target group. If young people can be introduced to good sporting habits, they are more likely to continue through life and up through the sports-development continuum stages. This can increase their fitness, fun, healthy lifestyle and socialisation skills.

The Youth Sport Trust (YST) focuses on young people from 18 months to 18 years, providing the tools required for the delivery of high-quality PE and school sport. It encourages young people of both sexes, including those with disabilities, and gifted and talented athletes to thrive, as well as providing support to teachers and others working with young people. Go to the Youth Sport Trust website at www.youthsporttrust.org to find more about how it is targeting young people.

The over-50s

There are more people in this age group in the UK than ever before, so it is a key target area. People are living longer, but also, because of the recession of 2009 and fewer good pension schemes, many more are working to 65, so there is a greater need for them to stay fit.

Schemes aimed at this group are mainly focused at the participation level of the sports-development continuum and most are run by local authorities. A key element is the social factor. Examples include Havant Borough Council's over-50s exercise class – advertised as 'for the active older person, to condition the heart and lungs and maintain mobility, strength and balance' – the average participant is nearer 80 than 50! Newcastle's over-50s can join swimming, gym and multi-activity

sessions. Many schemes offer a discount card. Assess what your local authority offers for the over-50s.

Disabled people

Since the early 1990s and the Disability Discrimination Act 1996, progress has been made for disabled people in terms of acceptance, funding, sports-development schemes and equality of access to sports facilities.

Black and minority ethnic groups (BMEs)

Black athletes are well known in sport, but other ethnic groups in the UK do less well in terms of sports participation. This is due to a range of factors such as poverty, lack of facilities, coaching or knowledge about UK sports. Extra support helps people to break through these barriers. Sports-development schemes can be a way of bringing groups together, helping to create understanding and relieve racial tensions. Many County Sports Partnerships have declared their commitment to addressing racial discrimination by signing the Racial Equality Charter for Sport. This charter promotes Sporting Equals, a national initiative to promote racial equality in sport in England. Why not check if your CSP has signed up.

Britain's Black and Minority Ethnic (BME) population is estimated to be around 11 million, but fewer than 1 in 5 members of some BME communities are participating in physical activities even once a month (see Table 6.1). Some 92 per cent of South Asian women do not take part in the recommended levels of activity, compared to 55 per cent of all women.

Ethnic minority and percentage participating in sport		National average percentage of people participating in sport
Bangladeshi	30%	
Pakistani	31%	46%
Black Caribbean	39%	

Table 6.1: Black and ethnic minority levels of sporting activity Source: Sport England

Many teams in the UK play in the true multicultural sense.
1. Why is it so important to embrace multi-culturism in sport?
2. Why do some people hold racist views?
3. How do you think racist chants at football matches affects players?

Asian role models are almost non-existent in professional sports development, as they have not been able to establish a foothold within the system, for example as PE teachers, sport and leisure centre managers or coaches. This is a key issue, according to www.sportingequals.org.uk (2009). Why do you think this is so?

Activity: Quiz

1. Give a clear definition of what a target group is in sports-development terms.
2. Give three examples of a target group.
3. Sum up the benefits of the types of campaigns like the ones given as examples of good work with BME groups and disabled athletes.
4. Explain what difficulties might arise in each case.
5. What improvements could you suggest to help target groups?

Assessment activity 6.2

You are a local sports-development officer researching the barriers to participation for target groups in your local community. You have been asked to present a short report to your department head which:

1. Describes barriers to participation for individuals at each level of the sports-development continuum, using three different examples drawn from at least three target groups. **P2**

2. Explains why barriers to participation occur for at least three different target groups in three different sports. Show how these can occur at different levels of the sports-development continuum. **M2**

3. Analyses why the barriers to participation occur for varying target groups at all levels of the sports-development continuum and provide realistic recommendations for how these might be overcome. **D1**

Grading tips

P2 You must be able to show a basic understanding in describing the barriers you select for each stage of the continuum and each target group. Real working examples will help here. Ensure you choose different sports, as that will determine your grade as well.

M2 To meet M2 criteria the work you produce will demand a bit more in terms of the quality of your evidence and its complexity, so pay attention to detail in your responses. Explaining means showing that you know why something happens and can describe it clearly.

D1 To meet D1 you will need to show in-depth understanding, use appropriate terminology well and have a really thorough approach. Above all, you must analyse, which means breaking up the components of the question and responding to them with critical insight. In other words, you need to have the ability to see important points that others miss, as well as identifying faults and making realistic suggestions as to how something could have been done better.

PLTS

Describing the barriers could develop your ability as an **independent enquirer**, discussing issues with your colleagues will help you to become an **effective participator**, and meeting the deadlines for submitting your work will make you a better **self-manager**.

Functional skills

You may create evidence for **ICT** skills depending on how you prepare your work, and for **English** skills as you discuss personal experiences or put questions to a guest speaker.

2. Know the key providers of sports development

The range of sports-development providers is quite diverse and it is valuable that you have good knowledge of them. Together with the agencies they interact with to deliver sports-development programmes, they create a framework of providers.

2.1 Providers

Types and levels of providers include:

- national organisations
- local authorities
- governing bodies
- voluntary organisations
- private sector providers
- professional providers.

National organisations

Sport England is the government agency responsible for building the foundations of sporting success, by creating a world-leading community sport system of clubs, coaches, facilities and volunteers.

Sport England want to create a vibrant sporting culture working in partnership with national governing bodies, their national partners, the HE/FE sector, local government and community organisations.

Their focus is around three outcomes – growing and sustaining the numbers of people taking part in sport and improving talent development to help more people excel.

Sport England have set themselves five targets which will see them deliver these outcomes:

Grow – One million people taking part in more sport and more children and young people taking part in five hours of PE and sport a week. These targets account for 15% of Sport England's investment.

Sustain – More people satisfied with their sporting experience and 25% fewer 16-18 year olds dropping out of a least nine sports – badminton, basketball, football, hockey, gymnastics, netball, rugby league, rugby union and tennis. These targets account for 60% of Sport England's investment.

Excel – Improved talent development in at least 25 sports. These target accounts for 25% of Sport England's investment.

How do these aims reflect the levels in the sports-development continuum?

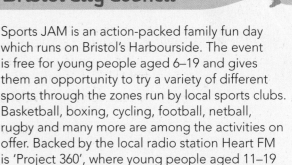

Take it further

In small groups, identify the values and key elements in sports coach UK's principles of operation, then try to break them down into a list you could use for a PowerPoint presentation. More information can be found at www.sportscoachuk.org.

Sports coach UK is a charitable organisation dedicated to the development of coaches and coaching throughout the UK. It provides a central resource of expertise, advice and support for its sports-development partners and helps to train coaches. It works with funding agencies and sports governing bodies, local authorities and other sports agencies that have an interest in coaching and its development.

The Youth Sport Trust (introduced on page 158) was established in 1984 to support the education and development of young children through sport and physical education. As well as setting up the TOP programmes, the organisation has developed a number of creative and innovative projects for young people aged 18 months to 18 years, which focus on specific issues including:

- social inclusion
- encouraging more teenage girls to take part in PE and sport
- playground development in primary schools to tackle social exclusion issues

Case study: Bristol City Council

Sports JAM is an action-packed family fun day which runs on Bristol's Harbourside. The event is free for young people aged 6–19 and gives them an opportunity to try a variety of different sports through the zones run by local sports clubs. Basketball, boxing, cycling, football, netball, rugby and many more are among the activities on offer. Backed by the local radio station Heart FM is 'Project 360', where young people aged 11–19 can take part in activities such as parkour, urban dance, BMX and skateboarding. SportsJAM is a city council partnership with Access Sport. (*Source:* www.bristol.gov.uk, 2009.)

- Do you have something similar in your town?
- Which target groups can you identify here?
- What does having the radio station on board bring to the scheme?

- supporting gifted and talented children and young people.

The Youth Sport Trust has formed partnerships with sponsors to help sports development, for example with Sainsbury's and its Active Kids campaign, Lloyds TSB and National School Sports Week, and Sky Sports Living for Sport.

Local authorities

Local authorities (LAs) are councils or metropolitan boroughs. They play an important role in sports development because they are concerned with all types of target groups in the community. Providing sporting and leisure facilities helps to make the community healthier and more inclusive.

Some local authorities tackle this on a large scale and have teams of sports-development officers running a range of programmes to meet the community's needs. Others have more specific programmes such as GP referral schemes or disability sports.

Another feature of LAs' work in sports development is through partnership schemes. They often join up with other social service providers and organisations, such as:

- health authorities to run health schemes
- voluntary clubs and groups to aid their sports development

- police and other welfare agencies to help reduce crime and exclusion
- charities and neighbourhood groups who work in disadvantaged areas.

(See the Bristol City Council case study.)

Remember

LAs also have many facilities at their disposal to run sports-development schemes, such as leisure centres, parks and swimming pools, but budgets will vary.

Governing bodies

Governing bodies of sport (GBs) are organisations that oversee a particular sport in terms of its management, rules, structure and development. They operate locally, regionally, nationally and internationally. Using football as our example, we can illustrate these levels and strategies as follows (see Figure 6.4).

International

Football is governed by FIFA, the International Football Federation. Football in Europe is governed by EUFA, the European Union Football Association. Both organisations have similar aims for the sport in terms of its development, which can be summarised as promoting, protecting and developing the game of football. Look at the following websites for more information on FIFA and EUFA: www.fifa.com and www.uefa.com. Compare their mission statements and purposes.

National

National Governing Bodies (NGBs) exist for most sports in each country and usually have 'mission or vision statements' which in turn drive their aims and objectives. For example see the English Football Association's vision statement for 2008-12: www.thefa. com. Their intended outcomes are similar to sports-development aims everywhere: for young people to be healthy, stay safe, enjoy and achieve, make a positive contribution, and achieve economic well-being. The FA National Game Strategy sets out its purpose, values, strategic goals and targets – with four key goals:

- growth and retention – increasing the number of players and addressing retention
- raising standards and addressing abusive behaviour – creating a safe and positive environment
- developing better players – focusing on improving the quality of the 5–11 age group
- running the game effectively – leading and governing the game.

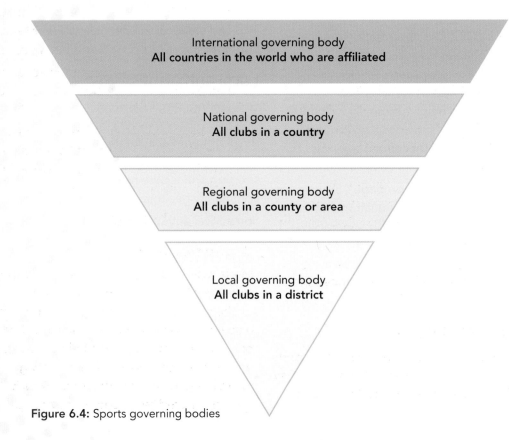

International governing body
All countries in the world who are affiliated

National governing body
All clubs in a country

Regional governing body
All clubs in a county or area

Local governing body
All clubs in a district

Figure 6.4: Sports governing bodies

Regional

Continuing the football theme we should see a reflection of the GB and NGBs' sports aims filter down to lower levels. For example, The North Riding County Football Association's development plan has many features that reflect these principles, values and aims:

- mini-soccer for children
- girls' and women's football development
- equality and inclusiveness
- ethnicity and disability partnership.

Local

The Scarborough & District Junior Football Association reflects these development aims locally, with themes coming down from the FA strategy of:

- equality of access
- support for player development
- caring coaches.

> **Remember**
>
> GBs operate at different levels and geographical locations (local, regional, national and international). Figure 6.4 shows the structure this creates.

Voluntary organisations

These are often known as the 'grass roots of sport', as they represent the wide variety of sport that goes on at a recreational and basic competitive level in the UK. This is achieved through low-cost participation supported by volunteers giving their time freely and sometimes by grants of money from Sport England, the local authority or sponsors.

Volunteers often join to take part in refereeing, administration, coaching and running club committees or just making the tea! Sports club volunteers (unsung heroes) may be eligible for awards for their dedication to sport.

Are there any weaknesses in relying on volunteers and grants?

Private-sector providers

Private-sector businesses normally get involved in sports development to further their business interests, but they often give benefits to local communities. Sports and participants can still gain from these types of businesses as they might provide new venues and sponsorship and administer leagues, or run activity camps.

According to 'sport and development.org' 2009, experience in creating and sustaining partnerships between NGBs and the private sector in sport and development shows that real partnership is the same as 'co-creating', in which both stakeholders share in efforts towards social change, as well as healthier people and stronger communities.

Some businesses get involved with sport as sponsors. For example, the Institute of Sports Sponsorship – on behalf of the government and Sport England – manages Sportsmatch, a business-sponsorship incentive scheme for grass-roots sport (see page 160 and www.sports-sponsorship.co.uk).

Much funding for the Organising Committee of the 2012 Olympics comes from the private sector. A total of £2 billion will be raised from sponsorship, broadcasting rights and selling merchandise.

Professional providers

These are individuals and organisations that operate in the area of sports development. Some are specialists in one sport and travel from location to location, while others stay at one centre or venue. Professional providers include:

- independent coaches who work for several clubs, such as a gymnastics or swimming coach
- self-employed developers or coaches who are employed by local centres for mini-soccer, netball or tennis coaching.

Professional providers often need to be licensed or approved by a GB. They must have insurance and a Criminal Records Bureau (CRB) check if they want to work with children or young people.

Associated benefits

Cross-cutting agendas

Many sports-development providers work in partnership with other agencies, each trying to achieve something on their own agenda. A scheme in a poor area might help local people and welfare services. It might also bring down crime rates (and help police) as young people are kept busy while participating. The scheme might bring a sense of pride to the area or a new image if it is sponsored by a good private company.

Improving performance

Improvement in performance is always desirable, regardless of the level of the sports-development continuum at which the scheme is operating. For example: beginners could advance to novice, intermediate to accomplished, recreationalist to competitor, competitor to champion. Performance might be improved in terms of speed, agility, strength, dexterity and teamwork. It might also lead to a place in an academy or school of excellence.

Opportunity

This benefit most often applies to areas where there is low provision in terms of teams, activities, facilities or coaching. Once an opportunity is provided for people to participate, it is hoped they will be motivated to continue. Many stories exist of young players emerging from poor areas through sports-development schemes. Such schemes allow them to show their talents, which means they can be identified and offered further opportunities.

Healthy lifestyles

Sports-development programmes should contribute to healthy lifestyles as they involve activity. Many schemes might spark people's desire to exercise more often through a sport. The better programmes also include diet and nutrition guidance, especially at elite level. The theme that generally runs through sports-development schemes is often aimed at lifelong learning and activity.

Activity: Benefits

In small groups, sum up the benefits that sports-development schemes and providers can bring. Create a diagram to illustrate them. List some other issues that might be negatives or constraints for these schemes.

2.2 Structure

It is important to understand how sports-development providers organise themselves to help them function effectively. All organisations have a structure or set-up that staff should follow to help deliver their programmes. This gives lines of communication and authority, defines roles and makes links to outside organisations (see Figure 6.5).

Four main types of organisational style are explored in this section: committees, working groups, forums and consultation groups. Each has its own merits and features, but they all need to work democratically in order to be successful.

Committees

These are most common in the voluntary sector. For a small club offering sports development, committees would be made up of around three people: a chairperson or captain having overall leadership, a treasurer looking after financial affairs, and a secretary doing the administration and communications work. A fourth person looking after child welfare might also be appointed. Committees make most of the decisions for the club (see Figure 6.5)

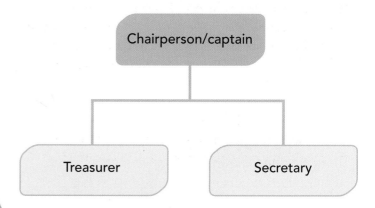

Figure 6.5: The structure of a simple committee. Note that the lines represent lines of authority and communication, which help to keep the post holders focused on their roles, but in touch with others – a 'functional approach'

Working groups

Working groups are a looser arrangement than a committee and are often found where many organisations work in partnership. They function by each partner sending a representative to work with the others in the group. This ensures every interested party is kept informed and able to achieve the aims set out for the scheme. They don't usually have decision-making powers (see Figure 6.6).

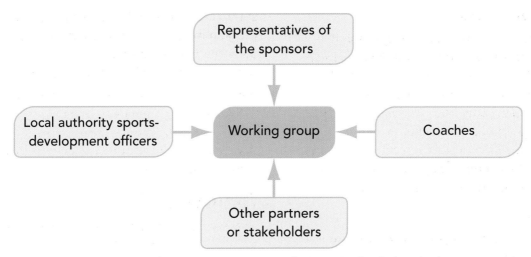

Figure 6.6: Working group arrangements for a sports-development scheme

Forums

These are sets of people who tend to be experts on the issues involved with sports development. Forums meet to discuss issues or problems and to put forward ideas for sports development. They are not the organisation that will implement the changes, but more like the 'think tank' that gives ideas for others to follow. See Figure 6.7 for a list of people who might attend a forum meeting.

Consultation groups

These can be large groups as they tend to be used for consulting a range of people who might be involved in a scheme for sports development. This allows a well-informed set of decisions to be made, but it may act slowly.

The participants who might be consulted include local politicians, county sports partnerships, community sports networks or representatives (reps), club reps, social services, the police, sports governing bodies, experts in planning events or disability sports, sports scientists, tutors, volunteers, safety experts, sports centre managers, health authority reps and professional bodies in sport. See Figure 6.8 on page 166 to see the role consultation groups play in a sports-development scheme.

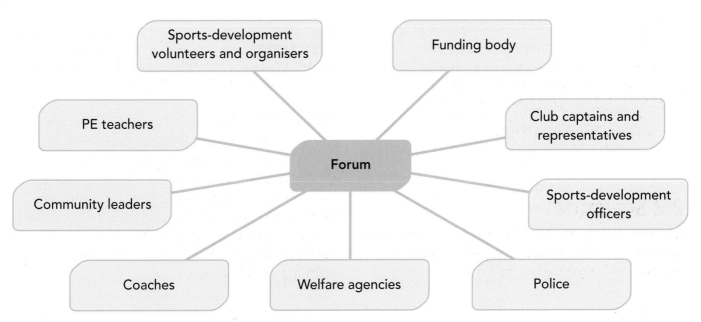

Figure 6.7: Those who might attend a forum meeting

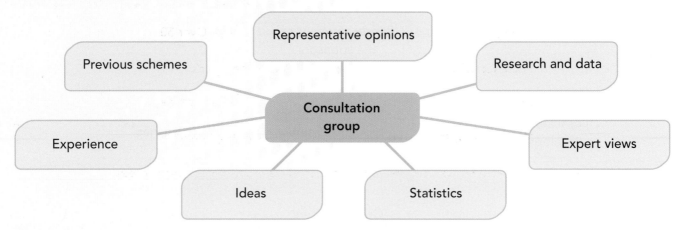

Figure 6.8: The inputs to a consultation group in creating a sports-development scheme. Can you identify appropriate sources for each input?

2.3 Roles

Providers

Sports development has many contributors as we have seen, all with diverse aims, dimensions, individuals and organisational set-ups. This inevitably leads to a range of different schemes and approaches. These are classified as follows to help you understand their nature.

The first style of delivery is called enabling. This means the provider responds to participants' needs by providing facilities or resources to give people the opportunities they need to take part.

Another type of delivery is known as facilitating (or empowerment). This might involve motivating and helping people, so that by the end of the facilitation period they are able to look after themselves and keep the scheme going without the help of others.

Both **enabling** and **facilitating** focus on the participants running the club or team by themselves in the long run.

Direct delivery sports-development schemes are carried out directly by professional sports developers, such as those done by local authority officers or coaches employed by large clubs.

Strategic delivery links into other, large-scale plans and is sometimes called an integrated approach. An example of this would be a strategy which links the healthy living and lifelong learning aims of the government, such as Natural England's Walking for Health scheme. Learn more at www.whi.org.uk. Local authorities might also use this style to meet objectives in their local plans.

Operational level programmes deal with the people concerned directly, such as disaffected youngsters or Asian women. Such a scheme would be tailored and delivered locally, but it might be put into action in several areas at once. Operational schemes tend to be delivered by professionals or leaders with community knowledge.

Sports-development workers can be asked to act in an **advisory** role. For example, a sports centre might wish to run a disability basketball team, but has no one on the staff who could do this. They might need guidance on safety factors and requirements for disabled athletes from a national disability organisation such as the English Federation of Disability Sport, Disability Sport Wales, Capability Scotland or the Disability Federation of Ireland.

Key terms

Enabling providers – an enabling programme provides facilities or resources to enable participants to play, start up a club or improve their skills.

Facilitating providers – helping a sport or target group by providing coaches or courses in administration and refereeing.

Direct delivery providers – delivery of a programme directly by professional sports developers.

Strategic providers – a programme that links to other, large-scale plans and may be called an integrated approach.

Operational providers – programmes that are run at club level and are tailored and delivered to the clubs.

Advisory providers – helping an organisation that has never run a sports-development scheme for a certain target group before and needs some advice.

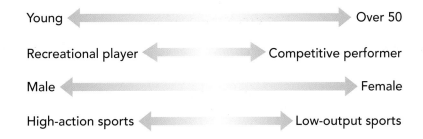

Figure 6.9: Some spectrums of participation which show the diversity of provision needed

Participation

Sports-development organisations may fulfil a role that focuses on the participation level of the continuum by helping to increase the numbers of people who actually take part. These can be across age ranges, ability levels, gender and sports (see Figure 6.9). This is the most prevalent type of scheme in the UK at present, with most funding being dependent on the scheme achieving an increase in participation. Organisations bidding for funding would virtually have to guarantee this as a target.

Activity: 'Active People'

The 'Active People' survey which identifies how participation varies from place to place and between different groups in the population, has been going on in phases since 2005. It aims to assess whether we are slowly shifting to become a more active and health conscious society.

Carry out your own research on the 'Active people website through the Sport England website to identify:
- current major trends
- data for your town or area
- rates for three sports you like.

Performance

For organisations dealing more with the performance end of the sports-development continuum, a more targeted or sports-specific approach is followed.

These are sometimes known as methods aimed at 'excellence', the highest level of the continuum, and something that will receive a lot of focus in the period running up to the London Olympics.

Key organisations at this level try to work in harmony to develop talent. Here are some websites where you can expand your knowledge of these further:
- UK Sport – www.uksport.gov.uk
- LOCOG – The London Olympic Organising Committee www.london-2012.co.uk
- BOA – The British Olympic Association www.olympics.org.uk
- EIS – The English Institute of Sport www.eis2win.co.uk.

Many GBs are using a similar model to develop players' performance – Long Term Athlete Development (LTAD). LTAD is about achieving optimal training, competition and recovery throughout an athlete's career, particularly in relation to the important growth stages in young people. These have been used by Dr Istvan Balyi to devise a staged framework for player development. The four stages – FUNdamentals, Learning & Training to Train, Training to Compete, and Training to Win are described in Table 6.2 on page 168. While much of it may be new to some people, most practitioners agree that these concepts should underpin the development of sport in the UK and become the common language of sports development. Further details on LTAD concepts are obtainable from sports coach UK.

If you look at how England Basketball apply LTAD, you can see the stages and content for each age set in Table 6.2 on page 168.

FUNdamental	Learning & Training to Train	Training to Compete	Training to Win
Chronological/biological age Male & Female: 6–10 yrs	Chronological/biological age Male: 10–15 yrs Female: 10–14 yrs	Chronological/biological age Male: 15–18 yrs Female: 14–18 yrs	Chronological/biological age Male: 18 yrs Female: 17 yrs
Fun & participation General, overall development Athleticism: ABCs of running, jumping and throwing ABCs of movement: Agility, Balance, Coordination and Speed Speed, Power and Endurance through Fun and Games Correct running, jumping and throwing techniques Medicine ball, Swiss ball and own body exercises for strength Introduction to simple rules and ethics of sport	Emphasis on general physical conditioning Shoulder, elbow, core, spine and ankle stability Fundamental technical skills, progressively more specific skills towards the end of the stage Fundamentals of tactical preparation Participation in complementary sports Individualisation of fitness and technical training Introduction to mental preparation Fundamentals of 'ancillary capacities'	Sport and individual specific physical conditioning Shoulder, elbow, core, spine and ankle stability Sport-specific technical and playing skills under competitive conditions Advanced tactical preparation Individualisation of technical – tactical skills Advanced mental preparation Sport and individual specific 'ancillary capacities'	Maintenance (or possible improvement) of physical capacities Shoulder, elbow, core, spine and ankle stability Further development of technical and playing skills Modelling all possible aspects of training and performance Frequent prophylactic breaks All aspects of training individualised Develop further 'ancillary capacities'

Table 6.2: Overview of long-term athlete-development stages Can you identify each level of the continuum?

Source: www.englandbasketball.co.uk, 2009

Sports-development officers

These are professional, qualified individuals who work for clubs and local authorities. They have to be versatile and able to manage budgets, participants, resources and venues for diverse schemes and a range of purposes. They can be classified in three main groups:

- Sport-specific – a specialist who is employed to focus on the development of one particular sport such as netball.

- Non-sport specific – the most versatile, as they may work with clients in different sports for different purposes, such as in deprived areas with few resources. Cross-cutting agendas are common in this area of work.

- Community – this type of officer will have a remit to work with different age groups and abilities in local communities and is likely to incorporate aims such as participation.

Volunteers

This is the largest category, since it includes everyone who gives their time freely to support and develop a sport or club. There are thousands around the UK, who coach and run teams, fund-raise and generally keep sport going at grass-roots level. Many are unqualified, enthusiastic amateurs. Obviously where they work with young children they need to be CRB checked, if they are going to coach they need to get qualifications, and if they need to hire premises or playing areas they need finance. So they are often dealing with the same issues as professionals, and most do a great job for sports development.

3. Understand how quality is measured in sports development

Quality should be an organisation-wide approach to meeting customer needs, but within a budget and in the most sustainable way. The starting point for this is knowing how you are performing as an organisation and building up the best features you can towards accepted standards.

Standards of performance are usually laid down by national organisations or independent bodies so that comparisons can be made. Most schemes try to measure quality in the hope that this can be continuously improved on.

3.1 Methods

A range of measures is available for sports-development providers to assess themselves or be assessed by independent inspectors. This allows them to get a measure of the quality and effectiveness of their provision. It is important that whatever method is applied, it is as objective as possible and gives a true picture of the organisation's position and delivery. The best schemes are nationally recognised ones.

Benchmarks

These are targets or standards set to enable organisations to compare themselves. This means making comparisons with other similar organisations or against standards set

nationally in order to compare performance and delivery, for example. A **quality system** or scheme encourages this process of assessment, so that providers can aim to continuously improve their services.

Key term

Quality systems – methods of management and evaluation.

Quest

Quest is a national quality system that can be used for assessing the management of sports-development schemes. Quest is an industry standard developed by Sport England and measures specific elements of sports-development work including research, management, customer service and partnership working.

Quest is aimed at sports-development units in local authorities, governing bodies and voluntary organisations. Sports-development organisations can use either a self-assessment/improvement programme or submit themselves for an independent external assessment in their pursuit of an award. The administration of the scheme is overseen by an independent consultancy to ensure it is fair.

Quest operates a grading system based on the following scores:

- to be registered, a score of above 60 per cent is needed
- to achieve highly commended, the score needs to be between 75 per cent and 84 per cent
- an excellent score is 85 per cent and above.

The assessment is based on criteria such as:

- objectives and the actions targeted at achieving these
- timekeeping, workmanship and coaching
- quality of equipment
- problem-solving techniques
- organisational culture – elements of pride, professionalism and standards.

You can find out more information about the Quest scheme from its website at www.quest-uk.org.

Investors in People (IiP)

The Investors in People (IiP) award follows many of the same principles as Quest. It focuses on organisations attaining standards for training and development of their staff, which in turn help in achieving the objectives of the sports-development unit. During the process, you would expect participants to benefit too.

The IiP standard provides a national framework for improving performance and competitiveness. It involves a planned approach to setting and communicating objectives, and developing people to meet these objectives. The scheme provides:

- the opportunity to review current policies and practices against a recognised benchmark
- a framework for planning future strategy and action
- a structured way to improve the effectiveness of training and development activities.

It is based on:

- a commitment to invest in people, such as by providing training
- effective planning to set down how skills, individuals and teams are to be developed to achieve these goals
- effective action being taken to develop and use necessary skills
- evaluating the outcomes of training and development for individuals' progress towards goals, such as checking that what was planned has been achieved.

Learn more at www.investorsinpeople.co.uk.

Charter Mark

Charter Mark is an award that can be attained by any public-sector organisation or department, such as a museum or even a refuse collection. It is an easy-to-use quality system designed to help everyone in the organisation focus on and improve customer service. Achievement of the standard is recognised by awarding the right to display the prestigious Charter Mark logo, which is much sought-after by sports-development units in the public sector. (This became Customer Service Excellence from 2009.)

The publicity material about the award says that Charter Mark is more about achieving a change of culture (to help target groups) than winning a trophy, but change and improvement must be ongoing. Those seeking an award have to demonstrate that:

- they offer choice to their customers so that a wide range of needs are catered for
- participants and staff are consulted on where choices can be made, and communities have a say in the design and delivery of local sports-development programmes
- continuous improvement is sought, which means new targets are set every year at a slightly higher level or lower cost.

To achieve the award, sports-development units have to show that staff are involved in planning services and are encouraged and given the power to put things right wherever possible.

Take it further

Inspection prep

In pairs, discuss what sports-development teams would need to do to prepare for an inspection by IiP, Quest or Charter Mark.

Clubmark

Clubmark was introduced in 2002 by Sport England. It is a cross-sport quality award for clubs with junior sections. The scheme demonstrates to partners, parents and young people that Clubmark accredited clubs are:

- active – getting the best out of young people
- accessible – giving everyone a sporting chance
- accredited – the Sport England mark of high quality.

The aim of Clubmark is to provide more and better opportunities for children and young people to participate in sport in their local communities. The award shows that a sports-development scheme at a club is safe, effective and child-friendly. It gives a new nationally adopted set of standards for national governing bodies (NGBs) of sport. Sports clubs have to set and meet standards that will lead to better-quality provision for children and young people.

The scheme applies across a wide range of sports. It is promoted nationally to enable parents, carers and young people to quickly recognise a club that is committed to providing a quality experience.

Clubmark sets out standards for:

- duty of care and child protection
- coaching and competition
- sports equity and ethics
- club management.

Internal or self-assessment

It is possible to achieve all the quality scheme awards described above through internal audits or inspections, which can be set up in-house. For example, Quest can be tackled this way through self-assessment evidence. Sports-development units assess their delivery in comparison to industry standards and best-practice information provided in the Quest guidance pack.

Remember

Internal audits differ from external audits. They are less objective (less independent) and more open to bias.

External audits

These take place under inspection from independent outsiders (hence external). External audits help to ensure objectivity and consistency in assessment. Quest, IiP, Charter Mark and Clubmark are all based on external audits.

Swim 21

This is a very good example of a club development model – a planning and quality management system designed to be followed by clubs to ensure they focus on swimming needs. Visit the ASA website to learn more at: www.britishswimming.org.

Purpose

Measure improvement

The main purpose of all these accreditation schemes is to help sports-development organisations to see some improvement in their delivery in order to achieve high standards.

Continuous improvement

Continuous improvement is always desirable. Improvements may only be possible in small steps, but they should still be rewarded. Some of the awards have scales and percentages at each stage so that even small improvements can be identified.

Standardisation

Standards ensure that sports-development units have something to aim for or refer to if they are not sure how to deliver an aspect of sports development. Standards might involve the quality of child protection offered, level of coaching or types of resources required.

Advantages

Benchmarking

The first advantage of quality schemes is that sports-development units can compare how they work and what they achieve with others around the UK. This is called benchmarking.

Take it further

Carry out some research to identify how the Sport England national benchmarking system works.

Accessing funds

A quality award helps to obtain funding for sports development as it assures the awarding body that the club or team that has been given the funding has achieved certain standards, it is reputable and that it is likely to use the funding well.

Quality delivery

Quality systems delivery should benefit participants, the organisation, staff and any other stakeholders or partners such as members of the community.

Recognition

Recognition of having a quality award will result in good press reports, being able to show their logo creating a good reputation among colleagues and with the public. This is called a 'virtuous spiral'.

Activity: How does a quality scheme help?

Write down how a quality scheme could benefit each of the following:

- participants
- organisations
- staff.

Disadvantages

A quality system does not solve all working practice problems and there may be a number of disadvantages in getting a system up and running, for example:

- The overall costs of putting a system in place may be too high.

- There may be problems with getting staff fully involved. They may feel they have to work harder or differently without a pay rise or bonus.

- It may be too tough for some staff members who are trying to make fewer mistakes and their motivation may suffer.

- Officers are expected to be creative and flexible, and to stick to a system for delivery. This might prove difficult for some.

- New ideas and improvements are expected without any additional reward.

- Confidence needs to be built so that staff are not afraid to speak up.

- The sports-development unit's culture may have to change and move away from familiar working practices.

- Everyone in the staff team needs to be involved, from top to bottom in the club or facility.

Cost

The overall costs of putting a system in place; this can range from the paperwork involved to computer software or new resources.

Time

It takes time to train staff, plan systems and implement and resolve any operating problems.

Expertise

Another hurdle may be in creating expertise where none existed before, such as customer or disability care.

How do you overcome any barriers?

Assessment activity 6.4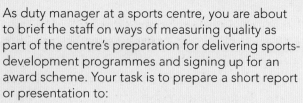

As duty manager at a sports centre, you are about to brief the staff on ways of measuring quality as part of the centre's preparation for delivering sports-development programmes and signing up for an award scheme. Your task is to prepare a short report or presentation to:

1. Give an explanation of two methods of measuring quality in the provision of a sports-development programme, giving some examples. **P4**

2. Give an evaluation of two methods of measuring quality in the provision of sports-development schemes using real examples. **M3**

Grading tips

P4 Remember that quality is measured by 'valuable features' that make the scheme better. It would be good if your explanations and examples are drawn from real schemes to show you really understand what you are describing. Be sure you include the purpose of the method and any advantages or disadvantages. A SWOT analysis might work as a summary.

M3 It is important to say why your chosen methods of evaluating quality are effective. Try to choose several criteria for evaluation and back them up with good examples and maybe even recommendation. A SWOT analysis might work as a summary tool.

PLTS

Researching your examples will develop your skills as an **independent enquirer**.

Functional skills

You may create opportunities for **ICT** skills evidence as you prepare and present your work.

4. Know about sports development in practice

You have learned that sports development is a dynamic sector with many initiatives, schemes and campaigns. You need to know about a selection of current initiatives as well as the practical dimensions of running programmes and the skills staff need. Here are some further ideas with a range of questions linked to the more practical dimensions.

4.1 Current initiatives

London 2012

Working towards London's Olympics and Paralympics in 2012 has given great impetus and focus to many sports, facilities and individuals in the UK. Preparation through sports development means finding talent and ensuring that coaching, facilities and finance are in place. Here are a few examples.

- Buckinghamshire local authority has set up a scheme called BuckSport, which has begun developing proposals for a talent development programme for Buckinghamshire athletes leading towards London 2012.

- The five London boroughs linked to the 2012 Olympic Games have teamed up to submit a 10-year, £70 million funding bid to support sport and businesses in the area. Greenwich, Hackney, Newham, Tower Hamlets and Waltham Forest plan to use the Games as a catalyst to secure training and employment opportunities for local people, as well as long-term sport and business growth.

Discuss what would be the difficulties in putting such a huge sports-development bid together.

The Newham sports-development plan has also identified some issues that need to be tackled with this ambitious sports-development scheme:

- poverty and deprivation
- unemployment
- poor health
- low participation rates
- low volunteer rates
- a wide ethnic mix.

Funding initiatives for programmes

Awards for All is a funding scheme for many things, including sports development. It is supported by the Arts Council of England, the Big Lottery Fund, the Heritage Lottery Fund and Sport England. Grants are awarded of between £300 and £10,000 for people to take part in art, sport, heritage and community activities, and projects that promote education, the environment and health in the local community. Support for sport-related activities may be given for:

- improved rural and urban environments which communities are better able to access and enjoy
- healthier and more active people and communities.

The Big Lottery Fund has been integrated into the Scottish Government's launch of the 2014 Commonwealth Games Legacy blueprint document. Through its 2014 Communities grant programme the Big Lottery Fund plans to contribute £6.8 million towards creating a lasting legacy from the Commonwealth Games.

Lottery Fund Scotland Director, Dharmendra Kanani, said:

'We have allocated £1.3m up to 2010 and plan to allocate a further £5.5m leading up to Glasgow 2014. We want to increase the number of people taking part in sport or physical activity at a grass roots level but also want to promote the benefits of volunteering. We have already awarded more than 200 grants with activities ranging from sea kayaking in Orkney to dance classes in Glasgow. What it is important to realise is that all of these groups are making the link that a small amount of money can make a huge difference to health and well-being. We will be learning the lessons of how our funding is being spent and plan to adapt the programme to best meet the needs of the public in the months and years to come.'
Source: www.biglotteryfund.org.uk, 2009

Every year BIG gives out millions of pounds from the National Lottery to good causes. The money goes to community groups and to projects that improve health, education and the environment. Big Lottery Fund and the Secret Millionaire have teamed up to give viewers of the programme a chance to help local c· groups secure funding through BIG's new Millionaire Fund.

Private-sector programmes

These are more likely to focus on regeneration and facility-building schemes because this is where the private sector is most likely to get a good return on any investment. This idea was at the heart of the Manchester Commonwealth Games and is also driving the 2012 strategy for London. Private-sector involvement usually increases jobs and training, which helps to develop local skills in such areas as coaching, volunteering and sports administration. Local people can also set up sports-related businesses to benefit from events such as souvenir and sports shops or supply services to sports businesses such as food, training or IT help.

Providers

Local authority sports-development programmes are often linked to local community plans and are therefore of strategic importance for local councils. For example Wigan Leisure and Culture Trust employs a dedicated team of sports-development professionals. The team of eight, managed by the senior sports-development officer, works across the whole borough through targeted generic and sports-specific programmes. This is a common approach.

Take it further

Governing body sports development

You have already looked at England Basketball on page 168. Carry out some research to assess how other major governing bodies structure their schemes such as the England Netball plan, the Rugby Football Union plan or the British Rowing plan.

Voluntary clubs

Voluntary clubs are supported by many agencies such as funding bodies and local authorities, to help them to develop and become sustainable. Here are two examples:

1. Many borough councils' recreation departments or sports-development teams provide a range of support and advice to voluntary-sector groups, sports clubs, village halls and parish councils on potential funding and project planning schemes. This is a public/voluntary scheme. Can you find one near you?

2. Some district councils offer financial assistance to support local community organisations in its efforts to provide facilities, equipment and services for sport and recreation. Grants are also available to individuals who have achieved or seek to develop a standard of excellence in sport. Can you find one near you?

Voluntary clubs can find funding, guidance and support for almost anything they want to do. Whether it is player development from a national governing body, coach improvement from sports coach UK, new buildings with a Sport England grant, umpiring and refereeing courses from an NGB or setting up a new club with local business help, professional support is there. Voluntary clubs work mostly with those groups low on the sports-development continuum, leaving the elite and performers to governing bodies, UK Sport and the English Institute of Sport.

Partnerships

Most city councils work in partnership with a wide range of organisations including the Primary Care Trust, Connexions, voluntary clubs, Sure Start, the Youth Offending Team, healthy living centres and the police, to create sports-related strategies and projects in their area. Sports-development teams are often at the heart of this as the deliverers and co-coordinators. For example, Hull City's Pride, Passion and Participation strategy from 2008 to 2013 sets out an agenda for the Hull's Community Sport Network to improve the quality of sport and active recreation opportunities for all city residents.

A range of individuals and agencies such as sport, health, education and community groups as well as residents have been consulted to develop a long-term strategy to improve opportunities for sport and active recreation in the city.

Source: www.hullcc.gov.uk, 2009

By now you should have a good idea of the three key areas that sports-development workers focus on. However, here is a brief summary to remind you.

- **Target groups** are specific groups of people who will benefit most from an initiative. Quickly list five from this unit.

- **Sport-specific** initiatives involve individual sports such as squash that would benefit from a boost.

- The **location** of an initiative may involve deprived areas with few facilities, such as run-down city estates.

Activity: What does a project do?

Using the examples of the schemes given in this unit and those from your own research, draw a table like the one below to summarise each project's typical areas of work (if a specific sport is identified) and the location.

Project	Area of work/Target group	Specific sport	Location

Areas of work

By now you should have a good idea that sports-development officers work in very diverse areas, with many types of people with a mixture of underlying agendas and development aims. Two of the most common are:

- **Target groups** – These are specific groups of people who will benefit most from an initiative.
- **Sport specific** – Individual sports that would benefit from a boost through an initiative, such as skiing.

Use these to tackle the activity above.

Location

The location of an initiative can be crucial to the success of the scheme – the closer it can be run to the target group the better take-up there will be, but of course the facilities have to be suitable for the sport.

Effectiveness and efficiency

All areas of sports-development work and investment should be evaluated. Sports-development schemes must show they give value for money and make good use of resources. They must also show they are efficient, with increasing accountability and public spending cuts, because of the recession in 2008/9. Accounting for all expenditure and showing the real benefits for participants are key issues for the officers involved.

One key point to remember is that the officers must be good at writing funding bids in order to get them accepted by funding organisations. This condition often underpins any initiatives.

New governments can also impose new performance criteria.

Activity: What problems might occur?

Analyse the flow chart below to identify problems that could occur at each stage.

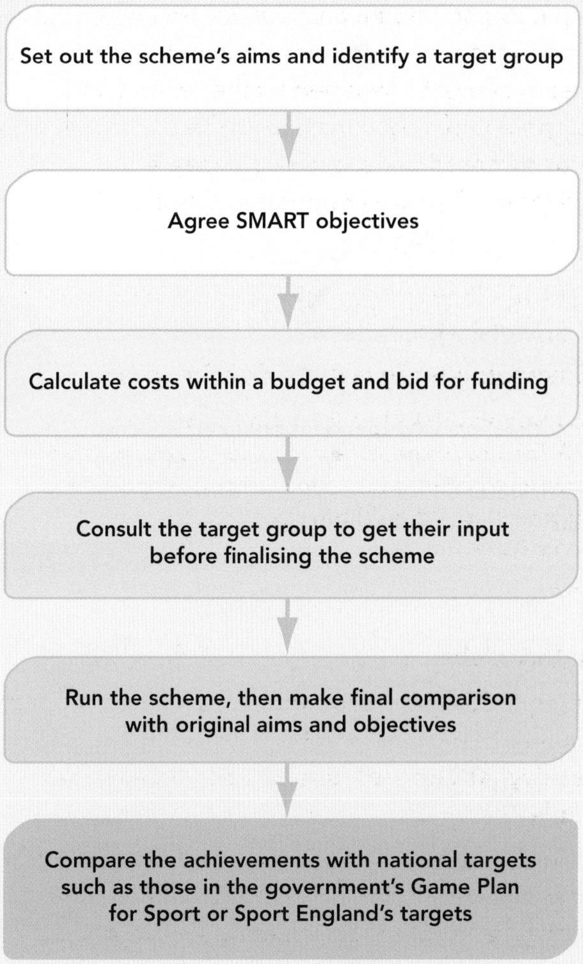

Set out the scheme's aims and identify a target group

↓

Agree SMART objectives

↓

Calculate costs within a budget and bid for funding

↓

Consult the target group to get their input before finalising the scheme

↓

Run the scheme, then make final comparison with original aims and objectives

↓

Compare the achievements with national targets such as those in the government's Game Plan for Sport or Sport England's targets

Figure 6.10: Flow chart showing targets

Assessment activity 6.5

 P5 M4 D2 · BTEC

You work for a County Sports Partnership and are responsible for advising on sports-development schemes for a region of England. You have been invited by a local college to give a talk on the range of sports-development initiatives in your area. The requirements are shown below.

1. Describe two different sports-development initiatives from any sector. **P5**

2. Compare and contrast two different sports-development initiatives from two different providers, giving strengths and areas in which you think they might improve. **M4**

3. Choose two different sports-development initiatives from different sectors in different sports and at different levels of the continuum if you can. Analyse these using quality- and performance-related criteria and the grading tips below, and make realistic recommendations for improvement. **D2**

Grading tips

P5 To give variety, breadth and depth, try different levels of the sports-development continuum and for different sports.

M4 Simply describing the sports-development scheme will not be good enough: you must go on to compare and contrast specific factors such as purpose, agendas, level, the organising body, type of scheme and quality levels. This means reviewing the initiatives and drawing some conclusions about what makes the initiative so effective in its strengths and what problems might need improvements.

D2 Offering effective examples and reasons for your judgements or comments will help you to gain a higher grade. The highest level of skill for you to aim for is analysis. This means picking out relevant factors and issues and saying what effects these might have, then building on these for your recommendations for improvements.

PLTS

Researching and presenting your work may develop your skills as an **independent enquirer**, working with others will help you progress as an **effective participator** and analysing the initiatives will increase your skills as a **creative thinker**.

Functional skills

Depending on how you formulate and present your work, there should be ample opportunity to find evidence for **ICT** skills. **Mathematics** skills can be evidenced by making calculations related to quality measurements and **English** skills can be evidenced through debating, researching and discussing projects or through writing documents.

Mike Squires

The East Riding of Yorkshire Sports Development Service

The East Riding of Yorkshire Sports Development Service is based in Beverley, just north of Hull, but also covers a large rural area. Its aim is to 'enable and support the development of quality sports, play and physical activity opportunities,' so officers need to be aware of cross-cutting agendas and the needs of a diverse population.

They tackled a shortage of good coaches in the area by using a scheme that comes under the umbrella of the Community Sports Coaches (CSC scheme), which aims to ensure that a number of qualified CSCs are working at a local level.

Mike Squires from the sports-development service says:

The underlying issue we had to address was the national target of increasing adult participation in sport by 1 per cent year on year.

The Sport and Play Development Service was successful in gaining a £200,000 grant for their area from Sport England and appointed six full-time Community Sports Coaches to deliver a wide range of activities. All six posts are mainly multi-sports and each has a second specialism: disability, healthy lifestyles, outdoor adventure, street sports, rural areas and coastal areas. Clearly sourcing funding was crucial for this scheme.

They developed a range of activities which included:

- community-based adult disability clubs
- women's circuits classes
- youth diversionary programmes
- school holiday programmes
- beach sports/festivals
- falls prevention programmes
- migrant sessions
- healthy-living programmes.

Think about it!

1. Part of their evaluation was to assess what difference they made. Assess the statistics below and draw some conclusions about the scheme's success in reaching the wider community.

   During 2008–2009:
   - 4,814 participants have accessed activities, of whom: 976 were women; 1,003 were over 45; 2,543 lived in a deprived area; 888 had a disability.
   - 444 participants were new to sport in the last 12 months
   - 26,924 places were taken on all activities.

2. Based on their first-round efforts, the team set some targets for the next. How realistic do you feel these are and how would you evaluate them?
   - Sourcing funding to continue four of the CSCs
   - Developing and delivering the Active in Age programme
   - Varying and increasing the women's circuit training sessions in rural areas
   - Running more community-based adult disability sessions
   - Increasing the provision of activities with migrant communities.

Just checking

1. How many levels does the sports-development continuum have and what are they?
2. Name three long-standing target groups.
3. Name four barriers to participation.
4. Chose one barrier for a particular target group and make recommendations on how it could be overcome.
5. Devise a classification system for providers to help you clarify who they are. Give examples.
6. Describe four ways of structuring a sports-development initiative.
7. Select three roles of providers and compare and contrast them.
8. What are audits, quality awards and benchmarking?
9. Name three advantages of quality awards and three difficulties that might be encountered.
10. How might you assess the effectiveness and funding of a scheme?
11. What are the key differences between a local scheme and national strategy?
12. Describe three key differences between public, private and voluntary schemes of sports development.
13. What issues might emerge if funding were to be scarce for elite or grass-roots participants?
14. How important is quality for the success of a scheme?

Assignment tips

- Make sure you fully understand the key concepts and terminology before you begin any research.
- It is important that you understand why organisations invest in sports development.
- If you can't get a guest speaker to come in and talk to you, why not arrange an interview with a SD officer to help you.
- You may be able to use the London Olympics and Legacy period to find examples for your assignments.
- Personal experiences or involvement (volunteering) might give you a useful 'inside track' on local initiatives.
- Website searches should help you find sports development strategies at national level.
- Keep any recommendations you make realistic and achievable.
- Make sure you structure your work in a logical way to cover all the points requested.

7 Fitness testing for sport and exercise

Fitness is vital for success in sport, and fitness testing plays a valuable role in the development of fitness levels. Sports performers participate in fitness tests in order to determine their baseline measures and training needs. Fitness testing is built into the elite performer's training regime so that they can push their bodies to the maximum, recording progress and fitness gains.

Results from fitness tests are used to predict performance potential and provide feedback on the effectiveness of a training programme. Coaches can use results to identify the performer's strengths, areas for improvement and types of training needed to achieve optimum performance.

Fitness testing is also carried out in health clubs where instructors screen clients for contraindications to exercise, administer fitness tests, and use the results to design exercise programmes that meet the clients' personal goals. When conducting fitness assessments, instructors adhere to strict health and safety procedures, test protocol guidelines, and can identify those clients requiring medical referral.

In this unit you will gain experience of a range of laboratory- and field-based fitness tests. You will administer these tests, providing feedback to an individual on their fitness levels. You will conduct health screening techniques and health monitoring tests for two contrasting individuals, interpreting the results, and provide recommendations for lifestyle improvement.

Learning outcomes

After completing this unit you should:

1. know a range of laboratory-based and field-based fitness tests
2. be able to use health screening techniques
3. be able to administer appropriate fitness tests
4. be able to interpret the results of fitness tests and provide feedback.

Assessment and grading criteria

This table shows you what you must do in order to achieve a pass, merit or distinction grade, and where you can find activities in this book to help you.

To achieve a **pass** grade the evidence must show that the learner is able to:	To achieve a **merit** grade the evidence must show that, in addition to the pass criteria, the learner is able to:	To achieve a **distinction** grade the evidence must show that, in addition to the pass and merit criteria, the learner is able to:
P1 describe one test for each component of physical fitness, including advantages and disadvantages **Assessment activity 7.1, page 200**	**M1** explain the advantages and disadvantages of one fitness test for each component of physical fitness **Assessment activity 7.1, page 200**	
P2 prepare an appropriate health screening questionnaire **Assessment activity 7.2, page 204**		
P3 devise and use appropriate health screening procedures for two contrasting individuals **Assessment activity 7.2, page 204**		
P4 safely administer and interpret the results of four different health monitoring tests for two contrasting individuals **Assessment activity 7.2, page 204**	**M2** describe the strengths and areas for improvement for two contrasting individuals using information from health screening questionnaires and health monitoring tests **Assessment activity 7.2, page 204**	**D1** evaluate the health screening questionnaires and health monitoring test results and provide recommendations for lifestyle improvement **Assessment activity 7.2, page 204**
P5 select and safely administer six different fitness tests for a selected individual recording the findings **Assessment activity 7.3, page 207**	**M3** justify the selection of fitness tests commenting on suitability, reliability, validity and practicality **Assessment activity 7.3, page 207**	
P6 give feedback to a selected individual, following fitness testing, describing the test results and interpreting their levels of fitness against normative data **Assessment activity 7.4, page 208**	**M4** compare the fitness test results to normative data and identify strengths and areas for improvement **Assessment activity 7.4, page 208**	**D2** analyse the fitness test results and provide recommendations for appropriate future activities or training **Assessment activity 7.4, page 208**

How you will be assessed

This unit will be assessed by an internal assignment that will be designed and marked by the staff at your centre. Your assessment could be in the form of:

- practically assessed activities
- laboratory reports
- presentations
- case studies
- written assignments.

Damian Silva, 17-year-old gymnast

This unit gave me an insight into conducting a client health fitness assessment and the knowledge, understanding and skills needed to perform well. Having studied the Edexcel BTEC Level 2 Diploma in Sport, I had some experience of fitness testing and had participated in fitness tests like the multi-stage fitness test and step test. In this unit we covered other fitness tests which I hadn't experienced before like the Wingate test of anaerobic power – which really pushes you to your max! We looked at the advantages and disadvantages of fitness tests and why different clients might need different types of test.

The thing I enjoyed most was working with clients in a real-world setting and administering health screening techniques, health monitoring tests and fitness tests. It was challenging giving detailed feedback to clients on what their results meant and how they could improve.

By studying this unit I've gained some great practical experience in assessing people's fitness and it has helped me to develop my confidence and skills when working with people.

Over to you

- **What areas of this unit might you find challenging?**
- **Which section of the unit are you most looking forward to?**
- **What preparation can you do in readiness for the unit assessment(s)?**

1. Know a range of laboratory-based and field-based fitness tests

Think about the different fitness tests you have observed or participated in, perhaps through your local sports club or through another programme of study. What were the advantages and disadvantages of the tests? Think about factors like cost, time and equipment required. Write a list and discuss in pairs or small groups.

1.1 Fitness tests

To safely and effectively administer laboratory-based and field-based fitness tests, you need good knowledge and understanding of tests for different components of fitness, and the procedures and protocols to follow. You'll need to be aware of the advantages and disadvantages of different fitness tests and the implications these have for test selection and administration. In this section you'll gain practical experience of different fitness tests, the standard methods to follow and how to interpret test results. You will look at the advantages and disadvantages of fitness tests and how these need to be taken into account when selecting appropriate tests to administer to a client. In particular, you will look at the following test methods for these different components of fitness:

Component of fitness	Fitness test
Flexibility	Sit and reach
Strength	Grip strength dynamometer 1 repetition maximum (1RM)
Aerobic endurance	Multi-stage fitness test Forestry step test 1.5 mile run test 1 mile walk test
Speed	35 metre sprint
Power	Vertical jump Wingate test
Muscular endurance	1 minute press-up 1 minute sit-up
Body composition	Skinfold testing (Durnin and Womersley, 1974) Bioelectrical impedance analysis

Table 7.1: The different components of fitness and types of fitness tests

Flexibility – the sit and reach test

This test is an indirect measure of static flexibility. Its aim is to measure trunk forward flexion, hamstring, hip and lower back range of motion. A standard sit and reach box is used.

1. Perform a short warm-up prior to this test. Don't use fast, jerky movements as this may increase risk of injury. Remove your shoes.

2. Sit with your heels placed against the edge of the sit and reach box. Keep your legs flat on the floor, i.e. keep your knees down.

3. Place one hand on top of the other and reach forward slowly. Your fingertips should be in contact with the measuring portion of the sit and reach box. As you reach forward, drop your head between your arms and breathe out as you push forward.

4. The best of three trials should be recorded.

Rating	Males (cm)	Females (cm)
Excellent	25+	20+
Very good	17	17
Good	15	16
Average	14	15
Poor	13	14
Very poor	9	10

Table 7.2: Interpreting the results of the sit and reach test

Alternative direct methods used to measure static flexibility include use of a goniometer or a Leighton flexometer. These devices can be used to measure joint range of movement (ROM) with norms available for interpretation of ROM achieved at the neck, trunk, shoulder, elbow, radioulnar, wrist, hip, knee and ankle joints.

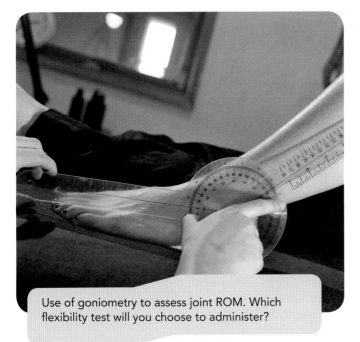

Use of goniometry to assess joint ROM. Which flexibility test will you choose to administer?

Static strength – grip strength dynamometer test

This measures the static strength of the power grip-squeezing muscles, where the whole hand is used as a vice or clamp. A grip dynamometer is a spring device – as force is applied, the spring is compressed and this moves the dynamometer needle which indicates the result. Digital dynamometers are also available.

1. Adjust the handgrip size so that the dynamometer feels comfortable to hold/grip.
2. Stand with your arms by the side of your body.
3. Hold the dynamometer parallel to the side of your body with the dial/display facing away from you.
4. Squeeze as hard as possible for 5 seconds, without moving your arm.
5. Carry out three trials on each hand, with a 1 minute rest between trials.

Rating	Males aged 15–19 (kg)	Females aged 15–19 (kg)
Excellent	52+	32+
Good	47–51	28–31
Average	44–46	25–27
Below average	39–43	20–24
Poor	<39	<20

Table 7.3: Interpreting the results of the grip strength dynamometer test

Dynamic strength – bench press 1 repetition maximum (1RM)

The bench press 1 repetition maximum (1RM) is a test of the dynamic strength of the bench pressing pectoral muscles of the chest. It is a dynamic test used to assess upper body strength. The test can be safely carried out using a bench press resistance machine.

1. An informed consent form must be completed before undertaking this maximal test. An example of a consent form is shown on page 184.
2. Carry out a standard warm-up and stretching of the major muscle groups.
3. Determine a comfortable weight to start to press.
4. Breathe out on exertion, i.e. as the weight is lifted. Ensure you don't hold your breath as this will cause an increase in blood pressure.
5. Each bench press weight successfully lifted should be noted.
6. Allow a 2 minute rest between trials before increasing the weight by 5–10 lb.
7. Continue this protocol until a maximum weight is successfully lifted. This is recorded as your 1RM.
8. Perform a standard cool down.
9. Divide your 1RM result (lb) by your body weight in lb. Use the table below to interpret your results.

Rating	Males (1RM lb/lb body weight)	Females (1RM lb/lb body weight)
Excellent	>1.26	>0.78
Good	1.17–1.25	0.72–0.77
Average	0.97–1.16	0.59–0.71
Fair	0.88–0.96	0.53–0.58
Poor	<0.87	<0.52

Table 7.4: Interpreting the results of the bench press 1RM test

Remember

If you measure your body weight and weight lifted in kg, convert these figures to lb by multiplying by 2.2.

To use the interpretation table above divide the weight lifted in lb by your body weight in lb.

INFORMED CONSENT FOR STRENGTH TESTS

FITNESS TESTS TO BE UNDERTAKEN
• **1-RM for Chest** • **1-RM for Back** • **1-RM for Legs**

1. The purpose of these tests is to determine the maximal strength of the muscle groups used.
2. The participant will carry out standard warming-up and cool down procedures for the test.
3. The participant will be required to perform a one-repetition maximum (1-RM) for the tests cited above.
4. All participants will receive method details in full.
5. The tutor/assessor is available to answer any relevant queries which may arise concerning the test.
6. The participant is free to withdraw consent and discontinue participation in the test at any time.
7. Only the tutor/assessor and participant will have access to data recorded from the test which will be stored securely. Participant confidentiality is assured.

I FULLY UNDERSTAND THE SCOPE OF MY INVOLVEMENT IN THIS FITNESS TEST AND HAVE FREELY CONSENTED TO MY PARTICIPATION.

Participant signature: _____   Date: _____

Tutor/assesssor signature: _____   Date: _____

I (insert participant name)**, UNDERSTAND THAT MY PARENTS/GUARDIAN HAVE GIVEN PERMISSION FOR ME TO TAKE PART IN THIS FITNESS TEST, WHICH WILL BE SUPERVISED BY** (insert tutor name) **. I AM PARTICIPATING IN THIS FITNESS TEST BECAUSE I WANT TO, AND I HAVE BEEN INFORMED THAT I CAN STOP THE TEST AT ANY TIME WITHOUT ANY ISSUES ARISING.**

Participant signature: _____   Date: _____

Assesssor signature: _____   Date: _____

Parental/Guardian Signature: _____   Date: _____

Figure 7.1: Example of an informed consent form for strength tests

Aerobic endurance – multi-stage fitness test

This test is used to predict your maximum oxygen uptake (aerobic fitness) levels and is performed to a pre-recorded audio tape. It should be conducted indoors, usually in a sports hall using two lines (or cones) placed 20 metres apart.

1. Perform a short warm-up.

2. Line up on the start line and on hearing the triple bleep run to the other line 20 metres away. You must reach the other line before or on the single bleep that determines each shuttle run.

3. Don't get ahead of the bleep – you need to make sure you turn to run to the other line on the bleep.

4. You will find that the bleeps get closer and closer together, so you'll need to continually increase your pace.

5. Continue to run to each line. A spotter is used to check you have reached each line in time with the bleep. If not, you will receive two verbal warnings before being asked to pull out of the test.

6. Continue running until you are physically exhausted, i.e. you have reached maximum exhaustion, at which point your level and shuttle reached is recorded.

7. Use Table 7.5 to predict your maximum oxygen consumption (ml/kg/min).

8. Use Table 7.6 on page 186 to interpret the maximum oxygen uptake result.

Level	Shuttle	VO$_2$ max	Level	Shuttle	VO$_2$ max	Level	Shuttle	VO$_2$ max	Level	Shuttle	VO$_2$ max
4	2	26.8	10	2	47.4	15	2	64.6	19	2	78.3
4	4	27.6	10	4	48.0	15	4	65.1	19	4	78.8
4	6	28.3	10	6	48.7	15	6	65.6	19	6	79.2
4	9	29.5	10	8	49.3	15	8	66.2	19	8	79.7
5	2	30.2	10	11	50.2	15	10	66.7	19	10	80.2
5	4	31.0	11	2	50.8	15	13	67.5	19	12	80.6
5	6	31.8	11	4	51.4	16	2	68.0	19	15	81.3
5	9	32.9	11	6	51.9	16	4	68.5	20	2	81.8
6	2	33.6	11	8	52.5	16	6	69.0	20	4	82.2
6	4	34.3	11	10	53.1	16	8	69.5	20	6	82.6
6	6	35.0	11	12	53.7	16	10	69.9	20	8	83.0
6	8	35.7	12	2	54.3	16	12	70.5	20	10	83.5
6	10	36.4	12	4	54.8	16	14	70.9	20	12	83.9
7	2	37.1	12	6	55.4	17	2	71.4	20	14	84.3
7	4	37.8	12	8	56.0	17	4	71.9	20	16	84.8
7	6	38.5	12	10	56.5	17	6	72.4	21	2	85.2
7	8	39.2	12	12	57.1	17	8	72.9	21	4	85.6
7	10	39.9	13	2	57.6	17	10	73.4	21	6	86.1
8	2	40.5	13	4	58.2	17	12	73.9	21	8	86.5
8	4	41.1	13	6	58.7	17	14	74.4	21	10	86.9
8	6	41.8	13	8	59.3	18	2	74.8	21	12	87.4
8	8	42.4	13	10	59.8	18	4	75.3	21	14	87.8
8	11	43.3	13	13	60.6	18	6	75.8	21	16	88.2
9	2	43.9	14	2	61.1	18	8	76.2			
9	4	44.5	14	4	61.7	18	10	76.7			
9	6	45.2	14	6	62.2	18	12	77.2			
9	8	45.8	14	8	62.7	18	15	77.9			
9	11	46.8	14	10	63.2						
			14	13	64.0						

Table 7.5: Predicted maximum oxygen uptake values for the multistage fitness test (ml/kg/min)

Rating	Males (aged 15–19) (ml/kg/min)	Females (aged 15–19) (ml/kg/min)
Excellent	60+	54+
Good	48-59	43-53
Average	39–47	35–42
Below average	30–38	28–34
Poor	<30	<28

Table 7.6: Interpreting maximum oxygen uptake results (VO_2 max, ml/kg/min)

Aerobic endurance – forestry step test

Developed in 1977 by Brian Sharkey, this test is a modified version of the Harvard Step test. It is widely used in fitness selection procedures (for example, by the police) and predicts aerobic endurance levels.

A different bench height is used for males and females. For males, the height of the bench should be 40 cm (15.75 in.), for females, 33 cm (13 in.). The stepping rate of 22.5 steps per minute is the same for both males and females, which means the metronome should be set at a cadence of 90 beats per minute.

1. Stand directly facing the bench and start stepping in time with the beat of the metronome. As soon as you start stepping, the tester will start the stopwatch.

2. Keep to the beat of the metronome, which means you will put one foot onto the bench, then your other foot, then the first foot will be lowered to the floor, then your other foot, i.e. 'up', 'up', 'down', 'down'.

3. Straighten your legs when you fully step up onto the bench.

4. Keep stepping for 5 minutes, at which point the tester will stop the metronome and you will need to sit down immediately and locate your radial pulse.

5. At 5 minutes and 15 seconds (15 seconds after you have sat down) you will need to count your pulse for 15 seconds (stopping at 5 minutes and 30 seconds).

6. Record your 15 second pulse rate and perform a short cool down.

Use the tables to obtain your non-adjusted aerobic fitness level:

- Use either Table 7.7 or 7.8 (depending on your gender) on pages 187 and 188 to locate your 15 second pulse in the 'Pulse count' column and your body weight (to the closest kg). You will find your non-adjusted aerobic fitness level (in ml/kg/min) where these two values intersect.

- Next, adjust your fitness level to take into account your age, which will provide a more accurate prediction of your aerobic endurance. In Table 7.9 on page 188, locate your nearest age in years (left-hand column) and locate your non-adjusted aerobic fitness level (fitness score) along the top. You will find your age-adjusted fitness level (ml/kg/min) at the point where these two values intersect.

- Use Table 7.10 on page 189 to interpret your aerobic fitness level.

Pulse count	Maximal oxygen consumption (VO_2 max)												
45	33	33	33	33	33	32	32	32	32	32	32	32	32
44	34	34	34	34	33	33	33	33	33	33	33	33	33
43	35	35	35	34	34	34	34	34	34	34	34	34	34
42	36	35	35	35	35	35	35	35	35	35	35	34	34
41	36	36	36	36	36	36	36	36	36	36	36	35	35
40	37	37	37	37	37	37	37	37	35	35	35	35	35
39	38	38	38	38	38	38	38	38	38	38	38	37	37
38	39	39	39	39	39	39	39	39	39	39	39	38	38
37	41	40	40	40	40	40	40	40	40	40	40	39	39
36	42	42	41	41	41	41	41	41	41	41	41	40	40
35	43	43	42	42	42	42	42	42	42	42	42	42	41
34	44	44	43	43	43	43	43	43	43	43	43	43	43
33	46	45	45	45	45	45	44	44	44	44	44	44	44
32	47	47	46	46	46	46	46	46	46	46	46	46	46
31	48	48	48	47	47	47	47	47	47	47	47	47	47
30	50	49	49	49	48	48	48	48	48	48	48	48	48
29	52	51	51	51	50	50	50	50	50	50	50	50	50
28	53	53	53	53	52	52	52	52	51	51	51	51	51
27	55	55	55	54	54	54	54	54	54	53	53	53	52
26	57	57	56	56	56	56	56	56	56	55	55	54	54
25	59	59	58	58	58	58	58	58	58	56	56	55	55
24	60	60	60	60	60	60	60	59	59	58	58	57	
23	62	62	61	61	61	61	61	60	60	60	59		
22	64	64	63	63	63	63	62	62	61	61			
21	66	66	65	65	65	64	64	64	62				
20	68	68	67	67	67	67	66	66	65				
Weight (kg)	54.5	59.1	63.6	68.2	72.7	77.3	81.8	86.4	91	95.4	100	104.5	109

Table 7.7: Forestry non-adjusted aerobic fitness values (ml/kg/min) for **males**

Pulse count	Maximal oxygen consumption (VO_2 max)											
45										29	29	29
44								30	30	30	30	30
43							31	31	31	31	31	31
42			32	32	32	32	32	32	32	32	32	32
41			33	33	33	33	33	33	33	33	33	33
40			34	34	34	34	34	34	34	34	34	34
39			35	35	35	35	35	35	35	35	35	35
38			36	36	36	36	36	36	36	36	36	36
37			37	37	37	37	37	37	37	37	37	37
36		37	38	38	38	38	38	38	38	38	38	38
35	38	38	39	39	39	39	39	39	39	39	39	39
34	39	39	40	40	40	40	40	40	40	40	40	40
33	40	40	41	41	41	41	41	41	41	41	41	41
32	41	41	42	42	42	42	42	42	42	42	42	42
31	42	42	43	43	43	43	43	43	43	43	43	43
30	43	43	44	44	44	44	44	44	44	44	44	44
29	44	44	45	45	45	45	45	45	45	45	45	45
28	45	45	46	46	46	47	47	47	47	47	47	
27	46	46	47	48	48	49	49	49	49	49		
26	47	48	49	50	50	51	51	51	51			
25	49	50	51	52	52	53	53					
24	51	52	53	54	54	55						
23	53	54	55	56	56	57						
Weight (kg)	36.4	40.9	45.4	50.0	54.5	59.1	63.6	68.2	72.7	77.3	81.8	86.4

Table 7.8: Forestry non-adjusted aerobic fitness values (ml/kg/min) for **females**

Fitness score		30	31	32	33	34	35	36	37	38	39	40	41	42	43	44	45	46	47	48	49	50
Nearest age	15	32	33	34	35	36	37	38	39	40	41	42	43	44	45	46	47	48	49	50	51	53
	20	31	32	33	34	35	36	37	38	39	40	41	42	43	44	45	46	47	48	49	50	51

(cont.)

Fitness score		51	52	53	54	55	56	57	58	59	60	61	62	63	64	65	66	67	68	69	70	71	72
Nearest age	15	54	55	56	57	58	59	60	61	62	63	64	65	66	67	68	69	70	71	72	74	75	76
	20	52	53	54	55	56	57	58	59	60	61	62	63	64	65	66	67	68	69	70	71	72	73

Table 7.9: Age-adjusted fitness levels

Example 1: If your age is 16 years and you score 36 on the step test, your age-adjusted score is 38.

Example 2: If your age is 20 years and you score 65 on the step test, your age-adjusted score is 66.

	Fitness category						
	Superior	**Excellent**	**Very good**	**Good**	**Fair**	**Poor**	**Very poor**
Age and gender	Maximum oxygen consumption (ml/kg/min)						
15-year-old male	57+	56–52	51–47	46–42	41–37	36–32	<32
15-year-old female	54+	53–49	48–44	43–39	38–34	33–29	<29
20-year-old male	56+	55–51	50–46	45–41	40–36	35–31	<31
20-year-old female	53+	52–48	47–43	42–38	37–33	32–28	<28

Table 7.10: Aerobic fitness levels

Aerobic endurance – 1.5 mile run test

This test is best performed on an indoor athletics track, or use an outdoor track on a day when weather conditions will not adversely affect test results.

1. Perform a warm-up and stretching of major muscle groups.
2. On the starter's orders, run a distance of 1.5 miles as fast as you can.
3. Record the time taken.
4. Perform a standard cool down and stretching of major muscle groups.

To interpret the results:

- use Table 7.11 to provide an estimate of maximal oxygen consumption (VO$_2$ max ml/kg/min) according to the time taken to complete the run
- then use Table 7.6 on page 186 to obtain the fitness rating.

Time (mins) for 1.5 mile run	VO$_2$ max (ml/kg/min)	Time (mins) for 1.5 mile run	VO$_2$ max (ml/kg/min)
<7.31	75	12.31–13.00	39
7.31–8.00	72	13.01–13.30	37
8.01–8.30	67	13.31–14.00	36
8.31–9.00	62	14.01–14.30	34
9.01–9.30	58	14.31–15.00	33
9.31–10.00	55	15.01–15.30	31
10.01–10.30	52	15.31–16.00	30
10.31–11.00	49	16.01–16.30	28
11.01–11.30	46	16.31–17.00	27
11.31–12.00	44	17.01–17.30	26
12.01–12.30	41	17.31–18.00	25

Table 7.11: Results of the 1.5 mile run test

Take it further

Amazing VO$_2$ max!

Cross country skiers and cyclists have some of the highest maximum oxygen uptake values ever reported. Check out the levels they have reached in Table 7.12. Spain's Miguel Indurain, the road racing cyclist and Tour de France winner, also had a reported resting heart rate of 28 beats per minute. How does your VO$_2$ max and resting heart rate compare?

VO$_2$ max (ml/kg/min)	Athlete	Gender	Sport/event
96.0	Bjorn Daehlie	Male	Cross country skiing
92.5	Greg LeMond	Male	Cycling
88.0	Miguel Indurain	Male	Cycling
85.0	John Ngugi	Male	Cross country runner
73.5	Greta Waitz	Female	Marathon runner
71.2	Ingrid Kristiansen	Female	Marathon runner
67.2	Rosa Mota	Female	Marathon runner

Table 7.12: Elite maximum oxygen uptake values

Aerobic endurance – 1 mile walk test

This low intensity test is used to predict maximum oxygen uptake and, because of the non-stressful nature of the test, it can be particularly useful in assessing those who are unfit. The test is best performed on an indoor athletics track, or use an outdoor track on a day when weather conditions will not adversely affect test results.

1. Perform a warm-up.

2. On the starter's orders, walk a distance of 1 mile as fast as possible.

3. Record the time taken and convert to decimal minutes:

   where: decimal minutes (t) = [min + (s/60)]

4. On crossing the finishing line, take pulse rate for 15 seconds.

5. Convert the 15 second pulse into heart rate (beats/minute):

   where: 15 second pulse rate x 4 = beats per minute

6. Use the equation **below** to predict maximum oxygen uptake (VO_2 max l/min)

$$VO_2 \text{ max (l/min)} = 6.9652 + (0.0091 \times wt) - (0.0257 \times age) + (0.5955 \times gender) - (0.2240 \times t) - (0.0115 \times HR)$$

Where:
- wt = body weight (lb)
- age = years
- gender = 0 = female; 1 = male
- t = time in decimal minutes
- HR = heart rate (beats/minute)

Key terms

Absolute VO_2 max – maximum oxygen consumption expressed in litres per minute (l/min).

Relative VO_2 max – maximum oxygen consumption expressed relative to the individual's body weight in kg. The units of relative VO_2 max are ml of oxygen per kilogram of body weight per minute (ml/kg/min).

Case study: Conducting the 1 mile walk test

Paul is a 19-year-old male who completed the 1 mile walk test in a time of 13 minutes and 26 seconds. His body weight is 174 lb. On crossing the finishing line, Paul's 15 second pulse was 29.

Calculate Paul's maximum oxygen uptake (VO_2 max ml/kg/min).

Workings

- To convert 13.26 to decimal minutes (where decimal minutes (t) = [min + (s/60)])

  = [13 + (26/60)] = 13.43 decimal minutes.

- To convert the 15 second pulse into beats per minute

  = 29 x 4 = 116 beats/minute.

- Use the equation to predict maximum oxygen uptake (VO_2 max ml/kg/min):

  VO_2 max (l/min) = 6.9652 + (0.0091 x wt) – (0.0257 x age) + (0.5955 x gender) – (0.2240 x t) – (0.0115 x HR)

  Therefore:

  VO_2 max (l/min) = 6.9652 + (0.0091 x 174) – (0.0257 x 19) + (0.5955 x 1) – (0.2240 x 13.43) – (0.0115 x 116)

  VO_2 max (l/min) = 4.31

- Convert **absolute VO_2 max** (l/min) to **relative VO_2 max** (ml/kg/min):

  VO_2 max (ml/kg/min) = [(4.31 x 1000) ÷ Body weight (kg)]

  Therefore:

  VO_2 max (ml/kg/min) = [(4.31 x 1000) ÷ 79 kg] = 54.6 ml/kg/min

- Using Table 7.6 on page 186, Paul's fitness rating is good.

1. How does your predicted VO_2 max from the 1 mile walk test compare to normative data?

2. How do your results compare to data for elite performers?

3. How do your results compare to those of your peers?

4. Calculate your results and discuss in small groups.

Maximal treadmill tests

Maximal treadmill tests require participants to exercise until physical exhaustion is reached. Informed consent is required prior to undertaking the test. Tests are performed on a motor-driven treadmill which can be adjusted for both incline and speed, and specialist equipment is required to collect and measure respiratory gases.

Maximal treadmill test methods are usually continuous and progressive in nature, where at prescribed time intervals, the tester will increase the percentage of incline and/or the speed of the treadmill. Due to the physically stressful nature of maximal treadmill tests, they are not suitable for certain people, for example, the elderly.

Remember

During maximal treadmill testing, maximum oxygen uptake (VO$_2$ max) is reached when:

- the individual reports a Rating of Perceived Exertion (RPE) of 20 (Borg 6–20 RPE scale)
- there is less than 150 ml/min increase between exercise workloads
- blood lactate is greater than 8 mmol/l.

Speed – 35 metre sprint

The test is best performed on an indoor athletics track, or using an outdoor track on a day when weather conditions will not adversely affect test results.

1. Perform a warm-up.
2. Three people should keep time for the sprint, using stopwatches capable of measuring to one-tenth of a second.
3. Line up on the start line, in a standing start position.
4. As soon as you start sprinting, the timers will start their stopwatches.
5. Sprint as fast as you can, crossing the 35 metre line.
6. When you cross the 35 metre line, the timers will stop their stopwatches.
7. Your time for the sprint is recorded to the closest tenth of a second. An average result can be taken from the three timers.
8. A maximum of two to three trials are performed in one day. Allow at least 3 minutes recovery between trials. A third trial should only be performed if the difference in times between your first and second trial is greater than 0.20 seconds.

9. The best time from your two or three trials is recorded as your 35 metre sprint result.
10. To prevent muscle soreness, perform a cool down followed by static stretching.

Rating	Males (s)	Females (s)
Excellent	<4.80	<5.30
Good	4.80–5.09	5.30–5.59
Average	5.10–5.29	5.60–5.89
Fair	5.30–5.60	5.90–6.20
Poor	5.60+	6.20+

Table 7.13: Interpretation of results from the 35 metre sprint test

Anaerobic power – vertical jump test

This is a test of the anaerobic power of the quadriceps muscle group. A standard vertical jump board is used for the test, which may digitally record the jump height, or alternatively gymnast's chalk may be used.

1. Perform a short warm-up prior to the test.
2. Stand with your dominant side against the board, feet together, and reach up as high as you can to record your standing reach height.
3. Only one dip of the arms and knees is permitted; make the jump while simultaneously touching the vertical jump board at the peak of your jump.
4. Perform three trials. No rest is required between trials. The time taken to observe and record the height of the jump is all that is needed for recovery between consecutive trials.

To obtain the results of this fitness test, a nomogram can be used. Use the Lewis nomogram to predict the power of your quadriceps in kgm/s.

- Plot the difference (D) between your standing reach height and your best jump height (cm) on the nomogram line (D).
- Plot your weight in kilograms on the nomogram line (Wt).
- Using a sharpened pencil and ruler, join up the two plots, which will cross over the power line (P) to give a prediction of the anaerobic power of your quadriceps muscles (in kgm/s).

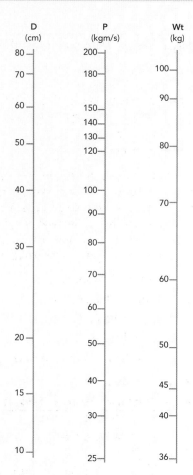

	D (cm)	P (kgm/s)	Wt (kg)

Figure 7.2: Lewis nomogram

Rating	Males (kgm/s)	Females (kgm/s)
Above average	105+	90+
Average	95	80
Below average	<85	<70

Table 7.14: Interpretation of anaerobic power results from the vertical jump test

Anaerobic power – Wingate cycle test

The Wingate cycle test predicts the anaerobic power of the quadriceps muscle groups using a 30 second all-out maximal sprint on a mechanically-braked cycle ergometer (for example, Monark 824E). The test was developed by scientists at the Wingate Institute in Israel.

1. Informed consent is required before participating in this arduous test.

2. You will need to wear a heart rate monitor for the warm-up. You need to cycle for between 2 and 4 minutes at an intensity sufficient to cause the heart to beat at 150–160 bpm. During the warm-up include two or three all-out bursts of cycling for 4–8 seconds each.

3. Following the warm-up you should rest for approximately 3 to 5 minutes during which you can carry out stretching of the major muscle groups.

4. Measure your body weight in kg. To calculate the weight to add to the cycle ergometer basket, use this formula:

   weight to add to basket = body weight x 0.075 minus 1 kg for the basket weight
   = weight to add to basket

- On command from the timer, pedal as fast as possible to overcome the inertia of the flywheel. The weight will then be lowered onto the basket.

- When the final load has been added to the basket, timing will commence. Continue to pedal as fast as possible for 30 seconds.

- An assistant will note the revolutions per minute (RPM) achieved for each 5 second period. This can be noted electronically from the cycle ergometer display.

- The subject will require motivation from peers to help them continue to sprint on the bike as fast as possible and keep the pedals turning for the full 30 seconds of the test.

- For cool down, and to minimise the risk of fainting, continue cycling with no load on the basket, for 2 to 3 minutes after the test. The subject will need to be given help from assistants to get off the bike and should then, as a precaution, assume the instructed recovery position.

- This is an extremely arduous test, requiring an all-out maximal effort. Tutors should be aware that such effort may cause participants to faint or be sick following the test and should ensure that procedures are in place should this happen.

Case study: Conducting the Wingate cycle test

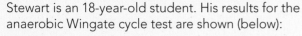

Stewart is an 18-year-old student. His results for the anaerobic Wingate cycle test are shown (below):

Calculation of weight to add to cycle ergometer basket:

Stewart's body weight	= 70 kg
Weight to add to basket	= Body weight x 0.075
	= 70 x 0.075
	= 5.25
Minus 1 kg for basket weight	= 4.25

Revolutions per minute for each 5 second period:

Time (s)	RPM
5	115
10	118
15	118
20	109
25	106
30	105

Calculation of anaerobic power:

anaerobic power (W) = total weight on basket (kg) x revolutions x 11.765

Time (s)	Anaerobic power (w)
5	5.25 x (115/60 x 5) x 11.765 = 592.0 W
10	5.25 x (118/60 x 5) x 11.765 = 607.4 W
15	5.25 x (118/60 x 5) x 11.765 = 607.4 W
20	5.25 x (109/60 x 5) x 11.765 = 561.0 W
25	5.25 x (106/60 x 5) x 11.765 = 545.6 W
30	5.25 x (105/60 x 5) x 11.765 = 540.5 W

Calculation of total revs in 30 seconds:

Time (s)		5s revs
5	115/60 x 5	9.58
10	118/60 x 5	9.83
15	118/60 x 5	9.83
20	109/60 x 5	9.08
25	106/60 x 5	8.83
30	105/60 x 5	8.75
Total revs		55.90
		= 56 (closest rev)

Anaerobic capacity = total revs in 30s x 6m*
(kgm-30s)   x force (kg)

= 56 x 6 x 5.25

= 1764 (kgm-30s)

*This is dependent on the cycle ergometer used. For a Monark cycle ergometer, one revolution of the flywheel is equal to a distance of 6 metres. For a Tunturi cycle ergometer, the flywheel travels through 3 metres for each pedal revolution. Insert the appropriate figure for the type of ergometer used.

Calculation of anaerobic capacity:

Calculation of anaerobic capacity (W)

= kgm-30s/3

= 1764/3

= 588 W (average mean power)

Calculation of power decline:

$$100 \times \frac{(\text{peak anaerobic power} - \text{low anaerobic power})}{\text{peak anaerobic power}}$$

= % fatigue rate

$$= 100 \times \frac{(607.4 - 540.5)}{607.4} = 11.0 \text{ \% fatigue rate}$$

1. Undertake the maximal anaerobic Wingate cycle test.

   From your results, calculate:

   a) peak anaerobic power (W)

   b) anaerobic capacity (W) – your average mean power

   c) your power decline (percentage of fatigue rate).

2. Plot a graph to show your data results. On the Y-axis plot anaerobic power (W) achieved for each 5 second period (plot time in seconds on the X-axis).

3. Show your average mean power (w) by drawing a straight line across your graph intersecting the Y-axis at your power result.

   a) What is your average mean power result (w)?

   b) How do your anaerobic power results compare to those of your peers?

4. A high peak anaerobic power and low fatigue rate indicates an individual who has good anaerobic power. Discuss and compare your results in small groups.

Muscular endurance – press-up test

This test is used to assess the endurance of the muscles of your upper body.

1. Position yourself on a mat, with your hands shoulder width apart and arms fully extended.

2. Next, lower your body until the elbows are at 90 degrees.

3. Return to the starting position, with your arms fully extended.

4. Make sure your push-up action is continuous, with no rests in between.

5. The total number of press-ups is recorded for 1 minute.

Due to reduced upper body strength, females may choose to use a modified press-up technique. The positioning is similar to the standard method, but in the starting position a bent knee position is assumed.

Rating	Males	Females
Excellent	45+	34+
Good	35–44	17–33
Average	20–34	6–16
Poor	<19	<5

Table 7.15: Interpretation of results from the full body press-up test

Rating	Number of reps
Excellent	39+
Good	34–38
Average	17–33
Fair	6–16
Poor	<6

Table 7.16: Interpretation of results from the modified press-up test

📱 Muscular endurance – sit-up test

This test assesses the endurance and development of your abdominal muscles.

1. Lie on a mat with your knees bent, and feet flat on the floor, with your arms folded across your body.

2. Raise yourself up to a 90 degree position and then return to the floor.

3. Your feet can be held by a partner if you wish.

4. The total number of sit-ups is recorded for 1 minute.

Rating	Males	Females
Excellent	49–59	42–54
Good	43–48	36–41
Above average	39–42	32–35
Average	35–38	28–31
Below average	31–34	24–27
Poor	25–30	18–23
Very poor	11–24	3–17

Table 7.17: Interpretation of results from the sit-up test

Body composition – skinfold testing

Skinfold testing can be used to predict percentage of body fat. A relationship exists between subcutaneous, internal fat and body density. Skinfold testing for the prediction of percentage of body fat is based on this relationship. In this section you will be using Durnin and Womersley's (1974) generalised prediction equations to predict your percentage of body fat.

For males and females, skinfolds are taken on the following four sites:

1. **Biceps** – a vertical fold on the anterior surface of the biceps muscle midway between the anterior axillary fold and the antecubital fossa.

2. **Triceps** – a vertical fold on the back midline of the upper arm, over the triceps muscle, halfway between the acromion process (bony process on the top of the shoulder) and olecranon process (bony process on the elbow). The arm should be held freely by the side of the body.

3. **Subscapular** – a diagonal fold taken at a 45 degree angle 1–2 cm below the inferior angle of the scapulae (point of the shoulder blade).

4. **Suprailiac** – a diagonal fold above the crest of the ilium, taken in the anterior axillary line above the iliac crest (just above the hip bone and 2–3 cm forward).

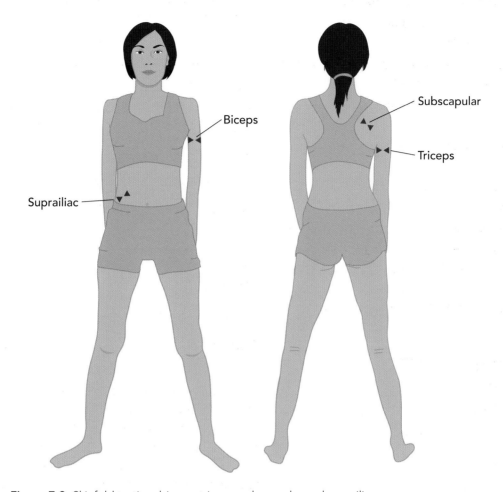

Figure 7.3: Skinfold testing: biceps, triceps, subscapular and suprailiac

Following a standard method will help ensure your results are valid. You will need skinfold calipers (such as Harpenden or Slimguide) to take the skinfolds as well as a tape measure and pen to mark each site. Work in pairs or small groups for skinfold testing.

1. Measurements should be taken on dry skin on the right side of the body. Exceptions to this would be if the participant has a tattoo or deformity on the site location, which means the left side of the body would need to be used.

2. The participant should keep their muscles relaxed during the test.

3. Mark each skinfold site with a pen and use a tape measure to find the midpoints.

4. Grasp the skinfold firmly between your thumb and index finger and gently pull away from the body. The skinfold should be grasped about 1 cm away from the site marked.

5. Place the skinfold calipers perpendicular to the fold, on the site marked, with the dial facing upwards.

6. Maintaining your grasp, place the calipers midway between the base and tip of the skinfold and allow the calipers to be fully released so that full tension is placed on the skinfold.

7. Read the dial of the skinfold calipers to the nearest 0.5 mm, 2 seconds after you have released the calipers. Make sure you continue to grasp the skinfold throughout testing.

8. Take a minimum of two measurements at each site. If repeated tests vary by more than 1 mm, repeat the measurement.

9. If consecutive measurements become smaller, this means that the fat is being compressed, and will result in inaccurate results. If this happens, go to another site and then come back to the site to be tested later.

10. Make sure you record each measurement as it is taken.
11. The final value is the average of the two readings (mm).

Calculation of percentage of body fat

1. Add up the results for the four skinfolds (mm).
2. Insert them into the body density calculation (see Table 7.18) according to gender:

   males (16–19 years)
   body density (d)
   = 1.162 – [(0.063) ($\sum$ log of four × skinfolds)]

females (16–19 years)
body density (d)
= 1.1549 – [(0.0678) ($\sum$ log of four × skinfolds)]

3. Next, complete the following calculation for the prediction of percentage of body fat:

$$\left[\frac{(4.57)}{d} - 4.142\right] \times 100 = \% \text{ body fat}$$

Rating	Males % body fat (16–29 years)	Females % body fat 16–29 years
Very low fat	<7	<13
Slim	7–12	13–20
Acceptable	13–17	21–25
Overweight	18–28	26–32
Obese	28+	32+

Table 7.18: Interpretation of percentage of body fat results

Hydrodensitometry or underwater weighing is often thought of as the best method for the prediction of percentage of body fat. Many universities have underwater weighing tanks so that learners can undertake practical assessments to predict their percentage of body fat.

- Use the Internet or textbooks to research the rationale behind hydrodensitometry.
- Find out about the specialist equipment needed, what the test method involves and how it works.

Body composition – bioelectrical impedance analysis (BIA)

Bioelectrical impedance analysis (BIA) is a method used to predict the percentage of body fat of an individual. A BIA machine is required to conduct the test (for example, Bodystat 1500). The method is based on the fact that fat free mass in the body (muscle, bone, connective tissues) conducts electricity, whereas fat mass does not. Therefore, the higher the resistance to a weak electrical current (bioelectrical impedance), the higher the percentage of body fat of the individual.

1. Hydration levels can affect validity of test results. To ensure the test is valid, the subject should not:
   - exercise for 12 hours prior to the test
   - drink or eat within 4 hours of the test
   - drink caffeine prior to the test.
2. The subject should urinate 15 to 30 minutes before conducting the test.
3. The subject should lie down and remove their right sock and shoe.
4. Place the BIA electrodes on the right wrist, right hand, right ankle and right foot.
5. Attach the cable leads (crocodile clips) to the exposed tabs on the electrodes.
6. Enter data into the BIA machine (for example, the subject's age, gender, height, weight and activity level).
7. The test only takes a few seconds. The subject should lie still as the weak electrical current is passed through their body.
8. The percentage of body fat test result will be shown on the LCD display of the BIA machine.

1.2 Fitness tests: advantages and disadvantages

The best way to understand the advantages and disadvantages of different fitness tests is to gain first-hand experience by direct participation. By participating in fitness tests yourself you can gain knowledge and understanding of:

- why some tests might not be as valid and reliable as others
- how factors which affect test **reliability** and **validity** can be controlled or reduced
- other test advantages and disadvantages such as cost, time, equipment, practicality and the skill level required of the person administering the test
- the implications of the test advantages/disadvantages for test selection and administration.

Key terms

Reliability – the consistency and repeatability of the results obtained. That is, the ability to carry out the same test method and expect the same results.

Validity – the accuracy of the results. This means whether the results obtained are a true reflection of what you are actually trying to measure.

Maximal versus submaximal fitness tests

One of the main considerations is whether the fitness test you have conducted is maximal or submaximal.

The advantages and disadvantages of maximal fitness testing

A maximal fitness test requires the individual to make an 'all-out' effort with measurements taken at the all-out effort stage. Examples include maximal treadmill tests for the measurement of maximum oxygen consumption.

If the individual is able to reach their true maximum, then results obtained are more valid compared to submaximal testing, because physiological data is

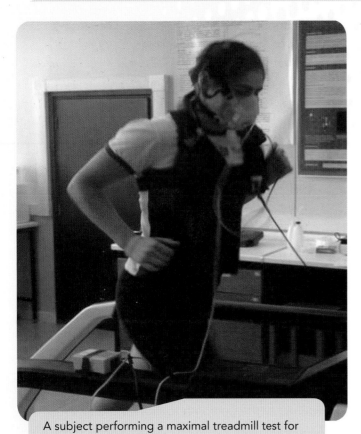

A subject performing a maximal treadmill test for measurement of maximum oxygen uptake. Could you reach your VO$_2$ max?

actually *measured* as opposed to 'predicted'. However, there can be difficulty in ensuring the individual is exerting maximal effort, and there are issues around motivating individuals to achieve their true maximum. There is the possibility of overexertion with some individuals and their more 'risky' nature means maximal tests are not appropriate for everybody. Maximal testing requires informed consent.

The advantages and disadvantages of submaximal fitness testing

A submaximal fitness test means that the individual performs the test at less than their maximal effort. Submaximal fitness tests require projection or extrapolation of data to estimate the individual's maximal capacity. Examples include the Astrand cycle ergometer test of aerobic fitness. Submaximal fitness tests are less 'risky' in nature and can be applied to a wider variety of populations. However, results only give a prediction, not a measurement. The extrapolation

of data is made to an unknown maximum and small inaccuracies or uncontrolled variables can result in errors in prediction of the maximum because these are magnified by the process of extrapolation.

Now we'll go on to consider some of the advantages and disadvantages of fitness tests you will be familiar with.

Flexibility: sit and reach test – advantages and disadvantages

Advantages

- It is easy to complete – can use a bench and ruler if a sit and reach box is unavailable.
- The test is quick to administer.
- Published tables of norms are available.
- Modified tests exist which take into account the distance between the end of the fingers and the sit and reach box.

Disadvantages

- The test is assumed to be valid for all populations. However, research by Jackson and Baker (1986) reported that sit and reach results for 13–15-year-old girls were only moderately related to hamstring flexibility and poorly related with measures of total, upper and lower back flexibility. They concluded that the sit and reach test does not validly assess lower back flexibility in teenage girls.
- There is the potential for inconsistency of test methods. Has a warm-up been allowed or not?
- Performance may be influenced by length or width of the body segments (Wear, 1963).

Aerobic endurance: step test – advantages and disadvantages

Advantages

- There is minimal cost.
- It can test large numbers of subjects at once.
- There is no need for calibration of equipment.
- It provides good predictions of aerobic endurance as long as subjects keep good time with the metronome.

Disadvantages

- Reliability and validity of the test depend on the correct stepping technique being used, which can be difficult for the subject to maintain.
- The stepping technique can be affected by length and proportion of the subject's legs.
- Any changes in technique can affect the work done by the subject. For example, not keeping up with the set stepping rate (dictated by a metronome), not maintaining the correct stepping rate throughout the test, not achieving correct leg extension as the subject steps up onto the bench.
- Efficiency of stepping may vary due to differences in hip angles and leg length when using a fixed bench height for all subjects.
- It is difficult to make ancillary measurements.
- It is difficult to accurately record your own radial pulse for fitness prediction.
- It is not suitable for certain populations, for example, the elderly.
- There is a risk of tripping if the step test is maximal (as exhaustion approaches).
- Well-motivated subjects are needed for maximal testing.
- The specificity of the step test favours sports performers who make endurance demands of the leg muscle groups (for example, cyclists and runners).

Accuracy of the step test: how can results be improved?

With any fitness test you need to be aware of **test variables** and how these can be controlled or reduced. Taking the step test as an example, test validity will improve if subjects have the opportunity to practise the stepping technique before the data is collected. This way, you will be able to make sure and check that the subject is aware of the correct timings and technique for stepping, i.e. full leg extension is achieved. The subject will also be able to practise locating and taking their radial pulse.

Key term

Test variable – this is any factor which could affect the validity and/or reliability of fitness test results.

Many of the published step tests that you will be familiar with use a standard bench height, which is sometimes different for males and females. However, the ideal would be for step test methods to alter the bench height to suit individual differences in the hip angles or leg length of subjects, thus ensuring efficiency of stepping movement.

Aerobic endurance: cycle ergometry tests – advantages and disadvantages

Advantages

- They can test a wider variety of populations.
- The subject is seated, which helps with taking ancillary measurements (for example, blood pressure).
- The digital display of the ergometer helps ensure correct revs/minute.
- There is a conversion of external work rate into approximate power demand.
- The seat height can be altered to suit individual differences in leg length to ensure efficiency of movement.

Disadvantages

- Subjects are tested individually, so it can be time-consuming.
- Loadings must be adjusted for differences of body mass.
- The equipment is expensive.
- There is overloading of the quadriceps at higher intensities of effort. Maximum effort can be prevented by local muscular fatigue rather than a general exhaustion of the cardiorespiratory system.
- There can be difficulty in dismounting from the ergometer in an emergency.
- The tests favour cyclists.

Cycle ergometry fitness tests are considered more accurate than stepping tests. This is because fewer variables need to be controlled than in step tests, for example, the pedalling rate is more accurately controlled than the stepping rate. The pedalling rate is shown on the digital display of the ergometer, and a metronome can also be used to help the subject with revs/minute timing. The cycle ergometer seat height can be altered according to the leg length of the subject, whereas for step tests a standard bench height is used. Therefore cycle ergometry tests enable subjects to perform more efficiently, leading to improved accuracy of test results.

The preferred method for maximal aerobic endurance testing is a graded treadmill test; higher values are obtained when a large muscle mass is involved in testing, resulting in improved accuracy of results. Individuals are not affected by local muscular fatigue; and provided they are well motivated, they can reach their maximal exhaustion of the cardiorespiratory system. During graded treadmill testing, VO_2 max is reached when:

- the individual reports a Rating of Perceived Exertion (RPE) of 20 (Borg 6-20 RPE scale)
- there is less than 150 ml/min increase between exercise workloads
- blood lactate is greater than 8 mmol/l.

Activity: Fitness test – advantages and disadvantages

Work in pairs or small groups. Choose a fitness test that you are familiar with, for example, the multi-stage fitness test.

- List the test advantages and disadvantages. Think about practicality, cost, ease of administration and potential issues like keeping in time/turning with the bleeps and motivation levels of subjects.
- Discuss the advantages and disadvantages you have listed and how test variables could be controlled or reduced.

Assessment activity 7.1

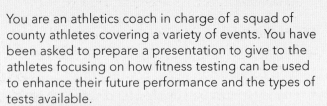 **P1** **M1** **BTEC**

You are an athletics coach in charge of a squad of county athletes covering a variety of events. You have been asked to prepare a presentation to give to the athletes focusing on how fitness testing can be used to enhance their future performance and the types of tests available.

1. Describe one test for each component of physical fitness, including advantages and disadvantages. **P1**
2. Explain the advantages and disadvantages of one fitness test for each component of physical fitness. **M1**

Grading tips

P1 To attain P1 provide a clear description of each test that includes all the relevant features, together with their advantages and disadvantages. Think of your description as if you are 'painting a picture with words'.

M1 To attain M1 provide details and give reasons and/or evidence to clearly support the advantages and disadvantages you have put forward. Draw examples from personal experience of participation or observing others performing the tests. Use research evidence to support the points you are making. Don't forget to cite references in text as well as in an overall references section to support your work.

PLTS

Describing and explaining the fitness tests for each component of physical fitness and preparing a presentation on the topic will develop your skills as an **independent enquirer**.

Functional skills

When you are discussing how to test each component of physical fitness, you can provide evidence of your **English** skills.

2. Be able to use health screening techniques

2.1 Health screening procedures

Questionnaires

Health screening involves collecting information regarding an individual's current physical activity levels, dietary habits and lifestyle. Health screening questionnaires can be used to collect such information. Questionnaire results identify those who have risk factors of heart disease and highlight where lifestyle changes are required.

Health screening questionnaires are likely to contain specific questions relating to the following areas:

- physical activity history
- current physical activity levels
- injuries
- personal training goals
- alcohol consumption
- smoking
- stress levels
- dietary habits.

Client consultation

During the screening you'll need to ensure the individual feels at ease – develop a rapport, keep them fully informed and show discretion. Remember that it is just as important to listen to your client as it is to ask questions. Be aware of your body language and the non-verbal messages you are giving out. Finally, you must clearly communicate your findings and the implications of these.

Client confidentiality

During the health screening process, a client will provide you with information relating to their personal health and fitness. In addition to this, you will also collect data and information from the health monitoring tests and administration of fitness tests.

Such personal data and information must be treated with the utmost care. It is your responsibility to maintain client confidentiality by ensuring that:

- such records are used and viewed only by yourself as the fitness instructor, and your supervisor/assessor (your clients should be made aware of this)
- your records are kept securely – they must not, at any time, be left in a public place and electronic records should be password protected
- the contents of the health screening and fitness assessment are not discussed in public with anyone else including your family or friends.

> **Remember**
>
> Medical and health records are confidential documents which contain sensitive data. It is your responsibility to ensure you maintain client confidentiality at all times when you have direct knowledge of, and/or access to, information which is confidential. Disclosing information about your client(s) to anyone who does not require it is a breach of their confidentiality.

Informed consent

Before administering any health or fitness tests, the individual to be tested should complete an informed consent form. This is documented evidence that shows that you have provided the individual with all the necessary information to undertake the tests. The individual to be tested will need to complete an informed consent form to confirm that they:

- are able to follow the test methods
- know exactly what is required of them during testing
- have fully consented to their participation in the fitness tests

Conducting health screening: what checks will you carry out?

- know that they are able to ask you any questions relating to the tests
- understand that they can withdraw their consent at any time.

The consent form should be signed and dated by:
- the individual to be tested (the participant)
- their parents/guardians (if under 18)
- you (the tester)
- a witness (usually your tutor/assessor).

Coronary heart disease risk factors

The five major coronary risk factors are:

1. high blood pressure (hypertension), where on at least two separate occasions:
   - systolic blood pressure is higher than 160 mmHg
   - diastolic blood pressure is higher than 100 mmHg
2. cholesterol is higher than 6.20 mmol/l
3. cigarette smoking
4. diabetes mellitus
5. a family history of coronary heart disease in parents or siblings prior to age 55 years.

Medical referral

Questionnaire results and results from health monitoring tests can be used to identify risk factors and those individuals requiring referral to their GP. Factors for medical referral include: heart conditions, chest pain, breathlessness, high blood pressure (hypertension), diabetes mellitus, pregnancy and bone or joint problems.

2.2 Health monitoring tests

Health monitoring tests include heart rate, blood pressure, lung function, waist-to-hip ratio and body mass index (BMI).

Heart rate (HR)

This can be measured manually via the radial artery in the wrist or via a digital blood pressure monitor. Heart rate is measured in beats per minute (bpm).

The average resting heart rate for a male is 68 bpm and for a female is 72 bpm. Males generally have larger hearts than females, which can pump a greater volume of oxygenated blood around the body, thus the average resting heart rate for a male is lower compared to females. A high resting heart rate (tachycardia) is >100 bpm.

Blood pressure (BP)

Blood pressure can be measured using a digital blood pressure monitor, which provides a reading of blood pressure as: **systolic blood pressure/diastolic blood pressure** (mmHg).

Key terms

Blood pressure – can be measured using a digital blood pressure monitor, which provides a reading of blood pressure in mmHg (millimetres of mercury).

Systolic blood pressure – the highest pressure within the bloodstream, which occurs during each beat when the heart is in systole (contracting).

Diastolic blood pressure – the lowest pressure in the bloodstream, which occurs between beats when the heart is in diastole (relaxing, filling with blood).

Rating	Blood pressure reading (mmHg)
Average (desirable)	120/80 mmHg
Above average (borderline)	140/90 mmHg
High blood pressure (hypertension)	160/100 mmHg*

* An individual should seek advice from their GP if BP is >160/100 mmHg on at least two separate occasions.

Table 7.19: An interpretation of BP results

Lung function

Spirometry can be used to monitor health and to check if an individual is suffering from chest or lung problems. A spirometer is a hand-held device which can be used to measure the volume of air that you can blow out against time, which provides information about your lung function. To undertake spirometry:

- enter your age, gender and height into the spirometer
- wearing a noseclip, take a deep breath in and then tightly seal your lips around the mouthpiece of the spirometer
- blow out as hard and fast as you can until your lungs are completely empty
- repeat the spirometry test again to ensure reliability of results.

The spirometer will compare and interpret your results according to the values predicted for your age, gender and height. Spirometry can be used to obtain various readings including the following.

- **Forced Vital Capacity (FVC):** the total volume of air that you can expire following maximal inspiration
- **Forced Expiratory Volume in one second (FEV1):** the total volume of air that you can expire within one second
- **Ratio of FEV1 to FVC (FEV1/FVC or FEV%):** from the total volume of air that you can expire, this is the proportion that you are able to blow out in one second

- **Peak Expiratory Flow (PEF):** the maximal speed (flow) resulting from a maximally forced expiration following maximal inspiration.

Spirometry can help diagnose and monitor conditions such as chronic obstructive pulmonary disease (COPD), asthma and pulmonary fibrosis. A narrowing of the airways reduces the amount of air that you are able to blow out. In general, you are likely to be suffering from a disease which causes narrowing of the airways if:

- your FEV1 is less than 80 per cent of the predicted value according to your age, gender and height
- your FEV1/FVC ratio is 0.7 or less.

Waist-to-hip ratio

This ratio can determine levels of obesity and those at risk of heart disease. Use a tape measure placed firmly against the individual's skin to measure the waist circumference in centimetres at the narrowest level of the torso. Next, measure the individual's hips by placing the tape measure at the maximum circumference of the buttocks. Make sure the tape measure is level when taking measurements. Divide the waist measurement (cm) by the hip measurement (cm) to obtain the waist-to-hip ratio.

Body Mass Index (BMI)

BMI is a measure of body composition in kg/m^2 and is used to determine to what degree someone is overweight. It is only an estimate, as the test does not take into account the individual's frame size or muscle mass. Research shows a significant relationship between high BMI and incidence of cardiovascular disease, and high BMI and diabetes.

To obtain BMI, measure the individual's body weight (kg) and height in metres, and calculate the BMI as: kg/m^2.

For women, a desirable BMI is 21–23 kg/m^2. For men, a desirable BMI is 22–24 kg/m^2. The risk of cardiovascular disease increases sharply at a BMI of 27.8 kg/m^2 for men and 27.3 kg/m^2 for women.

Assessment activity 7.2

You have been asked to undertake health screening procedures and safely administer four different health monitoring tests for two contrasting individuals. They need to be quite different in terms of their fitness levels and lifestyles. For example, you could ask a peer (someone who trains and competes regularly) and you could ask an older individual (perhaps a relative who doesn't participate in regular physical activity).

1. Prepare an appropriate health screening questionnaire. **P2**

2. Devise and use appropriate health screening procedures for two contrasting individuals. **P3**

3. Safely administer, and interpret the results of, four different health monitoring tests for the two contrasting individuals. **P4**

4. Describe the strengths and areas for improvement for the two individuals using information from their health screening questionnaires and health monitoring tests. **M2**

5. Evaluate the health screening questionnaires and health monitoring test results and provide recommendations for lifestyle improvements. **D1**

Grading tips

P2 To attain P2 think about the range of topics you need to cover in your questionnaire. Consider different ways of presenting your questionnaire and the types of question you could use, for example, open/closed.

P3 To attain P3 the individuals selected need to be *contrasting*. For example, you could choose to test an elite/county level sports performer and an individual who doesn't train. Your two clients will need to complete your self-designed health screening questionnaire and informed consent forms. You will need to show evidence of conducting the client consultation, including an awareness of coronary heart disease risk factors and the need for medical referral.

P4 To attain P4 you need to safely administer four different health monitoring tests for your two contrasting individuals and interpret

their results against normative published data, defining what their results mean.

M2 To attain M2 use the results from the clients' health screening questionnaires and health monitoring tests in order to describe their strengths and areas for improvement. In doing this you should compare their responses from the screening questionnaires and results from the health monitoring tests against normative published data and accepted health ranges.

D1 To attain D1 you need to evaluate their responses to the screening questionnaires and results from the health monitoring tests conducted, reviewing the information and then bringing it together to form your conclusions for each client. You will need to provide valid recommendations of how each client can improve their lifestyle, giving evidence for your views or statements.

PLTS

During the health screening, if you identify questions to answer and problems to resolve you can develop your skills as an **independent enquirer**. If you generate ideas, explore possibilities and ask questions to extend your thinking you can develop skills as a **creative thinker**.

Functional skills

By researching and preparing a health screening questionnaire, and recording the results of health monitoring tests, you could provide evidence of your **ICT** skills. By interpreting the results of your health monitoring tests, you can develop your **Mathematics** and **English** skills.

3. Be able to administer appropriate fitness tests

In this section you'll need to select and safely administer six different fitness tests for a chosen individual, recording the findings.

3.1 Fitness tests and their administration

You need to develop and apply your skills in assessing fitness to be able to select and administer, in a safe and effective manner, six different fitness tests for a chosen individual. Refer back to the fitness tests covered on pages 182–200 of this unit.

You must be able to successfully prepare for six different tests. In your preparation you will need a clear understanding and justification of why you have selected these particular tests for your chosen individual, together with an understanding of the validity, reliability and practicality issues of the tests that you are to administer (refer back to Section 1.2 on pages 197–200). It is important that you have a sound understanding of the purpose of each test and be fully confident in how you will administer it.

Following fitness testing, when you give feedback to the individual, you will be able to apply your knowledge and experience to describe what their fitness results mean, interpreting their levels of fitness against normative published data (population norms). This will provide the individual with baseline fitness measures from which you can put forward recommendations and suggestions for future activities and/or training methods which will help them to improve their fitness levels.

> **Remember**
>
> Before you administer any fitness test, it is extremely important that pre-test procedures are followed.

Pre-test procedures

As previously stated, before administering any fitness tests, the individual to be tested should complete an informed consent form (refer back to page 184).

Prior to testing, equipment should be checked carefully. It is also essential that you calibrate any equipment you will be using. This means checking (and if necessary adjusting) the accuracy of fitness testing equipment before it is used by comparing it to a recognised standard. If equipment isn't correctly calibrated it could lead to inaccurate (invalid) results.

> **Activity: Informed consent**
>
> Use the Internet to find examples of informed consent forms. Following the guidelines outlined (see Section 2.1 on pages 201–202), design your own informed consent form that is appropriate for the fitness tests you have selected to administer for the individual.

Test sequences and protocols

To conduct a fitness assessment and administer fitness tests in a professional, safe and valid manner, you need to ensure that you are fully familiar with the test procedures and protocols. This means that you have had sufficient time to practise the administration of each fitness test method, and how to collect and interpret data results before you go on to administer the tests for an individual.

> **Remember**
>
> - For effective administration of fitness tests you need to be well practised and very familiar with the test methods. If you are well rehearsed in techniques, your results are more likely to be valid and reliable.
> - Good planning will help you to feel more confident in administering fitness tests, particularly if you are administering tests to an individual you don't know.
> - You will need to use published data tables to interpret results and give feedback to the individual.
> - Practising test procedures and protocols will give you more experience in how to interpret results obtained. Results should be interpreted in a valid, effective and appropriate manner.

Recording test results

You'll need to be well planned and organised throughout the administration of the fitness tests. Use an appropriate data collection sheet to record the individual's results as you go along (see Figure 7.4). Ideally, for reliability of results, all fitness tests selected should be repeated. However, owing to availability of time this may not be possible, and you may need to take this factor into account when giving feedback to the individual.

Use the correct units of measurement for the fitness tests you have chosen to administer. For some fitness tests you may need to use tables to process raw data before you can interpret what the test results mean and provide feedback to the individual. For example, the multi-stage fitness test result is recorded as the level and shuttle achieved. Use a conversion table to look up the predicted aerobic fitness level (VO$_2$ max,

ml/kg/min) for the level and shuttle obtained (for example, see Table 7.5 on page 185). You can then provide feedback to the individual on their VO$_2$ max result, and by using a published data table you can let them know their fitness rating and what this means (for example, see Table 7.6 on page 186).

Reasons to terminate a fitness test

Individuals should be closely monitored while they are undertaking fitness tests. Reasons to terminate a test include your subject:

- requesting to stop the fitness test
- reporting chest pain
- experiencing severe breathlessness, wheezing
- showing signs of poor circulation, for example, pale, cold clammy skin
- showing signs of poor coordination, confusion and/or dizziness.

Administering fitness tests – recording test results

Name:

Age (yrs/mths):

Height (m):

Weight (kg):

Body mass index (BMI kg/m²):

Informed consent form completed (*insert date*):

Fitness component	Fitness test [insert 6 different fitness tests]	T1	T2	Av. result	Units	Interpretation of test results (rating)
Flexibility	Sit and reach				cm	
Strength	Handgrip dynamometer				kg	
		Result				
Aerobic endurance	1.5 mile run test				ml/kg/min	
Speed	35 metre sprint				s	
Muscular endurance	1 minute sit-up				Number of reps	
Body composition	Bioelectrical impedance analysis (BIA)				% body fat	

Figure 7.4: A fitness testing data collection sheet

Assessment activity 7.3

You need to conduct a fitness assessment and administer fitness tests to an individual. You could use one of your subjects from Assessment activity 7.2.

1. Select and safely administer six different fitness tests for a selected individual recording the findings. **P5**

2. Justify the selection of fitness tests commenting on suitability, reliability, validity and practicality. **M3**

Grading tips

P5 To attain P5 ensure you have documented evidence of how you have administered the tests, for example, that you have followed pre-test procedures, have completed informed consent form(s), have used disclaimers where appropriate etc. You will also need to show evidence of documenting results, e.g. see Figure 7.4 on page 206.

M3 To attain M3, in your feedback to the individual, justify why you selected the fitness tests you did. Why were these the most appropriate for the individual? In your selection of the fitness tests, did you take into account their goals, needs and general level of fitness? Give reasons or evidence to support your views and how you arrived at these conclusions.

PLTS

If you identify questions to answer and problems to resolve in your selection and safe administration of six different fitness tests for a selected individual, you can develop your skills as an **independent enquirer**.

Functional skills

When conducting the fitness assessment, if you use the Internet to search for published data tables and follow safety and security practices for client confidentiality, you can develop your **ICT** skills. Through the selection and safe administration of six different fitness tests for a selected individual, you can develop your **English** skills. When recording data results, you can develop your skills in **Mathematics**.

4. Be able to interpret the results of fitness tests and provide feedback

4.1 Interpret results against normative data

Data interpretation tables presented earlier in this unit can be used to aid your interpretation of test results against normative data. You can also use published data interpretation tables to compare judgements against data for sports performers and elite athletes. Your choice in selection of data tables for interpretation of fitness test results will depend on your selected individual, their needs and personal goals. However, most individuals will be interested to know how they compare against normative data (population norms).

4.2 Feedback

Having administered six different fitness tests for an individual, you now need to provide feedback to the individual regarding their test results, discussing what they mean and giving your recommendations for future activities or training. Your feedback may be given verbally to the individual, supported by a written copy of their data results and interpretation of their levels of fitness against normative data. You may be asked to adopt the role of a fitness instructor and conduct the fitness assessment as would be expected in a real-life vocational context. Your centre of learning will provide you with advice and guidance on how they would like you to present your assessment evidence.

In your feedback, recap the tests carried out and why these particular tests were appropriate for the individual. Discuss in detail their data results and what these mean in terms of their fitness levels. Complete your feedback by discussing the strengths, areas for improvement and your recommendations for appropriate future activities or training. Give the individual the opportunity to ask questions about your statements or views, and be prepared to justify your reasoning.

Assessment activity 7.4

You now need to provide verbal face-to-face feedback to the individual tested.

1. Following fitness testing, give feedback to a selected individual, describing the test results and interpreting their levels of fitness against normative data. **P6**

2. Compare the fitness test results to normative data and identify strengths and areas for improvement. **M4**

3. Analyse the fitness test results and provide recommendations for appropriate future activities or training. **D2**

Grading tips

P6 To attain P6 interpret and describe the results from the six fitness tests the individual has completed in your verbal feedback to them.

M4 To attain M4 use published data tables to interpret their fitness levels against normative data according to the individual's age and gender. Use the individual's completed data collection form to aid your discussion.

Use data interpretation tables to help make comparisons and verbally highlight their strengths and areas for improvement.

D2 To attain D2, in your analysis, relate the individual's results back to the fitness components tested. Use test results and information collected about the individual to provide your recommendations for appropriate future activities or training and give your reasons for these recommendations.

PLTS

In your feedback to the individual, if you analyse and evaluate information, judging its relevance and value, supporting your conclusions using reasoned arguments and evidence, you can develop your skills as an **independent enquirer**. If you adapt your behaviour to suit different roles and situations, showing fairness and consideration to others, you can develop your skills as a **team worker**. If you assess yourself and others, identifying opportunities and achievements, you can develop your skills as a **reflective learner**.

Functional skills

When you interpret your client's fitness test results, you can show evidence of your **ICT**, **Mathematics** and **English** skills.

Frieda Peterson
Senior fitness and lifestyle coach

Frieda is 21 and works in a private health and fitness centre. She is responsible for: instructing clients in the gym; undertaking health screening and client fitness assessments and designing personal coaching programmes; monitoring and evaluating client progress towards meeting goals and objectives and contributing to the club's programme of promoting lifestyle and health awareness.

'Each day is different depending on my schedule and whether clients require health screening and monitoring tests and/or a fitness assessment.

Individual one-to-one client consultations begin with a comprehensive screening process where the client completes questionnaires covering their medical, physical activity and lifestyle history.

We also look closely at diet. I then carry out health monitoring tests like blood pressure and lung function and give the client feedback on their results and the implications for future health. Health screening is usually followed by an assessment of their fitness. The club has a purpose-built fitness centre where we can carry out several tests for the different components of fitness. I then meet with the client to give feedback on their fitness test results and health monitoring and to discuss and agree their training goals. I then design a personal programme for the client to work to and closely monitor their progress throughout. Every six weeks or so, a client will book in with me for a reassessment of their health and fitness.

My other duties involve organising our internal programme of lifestyle and health awareness. This involves coordinating visits, events and guest speakers covering a range of topics from healthy eating to how to reduce stress levels. Last month a local GP visited and carried out free cholesterol testing for our club members. A lot of people just aren't aware of the damage they can do to their body through poor diet and lack of exercise.

You need good communication skills for this job and to be able to motivate people, develop a rapport and lead by example. I find the job very rewarding. Providing good education helps people to recognise where they may need lifestyle improvement and my role is to help clients to implement positive lifestyle changes.'

Think about it!

- What areas have you covered in this unit that provide you with the knowledge and skills used by a fitness and lifestyle coach?
- What further skills might you need to develop?

Just checking

1. The sit and reach test is an indirect measure of static flexibility. Name two direct measures of static flexibility.

2. Give two advantages and two disadvantages of the 1 repetition maximum bench press test.

3. What is the difference between absolute and relative VO_2 max?

4. Stacey weighs 65 kg. She completes the vertical jump test and achieves a difference of 30 cm between her standing reach and jump height. What is Stacey's predicted anaerobic power (kgm/s)?

5. Skinfold testing for the prediction of percentage of body fat is based on the existence of what relationship?

6. State two factors which affect body fat.

7. Why is it important not to exercise or drink caffeine prior to the bioelectrical impedance analysis test?

8. Why is health screening important?

9. Tom weighs 77 kg and his height is 1.83 m. What is Tom's BMI (kg/m^2) and how would you interpret the result?

10. Becky reaches level 8 shuttle 2 on the multi-stage fitness test. She is 17 years old. Interpret her test result.

edexcel

Assignment tips

- The Internet has a wealth of information on health screening procedures. Check out the different types of health screening questionnaires available to give you some ideas for the design of your own questionnaire.

- Speak to practitioners with experience of conducting health screening procedures. Examples include health fitness instructors, personal trainers and GPs. Check to see whether your local pharmacy conducts health screening and the methods they use.

- Search the Internet for published data interpretation tables for the fitness tests you intend to administer. Having more than one data source for interpretation of test results can help you provide comprehensive and detailed feedback to the individual.

- When administering the six different fitness tests for an individual, you should also consider any sports they participate in. Do they excel in a certain sport? If so, are there sport-specific fitness tests you can administer?

- By employing sport-specific fitness tests the results obtained will be a more accurate reflection of the individual's physiological sporting demands. For example, if the individual is a keen cyclist, you could use cycle ergometer tests to predict their aerobic endurance and anaerobic power. By doing this you will be testing the specific working muscles that the individual uses regularly in their sport, thus leading to greater accuracy of results.

Credit value for each unit: 10

8 & 9 Practical team sports & practical individual sports

The desire to participate in sports continues to grow. People are becoming more aware of the lifelong benefits of a healthy lifestyle, and the legacy of the UK's successful Olympic bid will provide more opportunities for those wanting to take part in sport.

Sport gives individuals an opportunity to push themselves to the limits. This is what motivates them to aim for the perfect performance and achieve the highest accolades. Units 8 and 9 introduce the skills, techniques and tactics required in selected sports. You will have to demonstrate application of these in each of your selected sports. You will also examine the application of the rules of team and individual sports, the methods used to assess sports performance and how to use performance assessments to further develop team or individual performance.

Learning outcomes

After completing this unit you should:

1. know the skills, techniques and tactics required in selected team/individual sports
2. know the rules and regulations of selected team/individual sports
3. be able to assess your own performance in selected team/individual sports
4. be able to assess the performance of others in selected team/individual sports.

211

Unit 8 and Unit 9 Assessment and grading criteria

This table shows you what you must do in order to achieve a pass, merit or distinction grade, and where you can find activities in this book to help you.

To achieve a **pass** grade the evidence must show that the learner is able to:	To achieve a **merit** grade the evidence must show that, in addition to the pass criteria, the learner is able to:	To achieve a **distinction** grade the evidence must show that, in addition to the pass and merit criteria, the learner is able to:
P1 describe skills, techniques and tactics required in two different team/individual sports **Assessment activity 8.1 page 220** **Assessment activity 9.1, page 221**	**M1** explain skills, techniques and tactics required in two different team/individual sports **Assessment activity 8.1, page 220** **Assessment activity 9.1, page 221**	
P2 describe the rules and regulations of two different team/individual sports, and apply them to three different situations for each sport **Assessment activity 8.2, page 230** **Assessment activity 9.2, page 230**	**M2** explain the application of the rules and regulations of two different team/individual sports, in three different situations for each sport **Assessment activity 8.2, page 230** **Assessment activity 9.2, page 230**	
P3 demonstrate appropriate skills, techniques and tactics in two different team/individual sports **Assessment activity 8.1, page 220** **Assessment activity 9.1, page 221**		
P4 carry out a self-analysis using two different methods of assessment identifying strengths and areas for improvement in two different team/individual sports **Assessment activity 8.3, page 239** **Assessment activity 9.3, page 241**	**M3** explain identified strengths and areas for improvement in two different team/individual sports, and make suggestions relating to personal development **Assessment activity 8.3, page 239** **Assessment activity 9.3, page 241**	**D1** analyse identified strengths and areas for improvement in two different team/individual sports, and justify suggestions made **Assessment activity 8.3, page 239** **Assessment activity 9.3, page 241**
P5 carry out a performance analysis using two different methods of assessment, identifying strengths and areas for improvement in the development of a team/an individual in a team/an individual sport **Assessment activity 8.4, page 240** **Assessment activity 9.4, page 242**	**M4** explain identified strengths and areas for improvement in the development of a team/an individual in a team/an individual sport, and make suggestions relating to development of a team/an individual **Assessment activity 8.4, page 240** **Assessment activity 9.4, page 242**	**D2** analyse identified strengths and areas for improvement in the development of a team/an individual in a team/an individual sport, and justify suggestions made **Assessment activity 8.4, page 240** **Assessment activity 9.4, page 242**

How you will be assessed

Your assessment for each of these two units can be in the form of:

- video showing you applying the appropriate rules, skills, techniques and tactics for selected team or individual sports
- logbooks with records of your achievements and development in each practical team or individual session
- observation records of your performance as a player in selected team or individual sports
- written summaries of the rules, regulations and scoring systems for selected team or individual sports
- written peer- and self-analysis and assessments of your performance in selected team or individual sports
- video showing analysis and assessments.

Team sports: Tom Dawson, 22-year-old schoolteacher

I completed a BTEC National Diploma before gaining a degree in Sports Coaching at university. At school I loved playing sport, and through completing this unit I learned more about the application of the rules and the techniques required to play a sport. This unit gave me a greater appreciation of development, and the things I learned have been really useful now that I am trying to develop young children every day as a teacher.

Part of my development plan was to obtain as many sports coaching awards and certificates as possible, and I started doing this as soon as the college offered us the opportunity to complete the Football Association Level 1 coaching award. After that I got the bug and now have a whole host of coaching awards, which has really helped with teaching.

I am now teaching this unit to my students and trying to communicate the importance of gaining knowledge of all sports, not just one!

Over to you

- **What team sports did you play at school?**
- **For each one, describe the scoring system and major rules.**

Individual sports: Lisa Stockdale, 18-year-old degree student

I have always wanted to be a sports therapist and I believe that this is because of the enthusiasm passed on to me from my PE teacher at school. I enjoyed the practical part of PE lessons, but used to worry that I would play less after I left school because of the lack of organised sport available.

When I discovered that the BTEC National Diploma in Sport at my local college included practical sports as well as the theoretical units, I was keen to complete this course.

At school, I was never as good at sports as some of the other students, but this course has allowed me to continue to play and to learn more about the skills, techniques and tactics of different individual sports and achieve the highest grade possible, without having to be a fantastic performer.

I play badminton at university and I feel the knowledge that I have gained from the course has given me the confidence to play with high-level performers. I hope to continue playing throughout university and beyond.

Over to you

- Examine the provision for playing individual sports in your locality.
- What clubs are there and who do they provide activities for (e.g. beginners, intermediate, advanced)?
- Discuss why sports participation levels drop when children leave school.

1. Know the skills, techniques and tactics required in selected team/individual sports

Warm-up

Team and individual sports

1. Make a list of team/individual sports.
2. Select two of these and list the required skills and techniques in each one.
3. For each sport, identify five elite performers.
4. List the strategies and tactics used to defend and attack in each of your selected team/individual sports.

The earliest evidence of sport includes *tsu chu*, a form of football played in China over 3,000 years ago, and the Ancient Greek Olympics. The Olympics were revived in 1896, and are now enjoyed by participants and spectators from all over the world.

Sport could be defined as 'an organised competitive physical activity, governed by set rules and regulations'. This definition clearly includes sports such as tennis, badminton, athletics and gymnastics, but leaves others such as snooker, pool and darts open to debate.

The debate will continue to grow as the popularity of these sports increases. Often as a sport grows, an international governing body is established to govern its rules, and this is often a determining factor in its classification.

Key term

Sport – the *Oxford Concise Dictionary* defines sport as 'An activity involving physical exertion and skill in which an individual or team competes against another or others for entertainment.'

Sports can be classified as athletic, gymnastic, and games, and as team and individual sports. They can then be divided further, for example within the 'games' category there are net and wall games, invasion games, striking and fielding games, combat games, target games, track athletics and field athletics.

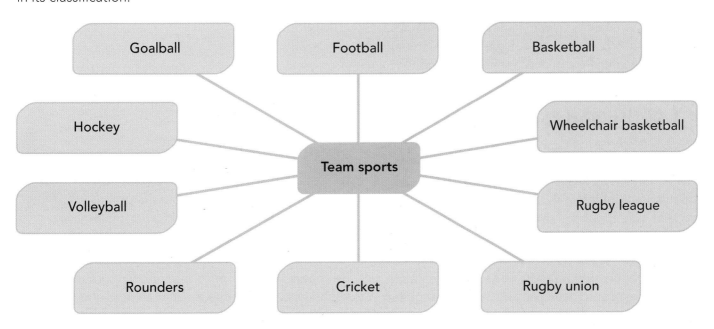

Figure 1: Team sports

215

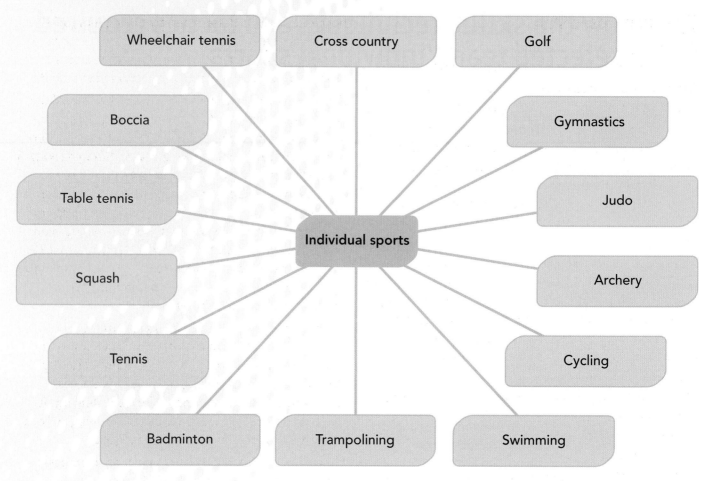

Figure 2: Individual sports

In this unit you will examine both team and individual sports. A team sport involves competition between teams of players with a shared goal of winning. Team sports require athletes to work together to obtain this goal. They are complex, with highly structured rules. An individual sport involves a single athlete competing against other athletes or another single performer. In most individual sports there can only be one winner.

1.1 Skills and techniques

Skills

Skill is defined by Knapp as 'The learned ability to bring about predetermined results with maximum certainty, often with the minimum outlay of time or energy or both.'

A skill in sport is the ability to produce a combination of movements using a variety of muscles and joints to produce a coordinated action. Skills are acquired through learning, and mastered through practice and observation. Athletes develop skills through support and feedback from experienced and knowledgeable coaches and/or athletes. Mastering a skill means being able to continually produce it successfully with little effort.

Skills vary, however some can be transferred from sport to sport. For example, an athlete who masters the skill of catching when receiving a pass in rugby can transfer this skill to other sports that involve catching, such as basketball, cricket or netball.

Activity: Skills transfer

Think of some other sports where skills can be transferred to enhance an athlete's performance.

Skills have been classified into different groups using continuums with opposites at either end and gradually changing characteristics between them.

Open and closed skills

Skills can be classified according to the environment in which they are performed. They may be open or closed.

Open skills are those which the athlete is constantly adapting, according to what is happening around them.

An example of an open skill in a team sport could be when a footballer is dribbling a ball, unaware of the location of all the members of the opposing team. Defenders will challenge the player to try to get possession of the ball. The decisions that the player dribbling the ball will make will depend on the actions of the opponents.

An example of an open skill in an individual sport could be a return in badminton: the receiver is unaware where the shuttlecock will be played by the returnee, so will have to react to their opponent's moves in order to select an appropriate return. The choice of the return shot will also be affected by the position of the opponent on the court.

Closed skills are pre-learned patterns of movements which the athlete can follow with very little reference to the surrounding environment.

An example of a closed skill in a team sport is a rugby player taking a conversion during a match. The movement pattern remains the same every time the player performs the skill.

An example of a closed skill in an individual sport is when an archer takes aim, pulls back the bowstring and releases the arrow towards the target.

We also classify skills by the pace with which the athlete controls the timing of an action. Skills are said to be self-paced, externally paced, or somewhere between the two.

Self-paced skills are those where an athlete controls the timing of the execution of the skill. An example of a self-paced skill in a team sport might be a serve in volleyball: the server decides when to start the action; the timing may depend on the location of the opponents and the readiness of the server.

An example of a self-paced skill in an individual sport might be a golf shot: the golfer determines when to start the swing, and may choose to wait until a gust of wind has dropped prior to taking the shot.

Externally-paced skills are those in which the timing of the skill is determined by what is happening elsewhere. For example, when applying a pass in hockey, the skill is determined by the location of players on the same team and the opposing team. Likewise, a windsurfer will have to alter the angle of his/her sail, depending on the direction of the wind.

For some skills the athlete can control the start of the action, but thereafter the movement takes place at an externally set pace. An example from a team sport would be a goalkeeper making a save during a football game: the goalkeeper will decide when to dive towards the ball, but once the decision is made, the goalkeeper no longer has any control over the speed at which she/he travels towards the ball. An example from an individual sport might be a 10-metre board diver who decides when to start the dive, but having left the board is unable to control the rate at which she/he heads towards the water.

To achieve success in sport, an athlete has to successfully master a range of skills. For example, a basketball player will have to perform the following skills successfully: dribbling, passing, free throws, jump shots, lay-ups, rebounds, blocking, stealing. A tennis player must successfully perform serves, volleys, forehands, backhands, slices and top spins.

Modern technological advances have affected sport just as much as other aspects of our lives.

Fine and gross body involvement

Skills can also be classified by the muscles involved. On this continuum, skills are defined as fine and gross.

Fine skills involve small movements of specific parts of the body. For example, taking a close-range shot at goal in netball will only require the goal shooter and goal attack to move their fingers and wrist to produce the required skill. An individual shooting a rifle on a shooting range will only have to move their trigger finger.

Gross skills involve large muscle groups and movement from the whole body. An example of this form of skill in a team sport is the bowling action in cricket, while an individual example is the javelin throw.

Continuous, discrete or serial skills

Continuous skills are those which have no obvious beginning or end; they can be continued for as long as the performer wishes, with the end of the skill becoming the beginning of the next, for example, running.

A **discrete skill** has a clear beginning and end. The skill can be repeated, but the athlete will start the full action again in a controlled and timely manner. An example of a discrete skill in a team sport is a rugby conversion, while an individual example is a golf putt.

A **serial skill** is a series of discrete skills put together to produce an organised movement. The order of the movement is often important, but the requirements of each part of the skill will require specific development. An example from a team sport is when a footballer dribbles with the ball, steps over it to beat a defender and then shoots at goal at the end of the movement. An example from an individual sport is a gymnastic tumble.

In groups, identify whether a golf shot is:

- an open or closed skill
- a fine or gross skill
- a self-paced or externally paced skill
- a continuous, discrete or serial skill.

List the skills in your own sport and identify which categories they fall into.

An athlete needs to understand the requirements of the skills in their sport and the correct application of each one, and must remember that coaching and practice are key elements in improving their performance and their ability to perform the necessary skills. Even the greatest athletes continually seek to improve their performance, through attending coaching sessions and listening to the advice of their coach.

Footballer Wayne Rooney taking advice from his manager, Alex Ferguson. Listening to advice is a key process in the development of an athlete.

Golfer Sergio Garcia on the follow-through of an approach shot to the green during a competition.

Techniques

A **technique** is the way an athlete performs a skill. In some sports, players use different techniques to produce the same outcome. For example, David Beckham and Cristiano Ronaldo have different techniques when taking direct free kicks, and Andy Murray and Rodger Federer will have different serving techniques.

The most effective way to consider a technique is to consider how the skill can be broken down. For

Key term

Technique – a way of undertaking a particular skill.

example, a long lofted pass can be broken down into its component actions as follows: run-up (preparation stage), alignment to the ball, feet position, body position, contact with the ball and follow-through. An example from an individual sport might be a tennis serve broken down into its component actions: feet position and movement, body position, action of the racket-holding arm, action of the other arm, ball toss, racket swing and follow-through.

Breaking down skills like this develops athletes' understanding of how to improve their application of each skill. The technical elements for each component will be different for each individual, but the components of the skill will remain the same.

Tactics

Tactics are the skills a player uses in any type of sport to be able to win, for example during a hockey or tennis match, each team or player will apply specific tactics and strategies to try to beat and outwit their opponent(s).

While techniques are the way we apply skills in a selected sport, tactics are how we apply skills successfully in competitive situations. The most skilful and talented performer can lose if they do not apply the skills strategically in specific situations.

Tactics in sport are mostly concerned with attacking and defending. Factors that affect tactics include the opposition, the playing conditions and possibly the timing of the game, match, or tournament in a season. Some tactics are determined before the event starts, these often target a player's or a team's weaknesses. Pre-event tactics can include carrying out research on an opposing player or team.

Tactics are often categorised into attacking strategies, used to attack opponents, and defensive strategies, used to prevent opponents scoring points or gaining ground. Each sport has strategies for attacking and defending, for example in a game of netball, one

team may spot a weakness in one of the opposing players and as a team try to exploit this to gain an advantage. On the other hand, if a netball team is suffering because of a particular player in the opposing team, changes may be made to mark that player very closely. Likewise, in a game of tennis a serve could be seen as an attacking shot, but the application of the skill alone cannot guarantee this. The player performing the serve may adjust their serve to disadvantage their opponent.

It can be difficult to coach athletes in applying tactics in a competitive environment. Such knowledge is developed through experience, although coaches try to develop the knowledge and ability to apply appropriate strategies through simulating specific practices. When athletes have experienced specific scenarios, they will be able to react appropriately.

Key term

Tactics – the skills and strategies a player uses in any type of sport to be able to win, for example during a hockey or tennis match, each team or player will apply specific tactics and strategies to try to beat and outwit their opponent(s).

Remember

The main factors affecting the application of tactics in team and individual sports are:

- attacking and defending
- the situation in the game – are you winning or losing?
- your own/team's strengths – what parts of the race/game are you stronger in and which parts of your game are weaker?
- your opponents' strengths and weaknesses.

Assessment activity 8.1: Skills, techniques and tactics of selected team sports

You should now complete a number of practical sessions for at least two team sports. In each session you should be introduced to a skill, technique and tactic for a sport. Your tutor should support you in understanding the correct application of each skill, technique and tactic in each of your selected sports.

1. For each session you participate in, you should complete a practical log or diary in which you describe the skills, techniques and tactics required in two different team sports. **P1**

2. In order to achieve the M1 criteria, in your practical logs you must also explain the skills, techniques and tactics required in two different team sports. **M1**

3. At the end of each session you should also ensure that you demonstrate the appropriate skills, techniques and tactics in at least two different team sports. **P3**

Grading tips

P1 After each session, complete your practical log/diary booklet.

Ensure you make notes regarding the correct application of each skill/technique.

Record your performance in each sport when applying specific defending and attacking strategies.

M1 In your diary, explain how the effective use of each skill can develop performance in a competitive situation.

P3 Record your application of each technique/skill.

Describe the different strategies used within each selected team sport.

PLTS

Researching the skills and techniques appropriate to two team sports will develop your skills as an **independent enquirer**.

Functional skills

When completing a written practical log describing techniques, skills and tactics covered within each practical session for each team sport, you will develop your **English** writing skills.

Assessment activity 9.1: Skills, techniques and tactics of selected individual sports

You should now complete a number of practical sessions for at least two individual sports. In each session you should be introduced to a skill, technique and tactic for a sport. Your tutor should support you in understanding the correct application of each skill, technique and tactic in each of your selected sports.

1. For each session you participate in, you should complete a practical log or diary in which you describe the skills, techniques and tactics required in two different individual sports. **P1**

2. In order to achieve M1 criteria, in your practical logs you must also explain the skills, techniques and tactics required in two different individual sports. **M1**

3. At the end of each session you should also ensure that you demonstrate the appropriate skills, techniques and tactics in at least two different individual sports. **P3**

Grading tips

P1 After each session, complete your practical log/diary booklet.

Ensure you make notes regarding the correct application of each skill/technique.

Record your performance in each sport when applying specific defending and attacking strategies.

M1 In your diary, explain how the effective use of each skill can develop performance in a competitive situation.

P3 Record your application of each technique/skill.

Describe the different strategies used within each selected individual sport to defend and attack.

Ask your tutor to complete a witness statement that records your achievements.

PLTS

Researching the skills and techniques appropriate to two individual sports will develop your skills as an **independent enquirer**.

Functional skills

When completing a written practical log describing techniques, skills and tactics covered within each practical session for each individual sport, you will develop your **English** writing skills.

2. Know the rules and regulations of selected team/individual sports

2.1 Rules and regulations

As mentioned earlier in the unit, a sport must have governed rules and regulations. These are organised and regularly updated by the appropriate governing bodies at the highest level, and are then enforced by officials who represent the governing bodies, both national and international. An athlete needs to be aware of the rules and regulations of any sport in which they participate.

Researching the rules and regulations of their sport can help to make players more competent and better role models for others. The better an athlete understands the rules and regulations of their sport, the more they will appreciate the work of the officials who implement them.

In team sports, the number of participants per team is restricted and in order for a game to be as equal as possible it is usual for each team to have equal numbers of players. For example, in a game of rugby union, each team is allowed to start with a maximum of 15 players; a side starting with fewer players will be at an obvious disadvantage. Each team has to rely not only on the application of skills from individual players but also on teamwork and the correct tactics. The rules, laws and regulations of a sport are set to provide players with standards to adhere to and ensure that they all play fairly.

Some rules do not differ much from sport to sport, for example in rugby league and rugby union the rules regarding losing control of the ball and knocking the ball forward are similar; likewise in table tennis and tennis the rules regarding the number of times a ball is allowed to bounce are similar. However, most sports' rules differ quite considerably. This section will look at some components of sports which remain constant although varying from sport to sport. This includes the start of a competition, scoring or methods of victory, the competitive environment and time. These are examples of rules which are managed and maintained by national governing bodies (NGBs) and international sports federations (ISFs).

The rules and regulations of sports are normally established and governed by the NGB and when appropriate by ISFs.

Team sport	National governing body	International sports federation
Football	The Football Association	Fédération Internationale de Football Association (FIFA)
Rugby Union	The Rugby Football Union	International Rugby Board (IRB)
Rugby League	The Rugby Football League	Rugby League International Federation (RLIF)
Volleyball	English Volleyball Association	Fédération Internationale de Volleyball (FIVB)
Basketball	England Basketball	Fédération Internationale de Basketball (FIBA)
Hockey	England Hockey	International Hockey Federation (FIH)
Cricket	England and Wales Cricket Board	International Cricket Council (ICC)
Rounders	Rounders England	National Rounders Association (NRA)
Netball	England Netball Association	International Federation of Netball Associations (IFNA)
Lacrosse	English Lacrosse Association	Federation of International Lacrosse (FIL)

Table 8.1: The national governing body and international sports federations for ten team sports

Individual sport	National governing body	International sports federation
Boxing	Amateur Boxing Association	International Boxing Association
Badminton	Badminton England	Badminton World Federation
Judo	British Judo Association	International Judo Federation
Gymnastics	British Gymnastics	Fédération Internationale de Gymnastique
Athletics	UK Athletics	International Association of Athletics Federations
Cycling	British Cycling	Union Cycliste Internationale
Rowing	British Rowing (formerly Amateur Rowing Association)	Fédération Internationale des Sociétés d'Aviron
Tennis	Lawn Tennis Association	International Tennis Federation
Sailing	Royal Yachting Association	International Sailing Federation
Table tennis	English Table Tennis Association	International Table Tennis Federation

Table 9.1: The national governing body and international sports federations for ten individual sports

Take it further

Find and research the website and location of each of the national governing bodies listed in the two tables – if your sport is not listed, research its NGB and ISF.

NGBs work closely with international sports federations to ensure that the rules, structure and development of a sport are managed appropriately.

In the past decade a number of sports have undertaken some changes to the rules and regulations to make them more entertaining for spectators. For example, in 1992 FIFA adapted the laws of football regarding allowing a goalkeeper to pick up a ball that has been passed back to them by a player on the same team, and in 2006 the Badminton World Federation adapted its method of scoring to ensure that for every successful shot a point was awarded to the player(s) who completed it. The process of changing the rules requires a trial period; once the ISF agrees that the rule change was appropriate, the change is sanctioned, the rules and laws of the sport amended and the appropriate information passed to the national governing bodies. This information would be expected to be passed on to officials, clubs, coaches, performers, teachers and spectators, and applied in all future competitions and events.

In most sports, rules and regulations are updated regularly, and it is the responsibility of everyone involved in a sport to have a thorough knowledge of these changes.

The rules and laws decided by national governing bodies and international sports federations determine how a sport can be won or lost. All sports have different rules, regulations and laws, however the goal in all sports is to achieve and win.

The assessment that you will carry out as part of Unit 8 will require you to describe the rules for two selected team sports, and for Unit 9, you will be asked to describe the rules of two individual sports. The text below will introduce you to some categories that the rules of your chosen sports will fall into. However, there will be other rules in the sports you describe, that will be fundamental to how they are played. You must ensure that your descriptions include the core rules and regulations.

2.2 The start of a game/race/competition

Any competition has to have a clear beginning and end. In all sports, the start will be administered by an official who will tell the players when to begin. For example, in a game of basketball a player from each of the two teams will compete to gain possession through participating in a tip-off conducted by the umpire. Before a game of cricket, the umpire must allow the captain from one of the two teams to decide who is going to start the batting or the bowling: this is decided by a toss of a coin. The winner of the toss then decides whether their team will bat or bowl first. In a 100-metre sprint race the start is controlled by the starter: the athletes will go when they hear the gun or starting signal. Before a tennis match, the umpire tosses a coin, and the winner of the toss chooses whether to serve first, and which side of the court to start the game.

2.3 Scoring

In some sports, scores are given for achieving a goal, while in others success is assessed by a time or a distance. The points, games, time, or distance determine who wins and who loses.

A cricket team will win a game if they score more runs than the opposing team. There can be restrictions on the number of overs a team may bowl in order to obtain a set number of runs (limited overs cricket) but some matches (test matches) can have unlimited overs but are restricted to a set number of days. In a sailing regatta, the winner will be the team which completes the race in the fastest time. A 100-metre sprinter will win the race by attaining a faster time than all the other athletes in the race. In tennis, on the other hand, a player has to win a certain number of points to win a game, a certain number of games to win a set and a certain number of sets to win the overall match.

Scoring in a team sport e.g. Cricket

Below is an example of how to score runs in cricket. The rules regarding scoring are set by the International Cricket Council (ICC) and governed in England by representatives (officials) of the England and Wales Cricket Board (ECB).

In cricket, teams score by obtaining units called runs. A run is completed when a batsman hits the ball and then runs to the other end of the cricket pitch, getting past the **crease**.

The non-striking batsman also has to run to the opposite end. The batsmen can run as many times as they like, but they may be out if a fielder hits their **stumps** with the ball before the batsmen reach the crease.

Runs can also be scored in the following ways.

- Boundaries are scored when the ball is hit and touches or goes past the outer edge of the field.

Key terms

Crease – in cricket a bowling crease, a popping crease and two return creases are marked in white at each end of the pitch. Bowlers must bowl within these limits and batsmen must remain within the area to ensure they do not get stumped or run out. Within this area the batsman is safe from being run out and stumped.

Stumps – three sticks of equal size around 90 cm tall, with 5 cm separating them. Bails (small pieces of wood) are balanced on top of the stumps.

- Four runs are scored when the batsman hits the ball and it hits the ground before reaching the outer edge of the boundary.
- Six runs are scored when the ball is hit and goes over the boundary without touching the ground.
- No-balls, when the bowler oversteps the crease, bowls in a dangerous manner or incorrectly. A no-ball is worth one run (it can be worth more, depending on the competition rules).
- A wide is scored when the ball goes outside the line of the pitch before coming in line with the batsman. This is also worth one run (it can be worth more, depending on the competition rules).
- A leg bye is scored when the ball hits the batsman but doesn't come into contact with his bat and he then proceeds to run.
- A bye is scored when the batsman runs without the ball having come into contact with the batsman or his bat.

Scoring in an individual sport e.g. Tennis

Below is an example of how a tennis match is scored, following the rules set by International Tennis Federation (ITF) and governed in the UK by the Lawn Tennis Association (LTA).

In tennis, points are awarded as follows:

- **Love** is called when a player has **no** points
- **Fifteen** is called when a player has won **one** point in a game
- **Thirty** is called when a player has won **two** points in a game
- **Forty** is called when a player has won **three** points in a game
- **Game** is called when a player has won a **fourth** point or **winning an advantage** from a deuce – see below.

The server's score is always given first. So for example if a server wins the first point of a game, the score will be **fifteen – love**. However, if the server then loses the next two points the score will be **fifteen – thirty**.

Deuce

During a game, if the players score three points each, instead of being forty-all, the score is said to be deuce. The game then continues until one of the players has won the game by two clear points. If the server wins a point at deuce, the score is advantage to the server, who then needs to win another point. If the server fails to win the next point, the score then returns to deuce.

Set

To win a set, a player must win six games. In an 'advantage' set (these are only used in grand-slam events, when a game goes into a final set), if the score reaches five-all, the player must win the set by two games ahead to win (so a game could go on to 9–7 if appropriate, as when Rafael Nadal beat Roger Federer in the 2008 Wimbledon Championship). In a 'tie-break set' if the score reaches six games-all, a tie break is played.

Match

The maximum number of sets in a match is five for men and three for women. Normally both men's and women's tournaments (apart from major tournaments) are played for the best out of three sets. However, tournament organisers decide on the number of sets per match.

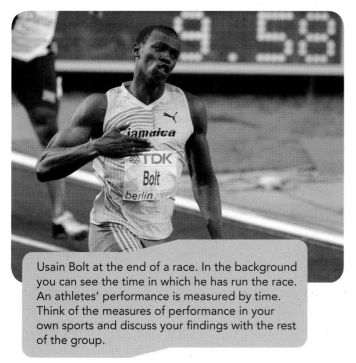

Usain Bolt at the end of a race. In the background you can see the time in which he has run the race. An athletes' performance is measured by time. Think of the measures of performance in your own sports and discuss your findings with the rest of the group.

2.4 Boundaries for participation

The area where sport is played may have many names, such as court, pitch, ring, course or track.

In order for a sport to be governed and the rules to be administered by officials, a set boundary is often required. In most sports this will be a closed environment such as a football pitch, basketball court or rugby pitch in team sports, and tennis court, badminton court or boxing ring in individual sports. In some sports the boundaries are more open, although there are still restrictions regarding the route or course an athlete has to take. For example, a sailing race will have limited boundaries and a specific route, but due to the nature of the event the boundaries are flexible.

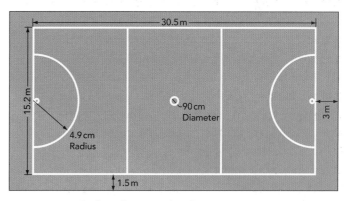

Figure 3: Netball pitch. Example of a competitive environment where athletes are expected to perform within the boundaries as stated by the NGB or ISF

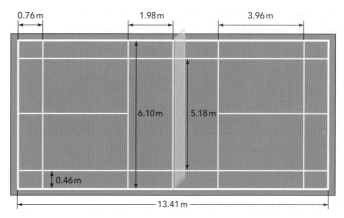

Figure 4: Tennis court. Think of the boundary within which you are confined to participate in your individual sport – draw and label the competitive environment for your sport

2.5 Facilities and equipment

As mentioned earlier in this unit, sports have specific boundaries within which their rules apply. These boundaries remain the same, although some sports can be played both inside and outside them, and the surfaces may differ. For example, association football can be played on either grass or third-generation grass surfaces, and tennis can be played on a variety of surfaces in a variety of facilities (indoor or outdoor). However certain surfaces, such as clay, are generally only suitable for outdoor use, whereas other surfaces are used both indoors and outdoors, e.g. hard court.

Sometimes rules have to be amended to suit the competitive environment, and players and officials must be aware of the rules regarding the use of different facilities. Before a match or event takes place, it is the responsibility of the official in charge to ensure that the facility is suitable. Some sports require a lot of equipment, such as American football, while sports such as volleyball require very little. The equipment must also meet specific rules and regulations.

As technological developments affect sports equipment, governing bodies must approve new products to ensure that they will not give users an unfair advantage. For example, when Adidas introduced its 'Predator' football boots, FIFA initially conducted a number of tests to ensure that they did not give too much of an advantage to any player wearing them. The boots could only be used in competitions after FIFA had approved them. Likewise, when metal woods were first introduced to golf, the Professional Golf Association banned them from all major competitions until testing had been carried out.

2.6 Time

Many team sports limit the length of time a game/match can last. Some include breaks, to give the players a rest and to allow coaches and managers the opportunity to discuss the application of tactics and strategies.

In basketball there are four quarters or two halves; the amount of time per quarter/half depends on the age of the players. If a match ends in a tie, extra time, called 'overtime', is added in order for one of the two teams to win the match.

The rules of some sports demand that there must be a winner at the end of a match, whereas in other sports, such as hockey, if a match ends with an equal score on both sides, a draw will be declared, equal points will be awarded to each team and added to a tally of points. The formulations of these points are governed by the appropriate NGB.

Few individual sports have time constraints, although some combat sports such as boxing and judo do. In boxing, a set number of rounds are agreed (a maximum of twelve is allowed for championship matches, though amateur bouts usually have four). If a bout goes the full number of rounds, the winner will be the boxer who has landed the most punches and obtained the most points (awarded by the officials/adjudicators). Sometimes a winner may be declared before the end of the allocated time; this could be due to a knockout or a stopped fight by the ring or match official.

2.7 Officials

Sports may have referees, umpires, judges, starters or timekeepers, each of whom has clear roles and responsibilities regarding the application of the rules and regulations.

Child protection

At the start of their career, officials will tend to work with younger performers, hence they need to be aware of child protection and the importance of safeguarding children at all times. As well as keeping them free from injury, an official should be aware of the signs and symptoms of child abuse (see Unit 5 Sports coaching page 123) and understand what to do if they notice anything suspicious. Anyone working with children must undergo the appropriate checks, which will be carried out by the organisers of the competition or the league. For more information on child protection in sport, see Unit 5 Sports coaching.

Health and Safety

A key responsibility of an official is managing the safety of everyone involved in a competitive situation. When working with anyone under 18 this responsibility becomes a legal obligation of a duty of care. They should ensure that the playing area meets the required regulations as stated in the sports rule book. Prior to starting a competitive situation, the referee will check the pitch, equipment and players. If they notice any hazards or risks to the participants, they will ensure that appropriate amendments are made. For more information on health and safety in sport, see Unit 3 Assessing risk in sport and Unit 5 Sports coaching.

Insurance

Officials are required to have appropriate insurance cover to participate in physical activity as well as to officiate a sport. An official has complete control over a group of athletes when refereeing/umpiring, so is responsible for their safety while they are under his or her supervision. If an athlete is injured during a competition and the official has not applied the laws/rules of the sport, the official could be considered liable for the accident and could be deemed negligent.

Activity: Health and safety

For the sport you play, list the checks that the head official will carry out before the start of a competitive situation and what sanctions or actions they will carry out if they find specific risks or hazards.

Administration

In some sports, the referee/umpire also has to carry out appropriate administration during and on completion of the competitive situation. They may have to keep a scorecard and submit the completed paperwork to the competition organiser or the NGB on completion of the match. The scorecard is so important in some sports that a designated official is appointed to complete it. For example, in cricket the official in control of completing the scorecard is in their own right part of the officiating team. Similarly in basketball, the table officials are responsible for scoring and recording player and team fouls. In other instances the official may be required to submit a match/game report, possibly because specific rules have been broken and sanctions may have been taken against specific performers.

2.8 Unwritten rules and etiquette

Unwritten rules and **etiquette** are the ethics and values which all athletes are expected to follow, both in training and in competitions. The concept of fair play revolves around equality, not just the desire to succeed. The founder of the modern Olympics, Baron de Coubertin, is believed to be one of the earliest exponents of the concept of sportsmanship; his words express the importance of a moral intention in all sports:

'The most important thing in the Olympic Games is not to win but to take part, just as the most important thing in life is not the triumph but the struggle.'

Key term

Etiquette – the rules that govern how people behave with others – in sport, etiquette is also known as sportsmanship and fair play.

The rules, regulations and laws of sport are written down and provided for all participants and officials, as well as the spectators. They exist to define what constitutes a victory. There are other rules which are not governed but which all sports performers are nevertheless expected to observe.

Sportsmanship is the belief that all athletes should conform to both the written and unwritten rules of their sport. Fair play means treating an opponent as an equal, and adhering to the rules at the same time as striving to win.

Remember

The concept of fair play includes:

- respect towards other players
- respect towards coaches and spectators
- respect towards officials
- playing within the rules of the sport
- equality for all players.

Case study: Unit 8
The unwritten rules in team sports

Paolo di Canio against Everton

In a Premier League clash in 2000, Paolo di Canio (West Ham United) displayed an unexpected but welcome example of sportsmanship. In injury time, Paul Gerrard, the Everton goalkeeper, went down injured in the penalty area. West Ham continued playing and Trevor Sinclair crossed the ball to di Canio in front of an open goal. Instead of tapping it in to score the winner, di Canio caught the ball and signalled that the writhing Gerrard, who it later turned out had only twisted his knee, needed some urgent attention. This earned him a standing ovation from supporters.

1. What unwritten rules do you think were applied in this situation?
2. Can you identify any other acts of sportsmanship that have been applied in team sports recently?
3. Do you think there is a place for sportsmanship and fair play in team sports today?
4. Discuss the phrase 'Winning isn't everything, it's the only thing.' Do you agree, if yes, why? If not, why not?
5. Can you identify five ways people can cheat in team sports?

Case study: Unit 9
The unwritten rules in individual sports

During the 1964 Winter Olympics in Innsbruck, the British two-man bobsled team, led by Tony Nash, completed its first run placing second overall. Then Nash discovered a broken bolt on the sled, which put them out of the competition. At the bottom of the hill, the Italian bobsled driver Eugenio Monti, (who was lying in first place), heard of their plight and, without hesitation, removed the bolt from his own sled and sent it to the British team at the top of the hill. Nash's team fixed their sled and clinched gold. Monti took the bronze and later commented, 'Tony Nash did not win because I gave him a bolt. Tony Nash won because he was the best driver.'

1. What unwritten rules do you think have been applied in this scenario?
2. Can you identify any other acts of sportsmanship which have been applied in individual sports recently?
3. Is there a place for sportsmanship and fair play in individual sports today?
4. Discuss the phrase 'nice guys finish last'. Do you agree, if yes, why? If not, why not?
5. Can you identify five ways people can cheat in individual sports?

2.9 Situations

Every athlete needs to have a good knowledge of how the rules are applied in various situations within their sport. This will give them the necessary understanding of what actions are within the rules and which are illegal. It will also explain any sanctions that may be imposed when they or another player breaks the rules.

A greater understanding of the rules and regulations will increase athletes' appreciation of the officials within the sport and the job they do. All sports demand a high level of respect towards the officials who enforce the rules in competitive situations, and in many sports, any athlete who fails to respect these individuals can expect to have sanctions imposed on them.

Activity: Unit 8 Applying the rules in team sports

For each of the team-sport situations described in the table below, say what sanctions and actions an official would impose.

Sport	Situation
Football	A defender commits a foul on an attacker in the defender's penalty area and prevents a goal-scoring opportunity.
Rugby Union	The fullback knocks the ball on in the goal area.
Cricket	A fielder catches the ball on the boundary, then steps over the boundary with the ball still in his grasp.
Basketball	The final buzzer goes to signal the end of the match and a shot that was made prior to the buzzer is scored.
Volleyball	A team serves and the referee has noticed that the receiving team has one extra player on their team.

Activity: Unit 9 Applying the rules in individual sports

For each of the individual-sport situations described in the table below, say what sanctions and actions an official would impose.

Sport	Situation
Badminton	The shuttlecock lands before the service line when the server is attempting a short serve during a competition.
Athletics	An athlete makes a false start during a 100-metre heat in the Commonwealth Games.
Tennis	One of the players is injured at the change of ends.
Boxing	A boxer hits their opponent below the waistline during an amateur bout.
Swimming	A swimmer makes a false start at the start of a 100-metre butterfly final in the Olympics.

Assessment activity 8.2

Rules and regulations and the correct application of the rules in team sports

In order to support the development of selected team sports, the sports-development department at a local authority is trying to increase young adults' awareness of the rules and regulations of these sports.

1. Select two team sports and describe their rules and regulations in the form of a promotional leaflet.

2. In addition, you should provide an information video which demonstrates how to apply the rules of each of your two chosen sports to three different situations. Ensure that you provide a voiceover describing the correct application of the rules in each situation. **P2**

3. In order to meet the requirements of M2 in your video voiceover, you must explain the application of the rules and regulations of two different team sports in three different situations. **M2**

Grading tips

P2 Summarise the major rules and regulations of two team sports.

Select three situations for each team sport, and describe how the rules are applied in each situation by appropriate officials.

Describe possible sanctions and the specific rules which have been broken.

M2 Explain the actions of each of the officials involved in the decision-making process, including hand signals and methods of communication.

PLTS

Considering how to apply the rules to three different situations for each sport will develop your skills as a **creative thinker**.

Functional skills

When you are searching the Internet for the rules and regulations of selected sports, you will be developing your **ICT** finding and selecting information skills.

Assessment activity 9.2

Rules and regulations and the correct application of the rules in individual sports

In order to support the development of selected sports, a local high school is trying to increase students' awareness of the rules and regulations of some individual sports.

1. Select two individual sports and describe their rules and regulations in the form of a promotional leaflet.

2. In addition, you should provide an information video which demonstrates how to apply the rules to three different situations in each of your two chosen sports. Ensure that you provide a voiceover describing the correct application of the rules in each situation. **P2**

3. In order to meet the requirements of M2 in your video voiceover, you must explain the application of the rules and regulations of two different individual sports in three different situations. **M2**

Grading tips

P2 Summarise the major rules and regulations of two individual sports.

Select three situations for each individual sport, and describe how the rules are applied in each situation by appropriate officials.

Describe possible sanctions and the specific rules which have been broken.

M2 Explain the actions of each of the officials involved in the decision-making process, including hand signals and methods of communication.

3. and 4. Be able to assess your own performance and the performance of others in selected team/individual sports

Athletes are constantly seeking to develop and improve their performance. A pivotal person in this process is the coach. However, as an athlete develops, they should also take responsibility for their own development.

In order to develop, athletes must be made aware of the correct applications of skills and techniques in their sport. They also need to learn the correct use of strategies and tactics in competitive situations. This knowledge may be developed through observing elite performers and also through feedback from their coaches.

As an athlete becomes more reflective about their performance, they should follow the performance cycle shown in Figure 5.

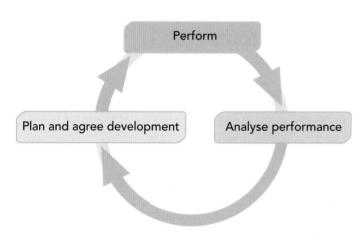

Figure 5: The performance cycle

In this section of the unit, you will examine a variety of methods that you can use to assess the performance of other athletes, but more importantly, you will learn how to assess your own performance and draw conclusions from your findings regarding self-development in individual sports.

3.1 and 4.1 Self-analysis and performer analysis

To support their own development an athlete must demonstrate effective analysis skills. Analysis of performance is the ability to observe and make appropriate judgements, including the technical and tactical elements of a specific performance.

An athlete should be able to identify strengths and prioritise performance targets for their own and other athletes' development.

In order to complete an effective analysis of performance, the observer needs to have a clear understanding of what to expect from an athlete at each stage of their development. Analysis requires the observer to assess any faults from what they see in the whole performance, a skill which takes time and experience to develop.

Take it further

Think about the last time you watched sport on television – did you make a judgement about an athlete's performance? If you made a negative judgement, who or what were you measuring the performance in question against?

Even the greatest athletes have weaknesses which may not be spotted by everyone; even their own coaches may not spot their faults. That is why elite athletes may change coaches or seek support from others, or build a team of coaches to work on specific parts of their performance.

Video analysis is an excellent way to assess performance. A recording is an objective record of what happened during the performance, which can be used as a basis for detailed analysis. The athlete or observer can study their earlier perceptions, thoughts, and decisions about the performance and draw appropriate conclusions regarding strengths and areas for development and improvement.

Specific to sport

When analysing the performance of an individual athlete, the assessor/observer should be aware of the demands of the sport they are assessing. For example, the skills and physical requirements of basketball and football, or of snooker and boxing, are very different and the assessor/observer will have to take this into account in order to make an appropriate judgement on the performance.

Application of skills

When carrying out an assessment the assessor/observer must understand the correct application of each skill ('the perfect model'). Without this understanding, the quality of feedback will be limited. For example, when assessing netball an assessor/observer should be able to compare the application of the players' skills, techniques and tactics to an ideal application of the technique/skill being observed. This comparison against an ideal will enable the assessor/observer to examine the performance for strengths and areas for improvement. If the assessor/observer is unable to spot any weaknesses in the performance, then the athlete should consider consulting a more knowledgeable and experienced coach/assessor/observer.

Techniques analysis and assessment

The skills in many sports are built up of complex contractions and actions, such as the volleyball serve or the tennis serve. To gain a greater understanding of these skills, they are broken down into smaller stages to allow a clear assessment of each stage of the technique.

This method of analysing an athlete's skills may require the assessor/observer to slow the action down (video analysis would be helpful here) and assess each part of the technique. For example, at full speed the service of a volleyball or tennis player may look fine, however slowing it down may show that the ball toss is too far away from the body of the server, which may weaken the player's overall performance.

Technological advances have developed the ability of coaches and analysts to assess performance, see the section on innovation in Unit 5 Sport Coaching (page 120).

Tactical analysis and assessment

It is important when analysing an athlete's performance that the assessor/observer understands the tactics and strategies. They should compare the performance they are watching against an ideal. The athlete must understand what is required and be able to execute the strategy effectively.

Achievements

When analysing the performance of an athlete or a team, it may be useful to look at their previous achievements, which are likely to form an impression prior to the observation. An assessor/observer may find it helpful to look back at recent matches to see if there is a pattern in the wins/losses, and whether this is related to the performers' physical attributes.

Such information may not always be helpful, but it may help to paint a picture prior to any assessment of performance.

> **Remember**
>
> The famous sporting cliché 'You're only as good as your last performance.'

Strengths

The feedback collated during the observational analysis should be drawn from the observer's subjective and objective views. The subjective views are their opinions of the performance and the objective views may come from data compiled during the observation. With this information, the observer should be able to identify the strengths of the performer observed.

Areas for improvement

Like the strengths identified during a performance analysis by an assessor or self-analysis by the athlete, areas for improvement should be identified from the observations made regarding the performance and, if appropriate, the data produced from the observation.

For example, in the 2006/2007 season, Manchester United won the Premier League title. The following season 2007/2008, they retained this title and added the Champions League title to it, proving that even the best teams continually seek to improve.

Likewise, who would have thought that Usain Bolt could have run the 100 metres any faster than he did in the Beijing Olympic final in 2008? However, by developing elements of his performance throughout a season, he managed to beat his own world record in the World Championships in Berlin in 2009.

3.2 and 4.2 Assessment methods

There are four areas of performance to assess: the physical, psychological, technical and tactical demands placed on a performer in a competitive situation. The methods used to assess sports performance are important if weaknesses are to be identified and worked on. To ensure that the best results are obtained from the analysis, the assessor/observer should select the most appropriate assessment method. The method may depend on the sport, the area of performance being analysed, their knowledge of the sport and even of the player(s) they are observing.

Objective performance data

An observer/assessor may choose to assess a team's or individual's performance 'live' at a training session or competition, or on video after the event.

Some observers/assessors like to make assessments by collating statistical data on a performance in a competitive situation. This data can take many different forms, and will allow the performer to make an objective assessment based on the use of numerical data or statistics. For example, if during a football match a team has 15 shots at goal, only three of which are on target, the observer/assessor may conclude that the team need to work on shooting. This data can be collated for teams, but is also used to assess the effectiveness of individual players within a team and athletes in individual sports, for example if a boxer landed 37 left jabs out of 43 attempts and only 23 right jabs out of 53 attempts in a bout, the observer/assessor may conclude that the boxer's strength is their left jab and their weakness is their right.

It is possible to collect objective performance data using notational analysis. This enables an observer/assessor to record data by completing tallies. See Table 9.2, which shows how notational analysis could be used to assess the effectiveness of a tennis player's first and second service during a game.

Number of first serves in	Number of first serves out
HHT HHT HHT HHT II	HHT HHT HHT HHT HHT HHT IIII
Number of second serves in	Number of double faults
HHT HHT HHT HHT HHT HHT II	II

Table 9.2: How notational analysis could be used to assess the effectiveness of a tennis player's first and second service during a game

From this data the observer/assessor would conclude that this tennis player needs to develop their first service. However, this information can be used to highlight the issues that may be encountered when

using objective performance data: the player may have hit 22 aces from each of the first serves they landed, and therefore the first serve may not be as much of a weakness as the data suggests.

Table 8.2 shows how notational analysis could be used to assess the effectiveness of a footballer's passing ability.

Completed passes in the final third	Failed passes in the final third
HHT HHT HHT HHT II	HHT HHT HHT HHT HHT HHT IIII

Table 8.2: How notational analysis could be used to assess the effectiveness of a footballer's passing ability

From this data the observer/assessor would conclude that this footballer needs to develop their passing in the final third of the pitch in order to improve their own performance and that of the team. Again, this information can be used to highlight the issues that may be encountered with objective performance data: the player may have completed 22 passes and set up three goals from three of the passes they completed. The 34 incomplete passes may have been the result of excessive marking from the opponents after the impact of the earlier passes on the game, so the player's passing ability may not be as much of a weakness as the data suggests.

The collation of data does not always assess technical efficiencies, as it does not include observation.

Activity: Unit 8 Team sport data analysis

In groups of two or three, watch a game of football and record simple information such as:

- successful passes
- shots on target
- shots off target
- number of corners
- successful tackles
- goals scored
- goals conceded.

Analyse the data you have collected. What does it show? Discuss the findings with the rest of your group, then:

1. Discuss what was good about the method of objective data analysis that you used.
2. What problems did you encounter?
3. How could the information you collate in the future be more accurate and effective for the analysis you have to complete?

Activity: Unit 9 Individual sport data analysis

In groups of two or three, watch a game of badminton and record simple information such as:

- successful forehand returns
- successful backhand returns
- number of serves
- number of successful serves
- points won on service
- points won on return of serve.

Analyse the data you have collected. What does it show? Discuss the findings with the rest of your group, then:

1. Discuss what was good about the method of objective data analysis that you used.

2. What problems did you encounter?

3. How could the information you collate in the future be more accurate and effective for the analysis you have to complete?

Many performance observations and assessments combine objective performance data and subjective observations. For example, an observation of a basketball player may include notational analysis of their application of each skill during a match, then the coach may observe their performance and compile feedback based on both these things.

Use of technology

Over the past decade a range of technology has been introduced to support the process of assessment.

Prozone is a computer program that analyses performance and generates data. It can provide post-match performance information for both home and away games, allowing the assessor/observer to analyse every aspect of team and player performance.

Prozone provides post-match analysis that enables coaches to supplement their own subjective observations with objective performance data.

Take it further

For more information regarding Prozone and its use in a variety of sports, visit the Prozone website: www.prozonesports.com.

Subjective observations

Subjective observations and assessments of a team or an individual are based on the observer's/assessor's judgements, interpretations, opinions and comparison against an ideal performance.

Observation analysis is a popular technique for assessing performance and effective application of skills, techniques and tactics. All coaches need to be effective observers, to enable them to identify strengths and weaknesses during performance.

Observation analysis should be used to identify the needs of a team or individual, and should inform a coach's plans to develop performance. An observer's/assessor's full analysis of overall performance should form the basis for a training programme with the aim of addressing the most significant weaknesses.

An example of how Prozone can be used to analyse the performance of a player/team in action.

Discuss how this could be used to develop a player's performance.

Can you think of any other technology that could support the assessment of a player?

An example of how Dartfish can be used to freeze the performance of a player in action.

Discuss how this could be used to develop a player's performance. Can you think of any other technology that could support the assessment of a player?

Another technological advance that can be used to assess the effective application of skills and techniques in sport is Dartfish technology. This program can slow down a movement and freeze-frame each component of a skill to enable an assessor/observer to assess the effective application of a technique at each stage.

Kandle technology is another form of video analysis software which is used to support coaches' observation of performance. The more complex the skill, the greater the requirement for software to enable sports coaches to analyse it in greater detail.

SWOT (strengths, weaknesses, opportunities, threats) analysis

SWOT analysis is used to evaluate the strengths, weaknesses, opportunities and threats involved in the performance of a player or team. The observer should understand the performance demands of the sport they are analysing. Normally, only experienced coaches carry out this process, although as athletes develop it is beneficial for them also to carry out SWOT analyses so that they can compare and contrast their findings with those of their coaches and agree on targets for future performance.

Strengths – the observer/assessor should identify the player's or team's strengths in a SWOT grid like Table 8.3. This information could come from objective data or subjective observations. The coach should compare the

Remember

When assessing the performance demands of a sport, it is important that all four key elements of the performance are assessed: physical, psychological, technical and tactical.

performance against an ideal model for each performance demand. It is important the observer/assessor has clear criteria against which to assess the performer(s) when carrying out the performance and SWOT analysis.

Weaknesses – with the support of the data, the assessor/observer should identify any weaknesses such as technical inefficiencies in the performance of specific skills, or the incorrect application of tactics and strategies in a game or a simulated practice.

Opportunities – the assessor/observer should note any opportunities that the player or team have to develop their performance, such as access to training sessions or specific coaches to support technical development. It may also include information about any opponent(s), such as objective data on previous performances (times, results, etc.) or subjective assessments of their effectiveness, possibly in the form of a scouting report.

Threats – the assessor/observer should identify any short- or long-term threats to the performance of the player or team.

Strengths	Weaknesses
• Good defensive organisation	• Inconsistent results
• Excellent centre (country standard)	• Space awareness
• High fitness levels for all sports performers	• Poor shooting
Opportunities	**Threats**
• Developed attacking tactics	• Opponents have two county netball players: wing attack and goal attack
• Opponents are weak in attack	• Mental strength – easily frustrated after a poor performance
• Recently appointed new head coach (very experienced with lots of ideas)	• Relegation from the league

Table 8.3: SWOT Analysis of West Side Netball Team

Strengths	Weaknesses
• Good overhead clear	• Inconsistent short and long serve
• Good agility on the court	• Poor backhand technique, clear, smash and drop shot
• Excellent court coverage	• Late to react to opponent's position on the court
• High fitness levels	• Poor shot selection
Opportunities	**Threats**
• Developed short serve through intensive coaching sessions	• Opponent is a better player
• Opponent also has a poor drop shot	• Mental strength – easily frustrated after a poor shot
• Ability to move around the court gives performer an advantage when returning shots and generating rallies	• Wrong shot selection in long rallies

Table 9.3: SWOT Analysis of Darren Milner, badminton player

Testing

Tests can give an objective picture of an athlete within a team's current performance levels. For example, psychometric tests may be used to assess an athlete's mental state, and fitness tests may be used to assess the physical and skill components of fitness required.

An example of a psychometric test is the 'profile of mood states' test (POMS). This measures an athlete's mood during training and can indicate whether they are overtraining. It is predominantly used for athletes who are looking jaded in performance or showing a lacklustre attitude when training, and is designed to examine the reasons behind the problems. Unit 7: Fitness testing for sport and exercise (page 179) discusses a variety of tests used to measure athletes' fitness levels.

Interviews

One of the easiest methods of analysing performance is to interview an athlete after a training session or a competition. This gives valuable feedback on how they felt their performance went, and what areas of their performance they feel require further development and improvement. Using the athlete's own views on their personal strengths and areas for improvement will allow them and their coach to develop training strategies to help future performances.

Performance profiling

In order to complete a full assessment of their performance, an athlete may choose to carry out a performance profile: a full assessment of the technical, tactical, physical and psychological requirements of their sport.

A performance profile uses a variety of assessment methods including notational analysis and performance observation. The assessor/observer will award a grade or mark which should be set against an achievable target performance or goal relating to the athlete's development.

It is important for athletes and coaches to have realistic expectations regarding developmental goals. For example, a 10-year-old footballer may compare their performance against that of another player in the same league who is the top goal scorer in the league, so on a scale of 1 to 10, 1 may be a player who has scored no goals in the season, while 10 may be a player who has scored 30 goals. It would not be realistic to compare their performance to that of Wayne Rooney because of the difference in age, ability and skill levels.

Similarly, a golfer who has a handicap of 16 may compare their performance against a golfer who has an 8 handicap, so on a scale of 1 to 10, 1 may be a 16 handicap while a 10 may be compared to a 4-handicap golfer. It would not be realistic to compare their performance to that of Tiger Woods, because of the difference in ability and skill levels.

When coaching beginners, a sports coach will need to complete a performance profile to determine which elements of their performance require development. As an athlete develops in age and ability, the performance profile should be completed by both the coach and the athlete. After the completion of the performance profile, both athlete and coach should discuss the findings and agree a plan that can be followed to develop any technical, tactical, psychological or physical weaknesses in their performance.

3.3 and 4.3 Development plan

Following a performance analysis, the player or team and the observer/assessor should agree a development plan which takes into account the findings from the analysis. This is essential, as without a development plan and agreed goals and targets for future performance, an athlete's or team's performance could plateau.

Aims and objectives

Before formulating a development plan, a team/player and coach should agree clear aims. These should consist of things they would like to achieve, e.g. promotion to the higher league, or improving sprint starts, by the start of next season.

In order to achieve their aims, a team or athlete will also need to have objectives that express how they will meet each of their aims. Each aim will need to have an objective, e.g. 'In order to improve our league position we will have to work on defending', or 'To improve my sprint start I am going to have to work on my reaction time and leg power.'

Goals

After the completion of performance assessments and player or team analysis, the observer and the team should agree specific goals for future development. Goal-setting should be used by individuals and teams to increase their motivation and confidence for future sports events. Goal-setting should be the first stage of the planning process for any team and coach, as through setting goals they can set clear targets for personal development. Goals should provide both direction and motivation. Goals are often set over various periods of time: teams can set short-, medium-, and long-term goals.

Short-term goals are set over a short period, between one day and one month. A short-term goal could be a target that a team or performer wishes to achieve after the next training session, or a specific technique they would like to develop by the end of the next month.

Medium-term goals should progressively support the team or individual achieving the long-term goals. These goals can be measured at specific points within a season.

Long-term goals are set for and with a team or individual to help them determine where they want to go, what they want to achieve and the best way of getting there. A coach should use these goals to shape their coaching schedule for a season or longer if appropriate.

SMART targets

Wherever objectives and goals are set for teams or individuals, they should be SMART:

- **S**pecific – the goals set should be as precise and detailed as possible for the team or individual.

- **M**easurable – the goals set should define a method of measuring the success of the team or individual. They should set achievement targets – what by when?

- **A**chievable – the goals set should be able to be attained within a set period of time and should be relevant for the team or individual.

- **R**ealistic – the goals set should be appropriate for the team or individual.

- **T**ime-bound – ensure you agree a timescale, even if it includes mini-targets for athlete development (short-, medium- and long-term goals).

Opportunities

Formulating a plan for future development may open new doors for teams' and individuals' personal development as well as sporting achievement.

It may be a requirement or an agreed target that an athlete will attend courses and obtain qualifications that involve them learning new skills and techniques, or developing knowledge about a specific area of their sport. They might learn about the treatment and prevention of sports injuries, technical requirements of a sport, sports nutrition or tactical development.

Take it further

In your own sport, find out about appropriate courses and/or qualifications an athlete could take to improve their knowledge about the areas listed below. Give the name of the course, provider, location and cost.

- treatment and prevention of sports injuries
- technical requirements of a sport
- sports nutrition
- tactical development.

For example, if an athlete has suffered a number of injuries, their coach may think it would be beneficial for them to attend a sports injury and rehabilitation course where they will learn about different methods of treating sports injuries, and where they may also learn how to avoid or prevent injuries. By completing these courses an athlete can increase their portfolio of qualifications.

The development plan agreed between the coach and the team may also introduce a team or individual to new methods of training and possibly new coaches. This may freshen up the current methods and develop further motivation. It may also provide an opportunity to develop overall performance.

Possible obstacles

Although the development plan produced for a team or individual may cover every possible eventuality and provide some excellent opportunities, unforeseen circumstances may arise and hinder progress towards attaining the set goals. These could include:

- injury and illness
- bad weather
- lack of funding
- failure to qualify for competitions/events
- family pressure
- peer pressure.

When participating in a training programme, athletes should be given every opportunity to meet their goals and targets. Athletes can seek support from within their club, or from their sport's NGB if appropriate. This support may deflect any obstacles that threatened to prevent them attaining the targets set.

Assessment activity 8.3: Self-analysis in team sport

A local sports team has asked you for support regarding their performance. Their manager would like you to show the players what a performance analysis is, what it entails and how feedback is used to develop performance.

1. The manager would like you to carry out a self-analysis using two different methods of assessment, identifying strengths and areas for improvement in two different team sports. **P4**

2. In order to meet the requirements of M3 in this task, in addition to the requirements of P4, in your summary of the assessments you must explain identified strengths and areas for improvement in two different team sports, and make suggestions relating to personal development. **M3**

3. Finally, in order to meet the requirements of D1 in this task, in addition to the requirements of P4 and M3, you must analyse identified strengths and areas for improvement in two different team sports, and justify suggestions made. **D1**

Grading tips

P4 Record your performance in two selected team sports in competitive situations.

Select two methods of assessment to analyse your performance in two team sports.

Observe your performance in two team sports and comment on the strengths and areas for future development.

M3 Summarise your findings in a conclusion, explaining the identified strengths and weaknesses and summarising the methods for addressing the areas of development for two team sports.

D1 For each team sport:

- produce a development plan for your own performance
- set aims and objectives for the development plan
- set appropriate long-, medium- and short-term goals
- identify SMART targets for development
- identify opportunities for development
- identify possible obstacles to achieving the goals set.

PLTS

When you are carrying out a self- or peer-analysis using two different methods of assessment, identifying strengths and areas for improvement in two different team sports, you will develop your skills as a **reflective learner**.

Functional skills

Completing a notational analysis of your own or another team's practical performance will develop your **Mathematics** skills.

Assessment activity 8.4: Peer-analysis in team sports

After the completion of your own self-assessments, the manager of the local sports team would now like you to complete a performance analysis and development plan for his team.

1. He wants you to carry out a performance analysis using two different methods of assessment, identifying strengths and areas for improvement in the development of a team in a team sport. **P5**

2. In order to meet the requirements of M4 in this task, in addition to the requirements of P5 in your summary, you must explain identified strengths and areas for improvement in the development of a team in a team sport, and make suggestions relating to development of a team. **M4**

3. Finally, in order to meet the requirements of D2 in this task, in addition to the requirements of P5 and M4, you must analyse identified strengths and areas for improvement in the development of a team in a team sport, and justify suggestions made. **D2**

Grading tips

P5 Record the performance of a selected team from a team sport.

Select two methods of assessment to analyse the team's performance and assess their performance from a recording.

Observe the team's performance and comment on the strengths and areas for their future development after your assessment.

M4 Summarise your findings in a conclusion – explaining the identified strengths and areas for development and suggesting how the team could develop.

D2 Produce a development plan to help the team improve their skills, techniques and use of tactics.

- Set aims and objectives for the team.
- Set appropriate long-, medium- and short-term goals for the team.
- Identify SMART targets for the team's development.
- Identify opportunities for the team's development.
- Identify possible obstacles that may prevent the team achieving the goals set.

PLTS

When you are carrying out a self- or peer-analysis using two different methods of assessment, identifying strengths and areas for improvement in two different team sports, you will develop your skills as a **reflective learner**.

Functional skills

Completing a notational analysis of your own or another team's practical performance will develop your **Mathematics** skills.

Assessment activity 9.3: Self-analysis in individual sports

In order to support the development of gifted and talented athletes at their school, a local sports college has asked you to demonstrate how performance analysis can be used to develop performance.

1 The college would like you to carry out a self-analysis using two different methods of assessment, identifying strengths and areas for improvement in two different individual sports. **P4**

2. In order to meet the requirements of M3 in this task, in addition to the requirements of P4 in your summary of the assessments, you must explain identified strengths and areas for improvement in two different individual sports, and make suggestions relating to personal development. **M3**

3. Finally, in order to meet the requirements of D1 in this task, in addition to the requirements of P4 and M3, you must analyse identified strengths and areas for improvement in two different individual sports, and justify suggestions made. **D1**

Grading tips

P4 Record your performance in two selected individual sports in competitive situations.

Select two methods of assessment to analyse your performance in two individual sports.

Observe your performance in two individual sports and comment on the strengths and areas for future development.

M3 Summarise your findings in a conclusion, explaining the identified strengths and weaknesses and summarising the methods for addressing the areas of development for two individual sports.

D1 For each individual sport:

- produce a development plan for your own performance
- set aims and objectives for the development plan
- set appropriate long-, medium- and short-term goals
- identify SMART targets for development
- identify opportunities for development
- identify possible obstacles to achieving the goals set.

PLTS

When you are carrying out a self- or peer-analysis using two different methods of assessment, identifying strengths and areas for improvement in two different individual sports, you will develop your skills as a **reflective learner**.

Functional skills

Completing a notational analysis of your own or another individual's practical performance will develop your **Mathematics** skills.

Assessment activity 9.4: Peer-analysis in individual sports

After the completion of your own self-assessments, the sports college would now like you to complete a performance analysis and development plan for one of their gifted and talented sports performers.

1. They would like you to carry out a performance analysis using two different methods of assessment, identifying strengths and areas for improvement in the development of an athlete in an individual sport. **P5**

2. In order to meet the requirements of M4 in this task, in addition to the requirements of P5 in your summary, you must explain identified strengths and areas for improvement in the development of an athlete in an individual sport, and make suggestions relating to the development of an individual. **M4**

3. Finally, in order to meet the requirements of D2 in this task, in addition to the requirements of P5 and M4, you must analyse identified strengths and areas for improvement in the development of an athlete in an individual sport, and justify suggestions made. **D2**

Grading tips

P5 Record the performance of a selected athlete from an individual sport.

Select two methods of assessment to analyse the individual's performance and assess their performance from a recording.

Observe their performance and comment on the strengths and areas for future development after your assessment.

M4 Summarise your findings in a conclusion, explaining the identified strengths and areas for development and suggesting how the athlete could develop in the selected sport.

D2 Produce a development plan to help the athlete improve their skills, techniques and use of tactics in the selected sport.

- Set aims and objectives for their development plan.
- Set appropriate long-, medium- and short-term goals for the athlete.
- Identify SMART targets for the athlete's development.
- Identify opportunities for the athlete's development.
- Identify possible obstacles that may prevent the athlete achieving the goals set.

PLTS

When you are carrying out a self- or peer-analysis using two different methods of assessment, identifying strengths and areas for improvement in two different individual sports, you will develop your skills as a **reflective learner**.

Functional skills

Completing a notational analysis of your own or another individual's practical performance will develop your **Mathematics** skills.

Darren Singh
Voluntary sports leader

Darren is a voluntary sports coach for a local mixed hockey team. While studying on the BTEC National in Sport at a local college Darren completed both Unit 8 and Unit 9. The practical units developed Darren's appreciation of the skills, techniques and tactics required to play a wide variety of team and individual sports. Before attending college and while at college Darren had always enjoyed playing hockey for a local team but had no intention to run one of the many teams at his club.

Through developing more of an appreciation of the sport while studying at college Darren became more involved at his local club and started to help one of the club coaches out. Initially Darren's role was as an assistant coach but as his confidence grew he became more and more involved. Eventually the head coach at the club asked Darren if he would be interested in completing some coaching courses which Darren accepted.

After completing his Level 1 assistant coaching award Darren started to become more involved in the delivery of training sessions and more recently the head coach has approached Darren again and asked him to be more involved in the analysis of some of the senior players at the club. In order to do this Darren will need to observe the senior team and make subjective judgements on the performances and provide feedback to the head coach on the performance of specific team players.

Think about it!

To support Darren to complete his performance analysis:
- List the core skills and techniques required to play hockey.
- List the tactics which he will need to use when observing the senior team.
- Provide two different methods of assessment that could be used to analyse the performance of these performers at the hockey club.
- Describe the strengths and weaknesses of each method of assessment.

Just checking

1. Define 'sport'.
2. What is a skill?
3. What is an open skill?
4. What is a discrete skill?
5. What is a serial skill?
6. What is a gross skill?
7. What is a technique?
8. What is a tactic?
9. What is an externally paced skill?
10. List five team sports and five individual sports.
11. What are the national governing bodies for each of the sports on your lists?
12. What four factors determine the performance demands of a sport?
13. What does SWOT stand for?
14. What is a subjective assessment?
15. Name two different types of objective data assessments used to analyse sports performance.

Assignment tips

- To complete Unit 8 or 9 successfully you will need to develop your knowledge about individual or team sports. In order to do this you should try to observe a variety of different sports in action. Observe a number of sports and make a list of the skills, techniques and tactics required to perform each sport.

- You are also required to perform in two team or two individual sports to complete either Unit 8 or 9 successfully. Each session that you participate in should cover a skill, technique and tactic required to perform effectively within that sport: you will be required to describe and demonstrate effective application of each of these skills, technique and tactics.

- You should learn the rules and regulations of each sport and develop your ability to apply these rules during competitive situations. You should observe officials from your selected sports in action.

- Ensure you enjoy the opportunities you will be given to participate in practical sessions and to develop skills which you may not have been introduced to before now.

- Develop an understanding of performance analysis through practice and observation. Try to get a model in your mind of an elite sports performer applying each skill, technique and tactic and use this to analyse performance.

- Be confident to observe other sports performers participating in your selected sport and comment on the effective application of each skill, technique and tactic.

- Remember to carefully consider which methods of analysis you will use to assess the effectiveness of yourself and other sports performers.

- When carrying out self-analysis you should first ask someone to visually record your performance in each sport and then watch back the performance comparing yourself to the model performance.

- Research the variety of coaching courses available in your selected sports. Also examine other courses and methods which could be used to develop your skills as a sports performer and develop your knowledge of the sport. You could discuss these with the coaches/tutors who deliver the sessions to you.

- Complete a Level 1 coaching award to support your development of the required skills, techniques and tactics required to perform effectively in your selected sport.

- Ensure that you read the assignment briefs properly. Take your time and ensure you are happy with the task you have been set. If not ask your tutor for additional assistance.

- Make sure you attempt all parts of the assignment briefs. If you only attempt the pass criteria then you can only achieve a pass grade. Think big and try to complete all of the assignment.

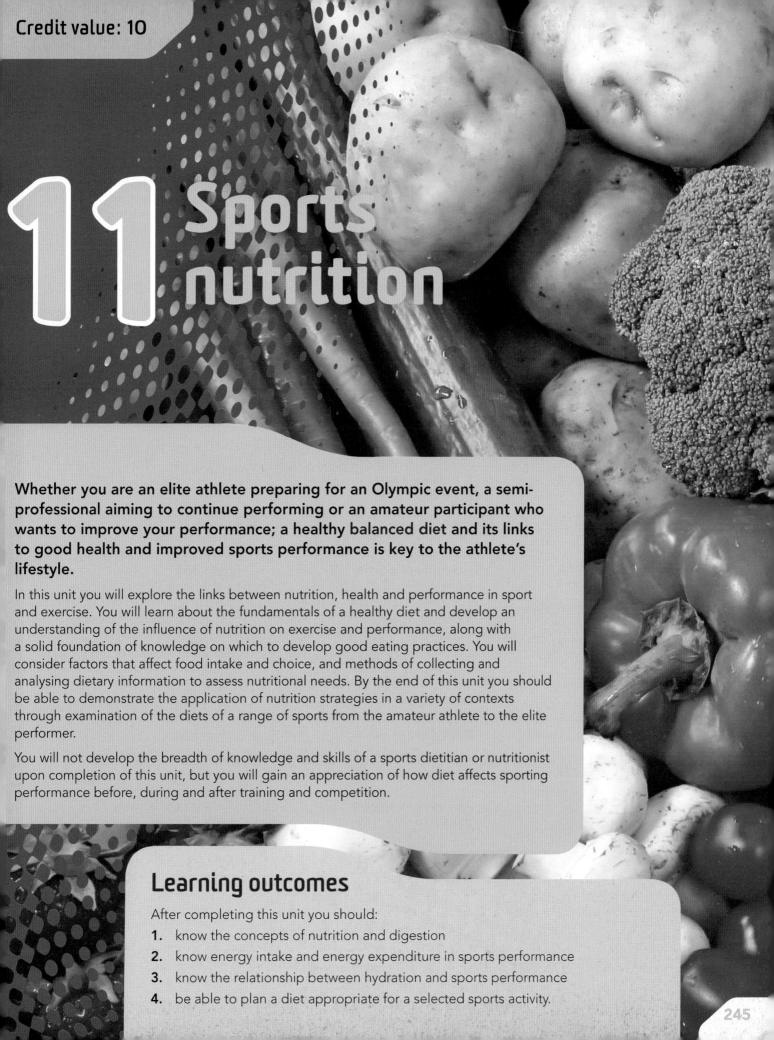

11 Sports nutrition

Credit value: 10

Whether you are an elite athlete preparing for an Olympic event, a semi-professional aiming to continue performing or an amateur participant who wants to improve your performance; a healthy balanced diet and its links to good health and improved sports performance is key to the athlete's lifestyle.

In this unit you will explore the links between nutrition, health and performance in sport and exercise. You will learn about the fundamentals of a healthy diet and develop an understanding of the influence of nutrition on exercise and performance, along with a solid foundation of knowledge on which to develop good eating practices. You will consider factors that affect food intake and choice, and methods of collecting and analysing dietary information to assess nutritional needs. By the end of this unit you should be able to demonstrate the application of nutrition strategies in a variety of contexts through examination of the diets of a range of sports from the amateur athlete to the elite performer.

You will not develop the breadth of knowledge and skills of a sports dietitian or nutritionist upon completion of this unit, but you will gain an appreciation of how diet affects sporting performance before, during and after training and competition.

Learning outcomes

After completing this unit you should:
1. know the concepts of nutrition and digestion
2. know energy intake and energy expenditure in sports performance
3. know the relationship between hydration and sports performance
4. be able to plan a diet appropriate for a selected sports activity.

245

Assessment and grading criteria

This table shows you what you must do in order to achieve a pass, merit or distinction grade, and where you can find activities in this book to help you.

To achieve a **pass** grade the evidence must show that the learner is able to:	To achieve a **merit** grade the evidence must show that, in addition to the pass criteria, the learner is able to:	To achieve a **distinction** grade the evidence must show that, in addition to the pass and merit criteria, the learner is able to:
P1 describe nutrition, including nutritional requirements using common terminology associated with nutrition **Assessment activity 11.1, page 257**		
P2 describe the structure and function of the digestive system **Assessment activity 11.1, page 257**		
P3 describe energy intake and expenditure in sports performance **Assessment activity 11.2, page 263**	**M1** explain energy intake and expenditure in sports performance **Assessment activity 11.2, page 263**	
P4 describe energy balance and its importance in relation to sports performance **Assessment activity 11.2, page 263**	**M2** explain the importance of energy balance in relation to sports performance **Assessment activity 11.2, page 263**	**D1** analyse the effects of energy balance on sports performance **Assessment activity 11.2, page 263**
P5 describe hydration and its effects on sports performance **Assessment activity 11.3, page 266**		
P6 describe the components of a balanced diet **Assessment activity 11.4, page 276**	**M3** explain the components of a balanced diet **Assessment activity 11.4, page 276**	
P7 plan an appropriate two-week diet plan for a selected sports performer for a selected sports activity **Assessment activity 11.4, page 276**	**M4** explain the two-week diet plan for a selected sports performer for a selected sports activity **Assessment activity 11.4, page 276**	**D2** justify the two-week diet plan for a selected sports performer for a selected sports activity **Assessment activity 11.4, page 276**

How you will be assessed

This unit will be internally assessed by a range of assignments that will be designed and graded by your tutor. Your assignment tasks will be designed to allow you to demonstrate your understanding of the unit learning outcomes and relate to what you should be able to do after completing this unit. Your assignments could be in the form of:

- presentations
- practical tasks
- written assignments and case studies
- a logbook or portfolio of evidence.

Sample assessment activities are included throughout this unit as an example of how you might achieve these learning outcomes.

Harry Archer, an academy rugby player

In this unit I learned how to predict my nutritional requirements and analyse my intake. I worked with my peers to research different diets for different sports and devise nutritional strategies to be implemented before, during and after exercise to optimise performance. I particularly enjoyed evaluating my eating and exercise patterns and planning to improve my nutritional intake. As a rugby player I am concerned about my body mass and size. I now understand the concept of energy balance and its implications on my desire to gain weight, and how I can achieve this through sensible dietary manipulation. I now enjoy a healthier diet and have more energy for my training programme.

Over to you

- **What areas of this unit are you most looking forward to?**
- **How might you apply some of the learning you acquire in this unit to impact on your health, performance or both?**

1. Know the concepts of nutrition and digestion

Factors that affect food intake and choice

Take a few minutes to think about the factors that might influence your food intake and choice. If you can think of 10, this is good going, and 20 or more is excellent. Awareness of these factors will assist you in formulating realistic and achievable dietary goals and plans when meeting some of the assessment requirements of this unit.

All activity stimulates your body's need for fuel and fluid. Knowledge of the nutrients your body requires, along with their different functions, provides the basis for the science of **nutrition**.

Remember

There should be no conflict between eating for health and eating for performance.

1.1 Nutrition

Foods contain varying amounts of the nutrients carbohydrate, protein, fat, vitamins, minerals, fibre and water.

Macronutrients

Nutrients in food are categorised according to the relative amounts required by your body. Carbohydrate, protein and fat are termed **macronutrients**, as they are required in relatively large amounts on a daily basis. These nutrients are also the energy-providing nutrients of your **diet**.

Carbohydrates

Carbohydrates form your body's most readily available source of energy and can be accessed rapidly. One gram of carbohydrate provides approximately 4 kcal of energy. Carbohydrate foods are divided into two basic types and are generally known as either simple or complex.

Simple carbohydrates are essentially sugars. They are formed from single and double sugar units and

Why is it important to have a balanced diet in order to stay healthy?
Discuss your ideas with your peers and tutor.

Longer chains of simple sugar units are called polysaccharides or complex carbohydrates. These allow large quantities of glucose to be stored as starch in the cells of plants or as glycogen in the muscles and liver of animals. All carbohydrate consumed ends up as glucose to provide energy.

Complex carbohydrates are an important source of energy since they are broken down slowly in your body to release energy over longer periods. They should form the largest percentage of your total carbohydrate intake. Unrefined sources such as wholemeal bread, wholegrain rice and pasta are preferable as they also contain a higher nutritional value by way of micronutrients and fibre.

are easily digested and absorbed to provide a quick energy source. The simplest carbohydrate unit is the monosaccharide, the most common of which is glucose. *Saccharide* means sugar, *mono* means one, therefore a monosaccharide is a single sugar unit. Glucose is used to produce adenosine triphosphate (ATP), the compound required for muscle contraction.

Other monosaccharides include fructose, also called fruit sugar as it is found in fruits and vegetables, and galactose, found in milk. Monosaccharides mostly occur combined in carbohydrates. Two monosaccharides together form a disaccharide or double sugar. The most common disaccharide is sucrose or table sugar. Others include lactose (found in milk) and maltose (found in cereals).

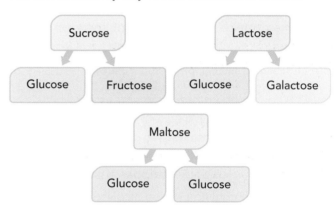

Figure 11.1: Double sugars or disaccharides and their monosaccharides

What sources of carbohydrate do you regularly consume in your diet?

After you eat foods containing carbohydrate your blood sugar level rises, stimulating the pancreas to secrete the hormone insulin. The role of insulin is to normalise blood sugar levels and aid the transport of glucose from the blood to the cells. Glucose is then used directly by the cells for energy or stored as glycogen in your liver and muscles. Glycogen is a crucial source of glucose for fuelling activity.

Simple	Complex
Sugar, syrup, jam, honey, marmalade, sugary fizzy drinks, boiled sweets, fudge, fruit juice, sports drinks, energy gels	Bread, bagels, crispbread, crackers, rice, pasta, noodles, couscous, potatoes, breakfast cereals, pulses, root vegetables

Table 11.1: Simple and complex carbohydrates

Around 80 per cent is stored in your muscles while the rest is stored in your liver, with a small amount of circulating blood glucose. Excess carbohydrate not required to replenish glycogen stores is converted to fat and stored in your body's **adipose tissue**.

Carbohydrate can only be stored as glycogen in limited amounts – approximately 375–475 grams in the average adult, equivalent to approximately 1,500–2,000 kcal. Day-to-day stores of glycogen are influenced by dietary carbohydrate intake and levels of physical activity or training. Regular exercise can encourage your muscles to adapt to store more glycogen. This is an important training adaptation for elite athletes, particularly in endurance-type sports.

Remember

The intensity and duration of exercise influence the rate and amount of glycogen usage. The harder the exercise and the longer its duration, the greater the depletion of glycogen.

Proteins

Proteins are essential to maintaining optimal health and physical performance. The smallest units of proteins are amino acids. It is not necessary for you to be familiar with the names and functions of the individual **amino acids**. The body needs all 20 amino acids to be present simultaneously for protein synthesis to occur, to sustain optimal growth and functioning. Different proteins contain different numbers and combinations of amino acids. The eight that your body is unable to make are called essential amino acids (EAAs) – they are a necessary part of your diet. The remaining amino acids are called non-essential – your body is able to synthesise these if all the essential ones are present.

Key terms

Adipose tissue – commonly referred to as fat tissue, is a type of connective tissue that serves as the body's most abundant energy reserve.

Amino acids – the building blocks of proteins.

The chief role of protein in your body is to build and repair tissue. Proteins may also be used as a secondary source of energy when carbohydrate and fat are limited, such as towards the end of prolonged endurance events or during severe energy restriction that may accompany dieting.

Proteins, like carbohydrates, have an energy value of approximately 4 calories per gram. Unlike carbohydrate and fat, excess protein cannot be stored in your body. All proteins carry out functional roles, so daily protein ingestion is required. If your protein intake exceeds requirements to support growth and repair, excess is used to provide energy immediately or converted to fat or carbohydrate and stored.

Protein foods are classified into two groups (see Table 11.2). The value of foods for meeting your body's protein needs is determined by their composition of amino acids. Foods that contain all of the EAAs are known as first-class or complete proteins. These are mainly of animal origin like eggs, meat, fish, milk and other dairy products, and soya. Foods that are lacking in one or more of the EAAs are called second-class or incomplete proteins. These come from plant sources such as cereals, bread, rice, pasta, pulses, nuts and seeds. Vegetarians and vegans must ensure that they eat a variety of these in careful combinations to ensure adequate intake of all EAAs; for example, beans and wheat complement each other well.

In the context of sports performance does the typical UK diet contain adequate amounts of protein?

Complete	Incomplete
Meat, poultry, offal, fish, eggs, milk, cheese, yoghurt, soya	Cereals, bread, rice, pasta, noodles, pulses, peas, beans, lentils, nuts, seeds

Table 11.2: Protein foods

Fats

Fat is an essential nutrient. Triglycerides form the basic component of fats. Each triglyceride consists of a glycerol molecule with three fatty acids attached. When triglycerides are digested and absorbed by your body they break down into these two substances. Fats are obtained from animal and vegetable sources and are of two main types: saturated and unsaturated.

Fatty acids contain chains of carbon atoms to which hydrogen atoms attach. The number of hydrogen atoms relative to the number of carbon atoms determines whether a fatty acid is classified as saturated or unsaturated. If all the carbons are associated with two hydrogens, the fat is saturated, but if one or more of the carbons is without hydrogen then the fat is unsaturated. Unsaturated fatty acids can be of two kinds: monounsaturated and polyunsaturated.

All fats in your diet are a mixture of these three fatty acid types (see Table 11.3 on page 252). Fats that contain mostly saturated fatty acids are generally solid at room temperature, like butter and ordinary margarine, and are usually found in meat, eggs and dairy foods. The two exceptions are palm and coconut oil, which are plant sources. Fats composed mainly of unsaturated fatty acids are usually liquid at room temperature, like olive or sunflower oils.

Most dietary experts recommend cutting back on fat intake. This is sound advice for athletes as it allows them to consume a greater proportion of energy intake from carbohydrates to maintain glycogen stores, to support training and competition.

The primary function of fats is to provide a concentrated source of energy, forming your body's largest potential energy store. Even the leanest of individuals will have large amounts of energy stored as fat. Fat is more than twice as energy-dense as other macronutrients, yielding 9 calories per gram.

Fats protect and cushion your vital organs, provide structural material for cells and act as an insulator. Animal fats are a source of the fat-soluble vitamins A, D, E and K. Fats add flavour and texture to foods, which can be the reason for over-consumption.

Saturated	Monounsaturated	Polyunsaturated
Full-fat dairy products, butter, hard margarine, lard, dripping, suet, fatty meat, meat pies, pâté, cream, cakes, biscuits, chocolate, coconut, coconut oil	Olive oil, olive oil spreads, rapeseed oil, corn oil, peanuts, peanut butter, peanut oil	Soft margarine, low-fat spreads labelled high in polyunsaturated fats, sunflower oil, safflower oil, soya oil, oily fish, nuts

Table 11.3: Sources and types of fat in the diet

Micronutrients

Vitamins and minerals are referred to as micronutrients as they are required in much smaller amounts – some in minute quantities. Despite your relatively small requirements for these nutrients, many play a critical role in regulating chemical reactions in your body.

Vitamins

Vitamins are vital, non-caloric nutrients required in very small amounts. They perform specific metabolic functions and prevent particular deficiency diseases.

Most vitamins required to maintain health cannot be produced by your body and must be supplied by your diet. The exceptions are vitamin D, which your body is able to synthesise by the action of sunlight on the skin, and vitamin K, which can be produced by the bacteria of the large intestine. Vitamins play essential roles in regulating many metabolic processes in your body, particularly those that release energy. They also support growth and the immune and nervous system functions, and some are involved in producing hormones.

Vitamins are obtained from a variety of plant and animal sources and are broadly grouped depending on whether they are fat- or water-soluble. Vitamins A, D, E and K form the fat-soluble group, with the B vitamins and vitamin C making up the water-soluble group.

Specific vitamins have specific functions and are required in differing amounts. Individual requirements are determined by age, sex, state of health and levels of physical activity. The UK Department of Health has set **Dietary Reference Values (DRVs)** for all nutrients for different groups of healthy people. The Reference Nutrient Intake (RNI) value should meet the needs of 97 per cent of the population. A balanced and varied diet with an adequate energy content should supply sufficient intake of all vitamins.

It is important to note that large amounts of some vitamins can be harmful to health. This is particularly true for the fat-soluble vitamins, as they can be stored in your body. The only situation in which large doses of any vitamin may be beneficial is when the body has a severe deficiency of a particular vitamin or is unable to absorb or metabolise vitamins efficiently.

Remember

Individual vitamin requirements vary and are determined by age, sex, state of health and physical activity level.

Supplementation with high doses of any vitamin should always be medically supervised and not self-prescribed.

- All fat-soluble vitamins have a number of common features. As the term suggests, they are found in the fatty or oily parts of foods. Once digested they are absorbed and transported in the lymph and ultimately reach the blood. As a result of their insolubility in water, they are not excreted in the urine and can accumulate in the liver and adipose tissue.

- Water-soluble vitamins consist of the B vitamins and vitamin C. Many of the B vitamins serve similar functions, facilitating the use of energy within your body. Excesses are excreted via the urine, so your body has only limited stores, necessitating regular intakes. It should be noted that many of these vitamins are destroyed by food processing and preparation.

Minerals

Minerals are non-caloric nutrients that are essential to life, and like vitamins they are required in small or trace amounts. Minerals are classified in terms of the relative amounts required by your body and can be placed broadly into two categories.

- Macrominerals such as calcium are required in relatively large amounts, sometimes as much as several hundred milligrams per day.

- Trace elements such as copper and selenium are required in much smaller quantities (micrograms per day).

All minerals are essential to health and form important components of your body such as bone, connective tissue, enzymes and hormones. Some play essential roles in nerve function and muscle contraction; others regulate fluid balance in your body. Levels of minerals are closely controlled by absorption and excretion to prevent excessive build-up. Some minerals compete with each other for absorption, especially iron, zinc and copper.

Fibre

Fibre is a complex carbohydrate. Non-starch polysaccharide (NSP) is the new scientific term for dietary fibre. NSP forms the main component of plant cell walls, which are the principal component of dietary fibre. They resist digestion by the stomach and small intestine and provide bulk which aids the transit of food through your digestive system.

Fibre is obtained from wholegrain cereals, nuts, pulses, fruits and vegetables. It is thought to help in both preventing and treating certain diseases including cancer of the colon, diabetes, heart disease and irritable bowel syndrome. A high-fibre intake plus a high-fluid intake also helps to keep your bowel functioning efficiently. Adequate amounts may also play a role in weight control by helping to achieve the feeling of fullness.

There are two types of fibre: soluble and insoluble. Soluble fibre can be found in oats, rye, barley, peas, beans, lentils, fruits and vegetables. This is important in the control of blood glucose and cholesterol. Insoluble fibre is found in wholewheat bread, rice and pasta, wholegrain breakfast cereals, fruits and vegetables; it is thought to be important in the prevention of bowel disorders. A healthy diet requires both types of fibre, with adults requiring around 18 grams in total per day.

Remember

Non-starch polysaccharide is the new scientific term for dietary fibre.

Nutritional requirements

The amount of each nutrient you need is referred to as the nutritional requirement. These differ depending on age, sex, levels of activity and state of health. Some nutrients are more essential during different stages of life, such as calcium in childhood and iron during pregnancy.

Essential and non-essential carbohydrates

To support health and performance, it is recommended that around 50–60 per cent of your total daily calorie intake is derived from carbohydrates. Greater intakes may be required by athletes in regular intense training. For example, a marathon runner or a triathlete may need to get 65–70 per cent of their total energy from carbohydrates.

However, the average sedentary individual will require around 50 per cent of total daily calorie intake to be supplied by carbohydrates, of which the majority should be from starchy sources. This would equate to around 250 grams per day for females and 300 grams per day for males. Table 11.4 estimates the carbohydrate requirements that can be prescribed based on activity levels.

Level of daily activity	Carbohydrate per kilogram of body weight (g)
Less than 1 hour	4–5
1 hour	5–6
1–2 hours	6–7
2–3 hours	7–8
More than 3 hours	8–10

Table 11.4: Carbohydrate requirements based on daily activity levels

Whether eating for health or performance, the best approach to achieving an adequate carbohydrate intake is to eat at regular intervals and ensure that all meals and snacks are centred around starchy carbohydrate foods. People with high carbohydrate requirements may need to eat more frequent meals and snacks or consume more simple carbohydrates to achieve their requirements.

Essential and non-essential protein

Active individuals have higher protein requirements in order to promote tissue growth and repair following training and competition. Overall, protein intake should represent between 12 and 15 per cent of your total daily energy intake. The misguided belief that additional protein will automatically help to build muscle has been perpetuated since the times of the ancient Greeks. Regular exercise does increase protein needs, but most people already eat enough protein. Athletes are likely to be eating more to meet increased calorie requirements, and therefore should already be eating enough to meet any theoretical increase in requirements.

Type of activity	Protein per kilogram of body weight (g)
Mainly sedentary	0.75–1.0
Mainly endurance	1.2–1.4
Mainly strength	1.2–1.7

Table 11.5: Daily protein requirements based on type of activity

Essential and non-essential fat

Surveys in the UK have shown that the average diet contains around 40 per cent of calories from fat, a level deemed by experts to be too high. It is recommended that fat intakes are reduced to 30–35 per cent of total calorie intake: around 70 grams per day for females and 90 grams per day for males. Of this, only 6–10 per cent should be from saturated fats. Athletes involved in regular intense activity may need to further reduce their overall fat intake to around 25–30 per cent of total energy consumed to achieve adequate carbohydrate intakes, but in absolute terms this may equate to the same quantity of intake as that of the sedentary individual, as athletes will be eating more calories to meet their increased energy requirements.

Common terminology

Recommended Daily Allowance (RDA)

Dietary standards have been used in the UK since World War II. The first set of standards focused on Recommended Daily Allowance (RDA), which aimed to prevent nutritional deficiency by recommending one intake target per nutrient. In the late 1980s, the government set up a panel of experts to review the RDAs of nutrients, and new Dietary Reference Values (DRVs) were established. The phrase 'dietary reference value' is an umbrella term that can be applied to any of the following measures of nutrient intake values:

- Reference Nutrient Intake (RNI)
- Estimated Average Requirements (EAR)
- Lower Reference Nutrient Intake (LRNI)
- Safe Intake (SI).

Optimal Level

It is thought that some recommended nutrient intakes may be too high or too low. The theory of optimal levels of nutrient intake is grounded in nutritional therapy and attempts to take more account of individual requirements, lifestyle and circumstances such as smoking and stress. Defining optimal nutrient intakes has presented nutrition scientists with considerable challenges. To determine an individual's optimum nutrient intake level requires biochemical screening through the analysis of blood or urine, which is not routine practice.

Safe Intake (SI)

Safe Intake (SI) is a term used to indicate the intake of a nutrient where there is insufficient scientific information to estimate the distribution of requirements within a population. It represents an intake that is thought to be adequate for most people's needs but not so high as to cause undesirable effects on health.

Estimated Average Requirements (EAR)

Estimated Average Requirements (EAR) are the most widely used value in assessing energy requirement. Many individuals require more than the EAR and many require less.

> **Take it further**
>
> To find out more about Dietary Reference Values, look at the Department of Health's *Report on Health and Social Subjects 41: Dietary Reference Values for Food Energy and Nutrients for the United Kingdom*, HMSO, 1991.

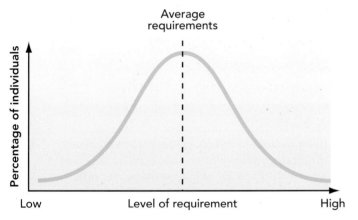

Figure 11.2: The normal distribution curve of nutrient requirements in a population. Where might athletes fit within this?

1.2 Digestion

You have already seen that food provides the energy and nutrients you need to stay alive and in good health. Before your body can make use of this energy and nutrients, the food has to be broken down to release them through the process of digestion.

Structure of the digestive system

Digestion starts in the mouth (**buccal cavity**). Your teeth and jaws crush and grind food to mix it with saliva, which contains the enzyme amylase that begins the breakdown of starch. You then swallow the food, which enters the **oesophagus**, the tube that connects your mouth to your **stomach**. The food bolus is squeezed along the oesophagus by the process of peristalsis. It takes around 3–6 seconds for food to travel from your mouth to your stomach. Your stomach acts as a large mixing bowl, churning the food into a liquid called chyme. Lining your stomach are cells that produce and release gastric juices containing enzymes and hydrochloric acid, which assist in the breakdown of the food and kill any bacteria present in it. Food normally remains in your stomach for 1–4 hours, but fluid may pass through much more rapidly.

From your stomach the chyme passes to your **duodenum** and then to your **small intestine**, a tube about 6 metres long. As the chyme enters your small intestine, it is mixed with more **digestive juices**, this time from the **pancreas**. Pancreatic juice contains bile made by the **liver** as well as **enzymes** to further assist the breakdown of carbohydrate, protein and fat. It is also alkaline to neutralise the acid from the stomach. Your **gall bladder**, a pear-shaped organ, stores and concentrates bile until it is required for digestion. Then it is released into your digestive tract to emulsify fats and neutralise the acids in partly digested food. Peristalsis continues to move the chyme through your digestive system to your **large intestine** (another long tube) and eventually the **rectum** and **anal canal**.

> **Key term**
>
> **Enzymes** – proteins that start or accelerate the digestive process.

As the chyme moves through your small intestine, vitamins, minerals, amino acids, fatty acids and sugars are absorbed by your intestinal wall. Lining the wall of your small intestine are finger-like projections known as villi, which increase the surface area available for absorption and speed up the process.

By the time the chyme reaches your large intestine, it is less fluid and has been reduced to mainly indigestible matter. Your large intestine does not produce any digestive enzymes but continues to absorb water. Bacteria in your large intestine produce vitamin K. The residue (faeces) left behind is eliminated (excreted) from your body through your anus. See page 256 for a diagram of the digestive system.

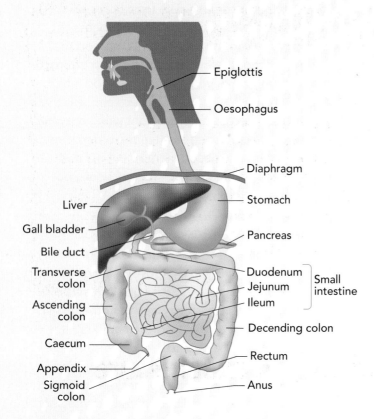

Epiglottis

Oesophagus

Diaphragm

Liver

Stomach

Gall bladder

Pancreas

Bile duct

Transverse colon

Duodenum ⎤
Jejunum ⎬ Small intestine
Ileum ⎦

Ascending colon

Caecum

Decending colon

Appendix

Rectum

Sigmoid colon

Anus

Figure 11.3: The digestive system

Function of the digestive system

Digestion

Digestion can be considered a multi-stage process following the ingestion of raw materials (the food you eat). It involves mechanical and chemical elements in the process that ultimately leads to enzymes in the gut breaking down the larger chemical compounds in your food into smaller compounds that can be absorbed by your body.

Absorption

This is the movement of digested food from your stomach and small intestine into your body tissues and blood. The process of absorption happens in the villi that line your small intestine. These finger-like projections provide a large surface area for absorption

to take place. Each villus has a network of capillaries to quickly absorb nutrients. Amino acids (from the breakdown of proteins) and glucose (from the breakdown of carbohydrates) enter your bloodstream directly. Fatty acids and glycerol (from the breakdown of fats) are taken up by your lymphatic system.

Excretion

Excretion is the removal of potentially poisonous end-products from metabolism, normally in your urine and faeces. In humans the main organs of excretion are the kidneys, through which urine is eliminated, and the large intestine, through which solid or semi-solid waste is expelled.

The kidneys

Your kidneys play a key role in keeping the composition of your blood constant by filtering it to remove excess water and waste products which are then secreted as urine. Every 24 hours your kidneys filter in the region of 150 litres of blood and produce around 1.5 litres of urine.

PLTS

Using a variety of sources to research the processes of digestion, absorption and excretion for Assessment activity 11.1 page 257 will demonstrate your skills as an **independent enquirer**. Evidencing the links between these processes will demonstrate your ability to think critically.

Functional skills

Using information communication technology (**ICT**) to produce your leaflet for Assessment activity 11.1 page 257 will develop your ability to access, search for and select ICT-based information and evaluate its fitness for purpose, and evidence your ability to present information in ways that are fit for the intended audience.

Assessment activity 11.1

1. Produce a leaflet for athletes, describing the importance of good nutrition to health and performance and introducing them to nutritional requirements and common terminology associated with nutrition. **P1**

2. Create a short PowerPoint presentation describing the structure and function of the digestive system. **P2**

Grading tips

P1 You must be able to describe nutrition and nutritional requirements using frequently used terminology. You should be familiar with guidelines recommended by public health sources.

P2 You need to describe the digestive system and be familiar with the enzymes that break down specific food sources, and you should evidence the links between digestion, absorption and excretion.

2. Know energy intake and energy expenditure in sports performance

2.1 Energy

Energy is obtained from the foods you eat and used to support your basal metabolic rate (the minimum amount of energy required to sustain your body's vital functions in a waking state), and all activity carried out at work and leisure.

Remember

- 1 calorie (cal) = 4.2 joules (J)
- 1 kilocalorie (kcal) = 4.2 kilojoules (kJ)
- 1 kilocalorie (kcal) = 1,000 calories (cal)
- 1 kilojoule (kJ) = 1,000 joules (J)

Measures

Energy is measured in **calories** or **joules**. As both these units are very small they are multiplied by 1,000 and referred to as **kilocalories** (the UK system) or **kilojoules** (the metric or international system).

Key terms

Calorie – the energy required to raise 1 gram of water by 1 °C.

Joule – 1 joule of energy moves a mass of 1 gram at a velocity of 1 metre per second. Approximately 4.2 joules = 1 calorie.

Kilocalorie – the energy required to raise the temperature of 1 kg of water by 1 °C. Equal to 1,000 calories and used to convey the energy value of food. Kilocalories are often simply referred to as calories.

Kilojoule – a unit of measurement for energy, but like the calorie the joule is not a large unit of energy; therefore kilojoules are more often used.

Sources

The potential fuel sources available to exercising muscles are listed below. Their relative value as fuels for activity differs. Protein may be used during prolonged periods of exercise and towards the latter stages of endurance events like the marathon, particularly if fat and carbohydrate as sources of fuel within the working muscles have become limited.

Fats

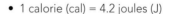

1 gram fat = 9.0 kcal = 38 kJ

Carbohydrates

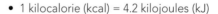

1 gram carbohydrate = 4.0 kcal = 17 kJ

Proteins

1 gram protein = 4.0 kcal = 17 kJ

Fat and carbohydrate are the main energy fuels for your exercising muscles. Exercising muscles prefer glucose as a fuel, particularly as the intensity of the activity being undertaken increases. When you exercise, your muscles use energy at a rate that is directly proportional to the intensity of your activity. If this energy is not replaced as it is used up, your muscles will be unable to maintain their rate of work and the intensity of the activity will need to be reduced or stopped.

Measuring requirements

Body composition

The most commonly used method of classification of body type is known as somatotyping, which recognises three basic body types:

- ectomorph – a slim build, long limbs, delicate bone structure, a low body fat and muscle content, and usually finds weight gain difficult
- endomorph – a heavy build, rounded shape, a tendency to gain weight, and generally finds weight loss difficult
- mesomorph – a muscular build and large bone structure.

Most of us have characteristics of each type to a varying degree, and although many women in particular want to be slim and ectomorph-like, it is important to note that it is impossible to alter your basic body type.

Lean body mass

Body composition refers to the lean body mass and body fat that make up total body weight. Lean body mass includes bone, muscle, water, connective and organ tissues. Body fat includes both essential and non-essential fat stores.

Percentage of body fat

People actively engaged in fitness regimes are often concerned about their weight, whether for performance or health reasons. Unlike basic body type, it is possible to alter body composition, with exercise generally having the effect of increasing lean body mass and decreasing body fat.

Methods of assessing percentage of body fat include:

- skinfold analysis
- bioelectrical impedance analysis
- hydrodensitometry (underwater weighing).

All these methods have most merit in measuring changes in body composition over time rather than absolute values. In order to minimise potential errors in measuring changes in body composition over time:

- always use the same method
- ensure the subject is assessed by the same person
- take repeat measurements at the same time of day.

Skinfold analysis

This technique uses callipers to measure the thickness of skinfolds at various anatomical sites, usually the biceps, triceps, subscapula and suprailiac crest. The sum of these measurements is used to calculate percentage of body fat, using equations or tables that take into account the subject's age and gender.

This is a relatively cheap and convenient method but it requires a high degree of skill. It is thought to be generally reliable if performed correctly.

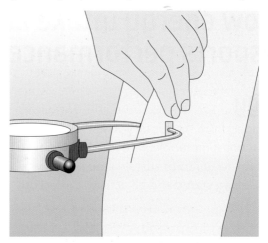

Figure 11.4: Skinfold callipers measure the amount of subcutaneous fat (fat immediately below the skin) in millimetres

Bioelectrical impedance analysis

Bioelectrical impedance analysis (BIA) is fast becoming a standard technique for assessment of body composition, particularly in the health and fitness sector. BIA machines provide a quick, easy and non-invasive method of estimating percentage body fat. Some equipment requires the attachment of electrodes to the hands and feet (Bodystat), others require the subject to stand on specially designed scales (Tanita) or to grip handles (Omron).

BIA measures resistance to the flow of an electrical current through the body, using the fact that different body tissues display different impedance to the flow of the current. Tissues that contain a large amount of water, such as lean tissue, provide a lower impedance than tissues such as bone and fat.

When using BIA techniques a number of assumptions have to be made, and equations applied, to obtain a body fat percentage figure. One potential drawback is that impedance measurements are related to the water content of tissues, so for accurate results subjects must be fully hydrated, and must abstain from exercise and substances which exert a diuretic effect – such as alcohol or caffeine – for at least 24 hours before the test. Invalid results may also be obtained for women immediately before or during menstruation, when the body's water content may be higher than normal.

Hydrodensitometry

This is considered to be one of the most accurate methods of assessing body composition. However, it is expensive and time-consuming and can be stressful as it requires the subject to be submerged in water. The technique measures body density that can be translated mathematically into percentage of body fat. It relies on Archimedes' principle of water displacement to estimate body density.

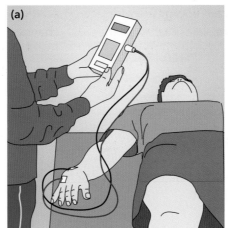
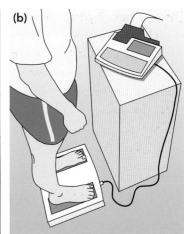
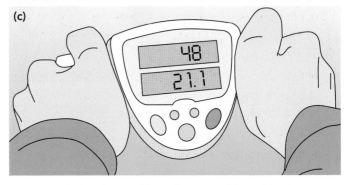

Figure 11.5: Bioelectrical impedance machines: (a) using electrodes, (b) foot-to-foot and (c) hand-to-hand

Take it further

Undertake an Internet search using the term 'body composition assessment'. Evaluate the range of body composition assessment products available in terms of affordability, ease of application and suitability for use with athletes. Be sure to investigate the methods of air displacement plethysmography and dual-energy x-ray absorptiometry.

Body weight

Body weight, more precisely referred to as body mass, is usually measured in kilograms. Some individuals have problems controlling their body weight, often resulting in obesity. Some sports are categorised based on body weight. Energy and nutrient requirements may also be expressed relative to body mass.

Direct and indirect calorimetry

Energy expenditure can be assessed by direct or indirect calorimetry, essentially through the measurement of heat production.

Direct calorimetry (DC) measures the actual amount of heat produced by the body. It uses an airtight chamber where heat produced by the subject warms water surrounding it.

Indirect calorimetry (IC) estimates heat production by measuring respiratory gases. The most common technique is via mouthpiece and Douglas bag collection or mouthpiece and gas analysis system, with energy consumption calculated from the amount of oxygen consumed. The consumption of 1 litre of oxygen equates to approximately 4.8 kcal of energy expended, assuming a mixture of fats and carbohydrates are oxidised.

Take it further

Using the Internet, investigate other measures of energy expenditure including doubly labelled water and motion analysers.

(a)

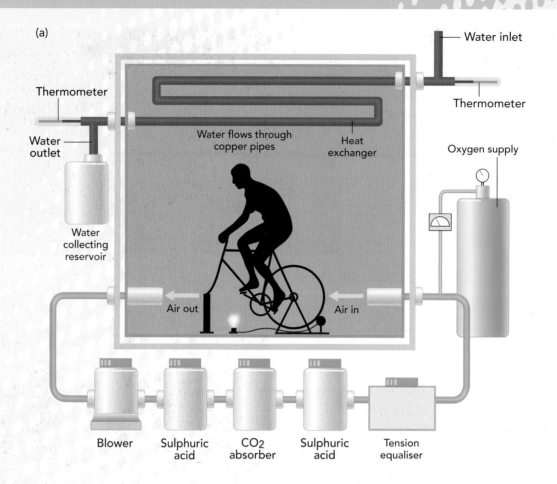

(b)

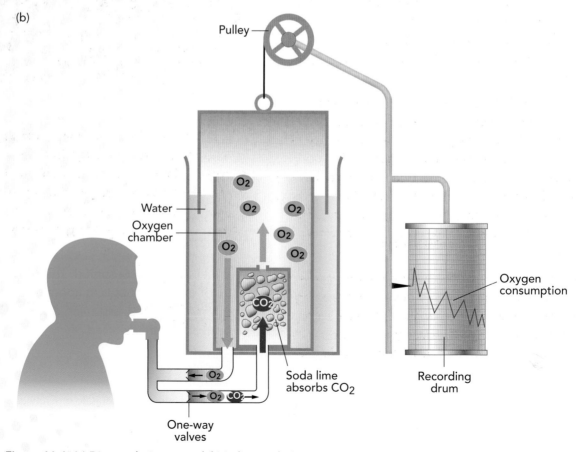

Figure 11.6: (a) Direct calorimetry and (b) indirect calorimetry

2.2 Energy balance

You are in energy balance when the amount of energy you take in as food and drink (energy input) equals the amount of energy you expend (energy output). You will neither be losing nor gaining weight. There are four major components to energy output: resting metabolic rate (RMR), dietary thermogenesis (DT), physical activity (PA) and adaptive thermogenesis (AT).

- Resting metabolic rate can account for 60–75 per cent of total energy output and represents the largest component of total daily energy expenditure. RMR is closely related to lean body mass and so is influenced by body composition. Muscle tissue is much more metabolically active than fat tissue. Gains in muscle mass will result in increases in RMR. RMR is also influenced by your age, sex and genetic background.

- Dietary thermogenesis refers to the energy expended above that of RMR for the processes of digestion, absorption, transport and storage of food. It is influenced by the calorie content and composition of your diet along with your individual nutritional status. High energy intakes and a regular eating pattern are thought to help maintain higher rates of dietary thermogenesis, while skipping meals and restrictive dietary practices lead to a reduction in this component of total energy expenditure.

- Physical activity represents the most variable component of your total energy expenditure. This is the additional energy expended above RMR and DT, and will contribute more to total daily energy expenditure in active individuals. Exactly how much it varies depends on how active your general lifestyle is, how often, how energetically, and for how long you participate in sport and exercise, and what type of activity it is.

- Adaptive thermogenesis is energy expenditure that occurs as a result of environmental or physiological stresses placed on your body, such as a change in temperature that may require you to respond by shivering or stress that causes anxiety or fidgeting.

Nutritional supplements are sometimes used to achieve and maintain energy balance. Investigate a range of supplements that make these claims.

When energy intake exceeds expenditure, this is referred to as **positive energy balance** and weight is gained. If intake is less than requirements, the additional energy required will be drawn from your body's fat reserves and weight will be lost. This is referred to as **negative energy balance**.

Remember

Energy balance is achieved when energy input equals energy output.

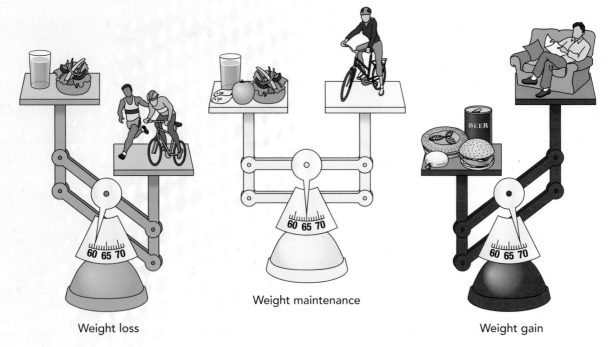

Figure 11.7: Energy balance

Basal metabolism

To estimate energy requirements, you first need to calculate basal metabolic requirements (BMR) in kilocalories per day using the data in Table 11.6.

	Age (years)	Basal metabolic requirements in kilocalories per day (W = weight in kilograms)
Males	10–17	BMR = 17.7W + 657
	18–29	BMR = 15.1W + 692
	30–59	BMR = 11.5W + 873
	60–74	BMR = 11.9W + 700
Females	10–17	BMR = 13.4W + 692
	18–29	BMR = 14.8W + 487
	30–59	BMR = 8.3W + 846
	60–74	BMR = 9.2W + 687

Table 11.6: Calculating basal metabolic requirements (Schofield et al., 1985)

Age

Your basal metabolism reduces with increasing age. After the age of 30, it falls by around 2 per cent per decade.

Gender

Males generally have greater muscle mass than females, so generally have a higher basal metabolic rate.

Climate

Exposure to hot or cold climates causes an increase in basal metabolism to maintain the body's internal temperature.

Physical activity

To estimate your total energy requirements you also need to consider your level of physical activity and training. The simplest method of estimating your total energy requirement is by multiplying your BMR by your **physical activity level (PAL)**. Calculating PALs requires you to make an assumption about the energy demands of both your occupational and non-occupational activity levels (see Table 11.7).

Activity: Skills

Using Tables 11.6 and 11.7, calculate your BMR and total daily energy requirements and record your answers in kilocalories per day.

Once you have calculated an estimate for your total energy requirement, you can predict your carbohydrate, protein and fat requirements. Remember that in general athletes will require an energy distribution of 50–60 per cent of calories from carbohydrate, 12–15 per cent from protein and 25–30 per cent from fat.

Non-occupational activity	Occupational activity					
	Light		Moderate		Heavy	
	Male	Female	Male	Female	Male	Female
Non-active	1.4	1.4	1.6	1.5	1.7	1.5
Moderately active	1.5	1.5	1.7	1.6	1.8	1.6
Very active	1.6	1.6	1.8	1.7	1.9	1.7

Table 11.7: Physical activity levels for three levels (adapted from Committee on Medical Aspects of Food and Nutrition Policy (COMA) 1991)

Assessment activity 11.2

1. Hold a group discussion to identify the range of sports participation in your class. In small groups, investigate the energy demands of some or all of these sports and prepare a short PowerPoint presentation to describe energy intake and energy expenditure in sports performance. **P3**

2. Produce a fact sheet for a specific sport to explain energy intake and energy expenditure in sports performance. **M1**

3. Consider the importance of energy balance in sport. Prepare a short PowerPoint presentation to support your views. **P4**

4. Explain the role of body composition assessment in the achievement and maintenance of energy balance in the athlete. **M2**

5. Analyse the effects of energy balance on sports performance. You could use some of the information you have collected in the Take it further activities in this section. **D1**

Grading tips

P3 You need to consider the importance of energy balance in sports performance.

M1 Consider the role of sports drinks, and energy gels and bars on achieving and maintaining energy balance.

P4 Describe energy balance and its importance to sports performance.

M2 Explain the importance of these measures in achieving and maintaining energy balance in the athlete.

D1 Consider examples from different sports and categories of athlete.

PLTS

Researching and analysing the importance of energy balance in a range of sports will develop you as an **independent enquirer** and **reflective learner**.

Functional skills

Discussing energy demands and interpreting energy balance and its importance in sports performance will develop your **English** skills in contributing to discussion, gathering arguments and opinions and making effective presentations.

3. Know the relationship between hydration and sports performance

During exercise, fluid requirements increase according to the type, duration and intensity of the exercise and the environmental conditions under which it is taking place. Understanding the relationship between hydration and sports performance is vital for achieving optimal performance in training and competition.

3.1 Hydration

Water is the main transport mechanism in your body, carrying nutrients, waste products and internal secretions. It also plays a vital role in temperature regulation, particularly during exercise, and aids the passage of food through your digestive system.

Water makes up around 50–60 per cent of your total body weight. Actual amounts vary depending on age, sex and body composition. Muscle has a higher water content than fat tissue, so leaner individuals have a higher water content than fatter individuals of the same body mass.

Water is lost from your body through a number of routes including urine, faeces, evaporation from the skin and expired breath. If water loss is high, your body becomes dehydrated. Under normal circumstances your body maintains a balance between fluid input and output. Table 11.8 illustrates the balance between water intake and water loss.

Signs and symptoms

Water is one of the most important nutrients. You cannot survive more than a few days without it. Losses may be as high as a litre per hour during endurance-type exercise, even higher in hot or humid conditions.

Fluid losses incurred by athletes during training and competition are linked to the body's need to maintain temperature within very narrow limits. During exercise, your body temperature rises and the extra heat is lost through sweating – evaporation of water from your skin's surface. If fluid lost through sweating is not replaced, there is a risk of dehydration and performance may suffer.

Dehydration

Dehydration can reduce strength, power and aerobic capacity. Severe dehydration can cause heatstroke and may be fatal. A loss as small as 2 per cent of body mass can be enough to begin to affect your ability to perform muscular work. For a 75 kg male this would be equivalent to a fluid loss of only 1.5 litres from the body. It is therefore important to minimise the risks of dehydration, and to note that thirst is a poor indicator of your body's hydration status. The warning signs for dehydration include:

- lack of energy and early fatigue during exercise
- feeling hot
- clammy or flushed skin
- not needing to go to the toilet
- nausea
- headache*
- disorientation*
- shortness of breath.*

* These are signs of advanced dehydration.

Daily water input		Daily water output	
Source	Millilitres	Source	Millilitres
Fluids	1,200	Urine	1,250
Food	1,000	Skin	850
Metabolism	350	Lungs	350
		Faeces	100
Total	2,550	Total	2,550

Table 11.8: Daily water balance for a sedentary 70 kg adult male

Hyperhydration

Hyperhydration is a state of increased hydration, producing a greater than normal body water content. Starting exercise in a hyperhydrated state can improve **thermoregulation**, improving heat dissipation and exercise performance. However, this area of sports science research needs to be further investigated.

Hypohydration

Hypohydration is a state of decreased hydration, producing a less-than-normal body water content. Hypohydration increases core body temperature, impairs the sweating response and causes skeletal muscle fatigue.

Superhydration

Superhydration is a state of hydration achieved by manipulation of the ergogenic aid glycerol. When ingested with large volumes of water (1–2 litres), glycerol has been shown to increase water retention in the body. This reduces overall heat stress during exercise in hot conditions, lowering heart rate and body temperature. However, not all glycerol studies have shown improvements in hydration or endurance performance and side effects may include headaches, dizziness, gastrointestinal upsets and bloating.

Fluid intake

To maintain water balance, a sedentary individual requires 2–2.5 litres of fluid per day, the equivalent of 6–8 cups. Around 10 per cent of your daily fluid requirements come from the metabolic processes that release water within your body. The other 90 per cent is derived from your diet. Approximately 60 per cent of this comes directly from fluids and the rest comes from food, particularly that with a high water content.

Pre-event

Athletes should be encouraged to begin fully hydrated and to drink plenty of water both during and after activity. Training should be used as the opportunity to practise fluid-replacement strategies that run smoothly in competitive situations. Drinking 300–500 ml of fluid 10–15 minutes before exercise is recommended.

Inter-event

Many factors can influence the effectiveness of fluid-replacement strategies during exercise. Fluid replacement can be accelerated by drinking still, cool drinks of a reasonable volume. They should not be too concentrated, and they must be palatable to drink. The more intense the activity, the more the absorption of fluid is slowed. Unpleasant symptoms experienced when drinking during exercise usually mean you started drinking too late and your body is already dehydrated. Drinking 150–200 ml every 15–20 minutes during exercise is recommended, especially if the exercise lasts longer than an hour.

Post-event

Weight and urine-colour checks are a useful and simple way of monitoring fluid status during and after training and competition. A weight reduction of 1 kg is equivalent to 1 litre of fluid loss. Frequent trips to the toilet to pass plentiful quantities of pale-coloured urine are an indicator of good hydration, whereas scant quantities of dark-coloured urine indicate poor hydration. These simple checks before and after exercise can be useful in determining fluid requirements post-training or during competition. As a guide, after exercise fluid losses should be replaced 1.5 times within the first 2 hours of recovery.

Sources
Water

Water is considered to be an adequate fluid suitable for most exercise, but some sports drinks may be useful if exercising at higher intensities for longer durations.

Sports drinks

Most sports drinks aim to provide three nutrients: carbohydrates to replace energy, water to replace fluid and **electrolytes** to replace minerals lost in sweat. The carbohydrate is usually glucose, fructose, sucrose or maltodextrins, which are all saccharides that are quickly absorbed. Sports drinks often contain a range of minerals and vitamins, but most often include the electrolytes sodium and potassium; both these macrominerals are lost in sweat. Sodium promotes the absorption of glucose and water. Magnesium is another mineral lost in sweat, and is present in water and most sports drinks.

Key terms

Thermoregulation – the ability to keep the body's temperature constant, even if the surrounding temperature is different.

Electrolytes – salts in the blood, for example, calcium, potassium and sodium.

Hypertonic

Hypertonic drinks contain over 8 per cent of carbohydrate and are absorbed more slowly. Although they provide a source of carbohydrate replenishment, they are not ideal for optimal rehydration and may need to be consumed with other fluids. These are best used in the recovery stage after exercise.

Isotonic

Isotonic drinks contain the same concentration of glucose to water as the blood: 4–8 per cent or up to 8 grams per 100 ml of water. They usually contain sodium, which makes them more quickly absorbed into the bloodstream. They are useful when exercise has been prolonged or during warmer weather. They can also be used before exercise.

Why is it important to minimise dehydration in sports performance?

Hypotonic

Hypotonic drinks have a lower concentration of carbohydrates and are more diluted than isotonic or hypertonic drinks. They contain less than 4 per cent

carbohydrate (4 grams per 100 ml of water) and are generally easily absorbed and well tolerated. Although water is adequate for non-endurance training or when sweat losses are small, these drinks may encourage fluid replacement through enhanced taste.

Take it further

Investigate a range of commercial sports drinks and evaluate their potential use before, during and after exercise.

Devise a simple 5-point plan to ensure that athletes maintain hydration during sport and exercise. You may use this plan later when formulating your diet plan for a selected sports performer.

Before	During	After
300–500 ml 10–15 minutes before activity	150–200 ml every 15–20 minutes	Based on body mass lost; replace losses 150%

Table 11.9: Fluid replacement strategies for exercise

3.2 Effects on sports performance

The greater the **frequency**, **intensity** and **duration** of exercise, the more important fluid replacement strategies become and the more likely that sports drinks will have a useful contribution to make in terms of effects on performance and **recovery**, by providing not only fluid but also energy. Sound nutritional strategies, including those relating to fluid replacement, may have their biggest contribution to make in allowing athletes to train consistently to meet the desired adaptations to training in terms of **specificity** and **progression**.

Assessment activity 11.3 P5 BTEC

Describe hydration and its effects on sports performance. **P5**

Grading tips

P5 You must show knowledge of the relevance of hydration and how it affects performance. Try to link your answer to the body's energy balance and the digestive process.

PLTS

Researching the effects of hydration on sports performance will develop you as an **independent enquirer**.

Functional skills

Developing and formulating your information into a leaflet, poster or PowerPoint presentation could evidence development of your **ICT** skills to present information in a way that is fit for purpose and includes text, tables and images.

4. Be able to plan a diet appropriate for a selected sports activity

4.1 Diet

To be able to plan a diet for a selected sports activity, you need to consider the physiological demands of the activity, the phase of training and the individual's needs. These will help you to plan a **balanced diet** across the food groups. This is also known as **sports nutrition**.

Balanced diet

Foods are popularly classed as good or bad, healthy or unhealthy, with **healthy eating** often viewed as a hardship or a chore. However, it is better to look at the overall balance of foods eaten as either healthy or unhealthy.

Key terms

Balanced diet – a diet that provides the correct amounts of nutrients without excess or deficiency.

Sports nutrition – the influence of nutritional strategies on sports performance during preparation for, participation in and recovery from training and competition.

Healthy eating – the pursuit of a balanced diet to support health and reduce the risks of chronic disease. Healthy eating principles should form the solid foundations on which athletes can build more specific nutritional strategies to support training and competition.

Fruit and vegetables

Bread, other cereals and potatoes

FLAKES

Milk and dairy foods

Foods containing fat
Foods containing sugar

Meat, fish and alternatives

Figure 11.8 A healthy plate – based on the Eatwell Plate

267

A simple guide to healthy eating:

- eat the correct amount to maintain a healthy body weight
- cut back on your fat intake, particularly fat from saturated sources
- eat plenty of foods with a high starch and fibre content
- don't eat sugary foods too often
- use salt sparingly and reduce your reliance on convenience foods
- ensure adequate intakes of vitamins and minerals by eating a wide variety of foods
- if you drink alcohol, keep within sensible limits
- enjoy your food and do not become obsessed with your diet or dieting.

Carbohydrates

To achieve optimal carbohydrate stores, athletes may need to top up with sugary sources that are more rapidly absorbed like sweets, dried fruit, fruit juice, and sugary or sports drinks.

As a guide, 4–5 grams of carbohydrate per kilogram of body weight should be sufficient if you do less than an hour's exercise each day, 5–6 grams per kilogram of body weight if you exercise for an hour a day, 6–7 grams for 1–2 hours per day and 8–10 grams per kilogram of body weight for heavy training exceeding 3 hours per day.

The best approach is to base all meals and snacks around starchy carbohydrate foods and eat at regular intervals. Glycogen – your body's store of carbohydrate – is replenished most efficiently within the first half-hour to 2 hours after exercise.

Fats

Fat provides a concentrated source of energy and is the predominant fuel for low-intensity activity. In the average UK diet, fat accounts for 40 per cent of total calorie intake. To promote good health it is recommended that intake is between 30 and 35 per cent. Those engaging in regular intense activity need to reduce this further to achieve recommended carbohydrate intakes.

Proteins

Many athletes believe they need to eat large amounts of meat, fish, eggs, pulses and dairy products to build muscle and increase strength, but in most cases this is not necessary. That can only be achieved by the appropriate training. Some of these foods are also high in animal fats, which should be reduced for long-term health. They may also leave no appetite for carbohydrate foods to provide sufficient energy stores to support training. Eating a normal varied diet and meeting energy (calorie) requirements should provide enough protein.

Active individuals require more protein per kilogram of body weight in order to promote tissue growth and repair. The International Olympic Committee's second Consensus Conference on Nutrition for Sport in 2003 recommended an intake of 1.2–1.7 grams per kilogram of body weight per day. The lower end of this range should cover the requirements of most endurance athletes, with the upper end meeting the needs of those engaging in more strength and power activities.

Water

Normal fluid requirements are in the region of 30–35 ml per kilogram of body weight per day, or 1 ml per calorie of energy requirement. Thirst is a poor indicator of dehydration, so drinking before the sensation of thirst is recommended to ensure adequate fluid status.

Fibre

Your daily requirement is 18 grams per day. Athletes with high carbohydrate requirements will need to manage fibre intake because consuming large quantities of fibre-rich carbohydrate food can make the diet bulky and filling, with the potential to limit overall food and energy intake.

Vitamins and minerals

Athletes often believe they need more vitamins and minerals than the average person. There is no doubt that an adequate supply is necessary for health, but whether regular exercise increases requirements is a different matter. The scientific consensus is that exercise does not particularly increase the need for micronutrients, although there may be a case for increased requirements of nutrients involved in energy metabolism. Generally, athletes will be eating greater quantities of food to meet increased energy requirements, and as a result will be automatically increasing vitamin and mineral intakes – as long as nutrient-rich foods are chosen.

4.2 Activities

Different activities require different dietary plans or strategies to optimise performance.

Aerobic

Aerobic or endurance activities will significantly challenge the athlete's energy and fluid stores. The longer and more intense the aerobic training or competition, the more depleted these stores are likely to become. A key goal for aerobic activities should be to maximise glycogen stores. Increasing carbohydrate intake during the 2 or 3 days before competition is a useful strategy. Carbohydrate supplements in the form of energy drinks, bars or gels may be a useful addition to the diet.

Endurance athletes should start exercise fully hydrated. The longer the duration of the activity, the more important it is to consume fluids during it. Sports drinks may be useful as they provide carbohydrate as well as replacing fluids.

Some aerobic activities may benefit from carbohydrate loading. The amount of glycogen available for storage in the muscles is related to the amount of carbohydrate consumed and the level and intensity of activity undertaken. For most sports, a diet consisting of 5–10 grams of carbohydrate per kilogram of body weight will maintain liver and muscle glycogen stores. However, the aim of carbohydrate loading is to increase the muscles' capacity to store glycogen above their normal level. This may be useful to athletes competing in endurance events that last longer than 90 minutes, such as marathon running, triathlons and endurance swimming. Although carbohydrate loading does not benefit all athletes, everyone regularly training and competing in sports should consume a high carbohydrate diet at all times and will benefit from a carbohydrate-rich meal or snack before training or competition.

Remember

The goal of carbohydrate loading is to increase the muscles' capacity to store glycogen above their normal level, usually in preparation for an endurance event.

Anaerobic

In anaerobic activities such as strength, power and sprint sports, the key role of nutritional strategies is to support the development of lean body mass (muscle) as well as to meet energy demands. Although carbohydrate requirements are not as great as for aerobic activities, they are still important. Combining carbohydrate with protein post-exercise promotes an **anabolic** environment and increases protein synthesis that helps to promote muscle development; however, excessive protein intake should be avoided. Some team sports may fall into this category.

Key term

Anabolism – the constructive metabolism of the body – the building of tissue.

Muscular strength and endurance

Many sports can fall into this category depending on the particular physiological demands of the sport. For example, high levels of muscular strength and endurance are required for team sports such as rugby as well as weight category sports such as judo. Nutritional demands will be dictated by the nature of the individual sport and participant requirements, but key nutrients in all cases are carbohydrate and fluid.

Flexibility

For sports that require a good deal of flexibility such as gymnastics, diving and figure skating, weight control is a serious issue. Evidence suggests participants in these aesthetic or appearance-orientated sports, where performance is subjectively evaluated by judges, may be more prone to eating-disorders. Leanness or a specific weight may be considered important for optimal performance, placing greater emphasis on what the athlete eats and how they look. However, it is important to remember that the fewer calories consumed, the fewer nutrients consumed. Calcium and iron intakes are reported to be particularly low in studies investigating the diet of female participants in these sports.

Healthy eating and Eatwell Plate principles apply to the planning of dietary intakes for these sports, but greater emphasis may be placed on a low-fat diet. However, this should not be at the expense of essential nutrients such as carbohydrate, protein, vitamins and minerals. Adequate fluid intake and hydration are also essential to maintain concentration for the technical demands of these sports.

Timing

Many athletes undertake a periodised programme of training. Periodisation represents the organised division of the training year and aims to prepare athletes for:

- achievement of an optimum improvement in performance
- a definite peak in the competition season
- main competitions within that peak.

Training undertaken within the programme is a form of stress to the body. If it is undertaken properly, the athlete adapts to that stress. Good nutritional practices are important in allowing the body to adapt and to deliver performance improvements.

Pre-season

For most sports, pre-season nutritional requirements need to take account of the frequency, intensity, duration and specificity of training. As training progresses in frequency, intensity and duration, it can be expected that the athlete's energy, carbohydrate and fluid requirements will increase. If energy and nutrient demands are not met, the athlete will increase their risk of injury and illness. In addition, reducing post-season weight gain is often a target of pre-season nutritional strategies.

Mid-season

Nutritional demands of the mid-season phase are focused on maintaining energy and fluid requirements as the competition schedule gets underway. During this time, less overall nutrition may be required but more attention may need to be placed on pre-event preparation and post-event recovery strategies to remain free from injury and illness.

Post-season

Post-season presents a window of opportunity where the athlete can relax dietary intake a little but unnecessary weight gain should be monitored. Energy and fluid requirements are likely to be at their lowest during this period.

Pre-event

Many of the principles of preparing for a competition mirror those of the training diet. A pre-competition

Choose a team sport and consider how the changing phases of the training and competition cycle impact on nutritional demands.

meal should aim to top up muscle and liver glycogen stores. Therefore, it should be rich in carbohydrate but low in fat and fibre and should contain a moderate amount of protein. It should be remembered that larger meals take longer to digest and that nervousness can result in delayed digestion.

Competition is not a time to experiment with new foods. The pre-event meal should be made of familiar foods and provide adequate fluids. Solid foods can usually be consumed with comfort up to 2 hours before an event, but liquid meals or carbohydrate drinks can be consumed up to 30–60 minutes before.

Athletes in events lasting longer than 90 minutes should be advised, where possible, to taper training in the week leading up to the event, include a rest day, and consume more carbohydrate and fluid than normal.

Inter-event

During training and competition, fluid loss is a major consideration. During intense training or competition isotonic sports drinks may be consumed. This may be beneficial especially if training or competition lasts longer than 60 minutes. During endurance or ultra-endurance events lasting longer than 4 hours, solid foods may be required. In these instances, energy bars or gels might be useful as a more concentrated source of carbohydrate.

Remember

Regular sports performers should be encouraged to practise their fluid and fuelling regimes in training to ensure that they do not run into any unexpected problems during competition.

Post-event

Good nutrition can make its greatest contribution in aiding recovery between training sessions. For the regular sports performer, performance improvements are the product of the body's adaptation to the demands of training. Sound nutrition has its biggest impact in supporting athletes in training consistently and effectively to achieve the desired adaptations.

What is consumed, how much and how soon after an intense workout or competition can all influence the recovery process. Sensible choices in terms of food and fluids will allow faster recovery for the next training session. It is important to refuel as soon as possible after each workout or competition. The longer refuelling is delayed, the longer it will take to fully refuel. Athletes may find it easier to have small, frequent meals and snacks at regular intervals to help to maximise glycogen synthesis.

To refuel efficiently, a high carbohydrate diet is required. Post-exercise carbohydrates that are easy to eat and digest are preferred. Athletes are advised to consume a high-carbohydrate (at least 50 grams) low-fat snack as soon as possible after training or competition, preferably within the first half-hour – when the muscles' capacity to refuel is greatest. They should eat their next meal, which should be rich in carbohydrate, within 2 hours.

After exercise, rehydration should start immediately. Drinks containing carbohydrates will also assist with energy and glycogen replacement. These may be particularly useful if the activity has been intense and resulted in a suppression of appetite and a reluctance to eat solid foods.

Case study: Meal plan

Jon is 16 years old and is competing in a national badminton tournament tomorrow. Considering Jon's overall nutritional requirements and the demands of his sport, suggest a suitable pre-competition meal plan and give some advice on how he might ensure that he keeps fuelled and hydrated during the tournament.

Suggest ways in which you might monitor or evaluate Jon's nutritional preparation for the competition and the impact of your advice on his performance.

4.3 Planning diets

Before you can safely and effectively plan and implement balanced eating programmes and nutritional strategies to support training and competition for others, you need to be able to critically evaluate your own eating habits and activity patterns and consider the relationship between them.

Keep a record of everything you consume for at least a 3-day period, which should include one weekend day. For a more detailed evaluation, record your intake for a full week.

Write down **everything** you eat and drink. Be as accurate and honest as possible, and be sure not to modify your usual intake at this stage, otherwise you will not be evaluating your typical diet. Carry your record with you at all times and record food and drink as they are consumed. You should describe:

- The type and quantity of food and drink consumed. Estimate the portion size using standard household measures, such as slices of bread, millilitres of fluid, tablespoons of vegetables, or give the weight.

- When and where the food or drink was consumed. These points are useful when assessing external factors that affect your dietary intake.

- Cooking methods and type of food preparation.

- Activity or exercise you took part in, including its duration and intensity (light, moderate or hard).

Compare your record to the Eatwell Plate model (see Figure 11.8 on page 267). Write a short report on your findings.

Is your diet better than you thought, or is there room for improvement?

Does your diet meet the demands you make on it as a result of any participation in sport and exercise?

Appropriate for selected activity

Athletes should pay careful attention to foods that can enhance, not hinder, their preparation for participation in and recovery from training and competition. Most athletes will obtain all the energy and nutrients they need by eating when they are hungry and choosing a balanced and varied diet.

Sports can be categorised into the following groups:

- multi-sprint or team sports, e.g. soccer
- strength sports, e.g. sprinting
- endurance and ultra-endurance sports, e.g. marathon running and triathlon
- weight category sports, e.g. boxing
- aesthetic sports, e.g. diving.

Each category requires sound nutritional strategies to support successful performance. Winning, avoiding injury and illness, and improving fitness are what matter to most competitive sportspeople. With the intermittent nature of team sports, the intensity at which they are performed can alter at any time. These changes are irregular and can be random, and may draw significantly on the body's glycogen stores. Performance may be impaired towards the end of a match if glycogen stores are running low. Weight-loss methods and restrictive dietary practices are often used by athletes in weight category and aesthetic sports, with potential dangers to both health and performance.

Appropriate for selected sports performer

There are a number of methods for collecting information on what people eat and drink. These include the 24-hour diet recall, the diet history or interview technique, daily food records or diaries, weighed food intake records and food frequency questionnaires.

With a partner, decide on an appropriate template for the purpose of recording all information relating to meal times, types of food and fluid consumed and cooking methods used.

1. **a)** Take turns to interview each other to recall all food and drink consumed in the past 24 hours. Use your template to record the details of your interview.

   b) What are the main advantages and disadvantages of this method of dietary intake recording?

2. **a)** Interview the same person again, but this time ask them to recall everything eaten and drunk in the past 7 days. Record the details using the same template.

   b) What are the main advantages and disadvantages of this method of dietary intake recording?

You may choose to use this technique to gain information on dietary intake of selected athletes. It is important when interviewing people to adopt a professional approach and to maintain confidentiality. Remember that an individual's food intake is a personal issue and should be handled sensitively. You should also ask if there are any medical factors such as diabetes or allergies that affect eating habits. These people should always be referred to a qualified professional for dietary advice.

- The 24-hour diet recall is quick and easy, but relies heavily on memory. The interviewer questions the subject about what he or she usually eats and drinks. It is useful in assessing the quality of food intake and may reveal imbalances such as a potentially high fat intake. However, it is rarely adequate to provide a quantitative estimate of nutrient intakes to allow for comparison with Dietary Reference Values.

- The diet history or interview is quick and easy to use, but again relies heavily on memory. The interviewer questions the subject about what he or she usually eats and drinks, but over a longer time period. Recollections usually underestimate intake and there is the danger of fabrication to impress the interviewer. The method is, however, useful in assessing the quality of dietary intake and may be able to reveal dietary imbalances in the same way as the 24-hour recall.

- Daily food record or diet diary: this can give a good overall guide to the types and quantities of food and drink consumed. At least 3 days should be recorded, including one weekend day to account for any different food patterns. For a more detailed picture, a 7-day record is recommended. With athletes, the record should include rest and competition days as well as training days.

- Weighed food intake: individual foods are weighed before consumption. This method is time-consuming and intrusive, and could lead to distortion of the overall pattern of foods consumed in order to make weighing and recording easier.

Assessment of needs

When developing sound eating habits and nutritional strategies to support training and competition, the following issues are important:

- the types of food eaten to support training and competition

- the timing of meals and snacks around training and competition

- ensuring a balanced diet is achieved in respect of all nutrients

- maintaining a sufficient fluid intake

- encouraging an adequate calcium and iron intake, particularly for females

- promoting long-term health and reducing the risk of chronic disease

- the problems of travelling to training and competition venues

- minimising the risk of injury and illness.

The nutritional requirements for different sports and individuals will vary according to:

- the type of sport and training methods undertaken

- the intensity of training or competition

- the duration of training or competition

- the frequency of training or competition

- the training status and fitness level of the individual.

The Eatwell Plate principles should be used to plan meals. These principles should form the foundations on which to develop more specific sports nutrition strategies. Athletes should eat sufficient carbohydrate and start refuelling as soon as possible after training, when muscle capacity to refuel is at its greatest. This may not coincide with traditional meal times. Eating may need to be fitted in around the training process, with smaller, more frequent meals and snacks being necessary. Snacks and fluids should be carried in the kit bag at all times.

Rest days are important, and should be used to recover from the stresses of training and competition. A high fluid intake should be encouraged. In many sports, post-match alcohol consumption is traditional, but it is important to rehydrate with other fluids before drinking alcohol. Where an injury has been sustained, alcohol consumption may delay recovery and should be avoided for at least 48 hours.

Weight gain

Weight can be gained by increasing the amount of fat or the amount of lean body mass. Both will register as increases in weight on the scales, but the results will be very different in terms of body composition. Gains in fat weight are relatively easy to achieve – as most people wishing to lose weight would testify – but gains in lean body mass can only be achieved as a result of adaptations to a progressive strength training programme, supported by an adequate diet.

Weight loss

Most athletes are concerned about either attaining or maintaining an optimal body weight. Weight-category sports include body-building, boxing, horse racing, martial arts and rowing. Participants in these sports must compete within a given weight range.

For some sports a low body weight may be crucial, which for some may be below their natural weight. These might be considered as weight-controlled sports, and include distance running, gymnastics, figure skating and diving. These sports may present challenges in maintaining a nutritionally adequate diet while reducing or maintaining weight. Inappropriate weight-loss practices include fasting or skipping meals, laxative abuse, bingeing and purging, and intentional dehydration by the use of sweatsuits or saunas. When most athletes talk about achieving weight loss, they usually mean fat loss, as losses in muscle mass may result in unfavourable changes in their power-to-weight ratio.

Muscle gain

When athletes talk about weight gain, they usually mean muscle gain. In this case strength training provides the stimulus for muscles to grow, while adequate nutrition provides the opportunity for them to grow at an optimal rate.

Rates of weight/muscle gain are dependent on genetics and body type. To gain strength and size, it is necessary to achieve a slightly positive energy balance – somewhere in the region of an extra 500 calories per day – and a protein intake of about 1.4–1.7 grams per kilogram of body mass. A high-protein diet, or supplementing with amino acids (common practice for many athletes wishing to gain muscle bulk and size) will not automatically lead to great increases in muscle size or strength. Achieving an adequate energy intake is more important.

Fat gain

In very few instances the athlete may wish to gain fat weight, such as in contact sports where additional body fat may provide extra protection.

Fat loss

When your diet provides more calories than your body needs for general maintenance and its current level of physical activity, the excess energy is stored in the form of body fat. The removal of excess fat is by a reversal of the processes that have stored this excess energy. If you burn more energy than you are consuming, the energy stored as fat will be broken down to provide energy.

Nutrition

Macronutrients

Performance in and recovery from exercise are enhanced by optimal nutrition. For most sports, carbohydrate requirements are likely to contribute 55–65 per cent of total energy intake, protein 12–15 per cent and the remainder coming from fat.

Micronutrients

Vitamin and mineral supplementation will not improve the performance of athletes whose diet is already adequate and varied. Those at risk of micronutrient deficiency are people who restrict energy intake, use severe weight-loss strategies or follow a high carbohydrate diet with low micronutrient density. Athletes should aim to consume diets that meet RNI values for micronutrient intakes.

Fibre

Athletes should aim to achieve fibre intakes in line with the sedentary population intake target of 18 grams per day.

Food groups

The Eatwell Plate is the UK's National Food Guide. Originally devised by the Health Education Authority as the Balance of Good Health, a simplified means of helping people understand healthy eating, it has been adopted by the Food Standards Agency. The model attempts to make following a balanced diet easier by identifying the types and proportions of foods required to achieve a healthy, balanced and varied diet, based around the five main food groups.

The model depicts a plate with divisions of varying sizes representing each of these five groups. Foods represented by larger divisions should feature in larger proportions in your diet, while those with the smaller shares should be consumed in smaller quantities or only occasionally (see Figure 11.8 on page 267).

This guide to healthy eating applies to most people in the UK, including those who engage in regular exercise and sport. It does not, however, apply to children under the age of five.

The key messages of the model are that you should aim to:

- base all your meals around starchy foods
- eat at least five servings of fruit and/or vegetables each day
- include milk and dairy foods, if possible three servings per day
- eat smaller portions of meat or fish, and try alternatives such as pulses
- limit your intake of foods with a high fat or sugar content.

Table 11.10 shows the recommended daily amounts and nutrients supplied by each of the main food groups.

Activity: Triathlon

Sayeed has recently taken up the triathlon. His usual diet consists of a macronutrient energy distribution of 40 per cent carbohydrate, 40 per cent fat and 20 per cent protein. He is about to enter his first major competition.

1. What effect could this macronutrient distribution have on his performance?

2. What practical advice could you offer to improve his diet?

3. What could Sayeed do in his preparation for the competition to help to delay fatigue?

Food	What is a serving?	Recommended amount per day	Main nutrients supplied
Grains and potatoes			
Bread, rolls, muffins, bagels, crumpets, chapattis, naan bread, pitta bread, tortillas, scones, pikelets, potato cakes, breakfast cereals, rice, pasta, noodles, couscous and potatoes	3 tbsp breakfast cereal, 1 Weetabix or Shredded Wheat, 1 slice of bread, ½ a pitta, 1 heaped tbsp boiled potato, pasta, rice or couscous	These should form the main part of all meals and snacks About a third of the total volume of food consumed each day	Carbohydrate, NSP (mainly insoluble), calcium, iron and B vitamins
Vegetables and fruits			
All types of fresh, frozen, canned and dried fruits and vegetables (except potatoes) and fruit and vegetable juices	1 apple, orange, pear, banana, 1 small glass of fruit juice, 1 small salad, 2 tbsp vegetables, 2 tbsp stewed or tinned fruit in juice	At least five portions per day About a third of the total volume of food consumed each day	NSP (especially soluble), vitamin C, folate and potassium
Oils			
Butter, margarine, cooking oils, mayonnaise, salad dressing, cream, pastries, crisps, biscuits and cakes	1 tsp butter or margarine, 1 tsp vegetable or olive oil, 1 tsp mayonnaise	These should be eaten sparingly and lower-fat options selected	Fat, essential fatty acids and some vitamins
Dairy			
Milk, yoghurt, cheese, fromage frais	1/3 pint milk, 1¼ oz cheese, 1 small carton yoghurt or cottage cheese	Two or three servings per day About a sixth of the total volume of food consumed each day	Protein, calcium, vitamins A and D
Meat, fish and alternative proteins			
Meat, poultry, fish, eggs, pulses, nuts, meat and fish products (e.g. sausages, beefburgers, fish cakes, fish fingers)	2–3 oz lean meat, chicken or oily fish, 4–5 oz white fish, 2 eggs, 1 small tin baked beans, 2 tbsp nuts, 4 oz Quorn or soya product	Two servings per day About a sixth of the total volume of food consumed each day	Protein, iron, zinc, magnesium and B vitamins Pulses provide a good source of NSP

Table 11.10: Food groups. How might the messages of the Eatwell Plate need to be adapted to meet the needs of a sports performer?

Sources

The sources of each food group are identified in Table 11.10, together with the main nutrients supplied by each food group.

Availability

Several factors influence food availability. These may include physical or environmental factors such as perishability and economic factors such as cost and budgeting priorities. Cooking skills and facilities, and nutritional knowledge, are also crucial factors in the provision and availability of food.

Assessment activity 11.4

1. Create a leaflet targeted at a specific sport to describe the components of a balanced diet to support performance. **P6**

2. Produce a short PowerPoint presentation targeted at a different sport to explain the components of a balanced diet to support performance. **M3**

3. Identify an athlete on whom you can undertake a dietary assessment (you may wish to consider your own diet if you are actively engaged in sport at a competitive level). Use the information you have gathered through the practical activities in this unit. Decide on an appropriate method for collecting information from your subject. **P7**

4. Analyse the information you have obtained and write a report which suggests, where necessary, appropriate modifications or improvements to support health and performance. Use a combination of manual and computer-based methods of processing and analysing nutrient intake information. **P7 M4 D2**

5. Plan a 2-week diet for your subject. Include advice on nutritional strategies to support preparation for, participation in and recovery from training and competition. **P7**

6. Explain the 2-week diet plan in terms of your selection of food and nutritional strategies. **M4**

7. Justify your food selection and nutritional strategies. Find ways of supporting your proposals by referring to relevant published material. **D2**

Grading tips

P6 You should consider the importance of carbohydrate, fat, protein, water, fibre, vitamins and minerals.

M3 You should explain the significance of the various nutrients in a balanced diet.

P7 You need to produce an appropriate 2-week diet plan for a named athlete. This should focus on aspects of achieving adequate fuelling and hydration.

M4 Explain your choice of food selection, fuelling and hydration strategies and their likely impact on training and competition performance. You should carefully consider the status of your athlete (amateur, semi-professional, elite) in explaining your 2-week plan.

D2 You need to justify your selection by being critical and looking for means to support your views. Do this with reference to relevant published material such as the ACSM (American College of Sports Medicine), Position Stand on Nutrition for Athletic Performance or the International Olympic Committee's Consensus on Nutrition for Athletes.

PLTS

Planning an appropriate diet for a selected athlete for a selected activity will develop you as a **self-manager**; interviewing your athlete, determining the physiological demands of their activity and evaluating their nutritional needs and intake will develop your skills as a **critical thinker** and **reflective learner**.

Functional skills

Calculating energy and nutrient requirements, interpreting food logs, devising menus and measuring body composition will require you to select and use a range of **Mathematics** skills to find solutions and advise on appropriate strategies to support training and competition.

Debbie Smith
Sports Nutritionist

I work as a freelance sports nutritionist. On a day-to-day basis I work with a range of athletes, from recreational to elite, to plan and advise on appropriate diets for their sport. I usually undertake a needs analysis interview with clients to ascertain relevant background information, particularly relating to factors that may affect their food intake and choice, and identify their nutritional and performance goals.

Another key element of my work is the assessment of adequacy of nutrient intake. For this athletes keep detailed diet and activity records that I analyse using nutritional analysis software. I then produce reports on their intake and feed this back to the athlete in a one-to-one consultation.

Most athletes, whatever their sport, will usually have weight-management goals, be it to lose, gain or maintain their current weight. It is recommended that if athletes have significant weight management concerns that they refer this to the sports nutritionist rather than trying to self-manage because without careful planning to the adjustments in intake that might be required nutritional inadequacies or imbalances might occur. Another key part of my work is the delivery of group education workshops, and I have from time to time undertaken supermarket visits and cooking sessions with clients.

The best thing about my job is educating clients to work out for themselves how to meet their dietary needs by increasing their knowledge of general nutrition and sport-specific nutritional strategies to aid performance.

Think about it!

If you are thinking about becoming a sports nutritionist:

- What knowledge and skills have you gained in this unit that provide you with an insight into the work of a sports nutritionist?
- What further knowledge and skills might you need to develop in order to pursue this career option?
- Try to spend a day shadowing a sports nutritionist at work, to see how they apply the theory you have learned in this unit.
- Ask a sports nutritionist about any professional training and accreditation that are necessary for the job.

Just checking

1. Define the term 'diet'.

2. Define the term Reference Nutrient Intake (RNI). What is the significance of this dietary reference value?

3. Draw and label a simple diagram of the digestive system.

4. Explain the term 'energy balance'.

5. Explain the components and the relative contributions of total energy expenditure.

6. Describe one method for estimating energy requirements.

7. List four routes of water loss from the body.

8. Because water losses are greater during exercise, athletes need to employ sound strategies for fluid replacement. What might be the signs and symptoms of dehydration and how might they be avoided?

9. What are the advantages and disadvantages of a high carbohydrate content in a sports drink?

10. Describe the skinfold analysis method of measuring body composition. Why is this one of the most widely used field techniques for assessing body composition in athletes?

11. List two micronutrients for special attention in the diet of athletes. Why might these be of particular concern in the diets of female athletes?

12. How soon do you need to eat after a hard training session and why is it so important to eat afterwards?

13. Describe the components of a balanced diet.

14. Describe how you might undertake an assessment of an athlete's nutritional needs.

15. What factors need to be taken into consideration when planning a diet for a selected sports activity?

edexcel

Assignment tips

- An awareness of the factors that affect food intake and choice, along with an understanding of the athlete's lifestyle and nutritional dilemmas they may face, will facilitate your ability to suggest realistic dietary plans to support sports performance.

- Being able to evaluate your own dietary practices and understand the links between your own diet, exercise and performance will help you meet the learning outcomes for this unit.

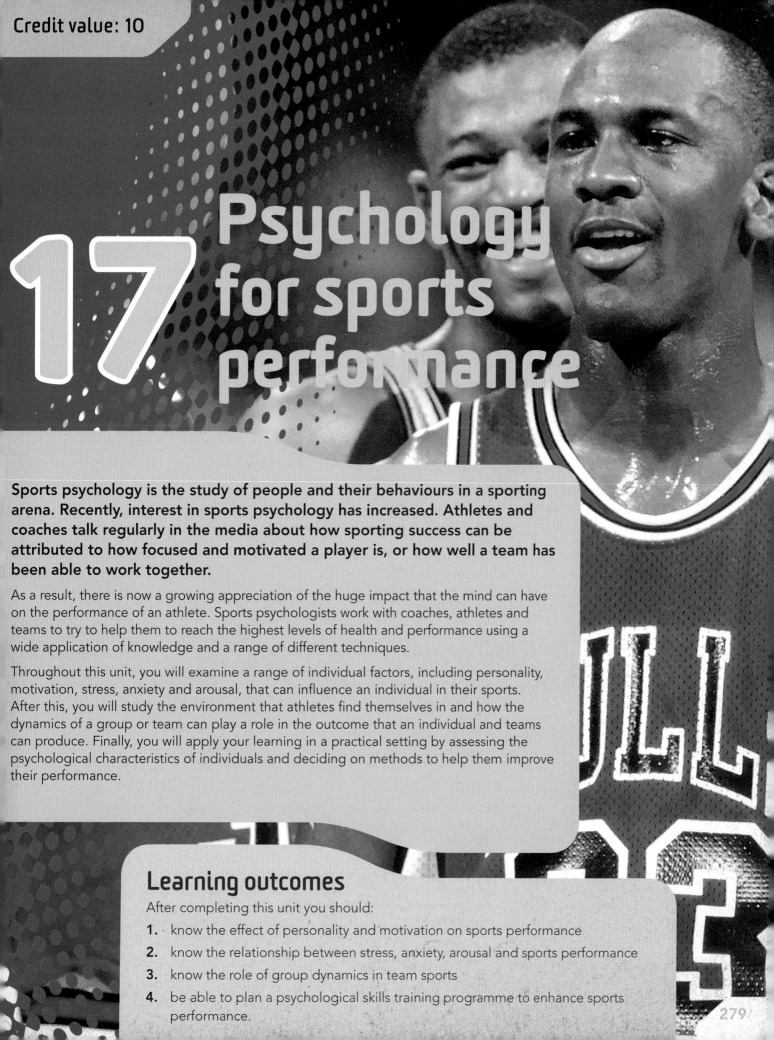

17 Psychology for sports performance

Sports psychology is the study of people and their behaviours in a sporting arena. Recently, interest in sports psychology has increased. Athletes and coaches talk regularly in the media about how sporting success can be attributed to how focused and motivated a player is, or how well a team has been able to work together.

As a result, there is now a growing appreciation of the huge impact that the mind can have on the performance of an athlete. Sports psychologists work with coaches, athletes and teams to try to help them to reach the highest levels of health and performance using a wide application of knowledge and a range of different techniques.

Throughout this unit, you will examine a range of individual factors, including personality, motivation, stress, anxiety and arousal, that can influence an individual in their sports. After this, you will study the environment that athletes find themselves in and how the dynamics of a group or team can play a role in the outcome that an individual and teams can produce. Finally, you will apply your learning in a practical setting by assessing the psychological characteristics of individuals and deciding on methods to help them improve their performance.

Learning outcomes

After completing this unit you should:

1. know the effect of personality and motivation on sports performance
2. know the relationship between stress, anxiety, arousal and sports performance
3. know the role of group dynamics in team sports
4. be able to plan a psychological skills training programme to enhance sports performance.

Assessment and grading criteria

This table shows you what you must do in order to achieve a **pass**, **merit** or **distinction** grade, and where you can find activities in this book to help you.

To achieve a **pass** grade the evidence must show that the learner is able to:	To achieve a **merit** grade the evidence must show that, in addition to the pass criteria, the learner is able to:	To achieve a **distinction** grade the evidence must show that, in addition to the pass and merit criteria, the learner is able to:
P1 define personality and how it affects sports performance **See Assessment activity 17.1, page 286**	**M1** explain the effects of personality and motivation on sports performance **See Assessment activities 17.1, page 286 and 17.2, page 290**	**D1** evaluate the effects of personality and motivation on sports performance **See Assessment activities 17.1, page 286 and 17.2, page 290**
P2 describe motivation and how it affects sports performance **See Assessment activity 17.2, page 290**		
P3 describe stress and anxiety, their causes, symptoms and effect on sports performance **See Assessment activity 17.3, page 297**		
P4 describe three theories of arousal and the effect on sports performance **See Assessment activity 17.3, page 297**	**M2** explain three theories of arousal and the effect on sports performance **See Assessment activity 17.3, page 297**	
P5 identify four factors which influence group dynamics and performance in team sports **See Assessment activity 17.4, page 303**	**M3** explain four factors which influence group dynamics and performance in team sports **See Assessment activity 17.4, page 303**	**D2** analyse four factors which influence group dynamics and performance in team sports **See Assessment activity 17.4, page 303**
P6 assess the current psychological skills of a selected sports performer, identifying strengths and areas for improvement **See Assessment activity 17.5, page 318**		
P7 plan a six-week psychological skills training programme to enhance performance for a selected sports performer **See Assessment activity 17.5, page 318**	**M4** explain the design of the six-week psychological skills training programme for a selected sports performer **See Assessment activity 17.5, page 318**	**D3** justify the design of the six-week psychological skills training programme for a selected sports performer, making suggestions for improvement **See Assessment activity 17.5, page 318**

How you will be assessed

This unit will be assessed by internal assignments that will be designed and marked by the tutors at your centre. Your assessments could be in the form of:

- written reports
- posters
- presentations
- practical observations of performance.

Danny Robins, a 17-year-old footballer

This unit has helped me to understand that there is more to getting ready for games than just training all the time. I enjoyed looking at different aspects of psychology that can be used to benefit sports performance and how I could use these to improve my own performance, both in training and in my matches.

There were lots of practical learning activities throughout this unit like learning how to do imagery and progressive muscular relaxation with athletes. These activities have helped me to understand the different techniques and know when to use them. Assessing my own psychological skills helped me to see the areas that needed improving, and practising the different techniques that I could use to improve these areas, like imagery, were the bits that I enjoyed doing the most.

Over to you

- **Which areas of this unit are you looking forward to?**
- **Which bits do you think you might find difficult?**
- **What do you think you will need to do to get yourself ready for this unit?**

1. Know the effect of personality and motivation on sports performance

The role of psychology in sport

Think about when you have played sport. Has there been a time when you have not played as well as you could have done, even though you had trained really hard? Has there been a time when you have got something wrong in a game even though you know how to perform the skill well? Why do you think this could be?

1.1 Personality

Personality and the potential effects it can have on sports participation and sports performance have been of interest to sport psychologists and researchers since the late 1800s. However, evidence on whether personality affects sports performance is still fairly limited and inconclusive.

1.2 Theories

There are a number of theories and approaches that have been suggested to try to explain personality and how it can influence sports performance. The main theories you will look at are:

- Marten's Schematic View
- the Psychodynamic Theory
- Trait Theory
- Situational Approach
- Interactional Approach.

Marten's schematic view

In this view, personality is seen as having three different levels that are related to each other:

- psychological core
- typical responses
- role-related behaviour (see Figure 17.1).

The **psychological core** is what people often call 'the real you' and is the part of you that contains your beliefs, values, attitudes and interests; these aspects are seen as being relatively constant or stable. **Typical responses** are the usual ways that you respond to the world around you or different situations you may find

yourself in. For example, you may always get angry and shout after being intentionally fouled in football because you feel that deliberate fouls are un-sporting behaviour, but you may be quiet and shy when you meet people for the first time because you don't want to overawe them. These are your typical responses to these situations and are often seen as good indicators of your psychological core.

Your **role-related behaviour** is often determined by the circumstances you find yourself in and this is the most changeable aspect of personality. Put simply, your personality changes as your perception of your environment changes. For example, in the same day

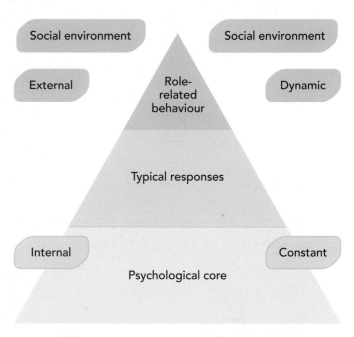

Figure 17.1: Martens' Schematic View of Personality (adapted from Chelladurai, 1990)

you might be captaining your college sports team where you show a lot of leadership behaviours, then working as an employee at your part-time job where you will have to follow a lot of instructions.

Psychodynamic theory

The psychodynamic approach to personality says that personality is made up of conscious and unconscious parts. The first part is called the 'id' which stands for instinctive drive. It is the part of your personality that is unconscious and makes you do certain things without thinking about them, for example, a sprinter on the start line in the Olympic final may feel so threatened by the expectations upon them that they respond with large levels of anxiety and their muscles automatically freeze. The second part of your personality, your **ego** is the conscious part. The final part is your **super ego**, which is your moral conscience. The effect of the ego and super ego can be seen in sport when a football player refuses to take a penalty in a penalty shoot out because they are worried about missing and letting their team down.

Rather than just looking at different parts of personality, the psychodynamic approach tries to understand the individual as a whole. This approach is not often used in sport as it focuses on the reasons for behaviour that come from within the individual and tends to ignore the athlete's environment. However, this theory is useful when sports psychologists try to explain behaviour as it helps us to understand that not all behaviour is under the conscious control of athletes.

What do you think will be going through the sprinter's mind as he prepares for this competition final?

Trait-centred views

Trait theories suggest that individuals have certain characteristics that will partly determine how they behave.

Traits are relatively stable aspects of personality and early trait theorists like Eysenck and Cattell argued that traits were mainly inherited. There are two main dimensions to personality:

- an introversion–extroversion dimension
- a stable–neurotic dimension.

Introverts are individuals who don't actively seek excitement and would rather be in calm environments. They tend to prefer tasks that require concentration and dislike the unexpected.

Extroverts tend to become bored quickly, are poor at tasks that require a lot of concentration and constantly seek change and excitement. Extroverts are less responsive to pain than introverts. Extroverts are said to be more successful in sporting situations because they can cope with competitive and distracting situations better than introverts.

Stable individuals are people who tend to be more easy-going and even tempered. Neurotic (unstable) people tend to be more restless, excitable, have a tendency to become anxious and are more highly aroused.

The conclusions are that trait views are too simplistic and that personality alone cannot predict success in a sporting environment. It can, however, be used to help explain why individuals choose certain sports.

Key term

Trait – a relatively stable and enduring characteristic that is part of your personality.

Remember

Although personality traits can be used with physiological and situational factors to try to predict who will do well in sport, there is no such thing as the right personality for all sports that will guarantee sporting success.

Situational-centred views

The situational approach is different from the trait theories approach as it says that behaviour is dependent on your situation or environment. It argues that this is far more important than traits.

There is some support for the situational approach in sporting behaviour, as individuals may be introverted – displaying characteristics such as tolerance and shyness – but may participate in a sport that requires them to be more extroverted and display characteristics like aggression in a sporting situation.

Remember

A situation can influence a person's behaviour but it cannot predict sporting behaviour. To be able to do this, you need to consider the individual's personality traits as well.

Social learning theory

Social learning theory suggests that personality is not a stable characteristic, but constantly changing and a result of our experiences of different social situations. It is unlikely that an individual will behave in the same way in different situations. The theory is that individuals learn in sporting situations through two processes: **modelling** and **reinforcement**. Modelling states that individuals are likely to model themselves on people they can relate to, like individuals in the same sport or of the same gender, and that as they observe their behaviour, they attempt to copy it. Reinforcement is important because if an individual's behaviour is reinforced or rewarded in some way it is likely that the behaviour will be repeated. Bandura, a leading psychologist, identified four main stages of observational learning that demonstrate how modelling influences personality and behaviour.

1. **Attention**: to learn through observation, the athlete must have a certain level of respect and admiration for the model they are observing. The amount of respect the athlete has for the model will depend on their status. If the model is successful, attractive and powerful they will hold the athlete's attention.

2. **Retention**: for modelling to be effective, the athlete must be able to retain the observed skill or behaviour in their memory and recall it when needed.

3. **Motor reproduction**: the athlete must be able to physically perform the task he or she is observing. The athlete needs time to practise the skill in order to learn how it should be performed.

4. **Motivational response**: unless the athlete is motivated, he or she will not go through the first three stages of modelling. Motivation is dependent on the amount of reinforcement (e.g. praise, feedback, sense of pride or achievement), the perceived status of the model and importance of the task.

Interactional view

To predict behaviour in a sporting situation, you need to consider how the situation and personality traits link and work together. This is known as the interactional approach to personality and sport behaviour.

The interactional approach is the view widely accepted by sports psychologists when explaining behaviour. This theory suggests that when situational factors are particularly strong, for example, during competitive sporting situations like penalty shoot-outs in football, they are more likely to predict behaviour than personality traits. The athlete who tends to be quiet and shy in an everyday situation is likely to run towards an ecstatic crowd screaming if he scores the winning penalty.

Personality types

Another approach in sports psychology suggests that personality traits can be grouped under two headings: type A and type B.

People with a **type A personality** tend to lack patience, have a strong urge for competition, a high desire to achieve goals, always rush to complete activities, will happily multi-task when placed under time constraints, lack tolerance towards others and experience higher levels of anxiety.

Type B personalities tend to be more tolerant towards others, more relaxed and reflective than their type A counterparts, experience lower levels of anxiety and display higher levels of imagination and creativity.

1.3 Effects on sports performance

There is no direct link between personality type and successful sporting performance. Some research has suggested that certain personality types may be more attracted to certain sports, but there is little to say that your personality will make you a better athlete.

Remember

Introverts tend to be drawn to individual sports like long-distance running, extroverts prefer team- and action-orientated sports like football. Psychologists think that extroverts are drawn to these types of sport because they offer high levels of excitement and stimulation, and the ever-changing, and unexpected environments required to keep them interested in the activity. Athletes that are towards the unstable or neurotic end of the scale experience high levels of over-arousal during the early stages of performance, which can lead to lower levels of performance.

Athletes versus non-athletes and individual versus team sports

Research implies that there is no such thing as a universal athletic personality. However, there are some differences between athletes and non-athletes; as well as between athletes in different types of sport. Compared with non-athletes, athletes who take part in team sports are more extroverted. When compared to non-athletes, athletes in individual sports tend to be more introverted. This suggests that in order to study the differences between athletes and non-athletes, you need to consider the sports the athletes play before reaching meaningful conclusions.

Elite versus non-elite athletes

Until recently psychologists thought that successful athletes display lower levels of depression, fatigue, confusion and anger, but higher levels of vigour. However, evidence which was used to draw these conclusions was insufficient because it was based on small numbers of athletes. More recent research shows that personality accounts for less than 1 per cent of the performance variation.

Type A versus type B

In sport, type A personalities are more likely than type B personalities to continue participating in a sport when the situation becomes unfavourable or when they are not motivated to take part.

Assessment activity 17.1

You are working with a youth sports team. The coach complains to you about some of his youth athletes, saying that they don't have the right personality to make it as athletes in his team.

Educate the coach about the role of personality in sport by preparing a short written report that looks at all of the different factors surrounding personality and environmental factors and their role in sports participation and performance.

1. Define personality and describe how it influences sport participation and performance. **P1**

2. Explain the different theories that try to explain the link between personality and sports participation and performance. **M1**

3. Explain how these theories try to explain that link. **M1**

4. Evaluate contrasting arguments that relate to the link between personality and sports performance. **D1**

Grading tips

P1 Make sure that you first describe what personality is and then give a brief overview of whether personality alone should determine whether or not people should be picked for sports teams.

M1 Use different theories and examples to explain how personality can influence sports performance.

D1 Make sure that you use a range of theories and supporting materials that give contrasting arguments so that you give as full a picture as possible to allow the coach to make an informed decision about their players.

PLTS

By exploring each of the different theories and judging their value when making your arguments, you can develop your skills as an **independent enquirer**.

Functional skills

By writing your report on personality and its effects on sports performance, you could provide evidence towards your **English** skills in writing.

1.4 Motivation

Most definitions of **motivation** refer to having a drive to take part and to persist in an activity. A sport-specific definition is the tendency of an individual or team to begin and then carry on with the activities relating to their sport. There are two main types of motivation: **intrinsic** and **extrinsic**.

Key terms

Motivation – the direction and the intensity of your effort; it is critical to sporting success.

Intrinsic – internal factors, such as enjoyment.

Extrinsic – external factors, such as rewards.

Intrinsic

Intrinsic motivation is when someone is participating in an activity without an external reward and/or without the primary motivation being the achievement of some form of external reward. Intrinsic motivation in its purest form is when an athlete participates in a sport for enjoyment. When people are asked why they play sport, if they reply with 'for fun', or 'because it makes me feel good' (or similar responses), they can be said to be intrinsically motivated.

There are three parts of intrinsic motivation:

- motivated by **accomplishments** – this occurs when athletes wish to increase their level of skill to get a sense of accomplishment

- motivated by **stimulation** – this refers to seeking an 'adrenaline rush' or extreme excitement
- motivated by **knowledge** – this means being curious about your own performance, wanting to know more about it and having a desire to develop new techniques or skills to benefit performance.

Extrinsic

Extrinsic motivation is when someone behaves the way they do because of some form of external mechanism. The most common forms of extrinsic motivation come through the use of tangible and intangible rewards. Tangible rewards are things that can physically be given to you, like money, medals and trophies, intangible rewards are non-physical things such as praise or encouragement.

For extrinsic motivation to be effective, rewards need to be used effectively. If the reward is given too frequently, it will be of little value to the athlete after a period of time, invalidating its potential impact on performance. A coach needs to have an in-depth knowledge of the athletes he is working with to maximise the effect of extrinsic rewards.

Extrinsic motivation can potentially decrease intrinsic motivation. If the extrinsic motivator is used as a method of controlling the athlete, generally intrinsic motivation will decrease. If the extrinsic motivator is used to provide information or feedback to the athlete, this can benefit intrinsic motivation. The way in which the athlete perceives and understands the original extrinsic motivator determines whether it will benefit or hinder intrinsic motivation.

Achievement motivation theory

Achievement motivation was proposed by Atkinson in 1964, who argued that achievement motivation comes from the individual's personality and is their motivation to strive for success. It is this drive that makes athletes carry on trying even when there are obstacles or when they fail. Atkinson grouped athletes into two categories: need to achieve (Nach) and need to avoid failure (Naf). Everyone has aspects of both Nach and Naf, but it is the difference between the two motives that makes up somebody's achievement motivation.

Take it further

The interaction of intrinsic and extrinsic motivation

A group of children are playing football, to the annoyance of an old man whose house they are playing outside. He asks them to stop playing but they carry on because they enjoy it so much. After a while, the old man offers them £5 each to play for him. As the children like playing anyway, they happily accept his offer. The next day, the children come back and play outside his house again. Just as before, he comes out and offers them money to play again but this time can only afford to pay them £4 The children agree to continue playing even though the amount is less than before. This pattern continues for the next few days until one day the old man comes out and says he can't afford to pay them anymore. Disgruntled, the children refuse to play if the old man isn't going to pay them.

1. What motivates the children to play initially? Is this intrinsic or extrinsic motivation?

2. At the end of the case study, what is the motivating factor for the children? Is this intrinsic or extrinsic motivation?

3. What effect has extrinsic motivation had on intrinsic motivation?

Attribution theory

In sport, **attribution** theory looks at how people explain success or failure. It helps you understand an athlete's actions and motivations.

Key term

Attribution – the reason you give to explain the outcome of an event.

Case study: Southern City U14 rugby team

Southern City is a U14 rugby team who have just been beaten 66–0 in their opening game of the season. When they got back to the changing rooms after the game, the coach asked the players why they thought they had lost so badly. The first player to speak said that the referee was rubbish and he gave tries that shouldn't have counted. A few players said that they lost because the other team were all bigger than them. The next player said that they lost because the other team cheated. After a little silence, a player said that they had lost because after they conceded the first try, the team stopped putting effort in and didn't believe that they could win. What does this case study tell you about the feelings and motivations of some of the players in the Southern City team?

In the case study, players explained the outcome using attribution. Attributions provide explanations for your successes or failures and fall into one of the following categories:

- stability – is the reason permanent or unstable?
- causality – is it something that comes from an external or an internal factor?
- control – is it under your control or not?

A table of types of attribution theory with examples that are often given after winning and losing is shown in Table 17.1 below.

Effects of motivation on sports performance

Motivation is an essential component of successful sports performance. However, if someone is so motivated that they won't stop, this can cause problems.

Positive

Someone who is motivated to play, perform and train at an optimal level will experience increases in performance. It is the role of athletes, coaches, managers and support staff to make sure the athlete is at optimal levels of motivation, without experiencing any negative side effects.

Negative

Being over-motivated can be a big problem for athletes. Athletes are often under pressure to perform at a high level, so feel the need to train more and more. However, over-motivation and a gruelling schedule can lead to **over-training**, **staleness** and **burnout**. Staleness can be a response

Key terms

Over-training – the athlete trains under an excessive training load, which they cannot cope with.

Staleness – inability to maintain a previous performance level.

Burnout – when an athlete strives to meet training and competition demands despite repeated unsuccessful attempts, and so tries harder. Can lead to the athlete no longer wishing to participate in activities they used to enjoy.

Type of attribution	Winning example	Losing example
Stability	'I was more able than my opponent' (stable) 'I was lucky' (unstable)	'I was less able than my opponent' (stable) 'We didn't have that bit of luck we needed today' (unstable)
Causality	'I tried really hard' (internal) 'My opponent was easy to beat' (external)	'I didn't try hard enough' (internal) 'My opponent was impossible to beat' (external)
Control	'I trained really hard for this fight' (under your control) 'He wasn't as fit as I was' (not under your control)	'I didn't train hard enough for this fight' (under your control) 'He was fitter than I was' (not under your control)

Table 17.1: Types of attribution with examples

to over-training. The key sign is that the athlete is unable to maintain a previous performance level or that performance levels may decrease significantly. Other signs and symptoms of staleness are that the athlete may suffer from mood swings and can become clinically depressed. Burnout happens when the athlete is trying to meet training and competition demands, and has often been unsuccessful so tries harder. When burnout occurs, the athlete finds they no longer want to take part in activities they used to enjoy. Burnout should not be confused with just dropping out because of being tired or unhappy. These negative effects of motivation affect not only players; they can also affect managers, coaches, match officials and team support staff.

Future expectations of success and failure

Expectations of future success or failure are linked to attribution theory. If you attribute to stable causes (such as skill), you are more likely to have expectations of future success whereas if you attribute to more unstable causes (like luck), you are more likely to have expectations of future failure.

Take it further

Attributions

How you attribute success or failure can affect your future expectations of sports performance. Why do you think this is?

Developing a motivational climate

The **motivational climate** is the environment in which an athlete finds themselves and how this affects their motivation positively and negatively.

A motivational climate that is focused on mastery of tasks – where athletes receive positive reinforcement and there is greater emphasis on teamwork and cooperation – will help develop motivation through improving the athlete's attitudes, effort and learning techniques. When an athlete is in an environment where there is a lot of focus on the outcome (where they feel they will be punished if they make mistakes, competition is strongly encouraged and only those with the highest ability will receive attention) this will lead to less effort and persistence from athletes and failure often attributed to lack of ability.

To develop an effective motivational climate, use the TARGET technique:

- **Tasks** – having a range of tasks that require the athlete to actively participate in learning and decision-making.
- **Authority** – giving athletes authority over monitoring and evaluating their own learning and decision-making.
- **Reward** – using rewards that are focused on individual improvement rather than comparing levels to other athletes.
- **Grouping** – giving athletes the opportunity to work in groups so that they develop skills in a group-based environment.
- **Evaluation** – focusing on an individual's effort and improvement.
- **Timing** – timing activities effectively so that all of the above conditions can interact effectively.

PLTS

By asking lots of different questions to explore all of the possibilities within the case study for Assessment activity 17.2 on page 290, you could develop your skills as a **creative thinker**.

Functional skills

Using ICT to independently select and use a range of theories of motivation for Assessment activity 17.2 on page 290, could provide evidence towards your skills in **ICT**.

Assessment activity 17.2

 BTEC

The coach of a local handball team has asked you to come to speak to Matt, a player he is struggling with. Matt is completely focused on winning trophies for their team and gets annoyed and frustrated when the team doesn't win. When the team loses, Matt says that it was the fault of the other players and bad luck. However, when the team wins he makes a point of telling everyone how well he has played.

Matt always seems to want to play when he is playing against teams that he knows he can beat, but he really doesn't like to play against teams when the players are just as good as him.

1. Describe the different types of motivation, and how they can influence sports participation and performance. **P2**

2. Explain the different theories that can be used to explain motivation. **M1**

3. Explain some methods that could be used to increase motivational climate. **M1**

4. Evaluate the relationship between motivation and sports participation and performance. **D1**

Grading tips

P2 Make sure that you define motivation and the different types of motivation. Look at how both intrinsic and extrinsic motivation influence sport performance. Describe each of the different theories of motivation and how people have tried to use them to understand motivation in sport.

M1 Use the attribution theory to explain how Matt's perception of success or failure can affect future expectations of sport performance. Explain how having a high need to achieve (Nach) or a high need to avoid failure (Naf) can affect sports performance and motivation to perform against certain individuals. Explain some methods the coach could use to increase motivational climate.

D1 Evaluate how intrinsic motivation can be affected by extrinsic motivation. Highlight strengths and limitations of each of the different theories of motivation. Discuss how and why the different suggestions to improve motivational climate can influence Matt both positively and negatively.

2. Know the relationship between stress, anxiety, arousal and sports performance

2.1 Stress

Lazarus and Follerman (1984) defined stress as: 'a pattern of negative physiological states and psychological responses occurring in situations where people perceive threats to their well-being, which they may be unable to meet.' Two terms have been introduced in sport to explain stress: eustress and distress.

Eustress is a good form of stress that can give you a feeling of fulfilment. Some athletes actively seek out stressful situations as they like the challenge of pushing themselves to the limit. This can help them increase their skill levels and focus their attention on aspects of their chosen sport. The benefit is that increases in intrinsic motivation follow.

Distress is a bad form of stress and is normally what you mean when you discuss stress. It is an extreme form of anxiety, nervousness, apprehension or worry as a result of a perceived inability to meet demands.

Key terms

Eustress – 'beneficial' stress that helps an athlete to perform.

Distress – extreme anxiety related to performance.

The effects of stress on performance

The effects of stress on performance are shown in the stress process flow diagram, Figure 17.2.

- At stage 1 of the stress process, some form of demand is placed on the athlete in a particular situation.

- At stage 2 the athlete perceives this demand either positively or negatively. It is at this stage that we start to understand how the negative perception of the demand can cause a negative mental state, a lack of self-confidence and a lack of concentration. If the demand is perceived as being too great, the athlete will feel unable to meet the demand (negative mental state and loss of self-confidence) and will then find it difficult to concentrate on what they will need to do to meet the demand.

- It is this perception that increases the arousal levels of the performer (stage 3). During this stage the athlete will experience heightened arousal, higher levels of cognitive and somatic anxiety and changes in their attention and concentration levels.

- Ultimately this determines the outcome of performance (stage 4).

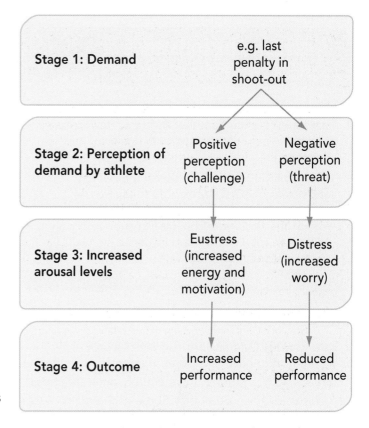

Figure 17.2: The stress process helps explain the relationship between stress, arousal, anxiety and performance

How can stress influence a snooker player when they're trying to pot the black?

Causes of stress

There are a number of individualised causes of stress. It is common to have a number of athletes in similar situations yet for them to have entirely different stress responses to those situations. Some of the main causes are discussed below.

Internal causes of stress include:

- illnesses like infections
- psychological factors, i.e. worrying about something
- not having enough sleep
- being overly self-critical or being a perfectionist, e.g. type A personality.

External causes of stress include:

- the environment in which you find yourself, e.g. too noisy, too quiet
- negative social interactions with other people, e.g. somebody being rude to you
- major life events, e.g. a death in the family
- day-to-day hassles, e.g. travel to and from games, training schedules.

Personal causes of stress are people who are significant in our lives – such as friends, family and partners – being a source of stress. Lifestyle factors like health and finance can also be sources of stress.

Occupational causes of stress are related to your job, e.g. lack of job satisfaction or unemployment. In a sporting situation, having a disagreement with a coach or a manager and subsequently being dropped from the team could cause you to suffer from stress.

Sports environments

There are two key aspects of sport performance that cause stress: the importance of the event you are taking part in and the amount of uncertainty that surrounds it. The more important the event, the more stressful it is. This doesn't mean that you have to be playing in a World Cup Final or sprinting in the 100-metre final in the Olympics; the importance of the event is specific to you. For example, someone who is playing their first mid-season game after a serious injury could show the same symptoms of stress as someone who is about to go in to bat in the last innings of a baseball game when the scores are tied and their team already have two outs. On the face of it, the mid-season game against a team you should beat would not be as important as the game-saving situation the baseball player finds himself in, but it is the importance that the individual attaches to the event that is key.

Symptoms of stress

When you are in a situation you find threatening, your stress response is activated. The way you respond depends on how seriously you view the threat, and the response is controlled by two parts of your nervous system: the **sympathetic nervous system** and the **parasympathetic nervous system**.

The sympathetic nervous system is responsible for the fight or flight response. It gives you the energy you need to confront the threat or run away from it. In order to do this, the sympathetic nervous system produces these physiological responses:

- blood diverted to working muscles to provide more oxygen
- increased heart rate
- increased breathing rate
- increased heat production
- increased adrenaline production
- increased muscle tension
- hairs stand on end
- dilated pupils
- slowed digestion
- increased metabolism
- a dry mouth.

Once the stress has passed, the parasympathetic nervous system begins to work. The parasympathetic system helps you to relax. It achieves this by producing the following responses:

- makes muscles relax
- slows metabolism
- increases digestion rate
- decreases body temperature
- decreases heart rate
- constricts the pupils
- increases saliva production
- decreases breathing rate.

Remember

A lot of people see the symptoms of stress as negative aspects when they play their sport, but without some of these responses your body would not be able to meet the demands of your sport.

2.2 Anxiety

Anxiety is a negative emotional state that is either characterised by, or associated with, feelings of nervousness, apprehension or worry. There are a number of causes of anxiety. These are largely the same as those covered earlier under the sources of stress.

There are two main types of anxiety: **trait anxiety** and **state anxiety**.

Trait anxiety is an aspect of personality and part of an individual's pattern of behaviour. Someone with a high level of trait anxiety is likely to become worried in a variety of situations; even non-threatening situations.

State anxiety is a temporary, ever-changing mood state that is an emotional response to any situation considered threatening. For example, at the start of a show-jumping event, the rider may have higher levels of state anxiety that settle down once the event begins. State anxiety levels may increase again when coming up to particularly high jumps and then be at their highest level when coming towards the final jump which, if they were to clear quickly and cleanly, would result in a win. There are two types of state anxiety:

- **cognitive state anxiety** is the amount you worry
- **somatic state anxiety** relates to your perception of the physiological changes that happen in a particular situation.

Key terms

Trait anxiety – a behavioural tendency to feel threatened even in situations that are not really threatening, and then to respond to this with high levels of state anxiety.

State anxiety – a temporary, ever-changing mood state that is an emotional response to any situation considered to be threatening.

Symptoms of anxiety

Cognitive state anxiety refers to negative thoughts, nervousness and worry experienced in certain situations. Symptoms of cognitive state anxiety include concentration problems, fear and bad decision-making.

When a performer's concentration levels drop, their performance decreases because of the number of mistakes they have made. As the performance levels decrease, the levels of anxiety increase further, as do arousal levels. These increased levels of arousal can then lead to increased levels of cognitive state anxiety, which can further increase the number of mistakes made in performance. The performer is now caught in a negative cycle that can harm performance.

Somatic state anxiety relates to the perception or interpretation of physiological changes (such as increases in heart rate, sweating and increased body heat) when you start to play sport. For example, an athlete could be concerned because they sense an increased heart rate if they have gone into a game less prepared than normal. This increase in heart rate is actually beneficial to performance, but the athlete can perceive it as negative. The symptoms of increased somatic state anxiety range from increases in heart rate, respiratory rate and sweating to complete muscle tension that prevents the athlete from moving (known as 'freezing').

Effects of anxiety on sports performance

Anxiety can adversely affect sports performance. It is seen as a negative mental state that is the negative aspect of stress. In skills that require a great deal of concentration such as golf putting and potting a ball in snooker, anxiety can lead to lower performance levels due to reduced concentration, attention levels, and coordination faults. In gross motor skills, anxiety can have a negative effect on performance due to factors like freezing and coordination faults. These negative effects of stress can lead to lower levels of performance, and as performance levels decrease further this can lead to a significant decrease in self-confidence.

Some symptoms of anxiety can be beneficial for sports performance, like increased blood flow, breathing rate and respiratory rate. These are physiologically beneficial, but if the athlete believes they are happening because of their inability to meet a demand, it is this perception that makes the symptoms negative.

Negative mental state

The definition of anxiety suggests that it is a negative mental state characterised by worry and apprehension. It is suggested that if this negative mental state becomes too great (i.e. you worry too much), your performance will suffer.

Constantly worrying about an event can make you think that you are not good enough to succeed (decreased self-confidence). This can make you feel like you are less likely to win (decreased expectations of success).

Heightened cognitive anxiety means there is an increase in nervousness, apprehension or worry. One of the things athletes worry about is failing. The problem with this is that once you start to worry about it, you are focusing on it. This increases the likelihood of it happening, i.e. if you worry about losing, you are more likely to lose. Heightened fear

of failure could result in negative physiological responses like hyper-elevated muscle tension and lack of movement coordination, which will also negatively affect performance.

2.3 Arousal

Arousal is referred to as a physiological state of alertness and anticipation that prepares the body for action. It is considered to be neutral because it is neither positive nor negative. It involves both physiological activation (increased heart rate, sweating rate or respiratory rate) and psychological activity (increased attention). Arousal is typically viewed along a continuum, with deep sleep at one extreme, and excitement at the other. Individuals who are optimally aroused are those who are mentally and physically activated to perform.

Key term

Arousal – the psychological state of alertness that prepares the body for action.

2.4 Theories of arousal

The relationship between arousal and performance is demonstrated through the following theories:

- drive theory
- the inverted U hypothesis
- the catastrophe theory
- the individual zones of optimal functioning (IZOF) theory.

Drive theory

The **drive theory** view of the relationship between arousal and performance is linear. This means that as arousal increases, so does performance (see Figure 17.3 on page 295). The more 'learned' a skill is, the more likely it is that a high level of arousal will result in a better performance. Therefore, drive theory is often summarised through the following equation:

Performance = arousal x skill

However, there is evidence to suggest that athletic performance is benefited by arousal only up to a certain point, after which the athlete becomes too aroused and their performance decreases.

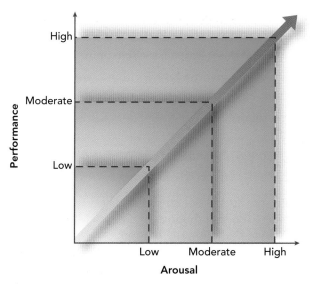

Figure 17.3: How does the drive theory explain the relationship between arousal and performance?

Inverted U hypothesis

The inverted U hypothesis differs from the drive theory. The inverted U hypothesis states that at optimal arousal levels, performance levels will be at their highest, but when arousal is either too low or too high, performance levels will be lower. It argues that at lower levels of arousal, performance will not be as high as it should be because the athlete is neither physiologically nor psychologically ready (e.g. heart rate and concentration levels may be too low). As arousal levels increase, so does performance, but only up to an optimal point. At this optimal point of arousal (normally moderate levels of arousal), the athlete's performance will be at its highest. After this optimal point performance levels will start to decrease gradually (see Figure 17.4).

Remember

The inverted U hypothesis states that arousal will only affect performance positively up to an optimal point; after this you will get a steady decrease in performance.

The inverted U hypothesis is more widely accepted than drive theory because most athletes and coaches can report personal experience of under-arousal (boredom), over-arousal (excitement to the point of lack of concentration) and optimum arousal (focus on nothing but sport performance). However, there has been some question over the type of curve demonstrated: does it give an optimal point, or do some athletes experience optimal arousal for a longer period of time?

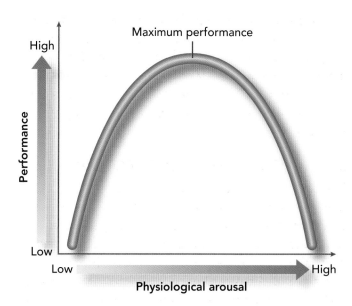

Figure 17.4: How does the inverted U hypothesis explain the relationship between arousal and performance?

Catastrophe theory

Catastrophe theory suggests that performance is affected by arousal in an inverted U fashion only when the individual has low levels of cognitive anxiety (see graph (a) of Figure 17.5 on page 296). If the athlete is experiencing higher levels of **cognitive anxiety**, and arousal levels increase up to the athlete's threshold, the player experiences a dramatic (or catastrophic) drop in performance levels (see graph (b) of Figure 17.5 on page 296).

The key difference between catastrophe theory and the inverted U hypothesis is that the drop in performance does not have to be a steady decline when arousal levels become too high. Catastrophe theory does not argue that cognitive anxiety is completely negative. The theory suggests you will perform at a higher level if you have a certain degree of cognitive anxiety because your attention and concentration levels increase; it is only when levels of cognitive anxiety are combined with hyper-elevated levels of arousal that performance levels decrease dramatically.

Key term

Cognitive anxiety – the thought component of anxiety that most people refer to as 'worrying about something'.

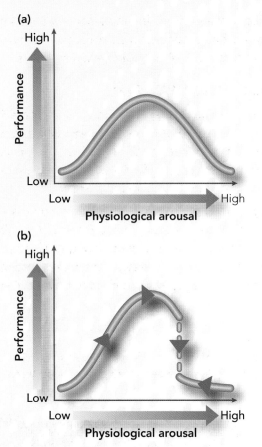

Figure 17.5: How does the Catastrophe theory (b) differ from the Inverted U theory (a)?

Individual zones of optimal functioning

Individual zones of optimal functioning (IZOF) theory states each person has different optimal levels of arousal and can remain in that zone of arousal for a period of time. As they can stay in the optimal level of arousal for a period of time, athletes can perform at a higher level of performance for a longer period of time. The main differences between the inverted U hypothesis and IZOF are as follows and are shown in Figure 17.6.

• Where the inverted U hypothesis sees arousal at an optimal point, IZOF sees optimal arousal as bandwidth.

• Where the inverted U hypothesis sees every athlete's optimal point at a mid-point on the curve, IZOF says the optimal point varies from person to person.

• IZOF and the inverted U hypothesis are similar in that they both propose that, after the optimal point of arousal, performance decreases gradually.

Activity: Arousal in sport

In pairs, produce a poster presentation explaining the four theories of arousal. Make sure you include the following information:

• a diagram and explanation of each theory

• practical, sport-based examples of each theory to develop your points

• the key differences between each theory

• a note about which theory you think is the most likely to explain the relationship between arousal and performance and why.

2.5 Effects of arousal on sports performance

Improvements and decrements in performance level

Arousal doesn't necessarily have a negative effect on sports performance – it can be positive depending on the perception of the athlete. If the changes due to arousal are interpreted by the performer as positive, this can have a positive effect on performance or prepare the athlete for their event (psyching up the performer). But, if the changes are viewed as negative,

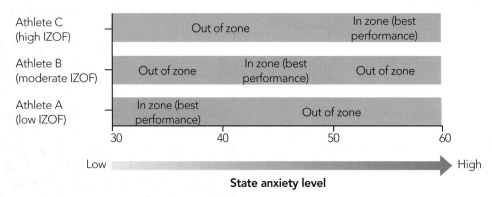

Figure 17.6: How does the IZOF explain the relationship between arousal and performance?

this can negatively affect performance or preparation for performance (psyching out the performer). Research carried out by Jones, Swain and Hardy in the 1990s suggests that if a coach can get the athlete to view the symptoms of anxiety and arousal as excitement rather than fear, performance will generally be facilitated.

Changes in attentional focus

During heightened states of arousal, the attentional field, which focuses attention and concentration, becomes narrowed. This means that the more aroused you become, the lower the number of relevant cues you can concentrate on. For example, in a game of netball, when at optimal states of arousal, the centre will be able to focus on the opposing player in possession of the ball as well as her position on the court and the position of other players. During heightened states of arousal, the centre may be able to focus only on the opposition player who has the ball and may disregard other important cues. Just as a heightened state of arousal can narrow the player's attention, it can also broaden it to the point where performance is decreased. In this scenario, the netball player would be concentrating on irrelevant information, like crowd noise, as well as the relevant game cues.

Increases in anxiety levels

Increases in arousal levels can lead to an increased awareness of symptoms of state anxiety, which leads to increases in both somatic and cognitive state anxiety. Whether this becomes a positive or negative influence is dependent on how the individual reacts.

Choking occurs in high-pressure situations, such as important events like waiting to putt in the Open. It is an extreme form of nervousness that negatively affects performance. It can be more apparent in the presence of significant others (e.g. parents, peers) or large audiences.

Key term

Choking – the whole process that leads to decreased performance, not just the decreased performance itself.

Assessment activity 17.3   P3 P4 M2   BTEC

You are working as an assistant to a sports psychologist and you have been asked to produce an educational poster that will help sports performers and coaches understand the relationships between stress, arousal, anxiety and sports performance.

1. Describe stress and anxiety. **P3**

2. Describe the causes, symptoms and effects of stress and anxiety. **P3**

3. Describe three different theories of arousal and the effect on sports performance. **P4**

4. Explain three different theories of arousal and the effect on sports performance. **M2**

Grading tips

P3 Prepare some coach- and athlete-friendly notes that describe stress and anxiety, their causes, symptoms and effects on performance; using sport based examples wherever possible.

P4 Describe three theories of arousal that you think provide the best explanations for the relationship between arousal and performance. Follow this up by describing the positive and negative effects of arousal on performance.

M2 Use sport based examples and advice for coaches and athletes to explain the different theories of arousal and the positive and negative effects of arousal on performance.

PLTS

Organising your time and resources and prioritising the work that you need to do will help you to develop skills as a **self-manager**.

Functional skills

Selecting, comparing, reading and understanding texts and using them to gather information, ideas, arguments and opinions could provide evidence towards your **English** skills in reading.

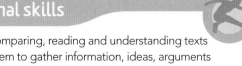

3. Know the role of group dynamics in team sports

3.1 Group processes

Groups or teams

There must be interaction between individuals in order for them to be classified as a group. This is characterised by communication over a period of time. The individuals need to get on (interpersonal attraction) and there needs to be some form of collective identity – the members of the group must perceive themselves to be a distinct unit that is different from other groups. The group must have shared goals, targets, norms and values, and be prepared to achieve these goals collectively. All of these characteristics are common in teams, but there are some key differences between a group and a team.

The main difference relates to the pursuit of shared goals and objectives, both within teams and for the individual.

For a group to be classed as a team, the members need to depend on each other and offer support to each other in order to try to achieve team goals, and the members will interact with each other to accomplish these goals and objectives.

3.2 Stages of group development

For a group of people to become a team, they must go through four developmental stages (Tuckman, 1965):

- forming
- storming
- norming
- performing.

All groups go through all stages, but the time they spend at each stage and the order in which they go through the stages may vary.

Once a team has progressed through the four stages, it does not mean that they will not revert back to an earlier stage. If key members leave, the team may revert back to the storming stage as others begin to vie for position within the team.

Forming

During the forming stage, group members familiarise themselves with other group members, get to know each other and try to decide if they belong in that group. During this stage, group members start to assess the strengths and weaknesses of other members, and start to test their relationships with others in the group. Individuals will get to know their roles within the group and will make decisions about whether or not they feel they can fulfil (or want to fulfil) their role within the group. Formal leaders in the group tend to be directive during the forming stage.

Storming

During the storming stage, conflict begins to develop between individuals in the group. It is common for individuals or cliques to start to question the position and authority of the leader, and they will start to resist the control of the group. Often, conflicts develop because demands start to be placed on the group members and because some individuals start to try to acquire more important roles. During the storming stage, the formal leader in the group tends to take

Michael Jordan once said 'Talent wins games; teamwork and intelligence wins championships.' What do you think his opinion is on the importance of team cohesion?

on more of a guidance role with decision-making and helps the team to move towards what is expected in terms of professional behaviour.

Norming

During the norming stage, the instability, hostility and conflict that occurred in the storming stage is replaced by cooperation and solidarity. Members of the group start to work towards common goals rather than focusing on individual agendas, and group cohesion begins to be developed. As group cohesion develops, group satisfaction increases (due to satisfaction from achieving tasks) and levels of respect for others in the group start to increase. In the norming stage, the formal leader will expect the group members to become more involved in the decision-making process, and will expect the players to take more responsibility for their own professional behaviour.

Performing

The performing stage involves the team progressing and functioning effectively as a unit. The group works without conflict towards the achievement of shared goals and objectives, and there is little need for external supervision as the group is more motivated. The group is now more knowledgeable, and able to make its own decisions and take responsibility for them.

3.3 Steiner's model of group effectiveness

Steiner's model was put forward to explain group effectiveness. It is described as:

Actual productivity = potential productivity
– losses due to faulty group
process

Actual productivity refers to how the team performs (the results they get and the level of performance they put in). Potential productivity refers to the perfect performance the team could produce based on the individual skill and ability of each athlete in the team and the resources available. Losses due to faulty group processes relate to the issues that can get in the way of team performance, preventing the team from reaching its potential performance. Losses are normally due to two main areas: **motivational faults/ losses** and **coordination faults/losses**.

Key terms

Motivational faults/losses – occur when some members of the team do not give 100 per cent effort.

Coordination faults/losses – occur when players do not connect with their play, the team interacts poorly or ineffective strategies are used. Generally, sports that require more interaction or cooperation between players are more susceptible to coordination faults or losses.

Activity: Motivational and coordination losses in volleyball

In a volleyball team, two players seem to be putting in little effort. When they are setting, they don't appear to be on the same wavelength as the other players on the team, and when they are blocking they don't seem to be putting a great deal of effort into their jumps. The other players on the team appear to be working harder to try to make up for this. However, despite their efforts, there is little interaction between spikers and setters.

1. Where are the coordination losses in this scenario?

2. Where are the motivational losses in this scenario?

3. What do you think would be your role as the coach to improve these faults?

Ringelmann effect

The Ringelmann effect is a phenomenon whereby as the group size increases, the individual productivity of the people in the group decreases, often by up to 50 per cent. It has been assumed that the Ringelmann effect is caused not by coordination losses but by motivational faults or losses. The Ringelmann effect can occur when people are not as accountable for their own performance – as the group gets larger, athletes can 'hide' behind other athletes and not get noticed.

Social loafing

Social loafing refers to when group members do not put in 100 per cent effort when they are in a group- or team-based situation. This is generally due to losses in motivation. Losses in motivation that cause social loafing are most evident when the individual contributions of group members are not identified or are dispensable. It can occur when some players seem to be working harder than others. Individuals who display social loafing often lack confidence, are afraid of failure and tend to be highly anxious. It is often the case that players who display social loafing do not feel they can make a useful contribution to overall team performance, which can be why they don't want to participate.

Interactive and coactive groups

Interactive teams require team members to work with each other in order to achieve a successful performance. Their successful performance is dependent on interaction and coordination between members.

Coactive teams require individuals to achieve success in their individual games, events or performances to achieve overall team success. There is no direct interaction between team members during the performance.

3.4 Cohesion

Cohesion is a dynamic process that is reflected in the tendency for a group to stick together and remain united in the pursuit of its goals and objectives:

- **Social cohesion** relates to how well the team members enjoy each other's company. In recreational sport, all of the players may get on well with one another and enjoy playing the game regardless of whether they win or lose.
- **Task cohesion** relates to how well group or team members work together to achieve common goals and objectives.

Although both types of cohesion influence performance to a certain degree, task cohesion is more closely related to successful sporting performance.

Creating an effective team climate

Team climate is a term that is used to describe how well the different players in the team get on. Creating the team climate is the responsibility of both the coach and the team.

To help build an effective team climate, the coach should:

- communicate effectively
- ensure everybody knows their role
- keep changes to a minimum
- encourage a group identity

- set both group and individual goals
- get to know their athletes.

Team members can also help to build an effective team climate by:

- being responsible for their own activities
- resolving conflict quickly
- trying as hard as possible
- getting to know each other
- helping each other.

3.5 Factors affecting cohesion

Carron's (1982) conceptual model of cohesion explains factors effecting cohesion (see Figure 17.7 on page 301). It says four factors can affect team cohesion:

1. environmental
2. personal
3. leadership
4. team.

Environmental factors

Groups that are closer to each other (in terms of location) and smaller tend to be more cohesive as the members have greater opportunities to interact and form relationships.

Personal factors

The individual characteristics of group members are important in group cohesion. If players are motivated to achieve the group's aims and objectives, are from similar backgrounds, have similar attitudes and opinions and similar levels of commitment, there will be more satisfaction among group members and the group is more likely to be cohesive.

Leadership factors

Leadership style, behaviours, communication styles and compatibility of the coach's and athlete's personalities are key leadership factors that affect cohesion.

Team factors

If the team can stay together for a long period of time, experience a range of successes and failures together and be involved in the decision-making process, the group is more likely to be productive and cohesive.

Figure 17.7: Carron's Conceptual Model of Cohesion (adapted from Carron, A.V. (1982). Cohesiveness in sport groups: Interpretations and considerations. Journal of Sport Psychology). How can the different factors influence cohesion, according to this theory?

Relationship between cohesion and performance

It is easy to say that the greater the level of cohesion, the higher the level of performance. Interactive sports like football and volleyball require direct interaction and coordination between players so cohesion (especially task cohesion) is important. Alternatively, coactive sports require little, if any, direct interaction or coordination. Cohesion has a greater influence on performance in interactive sports than it does on coactive sports, such as archery or golf.

3.6 Leadership

Qualities and behaviour

The best leaders can match their styles, behaviours and qualities to different situations. The following qualities will contribute to making a good leader:

- **Patience** – a good leader gives athletes time to develop their skills.
- **Self-discipline** – the leader should lead by example. If the leader expects players to always display professional standards, the players expect the same of the leader.

- **Intelligence** – a good leader is expected to come up with ideas and formulate plans, e.g. new tactics, to improve team performance.
- **Optimism** – the leader needs to remain positive and enthusiastic at all times, even when everything is negative, to motivate team members
- **Confidence** – to build confidence in the players and other colleagues, the leader needs to display confidence in him or herself. A good leader needs to give the people they work with the responsibility and capabilities to make decisions, and support them in the decisions they make.

Prescribed versus emergent leaders

Leaders are either prescribed or emergent.

- **Prescribed leaders** are those who are appointed by some form of higher authority. For example, Fabio Capello was appointed England manager by the FA.
- **Emergent leaders** are those who achieve leadership status by gaining the respect and support of the group. These leaders generally achieve their status through showing specific leadership skills or being particularly skilful at their sport. For example, Wayne Rooney emerged within the Manchester United team and became a leader of the team. He emerged because of his impressive performances, gaining the respect of others.

3.7 Theories of leadership

The four main theories of leadership are trait, behavioural, interactional and multi-dimensional. They are outlined below.

Trait theory

Trait theory (often referred to as the great man theory) suggests that there are certain personality characteristics that predispose an individual to being a good leader. It suggests that leaders are born, not made. This theory says that leadership is innate and a good leader would be good in any situation, not just his or her current domain. This approach has not had a great deal of support since the late 1940s and it is now generally accepted that there is no definitive set of traits that characterise a good leader.

Behavioural theory

Behavioural theories of leadership argue that a good leader is made, not born, and that anyone can be taught to be a good leader. The behavioural theory has its roots in social learning theory, and says people can learn to be good leaders by observing the behaviours of other good leaders in a variety of situations, reproducing those behaviours in similar situations and then continuing them if they are reinforced.

Interactional theory

Trait and behavioural theories to leadership place emphasis on the personal qualities of a coach. The interactional theory considers other factors that could affect the effectiveness of leadership, mainly the interaction between the individual and their situation. Two main types of leader are identified through the interactional theory:

- **Relationship-orientated leaders** are focused on developing relationships with individuals in the group. They work hard to maintain communication with members; always help to maintain levels of social interaction between members and themselves; and develop respect and trust with others. Relationship-orientated leaders are more effective with experienced, highly skilled athletes.
- **Task-orientated leaders** are more concerned with meeting goals and objectives. They create plans; decide on priorities; assign members to task; and ensure members stay on task, with the focus of increasing group productivity. Task-orientated leaders are more effective with less experienced, less skilled performers who need constant instruction and feedback.

Different athletes will have a preference for task-orientated or relationship-orientated leaders. In principle, a leader who gets the right balance between providing a supportive environment and focusing on getting the job done is the most effective leader. It is a leader's role to get to know their performers so they know where to concentrate their efforts.

Multi-dimensional model

The multi-dimensional model says the team's performance and satisfaction with the leader will be highest if the leader's required behaviours, preferred behaviours and actual behaviours all agree. This means that if the leader is required to act in a certain way in a certain situation and does so, and the group like the way the leader has acted, the group or team are more likely to be happy with their leader and higher levels of performance are likely to occur. This is shown in Figure 17.8 below.

- The behaviour required by the leader at the time is generally determined by the situation the leader is in and should conform to the norms of the group.
- The preferred behaviour is mainly determined by the people within the group or team. Their preferences are generally determined by factors such as personality of the athletes, experience of the athletes, skill/ability of athletes and non-sport related aspects like age and gender.
- The actual behaviour is determined by the characteristics of the leader, the situational factors and the preferences of the group.

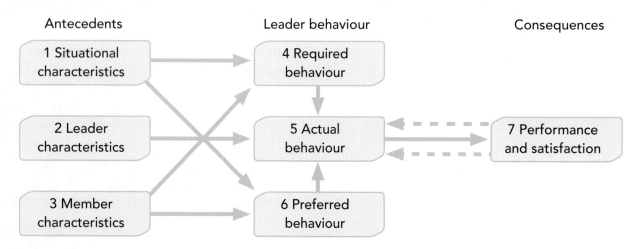

Figure 17.8: The multi-dimensional model of leadership (Weinberg and Gould, 2006 – adapted from Chelladurai, 1990). How do the different leadership factors interact to influence performance?

3.8 Styles of leadership

Autocratic

Autocratic leaders have firm views about how and when things should be done. They tend to be inflexible with their approach to the group. This type of leader dictates to the group who does what tasks and when to do them, and often dictates how the task should be done. They use phrases like 'do this', or 'do it how I said'. The leader does not seek the views and comments of people within the group, and rarely gets involved on a personal level with members of the group. This means members tend to be passive. When working with this type of leader, group members can stop working or work more slowly when the leader is not there, and have a tendency to become aggressive towards each other.

Democratic/consultative/group

This type of leader makes decisions only after they have been through a process of consultation with group members. They encourage the involvement of the group, adopt a more informal and relaxed approach to leadership and listen to ideas relating to the prioritisation and completion of goals and objectives. They are likely to use questions such as 'How do you think we can do this?', and 'Do you think this could work?'.

Democratic leaders maintain their status as leader by making the final decision based on the information collected from group members and their own thoughts and ideas. Generally, when the leader is not present, group members tend to continue working towards agreed goals and do not become aggressive towards each other when things start to go wrong.

Assessment activity 17.4   P5 M3 D2   BTEC

Imagine you are an assistant coach at a sports team. You have been watching one of your team's games trying to look at the different factors that can influence group dynamics and performance. You have been asked to prepare a presentation for the manager and coaches about your observations of the match, commenting specifically on the key factors you have identified that influence group dynamics and sports performance.

1. Identify four factors that influence group dynamics and performance in team sports. **P5**

2. Explain four factors that influence group dynamics and performance in team sports. **M3**

3. Analyse four factors that influence group dynamics and performance in team sports. **D2**

Grading tips

P5 You need to identify four factors which influence group dynamics and performance in team sports. These could be aspects of group processes, cohesion and leadership.

M3 You then need to follow this by explaining each of the different factors that you have identified.

D2 You must then say how and why the different group dynamics affected performance in that way.

PLTS

If you communicate the results of your observations effectively, you could develop your skills as a **reflective learner**.

Functional skills

By presenting the different factors that can affect group dynamics and team performance, you could develop your speaking and listening skills in **English**.

4. Be able to plan a psychological skills training programme to enhance sports performance

Although it is important for developing sports performance, some people don't practise their **psychological skills** as much as their physical skills. Have you ever walked off the field of play in disgust, having lost a game you thought you should have won? Have you ever turned up to a game and thought, 'I can't be bothered today'? Have you ever got to a crucial point in a game and your performance has sunk without you being able to explain why? These are situations where effective psychological skills training (PST) programmes might have helped you.

PST is the acquisition and development of a range of psychological skills that are designed to improve performance over a period of time. PST programmes involve three main phases:

- education – teaching the athlete why PST is beneficial
- acquisition – learning different psychological skills
- practice – providing opportunities to use techniques in competition.

PST programmes require you to conduct baseline assessments, plan the programme, take part in the programme, conduct reassessments and review the programme.

Key term

Psychological skills – qualities that the athlete needs to obtain through the PST programme.

Remember

Many coaches and sport psychologists use psychological skills training (PST) programmes to help sports performance.

4.1 Assessment for PST

Before deciding on the aims and objectives of the PST programme, you should perform an initial assessment of the psychological strengths and areas for improvement in your athlete. This can be achieved through:

- interviews – semi-structured interviews are often best
- questionnaires – to assess levels of different psychological factors in sport and the athlete's current psychological skills
- performance profiling – to help you to understand the athlete's and the coach's perception of performance and skills.

A good way of assessing your client's current psychological strengths and areas for improvement is to use a combination of methods. The use of self-assessment questionnaires is useful because motivation and adherence problems can occur if the athlete doesn't have an input into the PST programme at all stages.

Psychological strengths and weaknesses of the individual

As part of your PST programme, you should carry out an initial assessment to identify the current strengths and areas for improvement for the athlete you will be working with. There are a number of methods that you can use, but some common questionnaires can be found below.

Activity: Athletic coping skills inventory

Opposite is a copy of the ACSI–28 (Smith et al., 1995). Complete the questionnaire and analysis as follows:

- Read each statement and tick the response you most agree with (honestly!). Remember, there are no right or wrong answers and you shouldn't spend too much time on any statement.

- Work out your score for each subscale using the scoring system. Each scale has a range from 0 to 12, with 0 indicating a low level of skill in that area and 12 indicating a high level of skill in that area.

- Add up each subscale score to get a total score for psychological skills. Your total score will range from 0 to 84, with 0 indicating low levels of psychological skills and 84 signifying high levels of skill.

Statement	Almost never	Sometimes	Often	Almost always
1. On a daily or weekly basis, I set goals for myself that guide what I do.				
2. I get the most out of my talent and skill.				
3. When a coach or manager tells me how to correct a mistake I've made, I can take it personally and can get upset.*				
4. When I'm playing sports, I can focus my attention and block out my distractions.				
5. I remain positive and enthusiastic during competition.				
6. I tend to play better under pressure because I can think more clearly.				
7. I worry quite a bit about what others think of my performance.*				
8. I tend to do lots of planning about how I can reach my goals.				
9. I feel confident I will win when I play.				
10. When a coach or manager criticises me, I become more upset rather than feel helped.*				
11. It is easy for me to keep distracting thoughts from interfering with something that I am watching or listening to.				
12. I put a lot of pressure on myself by worrying about how I will perform.*				
13. I set my own performance goals for each practice or training session.				
14. I don't have to be pushed to practice or play hard; I give 100%.				
15. If a coach criticises me, I correct the mistake without getting upset about it.				
16. I handle unexpected situations in my sport very well.				
17. When things are going badly, I tell myself to keep calm and it works for me.				
18. The more pressure there is during a game, the more I enjoy it.				
19. While competing, I worry about making mistakes or failing to come through it.*				
20. I have my game plan worked out in my head long before the event begins.				
21. When I feel myself getting too tense, I can quickly relax my body and calm myself.				
22. To me, pressure situations are challenges that I welcome.				
23. I think about and imagine what will happen if I make a mistake.*				
24. I maintain emotional control regardless of how things are going for me.				
25. It is easy for me to direct my attention and focus on a single object or person.				
26. When I fail to reach my goals it makes me try even harder.				
27. I improve my skills by listening carefully to advice and instruction from coaches and managers.				
28. I make fewer mistakes when the pressure is on because I concentrate better.				

Use the following scale to calculate your skills:

For statements that **do not** have an asterisk (*) next to them:

- almost never = 0
- sometimes = 1
- often = 2
- almost always = 3.

For statements that have an asterisk (*) next to them:

- almost never = 3
- sometimes = 2
- often = 1
- almost always = 0.

Coping score ...... (sum your scores for statements 5, 17, 21 and 24). The higher your score on this scale, the more likely you are to remain calm, positive and enthusiastic when things go badly. You are more likely to be able to overcome setbacks in a performance situation.

Coachability score ...... (sum your scores for statements 3*, 10*, 15 and 27). The higher your score on this scale, the more likely you are to be receptive to guidance from your coaches or managers, and to concentrate on using their instructions to benefit your performance, rather than getting upset and taking the comments too personally.

Concentration score...... (sum your scores for statements 4, 11, 16 and 25). The higher your score on this scale, the less likely you are to become distracted by different things. You are also likely to focus on important aspects of your sport performance.

Confidence and achievement motivation...... (sum your scores for statements 2, 9, 14 and 26). The higher your score on this scale, the more likely you are to give 100 per cent in both competitive and training situations. You are also more likely to be confident in your skills and abilities, as well as being motivated by challenges.

Goal setting and mental preparation score ...... (sum statements 1, 8, 13 and 20). The higher the score on this scale, the more likely you are to set yourself effective goals and produce appropriate plans to achieve your goals. You are more likely to plan out your sport performance effectively.

Peaking under pressure score ...... (sum scores for statements 6, 18, 22 and 28). The higher your score for this scale, the more likely you are to find high-pressure situations challenging. It is likely that you will use them to help performance, as opposed to viewing them as threatening and allowing them to hinder performance.

Freedom from worry score ...... (sum scores for statements 7*, 12*, 19* and 23*). The higher your score on this scale, the less likely you are to put pressure on yourself by worrying about performance, making mistakes and what others think about your performance (particularly if you perform badly).

Total psychological skills score ...... (sum all of your subscale scores). The higher your score on this scale, the higher the level of psychological skills you have.

Activity: Competitive state anxiety inventory 2 (CSAI-2)

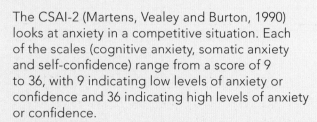

The CSAI-2 (Martens, Vealey and Burton, 1990) looks at anxiety in a competitive situation. Each of the scales (cognitive anxiety, somatic anxiety and self-confidence) range from a score of 9 to 36, with 9 indicating low levels of anxiety or confidence and 36 indicating high levels of anxiety or confidence.

Using the questionnaire below, assess your levels of cognitive state anxiety, somatic state anxiety and self-confidence:

- Complete the questionnaire during sport or think about a sporting situation you have been in.

- Read each statement and tick the appropriate number to the right of the statement (1 = not at all, 4 = very often).

- Indicate how you feel/felt at this moment in time. There are no right or wrong answers.

- Do not spend too much time on any one statement.

- Calculate levels of cognitive anxiety, somatic anxiety and self-confidence using the scoring system.

	Statement	1	2	3	4
1	I am concerned about this competition.				
2	I feel nervous.				
3	I feel at ease.				
4	I have self-doubts.				
5	I feel jittery.				
6	I feel comfortable.				
7	I am concerned I may not do as well as I should.				
8	My body feels tense.				
9	I feel self-confident.				
10	I am concerned about losing.				
11	I feel tense in my stomach.				
12	I feel secure.				
13	I am concerned about losing.				
14	My body feels relaxed.				
15	I am confident I can meet the challenge.				
16	I am concerned about performing poorly.				
17	My heart is racing.				
18	I'm confident about performing well.				
19	I'm worried about reaching my goals.				
20	I feel my stomach sinking.				
21	I feel mentally relaxed.				
22	I'm concerned that others will be disappointed with my performance.				
23	My hands are clammy.				
24	I'm confident because I mentally picture myself reaching my goal.				
25	I'm concerned I won't be able to concentrate.				
26	My body feels tight.				
27	I'm confident of coming through under pressure.				

To score the CSAI-2, add up all of the numbers you circled for the scores as outlined below to get a score for each of the different levels. Statement 14 is reverse scored (e.g. 4 = 1, 3 = 2, 2 = 3 and 1 = 4).

Cognitive state anxiety score .... (sum 1, 4, 7, 10, 13, 16, 19, 22 and 25)

Somatic state anxiety score...... (sum 2, 5, 8, 11, 14, 17, 20, 23 and 26)

Self-confidence ...... (3, 6, 9, 12, 17, 18, 21, 24 and 27)

Activity: Sport competition anxiety test

The Sport Competition Anxiety Test (Martens, 1977) was designed to assess levels of competitive trait anxiety. Although SCAT is a useful measure, it is a personality measure that shouldn't be used without taking into account an individual's situation.

Use the questionnaire below to assess your levels of competitive trait anxiety.

- Read each statement and choose the letter that describes how you usually feel when competing:

  A = hardly ever

  B = sometimes

  C = often feel this way.

- Tick the letter corresponding to your choice.
- Remember that there are no right or wrong answers. Try not to spend too much time on each question.

If you score high on the SCAT, this is an indicator that you are less likely to control anxiety and more likely to be nervous in competitive situations. If you score low on the SCAT, you are less likely to become nervous in competitive situations and more likely to cope with anxiety.

	Statement	A	B	C
1	Competing against others is socially enjoyable.			
2	Before I compete, I feel uneasy.			
3	Before I compete, I worry about not performing well.			
4	I am a good sports person when I compete.			
5	When I compete, I worry about making mistakes.			
6	Before I compete, I am calm.			
7	Setting a goal is important when competing.			
8	Before I compete, I get a queasy feeling in my stomach.			
9	Just before competing, I notice that my heart beats faster than usual.			
10	I like to compete in games that demand considerable physical energy.			
11	Before I compete, I feel relaxed.			
12	Before I compete, I am nervous.			
13	Team sports are more exciting than individual sports.			
14	I get nervous waiting to start the game.			
15	Before I compete, I usually get uptight.			

Work out your SCAT score using the following scale:

Disregard statements 1, 4, 7, 10 and 13

For statements 2, 3, 5, 8, 9, 12, 14 and 15, A = 1 point, B = 2 points, C = 3 points.

For statements 6 and 11, C = 1 point, B = 2 points, A = 3 points.

Activity: Sport anxiety scale

Smith, Smoll and Shutz (1990) used the multi-dimensional model of anxiety to design the Sport Anxiety Scale (SAS) so that they could measure levels of trait anxiety. The SAS measures worry and concentration disruption (cognitive anxiety) and somatic anxiety to give a total trait anxiety score.

Using the questionnaire below, assess your levels of trait anxiety as follows:

- Read each statement and circle the number that best describes how you usually feel prior to or during competition:

1 = never
2 = somewhat
3 = moderately
4 = very often.

- Remember that there are no right or wrong answers. Try not to spend too much time on each question.

- It's really important that you share your true reactions to the sport setting, don't be ashamed of admitting it if you feel nervous or worried!

	Statement	1	2	3	4
1	I feel nervous.				
2	I find myself thinking about unrelated thoughts.				
3	I have self-doubts.				
4	My body feels tense.				
5	I am concerned that I may not do as well in competition as I could do.				
6	My mind wanders during sport competition.				
7	While performing, I often do not pay attention to what's going on.				
8	I feel tense in my stomach.				
9	Thoughts of doing poorly interfere with my concentration during competition.				
10	I am concerned about choking under pressure.				
11	My heart races.				
12	I feel my stomach sinking.				
13	I'm concerned about performing poorly.				
14	I have lapses in concentration because of nervousness.				
15	I sometimes find myself trembling before or during a competitive event.				
16	I'm worried about reaching my goal.				
17	My body feels tight.				
18	I'm concerned that others will be disappointed with my performances.				
19	My stomach gets upset before or during performance.				
20	I'm concerned I won't be able to concentrate.				
21	My heart pounds before competition.				

Calculate your different values using the scales below:

Somatic trait anxiety score ...... (sum statements 1, 4, 8, 11, 12, 15, 17, 19 and 21)

Worry score ...... (sum statements 3, 5, 9, 10, 13, 16 and 18)

Concentration disruption score ...... (sum statements 2, 6, 7, 14 and 20)

Trait anxiety score ...... (sum scores from three scales above)

- The somatic anxiety scale ranges from a score of 9 to 36, with 9 being low somatic anxiety and 36 being high somatic anxiety.

- The worry scale ranges from a low level of 7 to a high level of 28.

- The concentration disruption scale ranges from a low of 5 to a high of 20.

- The overall trait anxiety levels range from a low of 21 to a high of 84.

These questionnaires are good objective measures of an individual's psychological state and can be used in real situations. Don't forget that one of the best ways to help the athlete you're working with is to get to know them; talking to your athlete is a good way to discover their psychological strengths and areas for improvement.

After your initial assessments with the athlete, you should complete a needs analysis. This is a document that outlines their main strengths and areas for improvement; how you can help them improve; and some initial suggestions of what they can do to improve. The needs analysis allows you to make your PST programme more effective by personalising it to your athlete. From this needs analysis, you can put together the aims and objectives of the PST programme in conjunction with the athlete, managers and coaches.

Needs analysis

Client's name Adrienne Robertson

Sports psychologist's name Mark Johnson

The following initial assessments were undertaken (*name the assessment methods and state what they were used for*)

1 ACSI-28 – Measure overall psychological skills

2 One-to-one interview – develop rapport with client

3 Performance observations – monitor client in performance environment

Results from assessment 1

Moderate psychological skills use

Low levels of confidence, low peaking under pressure

Results from assessment 2

Client said they sometimes lose confidence when they start to lose, they don't think that they can get back into the game

Results from assessment 3

Always lots of effort from client

Sometimes body language changes when they start to lose

Your main strengths are

High concentration levels, lots of effort during matches

Your main areas for improvement are

Low levels of confidence

You could improve your performance by using the following techniques

Imagery – rehearse positive situations

Breathing – Refocus/calm self in competitive scenario where you start to lose

Self-talk – use of positive statements relating to your ability

Figure 17.9: Example of a needs analysis form

Activity: Producing a needs analysis

Using the initial assessments you completed for the activities on the previous pages, produce a needs analysis for your partner using Figure 17.9 on page 310 to help you. Remember to report the results of your initial assessments to highlight the athlete's strengths and areas for improvements.

Identifying psychological demands of sports

Before starting to plan your PST programme, you need to identify the demands of the particular sport you are examining. Performance profiling is one way of doing this.

Performance profiling

Performance profiling has five main stages.

- **Stage 1: Identify and define key qualities for performance.** Introduce the idea by asking the client what attributes they think are important for top performance. When using performance profiling in a sports setting, the athlete could be asked to think of an elite performer and write down the athlete's qualities. Table 17.2 highlights some prompts that can be used with different clients.

  It will be useful for the client to record and define the qualities necessary for performance in a table format. This helps the client and practitioner to

develop an understanding of what the terms mean. To avoid misunderstanding the practioner must make sure the definitions used are devised by the client. They should aim for 20 key qualities. Tell them that there are no right or wrong answers.

- **Stage 2: Profile the practitioner's perceptions of the client's levels and profile the client's perceptions of their levels.** This is an assessment by you and the client of the current level of performance. You and the client write the 20 key qualities in each of the blank spaces around the outside of the circular grid. Each quality is given a rating from 0 to 10 (See Figure 17.10 on page 312).

- **Stage 3: Discuss the practitioner's and the client's profiles.** In this stage, you are using the results by interpreting the performance profiles by identifying perceived areas of strength and areas for improvement. When looking at the two profiles (shown in Figure 17.10 on page 312), if there are large differences between levels (a large difference is classed as two points or more), this should lead to a discussion between you and the client about why the different levels have been given.

- **Stage 4: Agree on goals and how they will be achieved.** You and the client need to agree on what you would like the client to achieve (i.e. set the benchmarks for each of the qualities). The results are used to set the goals to be achieved through the PST programme. Normally, each of these desired benchmarks will be at level 10 – any target level below this on the client's behalf would suggest that there is some form of resistance to achieving the ultimate level of performance.

Psychological	Physical	Attitudinal/character	Technical*
Confidence	Strength	Weight control	
Concentration	Stamina	Discipline	
Relaxation	Endurance	Determination	
Visualisation	Flexibility	Will to win	
Emotional	Power	Positive outlook	
Control	Speed		
Motivation	Balance		
	Reaction time		

Table 17.2: Examples of athlete qualities

*Technical skills are sport specific

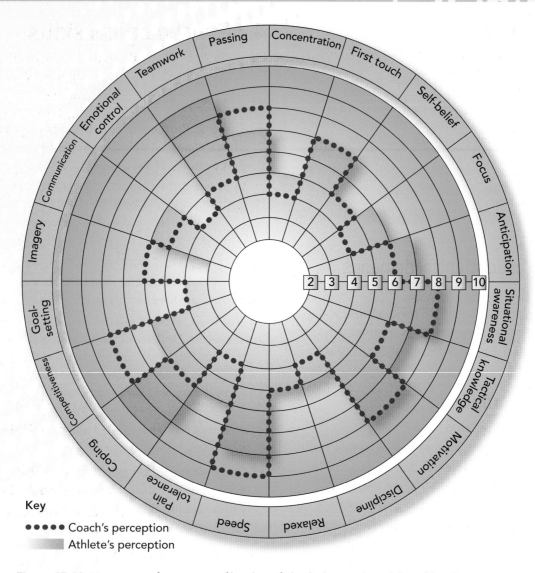

The segments around the wheel (clockwise from top): Passing, Concentration, First touch, Self-belief, Focus, Anticipation, Situational awareness, Tactical knowledge, Motivation, Discipline, Relaxed, Speed, Pain tolerance, Coping, Competitiveness, Goal-setting, Imagery, Communication, Emotional control, Teamwork.

Scale: 2 3 4 5 6 7 8 9 10

Key

●●●●● Coach's perception

▨ Athlete's perception

Figure 17.10: How can performance profiling benefit both the coach and the athlete?

Activity: Identifying differences of opinion

Using the profiles in Figure 17.10, identify which qualities have a mismatch in terms of the athlete's and the coach's opinions of performance levels.

- **Stage 5: Repeat the profiling to monitor progress**. Performance profiling can be repeated on a number of occasions to assess the client's progress. The aim is that the client will gradually progress further towards the outside of the scale (closer to the rating of 10). If the client does not make the desired progress, you and the client need to discuss why progress is not being made. Usually this is because the training programme didn't take into account a quality (errors in design of programme), you have different views on the importance of a quality (errors in communication and understanding) or the client has not put in the effort to achieve the improvements in performance.

Plan

The planning stage of a PST programme comes after conducting your needs analysis with the athlete. The strengths and areas for improvement you have identified will help you decide on the aims and objectives of the PST programme. During the planning stage you should consider the aims and objectives, targets, content, resources required and any other considerations relating to the athlete's personal circumstances.

Current situation

The current situation of the athlete can be assessed in a number of ways including inventories and questionnaires (such as ACSI-28, CSAI-2, SCAT and SAS), performance profiling and interviews. These help you get a picture of the athlete's current situation, which can be summarised in the needs analysis form.

Aims and objectives

The aims and objectives of the PST programme are what you and the athlete want to achieve through the programme.

Action plan to address aims and objectives

When you have decided on the aims and objectives of the PST programme, you should work with the athlete to prioritise them. The biggest areas for improvement or the skills that are most important to the athlete's performance are given the highest priority. After you have prioritised the aims and objectives, you need to produce SMART targets.

When producing a plan for any PST programme think about how much time should be spent on different aspects of the programme. If you are introducing new skills to the PST programme, then 15–30 minute sessions, in addition to physical practice sessions, 3–5 times a week are beneficial. Gradually, the aim is to move away from needing distinct sessions to allow the psychological skills to be integrated with normal practice, however this only becomes possible when athletes become more proficient in their new skills.

Daily and weekly content of the plan

The daily and weekly content should be decided by the consultant, coach and athlete together. This means the daily and weekly content has been decided on objectively and takes into account their different perspectives. Including the athlete in the decision of the daily and weekly content increases their motivation to adhere to the programme, as they will have invested time and effort in its design. The athlete will feel like they are in control which benefits motivation. Another important reason behind the inclusion of both the athlete and the coach is to ensure the daily and weekly content is manageable. You can also show how the PST programme fits with the normal training routine.

4.2 Psychological skills

Think about all of the times that you have heard an athlete being interviewed after they have lost a game and they have talked about losing focus or cracking under pressure. At some point during their career, all athletes will suffer from some form of lack of mental preparation or make an unlikely mistake. This is where Psychological Skills Training becomes important.

4.3 Motivation

Helping the athlete to increase their motivation to optimal levels is one of the most important aspects of the consultancy role of a sports psychologist.

Goal setting

Using the acronym SMARTS will help to set the right type of goals. SMARTS stands for:

Specific – goals should show exactly what needs to be done

Measurable – goals should be quantifiable

Achievable – the goals can be attained and are relevant

Realistic – goals should be within your reach

Timescale – there should be a reasonable timeframe

Self-determined – there should be input from the person for whom the goal is intended.

There are three types of goals:

- Outcome goals
- Performance goals
- Process goals.

Outcome goals

Outcome goals focus on the result of the event, like winning a table tennis match. This type of goal is often the least effective when it comes to motivation as your goal achievement is dependent on your opposition as well as the athlete themself. For example, an athlete could run a personal best in a 400-metre event but still finish last and if the outcome goal is always to win, then this could negatively influence their motivation, even though performance is improving. Spending too much time thinking about this type of goal just before or during competition can increase anxiety and decrease concentration, which can reduce motivation. However, this type of goal can improve short-term motivation. Think about when you have lost to somebody that you really wanted to beat. It probably spurred you on to train harder so you could beat them next time.

Performance goals

Performance goals focus on the athlete's performance and involve comparing their current performance to previous performances, so they are independent of other athletes and can give the performer a greater sense of control over the goal. Having greater control over goal achievement can be very beneficial for the athlete's motivation. An example of a performance goal would be improving pass completion percentage in football from 78 per cent to 85 per cent.

Process goals

Process goals are based on what the athlete has to do to be able to improve their performance. An example of this type of goal would be a basketball player wanting to improve their jump shot accuracy by making sure they release the ball at the height of the jump. This type of goal is useful for improving motivation as it gives a specific element of performance to focus on, which facilitates learning and development.

The key to using outcome, performance and process goals successfully is knowing which to use and when. It is hard for an athlete to focus on achieving process and performance goals without having a long-term outcome to aim for. Some studies have shown that using a combination of all three types of goal is better than using any single type of goal alone when wanting to improve motivation. There should also be a logical progression from short-term goals through to long-term goals.

Remember

The main reason athletes give for using goals is to help to provide direction and focus towards a task.

Performance profiling

Consider the use of performance profiling within any psychological skills training programme you design as it is one of the most common and effective techniques in sport psychology. As the athlete has a lot of control over the performance profiling process, this technique can be useful when wanting to increase motivation.

4.4 Arousal control

Progressive muscular relaxation

Muscle tension is one of the most uncomfortable and devastating symptoms of an over-aroused state and can severely hinder performance due to losses in coordination. It can lead to an increased risk of injury due to vastly decreased flexibility.

Progressive muscular relaxation (PMR) is an easy-to-use technique that helps reduce muscle tension. It increases an individual's awareness of their levels of muscle tension and, through the relaxation phase, helps distinguish between a state of tension and relaxation.

The technique involves tensing and relaxing groups of muscles in turn over the whole body. The process involves tensing a muscle group for five seconds, releasing the tension for five seconds, taking a deep breath and repeating. It is called progressive muscular relaxation because the athlete progresses from one muscle group to the next until all muscles have been tensed and relaxed.

Mind to muscle relaxation

The aim of mind to muscle relaxation is to train the muscles to recognise tension so they can be released and a relaxed state can occur. Common examples of mind to muscle relaxation techniques include imagery, PMR and autogenic training.

Autogenic techniques

Autogenic training is a type of self-hypnosis that helps to develop feelings of warmth and heaviness. This programme of self-hypnosis, uses a series of sentences, statements or phrases to focus attention on the different feelings the athlete is trying to produce.

A normal autogenic programme has six stages:

- Heaviness in the arms and legs, e.g. my left leg feels heavy.
- Warmth in the arms and legs, e.g. my right leg feels warm.
- Regulation of cardiac activity, e.g. my heart rate is normal.
- Regulation of breathing, e.g. my breathing rate is normal.
- Abdominal warmth, e.g. my abdomen feels warm.
- Cooling of the forehead, e.g. my forehead is cool.

Autogenic training is not used as widely as other techniques of arousal regulation simply because it takes several months to learn effectively and each session can last a long time.

Breathing control

When you start to experience increased pressure in sports situations, an automatic tendency is to hold your breath. Unfortunately this increases factors that are detrimental to performance, for example, muscle tension. The best time to use breathing control is in a sporting situation that lets you take a break.

Psyching up techniques

Psyching up techniques are frequently used to increase arousal levels for competition. Some of the more common techniques are discussed below.

1. Acting energised

How many times have you seen an American football player butt helmets with a teammate? What about when a tennis player wins a key point in tennis and screams at the crowd? These are examples of a technique known as acting energised. These actions have different common characteristics and involve the combination of quick and forceful movements, positive thinking and strong emotional releases.

2. Energising imagery

In the same way that imagery can be used to reduce arousal and anxiety, it can also be used to increase arousal. This can be achieved through the use of high-energy images of competition (e.g. a hard tackle in rugby), playing well (e.g. crossing the finish line first in a race) and high levels of effort (e.g. being able to lift a new weight in the gym).

3. Using music

The use of music increases arousal. Music can narrow a performer's attention and divert it from tiredness. Exciting music can increase body temperature, heart rate and breathing rate, all of which improves sport performance.

4. Imagery

This requires the athlete to think about an elite performer in their sport and remember how they have performed a particular skill. Visualising themselves performing that skill in their sport before trying to copy what they did will help the athlete to perform the skill. This is one example of imagery and how it is used by athletes to help them improve their technique.

Imagery can be used in other ways by athletes. Imagery is a polysensorial and emotional creation or recreation of an experience that takes place in the mind. It should involve as many of your senses as possible, as well as recreating emotions experienced through the activity you take part in. The most effective imagery uses the following senses:

- **Polysensorial** – involving as many of your senses in the imagery process.
- **Kinaesthetic** – concentrating on the feel of the movement.
- **Visual** – concentrating on the different things that you can see during the movement.
- **Tactile** – concentrating on the sense of touch throughout the movement.
- **Auditory** – concentrating on the different sounds that you associate with a sporting movement, e.g. hitting the sweet spot on a cricket bat.
- **Olfactory** – concentrating on the different smells that you associate with a sporting action, e.g. the smell of freshly cut grass on the first game of the season for your football team.

There are two main types of imagery in sport and exercise: **internal imagery** and **external imagery**.

Key terms

Internal imagery – imagining yourself doing something and concentrating on how the activity feels.

External imagery – imagining yourself doing something as though you are watching it on a film so that you can develop an awareness of how the activity looks.

Take it further

Imagery

Research the following theories behind imagery use and then try to justify why you would use imagery with athletes. Be sure to use coach-friendly terminology. You might find it useful to try to give some examples of how to apply the theory to different athletics events.

- Psychoneuromuscular Theory
- Symbolic Learning Theory
- Bioinformational Theory
- Attention–Arousal Set Theory

5. Mental rehearsal

Mental rehearsal is one aspect of imagery. It is a strategy for practising something in your mind before performing the task. The difference between mental rehearsal and imagery is that mental rehearsal does not take into account how the skill is rehearsed, or what senses and emotions are used throughout the skill. It is the cognitive rehearsal of a skill without any physical movement.

Using mental rehearsal in the lead up to, during, and after competition, as well as in practice settings, benefits skill practice and development. It gives the athlete the opportunity to practice 'what if' scenarios to assess whether something different would work in the same scenario. This is often combined with replaying the performance in their mind. The athlete goes through previous performances to detect errors using mental rehearsal.

Although not as effective as physically practising a skill, mental rehearsal is more beneficial than not practising the skill at all. It helps to develop neuromuscular patterns associated with different movements. It is important to rehearse both good and bad movement patterns so that you can get to know the difference between the two to develop the appropriate neuromuscular responses.

6. Controlling emotions

A cricket player is preparing to go out and bat in the Ashes Test series. He starts to visualise situations in the past where he has been bowled out against Australia and then starts to breathe deeply and change the image from being bowled out to successfully striking the ball and scoring combinations of quick singles, 4s and 6s. One of the benefits of using imagery is that you can imagine things that have gone wrong in previous performances (such as missing penalties, being bowled out, experiencing poor officiating). Then you can imagine yourself coping with these negative influences in a number of ways and being able to perform the task successfully.

7. Concentration

A golfer is waiting to putt to win the Masters at Augusta. He concentrates on the feel of the putter in his hand, the distance between the ball and the hole, the changes in the ground, the feel of the movement when he goes to stroke the ball and smell the green. He closes out any noises from the crowd so that he can listen to the contact of the club on the ball. A key aspect to concentration is being able to focus on relevant cues in your environment (e.g. things that directly affect your sports performance) and being able to close out factors that don't directly affect your sport performance (e.g. crowd noise and banners). By imagining what you want to achieve and what you need to be able to do to achieve it, you can prevent your attention from focusing on irrelevant aspects, and focus instead on relevant aspects.

8. Relaxation

A sprinter is in the start position in the final of the women's 100 metres at the Olympic Games. In this example, the athlete would imagine emotions associated with relaxation and, together with other techniques such as breathing exercises, could more effectively control anxiety, arousal and stress levels.

Activity: Relaxation imagery

Ask a friend to measure your heart rate and write it down before you read the following relaxation imagery script.

> Imagine yourself on a beautiful sandy beach. You are alone and everything is peaceful. Notice how the sand meets the clear blue water. Above, you can see only clear blue sky. You are walking towards the water and can feel the sand under your feet and between your toes. You can hear the waves as they reach the shore and you step into the sea. You can feel the cooling sensation on your feet and around your ankles and calves as you enter the water. Everything feels perfect. You can feel the warmth of the sun on your back and shoulders. You are completely relaxed and calm.

Record your heart rate again. Have you relaxed?

9. Pre-performance routines

These are routines that performers go through before a competition to help them focus attention, increase arousal or decrease arousal. Think about when you have seen a tennis player at Wimbledon before an important game serve. You will see them close their eyes, take a deep breath, bounce the ball and then start the serve. This is an example of a pre-performance routine.

4.5 Confidence building

Sports psychologists work with athletes to build up their confidence. For example, if a football player has been taking penalties for her team on a regular basis but keeps missing them, this could knock her confidence. A sports psychologist could work with the player, asking her to remember having a strong support foot placement, striking the ball hard, thinking about where exactly the ball should go, seeing the ball hit the back of the net and thinking about the joy experienced when scoring a goal. The sports psychologist would do this because when an athlete can picture themselves performing well in their mind, it helps to promote a sense of mastery, and increases their belief in their own ability to perform a task.

Self-talk

The main focus of self-talk is to convince yourself that you are good enough to play or perform well. Self-talk helps the athlete to build self-confidence. This should be done quite frequently. Everyone has, at some point, said to themselves 'Come on!' or 'You can do this!' when performing. It can be very effective.

For example, if a cricket player is having a very unsuccessful innings, and every ball he goes for he hits incorrectly or misses, he could find himself leaving balls he would normally attempt. If the player were to start saying to himself 'Think back to when you scored 100 against Australia. You concentrated on the flight of the ball, you watched the spin, you took into account the position of the fielders and you struck the ball well most times.' This would help his performance greatly, as he is concentrating on successful performances rather than negative ones.

Positive thinking

This is often used with other techniques such as imagery and PMR in order to increase the confidence of athletes during PST sessions. It is used regularly by athletes in different sports during the event to improve performance.

A golfer has a problem missing putts during important events and this has greatly knocked his confidence. He seems to miss most putts that are more than about six inches. When he approaches the shot the next time in competition, he automatically thinks 'Oh no, I hope I don't miss this one as well.' Positive thinking would be good here because the athlete would change the negative thought into a positive one. He could do this by thinking more about times when he has been successful in performance. Using phrases such as 'I *can* do this, I've done it a million times before. Relax.' After the event, the golfer could use imagery techniques to imagine putting from distances while using the positive thoughts to further enhance confidence.

Changing self-image through imagery

Imagery can be used to change self-image through increasing confidence. Through imagery, the athlete will be able to experience the feelings of success and will be able to come up with strategies as to how they can be successful in performance. As the performer sees that they can complete the performance successfully (if only in their minds), their levels of self-confidence will increase.

Assessment activity 17.5

1. Based on the initial assessments and needs analyses you have conducted for the earlier activities **P6**, produce a six-week plan for a PST programme. **P7**

2. Explain the programme to your client. **M4**

3. Justify why you have selected the different PST activities. **D3**

Grading tips

P6 Show evidence of assessing the current psychological skills of your performer by keeping all of your methods of assessing skills and the needs analysis form.

P7 Identify your performer's key areas for improvement and decide on six weeks' of psychological skills training that will help the performers develop these areas. Remember that the areas to develop may not always be the areas that have the lowest values on results.

M4 Provide an explanation of the design of the programme and of each of the activities that will be completed by the athlete as part of their skills training programme.

D3 Justify the design of the programme and the activities by saying how they will benefit the athlete and providing supporting evidence.

PLTS

By designing a psychological skills training programme and providing suggestions for your athlete to progress with their psychological skills training programme, you could develop your skills as a **reflective thinker**.

Functional skills

By working out all of the scores for each of the subscales on the different questionnaires and then comparing these to norm data for the different tests, you could develop your **Mathematics** skills.

Mark Johnson
Sports Psychologist

Mark works as a sports psychologist for an athletics club. One of Mark's key job roles is working with young athletes to help them develop their psychological skills.

'Sport presents lots of opportunities for young athletes to learn psychological skills alongside the physical skills that are required for their sport. Like most skills, some people manage to learn psychological skills more quickly than others do, but if you are prepared to spend the time to learn how to use the skill then it will be really beneficial for you.'

'One of the big advantages of teaching psychological skills alongside physical skills is that it can help athletes and their support teams (e.g. coaches and sports psychologists) to develop even better relationships because they will spend more time with each other. This can benefit the athlete's performance as the coach and the sports psychologist will develop more trust in each other's opinions and values which means that they can offer a better level of service to the athlete. One of the good things about working in this way is that I get to spend more time with the athletes and I can observe them more in competition and training. If I can do that, I get to see which athletes are developing well and which athletes are still struggling with things like stress, arousal and motivation.'

'One of the common problems that I face is when young athletes have low levels of motivation during their winter training. Often it is cold and dark, so some of the athletes don't really like to go to training and sometimes don't try very hard.'

Think about it!

- What techniques could you use to increase the motivation of the young athletes during winter training?
- How do you think these techniques would help to increase motivation?

Just checking

1. What is personality and how does it affect sports participation and performance?
2. What are the main theories that have tried to explain the relationship between personality and sports participation and performance?
3. What are the main arguments of each of these different theories and which is the most widely supported?
4. What is motivation and what are the different types of motivation?
5. What is the attribution theory and what are the different types of attributes we give?
6. What is stress and what are the different sources of stress?
7. What is the stress process?
8. What is arousal and what are the different theories that try to explain how arousal affects performance?
9. What is anxiety and what are the different types of anxiety?
10. What are Tuckman's stages of group development?
11. What is cohesion? Explain the key factors that can affect team cohesion.
12. What are the two main ways that team cohesion can be assessed?
13. What are some of the tools that you can use to plan and review a PST programme?
14. What are some of the different skills that you can incorporate in a PST programme and which areas of psychology will they benefit?

edexcel **:::**

Assignment tips

- Research tips – try to use as much supporting information as you can for this unit. This will be helpful in achieving higher grades in some cases. The Internet is full of websites based on sports psychology. You might want to try these:

  Athletic Insight (www.athleticinsight.com)

  Mind tools (www.mindtools.com)

  Zone of Excellence (www.zoneofexcellence.ca).

- Practise using the techniques. The key to being a good sports psychologist is knowing how to suggest and use different techniques with people based on the needs analysis. Try using some techniques in your own sport so that you become familiar with them.

Credit value: 10

27 Technical and tactical skills in sport

All sport requires a certain amount of technical ability. Tactics are needed to use this technical ability. Some skills belong to all sports like running, throwing, catching and jumping. Others belong to specific sports, for example a tennis serve, a golf swing or discus throw. Tactics are actions and strategies which are incorporated into sport and used to achieve a goal, which is usually to win.

All great athletes and players have tactical awareness. They think about factors such as the opposition and the importance of the game or event. You should always strive to improve, and this can be done by observing elite performers, and how they work with their coaches.

In this unit you will look at the technical skills and tactics associated with different sports and elite individual sports performers. You will then consider your own abilities during competition and over a period of time. Finally, you will think about your development technically and tactically, by producing a plan that aims to help you optimise your own sports performance.

Learning outcomes

After completing this unit you should:

1. understand the technical skills and tactics demanded by selected sports
2. be able to assess the technical and tactical ability of an elite sports performer
3. be able to assess your own technical and tactical ability.

Assessment and grading criteria

This table shows you what you must do in order to achieve a pass, merit or distinction grade, and where you can find activities in this book to help you.

To achieve a **pass** grade the evidence must show that the learner is able to:	To achieve a **merit** grade the evidence must show that, in addition to the pass criteria, the learner is able to:	To achieve a **distinction** grade the evidence must show that, in addition to the pass and merit criteria, the learner is able to:
P1 explain the technical and tactical demands of three contrasting sports **Assessment activity 27.1, page 335**	**M1** compare and contrast the technical and tactical demands of three contrasting sports **Assessment activity 27.1, page 335**	
P2 produce an observation checklist that can be used to assess the technical and tactical ability of a performer in a selected sport **Assessment activity 27.2, page 345**		
P3 use an observation checklist to assess the technical and tactical ability of an elite performer, in a selected sport, identifying strengths and areas for improvement **Assessment activity 27.2, page 345**	**M2** explain strengths and areas for improvement, in technical and tactical ability, of the selected elite sports performer, and make suggestions relating to development **Assessment activity 27.2, page 345**	**D1** justify development suggestions made for the selected elite sports performer regarding areas for improvement **Assessment activity 27.2, page 345**
P4 use an observation checklist to assess own technical and tactical ability, in a competitive or training situation for a selected sport, identifying strengths and areas for improvement **Assessment activity 27.3, page 353**	**M3** explain strengths and areas for improvement, in own technical and tactical ability in a competitive situation **Assessment activity 27.3, page 353**	
P5 complete a four-week log of own technical and tactical ability in a selected sport, identifying strengths and areas for improvement **Assessment activity 27.3, page 353**	**M4** explain identified strengths and areas for improvement of own technical and tactical ability in a selected sport **Assessment activity 27.3, page 353**	
P6 produce a development plan of own technical and tactical ability, based on identified strengths and areas for improvement **Assessment activity 27.4, page 356**	**M5** relate development plan to identified strengths and areas for improvement in own technical and tactical ability **Assessment activity 27.4, page 356**	**D2** justify suggestions made in personal development plan **Assessment activity 27.4, page 356**

How you will be assessed

This unit will be assessed by an internal assignment that will be designed and marked by your tutor. Your assessment could be in the form of:

- presentations
- written assignments
- case studies
- observational analysis
- video analysis
- practical work.

Benjamin Perez, 17-year-old club tennis player

This unit has helped me to understand through observation and video analysis the range of skills and tactics required to play a variety of sports. Selecting an elite performer and attending training sessions and live competitive matches enabled me to analyse their technical and tactical ability and gain a deeper insight into their strengths and areas for improvement.

By observing and analysing an elite performer I was able to use the knowledge and understanding gained to help me with my logbook and become more critical of my own performance.

I enjoyed working with my coach when devising practices to improve my personal performance and following this up with a development plan. My performance in competitive matches has improved and my club has asked me to assist with coaching the juniors now that I have achieved a National Governing Body Award.

Over to you

- **Which section of the unit do you think you will find most interesting?**
- **What preparation can you do for the unit assessment, e.g. logbook?**

1. Understand the technical skills and tactics demanded by selected sports

My greatest performance

Think of an elite athlete. List the skills and techniques they possess which have taken them to this level. Consider also their tactical awareness, fitness levels and ability to read the game.

How can this person improve their performance? In groups, discuss your findings and compare and contrast different elite performers.

What is this athlete's greatest achievement?

Key terms

Motor skills – skills associated with body movement. There are two types: gross motor skills and fine motor skills.

Gross motor skills – involve a low level of expertise and large muscular movements, for example sit-ups, with a low level of coordination needed.

Fine motor skills – highly controlled skills like drawing and writing. They are small and precise, take time to perfect and improve over time.

Cognitive skills – involve a person considering what they are doing. In sport this applies to tactics, making decisions quickly, planning and selecting how to play. In team sports, verbal skills are used to encourage and motivate players.

Perceptual skills – the major activities that transform an input into an output. From this information, an athlete will choose what is relevant and then act. Examples of perceptual skills include visual memory.

1.1 Technical skills

Skills in sport are the movements and actions needed to perform shots, strokes, jumps, throws, etc. Coordination is the skilful interaction of these movements. Balance is being able to maintain equilibrium.

A physical movement has a beginning and an end. This is not always clear. Skills can be divided into categories depending on how clearly the beginning and the end of the movement are defined. The categories are:

- continuous skills
- discrete skills
- serial skills.

Continuous skills

This skill has no obvious beginning or end and has a regular rhythm. Examples of technical skills under this heading include walking, running, swimming, rowing and cross-country skiing.

Walking

There are two phases of walking: brisk walking, and walking at a comfortable pace.

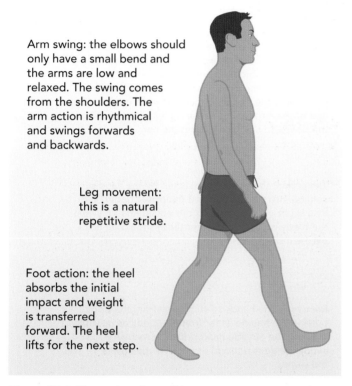

Arm swing: the elbows should only have a small bend and the arms are low and relaxed. The swing comes from the shoulders. The arm action is rhythmical and swings forwards and backwards.

Leg movement: this is a natural repetitive stride.

Foot action: the heel absorbs the initial impact and weight is transferred forward. The heel lifts for the next step.

Figure 27.1: The actions for walking

Running

Running can be divided into three phases: support, flight, and support. The support phases can be divided into front support and drive. Flight is divided into recovery, front swinging and back into support. This is a rhythmical continuous skill.

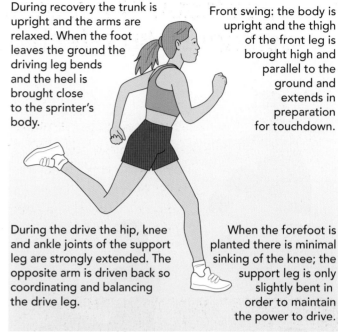

During recovery the trunk is upright and the arms are relaxed. When the foot leaves the ground the driving leg bends and the heel is brought close to the sprinter's body.

Front swing: the body is upright and the thigh of the front leg is brought high and parallel to the ground and extends in preparation for touchdown.

During the drive the hip, knee and ankle joints of the support leg are strongly extended. The opposite arm is driven back so coordinating and balancing the drive leg.

When the forefoot is planted there is minimal sinking of the knee; the support leg is only slightly bent in order to maintain the power to drive.

Figure 27.2: The actions for running

Swimming

A stroke in swimming has an arm action and a leg action; you must also consider the line of the body in the water and the timing of breathing.

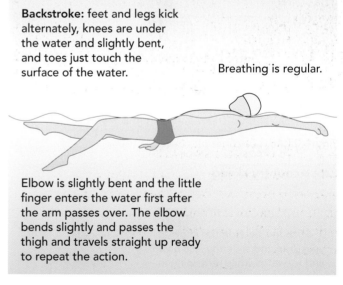

Backstroke: feet and legs kick alternately, knees are under the water and slightly bent, and toes just touch the surface of the water.

Breathing is regular.

Elbow is slightly bent and the little finger enters the water first after the arm passes over. The elbow bends slightly and passes the thigh and travels straight up ready to repeat the action.

Figure 27.3: The actions for swimming

Rowing

The actions of rowing occur in a smooth continuous cycle. The stroke can be divided into four sections: the catch, the drive, the extraction and recovery.

The catch: this phase is when the rower connects the blade to the water. This is performed by moving the feet away from the seat.

The drive: the rower drives both the legs and back together. The aim is to reach maximum force when the legs are about two-thirds down and the body is vertical. The rower draws the handle by maintaining the pressure which has been generated on the handle. From the point that the legs are flat the pressure in the fingers is maintained through to the end of the stroke. The rower thinks about moving the boat and not accelerating the oar.

Extraction: the blade is extracted by the handle coming into the ribcage and the rower begins this by a slight push down with the outside hand. When the blade is out of the water there should be no excess movement.

Recovery: the hands stretch away from the body, putting the handle as far from the body as possible keeping the outside hand grip. The recovery sequence does not end until the blade enters the water.

Figure 27.4: The actions of rowing

Cross-country skiing

1 Stick the poles in the snow at your side and slide the skis back and forwards while remaining in a stationary position to become used to the skis.

Put your hands through the pole straps.

2 Put one foot in front of the other letting the skis slide as if you were walking across an ice rink.

Plant your poles in a rhythmical manner, placing the left one in the snow at the end of a right foot glide and vice versa.

Gradually increase the speed and the gliding distance.

Figure 27.5: The actions of cross-country skiing

Serial skills

Serial skills are made up of discrete and/or continuous skills. This is a series of skills which follow each other in quick succession in an orderly sequence to become one movement.

Examples of serial skills include:

- high jump
- triple jump
- pole vault
- dribbling in football
- 400-metre hurdle race.

High jump

This serial skill can be divided into four phases.

- **Approach** – this run is J-shaped, straight for the first 3–6 strides and then curved for 4–5 strides. For the initial stride, the foot plants on the ball of the foot, the body leans slightly forwards, speed increases throughout the approach, the body leans naturally into the curve and the body is lowered in the penultimate stride.
- **Take off** – the foot plant is quick and flat with a 'down and back' action. The take-off leg is bent slightly and the knee of the free leg is driven up to horizontal and stopped. The body is vertical at the end of the take off.
- **Flight** – as the body gains height, the take-off position is held. The leading arm reaches up, across and over the bar. By arching the back and lowering the head and legs, the hips are raised over the bar. The head is brought up towards the chest to bring the legs clear of the bar.
- **Landing** – the head is drawn up towards the chest. The athlete lands on their shoulders and back, with knees apart.

Triple jump

This serial skill can be divided into four phases.

- **Approach** – 10–20 strides with a running technique similar to sprinting, increasing speed throughout the approach. The stride is increased towards the end of the approach.
- **Hop** – take off forwards, bringing the thigh of the free leg to a horizontal position and then draw the leg backwards. Keep take-off leg close to the body and cycle forward to extend and prepare for landing.

- **Step** – bring the thigh of the free leg forwards and upwards to be horizontal or higher. A double-arm swing is used and the trunk is kept in an upright position. Extend the free leg forwards and downwards. Plant the foot quickly.
- **Jump** – extend the take-off leg and use a double-arm action. Use the hang technique in the flight and extend the legs before landing. Collapse at contact.

Pole vault

There are five phases to this serial skill: approach and plant, take off, flight, flight off the pole and landing.

Dribbling in football

Jogging with the ball, when dribbling, is an example of a serial skill. A fake shot can be classed as an example of a discrete skill as the shot has a clear beginning and end. Therefore dribbling is a serial skill as it is made up of continuous and discrete skills.

- **Stop and go** – jog slowly with the ball, when the defender is alongside, burst pass them.
- **Cut back** – cut the ball back behind the body with the inside of the right foot. Plant the left foot to the side of the ball and then bring the right foot up to cut the ball back.
- **The fake shot** – bring the leg back as if to shoot. This can buy time.
- **Inside outside** – carry the ball a little to the inside with the inside of the foot on the ball. When the defender looks off balance or not ready, make a dash for the outside. This gives more space to cross the ball, make a pass or shoot.
- **Sole of the foot** – pull the ball back with the sole of the foot and burst away with a change of speed.
- **Scoop** – lift the ball over the defender's foot after making to go one way and then moving in the other direction.

400-metre hurdle race

There are four phases to this serial skill: sprinting, take-off, clearance and landing.

- **Sprinting** – athletes adjust the stride well before the take off.
- **Take off** – upright posture and forward drive. The hip, knee and ankle joints of the take off leg are fully extended and the thigh of the lead leg swings quickly to the horizontal position.

- **Clearance** – take off well in front of the hurdle. The lead leg is extended towards the hurdle with the foot flexed, shoulders are square and the lean depends on the height of the hurdler. The knee of the trail leg is kept high as it is pulled through and is brought down as quickly as possible after the hurdle.
- **Landing** – landing is on the forefoot, hips are over the landing foot. Contact with the ground is quick and the first stride away from the hurdle should be dynamic.

Discrete skills

This is the opposite of a continuous skill and has a clear beginning and end. It is performed in one clear movement.

Examples of discrete skills include:

- a golf swing
- a snooker shot
- board diving
- putting in golf
- a throw-in in football.

Golf swing

This can be broken down into stance, arm swing and body movement (the pivot).

Snooker shot

A snooker player should keep their body as still as possible when playing a stroke and concentrate on the cue brushing their chin as they push the cue through to strike the cue-ball. They should keep their eyes fixed on the spot where they have aimed the centre of the cue-ball to be when it strikes the object-ball, so they can see if they have hit it where they intended.

Board diving

This discrete skill can be broken down into a number of steps.

- Start with an erect and relaxed stance at the back of the board.
- Make a three-step approach – the third step should be the largest, with the weight on the step-off foot. The head is up, arms relaxed at the sides of the body and the eyes fixed on the tip of the board.
- Arms swing forward and up.

- Lift the knee of the other leg and leap up from the board off the jumping leg.
- Bring feet together in the air. Straighten legs and keep arms extended above the head.
- Drop down on the end over the springboard, landing toes first and then heels. Bend knees to cushion the impact. Swing arms down past the sides of the body and then begin to swing upward again. Fix eyes on the opposite end of the pool. The landing will push the springboard down.
- Spring up and out, swinging arms up and feeling the springboard pushing the body upwards, adding to the lift.
- Bend slightly at the waist as the body begins to fall. Bring hands together above the head and point them down towards the water.
- Enter the water hands first and let the body follow. The body should be streamlined with legs extended behind.

Putting in golf

This discrete skill can be broken down into a number of steps.

- Arms hang loosely and hold the putter lightly so both hang like a pendulum from the shoulder to achieve a smooth swing.
- Set up with the ball near the front foot, the club face square to the target line and eyes over the ball. It is important to keep hands level.
- Move the putter away smoothly, the arms hanging from the shoulders not the elbows or wrists. Keep the putter head as low to the ground as possible. Keep the putter on a line square to the target as it is swung back and then forth. Maintain tempo through the swing, accelerating slightly into the ball.
- Watch the putter head strike the back of the ball on the upswing, feeling almost as if the palm of the right hand is striking it towards the target. Follow through to the hole with the club, not the eyes.

Throw-in in football

This discrete skill can be broken down into a number of steps.

- Secure the ball with both hands, having the index fingers and thumbs as close as possible.
- Bring the ball over the head behind the ears with arms loose and elbows bent and out.

- Feet should be a little more than shoulder-width apart, with one foot in front of the other.
- Face the pitch.
- Bring the head, neck and trunk back, bending at the knees.
- Thrust the ball forward and this will result in the whole body going forward. Parts of both feet must remain on the ground at all times.
- Release the ball as it just goes past the head.

Activity: Skills

1. Select two sports. List six skills associated with each sport and decide whether they are continuous, discrete or serial.

2. Select one skill from each category. Can you explain why you have classified the selected skills as continuous, discrete or serial?

1.2 Tactics

Tactics appropriate to selected sports

Tactics are plans which are set up for a specific purpose during a performance or match. Tactics are involved in all sports. They can be discussed before a game situation and be part of the winning formula. However, the performer must be able to carry them out successfully. An example of a tactic in tennis would be to move your opponent around the court. A tactic in football might be the system you are to play. A player or team will go into a match with a strategy and the tactics will have been planned and employed to meet the objectives of the strategy. Of course, the player or team has to be allowed by the opponent to carry out the tactics.

Key term

Tactics – the skills a player uses in any type of sport to be able to win: for example during a hockey or tennis match, each team or player will apply specific tactics and strategies to try to beat and outwit their opponent(s).

Example 1: Volleyball

Many words are specific to a certain sport. In volleyball you will find the terms block, dig and set, as well as words found in other sports such as attack, defend, smash and volley. In volleyball you are not allowed to control the ball and move with it. Every contact is a rebound action.

All skills in volleyball begin with a mental process (cognitive skill) because before you can perform you must decide what action is required and then choose how to achieve it. All technical skills are actions and the player learns the basic mechanics of these actions. Having done this, the player is then exposed to a game situation where he or she will gather information and make tactical decisions. A player might have to assess the flight of a ball and then make a decision whether to use a volley or a forearm pass. To perform a skill well, the player must be in the right place at the right time, otherwise they cannot control the ball.

Positioning

Several skills can help you be in the right place at the right time.

- Being ready: this position shows physical and mental alertness, and is essential in volleyball (and indeed all sports).
- The 'ready' position:
  o feet shoulder-width apart
  o knees bent and inside the line of the toes
  o weight forward slightly over the knees
  o the spine straight
  o hands out in front of the body.

All movement in volleyball will begin with this 'ready' position. The hips and the eyes should remain parallel in order to judge the flight of the ball when it is moving. The five essential skills for the game are:

- the volley
- the forearm pass
- the serve
- the smash
- the block.

Activity: Ready position

Stand in the position shown in Figure 27.6 and then answer the following questions:

1. Can you move efficiently in any direction?
2. Can you think of other sports which would use the same 'ready' position?
3. What other similarities are there in these sports relating to skills?

Figure 27.6: The 'ready' position in volleyball

Choice of strokes and shots

The volley is a two-handed pass above the forehead. The flight is high and slow and, therefore, a beginner has a chance of assessing the flight of the ball and can move to make efficient and correct contact. The volley is an accurate pass.

The volley

The pass is used to set up an attack. A consistent contact point will come from:

- being ready
- being able to correctly judge the flight of the ball – where and when it will be at its highest point
- positioning the body behind and under the ball
- good flexibility of the knees upon ball contact
- knee extension
- using the whole body to complete the action.

The serve

The serve is used to start a game. This is the only skill in volleyball over which the player has complete control. An accomplished player will put pressure on the opponents through their serve by using more power or tactics. There are several different serves:

- the underarm serve
- the overarm serve
- the overarm float serve
- the overarm topspin serve
- the jump serve.

Variation

The smash is the principal attack shot in volleyball. The player runs in and jumps above and close to the net to hit the ball with one hand down into the opposite court. Variations that can be used include the following:

- smashing a high set cross-court, or down the line
- smashing a quick set
- hitting the ball off the block and out of court
- tipping the ball just over the block (similar to a drop shot in tennis).

Figure 27.7: The principal attacking shot in volleyball

Conditions

Conditions can be internal and external. Internal conditions may depend on the importance of a match in relation to your team's position in a league, or whether it is a cup game. Psychological factors like confidence, motivation, anxiety, focus and concentration are also conditions under which a match is played. Alternatively, you may be coming back from injury or key members of your team may be injured. Environmental conditions, for example the location of sport and recreation facilities, would come under this heading, as would issues such as the attitudes and behaviour of players. External conditions would also include the state of the court.

Take it further

With a partner, practise volleyball serves. Once you have accomplished the underarm serve, practise different ways of serving.

1. List the technical demands of the serves.

2. How would you classify the skills used in the serves?

Use of space

Developing tactics should accompany technical skills in any sport. In volleyball you should think about where and how it is best to attack and where you should stand in order to have the best opportunity to defend. The main aim of the defence is to prevent the ball being smashed down the centre of the court. The defence can stop this attack option when the block is used to defend the middle of the court against a powerful smash. Powerful attacks are made from above the height of the net and close to it. By being in this position, the attacker opens up the options for attacks and gives defenders the minimum amount of time to play the ball.

Example 2: Tennis

A tennis player must have good balance in order to be able to play at the top level. When a tennis player moves from being balanced to unbalanced, a sprinting action begins because they are forced to move their feet rather than fall. When a tennis player swings a racket, another part of the body, usually the arm, comes across to counter the movement of the racket arm. The player then retains control over the body, keeping the centre of gravity over their base of support. When a tennis player serves, the centre of gravity moves in the direction of the arm that is swinging upwards to toss the ball.

Positioning

Tracking the ball is important in tennis as players have to follow the movement of the ball in order to position themselves properly in relation to the ball. This is difficult if the ball is moving quickly or is very high or low. Throwing and catching the ball following a gentle arc pathway is the best way to initially follow the ball.

When a player is developing their strokes and techniques, they often run too far from the ball or too close. Many players who are looking to approach the net will hit their shot into the corners of the court to give themselves more time to position themselves at the net. However, an opponent who moves and can read the game well, will be able to position themselves in order to return the shot or even drive the ball past you. Hitting the ball deep but down the middle of the court will stop your opponent from hitting their return by using angles created by the approach. Therefore, hitting deep into the middle of the court will cut off the options available to your opponent.

Choice of strokes and shots

The technique used by less skilled players is the straight backswing. Few professionals use this as it is difficult to hit a ball with high velocity because the racket stops before it starts to move forward. The most common swing used by professionals is the small loop backswing. The body must prepare for the backswing by moving into the correct position. The foot on the racket side turns outwards and the hips and shoulders rotate. The back foot then pushes forwards. The upper limbs control the stroke but the power comes from timing and the lower limbs. The arm and the racket must generate speed before impact occurs in order to successfully hit through the tennis ball.

Example of a straight backswing. Practise a straight backswing and explain why the racket stops before it moves forward.

If a player stops their swing at impact, they will lose control of the shot and probably cause damage to themselves. Therefore, a good follow-through is necessary to make an effective shot and to avoid injury.

Variation

- **A forehand topspin drive** – when a player wants to attack they will hit the ball deep with topspin in order to push their opponent back, making it difficult for the opponent to return the ball.
- **A defensive lob** – involves hitting the ball high into the air and deep into the court. It is used when a player is out of position on the court, to give them time to recover their position on the court and be ready for the next shot.

Conditions

Conditions can affect technical and tactical demands, for example:

- a grass court is quick and the bounce is low
- a clay court is very slow, players can slide into their shots and the bounce is high
- a player may have to adjust their shot selections in order to cope with the glare of the sun or the direction of the wind.

Use of space

An attacking tennis player will approach the net at every opportunity. They need a good level of anticipation to know what their opponent will do next.

Advanced players will quickly identify their opponent's strengths and weaknesses and try to focus on these by making them hit as many shots as possible in areas they are least comfortable with. If successful, this will pressurise the opponent and affect their rhythm and concentration.

Example 3: Basketball

Basketball is a non-contact sport, therefore possession is important. The technical demands are strongly based around passing the ball.

- Passing must be accurate and players need to consider the direction of the pass and the effective use of movement and space.
- The speed of the pass is important. Aiming for optimum speed in a pass gives an opponent less time to intercept.
- A lob pass will allow a teammate time to move their body into a position to receive the pass.
- Players need to disguise their intentions when passing a ball. This comes from the technique of 'fast release' of the ball, using the wrist and fingers with minimum movement of the arms.

Pass	Description
Two-handed chest pass	Position your arms as if you have just caught the ball, elbows tucked in and fingers at the sides of the ball. Then extend your arms and push the ball away with your fingers. Step forward into the pass.
Two-handed overarm pass	A direct pass from a high point. It is excellent for a taller player when passing over a shorter opponent, and can be used if you are closely marked. The ball is passed with a vigorous snap of the wrist and fingers. You should not take the ball behind the shoulders.
Bounce pass	Similar to the chest pass, but you should lean forward slightly as you release the ball. The ball should bounce two-thirds of the distance between the passer and the receiver.

Table 27.1: Examples of passes made in basketball

Figure 27.8: The bounce pass should bounce two-thirds of the distance between passer and receiver

In basketball the ball often remains in play after a missed shot. This is called the rebound. A defender has two roles in these circumstances and needs to know how to block out an opponent by gaining the inside position between the basket and the attacker.

Positioning

Most play in basketball is tactical and requires good footwork. Positioning yourself between your opponent and the basket prevents an attacking player taking a straight route to the basket. Watch your opponent to see which way they might move, then block their path.

Defensive tactics in basketball include man-to-man marking or zonal defending, whereby individual defenders are responsible for certain areas on the court. The tallest player in the team operates close to the basket. The majority of free ball opportunities occur after a shot has been taken and missed. Success in gaining possession depends on gaining an advantageous position by blocking opponents and jumping for the ball.

Variation

Changes of hand and direction are used to dribble around a defender. You can switch the ball from one side of your body to the other, moving it from hand to hand. A change of hand goes with a change of direction. A high dribble is used to move from one end of the court to the other quickly. This is the same technique but a more upright stance. A low dribble is used when a player needs to avoid losing the ball. A roll is a change of direction used by an attacker to escape from a defender.

Dribbling

Dribbling in basketball has several purposes:

- to advance the ball up the court
- to move away from a crowded space
- to allow a player to travel with the ball
- to find a good position on the court to make an effective pass
- to get close to the opponent's basket.

The skills demanded in dribbling in basketball include:

- pushing the ball firmly towards the floor using the hands, wrists and arms
- controlling the height and speed of the bounce
- keeping your hand firmly on top of the ball
- being aware of the position of opponents and team mates on the court
- protecting the ball by keeping your head and body between the ball and your opponent.

Conditions

Conditions include team injuries, the pressure surrounding the game and the playing facilities.

Use of space

This is important for defending. The defender has to move quickly in order to cover the attacker as rapid changes of direction are made. Full court defences are called presses and the aim is to get more possession than the other team by forcing them into hurried shots and misplaced passes. If the attackers do get past the frontline defenders, then these defenders must use the space and sprint back to pick up their team mates again. Space can be created by pivoting. This is when you have the ball and want to take or keep the ball away from a close guarding defender. Take a step to the left on your left foot, your right foot remaining on the ground. Lift your left foot again and move it to the right away from the defender. Now you can dribble to the right and past the defender.

PLTS

Explaining the technical and tactical demands of three contrasting sports will develop your skills as an **independent enquirer**, **creative thinker**, **self-manager** and **effective participator**. (See Assessment activity 27.1 on page 335.)

Functional skills

By giving a presentation (see Assessment activity 27.1 on page 335) to explain the technical and tactical demands of three contrasting sports you can provide evidence of your **ICT** and **English** skills.

Assessment activity 27.1

P1 **M1**

You have been asked to give a presentation to a group of young athletes from the local sports academy. They have been studying various sports, particularly the factors relating to skills. Their tutors would like you to explain the technical skills and tactics used in a variety of sports. It would make the presentation more interesting if you could provide diagrams, demonstrations of performance technique and video clips. Your presentation must:

- Cover three contrasting sports of your choice.
- Explain the technical and tactical demands of these sports. **P1**
- To make the presentation more interesting, identify the fact that many skills belong to most sports but some skills are specific to a sport. Likewise, the tactical demands may be similar or very different.

- Explain the similarities and differences in relation to the technical and tactical demands of your three chosen sports. For example, explain the similarities and differences in shots, defence/attack and positioning. **M1**

Grading tips

P1 Your explanation must include all the relevant features of the skills used in three different sports, clearly identifying each specific technique. The tactical demands should also be explained. You must provide explanations and examples of the skills and the reasons why certain techniques and tactics are adopted in that sport.

M1 Compare and contrast the technical and tactical demands of three contrasting sports.

2.   Be able to assess the technical and tactical ability of an elite sports performer

2.1 Observation checklist

Performance profile

Performance profiling allows the performer and coach to focus on targets to improve performance. A performance profile:

- highlights perceived strengths and areas for improvement
- monitors change
- identifies any mismatch between the perceptions of the coach and the player
- analyses performance following a competition.

In order to assess an athlete's technical and tactical ability, the checklist will cover the following:

- technical skills
- selection of skills
- application of skills

- tactical awareness
- application of tactics
- ability to defend and attack
- shot selection.

The advantages of a checklist are that it is inexpensive and the information can be processed quickly. Producing a checklist or performance profile can be divided into the following stages:

1. Using the checklist/performance profile to identify the player's strengths and areas for improvement in their sport.
2. Explaining these strengths and areas for improvement.
3. Justifying the development suggestions for your chosen player.

Table 27.2 on page 336 is an example of a checklist for a sport. Many of the sections are transferable from one sport to another. The criteria can be marked from 1 to 3.

Player's name	Observer grade	Sport: football	Observer grade
Physical abilities:		**Technical skills:**	
Pace		**Heading:**	
Balance		Attacking the ball	
Endurance		Timing	
Work rate		**Shooting:**	
Tackling		Accuracy	
Jockeying		Selection	
Aggression		Technique	
Agility		**Receive and control:**	
Shielding and holding the ball		First touch	
Mental abilities:		Different surfaces of feet	
Motivation and determination		Open body on back foot	
Composure		Both feet	
Concentration		Shielding on front foot	
Awareness including tactical		Different parts of the body	
Creativity		**Passing:**	
Decision-making		Accuracy	
Attitude		Weight	
Self-confidence and belief		Timing	
Footwork:		Communication	
Both feet		Both feet	
Ball juggling		Different surfaces	
Turning skills		Selection of pass	
Dribbling skills		**Ability to defend:**	
Ability to attack:		Is the defender brave?	
Can the attacker exploit the defensive weakness?		Does the defender clear strongly?	
Can the attacker take opportunities to score?		Can the defender counter-attack?	
Can the attacker deliver good passes?		Can the defender take responsibility?	
Shot/stroke selection:		**Application of skills:**	
Pass, dribble, shoot when possible		Retain possession	
Create attacking moves		Support other players	
Tactical awareness:			
Make effective use of set play			
Vary the pattern of play			
Recall patterns of play			

Table 27.2: An example of an observational checklist

Mark out of 3: 1 = Good, 2 = Very good, 3 = Excellent

You can assess an athlete during live competition or training sessions, or through video or televised events. However, you must record without bias. If you are analysing live matches, it is difficult to observe every movement because of the speed of the game/sequence and you may miss important movements. Poor weather conditions may also pose problems.

You may have a smaller checklist associated with a specific area you want to assess, for example key skills and tactics. Observation could be focused on a particular period of time during a competition. You can read more about performance analysis on pages 130–31 in Unit 5 Sports coaching.

Having completed the checklists, you can then identify the strengths and areas for improvement.

Activity: Observation checklist

1. Using the ideas presented to you, design an observation checklist to assess the performance of a team or individual. Form groups if several of you are designing a checklist for the same sport.
2. Ensure that the checklist covers the following:
   - technical skills
   - selection of skills
   - application of skills
   - tactical awareness
   - application of tactics
   - ability to defend
   - ability to attack
   - shot selection.
3. Observe a colleague and test your checklist by analysing their skills. Does it give you all the information you need for assessing your chosen performer?

2.2 Elite performer

Professional athletes

A professional athlete is paid to perform in front of an audience. They must always function at the highest level, because if they do not, spectators will not want to pay to watch them. There are professional athletes in most sports.

National representatives

National representatives perform for their country in competitive situations. Elite performers would include national team members who have achieved or broken records in their sport.

National champions

National champions are the winners of those competitions, either for professionals or amateurs.

International champions

International champions are winners of worldwide competitions such as the Olympic Games, and can be professionals or amateurs.

2.3 Assessment

This next section will help you assess an elite performer by taking you through the steps that assist you in identifying the strengths and areas for improvement of your selected elite performer and how to advise them on development.

Competitive situation

Analysing an elite athlete in a competitive situation will give a more balanced picture of them because they are under pressure physically, psychologically and socially. Analysis from competitive situations can be used to provide feedback to help the athlete improve their performance.

Use of observation checklist or performance profiling

Your observation checklist is now going to be used to identify the strengths and areas for improvement of your selected elite performer. You may wish to use a performance profile (see the example in Table 27.3 on page 338).

Take it further

List as many qualities as you can that you feel are essential for elite performance in your selected sport. These may include technical, tactical, physical, mental and lifestyle factors, as shown in Table 27.3 on page 338.

Technical	Tactical	Physical	Mental	Lifestyle
Passing	Creating space	Speed	Determination	Diet
Shooting	Closing down	Stamina	Concentration	Hydration
Tackling	Communication	Flexibility	Setting goals	Positive attitude
Smash	System of play	Strength	Mental rehearsal	Preparation
Serve	Ability to play different systems	Power	Mental toughness	Punctuality

Table 27.3: An example of a performance profile

Experienced performers should select 6–8 targets to work on. Once these are identified, strategies should be put in place to achieve them.

Strengths

Specific skills

Elite performers can be defined as those in the top 5 per cent of their group.

- An elite performer has an innate ability in their sport and their technical and tactical ability is very strong.
- They must have a great desire to achieve. Their focus, discipline, self-control and concentration will be strong. They will be highly skilled and their tactics well planned and executed.
- They are confident performers and have high levels of energy, speed, strength and power.
- When things go wrong, elite performers persevere. Regular cardiovascular exercise raises their ability to cope.
- They are disciplined and should be high in self-control.
- An elite performer can put tactics and ideas into practice; they can experiment and dismiss movements that are not working.

When assessing an elite performer's skill level, you would identify qualities that show mental toughness – such as the ability to deal with pressure and anxiety. An example of a specific skill might be a footballer who has a talent for dribbling with the ball. This skill would unsettle opponents, leading to crossing and shooting opportunities and creating a positive attitude in the team.

Specific techniques

Technique is the way an action is carried out. Skills can be executed in a variety of ways. Technical requirements in sport include passing, shooting, receiving a ball, the golf swing, rowing and bowling in cricket. You will assess a performer's technique on the results it brings them. If the technique is successful for them, then the performer will stay with the technique.

Tactical awareness

Tactical awareness is the ability to make the correct choice of strategies and tactics relative to the strengths and weaknesses of the opposing player or team. Through having a game plan, an athlete can:

- control the structure of the game
- exploit the opposition's defensive weaknesses
- reduce the likelihood of conceding goals, points or runs
- avoid wasting energy
- increase the attempts on goals/opportunities to score points
- create more attacking moves
- make effective use of set plays
- vary the game.

When assessing an elite performer's tactical awareness you will consider the above factors.

Fitness levels

An athlete's fitness levels can be determined by a series of tests. Once fitness has been evaluated, the athlete and coach can consider:

- the effect of the present training programme
- whether the athlete needs to train harder
- the feedback between the athlete and the coach
- the objectives of the training programme
- the level of the competition the athlete is being prepared for
- the revising of the training programme.

Tests will not, however, predict what level of performance the elite athlete will achieve in a competitive situation. The results of fitness tests can motivate athletes to train harder and may also assist coaches and managers with decisions about bringing players back into full training or into competitive situations.

When observing and assessing an elite performer's fitness level, you will be aware that each sport makes different demands. Cycling, swimming and running demand a constant energy level, while football for example includes periods of jogging, walking, moderately paced running and short bursts of speed. When assessing your performer you will assess, for example, the continuous bursts of speed and how quickly the performer can recover. The greater the performer's aerobic and anaerobic power, the quicker they can recover from, and repeat, high-intensity bursts.

Ability to read the game

Elite performers will be able to read a game. This is a perceptual ability rather than a visual one. Elite performers will be able to:

- anticipate the opponent's movement direction or the pass or stroke which is to be made
- predict the outcome of a range of different situations, based on previous experience – for example, by recognising the potential passing/stroke/shot option open to the player in possession
- recall patterns of play.

Observation should enable you to assess how your elite performer reacts.

- Under pressure elite performers can recognise the body shape of an opponent and anticipate what will happen next.
- They can identify the critical players in a situation and pick out players who are less of a threat.
- They are aware of defensive and offensive patterns used by opponents and can recognise the evolving patterns.

Areas for improvement

You will need to consider all the following factors and decide whether your selected elite performer needs to improve in the following areas.

Attacking

When attacking, does the player take on the responsibility or pass it to someone else? Do they take every opportunity to attack? Areas for improvement may be in set play situations. Consider whether performers fulfil their roles; for example, is the attacker protected from a defender in order to have a clear shot on goal? Do the attackers create space, and when they pass is it a quality pass?

Attacking performers should:

- score points/goals
- create chances to score points/goals
- deliver good shots
- deliver good passes
- attempt to be the first to the ball
- shoot or attempt to win a point at every opportunity
- select the right shot/stroke
- be aware of teammates.

Defending

You may wish to consider the roles and responsibilities of defending, such as marking, challenging and blocking. There may be little understanding between the defenders. A player may have to spend more time developing defensive shots. Consider the following.

- Does the defender get caught out or is the opponent stopped from playing attacking strokes/shots?
- Is it man-to-man marking or zonal marking?
- Are the defenders brave?
- Are the clearances strong?
- Can the performer counter-attack?
- Does the performer take responsibility during set play?

Specific skills

An important function for coaches is to advise performers on how to perform skills correctly. This requires a good knowledge of the specific skills and analysis based on observation and assessment of these skills. Through correction of specific skills, the athlete's performance will be enhanced.

Specific techniques

Having identified skills for improvement, a coach would break down the skill to assess the athlete's technique. Most skills have four identifiable phases:

1. Initiation
2. Preparation
3. Execution
4. Follow-through.

Techniques are improved by identifying sub-phases, but these are integral parts of a phase.

Fitness

All athletes benefit from fitness training programmes. Fitness training can help the performer meet the physical demands of their chosen sport and maintain their technical abilities throughout a match, game or performance. There are three different types of fitness training.

- aerobic training
- anaerobic training
- specific muscle training.

 **Development**

Training

The principle of training dictates that it should be specific to the sport. Nevertheless, there are circumstances in which components of performance must be taken from a game context for targeted training. This is the case with strength training. For example, footballers and tennis players do not have to change their body shape like rugby players and bodybuilders.

Training should also focus on tactical needs. The choice of practices will give the coach and performer the opportunity to concentrate on detail.

Training may be to develop a specific skill. Here, the coach will give the performer a lot of feedback regarding any problems.

Training may also develop strength, power and speed. Strength refers to the neuromuscular system's ability to apply forces. Power is 'speed strength', that is, the ability to apply force quickly. Muscles will become stronger if they are exposed to more stress than they are used to. Speed is important to performers as it helps them to:

- perceive situations that require an immediate response
- take appropriate action immediately
- increase their ability to take this action.

For example, in certain situations a player has to produce force to perform an activity such as sprinting and a quick change in direction. You could assess the performer's change of activities: how often do they sprint and for how long? Do they recover quickly?

Resistance training should be included in training programmes to enhance and retain muscle strength. In order to achieve quick results, the muscles used

in individual sports will be trained specifically. This is called specific muscle training.

Aerobic training can be divided into three components:

- aerobic high-intensity training
- aerobic low-intensity training
- recovery training.

Aerobic training aims to increase the capacity of the oxygen transporting system and to increase muscle capacity during long periods of training. Aerobic training will also help the performer to recover quickly after a period of high-intensity exercise and put more effort into the next competition.

As the performer tires less easily, their technical performance will not deteriorate and concentration can be maintained throughout performance. Elite players need to have a high level of physical fitness. This can be assessed through observation during performance, performance tests, and physiological measures during simulated performance. You would assess the performer's fitness by their level of fatigue at the end of a performance. The aerobic system contributes most when the activity is low to moderate intensity; that is, jogging and running below maximum.

Anaerobic fitness training increases your ability to act quickly and produce power during high-intensity exercise, and also to increase your capacity to continuously produce power and energy through the anaerobic system. It is also important for recovery after a period of high-intensity exercise.

Why does a player have to produce force to perform an activity?

A coach should introduce surprises to break the monotony of training, but it is also important that performers go through well-known routines to strengthen areas in which they excel.

Competition

Competition can be introduced through training and matches. These increase elite performers' knowledge of their sport, allowing them to solve sport-related problems under pressure in competitive situations. In addition to their technical and tactical skills, an elite player will also be assessed on psychological factors such as concentration, confidence and attitude.

Top-level competitive performance has to be supplemented with a strength and conditioning process, so elite performers seek out coaches, nutritionists, fitness experts and psychologists to help them perform with maximum efficiency.

Specific coaching/coaches

The coach is responsible for creating learning situations in a performer's development. Their training programme and methods should always be interesting, stimulating and exciting. An athlete may suffer setbacks, and one of the many roles of the coach is to motivate the performer in spite of these. The coach has two main roles:

- to educate the performer to make the correct decision
- to equip the performer with the necessary skills to do this.

A coach should have a high level of knowledge of their sport and the application of this knowledge and skill is what separates the excellent coach from the average one. A coach can be assessed on their qualifications and past experiences, but they will be judged on the results of their performers. If an athlete's performance is to be enhanced, the coach's method of facilitating their learning is important. A coach should receive feedback about their strategies and methods. Most are looking for new ideas. When assessing an elite performer, a training session observation would identify strengths and areas for developing the coach.

Observational analysis

Athletes develop and improve through analysis of their performance. The characteristics of their game are examined alongside sports-specific assessments. Their strengths and areas for improvement can be identified and assessed as a means of improving their development. Research on elite performers includes:

- physical development
- psychological development
- sociological development.

These three factors need to be integrated and explored to find out what separates an elite sports performer from their counterparts.

Competitive performance can be examined through observation. Video evidence is valuable because it can be rewound, paused and slowed down, which makes analysing performance easier (see Units 8&9, pages 234–35).

Suggest tactics that are being discussed.

Observation can provide a wide range of data, from the modern computer tracking systems to the handwritten notation system. The observer can assess the performer's physical performance ranging from low-intensity movements (e.g. walking or jogging) to high intensity ones (e.g. sprinting). Observation can play a vital role in assessing fitness and in implementing specific training regimes, which may be broken down into skill and technique activities. The success rate of important match actions, for example serves, can be analysed and the results could mean a specific coach spending time with the performer developing this action.

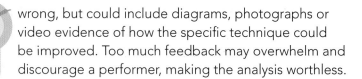

Activity: Observation

Observe 30 minutes of a competitive match.

1. Track a player, observing their technical and tactical skills, and record your findings in any form of notation.

2. In groups, discuss your findings.

3. Explain to each other your method of recording.

4. In your group, design a checklist that you could use for assessing an elite performer.

Assessment

Self-assessment is a widely recognised form of assessment. When using it, you must identify clearly the goals you have in mind and how you plan to achieve the assessment criteria for each of your targets.

- Identify what you need to improve.

- Decide how you are going to improve.

- Which criteria will you use to measure that improvement?

Performance profiling is not an assessment technique in itself. It can provide a basis for action when assessing what improvements are needed. Performance profiles can be structured and related to the objectives.

A checklist (a list where you mark specific features with a tick or cross according to whether you carried them out) is not the most complex form of observation, but is the most accurate, and is highly structured. Performance profiling and checklists will help you identify strengths and weaknesses, opportunities for improvement and threats that may hinder you.

Technical guidance

Following assessment, the purpose of evaluation is to give feedback. This should not be a list of what went wrong, but could include diagrams, photographs or video evidence of how the specific technique could be improved. Too much feedback may overwhelm and discourage a performer, making the analysis worthless.

Take it further

1. Ask your coach, teammate or tutor to observe you in a competitive situation. A checklist and/or performance profile can be used.

2. From the findings you are given, complete a SWOT analysis (see Units 8&9, page 235). Identify your strengths, weaknesses, the opportunities you may have to improve performance (for example coaches, courses) and what may hinder your progress (for example cost and travelling distance).

Can mental attitude influence your performance?

Nutritional guidance

An athlete's diet must contain all the nutrients needed for general well-being and also the extra stresses of training and competition. The essential nutrients include carbohydrates, protein, fat, vitamins, minerals and water. Part of a development process could involve examining a performer's intake of food and fluids. Different sports require certain types of food. Also, the amount of food an individual needs varies from person to person. Once a performer has identified the amount of calories used in a day, they can balance their food intake to equal this. To lose weight you would bring into your diet fresh fruit juice, cereals, yogurts, brown bread, lean meats, salads, fresh fruit and vegetables.

You can consider nutrition in more detail in Unit 11 Sports nutrition.

Figure 27.9: A balanced diet is essential for a performer to meet the demands of sport

Psychological guidance

Psychological guidance can be incorporated into a training programme and lead to enhanced performance. However, you cannot observe what is going on in a player's mind and sometimes performers do not want to discuss certain issues. Performance profiling can be used for assessing psychological factors as well as physical attributes. Profiling can evaluate strengths and areas for improvement and identify long-term goals for development.

The key psychological factors of an elite performer are:

- confidence
- concentration
- motivation
- a relaxed attitude
- arousal
- refocus after errors
- awareness and vision
- anxiety
- enjoyment.

There are several psychological factors associated with sports performance.

- Confidence is when you expect success because of your previous accomplishments. You have a positive interpretation of anxiety.

- Concentration is the ability to avoid distractions, which could mean blocking out the actions of your opponent, bad refereeing or umpiring, and fatigue.

- Motivation – great performers are highly motivated and tend to be optimistic. Sports psychologists have attempted to indicate the importance of motivation by suggesting that performance = skill × motivation.

An elite performer's motivation may come from within (intrinsic): they want accomplishment, achievement and challenge; or it may come from outside the individual (extrinsic) in the form of financial gain, trophies and fame.

- Anxiety can be overcome by improving confidence. Confidence gives positive feelings and a high level of confidence brings less stress in competition. Excess anxiety can cause underachievement. Why does a player miss an open goal? Because their muscles tense up when they are anxious.

- Arousal can be defined as the level of excitement a performer reaches. There is an ideal level, which allows players to perform at their best.

- Imagery is used to develop top-class professionals. The athlete visualises situations to help them practise skills, instil confidence and motivate them for competition or for coming back from injury. This can help to re-create positive experiences or picture new events to prepare for performance. It can become part of a training routine.

When assessing the psychological attributes of your elite performer, you will consider situations in which they show confidence or lack of it. Do they communicate well with other players and motivate themselves and others? Are there lapses in concentration or do they remain totally focused?

Target-setting can be used to improve the long-term performance of an elite performer. This develops a performer because it:

- draws attention to the important elements of the sports performer
- encourages the performer to focus their efforts
- makes the performer persist with their efforts
- encourages the development of new learning techniques.

Case study: Giving psychological guidance to improve competitive results

Ben, a tennis coach, wants to use performance profiling to improve a junior's performance.

	Ideal state	The junior's state	Difference	Multiply difference by 10 to form a %
Confidence	10	7	3	30
Concentration	10	8	2	20
Motivation	10	8	2	20
Enjoyment	10	6	4	40
Awareness	10	7	3	30
Attitude	10	6	4	40

Table 27.4: The junior's performance profile

1. a) How important is confidence to an elite player? Ben believes that this should be 10. What do you think it should be? Why?

   b) What would the junior's ideal state be for concentration? Ben believes it should also be 10. What do you think it should be? Why?

   c) How does the junior rate his confidence at the moment? He believes that it is only 7. Why might it be as low as this? Suggest how

   Ben could work with the junior to improve his mental attitude.

2. Identify the major areas that Ben needs to work on with the junior to improve tournament results. Suggest how Ben can develop these areas and explain why you have made these suggestions. How will your suggestions improve the junior's performance?

Fitness guidance

An athlete has to give 100 per cent. You have probably seen athletes at the end of a race, a match, a contest, with nothing left. They are exhausted. The main reason for this is a fall in glycogen stores in muscles. Performers should not train the day before competition. This will give them a higher level of muscle glycogen throughout a match/competition and appreciable levels remaining at the end of a race/game/contest. Fatigue brings a drop in performance capability, which will be an advantage to any opponent. Performers become slower in returning to positions and their work rate slows down.

Assessment activity 27.2

1. Your coach/tutor would like you to be aware of how assessment and feedback can develop an athlete. For this reason, he would like you to produce a checklist that could be used to assess the technical and tactical ability of an elite performer. **P2**

2. In order to improve your performance, your coach/tutor would like you to observe an elite sports performer of your choice. You may do this live, on television or on video or DVD.

Using the checklist you produced in task 1, identify realistic strengths and realistic areas for improvement. You may observe your performer as many times as you wish.

Working from your checklist, verbally describe to your tutor in a one-to-one discussion the strengths you identified in the performer and also the areas for improvement. Give as many relevant features as possible and think about what your performer could do to play a better game/contest. **P3**

Having completed the above task, your tutor would like you to go further and explain the strengths and areas for improvement in technical and tactical ability of your selected elite sports performer. Present your findings to your tutor or group, explaining your methods of assessment and clarifying points with diagrams, photographs and/or video.

In your recommendations, make suggestions relating to performer development. You should give details with reasons to clearly support your recommendations. The findings should be presented to your coach/tutor in the form of a short report. **M2**

Now extend the presentation and report by explaining why you have made the above recommendations. Using the evidence you have collected from your observations, what conclusions have you reached about the benefits your recommendations would bring to your elite performer if they were to include them in their training plan? Give reasons or evidence to support your conclusions. **D1**

Grading tips

P2 Ensure that your checklist can assess your performer's skills and how they are applied to the game: the performer's tactical awareness and how the tactics are applied, the performer's ability to defend, to attack and to select the right shots.

P3 Describe the performer's strengths including their level of skill, techniques, tactical awareness, fitness levels and ability to read the game. When you talk about areas for improvement, do not forget to describe how they could improve attacking, defending, certain skills and techniques and fitness.

M2 Explain the performer's strengths and areas for improvement, covering all the areas for P3. Make suggestions relating to development, considering the performer's training, competition, specific coaching and the type of coach the performer works with. Suggest how the performer could improve performance through observational analysis and improved nutritional, psychological and fitness guidance.

D1 Having explained the suggestions for development, justify your suggestions by explaining why you made them and what positive results they would have on the athlete's performance. How will your ideas and suggestions for improvement develop this athlete?

PLTS

Producing a checklist to assess the technical and tactical ability of an elite performer will develop your skills as an **independent enquirer**, **creative thinker** and **self-manager**.

Functional skills

Producing a checklist to assess the technical and tactical ability of an elite performer will provide evidence of your **ICT** and **English** skills.

3. Be able to assess your own technical and tactical ability

Through keeping a logbook, you will identify strengths and weaknesses in your own technical and tactical ability. These findings can then be used for your personal development plan.

3.1 Assessment

Competitive situation

There are several levels at which you can participate in sport.

- **Foundation level** – you participate mainly through school activities.

- **Participation level** – you participate regularly in sport by belonging to a team and playing for fun through competitive situations.

- **Performance level** – you compete for a club, your county or at regional level. You have been identified as having talent and have been selected to play at representative level.

- **Elite level** – you are at the highest level and may be a national team player, an Olympic competitor, champion or a professional.

Use of observation checklist or performance profiling

Competitive situation	Examples	Mark 1–10
Technical skills Do you understand the roles of your position? For example, if you are a defender, do you combine with other players to progress play from the back, do you support your teammates? Can you interchange positions, for example defender, midfield, attacker? Can you distribute the ball over short and long range? Can you mark, challenge, block and defend, head, control, receive, dribble, shoot, turn, cross the ball and communicate with teammates?	I operated as an attacker when coming forward from the back	6
Selection of skills Do you observe how the ball is coming to you? Do you know where your teammates and the opposition are placed? Do you select the right skill? Is the timing of the skill correct, and the pace and weight? Why have you made that choice considering the tactical objectives?	The cross led to a goal	
Application of skills Do you run and dribble with the ball, maintain possession and penetrate the defence, create attempts on goal, shoot, cross the ball frequently?	I scored a goal	
Tactical awareness How good are you at choosing the correct action in a game? Are you able to see the whole situation around you, evaluate and then make the right choice of action? Can you decide quickly which skill to use, the technique, where, when, how to use this skill and why your choice was the best option?	My free kick went into the wall	
Application of tactics Do you know how to prepare instantly to move from attack to defence and defence to attack? Can you move quickly from one system to another or adapt positions when a substitute is used?	I changed positions when the substitute came on	

Table 27.5: An example of an observation checklist

Activity: Observation checklist

Table 27.5 shows an example of an observation checklist. Assess your own technical and tactical ability and complete this, focusing on a competitive situation. You may adapt the checklist to suit your selected sport. Give examples of what you accomplished in a game and give a score out of ten.

Strengths

This section will help you assess your skill level, technique, tactical awareness, your ability to read a game and your fitness.

Specific skills

Because you are continuing to develop and change through growth, fitness levels and learning, your skill level can continue to develop. To continue to reproduce a skill by repeating an identical movement sequence would result in static and inflexible behaviour. In a quick and lively team game it is important that the performer continues to improve specific skills. A tennis player, for example, would assess their basic coordination pattern for a tennis volley and then practise movement patterns that would improve variables such as speed and force.

Specific techniques

When assessing your technique you are considering how the skill is performed. You might ask yourself whether the action was successful and how it can be improved. There are four phases to each action:

- initiation phase
- preparation phase
- execution phase
- completion phase.

By breaking down the skill, you can identify your strengths.

Tactical awareness

Before a match the performer will have discussed and decided on a tactical plan. It may be that tactical changes have to be made, for example as a result of an injury or a player being sent off. During a match situation the performer has a choice of action and must make decisions. During training sessions you will gain an insight into the tactical opportunities available during game situations. The performer can assess their strengths and acquire an in-depth understanding of the use of tactical skills through theoretical examination.

Fitness levels

Playing a match or game is the best overall test for an athlete. However, it is easier to assess fitness levels while training because they can be evaluated while performing defined activities. If fitness tests are to be reliable, the performer should be well rested, thoroughly warmed up and have clear instructions on how to perform the test. Tests should be performed at least twice before a result is considered.

Ability to read the game

It is important during competitive situations that you have the ability to read the game. Through video analysis the performer can assess how successful they are at reading the game. When assessing this ability, the following factors should be observed.

- Does the performer keep their head up and observe what is going on around them and where players are in relation to each other?
- Do they look before receiving the ball: do they anticipate the next pass and think ahead?
- Can they control the ball/pass/shot and move the ball away from pressure and create space?

The ability to read the game means having the imagination to know how your teammates or opponent(s) will react following each touch/shot/pass. The performer should assess their own insight into how various techniques can be used to control and play a shot/pass into different spaces.

Areas for improvement

Attacking

When identifying areas for improvement, the performer can consider individual attacking options and those of the team. For example, a basketball player might want to improve shooting, passing, getting free to receive a pass, creating space to allow players time to perform skills and moving to receive a return pass. In volleyball the player might want to improve a specific attacking skill, such as a smash or tip (a soft attack shot when the attacker plays the ball with the fingers just over the top or around the block, similar to a drop shot in tennis). Some performers like their opponents to attack. For example, tennis players will often make a mistake when they are continually forced to take the initiative in a rally.

An attacking system in football would mean playing the ball quickly up to strikers so that the game is taken into the opposition's 'defensive' area.

Defending

When assessing a player's defensive attributes weaknesses may be identified in the following areas:

- one-to-one situations
- preventing shots
- providing effective covering
- getting the ball back up the court/field quickly
- not applying enough pressure on opponents
- cutting off opponents' paths.

It is important that the performer gets back to their defensive position quickly to avoid attackers beating them.

Specific skills

There may be many reasons why a performer has to improve specific skills. It may be that they have not mastered a complex skill and need to master a more basic one first. Some performers may not have developed sufficient strength levels or the range of flexibility to execute certain skills. Having their coach identify areas for improvement and give regular reminders of the key points would encourage an athlete to practise a specific skill. The coach, when assessing areas for improvement, should consider the athlete's physical development as well as their technical development.

Specific techniques

The player or coach will observe and analyse performance in order to identify which phases of a technique need to be improved. Therefore, it is necessary to have a good understanding of the techniques required in the specific sport. Improving technique will come through comparing the way the performer executes the technique and the way it should be performed. It will be necessary to observe the technique several times before assessing how improvements can be made. A skill may not be 100 per cent technically correct but may still be effective: many top performers have unorthodox techniques but are nevertheless successful at their sport.

Fitness

Fitness training will help you to endure the physical demands of your sport and also maintain your technical ability. It can be divided into:

- aerobic training: high-intensity training, low-intensity training and recovery training
- anaerobic training: speed training and speed endurance training.

Specific muscle training can be divided into:

- muscle strength, e.g. training biceps using some form of external resistance
- muscle speed endurance, e.g. training the abdominal muscles using several repetitions of an appropriate exercise
- flexibility training, e.g. stretching the hamstrings.

You should improve your fitness in a games situation. In addition to training the specific muscle groups used in the sport, this will develop the technical and tactical skills similar to those needed in a competitive match. It also provides greater motivation for the performers. The physical demands of a competitive match will influence your fitness training programme, for example striker, defensive player, tennis player.

A good coach will continue to observe performers even after they have learned and mastered skills and techniques. Ongoing observation and analysis will enable the performer and the coach to identify strengths and areas for improvement.

3.2 Log

Diary of specific training sessions

A logbook is a diary of training sessions a performer has attended over a period of time. It should include:

- details of specific training sessions
- competition analysis
- areas for improvement
- specific practices.

The information below and on pages 349–352 will assist with your logbook. There are also examples of entries and performance profiles and match analysis game sheets (pages 349–351).

Training sessions for talented young people

You have been accepted on a football academy training plan and have been asked to keep a logbook for four weeks. Your logbook has to include:

- skills you have learned
- techniques and tactics you have covered
- your strengths and areas for improvement identified during competition and training
- some coach analysis after competition and training.

Your logbook will also include areas for improvement, such as:

- defending
- attacking
- fitness
- examples of specific practices that can be used to improve your performance.

Skills

Today, my coach observed me in a training situation. He was assessing key skills in order to target areas for improvement. My coach observed me for 30 minutes. This was divided into three ten-minute periods. The session was a training match between those invited on to the course and the academy players. I have included the data the coach collected about me in Table 27.6 below.

Figure 27.10: Extract 1 from logbook

	Time period		
	2–11 minutes	20–29 minutes	50–59 minutes
Ball watch: in attack	2	2	3
Ball watch: in defence	4	3	4
Look up and then decide whether to pass, run with the ball, dribble or shoot	4	3	3
Make a conscious pass to retain possession	2	2	3
Kick the ball towards the opponent's goal	3	4	4
Make a run towards the opponent's goal	3	3	4
Defend by running back towards own goal when possession is lost	4	4	3
Attempt to intercept passes	4	4	4
Deny the opposition space: close down, mark tightly	4	3	3

Table 27.6: Key skills chart

Key skills: 5 = Almost always, 4 = Often, 3 = Sometimes, 2 = Rarely, 1 = Hardly ever.

The coach recommended that this player intensified training relating to 'Make a conscious pass to retain possession' and 'Ball watch', particularly relating to attack.

	Initiation phase	Preparation phase	Execution phase	Follow-through phase
	Run-up	Retraction of kicking leg	Forward swing of kicking leg and contact	Follow through
Key observational features	Run-up used to gain speed Used an angled approach Normal running with arms used to balance	Body leans to the back and side Arms used to balance Kicking leg retracts to open out hip Arm on side of kicking leg is brought forward Eyes on ball	Twist is created in the trunk by counter-rotating the shoulders on the hips from a forward position to a backward position At contact, the knee is slightly flexed but extends through contact On contact, the foot is plantar flexed	The leg is raised for a high follow-through, gradually slowing down

Table 27.7: The penalty kick

Techniques and tactics covered

Today, our coach targeted shooting as a specific training point. I was in the group which concentrated on taking penalties. The penalty kick is a very important skill in football in which gaining high ball speed, as well as accuracy, is necessary. The coach showed us a video of an expert penalty performer and he encouraged us to watch the whole body movement and how the body is used to help the movement. The coach gave us some notes which I have included in Table 27.7 above.

Figure 27.11: Extract 2 from logbook

Today was a theory lesson about match tactics. The coach had a match analysis game sheet to go through with us. The data had been collected during our previous competitive game. It was interesting to discuss this data.
I have included just a section of this game sheet in Table 27.8 opposite.

Figure 27.12: Extract 3 from logbook

	Team	First half	Second half	Total
Entries into the attacking third	A	21	22	43
	B	26	30	56
Regained possession in the attacking third	A	6	4	10
	B	6	6	12
Effective crosses	A	1	2	3
	B	3	1	4

Table 27.8: A section of a match analysis game sheet. **Team A:** talented group on the course. **Team B:** academy players

Competition analysis

It is difficult to reproduce the stress of competition during normal training conditions. Therefore, it is important in training to focus on games with a strong competitive element. This can prepare the athlete for competitive situations.

Competition analysis can take many forms, for example analysis through peer- or self-evaluation, or post-event discussions between the athlete and their coach. Effective peer-analysis in a positive learning environment can stimulate learning, and you can benefit from both giving and receiving analysis from a competitive situation which identifies strengths and areas for improvement. Self-analysis increases the athlete's intrinsic motivation and leads to stronger achievement. Even the most talented athletes need coaches, who might, for example, question a technique, thereby provoking positive changes. Coaches have a great deal of knowledge about their sport; they can correct technique, provide motivation and help manage emotional stress through performance analysis.

Strengths and weaknesses during a competitive match

I really enjoyed myself today. My passing was brilliant. The practice really paid off. My crosses were accurate and we won. I ran and dribbled with the ball more frequently and the whole team was able to put more passes together. We created a lot more attempts on goal. I was really tired about 20 minutes before the end and I could work on my endurance in order to improve my performance levels.

Figure 27.13: Extract 4 from logbook

Specific skills	5	4	3	2	1
Specific techniques	5	4	3	2	1
Tactical awareness	5	4	3	2	1
Fitness levels	5	4	3	2	1
Ability to read the game	5	4	3	2	1
Attacking	5	4	3	2	1
Defending	5	4	3	2	1

Table 27.9: Match analysis – a sample

5 = Excellent, 4 = Very good, 3 = Good, 2 Average, 1 = Poor

The form of self-assessment shown in Table 27.9 can be used to identify strengths and areas for improvement and what you need to work on before the next game. Tick the box or circle the number that applies to you after a match. You might use the table several times to assess areas for improvement.

Coach analysis after competitions and training

The coach has asked me to include a profile checklist which he completed after competition and training (see Table 27.10).

Figure 27.14: Extract 5 from logbook

Technique	4
Fitness levels	3
Awareness of others	2
Ability to play as part of a team	2
Attitude and behaviour	4
Motivation	5
Speed	3
Ability	4

Coach's comments
Areas of strength: the performer is technically gifted with good natural ability. The performer is highly motivated and tries hard to please.
Areas for improvement: the performer tends to play as an individual and needs to learn that football is a team game. In the training plan for this player, speed can be worked on.
Performer's statement:
I accept the comments and will endeavour to work hard in the future to turn the above areas for development into key strengths.

Table 27.10: Profile checklist

5 = Excellent, 4 = Good, 3 = Satisfactory, 2 = Signs of weakness, 1 = Unsatisfactory

An athlete can evaluate their performance from the table above, and can use the information to improve training and competition through discussion with their coach. The weaker marks define areas for improvement, and the athlete and their coach will now work on fitness, awareness of others and ability to play within a team. A coach is able to objectively evaluate performance and use their knowledge and experience to improve an athlete's technical and tactical abilities.

Areas for improvement

Your logbook will help you identify areas for improvement. By considering Figure 27.15, you can examine the areas the performer and coach wished to develop.

> Date: March
>
> Place: Local tennis club
>
> Event: Club Junior Championships
>
> My opponent for this match was the club champion. I have played him twice before and lost both times. My game plan was to try to serve well in order for me to win my service games easily. If I managed to do this, I could then really attack on my opponent's service games and try to break their serve. I would concentrate on serving to their weakness rather than their strength.
>
> Match result: Lost 7/6, 7/6.

Figure 27.15: Extract 6 from logbook

The performer competed well for the majority of the time; this was reflected in the close score line. The plan succeeded in that they managed to hold serve but lost in two tie-break sets. They tried to impose their game rather than react to their opponent's game by trying to be the one who was dictating the rallies.

Attacking

At times, the performer was over-attacking and this led to some unforced errors creeping into their game. They must try to practise choosing the right time to attack the ball and learn to realise that, if the time is not right, they should wait for the correct opportunity.

Defending

The performer needs to be a little more consistent in their defence. At times, they were caught out of position on the court. This was due to fatigue.

Specific skills

They must work a little harder on their return of serve. Although they held their serve, which was the game plan, the performer was not successful at breaking their opponent's serve. This must be implemented more effectively for performance to improve.

Specific techniques

The performer must learn not to become nervous in tight game situations. This lost them the match because the opponent handled the situation better than them, particularly during the tie-breaks.

Fitness

The reason the performer was caught out of position was because they were tiring. The aim should be to increase fitness levels, particularly aerobic training.

Specific practices that could improve performance

Practices which will improve aerobic capacity in football.

- Warm-up – light jogging and specific stretching.
- Key factors – accelerate, receive the ball, play it back, spin and accelerate again.
- Cool down – jogging and stretches.

Practice will improve crossing.

- Warm-up – light jogging, side to side, stretches, jog high knees, flick heels, specific stretches.
- Key factors – position of the goalkeeper, eye on the ball, relaxed at the point of contact, and head over the ball, eyes on the ball.
- Cool down – light jog with specific stretches.

Practice will improve competitive edge.

- Use one half of a pitch.
- Use two full-sized goals.
- Play 8 × 8.
- After 4 minutes of play in the fourth period, the side in the lead at the end of the third period has a goal taken away from them every 2 minutes until the losing team scores.

In this way, the intensity is maintained and the team behind is still motivated to prevent further scoring.

Assessment activity 27.3

1. Ask your coach/tutor or teammate to video a sample of your performance in either training or competition to enable you to complete a self-analysis.

a) Consider the checklist you designed for Assessment 27.2, task 1.

   i   Adapt the checklist for your own sport.

   ii Use the checklist to assess your own technical and tactical ability. Watch the video of your performance as many times as you wish.

   iii From this analysis, identify your strengths and areas for improvement. Describe these to your coach/tutor or teammate. When you describe your strengths, include as many as possible. Look at the video carefully and consider all the factors on the checklist that you did well. What could have been better? Describe these to your coach/tutor. **P4**

b) For this task you will need to ask your coach/tutor or teammate to video a sample of your performance in a competitive situation. You may have already done so for task 1.

c) From analysis, explain the strengths and areas for improvement that you have identified in your own sport.

Present these findings in the form of a short presentation to your group or coach/tutor, using the video evidence to support your argument. Your explanation should include details of your strengths and reasons to support your decisions. Also, clearly explain your areas for improvement and state why you think these areas should be improved. **M3**

2. Complete a 4-week logbook while participating in your chosen sport. Design a front cover that identifies you, your sport, club and level of participation. Write words associated with your specific sport on the first page of your logbook.

The logbook needs to include as much detail as possible regarding your technical and tactical ability. You must identify both your strengths and areas for possible improvement. **P5**

3. a) Having completed your logbook in task 2 and identified your strengths and areas for development, explain each strength, stating why it is a particular strength in your chosen sport.

   b) Explain what impact improving your areas for development will have on your all-round performance. This is a written task. Within your explanations, present evidence to support your opinions regarding your strengths and areas for improvement in a selected sport. **M4**

Grading tips

P4 Ensure that your checklist covers technical skills, selection of skills, application of skills, tactical awareness and application of tactics. When you describe your strengths, give examples of skills and techniques and also examples of your tactical awareness, fitness levels and ability to read the game.

M3 Remember that you must assess yourself in a competitive situation. When you explain your strengths and areas for improvement, support your explanations with evidence.

P5 During training sessions you will cover skills, techniques and tactics in your selected sport. Make sure you provide evidence in your logbook of your tactical and technical ability from these sessions. You must also show evidence of assessments that identify your strengths during a competitive match. Ask your coach to assess you after a competition and in training and include these assessments in your logbook. Identify areas for improvement under the headings of attacking, defending, skills, techniques and fitness. Finally, include in your logbook practices which could improve your performance.

M4 Identify and explain in detail the strengths and areas for improvement of your own technical and tactical ability in a selected sport.

353

3.3 Development plan

How can you reflect on your performance and obtain **feedback**? This can be achieved through a development plan.

This is a structured plan that will be undertaken by you so that you can reflect upon your own performance and plan your personal development through **self-evaluation**. This plan will identify your goals and objectives and evaluate your progress in order to become a better sports performer. Having a development plan will:

- improve your performance
- give you a deeper understanding of how you can become a better performer
- encourage you to remain positive during your development.

When designing your development plan it is essential to use the SMART principle:

Specific

Measurable

Achievable

Realistic

Time-bound

Specific

This means that your development plan states a specific objective. For example, if a tennis player has a specific weakness with their backhand you could say that movement and racket preparation before ball impact is a weakness.

Measurable

This is how your performance will be measured. If, after training for the above example, your backhand percentage increases, then one can see that the training has worked.

Achievable

What you set out to achieve must be possible. You would not expect a beginner in tennis to quickly master the art of the topspin backhand.

Realistic

It must be realistic to achieve your set goal. Your goals are written down and a contract is made between you and the coach.

Time-bound

There should be enough time to complete the set development plan.

Targets

You have identified where you are now by assessing your strengths and areas for development. Now you need to plan exactly where you want to get to, what skills you need to get you there and how you will acquire the opportunities to do this by setting yourself targets. Putting your development plan into practice will mean recording and identifying your progress. Then you can reflect on your personal achievements and consider where you want to go next. Essentially, you need to **monitor** and **evaluate** whether you are progressing to or meeting your targets.

Key terms

Feedback – information about how you are progressing and whether your objectives have been met. It will also inform you whether or not your choice of objectives was correct. If you are not meeting your goals, then your training plan may be inappropriate. You can gather feedback from performance tests, competitive results, peers, your coach and assessments. Records of these could be added to your logbook.

Self-evaluation – using feedback from observation, performance tasks, your results and questionnaires to determine how well you have achieved your goals and objectives. If you have not achieved your objectives, then you can make meaningful changes. Through self-evaluation you can identify what you want to achieve and the appropriate methods of training to enhance performance.

Monitoring and evaluation – recording your progress towards achieving the set goals in your development plan and evaluation is about reaching conclusions and what you would then recommend for further improvement in future performances.

Improvement in technical weaknesses and tactical awareness

Through working with coaches performers can improve technical weaknesses and tactical awareness by devising specific practices in training which will lead to stronger performances in competitive situations.

Tactical awareness

By recording competitive situations the player is able to observe their own game and assess specific tactical situations. This will develop their understanding of tactical awareness.

Resources

Physical

When considering your development plan you will take into account the opportunities and equipment available at high-quality and safe facilities within travelling distance from where you live.

Human

The performer will take into account the opportunities available for coaching. Who, at their club, has the knowledge and experience to develop their performance, or can lead them towards better coaches? Are there coaching awards that they might access that would improve their technical skills?

Fiscal

A performer needs money to participate in sport. Club fees and also match fees can be high. The performer also needs money for equipment such as tennis rackets, tennis shoes, football boots, and for travel. There could be funds available for them and their club in the form of grants.

Courses

By attending courses the performer can not only improve their skills but also complete a National Governing Body coaching award in their specific sport. Through the Awards for All scheme, any organisation can attract funding. This enables individuals to have access to high-quality and safe facilities and high-quality coaching, allowing performers to progress to their best ability and to compete at the highest level. Performers can then improve their own and others' skills in a selected sport. Examples of courses include:

- Level 1 Certificate in coaching football – for anyone over 16 years of age with experience of participation in football who is looking for an introduction to the vocational area of coaching Association football.
- Volleyball Sport Course – a 4-hour course designed for those with little experience of teaching volleyball (or consider the Level 1 volleyball coaching certificate).
- Ist4Sport Level 1 Certificate in coaching rugby.

Coaches

A coach will design effective ways to explain important points to their performers. For example:

- What needs to be practised?
- When will it be practised?
- Where will it be practised?
- Who will be involved in the practice?
- How will it be practised?

Competitions

Competition can be introduced through training and matches. Competition develops performers not only technically but also improves concentration and confidence. As the performer progresses and becomes involved in more competition, finance is very important. Elite performers are often sponsored and win prize money. Sponsorship at local level means that nearby businesses sponsor performers but for this to happen the performers need to have been identified as having ability.

Take it further

1. Research the facilities and coaching opportunities within travelling distance of where you live, that could help you progress to reach your potential.

2. Research the coaching awards available to you in your selected sport in your local area.

   a) Which level of this award would you choose to access in order to improve performance?

   b) Which facilities are running these courses and how would you fund the course?

   c) Are there grants available?

Assessment activity 27.4

P6 M5 D2

 BTEC

1. You must produce a development plan in the form of a report. Your report will be sent to the head coach of your sports club. This will enable you to plan around your specific needs.

   In the report, identify your strengths and areas for development. Your plan will include current strengths and areas for improvement. This plan should include your targets, specific sport practices, courses which you can attend, competitions you can become involved in and coaching practice. **P6**

2. After completing your development plan in task 1, explain how the targets set, practices, courses and coaching are closely related to identified strengths and areas for improvement in your own technical and tactical ability and will make you a better performer. **M5**

3. You have made suggestions in your personal development plan on how to enhance your own performance in your selected sport. Now do the following.

   a) Review the information and make recommendations on how your development plan can be met.

   b) Explain how the targets, practices, courses, competitions and coaching are to be attainable.

   c) Assess the timescale for the completion and review of your plan.

   d) Give reasons or evidence to support your recommendations on how the development plan can be met and show how you arrived at your conclusions.

   e) Will your development plan improve personal performance? **D2**

Grading tips

P6 When selecting goals for your development plan based on your identified strengths and weaknesses, consider the word SMART. Also consider resources: where you can train, the equipment available, the quality of the coaching and the financial implications.

M5 Relate your plan closely to your needs. What strengths and areas for improvement in your own technical and tactical ability have you identified? Build your development plan around them.

D2 Justify the suggestions you have made in your development plan and show examples of how they could be attainable. Why, and how, do you think your targets will improve performance?

PLTS

Producing a development plan of your own technical and tactical ability, based on identified strengths and areas for improvement, will develop your skills as an **independent enquirer**, **creative thinker**, **reflective learner**, **team worker** and **effective participator**.

Functional skills

Using ICT systems to complete results and formulate charts or complete analysis of a sports performer in action will provide evidence for your **ICT** and **Mathematics** skills.

Edward Harris
Managing and coaching a football team

A past chairman has returned to a premiership football club following the resignation of the present one. The team has lost confidence and is in the relegation zone, and the manager accepts that only results will guarantee his future.

The chairman and coach worked together during the 2006/2007 season, and the chairman has stated that this coach will be in charge for the next match. A local newspaper quoted him as saying, 'It's not all about winning tomorrow, it's about playing well and getting a performance that will send fans home happy. We need to win enough games to stay in the Premier League.'

Since last December, the team has only won three games, and its four wins in the last 12 months is a paltry tally by any standards, but is it all the coach's fault? With the appointment of this chairman, the club is looking to stabilise. The chairman has said he will give his coach some time to sort out the club's on-field woes. He also wants to lose some of the club's 40 full-time professionals.

He hopes to offload at least ten players who are not premiership quality, in an effort to shrink the club's high wage bill. He is also trying to bring in some much needed investment to help cement the club's place in the Premier League.

Whether the chairman is successful or not is linked closely to the team's performance on the pitch, but steadying the financial problems should make the waters calmer for the team.

Think about it!

- What psychological guidance could you give these players in the current situation?
- Could you devise a training session which would focus on attack and goal scoring?
- Why is winning so important? Explain your answer.
- If you were the chairman, would you be satisfied with just a good performance? Why is the coach making this statement?
- What do you believe are a coach's main roles and how does a coach stay successful?
- What style of management brings success to a professional sports team? Discuss.
- Research any professional manager/coach. Discuss their style of management and the success it brings to the team.

Just checking

1. Describe the differences between continuous, serial and discrete skills. Give an example of each skill. Describe the skill and state why you have selected the specific skill to be classified as continuous, serial or discrete.
2. What do you mean by the word 'tactics'? If you were giving a team a talk before a match, what might you say about tactics?
3. Why is the 'ready' position so important in sport? Give an example of three sports in which the performer returns frequently to the ready position.
4. Why is positioning important in sport? Discuss positioning when defending and attacking.
5. Every shot/pass/stroke should have a purpose. Select a skill from sport and explain when you would use that skill – what is the purpose of the skill? Explain when you would consider the skill to be successful and when you would consider the skill to be unsuccessful.
6. The purpose of observation analysis in sports is to improve performance. Why would you use a checklist or performance profile to assess the technical and tactical abilities of a sports performer?
7. What do you mean by an elite performer? Name your favourite elite performer and explain the qualities possessed by this person which puts them into this category. Do you believe these qualities can be taught?
8. What factors would a coach and an athlete consider when discussing a training programme?
9. Discuss the roles and responsibilities of defenders and attackers in sport.
10. What is meant by aerobic and anaerobic training? Give examples of sports that would emphasise either or both training systems and explain why.
11. Why is competition so important in the development of sports performance?
12. What is the role of the coach in developing sports performance? Does knowledge alone make a good coach?
13. Why is video analysis so widely used by elite sports performers to develop performance?
14. How does nutrition affect sports performance?
15. What is the best way for you to improve sports performance? Is it through assessment? How does assessment help in your development plan?

edexcel :::

Assignment tips

Research
- Access the Internet. There is much information about the technical and tactical demands of different sports and elite performers and their training techniques.
- Newspapers and sports magazines often contain articles directly related to elite performers' training methods and schedules.
- Observe competitive matches on television, video/DVD.

Get active
- Visit training venues and observe selected elite performers and live competitive matches.
- Speak to your sports coaches about your logbooks and discuss methods for self-analysis.
- Discuss practices that will improve your performance.

Practice makes perfect
- Work with your coach to identify strengths and areas for improvement, and produce a development plan that will target areas for technical and tactical improvement. Set yourself achievable targets.
- Go on courses and discover what is available in your area and where you might get financial assistance.
- Remember: practice does make perfect!

28 The athlete's lifestyle

Success in sport is not just a combination of physical and mental skills or technical and tactical skills. An emerging athlete should consider their personal lifestyle and have knowledge of how this will affect their performance both during practice and during competition.

There are many areas that athletes should consider in order to be successful. The roles and responsibilities of modern athletes need to be understood, as well as the duties they are expected to undertake as part of their professional role. The emerging athlete will face many pressures when developing their talents, such as pressure on time to train and compete. Personal and financial sacrifices will be made along the road to success. Athletes must also consider their behaviour on and off the field, as many successful athletes will have their lives and lifestyles scrutinised by the media. Being able to cope with the associated pressures of being in the 'public eye' will allow an athlete to concentrate on competing at the highest level and not being distracted by outside, potentially negative influences.

An athlete should plan their long-term career and this unit will enable you to consider how to plan for the future and the opportunities that will enable you to maximise your chances of success both during and after your athletic career. This unit will also allow you to explore the factors that a successful coach will need to help them understand how to improve a team's or individual's performance.

Learning outcomes

After completing this unit you should:

1. know how lifestyle can affect athletes
2. know the importance of appropriate behaviour for athletes
3. know how to communicate effectively with the media and significant others
4. be able to produce a career plan.

Assessment and grading criteria

This table shows you what you must do in order to achieve a pass, merit or distinction grade, and where you can find activities in this book to help you.

To achieve a **pass** grade the evidence must show that the learner is able to:	To achieve a **merit** grade the evidence must show that, in addition to the pass criteria, the learner is able to:	To achieve a **distinction** grade the evidence must show that, in addition to the pass and merit criteria, the learner is able to:
P1 describe five different lifestyle factors that can affect athletes **Assessment activity 28.1 page 367**	**M1** explain five different lifestyle factors that can affect athletes **Assessment activity 28.1 page 367**	**D1** analyse five different lifestyle factors that can affect athletes **Assessment activity 28.1 page 367**
P2 describe the importance of appropriate behaviour for athletes **Assessment activity 28.2 page 375**	**M2** explain the importance of appropriate behaviour for athletes **Assessment activity 28.2 page 375**	**D2** justify the importance of appropriate behaviour for athletes **Assessment activity 28.2 page 375**
P3 describe strategies that can be used by athletes to help deal with three different situations that could influence their behaviour **Assessment activity 28.2 page 375**		
P4 describe the factors to be considered when giving two different types of media interview **Assessment activity 28.3 page 380**		
P5 describe the factors to be considered when communicating with significant others **Assessment activity 28.3 page 380**		
P6 produce a career plan covering an individual's career as an athlete and their career outside competitive sport **Assessment activity 28.4 page 384**	**M3** explain factors involved in career planning for an athlete **Assessment activity 28.4 page 384**	

How you will be assessed

This unit is assessed internally using a variety of methods designed by your tutors. Your assessments could be in the form of:

- written report
- case studies
- presentations
- interviews
- role play.

Jack Martin, 16-year-old footballer

This unit helped me understand that it takes more than training and fitness to become a successful footballer. I now realise that my lifestyle will have a huge impact on becoming a successful footballer.

I enjoyed looking at the different aspects of lifestyle and seeing how they can impact on my sporting performance. The unit also made me realise the lifestyle pressures that exist outside sport and the commitments needed to succeed. It was good to explore the lifestyle of famous footballers and compare them to mine and consider how they have achieved success.

The unit had lots of role play and practical aspects, which made it more exciting for me to study. I particularly liked looking at how the media can influence the public and how presentation both on and off the pitch is so important in making the right impression.

Over to you

- **Consider your own lifestyle. What aspects would you consider positive and what areas do you think could hinder sporting performance?**
- **How do you think that your lifestyle could improve to aid your own sporting performance?**
- **Why do you think that lifestyle is so important to an athlete?**

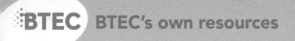

1. Know how lifestyle can affect athletes

Warm-up

Your lifestyle

Think of your own lifestyle and what pressures you have that may affect your ability to train or compete. Write down five factors that may take up your time outside of sport. Now consider how you can overcome these pressures in order to play sport.

1.1 Lifestyle factors

Being a successful athlete involves a huge commitment and many personal sacrifices. Lifestyle can play both a positive and negative role in achieving this success.

Leisure time

Leisure can be defined as time available for ease and relaxation or the freedom to choose a pastime or enjoyable activity. Athletes are advised to spend their leisure time doing things that are appropriate, such as resting and relaxing. However, some might choose to do inappropriate things like gambling or smoking.

Appropriate activities

Rest

Rest allows the athlete to unwind and is therefore important. Not only does it allow the body time to recuperate, it also offers a break from the mental pressures of training and competition. However, an emerging athlete has to combine their sport with education or a job to fund future financial security. This might have a significant impact on the amount of leisure time available, and it is common to 'juggle' to fit everything into daily life.

Relaxing

Relaxation can be active, like yoga or Pilates, or sedentary or non-active, like watching television or listening to music. Either way, it is important that an athlete finds time to relax and 'switch off'. This gives the mind and body time to relax, helping them to be prepared and focused when competing or training.

An athlete is likely to have taken up sport as a hobby. As the hobby progresses into a career, they may have a hectic lifestyle combining training, competition and travel with work or education. This will limit the amount of time available for them to switch off from the rigours of their sport. Athletes should carefully plan when and how they choose to rest, relax and unwind.

Inappropriate activities

Relaxation away from sport can come in many forms, most of them positive. However, certain activities can be described as inappropriate, especially for the elite or emerging athlete. Smoking, drinking alcohol – especially to excess – and gambling are likely to be viewed as bad habits. There is a danger that an elite athlete, who has both time and money, may have an excessive lifestyle. You are probably aware of a number of high-profile athletes who have had their lifestyles reported by the media, often with a focus on negative or inappropriate behaviour.

Alcohol

Alcohol is often used as a social tool and in sport it is sometimes used to celebrate a victory. Alcohol manufacturers often use sport as a marketing tool through sponsorship.

Unfortunately, drinking to excess presents both short- and long-term problems. It can lead to unruly and inappropriate behaviour, with crimes sometimes committed when drunk. In the long term, excessive alcohol use results in liver damage and can be fatal.

Drugs

Drugs can be divided into two main categories:

- **recreational drugs**
- **performance-enhancing drugs**.

Drug	Effect	Examples of abuse in sport	Side effects
Anabolic steroids	Increase power by increasing muscle strength and size Increase training time so athlete able to train harder and longer Used to help repair the body after training Increase competitiveness and aggression	• Power events such as shot put, javelin or weightlifting • Sprint events	• Liver disease • Certain forms of cancer • Fluid retention • Infertility • Hardening arteries increasing risk of coronary heart disease • Skin disorders
Beta blockers	Used to steady nerves and hand tremors	• Snooker • Darts • Archery • Shooting events	• Tiredness • Lethargy • Low blood pressure • Fainting • Breathing problems
Diuretics	Reduce body weight	• Horse racing • Boxing	• Dehydration • Muscle cramps • Kidney failure
Stimulants	Improve performance through increased awareness Athlete more physically aware Reduces fatigue	• Endurance-based sport	• Increased blood pressure • Increased heart rate • Paranoid delusions • **Anxiety** • Shaking and sweatiness • Sleeplessness and restlessness

Table 28.1: Examples of performance-enhancing drugs banned in sport

Key terms

Recreational drugs – drugs taken for social or recreational purposes, which generally alter the mind and body. Examples include alcohol, tobacco, cannabis, cocaine and heroin.

Performance-enhancing drugs – drugs used by athletes to improve performance. They are strictly forbidden in sport. Examples include anabolic steroids, nandrolone and diuretics. Athletes may be tempted to use performance-enhancing drugs in order to achieve success.

Anxiety – a negative form of stress that is characterised by long-term feelings of low confidence and poor concentration. Common symptoms will be a fear of failure and low self-esteem. Anxiety is likely to reduce the athlete's level of performance.

Common recreational drugs such as marijuana, cocaine or heroin are extremely dangerous and can have serious consequences for an athlete. Not only will performance be affected in the short term, with success unlikely, the risk of long-term damage to health is considerable. All athletes should avoid such drugs as there is no benefit to their use. It is common for athletes to be tested for both performance-enhancing and recreational drug use. If they test positive, athletes are likely to be banned from their sport for a long time or possibly life, as well as facing the risk of police prosecution. For example, the sprinter Dwain Chambers was found to have taken a banned substance and as a consequence was banned from competing for two years as well as receiving a lifetime ban from competing at the Olympic Games.

Doping refers to using performance-enhancing drugs. Their abuse has been well publicised, with many high-profile cases of athletes found using them. Some athletes take these to gain an unfair advantage over opponents. However, the consequences can have both long- and short-term health implications, as well as resulting in a ban from the sport.

Gambling

Gambling on sport is a multibillion-pound industry. Some sports, such as greyhound and horse racing, are dominated by gambling. The development of the Internet has allowed gambling to become more accessible and there has been a significant rise in the profile of this industry. It is now common for football teams to be sponsored by gambling companies.

Athletes are not allowed to gamble on events in which they are involved, and there are strict laws to enforce this. This is to prevent accusations of match-fixing, where the result is determined not by skill but by cheating.

Take it further

There is more information on the Gambling Act on the Gambling Commission's website at www.gamblingcommission.gov.uk.

High-earning athletes often gamble on sports in order to get the same thrill that they get when they are successful in their own performance. You will probably be familiar with a number of media cases where famous athletes have gambled large amounts of money at sporting events. Attention is often focused on the amount they bet and the amount of money lost.

Because betting is risky, it is easy to lose money quickly. Proper financial investment is a much better option.

Smoking

The dangers of smoking are widely publicised. In recent years the government has spent almost £23 million on campaigns aimed at preventing smoking among young people. Many young people are attracted to smoking as they see it as 'cool'. People often start smoking because of peer pressure.

Unruly behaviour

An athlete who is regularly in the media spotlight needs to consider their role as a sporting ambassador whom many young people will aspire to emulate. If media pictures show them smoking or behaving in an unacceptable or antisocial way, there is a possibility that children will copy them. Even amateur athletes should consider their behaviour during sporting competition and training, as well as away from the sports ground. Unruly behaviour will have a negative effect on their own image and that of their sport.

Activity: The importance of a positive image

In small groups, research two athletes who are portrayed positively in the media and two who are portrayed negatively. Explain why their behaviour can be viewed as positive or negative and the image this portrays to the public. What do you think are the effects on their sport? Prepare a short presentation using images to highlight your research.

Pressures

Peers

There are many demands on an athlete's time. Work, education, training and competition commitments mean that there is little time to socialise. What time there is might leave an athlete too tired to commit to other activities. However, the emerging or young athlete will feel pressure to meet friends. Combined with the pressure to achieve success through training and competition, this can be stressful. How can an athlete make sacrifices to be the best and maintain a healthy and rewarding social life? To achieve success, the emerging athlete has to work hard and train hard. Understanding and supportive friends are important if the athlete is to feel confident in their commitment.

Social life

An athlete will have many pressures that affect the amount of time available to spend with friends and family. However, it is important that time is spent relaxing in their company, away from the pressures of training and competition. The athlete's training programme should include time to relax and socialise.

Club

Playing for a club often puts additional pressure on an athlete. The club may wish the athlete to participate in extra training or to help other, younger athletes with their training. This will in turn put more pressure on them to fit in their own commitments both within and outside their sport.

Living away from home

Many young athletes have to leave home in order to train and compete at the highest level. Being away from friends and family can be daunting for a young athlete and they must be able to cope with these pressures.

Activity: Think it over

Imagine that you are required to live away from home in order to train and compete. List five things that you would need to able to do in order to cope with the pressure of being away. What would you miss most about home and how would you cope with this?

Training

Pressure is put on athletes to perform, both in training and in competition. Such pressure might come from coaches, tutors, parents, spectators, or the athlete themselves. One reason why athletes drop out of sport is stress. This is often the result of well-intentioned parents or coaches, who might set unrealistic goals. Athletes need to understand that mistakes are part of the learning process and should not be feared. Another pressure athletes face is being set goals which are not within their control.

Being able to deal with pressure is important if an athlete is to perform to the best of their ability. Training or performing when unwell or injured is likely to have a long-term damaging effect and should be avoided.

Overtraining will be unproductive and significantly increase the risk of injury. A successful athlete will develop coping strategies through experience and discussion with their coach, tutor or parents.

Competition

Athletes are likely to experience high pressure during competition. The desire to win – combined with factors such as spectators, the venue and other athletes (or the opposition) – all play a part in putting **stress** on the athlete. Being able to deal with this is important if the athlete is to compete to the best of their ability.

Key term

Stress – a mental or physical response to a situation that an athlete feels that they cannot cope with. Symptoms will be characterised by increased heart rate, a rise in blood pressure, muscular tension, irritability and depression.

Activity: Dealing with pressure

Consider a stressful situation you have encountered in your sport. How did it make you feel and how did you deal with it? List five ways in which you can deal with stress.

Financial

Spending

Athletes are likely to combine their sport with a job in order to reach their targets. Many sports are expensive, with costs of equipment, travel and accommodation having to be met by the athlete. Lottery funding might be available to cover the essential support services, such as coaching, training camps, competition and sport science. UK Sport also offers money to help with the essential personal living and sporting costs incurred while training and competing as an elite athlete. This is called an Athlete Personal Award (APA).

Saving

The career of an athlete can be relatively short, with second careers often undertaken at the end of a competitive career. It is essential that an athlete saves some of their income so that they have a source of money in the future. Savings accounts vary greatly, with some allowing tax-free investment while others offer immediate access to money. Either way, it is vital to have savings you can fall back on. Savings accounts can be set up and managed online, saving a great deal of time.

Investing

Investments are forms of saving designed for longer periods of time. Money is invested in the hope of making a profit on it. Investments can come in many forms, such as buying shares in a company, or buying property.

Sponsorship

Sponsorship is money or equipment given to an athlete or team by a company or individual. This allows the athlete to concentrate on their training rather than having to work full-time to support themselves. The influence of sponsorship on the modern development of sport has been massive. Sport is now big business, with large companies spending millions of pounds to sponsor events or individuals.

Roger Federer is one of the highest sports earners in the world with sponsorship deals worth in excess of $36 million a year. Why do you think Nike and Rolex are keen to sponsor Roger Federer and what are the benefits to them and to him?

Many companies want a high-profile athlete to endorse their product or company so that they gain media attention and, ultimately, sell more products. Companies such as Nike and Adidas invest millions of pounds in teams and individuals so that they wear their clothes. Such companies have been partly responsible for creating sporting icons such as Roger Federer and David Beckham.

Commercial companies recognise that elite sports stars can be fashion icons and role models, so are keen to use them in their advertising campaigns. This is particularly true of sportswear, which is now a fashion product rather than a sporting one.

On a smaller scale, a Sunday league football team might gain sponsorship from a local business in order to pay for their kit or match fees.

Tax

Paying tax on income can be stressful. A knowledge of what is required and how to do it is important. If you are on a fixed salary, tax should be deducted automatically before you receive your money. Any additional private work or self-employment involves declaring your income to HM Revenue and Customs.

An athlete in receipt of an Athlete Personal Award (APA) does not have to pay tax. However, if the government feels you are a professional athlete making a profit from sport, you will be taxed. If your sole income from sporting activities is your APA, you will not be considered to be a professional athlete, so your APA is not taxable. If, however, you have another source of income, you might be liable for tax. This is especially important if you receive money through sponsorship, in which case you might be taxed on your entire income.

Take it further

If you earn less than £6,475 from paid employment in a year, you do not have to pay income tax. For more information, go to the HM Revenue and Customs website at www.hmrc.gov.uk.

Insurance

Insurance can cover a number of things such as life, injury or property. For example, athletes may wish to protect expensive equipment against theft or damage. This means they will pay a fee or premium to a company, which in return pays to repair or replace the equipment if it is broken or stolen.

Take it further

Further information can be found on supporting athletes financially on the UK Sport website at www.uksport.gov.uk.

UK Sport is responsible for distributing Lottery and exchequer money to elite athletes in order to achieve world-class success. How do you think the money enables athletes to perform at their highest level?

Assessment activity 28.1: Lifestyle factors   **P1 M1 D1**

A new coach has been appointed at your club and is focusing on improving the performance of all the young athletes with the aim of coaching them to reach their maximum potential. The coach has spoken to each athlete and fully explained the importance of training and preparation. He has asked you to prepare a short PowerPoint presentation and handout describing how lifestyle can benefit or hinder performance. Your presentation should:

1. Describe the main lifestyle factors that can affect athletes. **P1**

2. Explain each of these factors in detail. **M1**

3. Use examples you have researched to fully analyse why each of these factors can aid or negatively affect performance. **D1**

Grading tips

P1 Lifestyle can have positive and negative effects on performance. You should consider your own sport and lifestyle and give examples.

M1 Consider why these factors are important and fully consider both the positive and negative aspects of lifestyle on an athletes' performance. Remember to use examples to support your findings.

D1 Consider why lifestyle can have a negative effect on performance and how you would address this if you were a coach.

Use the Internet to research examples of elite athletes who have their lives scrutinised by the media. How might this affect their performance?

PLTS

By researching and completing a short presentation, you are developing your skills as an **independent enquirer**, **creative thinker**, **reflective learner** and **self-manager**.

Functional skills

Using ICT to research examples of how lifestyle can affect performance and preparing a PowerPoint presentation and handout will give you practice at **English** and **ICT** skills.

2. Know the importance of appropriate behaviour for athletes

The way athletes conduct themselves during competition and training will influence sporting success. A positive attitude towards themselves and others is important if personal goals and targets are to be achieved. In this section, you will examine how appropriate behaviour both on and off the field of play is essential for sporting success. You will also look at a variety of situations in which you might find yourself and discuss how you would cope with them.

2.1 Behaviour

Conduct during competition and training

Adherence to rules

Ethics and **values** underpin all sporting performance. In sport, ethics include the idea of playing to the spirit of the rules of the game. Values might be enjoyment, personal satisfaction and health. An athlete should uphold these in both competition and training. An athlete has a duty to himself or herself as well as to the image of their sport, and as such must behave in an appropriate manner at all times. An athlete who has been highly publicised in 2010 for their off-field behaviour is England's football captain, John Terry. Consider how both his own reputation and that of his sport have been affected by these reports. What image does this portray?

Key terms

Ethics – moral principles or codes of conduct. For example, it is ethical to recognise when you have inadvertently broken a rule without anybody noticing: a goalkeeper who knows that the ball has crossed the goal line should tell the referee.

Values – ideals that form beliefs and actions. Athletes try to perform at their best in order to achieve success for their country or team. By recognising that they are competing not just for themselves, they are playing with positive values.

Respect for peers and others

An athlete's behaviour often comes under scrutiny from teammates, coaches and spectators. Behaving professionally and respectfully not only shows your personal values, but also that you value others. Sport can be frustrating, especially when you are performing below your best or when results are not favourable. Such frustration can cause an athlete to react badly to a refereeing decision or comments from spectators. However, this will have a bad impact on the athlete's image and the sport. They must always follow the rules and respect their peers and others. Athletes should never argue with officials, teammates, peers, spectators or opponents.

Appropriate clothing

Athletes should wear appropriate clothing and use safe and suitable equipment. Presenting the correct image is essential in sporting success.

Equal opportunities

Equal opportunities involve treating everybody equally and fairly, regardless of race, gender, age, disability or religion. Clear legislation is set out to prevent discrimination. To quote Sport England: 'Sports equity is about fairness in sport, fairness of access, recognising inequalities and taking steps to address them. It is about changing the culture and structure of sport to ensure that it becomes equally accessible to all members of society.'

Take it further

Sport England's website at www.sportengland.org.uk has more information about equity and inclusion in sport. You can also find out about its national initiative, Sporting Equals, which promotes racial equality in sport.

SPORT ENGLAND

Sport England is responsible for ensuring that people have access to sport regardless of their age, race or gender. How does Sport England work in your area? What facilities or schemes are organised and run by Sport England?

Following her gold-medal success at the 2004 Olympic Games, Dame Kelly Holmes has been appointed the National School Sports Ambassador. Why do you think she was chosen for this role?

Appropriate role models

Recent years have seen a rise in media coverage and the sponsorship of sports stars. Athletes must conduct themselves in a correct manner at all times, as they come under intense press scrutiny. Their private lives are often considered more newsworthy than their sporting successes. Sports stars can be positive ambassadors for their sports. They play an important role in introducing children to sport and so increase participation. Children imitate their heroes, both in the way they play and in the way they behave on and off the field of play. Athletes should consider that their actions can have both positive and negative consequences, for which they should be responsible. An example of an appropriate role model is goalkeeper David James and Portsmouth Football Club, who launched a campaign to help children learn about history through practical activities. Such campaigns are becoming increasingly common, with Premier League teams understanding the important role they have in the local community.

You do not have to be famous to be a role model. Younger and less experienced athletes might look at you and wish to copy your performance or style. Therefore, it is important that you conduct yourself in the right way.

Sports ambassadors

High-profile athletes often work within their local communities to provide encouragement to children and to act as sporting ambassadors. This is a positive experience for youngsters, and it also reflects well on the athlete. It is usual for the media to report this, raising the profile of both the athlete and their sport. These sessions might happen on a local basis, with local athletes working in schools and helping out with coaching, or they might take place on a national basis, with athletes endorsing specific nationwide campaigns. For example, David Beckham is an FA ambassador for the World Cup bid in 2018.

Celebrities

Many athletes have become sports stars or celebrities away from their sport. This means they are widely recognised by the general public and so their behaviour might be scrutinised. It is important that these celebrities behave in a positive manner at all times.

Enhancing the status of sport

All athletes can enhance the status of their sport by behaving in a positive manner, both on and off the pitch. The media report athletes' behaviour and it is vital that this enhances the image of the sport. By behaving positively and working with their local community, athletes can raise and enhance the profile of their sport via the local or national media. This in turn attracts children to the sport and increases participation at grass-roots level.

Encouragement of young performers to reach excellence

An athlete who has achieved sporting success is an excellent source of advice and information for emerging athletes. They will be able to share their experiences and to give training and competition advice. The elite athlete can act as a motivator or coach and further enhance the opportunities given to young performers.

Increasing participation for all

A positive role model in sport will have a positive effect on sports participation. Youngsters might try to copy their favourite sports stars and participate in the same sport, such as the Wimbledon Tennis Championships where the profile of tennis is raised via the media. People, especially children, see tennis stars and try to copy their performance at their local tennis courts. More participation today could mean more elite sports stars tomorrow.

An athlete who encourages children to participate is Kent County cricketer Rob Ferley. He regularly works with primary schools and takes cricket coaching sessions to encourage children to take up the sport. He also organises tours of the ground so they can see behind the scenes of a professional cricket club, as well as offering free tickets so they can watch the players in action.

2.2 Coping and management strategies

Being able to cope with a hectic and varied lifestyle is essential for sporting success. Athletes might find themselves in different situations, both on and off the field. They will have to develop coping strategies to deal with these situations. Failure to cope might result in an increase in stress and could have a detrimental effect on performance. Factors that might need to be considered by the athlete include:

- opposition
- spectators
- injury
- training and competition
- environment.

These factors should be addressed in advance so that a coping strategy can be developed. Research indicates that athletes should develop a range of cognitive and behavioural coping skills to manage the competitive stresses they face.

Mentoring and coaching

A mentor is an experienced and trusted tutor or coach. A coach will teach technical and tactical skills, and also understand their individual athletes. Being able to talk to an experienced athlete or coach helps the emerging athlete to understand sporting performance as well as how to deal with different situations. It should be possible to allocate time to work through and discuss problems with the coach so that a strategy can be developed. Discussing problems with your coach means that preventative measures can be adopted. The coach and athlete can discuss past, current or future performances and their concerns. It is important to be reflective and honest if the strategies are going to be successful.

Take it further

For more information on mentoring in sport, especially for new coaches, read *A Guide to Mentoring Sports Coaches*, published by Sports Coach UK (see www.sportscoachuk.org). Your local sports-development offices will also offer a wide range of courses and information on this important area.

Group and one-to-one discussions

To raise sporting performance, it is essential to discuss problems openly and honestly. The coach needs to have the awareness and skills to be able to understand the needs of the individual and of the team or group. Individual discussions are important so that the athlete can discuss private or confidential problems. Likewise, airing experiences or feelings as part of a group or team aids team cohesion and sporting performance. Group discussions allow athletes to express any problems, and coping strategies can be shared among the athletes or team members. Open discussions allow the coach to identify factors that might be affecting the team or individual performance.

Activity: Dealing with concerns

On your own, list any concerns or worries that may affect your performance in training or competition. For example, you may be worried about the effect of playing at a new ground. Remember to be honest in your self evaluation. Now speak to a coach or a group of other players and see whether they have similar concerns. How can you cope with these?

Change of lifestyle

Athletes make many sacrifices to reach their potential. Commitment to sport often leads to a pressure on other aspects of their lives, like family, friends, work or education. This feeling of lack of time or control can result in stress, which will in turn affect performance. Athletes should consider how they are going to cope with time pressures in their lives.

Change of routines

Sport involves changing routines, so planning can be difficult. Fixtures or competitions can involve travel, and it is normal to stay overnight in hotels. Athletes need to have a flexible approach in order to deal with their daily lives. They might experience an injury that will prevent them from training and competing, causing frustration and worry. Commitment and support from family, friends and employers helps the athlete to cope.

2.3 Situations

As an athlete, you are likely to find yourself in a variety of situations. These may occur during competition or training, or they may happen away from the sports arena. Being prepared to deal with these effectively means you can focus on your own performance, with the aim of producing a successful result. Situations may involve:

- teammates or colleagues
- coaches or managers
- opposition players
- spectators
- the media
- sponsors.

On and off the sports pitch or area

An athlete will often be at their happiest when they are participating in their sport. Too often, however, they have to spend time travelling or dealing with situations away from the field of play. People such as journalists might want to ask about past or future performances. This can cause frustration, as athletes are under pressure to either train or gain successful results. It is important to be able to deal with these situations in a professional way.

On the field of play, the opposition might try to affect your performance through negative comments or actions. 'Sledging' is the exchange of words with an opposition player to put them off their usual game. This is an attempt to 'psych out' an opponent, but is not in the spirit of the game.

Likewise, players may play aggressively with the intention of physically hurting the opposition. The rules or laws of the sport are designed to prevent this, with punishments to deal with offenders. The media regularly focus on the negative aspects of players' performances and behaviour. You are probably aware of examples where players have reacted badly to a challenge.

During competitions

It is important that athletes behave in an appropriate manner during competitions. Sport can be frustrating at times, but sportspeople must remember to conduct themselves in the correct manner. Officials may make decisions that you disagree with, or the opposition may make derogatory remarks, but you must always conduct yourself appropriately.

During training

Training is a time when you can practise with a coach or other team members. When certain situations occur that frustrate you, such as poor performance or a decision you disagree with, you may react badly. However, working with your teammates and coaches rather than criticising them will enhance your performance and reputation.

Travel to and from sports pitch or area

Many people may wish to speak to an athlete, perhaps when they are on their way to training or competition. To deal with this, athletes should allow a set amount of time to be interviewed before or after training or competition. During this time, they should answer questions in a helpful and professional manner.

Officials should always be treated with respect. What image does this give to fans?

Dealing with the media

The media (television, radio, newspapers and the Internet) are important to athletes as they provide a valuable opportunity for self-promotion and for the promotion of the athlete's sport. Dealing with the media effectively and professionally is vital to maximise opportunities.

There are three key reasons why an athlete will deal with the media:

- to promote themselves or to raise their personal profile
- to promote or raise the profile of the sport
- to promote a sponsor.

A press conference is a way of briefing the media on major issues, such as a forthcoming competition or the reaction to events that have taken place. Press conferences could take place before, during or after a competition, depending on the circumstances.

Athletes are likely to encounter the media in two main forms:

- broadcast, such as on television or radio
- written, such as in newspapers or magazines.

Many retired sportspeople have careers in both the broadcast and written media, offering their opinions on current issues and events.

Television

Television offers athletes the strongest opportunity to get their message across. Like radio, television can be an immediate outlet. It relies on many of the same techniques to deliver its messages, such as satellite links and studio editing. Television interviews can take place in a studio or at a venue as part of the outside broadcast unit. They may be broadcast live or pre-recorded.

Television covers sport across the same basic areas as radio and operates in the following formats:

- live coverage
- pre-recorded coverage
- studio-based items
- outside broadcast items
- news bulletins
- documentary programmes.

Radio

Radio is a flexible medium that operates 24 hours a day. It is also immediate because of its ability to turn around interviews and features quickly. Radio covers sport in three basic forms:

- live coverage of events
- news bulletins
- magazines and documentary programmes that look behind the scenes.

Radio gives minor sports a great opportunity to gain coverage, especially through local and regional radio.

Press

The written media include local newspapers, national newspapers and magazines. There is also an increasing number of specialist sports magazines, which offer athletes the chance to gain additional coverage. Sportspeople may also feature in more general lifestyle publications.

Roles in the written media can be broken down into four main areas:

- News reporters, who are looking for an eye-catching story. They often have a variety of sports to report and so will not be dedicated to one area. They may be sent to a local charity or sports event, or to an international event such as the Olympic Games. These stories might focus on a scandalous or negative aspect of performance rather than the achievements of the athlete or team.

- Sports reporters, who are generally supportive of athletes and their sport. They will not report on failures, but will usually have a balanced approach with the interest of sport at heart. Athletes should try to build a good relationship with these writers, as their articles can influence the public's perceptions.

- Columnists, who are looking for an overview. They write regular features about sport. Their role is to give their opinion and to provoke thought and debate.

- Feature writers, who cover the sport or the athlete in greater depth than sports reporters. If an athlete is a known winner or has a good story, feature writers may look to do a piece with them before a competition. On the other hand, feature writers may write afterwards if the athlete has emerged as a champion or something extraordinary has happened to them.

Dealing with the public

Athletes often have to deal with members of the public as part of competition and training. They also have to deal with fans, who might be aggressive or hostile towards them or their team. On the other hand, fans can be supportive, which often leads to improved performance. It is important that the athlete deals with these in a professional and effective way.

Many clubs employ a **public relations (PR)** officer who is responsible for dealing with the public and the media.

Disruptive and aggressive fans

Unfortunately in sport some spectators behave in an inappropriate or aggressive way towards the opposition's fans or the players themselves. Athletes can be subjected to personal verbal abuse, which may affect their performance. It is essential that sportspeople learn to ignore such comments and behaviour, and to focus on their sporting performance. Athletes should never engage with disruptive or aggressive fans as this may provoke them further.

Dealing with others

Athletes have to deal with many other people and organisations, including employers, match officials, managers, sponsors, agents and team colleagues. Being able to communicate and behave appropriately is fundamental to achieving sporting success.

Employers

Working with an employer in a professional and open manner allows the athlete to develop their career fully. The support of an employer who understands the needs of the athlete, means additional time can be spent on training, travel and competition. A flexible and open approach is beneficial to both parties: the employer has a dedicated worker while the athlete feels valued in their work.

Match officials

Match officials are an essential part of sport. Without officials, sport could not exist in the form that it does today. Match officials are in charge of the decisions within the competition in which the athlete is involved. Their decisions are final and must never be questioned by athletes. Pressurising an official to make a favourable decision is known as **gamesmanship** and is unacceptable in sport. **Sportsmanship**, on the other hand, means conforming to the rules of the sport.

Key terms

Public relations (PR) – manage communication between an organisation and the public to build, manage and sustain a positive image.

Gamesmanship – when an athlete 'bends' the rules to their advantage. Examples may include time-wasting, sledging or putting pressure on match officials.

Sportsmanship – playing fairly and to the recognised rules, for example shaking hands with the opposition, helping an injured opponent or congratulating a winner, player or team.

Club/regional/national coaches

Successful athletes work with a number of coaches in their pursuit of excellence. You may have worked with coaches at a variety of levels as your sporting career has developed. Athletes need to understand what each of these coaches demands and expects in order to reach collective sporting goals. Behaving in a professional manner will help you in your pursuit of success. All coaches will have the athlete's interests at heart and most are likely to be experienced in their chosen sport and will be supportive in the pursuit of excellence.

Agents

Athletes may feel that they need to have an agent as part of their support team. An agent would help them with:

- commercial and sponsorship opportunities
- contract advice
- managing external commitments.

The use of agents is common to athletes who feel that they do not have the time or expertise to maximise their commercial potential.

Managers

A team manager is in charge of making team selections, organising fixtures, and preparing kit and equipment prior to training and competition. As an athlete, you are supported by a manager who will help you as part of your training. The manager organises opportunities to help you improve, such as additional coaching or injury rehabilitation. The manager also decides on competition tactics before and during an event, and these decisions might affect you as an athlete.

It is important that a manager is treated with respect and honesty, even if you feel that a decision is affecting you personally. Managers have to make difficult but considered decisions that they feel are going to benefit all those concerned in the competition.

Sponsors

Sponsorship is a formal relationship between an athlete or team and a company. The business deal should be mutually beneficial to the sponsored individual and the sponsor. Most companies seek a return on their support or investment, ranging from goodwill within the community to increased media awareness of their products.

A successful sponsorship deal can be long-lasting and beneficial. It involves the athlete building strong, positive relationships with the sponsor. The longer the relationship lasts, the greater the value that can be gained from it.

The sponsor might make demands on the athlete's time in reward for publicity and money. The athlete should behave in a way that is likely to benefit the sponsor and portray them in a positive way, enhancing their reputation or company. Negative publicity through poor behaviour is likely to result in the sponsor withdrawing or cancelling their contract.

Other team colleagues

Being part of a team is a vital ingredient in many sports. Taking collective responsibility for success and failure is also part of being in a sports team. Working closely and striving to achieve the same goals for success allows a team to bond and perform at the optimum level. Therefore, as an athlete you should not blame team mates or individuals for bad results or mistakes.

PLTS

This activity (see Assessment activity 28.2 on page 375) will improve your skills as an **independent enquirer**, a **reflective learner**, a **team worker** and an **effective participator**.

By researching examples of abuse and the reasons for it, you can develop as an **independent enquirer**. By considering your own experiences you can develop as a **reflective learner**.

Functional skills

Using ICT to research examples of how lifestyle can affect performance (see Assessment activity 28.2 on page 375) and preparing a PowerPoint presentation and handout will help you gain evidence to meet functional skills in **English** and **ICT**.

Assessment activity 28.2

Successful athletes often have their lives scrutinised by the media, and too often negative behaviour is highlighted in the press and on television. Prepare a poster presentation that gives three examples of positive behaviour and three of negative behaviour.

1. You should describe each of these behaviours and give specific examples of how they are portrayed in the media. **P2**

2. Fully explain the image these behaviours portray to the public and how this may affect the athlete and the sport that they are involved in. **M2**

3. Now consider why behaviour is important and think about the effects of poor behaviour on both the athlete and the sport. You should fully justify the importance of appropriate behaviour both during competition and also away from the sports field. **D2**

4. Consider three different situations commonly found in sport where behaviour is important. Describe different ways in which the athlete will be able to deal with these and how a failure to do so may affect their behaviour. **P3**

Grading tips

Remember that behaviour should be considered not only during competition but also during practice and training. Don't forget that the people who help you with your sport, such as tutors, parents and coaches, will expect you to behave in a positive and appropriate manner.

P2 Make your presentation interesting by using specific examples of behaviour. Remember to consider both positive and negative behaviour.

M2 You must fully explain why each of these behaviours is important and its effect on the image of the athlete and the sport. Try to consider the long-term problems associated with poor behaviour.

D2 You should fully analyse the implications of both good and poor behaviour and explain why athletes should be ambassadors for their sport.

P3 Consider an athlete who is subjected to verbal abuse from visiting spectators every time they touch the ball or play a shot. How can they deal with such vocal attacks and what would be the consequences if they allowed these negative, derogatory comments to affect them?

3. Know how to communicate effectively with the media and significant others

3.1 Factors

Communicating accurately and clearly

There are verbal and non-verbal forms of communication. We communicate using speech, writing, body language or gestures. By communicating, we are giving information or knowledge. Being able to do this accurately and clearly is essential. It is a skill that can be developed with practice and has a significant effect on the learning process and sports performance.

Active listening skills

If you do not have listening skills your performance will suffer because you will not know what is expected in a task or situation. In sport, this might lead to confusion, frustration or injury. Clear lines of communication should be open between people who rely on one another to get good results.

Activity: Non-verbal communication

Watch a television presentation or interview with the sound turned off. What do you notice about body language? Does the speaker look open and confident or nervous or worried? List the different types of non-verbal communication you notice.

Asking questions

What someone says and what we hear can be amazingly different. We might make assumptions that can distort the information. It is useful to ask relevant questions, both to gain knowledge and to confirm understanding. Being able to ask such questions in an open and honest way will clarify key points as well as showing that you have an understanding of what is expected from you. Asking questions will also help develop your understanding of personal performance and allow you to discuss your short- and long-term goals with others.

More information is gained from open questions, which normally start with words such as why, what, how, where or when. A closed question is where a simple yes or no answer is sufficient.

Activity: Chinese whispers

In your class, sit in a circle. One person should start by whispering a statement into the ear of the person sitting next to them. This should be said only once. This person repeats the statement to the next person, making sure that nobody can hear them. Repeat this process until everybody has heard the statement. The last person should now say what they have heard to the rest of the group.

1. Was the final statement the same as the first statement?
2. If there was a difference, why has the message changed?
3. What could be the consequences of this in sport to an athlete or team?

Writing clearly and effectively

There are times when athletes have to write to people such as sponsors, managers, the media or coaches. Many people are intimidated by having to write. However, there are times when it is the best way to communicate, and there are other occasions when it is the only way to communicate. Remember that once something is in written form, it cannot be taken back. Communicating through words can be more concrete than verbal communication, with less room for errors and mistakes. This means that you should use accurate writing skills, and think about your spelling, grammar, punctuation, writing style and choice of words.

Today's technology makes letter-writing and other written forms of communication easier by providing reliable tools that check and correct misspelled words and grammar use.

Always check a letter or email thoroughly when you have finished writing it. Even when you think it is exactly what you want, read it through again before sending it. Check that there is nothing that could be misinterpreted.

Remember

First impressions matter: always proofread any written communication, checking spelling, grammar and punctuation.

Discussions

Throughout your sporting career, you will have discussions with others covering a wide range of subjects such as results, personal or team performance.

With coaching staff, managers, advisers, other athletes

You might find yourself having conversations with coaching staff, managers, advisers and other athletes. Such discussions allow you to share ideas and opinions, and can be useful in identifying how to improve performance. The key to a successful discussion is to be prepared, know what you want to say in a clear way and be able to listen to others. It is also important that you respect others, with everybody having the chance to put across their thoughts and ideas.

Preparation for communication

The old saying 'fail to prepare; prepare to fail' is true when discussing coaching, performance and communication. It is important to be prepared well in advance so that you know what to expect. Preparation might include research, scripts, prompt sheets and rehearsals, to prevent any poor or unexpected performance. This is essential when preparing to deal with the media, especially as part of a press conference or live broadcast interview. Athletes need to be able to convey information in a clear and concise manner to aid understanding and avoid any embarrassing or controversial moments.

Being prepared might include asking yourself:

- What questions will I be asked?
- How should I respond to these questions?
- How should I present myself at the interview?
- What should my appearance be at the interview?
- Who can I seek help and advice from?

Remember

People won't just be listening to what you say, they will be listening to *how* you say it. Be positive, open and clear, and remember not to let your body language become a distraction.

Purpose and content

Knowing the purpose of the interview beforehand will allow you to prepare in advance. You will need to research what questions are likely to come up, and what the answers should be. You should also prepare for the unexpected so that you are fully aware of the content of the interview or presentation.

Audience

Being aware of your audience means you can prepare a suitable presentation. The size and level of knowledge within the audience means you can talk at the correct level and aid their understanding.

Rehearsals

A good way of improving your presentation skills is to rehearse in advance. Read through your notes and presentation, so that when you have to do it for real you are familiar and confident with its content.

Scripts and prompt sheets

Scripts and prompt sheets can be used to refer to during a presentation. They will give you confidence if you feel that you might forget something. However, do not rely solely on these as you may end up simply reading a script rather than presenting the information.

Research

Research into the area that you have to present will give you valuable knowledge. This allows you to have the confidence to answer any additional questions that may arise.

Resources and information-gathering

Before you undertake a presentation, gather as much information as possible. This research might involve investigating the subject matter, as well as speaking to experts or people who can give specific advice. Remember to use all the resources available to you to prepare a professional interview or presentation.

Personal delivery

The ability to communicate effectively depends on many factors, including body language, style of communication, vocabulary and tone. Communication might also be affected by your appearance and the timing of your delivery.

Speaking to an audience can be exciting. However, lack of preparation can make even the best-intended presentation a poor experience. To ensure that you are effective, ask yourself:

- Why am I giving this presentation or interview?
- What do I want the audience to take away from the presentation?

Find out in advance how much time you will have to make your presentation. Divide this time into smaller parts, with each part tackling a specific element. All of the elements should reflect the overall objective of the presentation. For example, the first part should be an introduction.

Keep your presentation short and simple. Your audience will not remember every point, so highlight the most important parts.

Communication styles and body language

Your style of communication and **body language** will vary depending on who you are communicating with, your message and the situation you are in. You are no doubt aware of your own style of communication. There are three main styles:

- **passive** – where you put others' needs before your own and minimise your own self-worth
- **assertive** – where you stand up for your rights while maintaining respect for the rights of others
- **aggressive** – where you stand up for your rights but in doing so violate the rights of others.

Each of these has a direct effect on how you are perceived by others.

Key term

Body language – body movements or gestures such as hand gestures, smiling or nodding. Body language can help communication and shows whether someone understands or is acknowledging what you are saying. It is important to understand body language and how it affects the way you might be perceived. For example, yawning can show lack of interest, while keeping your arms crossed might indicate a lack of openness.

Language

It is essential when presenting information that you use the correct language: you should avoid slang and swearing. Your voice should be clear and words should be pronounced properly. Any difficult or unfamiliar words should be practised beforehand.

Speech

Use of technical vocabulary

Sport uses technical terms and specialist language to describe performance and techniques. Other athletes are likely to understand what you are saying, but non-athletes may be confused by technical jargon, so you should avoid it. Coaches should avoid using too many technical terms as athletes may be unsure about what is required, leading to confusion and poor performance.

Pace

For a presentation to be successful and for the audience to remain involved and interested, consider the pace at which you talk. If you speak too quickly, people will not be able to follow what you are saying. If you talk too slowly, people may become bored.

The way you dress is important. In a sports setting, appropriate attire may be training wear, kit or even a suit or blazer worn with a shirt and tie. What impression do the England rugby team give when wearing their team blazers?

Intonation and clarity

What you are saying might be affected by the intonation and clarity of your verbal communication. Intonation is the pattern and pitch of your voice, and clarity means how clearly you speak. People who speak very slowly in a non-expressive voice can be difficult to understand and uninspiring. Alternatively, someone with a lively, fast-paced voice may be difficult to understand as they speak too quickly. You should learn to use your voice in a way that creates interest and is easy to listen to.

Appearance

Remember that first impressions count. Someone meeting you for the first time will quickly form an opinion of you, based on your appearance, speech, body language and mannerisms. These first impressions can set the tone for the whole relationship that follows, so it is vital for successful communication that you look professional and act professionally.

You should also consider your grooming. A clean and tidy appearance is appropriate for most occasions. Hair should be clean and tidy, and tied back if long. Jewellery should be kept to a minimum. A professional appearance involves a clean shave for men and discreet make-up for women. Clean and tidy clothes and shoes are essential in making the right impression. Make sure your grooming is appropriate and helps you to feel 'the part'.

Timing

An athlete may be an ambassador or role model. Make sure you always get to appointments on time and well prepared. Plan to arrive early and allow flexibility for possible delays. Arriving early is the first step in creating a good first impression.

Requirements of different media types

Different media types require different information about the athlete. This might range from immediate post-match interviews through to lifestyle guides. Some forms of media – such as newspaper or radio interviews – allow athletes to prepare their responses in advance. Others put them on the spot during live interviews that can be broadcast around the world. Athletes must be prepared and confident in their ability to communicate with the many forms of media that exist.

3.2 Types of media interview

Television (local and national)

The media give athletes a valuable opportunity to promote themselves and their sport. Making sure that communication is clear and open is a skill that develops with practice and experience. Athletes may have to give interviews to journalists from local and national television, or attend press conferences to give their views on individual or team performances.

It is important to understand how to communicate verbally and non-verbally in a professional way. This will raise the profile of the athlete and their sport, and present them in a positive light. The British Olympic Association (BOA) produces an information sheet for athletes that gives advice on dealing with the media. Here is a summary of the main points.

- Be yourself.
- Show how you feel.
- Think before you speak.
- Be natural.
- Speak clearly and not too fast.
- Look the interviewer in the eyes.
- Be open.
- Enjoy it: people want to know about you.
- Be proud of your achievements.

Radio (local and national)

Many interviews are conducted by local or national radio stations, often immediately after a performance. Interviewers will expect you to be able to give a clear evaluation and opinion on sporting performance and it is important that you convey this in a clear and professional manner. Many radio interviews will be broadcast live, so it is essential that communication is precise and accurate, even though you may be tired or disappointed after an energy-sapping match or event.

Print media

Local newspapers

Local newspapers will be able to report on an individual's or team's performance. They may also seek to talk to those involved and get their pre- and post-match opinions. Local newspapers can be vital in raising the image and profile of an athlete or team, so it is essential that you communicate clearly with their journalists.

National newspapers

It is common for the national press to include a journalist's opinion on a team or individual athlete, and ex- or current players are also asked to give their professional opinion. It is essential that an athlete knows what they want to say before speaking to a journalist, particularly immediately after a match or event when they may be tired, disappointed or frustrated. Remember to take your time in listening to the question that has been asked and respond confidently and with consideration.

Specialist magazines

In recent years there has been a massive increase in specialist sports magazines, ranging from athletics through to activities such as climbing and mountain biking. Magazines regularly feature exclusive interviews with specific athletes, informing the public of their achievements and hopes for the future.

Club magazines

Club magazines are produced to inform athletes and sport club members of recent events, results and sport-specific news. They interview successful athletes on topics such as training, competition success and lifestyle away from sport.

3.3 Significant others

Employers

Emerging athletes are often employed outside their sporting careers and need a positive relationship with their employers. These athletes should communicate openly, professionally and with respect. They might need the employer to be flexible with their conditions of work in order for them to train, travel or compete.

Match officials

Match officials are an essential part of competitive sport. Athletes must respect officials' decisions during and after competition. Communication, both verbal and non-verbal, should be clear, open and respectful.

Take it further

On average, 7,000 referees quit football every year because of abuse from players and from the sidelines. The FA has created the Respect Campaign, which provides information for leagues, clubs, coaches, referees, players and parents from grassroots to elite football to ensure a safe, positive environment in which to enjoy the game. For more information, visit the FA website at www.thefa.com/Leagues/Respect.

Club/regional/national coaches

You have probably worked with coaches at a variety of levels as your sporting career has developed. Successful athletes work with a number of coaches, and need to understand what their coaches expect in order to reach collective sporting goals. It is important that your relationship with your coaches is professional, honest and open so that important goals and performances can be discussed and developed.

Agent

An agent normally looks after an athlete's personal affairs, such as contracts and sponsorship deals. They also organise events that athletes need to attend in order to raise their profile. For this to be successful, it is important that athletes can express what they want, to ensure that the agent understands their goals and aspirations.

Manager

A manager is responsible for an athlete's or team's sporting affairs and should be treated with respect and consideration. The manager often has to make difficult or unpopular decisions, such as selecting a team or dropping a player who has been under-performing.

This may cause frustration, but the player should remember to communicate their concerns or worries in a constructive manner.

Sponsors

Individual or event sponsors are an important source of income for athletes and sports. Athletes may be required to attend meetings with sponsors, so they should present themselves in the best light. They must be courteous and professional at all times and ensure that they communicate appropriately. Their verbal and non-verbal communication should show that they are interested and value the sponsor's contributions.

Other team colleagues

Being able to communicate openly and honestly with team colleagues is an important part of team success. All members should feel valued and that they are able to raise concerns or specific points with teammates, managers and coaches. An environment in which open communication and discussion are possible should be developed, and encouragement should be given to any players who might be under-performing. Athletes should never criticise other team members as this will have a negative effect on performance.

Assessment activity 28.3   P4 P5   BTEC

A successful athlete will often have to give interviews to the media. Being prepared for these in advance will help. Working in small groups, prepare a series of questions that you might be asked after a match or event. Now conduct two different types of media interview using the questions. You may wish to video this interview to recreate a television session, or write down the answers as though you are a journalist. Once you and your group have completed this, reflect on how it went and write down and describe the main factors that should be considered when giving different types of media interview. **P4**

Using this information, now consider the different factors that you should consider when communicating with other people in your sport, such as match officials, coaches, sponsors and team colleagues. **P5**

Grading tips

P4 Watch some sports interviews on television. What are the questions being asked and how well does the interviewee answer them? What impression do the answers give of the sport and the athlete being interviewed?

P5 Consider different types of communication, including non-verbal communication such as appearance and body language. Avoid jargon and technical language. Remember to be clear in what you are saying and be positive and enthusiastic.

PLTS

By preparing and completing a short interview, you are developing your skills as an **independent enquirer**, **creative thinker**, **reflective learner** and **team worker**.

Functional skills

Preparing questions for an interview and handout will give you practice in **English**.

4. Be able to produce a career plan

4.1 Career plan

Goal-setting

Being a successful athlete does not happen by chance. Sporting careers are usually well considered and well planned, with short- and long-term personal goals identified by the athlete and coaching team. Progress may be made from club to regional and national teams or competitions. This brings many aspects that will support success, as well as considerations about post-athletic careers when factors such as injury or loss of form might result in secondary careers being undertaken.

Short term

To successfully achieve a long-term goal, set smaller, short-term goals that build towards the long-term goal. Focus your efforts and energy into achieving these small goals. Remember to bear in mind the larger, long-term goal. If you are not sure how to do this, seek advice from experts and coaches. Talking to experienced athletes enables you to gain an invaluable insight into how they have achieved success. Coaches should help their athletes set career and performance goals, as well as encouraging them to achieve short-term goals.

Medium term

Medium-term goals usually last for between one month and six months and are a progression of short-term goals.

Long term

An athlete needs to have a long-term goal. Answers to the question 'What is it that you want to achieve?' might be 'to finish tenth or above at the end of season' or 'to have a batting average of at least 50 at the end of the season'. These are objective statements about specific, measurable achievements. Replies such as 'I want to win' or 'I want to be the best' say little about how to achieve these things, and they do not direct the athlete's behaviour.

Self- and needs-analysis

Being able to appraise yourself honestly is the foundation to future success and achievement. It is important for long-term success that athletes have

a clear vision of what they want to achieve before identifying how to accomplish this. You might find there is a gap between your performance and your goals: you should identify how you are going to bridge this gap.

SWOT analysis

It may be useful for athletes to perform a SWOT analysis. Originally this was a business concept used to plan and evaluate the strengths, weaknesses, opportunities and threats involved in any project or in a situation requiring a decision. Being clear and identifying each of these key areas will allow you to set long- and short-term goals both in terms of performance and also long-term athletic career planning.

Strengths What are your strengths?	Weaknesses What are your weaknesses or areas that you wish to develop?
Opportunities What are the opportunities for employment in your local area?	Threats What competition is there that may act as a barrier to your career planning?

Figure 28.1: An example of a SWOT analysis for an athlete

Short- and long-term career goals

Goal setting should follow the SMART principle, that is, goals should be:

- **S**pecific
- **M**easurable
- **A**chievable
- **R**ealistic
- **T**ime-bound.

Technical and practical skills

Within your sport, you possess a number of important technical skills, such as the ability to serve a tennis ball or kick a football accurately. Through practice, training and analysis, these skills will improve so that you can gain success either individually or as a team. Identifying the specific skills required will enable you to focus on how to improve. This is true for basic or key skills that will be important as part of your future career. You need to learn how to communicate with individuals or groups of people and how to deal with the media. In order to do this, you can seek specialist advice from experts or even enrol on college courses that specialise in a variety of communication or public-speaking methods.

Key and basic skills

Key and basic skills may include communication, interpersonal and organisational skills. These can be developed within sport as well as outside, and are an important part of development. The skills learned will help athletes both in their sport and after their competitive sports careers have finished. Skills such as numeracy and literacy should also be developed, as these are essential in all areas of life and work.

Athletic career planning

Achieving your goals will involve athletic training and life skills. Being able to identify practical skills that can be used to achieve personal targets is important to the athlete. Clear and time-defined planning is also important as this will indicate how and when such targets are achieved.

Current expectations as an athlete

As an athlete, you will no doubt have expectations of yourself and others in terms of sporting performance and how you see your sporting career developing. Being able to clearly identify specific expectations will help you to plan you career and set defined targets.

Key review dates

It is vital that athletes set clear and defined dates to review their career plans. These will help to identify specific targets and determine whether these have been achieved or not. Key dates should be realistic, although they can be flexible if circumstances dictate that they are unlikely to be achieved.

Transitions

Athletes experience many transitions and changes throughout their careers. These might include a change in coach, club or location, or a change in national or international status. There will also be the significant transition from participating in sport to the secondary, post-performance career.

Change of coach

There may be times during an athlete's career when they will have to change coach. This may be due to career progression or when representing different teams. It is important that athletes accept this transition and are able to continue to perform at their best levels.

Change of club

Changing club can be a difficult time for an athlete. They may be leaving friends or family and feel like they are the new person in the club. There are likely to be many unfamiliar faces and the prospect can seem daunting at first.

Achieving national and international status

As an athlete's career progresses, they may be selected to represent their region, county or country. This involves communication and working with a wide range of people including coaches, managers and the media. Being able to recognise how to achieve national and international status allows the athlete to identify key targets and how they can be achieved.

Contingencies

Sport can have many uncertainties. Clear and definitive planning does not prevent the unexpected happening, such as long-term or permanent injury, accidents or illness. You should consider what options are available after a performance career has ended and what skills and qualifications these might require.

Illness

An unexpected illness will prevent an athlete from performing or training. It may also be a setback in terms of competition preparation.

Accidents

As the nature of sport is often uncertain, accidents will occasionally happen, so it is important that there is a contingency in place. Accidents must be dealt with promptly and you should evaluate their impact on future training, practices and performances.

Permanent injury

Many sports careers are cut short due to permanent injury. If this happens, the athlete may feel uncertain of their future as most of their lives may have been dedicated to training and competition in their sport. It is important that athletes have a contingency plan and a future career plan in place.

Second career planning

Being faced with planning a career away from sport can be a daunting and stressful experience for athletes. For most of their adult lives, they will have been training and competing, and an uncertain future can lead to anxiety and stress. However, many of the skills gained in sport can be used in other occupations. Athletes tend to be highly motivated and committed: these are valuable traits in any industry, as are teamwork and leadership skills. Identifying which careers are available and the qualifications and experience needed will give athletes the direction needed in planning for the future.

Qualifications and experience

Most jobs or careers require qualifications and experience. As part of your career planning, you should identify the careers that interest you and the qualifications they require. Many careers will require you to study further at university and as such there are now hundreds of sports-related courses. Valuable insights can be gained by work experience, where you take on a job for a short period to see whether it is an area in which you would enjoy working.

Take it further

To apply for a place at university you must use the University and Colleges Admissions Service (UCAS). Here you will find information related to different higher education courses, finance and how to apply. Visit their web page at www.ucas.com.

Activity: Higher education sport courses

Using the UCAS website at www.ucas.com, research the different Higher Education sports courses that are available. Using this information, choose a specific course and find out the entry requirements. Discuss your findings with your tutors, class or careers adviser.

Career options inside and outside professional sport

Careers after sport can be found both within and outside professional sport. The skills found within sport can be transferred easily to many other employment areas. There are also many careers alongside current athletes. These can involve physiotherapy, sports nutrition, coaching and teaching, working in the media or sports development. Each of these key areas still involves close contact with sport and competition. An example of a former athlete who continues to work in sport is television presenter Gary Lineker. After a successful career in football where he captained the England team, Gary pursued a career in the media.

Coach

It is a natural progression for athletes to continue in their sport as a coach. There are opportunities to coach at all levels, from grass roots through to elite. A number of specific and progressive coaching courses are now available.

Teacher

Teaching can be undertaken at schools, colleges or universities. It is natural for sports teachers to have an active interest in sport and they often compete outside work. To be a teacher you must study to degree level in sports science or physical education and also hold a certificate in education. Study normally lasts for a period of three years in higher education.

Media

There are many jobs in the media such as a journalist or reporter. To undertake a career in this field, you should have a good command of written and spoken English and it is normal to study up to degree level.

Sports development

Sports development is concerned with getting various groups involved in sport, such as elderly or disabled people, or children. Local authorities normally target groups that are under-represented in sport and offer schemes or sessions to get them actively involved. Sports-development officers normally have a sports-related qualification as well as a range of coaching awards.

Physiotherapist

Athletes are often keen to become physiotherapists as they may have experienced injury during their careers. There are a number of courses available in the UK, but competition for places is stiff. A physiotherapist has to study to degree level and the course will involve working in general physiotherapy at a hospital. Sports injuries and rehabilitation are not studied in a physiotherapy undergraduate degree course.

Sports science support

The area of sports science is expanding as we try to improve athletic performance. Areas include biomechanics, psychology, fitness testing and physiology. Each of these areas is designed to offer athletes support and to improve their performance. Sports scientists normally study at university and often continue their studies afterwards in the form of research.

Assessment activity 28.4

As sport can be a short career due to injury or factors outside the athlete's control, it is important to have a clear career plan. List the jobs that are available in the sports industry and describe what qualifications and experience you need in order to pursue each one as a career. To help you, research a recognised athlete or someone you know and produce a career plan that describes their career as an athlete as well as their career outside competitive sport. **P6**

Explain the factors involved in career planning for an athlete. **M3**

Grading tips

P6 Speak to people you know in sport and ask them how they achieved their career successes. What qualifications did they need? Are they still studying now in order to improve?

M3 Consider the wide range of careers in sport and give examples of the skills and qualifications needed to undertake them. Remember that careers take a long time to achieve.

PLTS

By researching and creating a career plan covering an individual's career as an athlete as well as their career outside of competitive sport, you will develop your skills as a **creative thinker**.

Functional skills

Using ICT to research examples of careers in sport and preparing a PowerPoint presentation and handout will give you practice in **English** and **ICT**.

James Butterfili
PE teacher and semi-professional cricketer

James works as a PE teacher in a local school. However, he has managed to combine this with a semi-professional career as a cricketer. As an ex-professional, James is aware of the importance of training and practice. He is also aware of the importance of being able to commit to both his teaching role and his sport. Therefore James has to combine these two roles and find a suitable balance that allows him to commit to both.

Being able to plan and prepare is an essential skill that he has developed as well as being organised. James also has to consider his family commitments outside of work and cricket and each of these puts a tremendous amount of pressure on his time. James also understands the importance of positive behaviour both on and off the field, as he is a role model to young people both as a PE teacher and a cricketer. He should therefore aim to act appropriately at all times as any negative incidents will attract attention and can be damaging both to cricket to and his job as a PE teacher.

Think about it!

- What are the main pressures on James?
- Why must James behave appropriately while playing cricket?
- What might happen if James acted inappropriately?

Just checking

1. Describe the difference between appropriate and inappropriate leisure activities and explain why an athlete must understand these.
2. Why is appropriate behaviour important both on and off the field of play?
3. List five examples of negative behaviour seen in sport. How does this affect the image of the individual or teams involved and the sport?
4. What pressures exist in sport and how might these affect an athlete?
5. Describe three coping strategies that may help an athlete.
6. Why is the media important to the athlete?
7. What are the main factors that should be considered when giving an interview?
8. Why is career planning important to an athlete?
9. List five careers that an athlete may wish to pursue after their career.

Assignment tips

- Remember that athletes have a duty to their sport. When researching types of behaviour, look for positive behaviour as well as negative.
- Use your own experiences in sport to highlight positive and negative behaviour. Explain what happened and how you felt about it.
- Consider different ways in which to relax away from sport. Remember sport should be enjoyable.
- Talk to your tutors and coaches if you aren't enjoying your sport or if you feel under pressure. They will all be experienced and have plenty to teach you.
- Use websites to help you gather research material; they contain plenty of useful information.
- Ensure that you read the assignment briefs properly. Take your time and ensure you are happy with the task set for you. If not, ask your tutor for additional assistance.
- Give yourself plenty of time to research and plan your assignments.
- Make sure you attempt all parts of the assignment briefs. If you only attempt the pass criteria, this is all you will achieve. Think big and try it all. Talk to your tutor if you're not sure.

Glossary

Absolute VO$_2$ max – maximum oxygen consumption expressed in litres per minute (l/min).

Act of Parliament – these originate from a bill, which is considered by both houses of parliament. Once the content of the bill has been agreed, it receives Royal Assent and becomes an Act of Parliament.

Adenosine triphosphate (ATP) – a molecule that stores and releases chemical energy for use in body cells.

Adipose tissue – commonly referred to as fat tissue, is a type of connective tissue that serves as the body's most abundant energy reserve.

Advisory providers – helping an organisation that has never run a sports-development scheme for a certain target group before and needs some advice.

Aerobic – requiring oxygen.

Aerobic endurance – the ability of the cardiovascular and respiratory systems to supply the exercising muscles with oxygen to maintain the aerobic exercise for a long period of time, for example over two hours during a marathon.

Aim – something you want to achieve – a goal.

Amino acids – the building blocks of proteins.

Anabolism – the constructive metabolism of the body (the building of tissue).

Anaerobic – not requiring oxygen.

Anaerobic threshold – the point at which aerobic energy sources can no longer meet the demand of the activity being undertaken, so there is an increase in anaerobic energy production. This shift is also reflected by an increase in blood lactate production.

Anxiety – a negative form of stress that is characterised by long-term feelings of low confidence and poor concentration. Common symptoms will be a fear of failure and low self-esteem. Anxiety is likely to reduce the athlete's level of performance.

Arousal – the psychological state of alertness that prepares the body for action.

Articulation – the meeting of two or more bones.

Assistance exercises – focus on smaller muscle areas, only involve one joint and have less importance when trying to improve sport performance.

Attribution – the reason you give to explain the outcome of an event.

Balanced diet – a diet that provides the correct amounts of nutrients without excess of deficiency.

Barriers to participation – factors that prevent people from participating.

Benchmark scores – give a current fitness status against which to monitor adaptation within a fitness programme.

Blood pressure – can be measured using a digital blood pressure monitor, which provides a reading of blood pressure in mmHg (millimetres of mercury).

Body language – body movements or gestures such as hand gestures, smiling or nodding. Body language can help communication and shows whether someone understands or is acknowledging what you are saying. It is important to understand body language and how it affects the way you might be perceived. For example, yawning can show lack of interest, while keeping your arms crossed might indicate a lack of openness.

Burnout – when an athlete strives to meet training and competition demands despite repeated unsuccessful attempts, and so tries harder. Can lead to the athlete no longer wishing to participate in activities they used to enjoy.

Calorie – the energy required to raise 1 gram of water by 1°C.

Choking – the whole process that leads to decreased performance, not just the decreased performance itself.

Codified systems – general and permanent laws or regulations that are arranged in subject matter order by title or other major subdivision and section.

Cognitive anxiety – the thought component of anxiety that most people refer to as 'worrying about something'.

Cognitive skills – involve a person considering what they are doing. In sport this applies to tactics, making decisions quickly, planning and selecting how to play. In team sports, verbal skills are used to encourage and motivate players.

Collagen – the main protein of connective tissue.

Concentric muscle action – the muscle gets shorter and the two ends of the muscle move closer together.

Coordination faults/losses – occur when players do not connect with their play, the team interacts poorly or ineffective strategies are used. Generally, sports that require more interaction or cooperation between players are more susceptible to coordination faults or losses.

Core exercises – focus on large muscle areas, involve two or more joints and have more direct impact on sport performance.

Crease – in cricket a bowling crease, a popping crease and two return creases are marked in white at each end of the pitch. Bowlers must bowl within these limits and batsmen must remain within the area to ensure they do not get stumped or run out. Within this area the batsman is safe from being run out and stumped.

Cross-cutting agendas – sports development schemes can have more than one purpose, mixing sports aims with social or cultural ones.

Diastolic blood pressure – the lowest pressure within the bloodstream, which occurs between beats when the heart is in diastole (relaxing, filling with blood).

Diet – a person's usual eating habits and food consumption.

Direct delivery providers – delivery of a programme directly by professional sports developers.

Distress – extreme anxiety related to performance.

Duty of care – a legal obligation imposed on an individual, requiring that they adhere to a standard of reasonable care while performing any acts that could possibly harm others.

Dynamic flexibility – the range of movement that a muscle or joint can achieve when in motion.

Eccentric muscle action – the muscle increase in length while still producing tension.

Electrolytes – salts in the blood, for example, calcium, potassium and sodium.

Enabling providers – an enabling programme provides facilities or resources to enable participants to play, start up a club or improve their skills.

Enzymes – proteins that start or accelerate the digestive process.

Epinephrine – a chemical in the body used for communication between cells in the nervous system and other cells in the body. It works with norepinephrine to prepare the body for the 'fight or flight response'.

Ethics – moral principles or codes of conduct. For example, it is ethical to recognise when you have inadvertently broken a rule without anybody noticing: a goalkeeper who knows that the ball has crossed the goal line should tell the referee.

Etiquette – the rules that govern how people behave with others – in sport, etiquette is also known as sportsmanship and fair play.

Eustress – 'beneficial' stress that helps an athlete to perform.

External imagery – imagining yourself doing something as though you are watching it on a film so that you can develop an awareness of how the activity looks.

Extrinsic – external factors, such as rewards.

Extrinsic risk – something outside the body that may cause an injury.

Facilitating providers – helping a sport or target group by providing coaches or courses in administration and refereeing.

Fair play – playing as competitively as possible, but always within the rules of the sport as determined by the national governing body.

Fartlek (Swedish 'speed play') – a type of training that varies the pace at specific intervals and is usually applied to running. Continuous running at a steady pace is interspersed with changes in speed for varying durations.

Feedback – information about how you are progressing and whether your objectives have been met. It will also inform you whether or not your choice of objectives was correct. If you are not meeting your goals, then your training plan may be inappropriate. You can gather feedback from performance tests, competitive results, peers, your coach and assessments. Records of these could be added to your log book.

Fibroblasts – the most common cells of connective tissue, they produce secretions to build fibres.

Fine motor skills – highly controlled skills like drawing and writing. They are small and precise, take time to perfect and improve over time.

Fiscal resources – the financial costs of running coaching sessions, this may include facility and equipment hire and could include depreciation costs or loss or damage costs to the equipment of facility.

Flexibility – the ability of specific joint, for example the knee, to move through a full range of movement. As with muscular endurance, an athlete can have different flexibility levels in different joints.

Food – any substance derived from plants or animals containing a combination of carbohydrates, fats, proteins, vitamins, minerals, fibre, water and alcohol.

Formative assessment – takes place informally and should the development of a coach.

Free fatty acids – the parts of fat that are used by the body for metabolism.

Gamesmanship – when an athlete 'bends' the rules to their advantage. Examples may include time-wasting, sledging or putting pressure on match officials.

Gross motor skills – involve a low level of expertise and large muscular movements, for example sit-ups, with a low level of coordination needed.

Hazard – something with the potential to cause harm.

Health and Safety Executive (HSE) – the organization responsible for proposing and enforcing safety regulations throughout the UK.

Health surveillance – a strategy and method for employers to detect and assess systemically the adverse effects of work on the health of workers.

Healthy eating – the pursuit of a balanced diet to support health and reduce the risks of chronic disease. Healthy eating principles should form the solid foundations on which athletes can build more specific nutritional strategies to support training and competition.

Human resources – people involved in the delivery of a coaching session, e.g. coaches, assistant coaches, parents, spectators.

Inclusiveness – bringing in those who are not usually included.

Insertion – the end of a muscle that is attached to the movable bone.

Internal imagery – imagining yourself doing something and concentrating on how the activity feels.

Intrinsic – internal factors, such as enjoyment.

Intrinsic risk – a physical aspect of the body that may cause an injury.

Joule – 1 joule of energy moves a mass of 1 gram at a velocity of 1 metre per second. Approximately 4.2 joules = 1 calorie.

Jurisdiction – the right and power to apply the law.

Kilocalorie – the energy required to raise the temperature of 1 kg of water by 1°C. Equal to 1,000 calories and used to convey the energy value of food. Kilocalories are often simply referred to as calories.

Kilojoule – a unit of measurement for energy, but like the calorie the joule is not a large unit of energy; therefore are more often used.

Macronutrient – nutrient required by your body in daily amounts greater than a few grams, e.g. carbohydrates, fat and protein.

Mitochondria – organelles containing enzymes responsible for energy production. Mitochondria are therefore the part of a muscle responsible for aerobic energy production.

Monitoring and evaluation – recording your progress towards achieving the set goals in your development plan and evaluation is about reaching conclusions and what you would then recommend for further improvement in future performances.

Motivation – the direction and the intensity of your effort; it is critical to sporting success.

Motivational faults/losses – occur when some members of the team do not give 100 per cent effort.

Motor skills – skills associated with body movement. There are two types: gross motor skills and fine motor skills.

Muscular endurance – the ability of a specific muscle or muscle group to sustain repeated contractions over an extended period of time.

Muscle fibres – the contractile element of a muscle.

Myofibril – the contractile element of a muscle fibre.

Myoglobin – the form of haemoglobin found in muscles that binds and stores oxygen. Myoglobin is responsible for delivering oxygen to the mitochondria.

Norepinephrine – a chemical in the body used for communication between cells in the nervous system and other cells in the body. It works with epinephrine to prepare the body for the 'fight or flight response'.

Nutrition – the means by which your body takes in energy and nutrients in food to sustain growth and development, and to keep us alive and healthy.

Objective – how you are going to achieve your aim.

Operational providers – programmes that are run at club level and are tailored and delivered to the clubs.

Origin – the end of a muscle that is attached to the immovable (or less movable) bone.

Osteoporosis – a disease characterized by the loss of bone mass and a change in bone structure that makes bones porous and increases the risk of fracture.

Overtraining – the athlete trains under an excessive training load, which they cannot cope with.

Perceptual skills – the major activities that transform an input into an output. From this information, an athlete will choose what is relevant and then act. Examples of perceptual skills include visual memory.

Performance-enhancing drugs – drugs used by athletes to improve performance. They are strictly forbidden in sport. Examples include anabolic steroids, nandrolone and diuretics. Athletes may be tempted to use performance-enhancing drugs in order to achieve success.

Personal Protective Equipment (PPE) – all equipment (including clothing affording protection against the weather) which is intended to be worn or held by a person at work and which protects them from one or more risks to their health or safety, for example, safety helmets, gloves, eye protection, high-visibility clothing and safety footwear.

Personality – the sum of the characteristics that make a person unique.

Physical resources – the facility and equipment required to deliver the session.

Pliability – relates to the stretchiness of your muscles and connective tissue.

Power – the ability to generate and use muscular strength quickly over a short period of time.

Psychological core – the part of you that contains your beliefs, values, attitudes and interests.

Psychological skills – qualities that the athlete needs to obtain through the PST programme.

Public relations (PR) – manage communication between an organisation and the public to build, manage and sustain a positive image.

Quality systems – methods of management and evaluation.

Recreational drugs – drugs taken for social or recreational purposes, which generally alter the mind and body. Examples include alcohol, tobacco, cannabis, cocaine and heroin.

Relative VO$_2$ max – maximum oxygen consumption expressed relative to the individual's body weight in kg. The units of relative VO$_2$ max are ml of oxygen per kilogram of body weight per minute (ml/kg/min).

Reliability – the consistency and repeatability of the results obtained, That is, the ability to carry out the same test method and expect the same results.

Risk – the likelihood and severity of the harm that could occur as a result of the hazard.

Role-related behaviour – behaviour determined by the circumstances you find yourself in.

Self-evaluation – using feedback from observation, performance tasks, your results and questionnaires to determine how well you have achieved your goals and objectives. If you have not achieved your objectives, then you can make meaningful changes. Through self-evaluation you can identify what you want to achieve and the appropriate methods of training to enhance performance.

Speed – the ability to move a distance in the shortest time.

Sports-development continuum – a model that shows the different levels of sports development.

Sports nutrition – the influence of nutritional strategies on sports performance during preparation of, participation in and recovery from training and competition.

Sportsmanship – playing fairly and to the recognised rules, for example shaking heads with the opposition, helping an injured opponent or congratulating a winner, player or team.

Stakeholders – people who have an important share in something.

Staleness – inability to maintain a previous performance level.

State anxiety – a temporary, ever-changing mood state that is an emotional response to any situation considered to be threatening.

Static flexibility – the range of movement that a muscle or joint can achieve.

Statute – a written law passed by a legislative body.

Strategic providers – a programme that links to other, large-scale plans and may be called an integrated approach.

Strength – the ability of a specific muscle or muscle group to exert force in a single maximal contraction to overcome some form of resistance.

Stress – a mental or physical response to a situation that an athlete feels that they cannot cope with. Symptoms will be characterised by increased heart rate, a rise in blood pressure, muscular tension, irritability and depression.

Stretch reflex – the body's automatic response to something that stretches the muscle.

Stumps – three sticks of equal size around 90 centimetres tall, with 5 cm separating them. Bails (small pieces of wood) are balanced on top of the stumps.

Summative assessment – takes place formally to assess the performance of a coach. It is often used to assess ability – for example, when trying to attain a coaching qualification.

Systolic blood pressure – the highest pressure within the bloodstream, which occurs during each beat when the heart is in systole (contracting).

Tactics – the skills a player uses in any type of sport to be able to win, for example during a hockey or tennis match, each team or player will apply specific tactics and strategies to try to beat and outwit their opponent(s).

Technique – a way of undertaking a particular skill.

Test variable – this is any factor which could affect the validity and/or reliability of fitness test results.

Thermoregulation – the ability to keep the body's temperature constant, even if the surrounding temperature is different.

Trait – a relatively stable and enduring characteristic that is part of your personality.

Trait anxiety – a behavioural tendency to feel threatened even in situations that are not really threatening, and then to respond to this with high levels of state anxiety.

Triglycerides – the most concentrated energy source in the body. Most fats are stored as these.

Typical responses – the usual way that you respond to situations.

Validity – the accuracy of the results. This means whether the results obtained are a true reflection of what you are actually trying to measure.

Values – ideal that form beliefs and actions. Athletes try to perform at their best in order to achieve success for their country or team. By recognising that they are competing not just for themselves, they are playing with positive values.

Vasoconstriction – when the blood vessels widen in an attempt to increase blood flow.

Vasodilation – when blood vessels narrow and reduce blood flow.

Venules – have thinner walls than arterioles. They collect blood leaving the capillaries and transport it to the veins.

Viscous – the measure of resistance (thickness) of a fluid.

VO$_2$max – the maximum amount of oxygen that can be taken in by and be utilised by the body. Also, a measure of the endurance capacity of the cardiovascular and respiratory systems and exercising skeletal muscles.

Index